CULTURALLY COMPETENT PRACTICE

Skills, Interventions, and Evaluations

edited by

ROWENA FONG

University of Hawaii at Manoa

SHARLENE B. C. L. FURUTO

Brigham Young University–Hawaii

Allyn and Bacon

Boston ■ London ■ Toronto ■ Sydney ■ Tokyo ■ Singapore

Editor in Chief, Social Sciences: *Karen Hanson*
Editorial Assistant: *Alyssa Pratt*
Executive Marketing Manager: *Jackie Aaron*
Editorial Production Service: *Chestnut Hill Enterprises, Inc.*
Manufacturing Buyer: *Julie McNeill*
Cover Adminstrator: *Kristine Mose-Libon*
Electronic Composition: *Omegatype Typography, Inc.*

Library of Congress Cataloging-in-Publication Data

Culturally competent practice : skills, interventions, and evaluations / edited by Rowena Fong and Sharlene Furuto.
    p. cm.
    Includes bibliographical references and index.
    ISBN 0-321-05488-1
    1. Social work with minorities—United States. 2. Minorities—Services for—United States. I. Fong, Rowena. II. Furuto, Sharlene Maeda.
    HV3177.U2 C86 2000
    362.84'00973—dc21

                         00-052560

Printed in the United States of America
10 9 8 7 6 5 4 3 2   05 04 03 02 01

To our parents, who gave us being and the gift of heritage
To our colleagues, students, and clients, who give us insight and challenge
To all ethnic families and communities, who continue to give us vision
and determination

CONTENTS

PART III INTERVENTIONS SKILLS FOR INDIVIDUALS, FAMILIES, COMMUNITIES, AND ORGANIZATIONS

PART IV   EVALUATIONS SKILLS FOR INDIVIDUALS, FAMILIES, COMMUNITIES, AND ORGANIZATIONS

FOREWORD

We have now entered a new century, one in which people of color—First Nations people, African Americans, Latinos, and Asian and Pacific Islanders—will comprise the largest segment in the United States. Yet, income, educational, and other social inequities related to race, ethnicity, and gender continue to exist. In this context, it is increasingly important for the helping professions to develop strategies and methods for working effectively with communities of color. Culturally relevant methods may provide one means to build human capital and reduce or eliminate existing social inequalities.

Social work was one of the first of the helping professions to begin to address the needs for culturally relevant programs, policies, and services. Over thirty years ago social workers of color questioned the dominant practice paradigm that encouraged us to be culture-free and universal. We began to suggest that our discipline consider how gender, culture, sexual orientation, race, and other social identities affect the experiences, problems, and solutions of the communities with which we work. The earliest advocates of this view placed equal importance on issues of social justice and developing methods that were not only culturally relevant but also focused on advocacy, social development, and change. During these decades we have developed many models, including the ethnic-sensitive, cross-cultural, culturally competent, empowerment, and multicultural methods. As we have developed these models for practice, there has been no consistent view of how social workers should use a multicultural lens in their work.

It is in this context that this book is published. It contributes to our growing literature on cultural competence in two important ways. The breadth of this book is impressive. Much of our work on culture may provide a superficial or cursory view of different comminutes of color. However, in this volume the authors provide different views of different groups as they relate to different stages of practice and different levels of intervention. Therefore, there is much here for the practitioner or student to use in understanding *how* culturally competent practice relates to different groups in different ways. This book is a valuable tool for social workers to use throughout their practice.

However, the major contribution of this book is in the depth of the models presented. So often our views of culturally competent practice have been additive: Material related to culture and identity is fused or added to our existing ways of doing things. In this book, the focus is on integration and the development of new ways of doing things. The work described here is strengths-based and uses an empowerment framework to demonstrate how our practice can work toward social justice on many levels and with many different groups. A critical element of this model is practice that utilizes community strengths and assets and methods that are indigenous to different groups.

In looking at this book, I was struck by how far we as a profession have come in developing models for culturally competent practice. This book synthesizes much of our earlier work and moves us farther toward a "bicultural" or "multicultural" view of practice. The chapters in this book represent many of the finest scholars in this field and their work in this volume contributes significantly to the development of social work practice in general.

Lorraine M. Gutierrez

PREFACE

This book was designed to be useful for both the student and professional social work practitioner interested in becoming more culturally competent with the various major ethnic groups. While this book presents values, knowledge, and skills about four major ethnic groups—African Americans, Latinos/Hispanic Americans, First Nations Peoples, and Asians and Pacific Islanders—many of the underpinnings, minority worldviews, ethnic institutions, and resources can be transferred to other ethnic groups.

There are five parts to this book, each one laying the foundation for the subsequent parts: introduction, assessment, intervention, evaluation, and conclusions. The introduction section presents an overview of the book and begins with a historical background of cultural competence, what preceded it, and what it is. The second chapter fleshes out more fully cultural competence in terms of the major theoretical frameworks selected for this book: the ecological model, strengths perspective, and empowerment theory. The next four chapters discuss values and ethical dilemmas, one chapter for each of the ethnic groups in this book: African Americans, Latinos/Hispanic Americans, First Nations Peoples, and Asians and Pacific Islanders. The seventh chapter offers a general review of the overall attitudes, knowledge, and skills needed to become more culturally competent.

The second section looks at assessment with the four major ethnic groups on the micro, mezzo, and macro levels. Chapter eight describes assessment skills needed when working with African American individuals and families, while Chapter nine focuses on assessment skills useful when intervening with African American organizations and communities. Chapter 10 emphasizes assessment skills needed when working with Latino/Hispanic American micro and mezzo populations, and Chapter 11 focuses on assessment skills needed with Latino/ Hispanic American macro populations. Chapters 12 and 13 do likewise with First Nations Peoples, while Chapters 14 and 15 do so with Asians and Pacific Islanders.

Section three discusses intervention with the same four ethnic populations, again on the micro, mezzo, and macro levels in much the same manner as above. Chapter 16 proposes an Africentric way of intervention with individuals and families; Chapter 17 does the same thing on the macro level. Chapter 18 concentrates on micro and mezzo practice, and 19 expands to macro intervention with Mexican Americans and Hispanic Americans. Chapter 20 discusses at intervention with Native Americans on the micro and mezzo levels, and the next chapter does so on the macro level. Intervention with Asians and Pacific Islanders on the individual and family levels are reviewed in Chapter 22, while the focus is on Pacific Islander communities in Chapter 23.

The fourth section completes the problem-solving model by presenting skills needed to work in the area of evaluation. Chapter 24 covers evaluation with African American individuals and families and the following chapter looks at evaluation of

African American organizations and communities. The pattern is repeated for Chapters 26 and 27 with Latino/Mexican Americans, Chapters 28 and 29 with First Nations Peoples, and, finally, Chapters 30 and 31 with Asians and Pacific Islanders.

The last section briefly summarizes all the chapters and looks to cultural competence practice and research needs in the twenty-first century. In essence, this book attempts to describe briefly cultural competence in social work practice to the present and cultural competence in terms of theory and attitudes. Chapters regarding the knowledge and skills needed to work with ethnic groups in assessment, intervention, and evaluation are covered in depth, and the chapter concludes with future perspectives.

Many people have helped us put this book together. We thank those who, early on, encouraged us to write about what we know and feel—ethnicity, social work practice, and cultural competence—including many colleagues and practitioners in the field. We would like to acknowledge the many practitioners and scholars who have contributed to the profession of social work in the area of culturally competent practice, especially Dr. Doman Lum, Professor at California State University at Sacramento, one of many pioneers. Others to acknowledge and thank are those who gave input for the structure of the book, including the many chapter contributors. Support staff tirelessly helped and addressed many details, especially Hisae Tachi at the University of Hawaii and Jill Vasconcellos at Brigham Young Universty Hawaii. Family members contributed by being understanding and encouraging. Thank you Lee, Naomi, Daniel, David, Linda, Matthew, Michael, and Daniel. To others not named, we also say *mahalo nui loa.*

We also thank the following reviewers who made many insightful comments: Bob Blundo, University of North Carolina at Wilmington; Margaret Seime, Middle Tennessee State University; and Norma D. Thomas, Widener University.

CONTRIBUTORS

Gregory Acevedo, Ph.D., Temple University.

Maria Yellow Horse Brave Heart, Ph.D., Director and Co-founder of the Takini Network and teaches at the University of Denver.

Eddie F. Brown, D. S. W., Associate Dean for Community Affairs at Washington University in St. Louis, Missouri.

Colette V. Browne, Dr.P. H., University of Hawaii at Manoa.

Monit Cheung, Ph.D., University of Houston.

Julian Chow, Ph.D., University of California at Berkeley.

Edgar Colon, D. S. W., teaches at Southern Connecticut State University.

Alfrieda Daly, Ph.D., consults on organizational and community reforms to remedy institutional racism and other diversity issues.

Eddie Davis, D. S. W., Buffalo State College.

Wynetta Devore, Ed.D., Professor Emeritus at Syracuse University.

James Edmondson, M. A., Regional Leader for the NorthWest Regional Office of Casey Family Programs, based in Federal Way, Washington.

Loia Fiaui, Ph.D., is the ethno-cultural specialist for the Hawaii State Health Department and teaches at Hawaii Pacific University and Education America, Honolulu Campus.

Rowena Fong, Ed.D., University of Hawaii at Manoa.

Cynthia Franklin, Ph.D., University of Texas at Austin.

Sharlene B. C. L. Furuto, Ed.D., Brigham Young University-Hawaii.

Fernando Galan, Ph.D., University of Texas at El Paso.

Dorie J. Gilbert, Ph.D., University of Texas at Austin.

Darlene Grant, Ph.D., University of Texas at Austin.

Bethney N. Gundersen, doctoral candidate, teaching fellow at Washington University in St. Louis, Missouri.

Aminifu R. Harvey, D. S. W., the University of Maryland at Baltimore.

Altaf Husain, doctoral candidate at Howard University.

Valli Kalei Kanuha, Ph.D., University of Hawaii at Manoa.

Gwendolyn Epuni Kim, M.S.W., Unit Manager for the Queen Lili'uokalani Children's Center Windward Unit in Hawaii.

Patrick Leung, Ph.D., University of Houston.

Lorre G. Lewis, Ph.D., State University of New York at Buffalo.

Maxwell C. Manning, Ph.D., Howard University.

Jon K. Matsuoka, Ph.D., University of Hawaii at Manoa.

Crystal Mills, Ph.D., Eastern Michigan University.

Julio Morales, Ph.D., University of Connecticut.

Paula T. Tanemura Morelli, Ph.D., University of Hawaii at Manoa.

Lirio K. Negroni-Rodriguez, Ph.D., University of Connecticut.

Chet M. Okayama, M.S.W., social worker and cultural specialist at the Honolulu Division of Casey Family Programs in Hawaii.

Maria Elena Puig, Ph.D., Colorado State University.

Fariyal Ross-Sheriff, Ph.D., Howard University.

Ronald John San Nicolas, Ph.D., University of Guam.

Saundra H. Starks, Ed.D., Western Kentucky University.

Roberto Villa, Ph.D., Associate Dean at the School of Social Work at New Mexico Highlands University.

Hilary N. Weaver, D. S. W., State University of New York at Buffalo.

Karen Westbrooks, Ph.D., Western Kentucky University.

Michael Yellow Bird, Ph.D., Arizona State University.

Maria E. Zuniga, Ph.D., San Diego State University.

CHAPTER 1

CULTURALLY COMPETENT SOCIAL WORK PRACTICE: PAST AND PRESENT

ROWENA FONG

Culturally competent practice will be the concern for all social workers who engage in problem-solving situations with the growing number of ethnic minority clients in the twenty-first century. Within the last couple of decades, social work, as well as other professional disciplines, has been concerned with the cultural appropriateness and effectiveness of services offered to ethnically diverse clients. It is important that social workers, operating from an empowerment, strengths, and ecological framework, provide services, conduct assessments, and implement interventions that are reflective of the clients' cultural values and norms, congruent with their natural help-seeking behaviors, and inclusive of existing indigenous solutions.

Ethnic sensitivity and concerns related to cultural competency in social work, as evidenced by the abundance of literature, began developing in the 1970s and early 1980s, and terms relating to its concerns began to appear in the literature: *dual perspective* (Norton, 1978), *ethnic-sensitive practice* (Devore & Schlesinger, 1999), *cultural awareness, cross cultural social work, ethnic competence* (Green, 1982, 1995, 1999), and *process-stage approach with people of color* (Lum 1986, 1992, 1996, 2000). The 1990s brought additional terms: *ethnic competent practice* (Mokuau and Shimizu, 1991), *culturally diverse social work practice, culturally competent practice* (Lum, 1999), and *person-in-family-in-community* (Fong, 1997), *communicating for cultural competence* (Leigh, 1998), *biculturalization of interventions* (Fong, Boyd, and Browne, 1999), *critical cultural values* (Zayas, Evans, Mejia, & Rodriguez, 1997), and *cultural competence as an empowerment strategy* (Pinderhughes, 1995). These are but a few of the many new expressions indicating that social work as a profession continues to prioritize and prepare social workers to modify their practices to accommodate the needs of the ethnic minority clients they serve.

Affiliative disciplines, such as multicultural counseling and psychology (Dana, 1998; Ponterotto, Casas, Suzuki, & Alexander, 1995; Pope-Davis & Coleman, 1997;

Sue, Arrendondo, & McDavis, 1992; Suzuki, Meller, & Ponterotto, 1996) also strove to instill knowledge, values, and skills preparing professionals to be culturally competent to serve their diverse client population. The history of the cultural competency movement is said to have begun in 1980 by the American Psychological Association's (APA) requirement for professional competent practice (Lum, 1999). By 1991, the Association for Multicultural Counseling and Development (AMCD) approved a document emphasizing the need for multicultural counseling, which later resulted in the addition of thirty-one multicultural competencies being required in the APA's accreditation criteria (Sue, Arredondo, & McDavis, 1992). This has been critical in shaping the assessments and interventions for individuals and organizations. (Arredondo et al., 1996; Ponterotto et al., 1995; Pope-Davis & Coleman, 1997; Pope-Davis & Dings, 1995; Sue et al., 1998) It also has been critical in the advocating of "culturally responsive psychotherapies" in order to acknowledge ethnopsychologies (Vargas & Koss-Chioino, 1992, p. 3).

In areas relevant to social work, such as mental health and child welfare, it was important for children and families to receive services that were community-based and grounded in the clients' culture. An example in the field of mental health is the culturally competent system of care known as the Child and Adolescent Service System Program (CASSP), targeted to provide effective services for severely emotionally disturbed minority children (Cross, Bazron, Dennis, & Issacs, 1989). It offered major points along a cultural competency continuum in an organizational mental health system of care.

Cross-disciplines, such as family studies and family therapy, factored ethnicity into family-centered assessments and interventions (Ho, 1987; Lynch & Hanson, 1998; McAdoo, 1993; McGoldrick, Giordano, & Pearce, 1996; Okun, 1996). Interdisciplinary problem areas, such as substance abuse, also emphasized culture, as evidenced by the Center for Substance Abuse Prevention (CSAP), which has recently been promoting a Cultural Competence Monograph Series. The eighth installment of this collaborative series featured *Responding to Pacific Islanders: Culturally Competent Perspectives for Substance Abuse Prevention* (Mokuau, 1998). CSAP and the National Association of Social Workers (NASW) also produced a book, entitled *Cultural Competence in Substance Abuse Prevention* (Philleo & Brisbane, 1996). Other interdisciplinary efforts in cultural competency are in health, social, and human services, as evidenced by Lecca, Quervalu, Nunes, & Gonzales (1998), who published *Cultural Competency in Health, Social, and Human Services: Directions for the Twenty-First Century.* These are but a few of the many contributions to the profession of social work that further cultural competency.

While the past literature has directed scholars and practitioners to personal and professional development, a thorough reexamination of the approaches to treatment and the kinds of services social workers offer to clients of color is long overdue. With the growing numbers of ethnic minority clients, as well as the shift in social work practice from deficits to strengths solutions and empowerment of clients (Gutierrez, Parsons, & Cox, 1998; Pinderhughes, 1995; Saleebey, 1997), a reconceptualization of social work practice is warranted. This most likely will result in social work educators and practitioners recreating paradigms, models, and definitions to reflect the values and cultures different from the Euro-American world-view and norms espoused in standard social work practice methods. This chapter will briefly review concepts and models related to cultural competency and then propose changes to be made in current paradigms.

TERMINOLOGY AND PARADIGM SHIFT

The conceptual and definitional development of a cultural competent perspective has been evolving over the last two decades. One of the earlier notions was Norton's (1978) point that it was critical to see issues from two sides by having a "dual perspective." Social workers needed to be able to compare the perspective of the larger social system with the client's immediate family and community. Thus, they needed to become aware of and sensitive to alternative values, beliefs, and treatment systems important to the client systems. Cultural awareness and ethnic-sensitive practice in the 1980s prompted professionals working with ethnic minority clients to be ethnically sensitive to the client's ethnicity, social class, language, norms, customs, and help-seeking ways (Devore and Schlesinger, 1981). According to Devore and Schlesinger (1981, 1996, 1999), the ethnic-sensitive social worker is to be concerned with the interaction of ethnicity and social class as they affect life's problems and solutions. Social workers should examine the assumptions and the "ethnic reality" of the approaches offered to their clients. These authors warned and continue to advocate that the experiences and the world of the client, i.e., the context of their reality, was not to be ignored. To heed that warning, social workers should be empathetic to the client's reality and prioritize the awareness of ethnic identity, to acquire knowledge of the clients' cultures and their ethnic worlds, and to develop social work skills to implement the methods appropriate to the client's reality.

Green (1982, 1995, 1999) challenged and continues to advocate that social workers explore the help-seeking behaviors of clients. He argued that ethnic minority clients had their own ways of seeking and receiving assistance, including indigenous strategies, and delineated five ethnic competencies that were necessary for cross-cultural social work (1982, p. 54–58):

- Ethnic competence as awareness of one's own cultural limitations
- Ethnic competence as openness to cultural differences
- Ethnic competence as a client-oriented, systematic learning style
- Ethnic competence as utilizing cultural resources
- Ethnic competence as acknowledging cultural integrity

To integrate cultural resources and to acknowledge cultural integrity have been exhortations to social workers working with ethnic minority clients for nearly two decades (Davis & Proctor, 1989; Devore & Schlesinger, 1999; Lum, 2000; Zayos, Evans, Mejia, & Rodriguez, 1997). While these are important principles of practice, the next steps are to make sure that cultural resources are actually used. There needs to be a change of perspective that assumes the cultural values of the ethnic minority client and uses them to make assessments and match interventions. It is not appropriate or helpful to insist that ethnic minority clients who come from a value system differing from the Eurocentric worldview be subjected to interventions that are often incompatible with their cultural norms. Changes to current paradigms are needed. Based on Lum's (1986) comprehensive process–stage approach of culturally diverse practice, social work education advocated that a culturally competent social worker focus on awareness, knowledge, and skills. Soon inductive learning was recommended to further the worker's culturally competent ability (Lum, 1999). The call for inductive learning is important, and it should start with the worldview of the client and integrate agencies with the communities in which they reside.

While social workers are expected to change and educate themselves to meet the needs of their ethnic minority clients, it is imperative that agencies and organizations that provide these services also be examined for cultural compatibility. Green (1982, 1995, 1999), author of *Culture Awareness in the Human Services*, asserted that ethnic-competent practice involved acquiring a knowledge base, professional preparation, and appropriate interventions in order to compare and understand culturally different worlds. To bridge these worlds in social service delivery systems, cultural competencies, defined as a "set of culturally congruent beliefs, attitudes, and policies that make cross-cultural work possible" (Cross, Bazron, Dennis, & Issacs, 1989, p. 13), were also necessary at the macro level. In 1993, the Child Welfare League of America developed a "Cultural Competence Self-Assessment Instrument" whose purpose was to "help agencies measure their cultural competency in agency policy making, administrative procedures, and practices, and to allow them to comprehensively review and assess their operational and programmatic function" (p. vi). This assessment tool was developed to challenge the agencies and organizations to value diversity in governance, administration, policy development, and service delivery.

Valuing diversity, according to Lum and Lu (1997), is expected to be included in academic curriculum and professional training as the focus from ethnic sensitivity and cultural awareness moves toward multiculturalism and competency. Multicultural social work has been moving beyond ethnicity. In the 1990s the profession of multicultural counseling shifted cultural diversity to a competency-based practice, including gender and sexual orientation. This made an impact on social workers, whose own adoption of multiculturalism and cultural diversity was also shifting. The term *multicultural* was broadening in its definitional scope as well. Lum (1999) defines *cultural competency* as "the set of knowledge and skills that social workers must develop in order to be effective with multicultural clients" (p. 3). Multicultural social work addresses varying facets of culture, which include race, gender, age, sexual orientation, religion, and so on. While multicultural social work does include these factors beyond ethnicity, it is this author's stance that the work with ethnic diversity is still lacking in depth and needs further challenging. In this chapter and book the task of multicultural social work practice remains to deepen the interracial, interblending of cultures found within a single ethnic group. For example, interracial marriages, international adoptions, and foster care situations allow clients to experience multiracial/multicultural experiences. In these experiences, social workers need to be prepared in assessments and interventions to deal with the multiethnic identities and differing environments of clients. The knowledge of cultural competency that has been advocated in the past has focused on thinking and learning factual and descriptive knowledge about the client, with attributes presented as tangential to the functioning of the person or community. The value and belief systems that comprise traditions and cultural norms need to be presented as central to the ethnic client's functioning. New paradigms and models need to be created to instill the practice of adopting the client's values as the norms. Social workers need to start with the ethnic social environment of the client and use the larger, usually Euro-American norms only as they complement the client's ethnic reality.

THE PARADIGM OF MULTICULTURALIZATION

The culturally competent practice model, according to Lum (1999), focuses on four areas: (1) cultural awareness, (2) knowledge acquisition, (3) skill development, and (4) inductive learning. These four areas each make an important contribution to the culturally competent social worker in shaping attitudes, knowledge, skills, and directing ongoing learning. However, a shift in each of the areas is warranted in order to provide a culturally competent service focused solely on the client rather than the social worker and what he or she brings to the awareness of ethnicity. Historically, effectiveness of the helping relationship with the client system was dependent on the social worker's awareness of self and his or her ethnicity. The assumption was that, by being in touch with one's own ethnic identity or culture, it would make a social worker more sensitive and empathetic to the needs of the client. This assumption has been theoretically true for decades without any substantial evidence in practice. While it may help a social worker be more sensitive, it is critical that the social worker shift to understanding cultural values and the importance of them to the client.

Each social worker will value certain qualities from his or her upbringing and will cling to them because they are meaningful in his or her life. If social workers can empathize with the importance of values to a client, then perhaps the planning of social services will have a context and impelling force to operate. For example, Chinese traditionally value education and achievement. If a social worker comes from a background that values achievement and education, perhaps he or she will be able to remove the barrier of color and better understand the strength of valuing education and use it in planning services for someone who is Chinese. There are certainly differences between the values of social workers and their clients, but these differences no longer have to be a conscious or unconscious barrier. The understanding and appreciation of cultural values may allow for better helping relationships.

In the past, there were three skills in helping relationships: process, conceptualization, and personalization (Lum, 1999, citing Bernard, 1979). Presently, Lum (1999) has incorporated these skills into the assessment and intervention stages of his five stages of practice. In the assessment stage, Lum includes the assessment of cultural strengths and assessment conceptual skills, which "focus on cultural/ethnic group strengths and the use of indigenous sources of help" (1999, p. 179). Intervention process skills, Lum proposes, "implement the selection of culturally diverse intervention strategies" (1999, p. 179). These assessment and intervention skills are critical to culturally competent practice, but assessed cultural strengths need to have a direct impact on the choice of interventions. The assessed strengths of the client's cultural values should determine the design and planning of interventions. If the cultural strength of extended family is assessed, then recommending and implementing individual therapy may be contraindicated. If spirituality is central to the belief system of a culture, to omit or neglect it is no longer acceptable for culturally competent practice. Historically, social workers have ignored cultural values or, at best, we have been asked to "be aware" or "be sensitive" to them. Now it is mandatory that we know what they are for every client system of color with which we interact. To be culturally competent is to know the cultural values of the client system and to use them in planning and implementing services. Cultural values can no longer be treated as tangential; they must be the basis of services to ethnic minority clients. This requires culturally competent social work practice to shift to the strengths of the client, extracted from the cultural value system, as a means of identifying resources for empowerment. This shift mandates that knowledge acquisition, as included in Lum's cultural competency model (1999), be directly applied at the skill development stage.

Thus, an extension of Lum's model for culturally competent practice would be:

1. Cultural awareness: The social workers' understanding and the identification of the critical cultural values important to the client system and to themselves.

2. Knowledge acquisition: The social workers' understanding of how these cultural values function as strengths in the client's system.

3. Skill development: The social workers' ability to match services that support the identified cultural values and then incorporate them in the appropriate interventions.

4. Inductive learning: The social workers' continued quest to seek solutions, which includes finding other indigenous interventions and matching cultural values to Western interventions.

Fong, Boyd, and Browne (1999) promote the biculturalization of interventions, because making Asians, Pacific Islanders, or any non-Western client change to fit a Westernized environment or using Western interventions for adaptation purposes may not be a culturally acceptable solution. Instead, practitioners should be taking a part of the client's culture and adapting the Western interventions to accommodate and reinforce the client's worldview. A biculturalization of interventions model is proposed for both the assessment and intervention stages of the social work process. The five steps of the process are:

1. Identifying the important values in the ethnic culture that can be used to reinforce therapeutic interventions;

2. Choosing a Western intervention whose theoretical framework and values are compatible with the ethnic cultural values of the family client system;

3. Analyzing an indigenous intervention familiar to the ethnic client system in order to discern which techniques can be reinforced and integrated with a Western intervention;

4. Developing a framework and approach that integrates the values and techniques of the ethnic culture with the Western interventions; and

5. Applying the Western intervention, at the same time explaining to a family client how the techniques reinforce cultural values and support indigenous interventions (p. 105).

Although a change in the practice of developing interventions is important, it is also imperative that culturally competent practice includes the evaluation of organizations in communities. Gutierrez (1992) emphasizes that the empowerment of ethnic minorities happens at the macro level with organizational and community change. The Multicultural Counseling and Development psychologists and counselors (Sue et al., 1998, p. 120) have defined multicultural counseling competence as being able to:

- Develop experiences related to personal multicultural competence, such as reading literature, using cultural guides, attending cultural events, learning to ask sensitive cultural questions
- Develop experiences related to professional multicultural competence
- Develop and propose strategies for organizational multicultural competence

Multicultural counselors stress that multicultural competence will occur as change happens in the personal, professional, and organizational levels. In order to develop culturally appropriate intervention strategies, Sue and colleagues urge us

to free ourselves from traditional definitions of counseling and psychotherapy; to expand the boundaries of professional practice and the repertoire of interpersonal helping skills; to expand and use alternative helping roles; and to learn from indigenous models of healing (1998, p. 80).

The Multicultural Counseling and Development psychologists and psychotherapists advocate that their counselors be trained to use indigenous models of healing. Social work academicians are also educating their practitioners to include indigenous strategies of helping. This book makes cultural values the foundation of performing assessments, implementing interventions, and conducting evaluations. It also requires a biculturaliztion or multiculturalization of practice methods, incorporating the norms and practices of the appropriate ethnic groups, which can then be supplemented by Euro-American practices. This is the shift in perspective that needs to guide the development of cultural competency as the helping professions enter the twenty-first century.

REFERENCES

Arrendondo, P., Toporek, R., Brown, S., Jones, J., Locke, D., Sanchez, J., & Stadler, H. (1996). Operationalization of the multicultural counseling competencies. *Journal of Multicultural Counseling and Development, 24,* 42–78.

Bernard, J. (1979). Supervisor training: A discrimination model. *Counselor Education and Supervision, 19,* 60–68.

Child Welfare League of America. (1993). *Cultural competence self-assessment instrument.* Washington, DC: Author.

Cross, T., Bazron, B., Dennis, K., & Isaacs, M. (1989). *Towards a culturally competent system of care.* Washington, DC: CASSP Technical Assistance Center.

Dana, R. (1998). *Understanding cultural identity in intervention and assessment.* Thousand Oaks, CA: Sage.

Davis, L. & Proctor, E. (1989). Race, gender, and class: Guidelines for practice with individuals, families, and groups. Englewood Cliffs, NJ: Prentice Hall.

Devore W. & Schlesinger, E. (1981). *Ethnic-sensitive social work practice.* St. Louis: C. V. Mosby.

Devore, W. & Schlesinger, E. (1996). *Ethnic-sensitive social work practice.* Boston, MA: Allyn and Bacon.

Devore, W. & Schlesinger, E. (1999). *Ethnic-sensitive social work practice,* 5th ed. Boston, MA: Allyn and Bacon.

Fong, R. (1997). Child welfare practice with Chinese families: Assessment issues for immigrants from the People's Republic of China. *Journal of Family Social Work, 2,* 33–48.

Fong, R., Boyd, T., & Browne, C. (1999). The Gandhi technique: A biculturalization approach for empowering Asian and Pacific Islander families. *Journal of Multicultural Social Work, 7,* 95–110.

Green, J. (1982). *Culture awareness in the human services,* Englewood Cliffs, NJ: Prentice-Hall.

Green, J. (1995). *Culture awareness in the human services,* 2nd ed. Englewood Cliffs, NJ: Prentice-Hall.

Green, J. (1999). *Culture awareness in the human services,* 3rd ed. Boston, MA: Allyn and Bacon.

Gutierrez, L. (1992). Empowering ethnic minorities in the twenty-first century. In Yeheskel Hasenfeld (Ed.), *Human services as complex organizations* (pp. 320–338). Newbury Park, CA: Sage.

Guitierrez, L., Parsons, R., & Cox. E. (Eds.) (1998). Empowerment in Social work practice: A source book. Pacific Grove, CA: Brooks/Cole.

Ho, M. K. (1987). *Family therapy with ethnic minorities.* Newbury Park, CA: Sage.

Inglehart, A. & Becerra, R. (1995). *Social services and the ethnic community.* Boston, MA: Allyn and Bacon.

Lecca, P., Quervalu, I., Nunes, J., & Gonzales, H. (1998). *Cultural competency in health, social, and human services.* New York: Garland.

Leigh, J. (1998). *Communication for cultural competence.* Boston, MA: Allyn and Bacon.

Lum, D. (1999). *Culturally competent practice.* Pacific Grove, CA: Brooks/Cole.

Lum, D. (2000). *Social work practice and people of color,* 4th ed. Pacific Grove, CA: Brooks/ Cole.

Lum, D. & Lu, E. (1997). Developing cultural competency within a culturally sensitive environment. Paper presented to the Council on Social Work Education annual program meeting. Chicago, Illinois. March.

Lynch, E. & Hanson, M. (1998). *Developing cross-cultural competence,* 2nd ed. Baltimore, MD: Brookes.

McAdoo, H. (Ed.). (1993). *Family ethnicity: Strength in diversity.* Newbury Park, CA: Sage.

McGoldrick, M., Giordano, J., & Pearce, J. (1996). *Ethnicity and family therapy.* New York: Guilford.

Mokuau, N. (1998). *Responding to Pacific Islanders: Culturally competent perspectives for substance abuse Prevention.* Washington, DC: U.S. Department of Health and Human Services. Center for Substance Abuse Prevention. Cultural Competence Series, No. 8.

Mokuau, N. & Shimizu, D. (1991). Conceptual framework for social services for Asian and Pacific Islander Americans. In Noreen Mokuau. (Ed.), *Handbook of social services for Asian and Pacific Islanders* (pp. 21–36). New York: Greenwood Press.

Norton, D. (1978). *Dual perspectives: The inclusion of ethnic minority content in social work curriculums.* New York: Council on Social Work Education.

Okun, B. (1996). *Understanding diverse families.* New York: Guilford.

Philleo, J. & Brisbane, F. (1996). *Cultural competence in substance prevention.* Washington, DC: National Association of Social Work.

Pinderhughes, E. (1989). *Understanding race, ethnicity, and power.* New York: Free Press.

Pinderhughes, E. (1995). Empowering diverse populations as a basis of empowerment strategy. *Families in Society, 76,* 131–140.

Ponterotto, J., Casas, J. M., Suzuki, L., & Alexander, C. (1995). *Handbook of multicultural counseling.* Thousand Oaks, CA: Sage.

Pope-Davis, D. & Coleman, H. (Eds.). (1997). *Multicultural counseling competencies: assessment, education and training, and supervision.* Thousand Oaks, CA: Sage.

Pope-Davis, D. & Dings, J. (1995). The assessment of multicultural counseling competencies. In J. G. Ponterotto, J. M. Casas, L. Suzuki, & C. Alexander (Eds.), *Handbook of multicultural counseling* (pp. 287–311). Thousand Oaks, CA: Sage.

Saleebey, D. (1997). The strengths perspective in social work practice. 2nd ed. White plains, NY: Longman.

Sue, D., Arrendondo, P., & McDavis, R. (1992). Multicultural counseling competencies and standards: A call to the profession. *Journal of Counseling and Development, 70,* 477–486.

Sue, D., Carter, R., Casas, J., Fouad, N., Ivey, A., Jensen, M., LaFromboise, T., Manese, J., Poterotto, J., & Vazquez-Nutall, E. (1998). *Multicultural counseling competencies: Individual and organizational development.* Thousand Oaks, CA: Sage.

Suzuki, L., Meller, P., & Ponterotto, J. (1996). *Handbook of multicultural assessment.* San Francisco, CA: Jossey-Bass.

Vargas, L. & Koss-Chioino, J. (Eds). (1992). *Working with culture.* San Francisco, CA: Jossey-Bass.

Zayas, L. H., Evans, M. E., Mejia, L., & Rodriguez, O. (1997). Cultural competency training for staff serving Hispanic families with a child in psychiatric crisis. *Families in Society, 78,* 405–412.

CHAPTER 2

THEORETICAL FRAMEWORKS: ECOLOGICAL MODEL, STRENGTHS PERSPECTIVE, AND EMPOWERMENT THEORY

COLETTE BROWNE

CRYSTAL MILLS

The resurgence of interest in empowering the disenfranchised and poor in the United States has been tied to the liberal reform agenda, which has changed the face of poverty programming in the nation (see Zippay, 1995). Since the passage of the 1988 Family Support Act, there has been increased momentum for reforms that would link social supports to personal responsibility (Young, 1999). In his 1993 address to a joint session of Congress, President Bill Clinton pledged to "change the whole focus of our poverty programs from entitlement to empowerment" (Zippay, 1995, p. 263). In 1994, with the endorsement of Republicans, the idea of devolution had become a favored policy choice. States were given greater flexibility and responsibility in determining social agendas and designing and administering social programs (Young, 1999). In 1996, the Personal Responsibility and Work Opportunity Reconciliation Act was passed, and the Aid to Families with Dependent Children program was replaced with block grants to states to support Temporary Assistance for Needy Families (TANF). At the same time, specific Federal programs and initiatives such as "Empowerment Zones," "Strong Families/Safe Children," and "Kinship Care" have rolled out across the nation in support of this new agenda; all of them emphasize family and community decisions and responsibility. These initiatives have been supported by an ideologically diverse group of policymakers who are seeking solutions to a variety of social problems.

At a philosophical level, this new direction in government appears congruent with the social work value of self-direction. In practice, however, social workers have struggled with the definition of empowerment and how to incorporate capacity-building strategies into social work practice. As the nation's demographic profile continues to change, new issues and concerns come to the fore. Increasingly, social workers are confronted with issues related to multicultural, multirace, and multiethnic practice (Gutierrez, 1990). With the demographic shift toward an older U.S. citizenry, issues related to aging are of increased concern (Hooyman & Kiyak, 1999; Torres-Gil, 1992). Demographic data also detail the shrinking of the middle class, and growing numbers of poor Americans (Jansson, 1997), most of whom are women and children (Ozawa & Kirk, 1996) and, in addition, members of minority groups (Abramowitz, 1995). These demographic changes have not gone unnoticed by social work practitioners, who are charged with implementing empowering and capacity-building strategies among those who possess the least power and social resources in this nation (Guiterrez, Parsons, & Cox, 1998a & b; Ozawa, 1986; Torres-Gil, 1992).

The profession of social work has traditionally focused on assisting oppressed and vulnerable populations. Most often, consumers of social service are racial and cultural minorities who have been subjected to negative valuations and unequal treatment in U.S. society. Clearly, not all ethnic or cultural groups are subject to the same type of discrimination and oppression. Nonetheless, racial and cultural minorities face many difficulties that persons from the majority group do not (Morales & Sheafor, 1998). For many of these groups, negative valuation and oppression have been constant forces in their lives. These forces have become incorporated into family and community processes and have shaped the lives and limited the life chances of the poor and the oppressed (Solomon, 1976). Inadequate and substandard schools, poor housing, lack of employment opportunities, discrimination, and crime in the streets are their realities (Mokuau, 1991). Many of the poor see the members of their community fall victim to forces they cannot control, and are skeptical about their own abilities to control their fate. Social workers employed in agencies established to help marginalized and oppressed groups can end up feeling as powerless as the people they are attempting to assist.

Long recognized among social workers is the importance of understanding the multiple and complex interactions that exist among the individual, the family, and the greater community as a prerequisite for effective practice. In order to intervene in meaningful and beneficial ways on behalf of consumers, social work has recently focused its attention on the development of a theoretical and practice base built on three perspectives that shape the ways in which we view people and the methods by which we help them. These include the ecological model for understanding individual, family, and community behavior, the strengths perspective, and empowerment theory.

In this chapter, we will discuss the ways in which empowerment theory and the strengths perspective, building on the ecological model, can help social workers empower themselves and the consumers they work with. The conceptual framework provided by the ecological perspective, together with strategies and ideas from the strengths perspective and empowerment theory, has the potential to help social workers support the abilities and skills of individuals, families, groups, and communities to act on their own beliefs to improve their lives. Special attention will be given to the relevance of these strategies and ideas when working with racial/cultural minorities and oppressed groups.

THE ECOLOGICAL MODEL

> As opposed to other models of behavior used in social work practice that largely depend on ideas current in the allied social and behavioral sciences, the ecological model is one that grows directly out of our profession's dual commitment to the person and to the environment (Brower, 1988, p. 411).

In recent years, the ecological model has become the prevailing perspective for social work practice (Brower, 1988). Saleebey (1998) suggests that the ecological perspective is not a model or a theory that can be scientifically tested, but is, rather, a paradigmatic shift in how we look and think about practice. Similarly, Germain and Gitterman (1980) describe the ecological perspective as a useful "metaphor" that provides a set of categories to guide the way social workers think about cases. For the assessment process, it provides a sound conceptual framework for organizing and understanding case information and an adaptive view of individuals in continuous transactions with the environment. The ecological perspective attempts to capture the process of "dynamic equilibrium" in person-in-environment interaction (see Brower, 1988) through a set of explanatory principles: The individual actively manipulates the environment and environmental forces mold and shape the individual. As a conceptual framework from which to understand complex human transactions, the ecological perspective has received much recognition. Consequently, it stands out as the most influential and widely accepted generic framework for social work practice (Wakefield, 1996).

Roots and Definition of the Ecological Perspective

The ecological perspective in social work practice borrows from the science of human ecology (see Germain & Gitterman, 1995). The science of human ecology relates to the sensitive balance between humans and their environments and the ways in which such interactions can be enhanced. According to ecological theory, people are bound to the biotic (living) and abiotic (nonliving) elements in their environment by an intricate web of relationships (Ehrlich, Ehrlich, & Holdren, 1977). Interactions between individuals and their environment are thought to be critical for growth and survival. Embedded in the physical environment, humans interact with and modify the environment. Interdependence characterizes the relationship between the physical and biological elements of the environment. This interdependence led ecologists to coin the term *ecosystem* (short for *ecological system*) to describe the functional unit that contains all living and nonliving elements (see Ehrlich, Ehrlich, & Holdren, 1977).

The ecological perspective in social work extends the science of . **13**
ogy to social work practice (Germain & Gitterman, 1995). As in the natural .
the term *ecosystem* in social work is a combination of ideas from the ecologica.
spective and general systems theory (Wakefield, 1996). *Ecosystem* refers to a theore.
ical self-contained unit that represents a distinct community of interrelations.
Within this community of interrelations, elaborate systems and structures exist that
provide opportunity for individuals to meet their physical, psychological, social,
and spiritual needs. Needed supports, supplies, and stimulation flow from environmental systems and structures to the individual and the individual ventures out
into the environment to find opportunities for growth and development. The nature
of these dynamic, two-way transactions determines the "person-in-environment
fit." If the "fit" is good, transactions flow smoothly and the individual experiences
health and growth. Difficulty in the person-in-environment fit is thought to result in
problematic behaviors and/or situations (Germain, 1979; Wakefield, 1996).

Though the profession of social work has a historical commitment to the interactional and relational aspects of human problems—person-in-environment—the
ecological metaphor as a conceptual framework for practice was not introduced
until 1973 (Germain, 1973). The introduction of the ecological perspective provided social workers with a framework for understanding how the environment
affects and is affected by human development and functioning. It also made "clear
the need to view people and (their) environments as a unitary system within a particular cultural and historic context" (Germain & Gitterman, 1995, p. 816).

The ecosystems perspective brings with it principles of systems function that
help to guide the social worker's assessment of complex, reciprocal patterns of
exchange between the person (as a system) and systems in the environment. Systems theory emphasizes notions such as equifinality (change in one element in a
system reverberates throughout linked systems), homeostasis and equilibrium,
interconnectedness, and interdependence, suggesting complex, circular relationships between and among linked systems (see Wakefield, 1996). Ecosystem assessments embrace these notions through the assessment of circular causality. Such
assessments seek to capture the complexity of human phenomena through
dynamic interactional patterns (Germain & Gitterman, 1995; Wakefield, 1996).

Key Components, Principles, and Assumptions

The ecological perspective suggests that a sensitive balance exists between individuals and their environments and that this mutuality can be enhanced and maintained.
Key to the ecological perspective is the concept of "person-in-environment"—a
person is involved in constant interaction with various systems in the environment.
These systems include the family, friends, work, social services, politics, religious systems, goods and services, and educational systems. The person is portrayed as being
dynamically involved with each outside system (Hartman, 1979).

The assumption of the ecological perspective is that social work practice is
directed at improving the interactions between the person and the various environmental systems—"the person-in-environment fit." This direction for practice

requires an expanded focus in the assessment of problematic concerns and situations and in the development of intervention strategies. The ecological perspective provides a way for social workers to interpret and examine client situations by focusing on the interactions between individuals, systems, and the environment.

Germain (1979) suggests that the ecological perspective rests on an adaptive, evolutionary view of people in transaction with their environments. The following principles are derived from that view:

1. People live in an environment that includes air, water, and food, but it also includes elaborate structures through which humans meet their needs. Work systems, welfare systems, churches, and schools are all examples of such structures.

2. People must maintain a relationship with these structures in order to survive and grow.

3. People and their environments are continuously changing and accommodating one another. Supports, supplies, and stimulation flow to individuals from the environment, and people actively move out into the environment to find opportunities to develop.

4. People also have connections with the environment that are stressful and conflicted. Stress and conflict are part of the world of any living system.

5. Some sort of balance between stressful and supportive connections must be achieved if a person is to survive and develop.

The Ecological Model with Individuals, Families, Groups, and Communities

Each person's ecosystem is unique, with varying characteristics and patterns of influence. It is this uniqueness, the idiosyncratic patterns that develop in the individual's attempt to satisfy human needs and master developmental tasks within the ecosystem, that is important for social work assessment (see Bronfenbrenner, 1979; Hepworth & Larsen, 1990).

One conceptual model that has been employed to capture the ecosystems perspective and circular causality in practice settings uses four concentric circles, each delineating a system boundary. Influence between and among the various systems within the ecosystem is dynamic and reciprocal. Forces stemming from each system impact on and are impacted by the other systems (Bronfenbrenner, 1979).

The diagram in Figure 2.1 provides a simple, understandable way to conceptualize complex transactions and interactions within an ecosystem. The innermost circle denotes the individual as a system. To assess the functioning of the individual as a system, the social worker must consider dynamic interactions among biophysical, cognitive, emotional, developmental, motivational, and behavioral subsystems. Though all subsystems may not play a significant role in the identified behavior or situation, the individual strives for equilibrium among all subsystems. For example, as a person grows and develops, change produces disequilibrium. All subsystems make adjustments in response to change in an attempt to create renewed balance. Further, the principle of equifinality suggests that change in one part of a

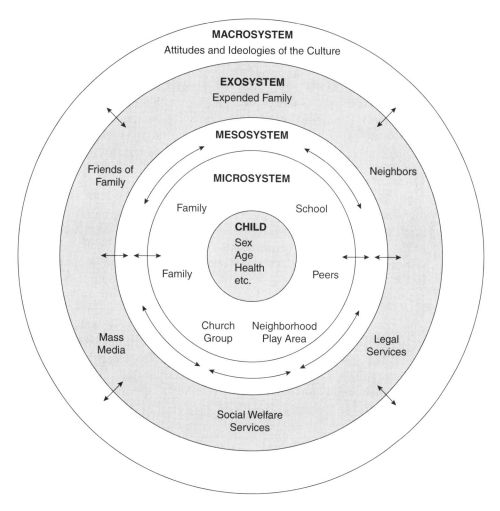

FIGURE 2.1   Bronfenbrenner's model of the ecology of human development. From Garbarino, 1982b, p. 648.

system may produce unexpected change anywhere in linked systems. Therefore, it is important to consider all subsystems in assessment. Overlooking relevant systems results in partial and/or erroneous understandings (see Hepworth & Larsen, 1990).

Moreover, the evaluation of individual function requires extensive knowledge about and consideration of other systems that impinge on the individual system. As illustrated in the diagram, the individual system is embedded in a microsystem that usually includes the family, neighborhood, school, and peers. Considerations in the assessment of family systems include rules, roles, composition, atmosphere, and structure. These characteristics govern interactional patterns, communication, problem solving, and decision making within the family system.

Family characteristics and function are influenced by the characteristics of each individual member, and each individual member is influenced by family characteristics and function and by every other member of the family. The more individual systems that are accommodated within the family system, the greater the level of complexity for the social work assessment.

Hartman (1979) suggests that looking at a family system ecologically leads a social worker to consider what may be an overwhelming mass of complex, interrelated information. To assist in organizing this complexity, Hartman developed a practice tool called the *EcoMap*. EcoMapping is a process of mapping exchanges and interfaces of a consumer system with other systems in its environment. The EcoMap conveys a lot of information in a simple way and is used primarily as an interviewing and assessment tool.

Because the family system is embedded in a community system, the boundaries and interface of the family system with other systems in the community are critical for the social work assessment (see Hartman, 1979). Educational systems, religious systems, social welfare systems, child care systems, and work systems are but a few of the various systems that may exist within a given community (grouped in the diagram under mesosystem, exosystem, and macrosystem). Each community has different physical characteristics, resources, and problems that may impact the family system or individual members of the family directly. The larger exosystems and macrosystems provide additional considerations for assessment that are related to the historical/cultural context that translate into larger societal values. Laws, policies, programs, and values determine to a large extent the environmental forces that will ultimately shape communities and the quality of life for families and for individuals.

The Ecological Model and Cultural Competence

Germain and Gitterman's (1995) discussion of niche and habitat appears particularly relevant in determining the significance of ecosystems theory for social work with oppressed and vulnerable groups. Oppressive niches and habitats create indirect and direct power blocks that reinforce powerlessness among vulnerable groups (Solomon, 1976). The ecological perspective directs the social worker to an assessment of environmental forces that diminish personal power and the development of strategies that will assist disempowered groups in developing a sense of personal power and gaining control over their lives.

A first step in this process for the social worker is developing an understanding of power dynamics and how powerlessness is reinforced through oppressive niches and habitats. A niche represents a unique place within the environment where, through dynamic transactions, the individual has a "fit." It refers to the status of a person in the social structure of the environment (Germain & Gitterman, 1995). More technically, the niche is that portion of the environment where the individual has made accommodation and is interdependent. The notion of niche has been equated with Lewin's notion of "life space," which is inclusive of all internal and external processes that are operative in a given situation (Brower, 1988). The primary difference is the notion that life space is time-dependent while niche is assumed to be somewhat stable over time (Brower, 1988).

In the United States, one's niche is dictated by both ascribed and achieved attributes. Ascribed attributes, such as gender, age, and ethnicity, have historically been powerful predictors of niche. Solomon (1976) discusses how attributes such as race and ethnicity may dictate a niche that does not support human rights and provides only limited opportunities for meeting needs and aspirations. Her thesis is that some individuals and groups, specifically African Americans, have been subjected to niches that are oppressive and create indirect power blocks. Indirect power blocks stem from negative valuations that stigmatize and isolate occupants. Solomon argues that one of the "more insidious . . . consequences" of niches that carry negative valuations is an "overriding sense of one's powerlessness to direct one's own life" (p. 13). This internalized powerlessness becomes incorporated into family processes, limits the development of skills, and reduces effectiveness in the performance of valued social roles (Solomon, 1976).

Similarly, oppressive habitats carry negative valuations that translate into the absence of vital resources and opportunities. Human habitats are places where people dwell. These include "physical layouts of urban and rural communities; physical settings of schools, workplaces, hospitals, social agencies, shopping areas, and religious structures; and parks and other amenities" (Germain & Gitterman, 1995, p. 818). Habitats evoke attitudes and behaviors that, in turn, shape and color the environment. For example, poor schools, lack of adequate housing, unemployment, crime, drugs, and violence in a community create a negative expectation set and living becomes a daily struggle to maintain a positive sense of self. Solomon argues that such habitats provide direct power blocks that are experienced on three levels: (1) inadequate services that lead to poor health and living conditions; (2) limitations placed on educational opportunities so persons with potential are not provided opportunities to develop it; and (3) material resources that are important for the performance of valued social roles are denied (p. 18).

A major advantage of the ecosystems perspective for social work with oppressed and vulnerable groups is its breadth. It moves the profession away from the tendency to focus on "individual pathology" and brings to the change effort knowledge of diverse systems, as well as an understanding of how personality, culture, age, gender, socioeconomic status, and experience shape transactions with the environment and reinforce oppressive niches (see Germain & Gitterman, 1995). It provides a conceptual framework from which to review and analyze complex transactions between and among the various systems. However, as noted in the literature, the ecosystems approach was built on the social work tradition of focusing on the problem (Weick, Rapp, Sullivan, & Kisthardt, 1989). Emphasis is placed on the ability to adequately assess difficulties in the "person-in-environment fit" and interventions are designed to improve the "fit" by reducing or eliminating negative transactions (Germain & Gitterman, 1980). This often translates into individual change to help the oppressed person to "fit" better into the dominant culture.

As we move into a discussion of the strengths approach and empowerment theory, "We must ask about the extent to which our efforts to help clients actually maintain the social system equilibrium that victimizes them" (Pinderhughes, 1983, p. 333).

STRENGTHS PERSPECTIVE

> The strengths perspective . . . subscribes to the belief that people have credible, though often untapped or unknown, resources for transformation and development (Saleebey, 1997, p. 176).

As Weick and colleagues (1989) have noted, the social work profession is one of many helping professions that has historically focused on a deficit, pathology model for understanding individual and community behavior. In contract, the strengths perspective/model assumes that consumers and communities have skills and resources that can be further developed and used to enhance functioning (Saleebey, 1997). In some ways, the idea of identifying strengths has always been part of the social work process, more in theory than practice, perhaps. The strengths model, however, requires a paradigm shift whereby social workers and other helping professions are called on to move away from pathologizing individuals, families, and communities (Rapp, 1998; Weick, 1983; Weick, Rapp, Sullivan, & Kisthardt, 1989). As described by Sullivan (1998), the strengths perspective is an alternative way of viewing people. Consumers of services are not viewed as "damaged" or having "deficits"; rather, they are viewed in relation to their potential. The focus is on "real life goals in real life settings." As an evolving model and approach to practice, the strengths perspective seeks to "define those factors affecting a person's life and the methods by which they can be altered" (Rapp, 1998, p. 24). Consumer goals, then, are self-directed, concrete, and growth-oriented, reflecting a focus on options and possibilities.

Roots and Definition of the Strengths Perspective

The emphasis on problems and pathology in social work practice established a conceptual trend that is still evident today. Historically, the profession supported this view: The process of client diagnosis emphasized individual weaknesses. While Jane Addams attempted to influence the profession with her view of the community's potential, Mary Richards's adoption of empirical methods and her evidence-based, outcome-oriented method of helping led to the importance of problem-defined interventions. The focus on problems was further supported by the introduction of psychoanalytic theory, which was adopted by many social workers. More recent directions in social work have embraced the ecological perspective discussed in the previous section (see Germain & Gitterman, 1980). According to these authors, the complex interactions between people and their communities can result in maladaptive strategies or difficulties, referred to as "upsets" in the "usual adaptive balance or goodness-of-fit." Rapp (1998) argues that the focus on "upsets" is equivalent to a subtle focus on individual and/or environment deficits, and that this focus persists today. According to Rapp, the emphasis on understanding these "upsets" insinuates that the "problem" is created either by characteristics of the individual or characteristics of the environment. This perspective results in problem-solving methods that too often focus on helping the individual adapt to the environment.

The strengths perspective was developed in response to some of the concerns with problem-focused methods. Since the late 1980s, there has been mounting attention in the social work literature to this perspective. Impetus for the strengths perspective derives from continued critique of the "problem focus" in social work on both a philosophical and a practical level (Saleeby, 1997; Weick, Rapp, Sullivan, & Kisthardt, 1989). Philosophically, the focus on problems and liabilities makes it difficult for the practitioner to embrace and express belief in individual and collective dignity, worth, strength, and potential. On a practical level, the focus on problems makes it difficult for consumers to believe in their ability to set their lives on course (Weick, Rapp, Sullivan, & Kisthardt, 1989).

In contrast to the problem-focused approaches, the strengths perspective in social work practice is congruent with the philosophical values of the profession (Weick, Rapp, Sullivan, & Kisthardt, 1989). Strengths-based practice acknowledges the positive attributes and strengths of consumers and seeks to enhance abilities. Strengths-based practice does not require that social workers ignore the problems (Saleebey, 1997). On the contrary, the problems that bring consumers to the attention of social work practitioners are real. However, these problems are not viewed by the practitioner as all-encompassing; rather, the social worker helps the consumer focus on possibilities, potentials, and the capacity for continued growth. In so doing, the practitioner empowers the consumer to resolve the problems. This perspective has been used with the mentally ill, substance abusers, and those on public assistance (see Rapp, 1998; Saleebey, 1997).

Over the past fifteen years, the strengths perspective has developed a number of values, principles, and methods that continue to be refined. While empirical testing of this approach has been somewhat limited, available data suggest that results from using the strengths perspective are better than the traditional approaches to serving people with mental illness (Kisthardt, 1993; Rapp & Chamberlain, 1985; Rapp & Wintersteen, 1989; Ryan, Sherman, & Judd, 1994).

Key Components, Prerequisites, and Assumptions

The key ideas of the strengths perspective found in the social work literature include the following:

1. All people have a reservoir of untapped, renewable, and expandable abilities (mental, physical, emotional, social, and spiritual) that can be used to facilitate change (Weick, Rapp, Sullivan, & Kisthardt, 1989).

2. The realization of abilities and accomplishments builds capacity and motivation, and diminishes concerns. People and communities can learn, grow, and change (Saleebey, 1997).

3. All people have the wisdom and capacity to determine the best healing and course of action for themselves (Weick & Pope, 1988).

4. Interventions must be built on client and community self-determination. Need is conceptualized as potential, not pathology, achievement, not problem solving (Rapp, 1998; Weick, Rapp, Sullivan, & Kisthardt, 1989).

5. In the complexity of life and living, what may appear to be wrong choices are a person's attempt to do what is best at the time (Weick, Rapp, Sullivan, & Kisthardt, 1989).

6. No professional is able to judge how a person should live his or her life (Weick, Rapp, Sullivan, & Kisthardt, 1989).

7. The goal of social work intervention is to hear what consumers have to say in order to appreciate their strengths and to collaborate with them to gain access to information, resources, and tools to resolve their own problems and achieve their aspirations, hopes, and dreams (see Weick & Saleebey, 1995).

8. Empowerment, or discovering the power that exists in people and communities, is a goal that people aspire to and that consumers and professionals collaborate to achieve. This is done through providing options and choices, building on individual and community confidence, and encouraging action; it is a desired state of the strengths approach (Rapp, 1998).

The Strengths Perspective with Individuals, Families, Groups, and Communities

The strengths perspective suggests that individuals, families, and communities have strengths that are to be supported, utilized, and matched to other resources so that people can reach their potential. More than just effective social work practice, it requires that all aspects of practice be reexamined and challenged, from the conceptualization of issues and need to intervention planning, implementation, and evaluation (Sullivan, 1998).

The literature identifies four major strategies for building a strengths approach with consumers: collaborating with consumers, providing enabling niches, giving voice to consumers, and exploiting community resources (Rapp, 1998; Weick, Rapp, Sullivan, & Kisthardt, 1989; Weick & Saleebey, 1995). When working with individuals, families, and groups, the social worker collaborates with them to reach their potential. The consumer is viewed as the expert, and by listening to what the consumer has to say, the social worker can appreciate the strengths and begin to understand the consumer's uniqueness. In this way, the consumer is elevated from a "passive recipient of services to the director of the process" (Sullivan, 1998). Sullivan (1998) further suggests that case management that incorporates the strengths approach "helps others reclaim full citizenship, replete with all of the rights and responsibilities that come with citizenship."

The achievement of desired consumer or community outcomes, such as quality of life, achievement of goals, sense of competence, life satisfaction, and/or empowerment, is enhanced by utilizing ideas from the ecological perspective together with the strengths approach. Taylor (1997) suggests that individual strengths, aspirations, competence, and confidence are either supported or not by niches and environmental strengths. As defined earlier in this chapter, enabling niches and habitats are those statuses and physical environments related to oppression that address individual and community factors and produce life bene-fits. Taylor differentiates entrapping niches from enabling ones. Entrapping niches stigmatize people, isolate and segregate them, give few resources or incentives to reach goals, offer few opportunities to learn new skills, and provide sparse resources. In contrast, enabling niches do not stigmatize or label people; rather, they provide adequate resources or incentives to reach goals and opportunities for learning new skills. It follows, then, that one strategy that may be employed by the practitioner in the strengths approach is to create and support enabling niches, thereby assisting consumers to help themselves. Using ideas from empowerment theory, "consciousness-raising," whereby the unequal access to power that too often results in entrapping niches is identified and confronted, may assist the practitioner in reducing the barriers to enabling niches. It can also be helpful to leverage professional associations, political leaders and coalitions, the media, and community leaders to develop and improve social policies that affect the oppressed and the poor (Germain 1979, Germain & Gitterman, 1995).

Another strategy that will help the practitioner use the strengths approach is to honor consumer stories. Often not told, sometimes not believed, usually not respected, consumer stories hold much potential for identifying strengths and pos-sibilities. If the practitioner is able to help consumers give voice to their personal stories, on an individual level, their strength and power in the helping relationship may be realized. In the telling of personal stories, both the consumer and the prac-titioner are able to recognize efforts, successes, and skills demonstrated in times of intense difficulty. The telling of stories also makes it possible to identify possible supports and communities of interest where the individual is respected and is able to blossom.

Exploiting and maximizing community strengths and resources is still another strategy that is used in the strengths approach. This strategy is built on the principle that considerable improvements in quality of life can only be achieved by capitalizing on community capacities (Kretzmann & McKnight, 1993). The strengths approach challenges communities to "move beyond the segregation impulse to embrace those who face serious challenges and to allow them to make their contribution to the human enterprise" (Sullivan, 1998: p. x). To accomplish this, it is important for the social worker to understand and note the community's assets, strengths, potential capabilities, and abilities. The mantra of the strengths approach community workers is: Every community is special and unique in its own way; every community has many strengths; and it is these strengths that must be mobilized in order to improve the life of that community.

The strengths perspective enters the arena of policy when social workers learn to deal with community stakeholders for resource allocation. Sullivan (1997) and Rapp (1998) describe strategies for community-based strengths practice. One is the data-based approach, whereby the community is mobilized to gather data, identify those who have a stake in the data, and instigate the group to act on the data. Another way is to create opportunities and options to fill concrete solutions to problems.

The Strengths Perspective and Cultural Competence

Many of the values and principles of the strengths perspective appear, at first reading, to be what all social workers do, as opposed to a new agenda for social work (Weick, 1992). Yet, not everyone appreciates the fact that the strengths perspective brings a new conceptual base to the profession. Saleebey (1997), for one, states that social work's emphasis on the strengths perspective is "little more than lip service," for the ideas of "centering practice on eliciting and articulating a client's internal and external resources has not been reasonably explicated as either an idea or practice" (p. 3). Rather, the continued emphasis in social work is on the client's weakness, deficits, problems, pathologies, and diseases. This focus on problem-based assessments encourages individualistic rather than ecological accounts of human predicaments and possibilities, which essentially disallows any societal responsibility for structural impediments to well-being, such as poverty, racism, and discrimination. Instead, once consumers become diseases and labels, they are then too easily discounted. This often leads, according to Saleebey, to a negative outlook about a consumer and the inability to see their hopes, possibilities, resilience, or resources.

   Much of the literature suggests that the oppressed themselves can internalize negative valuations and accept negative expectation (Freire, 1973; Solomon, 1976). After years of oppression and unmet need, identifying strengths can be quite challenging, especially when the consumer and the community doubt that they exist. Solomon (1976) offers a helpful differentiation that is often lost to those working with the needy and oppressed, the confusion between the concepts of strengths and power. Individuals, she states, "can be strong and have no power; empowerment oriented practice facilitates the process whereby individual strengths are transformed into collective power" (p. 34). People do have resources, although they may not recognize it. The strengths perspective, together with empowerment theory, works to help people recognize this fact, identify factors that serve as barriers to their well-being, and collaborate with others for new solutions.

EMPOWERMENT THEORY

> I saw nothing wrong with being who I was, but apparently many others did. My world grew larger but I felt I was growing smaller. I tried to disappear into myself in order to deflect the painful daily assaults designed to teach me that being an African American, working class woman made me less than those who were not. And as I felt small, I became quiet and eventually was silenced (P. H. Collins, 1991: p. xi).

These words, written by sociologist Patricia Hill Collins (1991), describe her childhood experiences with racism, sexism, and classism, which left her feeling disempowered and nearly without a voice. Too often, the oppressed experience feelings of powerlessness in their lives. The circumstances and events seem (and may in fact be) impossible to control (Gitterman & Shulman, 1986: Mokuau, 1990). But, as Solomon (1996) writes, the oppressed should have both a say and the right to have a say. Ensuring that the powerless not only speak their voice, but have it heard and respected, is a major challenge for the social work practitioner.

A critical focus of social work practice is empowering oppressed people to participate in the decisions that impact their lives, in fact, to have their say. Empowerment generally refers to the gaining of power by an individual, family group of persons, or a community. However, the definition of empowerment appears to depend on who is defining and using the term. In the social work literature, empowerment has been viewed at the personal/interpersonal level as the capacity of a person to influence the forces that affect his or her life. At a broader social/political level, empowerment has been viewed as a political process that benefits groups of people (see Breton, 1994). In this literature, it becomes clear that the definition and use of the term *empowerment* in the social work community is contingent on socio/political trends (see Zippay, 1995). Notwithstanding, two basic assumptions appear related to empowerment-oriented practice: (1) all human beings are potentially competent, even in extremely challenging situations, and (2) all human beings are subject to various degrees of powerlessness (Cox & Parsons, 1994, p. 17). Drawing from the ecological model, the social worker who incorporates empowerment principles into his or her work makes the connections between power and powerlessness when viewing the transactions between the consumer and his or her environment. These transactions, based on power dynamics, become critical for the assessment and subsequent intervention plans.

Definitions and Roots of Empowerment

Browne's (1995) review of the social work literature on empowerment identified three ways in which the term is generally defined: (1) as an intervention and product, (2) as a process, and (3) as a skill benefitting wide and diverse populations. The term *empowerment* was popularized in the 1970s by social work educator Barbara Bryant Solomon (1976). Her definition of *empowerment,* which is supported by Hegar and Hunzeker (1988) and McDermott (1989), describes both traditional and creative social work interventions and strategies that are especially effective with oppressed populations. Solomon argued that empowerment results when persons who belong to a stigmatized social category are assisted to develop and increase skills in interpersonal influence and the performance of valued social roles. As an intervention, empowerment begins with self-definition and self-esteem (Collins, 1991; Pinderhughes, 1983). Gutierrez (1990) viewed empowerment as a process rather than a product. In her work with women of color, women who were assisted in helping others developed enhanced capabilities. The empowerment of these women was a process whereby the focus on group empowerment increased group power and enhanced the functioning of individual members of the group.

Somewhat similarly, Pinderhughes (1983) viewed empowerment as a process in which the consumer's personal self-concept is nurtured and strengthened so that he or she is able to participate in collective action and change. Still others have defined *empowerment* as one of the major skills and responsibilities of those working in social welfare today (Mandell & Schram, 1985).

The roots of empowerment draw from a number of different, yet connected, life events and perspectives. Examples include the civil rights and black empowerment movements, the new left, nonviolent resistance (e.g., Gandhi), Chinese consciousness-raising, the African independence movements, liberation theory, the self-help movement, feminist theory, the disability rights movement, and gay and lesbian liberation (Simon, 1994). Each of these movements, theories, and philosophies, according to Simon (1994), "fueled the empowerment 'wing' of the profession" (p. 137). What each of these contributors have in common is the belief that powerlessness can be countered by personal journeys and action, community building, and social and political action.

Key Concepts, Principles, and Strategies

Regardless of whether one is practicing social work with individuals and families, at the community level, or in the policy and political arena, there exists a number of key concepts and strategies that characterize empowerment practice (Cox, 1991; Gutierrez, 1990; Parsons, 1991). As summarized by Gutierrez, Parsons, and Cox (1998b), they include:

1. The requisite attitudes, values, and beliefs around self-efficacy that extend from developing feelings of individual competency for the betterment of the community.

2. The validation of people's stories and the collective experience. It is in the sharing of self and personal experiences that one moves toward collective experience and action.

3. Knowledge and skills for critical thinking, access to information, and action based on critical analyses of structural forces that impact life and opportunity.

4. The importance of developing strategies for action that focus on individual and social change.

Moreover, Gutierrez, Parsons, and Cox (1998a, 1998b) also identify five central principles of empowerment practice. First noted is the imperative for social workers to provide a safe and supportive environment for the working relationship. It is through the working relationship that trust evolves and a sense of connection with the community emerges. Second, the social worker must seek to understand the consumer in the context of his or her environment. A consumer's cultural background provides important information for understanding and defining the issues, needs, strengths, and concerns. Third, the helping process must encourage empowerment via a relationship that promotes self-confidence, self-definitions, self-direction, self-respect, and self-control. Fourth, the value of the consumer's strengths is stressed through a collaborative style of helping. Finally, empowering practice requires workers to take on multiple roles such as broker, educator, advocate, and negotiator, and to teach new skills by modeling them in the helping relationship.

In addition to the concepts and principles outlined above, there are three generally recognized strategies for empowerment that work toward social justice and social change. They are: critical education and consciousness-raising, the democratization of the helping relationship, and a focus on client and community strengths, rather than problems (Guiterrez, Parsons, & Cox, 1998).

Empowerment Practice with Individuals, Families, Groups, and Communities

Empowerment practice is guided by the philosophy that interventions "should enhance mental, spiritual, and physical wellness, as well as social justice" (Cox & Joseph, 1998, p. 169). Empowerment works across fields of service, levels of practice, and with diverse populations. Consumer self-empowerment, as suggested by Simon (1994), "couples a client's pursuit of enhanced personal and social power with three interactive processes: . . . a firm sense of self worth . . . as a critically conscious and dignified member of . . . a stigmatized group, and a set of daily living and working skills that enable the person to survive and . . . thrive with greater authority, satisfaction and community than previously" (p. 162).

When working with individuals and families, empowerment strategies often emphasize teaching them about power dynamics and the systems in which they live (Pinderhughes, 1983). Pinderhughes suggests that it is important for consumers to understand the ways in which the social system supports or undermines their functioning as individuals and as a family. Social workers can facilitate these understandings by helping consumers to differentiate between difficulties stemming from the larger external environment and those that manifest at an individual level. Strategies to empower families, according to Pinderhughes, include the nurturance of the self, but also acknowledgment that change must occur on many levels. This approach requires that workers develop: (1) knowledge of themselves as participants in the societal projection process; (2) skills in using power on behalf of consumers and teaching consumers how to understand and use power; and (3) a readiness to share power with consumers (p. 338).

Specific implications exist for social workers working in culturally rich areas and with diverse groups. As Parsons, Gutierrez, and Cox (1998) note, consideration and respect for diversity include an understanding of how the consumer and worker, and his or her place in the social structure, can affect the problems, processes, possibilities, and outcomes. Thus, key strategies focus on educating both the consumer and worker in the development of mutual respect, a nonjudgmental approach, and collaborative processes to ensure that desired outcomes are reached. Empowerment-based social workers also seek to enlist their consumers as leaders in the development program and policy, and the evaluation of the effectiveness of outcomes.

A number of characteristics of empowerment-based practice with families has been suggested in the social work literature. Among these are "collaborative relationships between practitioners and family members, capacity building among families, and use of the resources and support that extended family members and non-kinship networks provide" (Hodges, Burwell, & Ortega, 1998, p. 161). In this way, families can be taught to utilize their own "strengths, gain access to needed resources, and develop life skills to function as a healthy family unit" (p. 161). These characteristics have special relevance for ethnic, minority, and cultural populations due to the multitude of potential negative environmental factors, such as racism, unemployment, poverty, and public health problems (Hodges, Burwell, & Ortega, 1998).

Empowerment practice is also useful from a group and community perspective. Guiterrez's (1990) definition focuses on the ways in which individual empowerment contributes to group empowerment and how increases in group power enhance the functioning of individual members. According to Hannah Arendt, a political feminist theorist, power and empowerment spring up whenever people come together and act. Legitimacy for power comes from the act of creating community (Arendt, 1958). A number of empowering processes have been suggested by Gitterman and Shulman (1986) to support empowerment-based practice with groups. Among the processes that have been suggested are the sharing of data, the "all-in-the-same-boat" phenomenon, strength in numbers, entering taboo discussion areas, mutual support and demand, and individual problem solving (p. 9). An example of empowerment-based community building was recently provided by Okazawa-Rey (1998) in her description of a self-help model used to empower African American grandmothers caring for their grandchildren. These grandmothers became involved in kinship care because the children's parents were involved in substance abuse behaviors. In describing the model, Okazawa-Rey details one strategy used at a community-based health care program that, working in partnership with their consumers, responded to the myriad needs of poor people of color in urban areas. This community-building approach was rooted in Afrocentric feminist epistemology, whereby Western male ideas of knowledge, truth, and leadership are confronted, resisted, and reconceptualized. A model of communication referred to as "call and response" was specifically adopted to empower the group members. In this method, each member speaks at will and anyone can then respond to the previous comment, a sign of commitment to the community's well-being. This type of exchange is "long extant in Afrocentric . . . tradition whereby power dynamics are fluid, and everyone has a voice, but everyone must listen and respond to other voices in order to be allowed to remain in the community" (Collins, 1991, p. 237). In using the call and response approach, the consumer's cultural background and experiences are honored and respected. Consumers are provided collective support and action, and their problems are analyzed from the structural inequalities that describe them (Okazawa-Rey, 1998). This exchange was far from a "gripe session." The grandmothers, who were all caring for their grandchildren with minimal financial resources, ended up collaborating with a state legislator in the passage of a bill that made it easier for grandparents in similar situations to receive payments and entitlements under the foster care system. This example shows how goal setting for empowerment practice can move from the personal to the interpersonal to the political (Parsons, Gutierrez, & Cox, 1998). Ann Weick (1994) has this to say about the relationship between personal power and power for the community good:

> Knowing that one has the ability to re-image her life is a fundamental aspect of personal power. To see things differently, to name things in new ways, is a source of power that is not given by others. It is a power, however, that can be shared with others, so that the act of seeing differently moves naturally into the realm of collective action. Once it is discovered and possessed, it serves as the seedbed for all other imaginings (p. 226).

Empowerment-based work in the community requires an understanding of power dynamics, group processes, interpersonal interaction, and organizational theory (Gutierrez, Parsons, & Cox, 1998a, p. 225; Hasenfeld, 1987). The challenge is to politicize and educate consumers, as well as social workers, to the value and potential of power. It is a well-understood fact that social workers use their power resources to influence outcomes in worker–consumer relationships. However, social work practice usually does not address the power of the agency over the performance of the worker. There tends to be an implicit assumption that social workers have sufficient autonomy and are able to buffer the worker–consumer relationship against agency intrusion. However, it is a fact that both worker and consumer interests are subordinated and shaped by organizational policies (Hasenfeld, 1987). Hasenfeld argues that agencies use power to shape the social work process. The agency sets the parameters of practice by controlling intake, case processing, and the termination of cases. However, the dynamics of power are such that, within the agency setting, some workers are able to "use their power advantage to improve the quality of their work by (controlling) . . . the type and number of clients they serve and by having greater access to sources of knowledge and expertise" (Hasenfeld, 1987, p. 477). When social workers have access to power resources within the agency, social work practice within the agency tends to be more effective. Workers who feel empowered are better able to empower consumers. Moreover, organizations that empower workers are more capable of empowering consumers and communities (Gutierrez, Glenmaye, & Delois, 1995).

Strategies that encourage empowerment practice in social work settings include: (1) the creation of an employment setting that provides for participatory management, (2) the ability of social workers to make independent decisions about their work, (3) support and open communication patterns with administrators, and (4) opportunities for skill development. Social work administrators and practitioners alike must commit themselves to the ideas and principles of democracy, equality and equity, social justice, nonviolence, and nonintimidation. Consumers like those grandmothers discussed by Okazawa-Rey (1998) understand well concepts like equality, equity, and social justice and the impact they have on their lives.

Empowerment practice does not ignore policy. It is important for social work professionals to examine research on social movements, social organizations, political economy, and political power to understand how to translate power from individual to collective levels (Gutierrez, Parsons, & Cox, 1998). Knowledge about policymakers and the policy process is essential for empowered action (Cox & Parsons, 1994). Social workers who are knowledgeable about and involved with the policy process are able to model this behavior for consumers. How to obtain information, how to understand both the formal and informal aspects of policy decisions, and how to analyze policy are just some of the skills that social workers must have and be able to model for consumers. In fact, these skills are requisite for empowerment practice on any level.

Empowerment Theory and Cultural Competence

As Solomon stated so many years ago, "empowerment work is not a panacea for the problems of the world or of social work practice" (1976, p. 33). Solas (1996), in his critique of empowerment, argues that a number of key assumptions, goals, and practices fundamental to empowerment are in fact less than empowering, and can actually perpetuate asymmetrical power relations between human service workers and consumers (p. 147). For example, practitioners are often assumed to have a more progressive worldview than consumers. However, this assumption may actually act to impede the empowerment of consumers. Additionally, practitioners often give the illusion of equality between themselves and the consumers with whom they work, especially when the authoritarian nature of the relationship is left unchallenged.

Solas suggests that there is a complex interplay between those that have and those that want. He suggests that social workers and consumers engage in a tentative discourse about the meaning of power in the helper–helpee relationship. When ethnic and cultural differences exist in the helping relationship, this discourse becomes even more important. The social worker and consumer must discuss the existence of any preconceived notions they may have about each other and the affect of such differences on their ability to collaborate (Davis & Proctor, 1989; Parsons, Gutierrez, & Cox, 1998).

Finally, the term *empowerment* itself holds different meanings for different people (Browne, 1995; Ewalt & Mokuau, 1995). Among certain oppressed populations, necessary components of empowerment, such as self-determination, should be reexamined. For example, Ewalt and Mokuau's writing on self-determination from a Pacific perspective highlights how varying definitions can impact assessment, goal setting, and intervention planning. A consumer whose culture values collective goal attainment, as opposed to individual goal attainment, cannot be criticized for an emphasis on group goals and norms. These authors recommend that the fundamental principles of social work, such as independence and self-determination, be scrutinized for cultural distortion (Ewalt & Mokuau, 1995).

A final thought for empowerment-based practice: Empowerment is not synonymous with devolution. It is not the transferring of governmental responsibility of the poor back to oppressed and vulnerable populations under the guise of "empowering communities." Poor communities and families still require assistance and resources. As Simon (1994) argues, "an empowered group of formerly disenfranchised people cannot be waived into existence by a cynical real politik that attempts to mask its systematic dismantling of the welfare state with oratory about the moral responsibility of individuals to take charge of their own lives" (p. 181). Empowerment is better realized on the community level when those with power, and the economic and structural institutions that support their power, commit themselves to the well-being of the greater community, instead of continuing the policy of domination that has benefitted only themselves (Simon, 1994).

SUMMARY

Neither practice, policy, nor national desire have alleviated or corrected existing inequalities that are too often determined by gender, race, ethnicity, age, and physical ability in U.S. society (Abramowitz, 1995; Dressel, 1988). The new political agenda that calls for personal responsibility does not address past transgressions, nor does it address the negative valuations that promote indirect and direct power blocks and inhibit empowerment among oppressed and marginal groups (Solomon, 1976). As many social workers have noted, the oppressed face onerous difficulties that the privileged and dominant do not (Longres, 1995; Ewalt & Mokuau, 1995). Problems, such as unemployment and underemployment, inaccessible and poor health care, failed schools, crime-ridden neighborhoods, inadequate and costly housing, discrimination, and lack of community-based resources, are faced daily by some groups. In many communities, the threat of violence is never far away, fueled by prejudice, ignorance, and fear. This stark and difficult reality can result in feelings of incompetence, hopelessness, and powerlessness (Solomon, 1976), can collude to institutionalize vulnerability and helplessness, but can also build individual and community strengths and numerous sites of resistance.

The complexity of forces that serve to disempower individuals and groups presents a major challenge for social work professionals, and the development of meaningful, empowering interventions with oppressed groups is a greater challenge. While the profession continues its struggle with these challenges, the new political agenda is moving forward. Welfare reform is rolling out across the nation. Programs and services are being reconceptualized to incorporate notions of local control and personal responsibility. The roles of social workers are changing, and more than ever the profession of social work needs to depend on a sound theoretical orientation and practice perspective to assist social service consumers in taking control of their lives.

The ecological perspective, together with ideas from the strengths perspective and empowerment theory, has the potential to assist social workers in understanding multiple and complex interactions between individuals, families, communities, and larger societal values, and developing culturally rich, empowering interventions. The ecological perspective helps social workers assess multiple interrelated and complex issues related to "person-in-environment." The strengths perspective shifts the focus from problems to possibilities, and emphasizes positive change. Finally, empowerment theory promotes understanding of power dynamics at all levels and suggests strategies to support consumer well-being and social justice.

REFERENCES

Abramowitz, M. (1995). From tenement class to dangerous class: Blaming women for social problems. In N. Van Den Bergh, (Ed.), *Feminist practice in the 21st century* (pp. 211–231). Washington, DC: NASW Press.

Arendt, H. (1958). *The human condition.* Chicago: University of Chicago Press.

Breton, M. (1994). On the meaning of empowerment and empowerment-oriented social work practice. *Social Work with Groups, 17,* 23–37.

Bronfenbrenner, U. (1979). *The ecology of human development.* Cambridge, MA: Harvard University Press.

Brower, A. (1988, September). Can the ecological model guide social work practice? *Social Service Review,* 411–429.

Browne, C. (1995). Empowerment in social work practice with older women. *Social Work, 40,* 358–364.

Chamberlain, R. and Rapp, C. (1991). A decade of case management: A methodological review of outcome research. *Community Mental Health Research Journal, 27*(3), 171–88.

Collins, P. H. (1991). *Black feminist thought: Knowledge, consciousness, and the politics of empowerment.* New York: Routledge.

Cox, E. O. and Joseph, B. H. R. (1998). Social service delivery and empowerment. In L. Gutierrez, R. J. Parsons, and E. O. Cox, (Eds.), *Empowerment in social work practice: A source book* (167–186). Pacific Grove, CA: Brooks/Cole.

Cox, E. O. and Parsons, R. J. (1994). *Empowerment-oriented social work practice with the elderly.* Pacific Grove, CA: Brooks/Cole.

Davis, L. and Proctor, E. (1989). *Race, gender, and class: Guidelines for practice with individuals, families, and groups.* Englewood Cliffs, NJ: Prentice-Hall.

Dressel, P. (1988). Gender, race, class: Beyond the feminization of poverty in later life. *The Gerontologist, 28,* 177–180.

Ehrlich, P., Ehrlich, A., and Holdren, J. (1977). *Ecoscience: Population, resources, environment.* San Francisco: W. H. Freeman.

Ewalt, P. and Mokuau, N. (1995). Self-determination from a Pacific perspective. *Social Work, 40* (2), 168–175.

Freire, P. (1973). *Pedagogy of the oppressed.* New York: Seabury.

Germain, C. B. (1973). An ecological perspective in casework practice. *Social Casework 54,* 323–330.

Germain, C. B. (1979). Introduction: Ecology and social work. In C. B. Germain (Ed.)., *Social work practice: People and environments* (pp. 1–22). New York: Columbia University Press.

Germain, C. B. and Gitterman, A. (1980). *The ecological model of social work practice.* New York: Columbia University Press.

Germain, C. B. and Gitterman, A. (1995). Ecological perspective. In National Association of Social Workers (Ed.), *19th encyclopedia of social work,* vol. 1. Washington DC: NASW Press.

Gitterman, A. and Shulman, L. (Eds.). (1986). *Mutual aid groups and the life cycle.* Itasca, IL: Peacock.

Gutierrez, L. (1990). Working with women of color. *Social Work, 35,* 149–154.

Gutierrez, L. (1992). Empowering clients in the twenty first century: The role of human service organizations. In Y. Hasenfeld (Ed.), *Human service organizations as complex organizations* (pp. 320–338). Newbury Park: Sage.

Gutierrez, L., Glenmaye, L., and DeLois, K. (1995). The organizational context of empowerment practice: Implications for social work administration. *Social Work, 40* (2), 249–258.

Gutierrez, L. M., Parsons, R. J., and Cox, E. O. (Eds.). (1998a). *Empowerment in social work practice: A source book.* Pacific Grove, CA: Brooks/Cole.

Gutierrez, L. M., Parsons, R. J., and Cox, E. O. (1998b). Creating opportunities for empowerment-oriented programs. In L. M. Gutierrez, R. J. Parsons, and E. O. Cox (Eds.), *Empowerment in social work practice: A source book* (pp. 220–223). Pacific Grove, CA: Brooks/Cole.

Hartman, A. (1979) *Finding families: An ecological approach to family assessment in adoption.* Beverly Hills, CA: Sage.

Hasenfeld, Y. (1987, September). Power in social work practice. *Social Service Review,* 469–483.

Hegar, R. L. and Hunzeker, J. M. (1988). Moving toward empowerment-based practice in public child welfare. *Social Work, 33,* 499–503.

Hepworth, D. and Larsen, J. (1990). *Direct social work practice: Theory and skills,* 3rd ed. Belmount, CA: Wadsworth.

Hodges, V., Burwell, Y., and Ortega, D. (1998). Empowering families. In L. M. Gutierrex, R. J. Parsons, and E. O. Cox (Eds.), *Empowerment in social work practice: A source book* (pp. 146–162). Pacific Grove: Brooks Cole.

Hooyman, N. and Kiyak, A. K. (1999). *Social Gerontology,* 5th ed. Boston: Allyn and Bacon.

Jansson, B. (1997). *The reluctant welfare state,* 3rd ed. Pacific Grove, CA: Brooks/Cole.

Kisthardt, W. (1993). The impact of the strengths model of case management from the consumer perspective. In M. Harris and H. Bergman (Eds.), *Case management: Theory and practice* (pp. 165–82). Washington, DC: American Psychiatric Association.

Kretzmann, J. B. and McKnight, J. L. (1993). *Building communities from the inside out.* Evanston, IL: Northwestern University.

Longres, J. E. (1995). Hispanics overview. In R. L. Edwards (Ed.), *Encyclopedia of social work,* 19th ed. Washington, DC: NASW Press.

Mandell, B. and Schram, B. (1985). *Human services: Introduction and intervention.* New York: Wiley.

McDermott, C. J. (1989). Empowering elderly clients in nursing home residents: The residents' rights campaign. *Social Work, 34,* 155–157.

Mellanby, K. (1973). The ecological tradition. In N. Calder, *Nature in the Round: A guide to environmental science.* New York: Viking Press.

Mokuau, N. (1990). A family-centered approach in Native Hawaiian culture. *Families in Society: The Journal of Contemporary Human Services, 71,* (10), 607–613.

Mokuau, N. (1991). *Handbook of social services for Asian and Pacific Islanders.* Westport, CT: Greenwood Press.

Morales, A. and Sheafor, B. (1998). *Social work: A profession of many faces,* 8th ed. Boston: Allyn and Bacon.

Okazawa-Rey, M. (1998). Empowering poor communities of color: A self help model. In L. M. Gutierrez, R. J. Parsons, and E. O. Cox (Eds.), *Empowerment in social work practice: A source book* (pp. 52–64). Pacific Grove: Brooks Cole.

Ozawa, M. (1986). Non-whites and the demographic imperative in social welfare spending. *Social Work, 31,* 44–445.

Ozawa, M. (1995). The economic status of vulnerable older women. *Social Work, 40,* 323–333.

Ozawa, M. and Kirk, S. A. (1996). Welfare reform. *Social Work, 20,* 194–195.

Parsons, R. J. (1991). Empowerment: Purpose and practice in social work. *Social Work with Groups, 14,* 37–43.

Parsons, R. J., Gutierrez, L. M., and Cox, E. O. (Eds.) (1998). A model for empowerment practice. In L. M. Gutierrez, R. J. Parsons, and E. O. Cox (Eds.), *Empowerment in social work practice: A source book* (pp. 3–23). Pacific Grove, CA: Brooks/Cole.

Pinderhughes, E. (1983). Empowerment for our clients and ourselves. *Social Casework, 31,* 331–337.

Rapp, C. (1998). *The strengths model: Case Management with people suffering from severe and persistent mental illness.* New York: Oxford University Press.

Rapp, C. and Chamberlain, R. (1985). Case management services to the chronically mentally ill. *Social Work, 30,* (5), 417–22.

Rapp, C. and Wintersteen, R. (1989). The strengths models of case management: Results from twelve demonstrations. *Psychosocial Rehabilitation Journal, 13* (1), 23–32.

Ryan, C. S., Sherman, P. S., and Judd, C. M. (1994). Accounting for case management effects in the evaluation of mental health services. *Journal of Consulting and Clinical Psychology, 62* (5), 965–74.

Saleebey, D. (Ed.). (1997). *The strengths perspective in social work practice.* (2nd ed) White Plains, NY: Longman.

Simon, B. L. (1994). *The empowerment tradition in American social work.* New York: Columbia University Press.

Solas, J. (1996). The limits of empowerment in human service work. *Australian Journal of Social Issues, 31* (2), 147–156.

Soloman, B. B. (1976). *Black empowerment: Social work in oppressed communities.* New York: Columbia University Press.

Sullivan, W. P. (1997). Reconsidering the environment as a helping resource. In D. Saleebey (Ed.), *The strengths perspective in social work practice* (2nd ed.). (pp. 148–157). New York: Longman.

Sullivan, W. P. (1998). Foreward. In C. Rapp, *The strengths model: Case management with people suffering from severe and persistent mental illness* (ix–xi). NY: Oxford.

Taylor, J. (1997). Niches and practice: Extending the ecological perspective. In D. Saleebey (Ed.), *The strengths perspective in social work practice* (2nd ed., pp. 217–228). New York: Longman.

Torres-Gil, F. (1992). *The new aging: Politics and change in America.* New York: Auburn.

Wakefield, J. (1996). Does social work need the eco-systems perspective? Part I. Is the perspective clinically useful? *Social Service Review, 70,* 1–32.

Weick, A. (1983). A growth-task model of human development. *Social Casework, 64* (3), pp. 131–137.

Weick, A. (1992). Building a strengths perspective for social work. In D. Saleebey (Ed.), *The strengths perspective in social work practice* (pp. 18–38). New York: Longman.

Weick, A. (1994). Overturning oppression: An analysis of emancipatory change. In L. V. Davis (Ed.), *Building on women's strengths: A social work agenda for the 21st Century* (pp. 211–218). Binghamton, NY: Haworth.

Weick, A. and Pope, L. (1988). Knowing what's best: A new look at self determination. *Social Casework, 69* (1), 10–16.

Weick, A., Rapp, C., Sullivan, W. P., and Kisthardt, S. (1989). A strengths perspective for social work practice. *Social Work, 34,* 350–354.

Weick, A. and Saleebey, D. (1995, March). Supporting family strengths: Orienting Policy and Practice toward the 21st century. *Families in Society,* Vol. 76, 141–149.

Young, A. (1999). *Welfare reform: Focus on children.* Detroit, MI: Skillman Center for Children.

Zippay, A. (1995). The politics of empowerment. *Social Work, 40,* 263–267.

CHAPTER 3

"WHENCE CAME THESE PEOPLE?" AN EXPLORATION OF THE VALUES AND ETHICS OF AFRICAN AMERICAN INDIVIDUALS, FAMILIES, AND COMMUNITIES

WYNETTA DEVORE

When W. E. B. DuBois (1967) asked, "whence came these people?" he was referring to the Negroes arriving in Philadelphia at the end of the nineteenth century. He implies that these new residents would have little to offer to the community. It was his contention that this mass of individuals and families, "scattered in every ward of the city" (p. 7), formed a class of social problems of their own as they joined other Negroes in the various wards of the city, particularly areas that had social problems already. He seemed to negate any contributions that they might offer, especially those who could be located in the working class. There appeared to be little interest in the contributions that these Negroes could make.

These contributions would be found in the values and ethical perspectives held by those individuals and families. It cannot be said that African American families hold values that differ from other ethnic groups. Each group will be influenced by its own history and experiences in and with the larger society. The implementations of values and ethical dispositions will be influenced by their own ethnic dispositions. Oppressed ethnic groups may have their values held up to ridicule. Yet, it will be long-held values and modes of ethical behavior that have been sustaining forces.

Considerable attention has been given to the values said to be held by African American families and communities. Pinderhughes (1982) presents a set of values held by African Americans that may conflict with values he called

33

American. Values in conflict may be the emphasis on collectivity, sharing, affiliation, obedience to authority, belief in spirituality, and respect for elders and the past (p. 109). To these may be added a commitment to family and children, education, work, role flexibility, and the church as a forum for spirituality. As this chapter proceeds, attention will be focused on the manner through which these values and ethics may be played out within the context of a society plagued by institutional racism.

We begin with the understanding that African American families are not homogenous. One cannot point to the African American family. No composite exists. Therefore, social workers must understand that African Americans will differ in style and composition, but will experience persistent racism. These oppressive practices build on the influences of slavery, the Great Migration, the Civil Rights Movement, and Affirmative Action Policy.

This understanding will serve the competent ethnic-sensitive social worker well. At the same time, each practitioner must come to understand his or her own ethnic history and the ethnic dispositions that influence their lives. A worker's positive or negative experiences with race and ethnicity will influence social work with members of other ethnic groups, particularly oppressed ethnic groups (Devore & Schlesinger, 1999). Social workers need to be wary of the myths and stereotypes that serve to denigrate African Americans. These myths and stereotypes have hindered positive race relations and competent social work practice. A definition of stereotypes and myths will inform explorations into the lives of African American individuals, families, and communities.

> **Stereotype:**   An exaggerated generalization of a category of people that persists, regardless of the evidence (Eitzen & Zinn, 1994: 299).

Derogatory images of African American families may be seen on cable television with reruns of "Good Times." This family has the beleaguered father, the overweight mother, an outrageous adolescent son, a nice sister, and a positive good neighbor. They live in the "projects," a code name for poor housing. "Moesha," a current offering, is an adolescent female surrounded by a loving, caring family and a good friend. The concern for values and ethical behavior is a continuing theme, and it is clear that family members love and value each other and will be present when needed (*Michigan Chronicle*, 1998).

> **Myth:**   A traditional or legendary story; a story that attempts to express or explain a basic truth (*Random House College Dictionary*, 1984). The *Rodale Synonym Finder* (1978) suggests words similar to *myth: legend, tale, tradition, absurdity,* or *fantasy.* Myths about irresponsible Black men who "make a baby and run," for example, have been challenged by fathers, who have assumed the role of single fathers looking to older adult males and females as models.

This chapter provides the historical context in which the demeaning stereotypes and myths related to the African American experience may find their roots.

WE HAVE STORIES TO TELL

Our own ethnic stories have been influenced by the group or groups into which we have been born. Stories help us to understand who we are, and, sometimes, who or what we wish to be. Family is the context in which we begin to understand and practice the values, traditions, and ethics that will sustain us in the larger society. The behaviors and stories help to solidify family cohesion.

Social work professional relationships begin with stories told by individuals, families, groups, or institutions. Mary Richmond (1917) explained that, when stories are shared with social workers, they become cases and, in that transition, they reflect "real experiences in the lives of real people."

Linda Brent's story, the "real life" story of a slave girl, was published in 1861 and is said to be "one of the last and most remarkable of its genre and also one of the very few written by a woman" (Teller, 1973). It is the first of my stories about the African American experience in the United States.

> I did not know that I was a slave until I was six years old. My father was a skillful carpenter and worked at his trade. But, he had to pay his mistress $200 a year to support himself. He wanted to save money to buy our freedom, made offers that were never accepted. We lived in a pleasant house even though we were slaves. I did not realize that I was a slave, a piece of merchandise trusted to my parents for safekeeping, and could be demanded of them at anytime. I had a younger brother. My maternal grandmother told me stories of her life as a slave. Her mother and her siblings were freed but captured during the Revolutionary War and sold again. Grandmother worked in a hotel, was a good cook, and allowed making nice crackers for sale, after her day's work was done. The profits bought the children's clothes. Her master died, she remained with the wife and her children were divided among the master's children, except for one eight-year-old son who was auctioned. Grandmother had saved $300 that she was forced to "loan" to the mistress. A slave being property could hold no property. When I was six years old my mother died, I lived with her mistress who taught me to read and spell. When she died I learned that she had willed me to her niece who was five years old. Her other slaves, my uncles and aunts were sold at auction. "These God-breathing machines were no more, in the sight of their masters, than the cotton they plant, or horses they tend (Brent, 1861, p. 6).

Linda Brent's story is of a real African family held in bondage in the United States. Sociologists and historians have commented extensively on the experience of slavery in the United States. Bennett notes that slave society revolved around the slave family, which was fragile at best. Marriages had no legal standing. The slave master would perform the ceremony or the custom of "jumping the broom" that would be decorated for the occasion.

Work has been established here as a special family value, but in bondage work could and would be demanded. A positive response was necessary for survival. Every member of the family worked: fathers, mothers, children, and the elderly. Women cut down trees, dug ditches, and plowed. The work of the elderly was less vigorous: feeding the poultry, cleaning the yard, mending clothes, or caring for the young or the sick.

Family was held in respect, but it was difficult for slave families to carry out expected family roles. Parents were denied the responsibility for providing food, clothing, and shelter when they were supplied by the master, their owner. A man lost the protector role when he could not protect his wife or children if they were subjected to beatings by owners or their representatives (Meir & Rudnick, 1970).

E. Franklin Frazier's (1948) conclusions call into question the value of children and their care. Women who were pregnant were offered no relief from work, nor were they cared for following childbirth if they were expected to return to work immediately after delivery. This practice of the owner was detrimental to mother and child. Even when some respite was given and infants were carried to the workplace, Frazier concluded that, because of the strain resulting from the immediate return to work, the limitations for breast-feeding, and other nurturing contacts, mothers had little opportunity to develop emotional attachments to their babies. This view may be countered with the observation that slave mothers did develop a deep and permanent love for their children and suffered immensely when they were separated (Gutman, 1976).

Slavery was an oppressive circumstance that tested the adaptive capacities of men and women for several generations. Gutman (1996) suggests that the focus on family was, at the same time, a focus on culture. Family socialization transmitted historically derived beliefs from generation to generation. "The assumption that slaves could not develop and maintain meaningful domestic arrangements denies the capacity and often serves to 'explain' why so many slaves and their immediate family descendants were 'disorganized' in their social life and 'pathological' in their individual behavior" (p. xxi).

Pejorative terms such as *disorganized* and *pathological* have lost currency in the present. Instead, we determine that African American families and individuals are "at risk," "a challenge to helping professionals," or that young African American males are a menace. In the end, both past or present terminology cast doubt about the status and ability of African American families.

MYTHS OF THE AFRICAN AMERICAN PAST

Myths about African Americans are abundant. This chapter will be limited to the counter positions held by Andrew Billingsley (1968) and Melville J. Herskovits (1958). Herskovits's work, *The Myth of the Negro Past*, challenges myths about African Americans that give support to the variations of racism that may be identified. Some of these myths contend that:

    1. *Negroes are naturally childlike, adjust easily and are happy with unsatisfactory conditions;* the myth presents professional with permission to take care and take charge of Negro "children" who are unable to make decisions on their own. Advocacy is unnecessary for people who are satisfied with a marginal existence.

2. *Negroes were unable to establish unity due to differences in language and customs and, even if they had the will, they were savage and low on the scale of human civilization. The behavior of their masters made it clear that they were the superior, so Negroes gave up their aboriginal traditions.* The value of family and community connectiveness led slaves to come together in sharing and self-help. West African experiences in self-government, sharing, collective activity, and religious worship became a mainstay in the new oppressive environment. Contributions to literature, the arts, and science by slaves and their descendants are significant. Other contributions are such as painting, sculpting and music. Each skill is an attribute shared with the larger society.

3. *The Negro is a man without a past.* John Hope Franklin (1967) and Lerone Bennett (1964) have written two comprehensive accounts of the Negro past. Bennett begins his work *Before the Mayflower: A History of the Negro in American;* Franklin's history is *From Slavery to Freedom.* Each provides a view of a Negro past with communities that had viable political and social institutions. A review of these, or other comprehensive historical accounts, provides social workers with resources that will enrich the body of knowledge related to the African American experience.

DuBois (1966) provides support to these myths when he charges the family with marital instability and the husband with desertion. The effect of this male behavior was to place women in charge of the family. Herskovits (1958) views this behavior as appropriate, an adaptation to oppressive institutional behavior that brutalized the family. Billingsley (1992) provides some grounding for a definition of the African American family. For Billingsley, the African American family is "an intimate association of persons of African descent who are related to each other by a variety of means, including blood, marriage, formal adoption, informal adoption or by appropriation sustained by a history of common residence in America" (p. 28).

Relying on Gutman's (1976) suggestion that family development and customs were based on "historically derived beliefs," Billingsley identifies West African family life practices that survived the trip into bondage. Several are presented here for consideration in light of our interest in family values and ethics.

1. *Descendant connection:* This pattern reflected the value of family connectedness; while not practiced so much in the present, families still call on their ancestors in times of distress.

2. *Types of marriages:* West African parents of the bride and groom made arrangements for the marriage of their children. This practice may be found in many ethnic groups. African American parents are not expected to arrange (select partners for their children) marriages. Still, they hope for an alliance that will benefit both families.

3. *Residential patterns:* In West African tradition the new couple would reside with one set of parents, or nearby. A positive response to this tradition (value) is difficult in a Western society, which may force the couple to move to distant places in search of employment. Modern technology—the telephone, e-mail, and other digital technologies can transmit images of family members and activities and provide links not available in the past. Family reunions of African American families are welcomed in the hotel industry as they support the value of family connections.

4. *Child care and protection:* Child welfare literature informs us of the wide range of child care practices in the United States. The foster care program of kinship care gives indications of the value of connectiveness in African American families. African American children in need of foster care will most often be placed with relatives. Aunts, siblings, cousins, or grandparents enter into formal agreements with public agencies in order for children to remain in the family where they are valued. Their parents have been charged with behavior that makes them unacceptable as parents.

5. *West African fathers:* They played an important role in the care of children. He held responsibility for the moral behavior of his sons and, along with his wife, consented to the son's marriage. In addition, he was responsible for making sure that his daughter's suitor could support her. Relationships between mothers and children were paramount and extended into adulthood. Sociological research literature and social work practice literature have increased their attention to African American men as fathers. McAdoo's work (1993) examined the role of African American fathers and found them to be diligent in their attempts to assume the roles of provider, decision maker, child socializer, and marital partner.

The patterns of close-knit families organized and connected to kin and community were highly functional for economical, social, and psychological life. These values were held by slaves who were stolen from West Africa. In bondage, they were able to be adaptable and flexible so that long-held values could sustain families during this experience of oppression and bondage.

Following the Civil War and emancipation, free men and women set about to take charge of the lives of their families. Barriers to progress were racism, lack of education, or skills. The next historical event, the Great Depression, would have a significant impact on the African American family. One needs to recall that we are considering the family within a social, individual, and historical context (Germain & Gitterman, 1996).

THE WALTER COACHMAN STORY AND THE GREAT DEPRESSION (CIRCA 1929)

Coachman was born the twelfth son in a family of thirteen children. His father worked for "old man" Whitelaw on a twelve-horse plantation outside Bennetsville. His mother was a forceful character who fought tooth and toenail to see that her children got some education. Walter went to a one-room Negro school some distance from his home where he learned to read, write, and figure. This skill enabled him [with support from his mother] to miscalculate as he delivered for Whitelaw. Hauling his bales to the gin at night the family came out "pretty good" that year. At 18 Coachman attended Allen College to study theology. Family finances were not good so he began to work for a [white] widow who had a wonderful garden. When not at school Walter and the widow developed a showplace and began to sell flowers. When Coachman told this story he was 41, his wife 30. He had four churches scattered throughout the county. He had a "piece of car" to travel to his several congregations. With about eight or nine dollars per week he bought a little farm where his wife took care of the garden and the chickens. The younger children did heavy work cutting wood and milking. Their older brother was away studying electricity. Coachman pledged to teach his children that kindness and consideration for the feelings of others will carry them far, and I impress on them the necessity for upholding the ideals of the race (Atwell, 1939).

We hear Mr. Coachman's story and, immediately, we are able to observe the implication of sustaining values and perspectives on ethics and behavior (could miscalculation of delivery of bales be an adaptation to oppression?). This family did not hold to the stereotypes attributed to African American families. The Coachmans were not disorganized. He was absent from the family in order to earn a living as a clergyman. Nor was the family unable to maintain a home; in fact, they purchased and assigned tasks of maintenance of their home according to age. This family lived a marginal existence, but owned their home. Mr. Coachman, the father, held regular employment, Mrs. Coachman maintained the home, and they educated their children. What problems they did have could only be exaggerated by the Depression.

The values held by slave families, undoubtedly the Coachman's parents, continued to hold during this phase of African history in the United States. Education was highly valued. It appears that Mrs. Coachman was the only family member who did not attend school. Yet, she, and her mother-in-law before her, honored and supported education for their children.

Mr. Coachman was very pleased that no member of the local African American community had ever been buried by the county, as were Caucasian neighbors. The practice of mutual aid had been institutionalized in burial societies. Community members made regular deposits and funds were available for burial. Families who found themselves "in the tight" were tided over by the larger community. Fairly well-to-do families did their best to help, but need often exceeded their means. Public relief was the very last resort.

Community mutual aid has been identified as a survival of African traditions that calls for a positive response to members of the community in need. Sharing, collectivity, and affiliation were the norm, the expected behaviors. Cooperation such as this was fundamental to West African agricultural enterprises and, like other community-based traditions, they were carried into bondage. These sustained the Coachman family during the immediate future.

The fall of the economy in 1929–1930 placed tenant farmers and sharecroppers in precarious positions. In 1932, Congressman George Huddleston, of Alabama, described the conditions of sharecroppers in his district. He reported that the Negro family's ability to survive, eat, and have shelter depended on the landlord, who supplied these in exchange for labor in planting and harvesting the crops. The current economic conditions in agriculture were such that the landlord was unable to finance tenants any longer. Both tenant and landlord were in need of assistance (Shannon, 1960).

Walter Coachman and his family could be self-sustaining, but southern tenant farmers and sharecroppers were in dire need, with their homes at risk. Families in the North had similar experiences with housing, which was scarce, in poor condition, and expensive. These conditions led to homelessness and overcrowding. It would appear that the community, with the value of mutual aid, supported overcrowded housing conditions as an alternative to homelessness. All would not find shelter, but an alternative was offered.

MIGRATION TO THE CITY PUSHED BY THE GREAT DEPRESSION

Families migrated to several northern cities, but researchers have focused on Philadelphia (DuBois, 1967) and Chicago (Drake & Cayton, 1945). (The pseudonym selected for Chicago was Bronzeville, a city that experienced the onslaught of the Depression.) People who had been employed regularly lost their positions. Panic and frustration resulted in unorganized demonstrations and boycotts that generated only a few jobs for colored people. Families were evicted. Thousands remained unemployed, and the families from the South only added to the number of distressed people. The collapse of cotton tenancy, discrimination, emergency employment, and relief compelled the movement North.

New families and long-time residents lived in flats with three to six rooms and shared space with boarders, lodgers, and relatives. In the doubling-up, much privacy was lost. Drake and Cayton (1945) defined "fragmented families" as young bachelors and young women living alone or sharing their apartments with footloose men. These families and many others moved from flat to house, house to flat, in search of affordable living quarters.

The WPA check was their only income. In Brownsville, as in other northern cities, Negro men looked to the WPA for assistance as they experienced unemployment. Isolation was experienced even in a crowded apartment. This living style negated the value of affiliation. Roomers had little to offer each other for joy and comfort; a gathering of friends gave little or no sense of affiliation. Later, Billingsley (1968) would describe the practice of shared housing as "augmented families," counting them as strengths. He pointed to these families as examples of the African American family's ability to adapt to historical and contemporary social conditions.

The reality of unemployed men seemed to support the myth that Negro women were matriarchs, who held the dominant role in family and marriage relations. Drake and Cayton (1945) reported that, "Negro men have never been able in mass to obtain good jobs long enough to build a solid economic base for family support" (p. 582).

Men without employment became wanderers as they searched for employment. The contention was that this behavior placed women in the position of responsibility for the family. Unable to provide a steady, dependable income, men looked to their wives and girlfriends, the only resource available at the time. These economic truths placed women in a powerless matriarch position. Matriarchs are said to be women who hold power equal to men in society. We have visions of mature, stately women, with control over family, mostly white upper-class families. Their pictures are sprinkled throughout the literature. Black women in Brownsville had few resources to control, they were powerless in relation to the fortunes of their families; tried and bent rather than stately

For families who could find employment, Brownsville had much to offer. Richard Wright's short story, (1963), "Lawd Today" describes a day in the life of Jake Jackson, a post office employee. This position placed Jake among the struggling middle class. Some had hoped to be professionals, but were unable to meet the educational expectations. Jake, and his wife Lil, are a small family troubled by Lil's illness, her abuse from Jake, racism, and Jake's anger. The day selected by Wright is February 12, Lincoln's birthday. Jake awakes from a dream that reveals his frustration and anger with the postal service. He climbs and climbs but cannot reach the top. He is always on the bottom and can hear the white boss's voice as a voice-over. Anger finds a short-term release as he heaps physical and mental abuse on Lil. Jake's anger, even with racism as a reasonable source, does not warrant his behavior. Such responses serve to perpetuate the stereotype of the irresponsible African American male who neglects his family, and, with that neglect, the value of family cohesiveness vanishes.

Other families in Bronzeville accepted the checks for rent and food delivered by caseworkers. They used commodities that were available and accepted health care at the public clinic. It was their expectation that prosperity would return, and it did. An industry to support the Second World War began to provide the employment needed.

The Depression presented a variety of experiences for U.S. families of all ethnic groups. (Germain & Gitterman, 1996). Social workers with an understanding of this position in the life course may be better able to work with older clients born during this era of social change. They may have experienced deprivation, unhealthy living conditions, urban and rural poverty, near-starvation, unemployment, relief, and the WPA. For members of oppressed ethnic groups, racism was always present. These experiences may serve as barriers to intervention, or strengths that reflect the value of family cohesiveness.

AFRICAN AMERICANS AND MIGRATION EXPERIENCES

Migration was first experienced by West Africans who were forced from their homes, taken into bondage, and transported in chains to another country. The second migration was planned by the slaves themselves. The goal was to escape slavery, by any means possible. Harriet Tubman was a leader of many attempts at freedom. This "Moses" led her people, fugitive slaves, toward the North and freedom. Impetus for the next migration movement was the Great Depression, but freedom in a new location was hard to come by. The United States of America proved to be unwilling to provide the release and relief they expected. Drachman and Halberstadt (1992) describe a framework for understanding the immigration process that is also useful for the migration that interests us. According to these authors, the movement from home to a new place by choice, as a refugee, or in bondage holds similar perils, including:

1. *Departure.* Leaving one's homeland is usually due to economic pressures (the Great Depression), social or political factors (refugees escaping war), and necessitates a loss of family, friends, and a familiar environment.
2. *Transit.* The journey for slaves included the terrors of the Middle Passage; for southern Negroes there were the anxieties about racist travel experiences and the question, what will it be like when we get there?
3. *Resettlement.* In this stage there are cultural issues to be addressed, for example, loss of religious rituals and language. Many other new arrivals to the United States of America also shared these experiences, but auctions placed slaves, as property, in the homes of the highest white bidders. Migrants of the Depression were not welcomed by the cities they selected. They found substandard, crowded living conditions, and scant employment. The most difficult task was adapting to the differences between their expectations and reality.

Goodwin (1990) listened to the stories of older African American residents of Chicago who had migrated from Mississippi between 1920 and 1960. Through their stories, Goodwin was able to determine that they or their families were pursuing the value of education that would increase the possibility for better employment opportunities. Some came soon after marriage, as a young family; women came to join their husbands. All wanted a better life, and social improvement, made possible by education, was a primary goal. In this transition, they held to the values of family and community cohesiveness.

Through many migration experiences, families held to traditional values, although there were African American social scientists who continued to perpetuate myths and stereotypes. Choosing to negate examples of resiliency and adaptability of this oppressed ethnic group, Pettigrew (1964) felt that poverty and migration served to maintain the mother-centered family of slavery. Poor housing, lack of recreation facilities, and urban disorganization made it impossible for these African Americans to meet the ideal (white) U.S. family pattern: a stable unit with a husband who worked and supported his family. By accepting the myth of the superiority of the white family, Pettigrew provided the foundation for the work of Daniel Partick Moynihan (1965).

The movement of large numbers of African American families from southern agricultural communities to northern or western industrial states has had a significant impact on the life course of individuals and families. Migration was an historical event that was the foundation for events in the individual and social time of individuals (Germain & Gitterman, 1996).

THE AFRICAN AMERICAN FAMILY:
BEYOND THE MOYNIHAN REPORT

The Case of National Action: The Negro Family (1965) was a U.S. Department of Labor publication that became known as the "Moynihan Report." The questionable conclusions about the status and future for African American families fueled a debate that continues today. Moynihan used the work of E. Franklin Frazier (1948) and Thomas F. Pettigrew (1964) to support his conclusions. Moynihan contended that after the Civil Rights Act of 1964, Negroes were expected to demand equal opportunity and recognition of their civil rights. He concluded in the report, "this will not happen for generations to come unless a new and special effort is made" (p. 29). The report cited the crumbling structures of the Negro family as the cause. With this indictment, the stage was set for a social policy that would "repair" the family. The so-called disrepair was said to represent a "tangle of pathology" caused by a forced matriarchal structure that was out of line with the (white) societal norm, in which the male was the public and private leader of the family.

More recent work (Ruggles, 1994; Tolnay, 1997) has revisited the data on African American family life. This data, unlike the anecdotal work of Frazier (1948), or Drake and Cayton (1945), has been generated by Bureau of the Census data, and leads to the conclusions that urban families with southern origins maintained traditional family patterns, that children lived with two parents, (more over, married women with their spouses), and there were fewer never-married women than early studies assumed. Tolnay (1997) provided no support for the notion that southerners carried a "dysfunctional family to the North," and Ruggles (1994) confirmed that single parenthood and children living with their parents was not a new family constellation. Indeed, the pattern was evident among free Blacks during the 1850s. Such myths and stereotypes are still challenged, and the value of family cohesiveness may be found in the work of scholars of the 1990s.

DIRECTIVES FOR ETHNIC-SENSITIVE PRACTICE

This chapter has presented a cursory view of historical events that have influenced the experiences of African Americans in the United States. Slavery, emancipation, civil disturbances, the civil rights movement, civil rights legislation, and the persistence of institutional racism have their impact on stories in the present.

The competent ethnic-sensitive social worker will consider the stories of Linda Brent, Walter Coachman, and Jake Jackson with contemporary stories. Two layers of understanding from the work of Devore and Schlesinger (1999) may inform the social worker's thinking. Layer two of the model calls for a "basic understanding of human behavior" that will generate questions such as: What is life like for an adult who is unable to find meaningful employment because of race? How does an adolescent male feel when it is clear that many white people, youth and adults, fear him when he walks by them in the mall? What is the level of anger generated by a middle-class suburban wife when the people she opens her door to assume that she is the maid?

An understanding of the impact of the ethnic reality (the juncture of ethnicity and social class) on the daily life of clients is the mandate of layer five. Social class and ethnic group membership will, too often, determine place of residence, available work, the education of children, as well as entry into some places of recreation or worship. In the stories that follow, families hold to the values suggested throughout this chapter.

FAMILY STORIES CIRCA 1990: MOTHER LOUISE, THOMAS AND MARTHA, AND SHIRLEY

Mother Louise has been an active member in her church for many years. Her energy belies her 82 years. Her age and wisdom have earned her respect as "mother" of the church. Her deceased husband worked as a porter on the railroad, providing her with an adequate income. Still, she was moderate in her spending. Ellen, her daughter and her only child, is an upper-level public health professional. Because her salary places her well within the middle class, she can afford a coop apartment, which she shares with her pre-adolescent daughter, Alice. A single mother, Ellen relies on her mother, Louise, to accompany Alice to after-school activities of music or dance lessons. Ellen does not worship with her mother, but Alice does attend worship with her grandmother on some occasions.

Mother Louise, Ellen, and Alice illustrate values that have sustained their family in the past. Louise is active in the church, with particular interest in the development of the children. A focus on the value of education has prepared Ellen for responsible professional employment. Mutual aid is an important part of their relationship, as Louise accompanies Alice to various after-school activities. Ellen monitors her mother's health even though she is healthy at 82. Companionship in public and private lives exemplify sharing and connectedness.

Thomas and Martha are a young couple with a teen-age son and preteen daughter. Karl, the son, is an excellent athlete; his sister, Carrie, wants to be an actress and tests herself in local theater. The family lives in an exclusive neighborhood outside Washington, D.C. The parents met at a university and were married after graduation. She is an artist and he is a director of photography at a nationally known news organization. Although they do not attend church regularly, they revere "the ancestors."

This family lives in a spacious home in the Washington, D.C. suburbs. The family is the center of life for both parents and children. Karl and Carrie are encouraged to use all of the educational resources that are available to them: Karl will enter a private school for boys and Carrie will remain in an excellent public school system, and they expect to go to college, as did their parents and grandparents. Nevertheless, social class and race are factors in the lives of both parents and children. The children have the support of their parents when they experience racism. The school social worker cannot assume that social class provides this family with a protective shield.

> **Shirley** was abandoned by her mother early in her childhood. Indifferent relatives passed her from one to another. In this movement, it did not occur to the family that school was an option. This benign neglect is evident in her present life circumstances. Substance abuse and promiscuity led to the birth of two children and a life in disarray, but her young family has found acceptance in a new community and a new view of her possibilities. She found marginal employment, did well, and was promoted to a more responsible position. Enrollment in a literacy program encouraged her to enroll in a community college. She has yet to be accepted, however, and plans to become a student in an adult literacy program. The children are doing well in school and are proud of their mother's accomplishments.

Shirley and her children have benefited from the African American value of collectivity, sharing, education, work, and religion. A grassroots community organization helped her to find and maintain employment, encouraged her educational pursuits, and cared for the children, who also attend school. Shirley is a woman who is beginning to sense her personal worth. Competent social workers, familiar with the layers of understanding, will understand the community's commitment to mutual aid, sharing, education, caring for children, and the augmented family (Billingsley, 1968), which is a resource that cannot be ignored.

The stories of Mother Louise, Thomas and Martha, and Shirley are offered to indicate that African American families will be found at all social class levels. At any level, they will not have the negative characteristics suggested by social science literature and the Moynihan Report (1965). Stereotypes perpetuated by these sources failed to understand the complexity and diversity of the African American family. The Social Work Code of Ethics calls on the profession to be more understanding than those who continually condemn African American families without considering the history of strengths, values, and ethical perspectives that have sustained these families. If we are to be competent ethnic-sensitive social work practitioners, we must begin to understand from "whence came these people."

REFERENCES

Atwell, F. D. (1939). I am a Negro. *American life histories: Manuscripts from the Federal Writers' Project, 1936–1940.* (On line) Available, Library of Congress.

Bennett, L., Jr. (1964). *Before the Mayflower: A history of the Negro in America,* rev. ed. Chicago: Johnson.

Billingsley, A. (1968). *Black families in white America.* Englewood Cliffs, NJ: Prentice-Hall.

Billingsley, A. (1992). *Climbing Jacob's ladder: The enduring legacy of African American families.* New York: Simon & Schuster.

Brent, L. (1861). *Incidents in the life of a slave girl.* New York: Harcourt Brace Jovanovich.

Devore, W. & Schlesinger, E. G. (1999). *Ethnic-sensitive social work practice,* 5th ed. Boston: Allyn and Bacon.

Drachman, D. & Halberstadt, A. (1992). A stage of migration framework as applied to recent Soviet émigrés. *Journal of Multicultural Social Work, 2* (1), 63–78.

Drake, St. C. & Cayton, H. R. (1945). *Black metropolis: A study of Negro life in a northern city,* vols. 1–2, rev. ed. New York: Harcourt, Brace, & World.

DuBois, W. E. B. (1967). *The Philadelphia Negro: A social study.* New York: Schocken.

Eitzen, D. S. & Zinn, M. B. (1994). *Social problems,* 6th ed. Boston, MA: Allyn and Bacon.

Franklin, J. H. (1967). *From slavery to freedom,* 3rd ed. New York: Alfred A. Knopf.

Frazier, E. F. (1948). *The Negro family in the United States,* rev. ed. Chicago: University of Chicago Press.

Germain, C. B. & Gitterman, A. (1996). *The life model of social work practice in theory and practice,* 2nd ed. New York: Columbia University Press.

Goodwin, E. M. (1990) *Black migration in America from 1915–1960: An uneasy exodus.* Lewiston, NY: Edwin Mellen Press.

Gutman, H. G. (1976). *The black family in slavery and freedom, 1750–1925.* New York: Pantheon.

Herskovits, M. J. (1958). *The myth of the Negro past.* Boston: Beacon.

McAdoo, J. (1993). The role of African American fathers: An ecological perspective. *Families in Society, 74,* 28–34.

Meir, A. & Rudnick, E. (1970). *From plantation to ghetto,* rev. ed. New York: Hill and Wong.

"Moesha" and Brandy . . . both winners. (1998, October 27). *Michigan Chronicle,* D1.

Moynihan, D. P. (1965). *The Negro family: The case for national action.* Washington, DC: U.S. Government Printing Office.

Pettigrew, T. F. (1964). *A profile of the Negro American.* Princeton, NJ: D. Van Nostrand.

Pinderhughes, E. (1982). Afro-American families and the victim system. In M. McGoldrick, J. K Pearce, & J. Giorando (Eds.), *Ethnicity & family therapy* (pp. 108–122). New York: Guilford.

Random House College Dictionary, rev. ed. (1984). New York: Random House.

Richmond, M. (1917). *Social diagnosis.* New York: Russell Sage Foundation.

Rodale, J. I. (1978). *The synonym finder.* Emmaus, PA: Rodale Press.

Ruggles, S. (1994). The origins of African-American family structure. *American Sociological Review, 59,* 136–151.

Shannon, D. A. (Ed.). (1960). *The great depression.* Englewood Cliffs, NJ: Prentice-Hall.

Teller, W. (1973). Introduction. In L. Brent, *Incidents in the life of a slave girl* (1861). New York: Harcourt Brace Jovanovich.

Tolnay, S. E. (1997). The great migration and changes in the northern Black family, 1940–1990. *Social Forces, 75* (4), 1213–1226.

Wright, R. (1963). Lawd today. In E. Wright and M. Fabre (Eds.), *Richard Wright Reader.* New York: Harper & Row.

CHAPTER 4

LATINOS: CULTURAL COMPETENCE AND ETHICS

MARIA E. ZUNIGA

During this new millenium, the Latino population will become the largest minority group in the United States (Hayes-Bautista, 1999). The within-group diversity for Latinos is becoming increasingly complex, as individuals and families immigrate from the diverse countries of Mexico, and Central and South America.

More social workers will need to know how to decipher the special needs of this diverse group due to their unique political, economic, social, and immigration histories. Workers must comprehend how to individualize their needs while being cognizant of the value, behavior, and belief systems that often characterize this group (Zuniga, 1998).

This chapter will elucidate how these complexities should be assessed to intervene with this population, using judgments that assure viable ethics. Some social workers assume that ethical issues only present for special occasions, that most actions do not involve moral questions. However, others feel that there are ethical implications or ethical aspects to almost every professional decision (Dolgoff & Loewenberg, 1985). The latter statement is assumed for professional intervention with Latino populations in this chapter.

Professionals must insure that their practice with all clients adheres to standards or ethical codes, such as the National Association of Social Workers (NASW) Code of Ethics (Hepworth, Rooney, & Larsen, 1997). Ethical standards guide professionals in their ability to determine the best form of practice. In today's society, issues of ethics are taking front stage. The paradox is that, at a time when interest in ethics is becoming highlighted, the moral fiber in society seems to be approaching an all-time low. Dolgoff and Loewenberg (1985) offer examples of corruption and scandals in government and industry. President Clinton, who was caught lying about sexual misconduct, has contributed greatly to this sense of a downturn in morality. A compounding factor is that the world is a place of rapid social and technological changes. The realities of cloning, multiple births, and harvesting human organs are challenging us to rethink moral and ethical themes. Ethical dilemmas are alive and well. They do not necessarily present themselves only for special occasions or in dramatic ways. Social workers must be schooled to address them in both the dramatic scenarios as well as in the mundane ways they comport themselves. Some of the ethical issues that erupt when working with diverse populations will be elucidated in this chapter. Before this is addressed, I will identify pertinent themes for Latino populations.

The next section will offer perspectives on the within-group diversity that comprises the population termed *Latino*. *Latino* is the preferred term as one that is self-applied, as compared to *Hispanic*, which is a term imposed by government entities in their census work.

DEMOGRAPHICS

According to the 1993 Census reports, Latinos constitute approximately 8.9 percent (22.8 million) of the population in the United States (Montgomery, 1994). The three largest groups are those of Mexican origin, Puerto Ricans, and Cubans. There are also many groups from Central and South America. (See Table 4.1 for Latino demographics.)

TABLE 4.1   **Latino Demographics**

Mexican origin	14.6 million	68.9%
Puerto Ricans	2.4 million	11.3%
Cubans	1.1 million	5.2%
Central & So. Americans	3.1 million	14.6%
		100.0%
Central Americans		
Salvadorians	42%	
Guatemalans	20.3%	
Nicaraguans	15.3%	
Hondurans	9.9%	
Panamanians	7.0%	
Costa Ricans	4.3%	
Other	1.1%	
	99.9%	
South Americans		
Columbians	36.6%	
Ecuadorians	18.5%	
Peruvians	16.9%	
Argentineans	9.7%	
Chileans	6.6%	
Other	11.7%	
	100.0%	

(Montgomery, 1994)

Mexico

Mexico, the country closest to the United States on its southern border, has unique geographic and political ties to the United States. Its extensive border provides the opportunity for international business and economic endeavors.

The United States–Mexican War and Treaty of Hidalgo, 1848, resulted in Mexico losing to the United States vast domains of land including what is now California, Texas, New Mexico, and Colorado. Economic woes in Mexico have periodically pushed migrants across its borders to the United States. This geographic and historical uniqueness has insured that the Mexican subgroup is the largest Latino population in the United States.

Puerto Rico

A unique aspect of the second largest Latino subgroup, Puerto Ricans, is their political history that has resulted in U.S. citizen status. Thus, migration themes for this group include the freedom of U.S. entry and exit unavailable to any of the other subgroups of Latinos. The United States retained Puerto Rico as an unincorporated territory after the Spanish–American War in 1848 ended 400 years of Spanish rule, imposing citizenship on Puerto Ricans (Montijo, 1985). Like Mexicans, who return to Mexico frequently, the ease and frequency with which many Puerto Ricans return to the island also promote cultural maintenance.

Cubans

The third largest group of Latinos are those of Cuban heritage. Due to the political turmoil that occurred with the takeover of Cuba by Fidel Castro in 1959, there have been waves of immigration that have contributed to this largely immigrant group. These waves include periods such as the Cuban Missile Crisis in 1962 and the Mariel boatlift to Key West in the 1970s. The sustained and substantive reliance on the Spanish language and Cuban cultural traditions have also promoted adherence to traditional culture, at least for those of the first and second generations.

Central Americans

The civil wars of the 1980s, in such areas as Nicaragua and El Salvador, pushed immigrants to the United States to seek political asylum. The unique political experiences, often the brutal realities of those who were subjected to torture or the mayhem that surrounded them during the civil war, contribute other assessment arenas that are critical to evaluate, especially for post-traumatic stress disorder. Some experts theorize that just the hazardous crossing experiences of the undocumented must be considered for the trauma and their long-term effects on these sojourners. Before examining these specific themes, an examination of the value motifs that often underpin the experiences of Latinos will highlight cultural perspectives for this group.

CULTURAL VALUES AND BEHAVIORAL NORMS

Values underpin the lifestyles of people and are a critical aspect of everyday life. For professionals in the human services, values must be comprehended as some of the core factors in the choices that people make. Thus, it is imperative that we comprehend the values that are the driving forces in our lives, so that we can consciously examine the implications of the value choices clients make and minimize the projection of our own values. This process provides the knowledge base we must utilize in making decisions that are ethically viable. Dolgoff & Loewenberg (1985), citing Siporin (1982), note that value judgments can be one of the various factors that mitigate sound ethical practice.

One of the fascinating aspects of the values of Latino groups is the mixture (*mestiaze*) that underpins their essence. Ramirez (1983) uses this *mestizo* term to address the mixture that evolved from the amalgamation of the peoples that we term *Latinos*. He refers to the genetic mixtures that resulted as the European colonizers, especially from Spain, mixed with the indigenous peoples of the Americas. When the Spaniards landed in the Americas, they already were a genetic, psychological, and cultural mix, including residues of centuries-old Moorish and Jewish influences in Spain (Cervantes & Ramirez, 1992).

In this chapter I will review seven key value stances necessary for clinicians to comprehend in their work with Latino clients.

Spirituality: The Cornerstone of One's Being

The concept of spirituality is not limited to the idea of church attendance or organized religion. Cervantes & Ramirez (1992) highlight concepts of spirituality, including that of Elkins (1988). Elkins broadens the concept of spirituality to include values that typically are outside of traditional religious practice, including a search for meaning, a sense of transcendence and mission in life, and a belief in the sacredness of life. Cervantes & Ramirez (1992) extend this definition to include " . . . a transcendent level of consciousness that allows for existential purpose and mission, the search for harmony and wholeness, and a fundamental belief in the existence of a greater, all-loving presence in the universe" (p. 104). They go on to add that this *mestizo* spirituality fosters a culturally sanctioned impetus towards wholeness, harmony, and balance that are reflected in one's relationship with self and family, as well as the broader community. This sense of balance is elucidated in reference to the family centeredness that epitomizes Latino values.

Family: The Core Principle in One's Life

This value stance evolved from both the Spaniards' Catholic-inspired reverence for the family as well as from the value of family that was inspired by the indigenous peoples of the Americas. This family orientation has resulted in a genuine respect for and trust in extended family relations (Cervantes & Ramirez, 1992). For many of the indigenous peoples in the Americas, there had been a mixture of matrilineal and patrilineal tribal governance, so the emphasis on male dominance was not a consistent value stance. However, research in California has found that, in general, both male and female Latino participants did not adhere to the stance that husbands should dominate, negating the traditional view of the Latino family as being husband-centered (Rubel, 1966). Rather, Latino families in Rubel's study were relatively egalitarian and supportive of women's rights (Hurtado et al., 1992). The extensive participation of women in the labor force has supported this role flexibility (Cromwell & Ruiz, 1979). However, for less acculturated families, traditional gender formats will very likely persist.

The California research also noted that the family plays an important role in Latino life, with the third generation valuing the family almost as much as the first generation (Hurtado et al., 1992). The central value of the family and extended family membership supports another Latino value stance, the related importance of the collective.

The Value of Community

Roland (1988) has examined values in many non-Western cultures and indicates that Latinos have a sense of familialism that results in a focus on the collective, which extends to valuing community life. The individualism that is the bedrock of many values in the United States is almost antithetical to many Latino persons, unless they have become very acculturated (Zuniga, 1988). In contrast, Latinos have a sense of collective that underpins values of *compradazco* (fictive kinship) as well as communal responsibility. The modern sense of community is operationalized by natural support systems that are woven into Latino communities (Valle & Mendoza, 1978) with the sense of responsibility for others even if they are not blood-related. Hurtado and colleagues (1992) offer the insight that the Mexican/Latino culture has deep historical roots as farmers who tended the land, origins that reinforce collective values. Often, the community focuses on giving to the young or children of that particular community.

The Value of Children

The role of children in Latino communities and families takes on added meaning or prominence as one examines Latino family life. In U.S. culture, people marry in concert with the romantic idea of falling in love. While this may also be true for Latinos, one marries to have children. The parent–child relationship has more importance than the marital relationship (Zuniga, 1998).

Although class dimensions and acculturation stages affect Latino values, and may color the value of children with a lighter tone, the overall fabric of Latino families is focused on children. Latino families continue to have larger families on average than mainstream U.S. families; 65 percent of Latino families have three members compared to the U.S. population of 57 percent of families with fewer than two members. Latinos have three times as many families with more than six members as compared to the majority population (Garcia & Marotta, 1997). Latino families have a strong commitment to socialize a child to be *bien educada* (well educated) when it comes to interpersonal relationships (Zuniga, 1998).

Interpersonal Relations: The Value of Respect

Research that has examined the behavior style of Latino children has noted that they tend to have a more field-sensitive cognitive style than children of other ethnic groups (Ramirez & Price-Williams, 1974). This field dependence is a heightened sensitivity to nonverbal interpersonal cues. What these children have learned from their family and community is that you interact with others in a warm and humanistic fashion so that proper interpersonal ritual is provided each person. This sense of being personable (*personalismo*) and respectful is the expected interaction.

An important area that carries on the family's expectation for respectful interaction is the cooperation or sense of sharing they instill in their children.

The Value of Cooperation versus Competition

The largeness of many Latino families teaches children the value of sharing one's resources. Similarly, the value of the collective teaches people to accomplish for the good of the community, rather than to exert one's individual needs. The value of sharing, despite the meagerness of one's resources, promotes the sense of the collective (Murillo, 1971). However, as acculturation changes affect these value stances, the individualism that is promoted in academic environments may become more influential, resulting in a more competitive mold for individuals of Latino heritage (Zuniga, 1998).

These value and behavioral norms are inclinations that may underpin the life perspective of Latino client systems. To what extent that perspective actually pertains to a Latino client will have to be ferreted out in thorough assessment processes. Yet, in examining demographic indices, there are major problems and issues that one must consider that could apply to an individual client.

THE SPECIAL STRESSES OF IMMIGRANTS

The Latino population has experienced a major increase in immigrants, especially those who are undocumented. Thus, the unique situations of this subpopulation are of particular concern to the human service worker. Padilla (1999) notes the variety of stresses this group encounters: separation issues from family, relatives, and country of origin; journeys that are often dangerous and of different durations; the relocation issues related to language and cultural incongruence; and practical aspects of finding housing and employment.

Many immigrants from Central American countries mired in the civil war lived with a low-intensity warfare, different from traditional wars, like World War II, in that it was characterized by random acts of terrorism. Thus, individuals, especially children, could not easily discern who was the enemy or friend (Melville & Lykes, 1992), adding another component to their anxiety.

For those who are undocumented, a critical stress is the fear of being found out and deported by *La Migra* (the immigration authorities). Salcido (1982) identifies the daily torment that undocumented immigrants experience as they fear detection and the subsequent toll on their psychological well-being.

Another kind of fallout caused by this large immigration is the antipathy towards immigrants that is growing in the United States, and the prevalent view that social problems, in such states as California, are the direct result of immigration growth (Hayes-Bautista, et al. 1992).

PRACTICE: ETHICAL DECISION MAKING

Due to the high levels of poverty that many Latino families experience, workers must assess to what extent they receive or have access to needed resources, including decent housing and health care. For example, the social worker must know the relevant social policy issues on utilization of health care programs that could jeopardize eligibility for legalizing their immigration status (Bellisle, 1999).

THE ORTEGA FAMILY

Lupe Ortega, age eighteen, became ill and nauseous in class. After some questioning by the school nurse, Lupe tearfully indicated she was eight weeks pregnant. She pleaded with the nurse and social worker not to tell her family.

The social worker, Ms. Middle, helped to reassure her. She had worked with Lupe since her junior year. She had even met Lupe's family when she made a home visit to help fill out financial aid packages for college applications. Lupe comes from a family of four children: two brothers, age seventeen and thirteen, and one sister, eight.

Mr. Ortega is from Nicaragua. When he was seventeen years of age he fled to Mexico because of the civil war in his country. He met Mariam, who was nineteen and living in Mexico. She had legal immigrant papers because she had lived in the United States with her family since childhood. She also spoke English well, and, after the birth of two children, she helped to get the family to the United States.

Lupe's main concern was that her family not know about her pregnancy. She felt her parents would become very angry. Lupe said she felt her mother would strongly oppose an abortion because her family is Catholic. Lupe indicates, however, that that is not the main reason she would not have an abortion. She really wants to keep her baby, but that would mean that she would have to face the anger and rejection of her parents, especially her father. In addition, her parents have often talked about getting legal status for her father and her so that they can seek employment without fearing apprehension by the Naturalization and Immigration Service. Now Lupe feels she has "messed up" and her pregnancy will just make family problems more difficult.

Ms. Middle thinks she understands exactly how Lupe feels, because, as a Catholic, she sees how the family would feel that an abortion would be wrong. However, she feels constrained by the ethical issues Lupe presents: the plea for confidentiality that Lupe is adamant about and the health care issues that could complicate the family's eligibility for legal status if Lupe uses public resources to have her baby. (Because her father is undocumented, he is paid under the table and does not receive any medical coverage through his employment.) Ms. Middle, as the school social worker, has gone out of her way the past two years to connect this student to college mentors and to refer her for leadership conferences and opportunities.

This case presents a variety of ethical issues. The issue of confidentiality stands out as the client insists that her family not discover her situation. The fact that her brother attends the same school may quickly challenge this need as the gossip mill takes over.

The issue of self-determination is a cardinal value in social work (Hepworth, Rooney, & Larsen, 1997). It is difficult to work with a teenager who demands that her family not be involved when the issues are so challenging. The following are some reflections that zip through the worker's mind as she listens to Lupe state her concerns.

> What a shame she is pregnant when she has such potential to go on to college and a professional career. All my work and effort with her for these past two years will just go down the drain with this pregnancy. Her family doesn't really value education, so what kind of help can she expect from them in the future? Her father may very likely throw her out of the house or maybe even hurt her. If she did obtain an abortion, that would simplify the whole situation. She would not have to deal with her family and neither would I. She could receive one of the scholarships she very likely will be offered, and can even go away to school so she can become her own person. How can I think of that as an option, when as a Catholic I don't believe in abortion. That's not the point. Lupe doesn't really feel abortion is a moral issue for her. But her family, if and when they found out she had an abortion, would challenge the school and they would be so furious at me.

We will examine the worker's reflections to discern how ethical issues are salient on many different levels. In addition, cultural diversity themes of pertinence will be elucidated to identify when ethical issues are relevant.

VALUE IMPOSITION

Workers must be cognizant of their values, and if and how they may be imposed on a client system. Linzer (1999) cites Levy (1973) in classifying values in social work as falling along three dimensions: (1) values can be preferred conceptions of people; (2) they may be preferred outcomes for people; or (3) preferred instrumentalities for addressing people. In Lupe's case, the worker has spent time and resources to support Lupe's academic goal of higher education. The student has shown motivation to achieve. These behaviors are based on the worker's and this student's value for education. For the worker, this value falls in the dimension of preferred outcomes for people. She has invested a lot of time in this student. Certainly, this value is particularly viable for women and for members of diverse groups. However, this value preference can challenge this worker with counter-transference themes. Is Ms. Middle really able to discern what this client needs at this time? Or, is she allowing her time-consuming efforts with this student and her own values to convolute the problem solving that must take place? Is she imposing her own preferences on this sticky situation? Despite Lupe's disappointing situation, what are the core issues and needs at this point for this client system?

Siporin (1982) identifies the various ways professionals can err, even when they are aware of ethical guidelines. For instance, they may allow value judgments or insufficient conscious use of self to weaken their ability to carry out ethical practice. Ms. Middle must recognize that her personal investments and personal values must be eradicated from her work with this teen. How can she look beyond her own preferences to see what is in the client's best interest?

RIGHT TO FREEDOM

One of the ways social workers are ethically bound to work with clients is to insure that they have access to resources and to inform them of their options. Dolgoff & Loewenberg (1985) identify two basic ethical issues in social work practice: freedom and power. They observe that we have two professional obligations to clients: "The obligation to provide professional help when needed or requested by a client in order to assure or improve that person's welfare. The obligation not to interfere with a client's freedom" (p. 23). While the option of an abortion would indeed appear to simplify many aspects of this teenager's situation, the worker cannot allow her own preferences to push the client in a particular direction. She must provide all the information about her options so Lupe can have the freedom to select her preference.

Yet, when the worker catches herself thinking about abortion as an option and then realizes that it is against her own personal views, she is still able to acknowledge that Lupe has to decide what is morally right for herself. The worker cannot assume that, because someone is Catholic, she will necessarily reject abortion as an option. In fact, a social worker may even be able to share her own personal values on such a sensitive area as abortion, when indicated, if it is an avenue for giving a client another perspective or option that might not otherwise be considered. The main ethical issue for the worker is not to share personal views if doing so will push the client in that direction, either through the worker's own insistence or the client's sense of pressure from the worker. Thus, Ms. Middle must not err either by not offering all the options or by pushing her own preference, because these behaviors interfere with a client's freedom.

IMPLICATIONS OF CHOICES

The importance of freedom in decision making also mandates enabling the client to discern the implications of each choice she might make. By assessing the implications for each option, the client will be able to be guided by her own judgment, her value preferences as well as political realities. For clients who are undocumented, it is especially critical to identify and evaluate the limitations and implications of their choices because they have far-reaching impact.

Ms. Middle must review with Lupe all her options. Helping a client thoroughly examine all the costs and benefits of having an abortion promotes free choice. There may be costs to this option that the worker may not consider if she is not from the cultural or racial group of the client. The worker should directly ask if there are cultural implications that might result from having an abortion. To frame this option within a cultural view may provoke a concern that could be sensitive in the client's decision making, but one the worker might not think to consider.

ASSURE OR IMPROVE WELFARE

If Lupe decides to have her child and obtain health care from the public arena, Ms. Middle must seek out all the information on how this might challenge her eligibility for legal immigration for herself or her father and brother. This is part of identifying all the implications for each choice a client is considering. Because the implications of choice-making related to public resources has become such a major issue for immigrants, the Clinton Administration issued policy statements in May 1999 to delineate what services immigrants were entitled to receive without jeopardizing their applications for immigration (Bellisle, 1999).

Workers have the ethical responsibility to clarify these kinds of issues so their clients' choices are informed. This enables the worker to fulfill both ethical obligations to clients that Dolgoff and Lowenberg (1985) emphasized: to help assure or improve a client's welfare and not to interfere with a client's freedom.

The worker must examine her own political views on immigration and how she feels about undocumented immigrants. The issue of legal status is a value-laden theme. Those who cross a border without documentation are seen by many as true criminals. Others are angry that they utilize resources like schools and health care (Hayes-Bautista, 1999).

Social workers are not immune to political sentiments, and must face the reality of how they truly feel about persons who are undocumented. This will insure that unconscious or preconscious feelings of antipathy do not cloud their ability to offer a client who is undocumented the full array of options to which they have a right, according to the NASW Code of Ethics.

For those social workers who feel strongly that the undocumented should not use this country's resources, they must remove themselves from those agencies that serve the undocumented. Or, in a particular case, they must refer the client to a worker who does not hold that bias. Otherwise, personal political views that disallow providing undocumented clients all their options for needed resources result in unethical professional behaviors.

Competency Issues

Several stereotypes were evident in Ms. Middle's thinking. Although she had met Lupe's family on one occasion, she did not believe they valued education. She felt it would be necessary for Lupe to "get away" from her family so as to become her own person. These sentiments exemplify the cultural stereotyping that often occurs when nonminority professionals interact with Latinos.

Often Latinos, especially those who are immigrants, want their children to benefit from the educational opportunities offered in this society. However, many of them are poorly educated. They are not knowledgeable about the format and expectations that characterize school systems in the United States. This lack of experience with and knowledge of educational systems is often misinterpreted as their devaluing education.

Another area where misinterpretations are made is about the traits and styles of Latino family systems. Often, professionals see the Latino family's interdependence as a liability, rather than the strength this cohesive system produces.

Ms. Middle shows concern that Lupe's father may even be physically violent with Lupe. As Falicov (1998) stresses, Latino parents do become very upset at a teen daughter's pregnancy that is out of wedlock. Again, this demonstrates a strength the family exhibits in its expectations for its daughters. But the ill feelings diminish as they welcome the birth of the child into their family system. The worker may be misinterpreting Lupe's fear by assuming that the father might be violent. The worker must individualize this family system and to assess and ask Lupe if the father is or has been violent. Could he become violent in this situation?

Because Ms. Middle has met the family only once, is she buying into her own stereotyping about Latino families and the assumed authoritarian stance of the father, coupled with the violence theme? Is she really wondering if this is, in fact, what Lupe's father is like?

Another area of misinformation and value imposition is the assumption that Lupe needs to get away from her family to become her own person. This value stance of the worker on the importance of individuation may stem from her own cultural style. For Latino families, the centrality of the family in the life of the individual must be readily entertained. It could be that Lupe wants "to get away." On the other hand, she may have mixed feelings about leaving her family system. The worker needs to help the client understand the implications of the choices she makes.

Should Lupe be able to have options for going to college away from home, it is incumbent on the worker to help Lupe process the implications of this choice. As Latinos acculturate, especially young people, they need to discern how choices present the potential for diminishing some values that may be important to them. Zuniga (1988) emphasizes the viability of helping persons comprehend how their choices impact their acculturation process. A cost–benefit analysis of their acculturation process enables them to recognize the value in becoming bicultural.

These examples of stereotyping, value imposition, failing to individualize Latino families, and failing to delineate implications of acculturation choices of members are all characteristics of professional practice that demonstrate cultural incompetence.

Professional groups such as psychologists, school counselors, and social workers have indicated concern about the ability of professionals to provide services that acknowledge and respect the values and style differences exhibited by diverse populations (Corey, Corey, & Callanan, 1988; Lum, 1999; Pedersen & Marsella 1982). In 1986, the American Psychological Association (APA) Committee on International Relations in Psychology held a symposium to address whether the APA's ethical principles were culturally encapsulated or ignored cultural differences. Pederson (1986), as noted by Corey and colleagues (1988), argued that the principles were in fact encapsulated. Pederson asserted that the codes were based on stereotyped values that represented only the dominant culture. The codes were grounded only on one single standard of normal and ethical behavior that did not include culturally defined alternatives. Lastly, the codes were technique-oriented, so they needed to be reformulated to be congruent with multicultural situations.

Ethical principles and codes for the American Association for Counseling and Development and the American Psychological Association were viewed as needing to incorporate the variety of principles that supported and viewed cultural competence as part of ethical practice. The National Association of Social Workers Code of Ethics highlights the need to be competent and the importance of social workers to be flexible in order to address the diversity they encounter (Hepworth, Rooney, & Larsen, 1997).

Thus, professional schools must train their students to be culturally competent. Professionals already in the field must insure that they receive the training to become competent with diverse populations. Professional schools that do not train students to be culturally competent are being unethical. Professionals who do not upgrade their skills to be competent with diverse groups are acting in an unethical manner.

CONCLUSIONS

This chapter has elucidated the traits and within-group differences and situational stressors that often characterize Latino populations. The unique needs and stresses that characterize undocumented members of the Latino population raise issues concerning ethical responsibility on the part of professionals like social workers. Examples of how cultural incompetence can disrespect the cultural and situational needs of Latino clients were illustrated in the Ortega family vignette. Ethical mandates related to the right to resources and the right to freedom were some of the principles used to offer perspectives on this cultural vignette. The urgency to insure that Latino and other diverse populations have human services that are offered in a culturally competent manner has been underscored by viewing cultural incompetence as unethical. Framing the need for culturally competent services as an ethical mandate elucidates the seriousness of how services are provided to poor, immigrant, and diverse populations.

REFERENCES

Bellisle, M. (1999, May 27). Policy on benefits is praised for clarity. *San Diego Union Tribune,* A-3.

California State Employment Development Department.(1986). Socio-Economic Trends in California, 1940–1980. Sacramento, CA: Author.

Cervantes, J. & Ramirez, O. (1992). Spirituality and family dynamics in psychotherapy with Latino children. In L. A. Vargas & J. D. Koss-Chioino (Eds.). *Working with culture: Psychotherapeutic interventions with ethnic minority children and adolescents* (pp. 103–108). San Francisco, CA:

Corey, G., Corey, M. S., & Callanan, P. (Eds.). (1988). *Issues and ethics in the helping professions,* 3rd ed. Pacific Grove, CA: Brooks/Cole.

Cromwell, R. & Ruiz, R. A. (1979). The myth of macho dominance in decision-making within Mexican and Chicano families. *Hispanic Journal of Behavioral Sciences, 1,* 355–373.

Dolgoff, R. & Loewenberg, F. (1985). *Ethical decisions for social work practice.* Itasca, IL: F. E. Peacock.

Elkins, D. (1988). On being spiritual without necessarily being religious. *Journal of Humanistic Psychology, 28* (4), 5–18.

Falicov, C. (1998). *Latino families in therapy: A guide to multicultural practice.* New York: Guilford.

Garcia, J. & Marotta, S. (1997). Characterization of the latino population. In J. Garcia & M. C. Zea (Eds.), *Psychological interventions and research with Latino populations* (pp. 1–14). Boston, MA: Allyn & Bacon.

Hayes-Bautista, D. (1999, March). Changing demographics and the new millenium: Implications for culturally competent social work training. Annual Program Meeting, Council of Social Work Education, San Francisco, California.

Hayes-Bautista, D., Hurtado, A., Valdez, R., & Hernandez, A. (1992). *No longer a minority: Latinos and social policy in California.* Los Angeles: UCLA Chicano Studies Research Center.

Hepworth, D., Rooney, R., & Larsen, J. R. (1997). *Direct social work practice: Theory and skills.* Pacific Grove, CA: Brooks/Cole.

Hurtado, A., Hayes-Bautista, D., Valdez, R., & Hernandez, A. (1992). *Redefining California: Latino social engagement in a multicultural society.* Los Angeles: UCLA Chicano Studies Research Center.

Levy, C. S. (1973). The value base of social work. *Journal of Education for Social Work, 9* (4), 35–42.

Linzer, N. (1999). *Resolving ethical dilemmas in social work practice.* Boston, MA: Allyn & Bacon.

Lum, D. (1996). *Social work practice and people of color: A process–stage approach,* 3rd ed. Pacific Grove, CA: Brooks/Cole.

Lum, D. (1999). *Culturally competent practice: A framework for growth and action.* Pacific Grove, CA: Brooks/Cole.

Melville, M. B. & Lykes, M. B. (1992) Guatemalan Indian children and the sociocultural effects of government sponsored torrorism. *Social Science & Medicine 34,* 533–548

Montgomery, P. A. (1994). The Hispanic population in the United States: March 1993 (U.S. Bureau of the Census, Current Population Reports, Series P 29–475). Washington, DC: U.S. Government Printing Office.

Montijo, J. (1985). Therapeutic relationships with the poor: A Puerto Rican perspective. *Psychotherapy, 22,* 436–440.

Murillo, N. (1971). The Mexican American family. In N. Wagner & M. Haug (Eds.), *Chicanos: Social and psychological perspectives* (pp. 97–108). Saint Louis: C. V. Mosby.

Padilla, Yolanda. (1999). Immigrant policy: Issues for social work practice. In P. L. Ewalt, E. M. Freeman, A. E. Fortune, D. L. Poole, & S. Witkin (Eds.), *Multicultural issues in social work: Practice and research* (pp. 589–604). Washington, DC: NASW.

Pederson, P. B. (1986). Are the APA ethical principles culturally encapsulated? Unpublished manuscript, Syracuse University. As cited in Corey et al. (Eds.), *Issues and ethics in the helping professions.* Pacific Grove, CA: Brooks/Cole.

Pedersen, P. & Marsella, A. J. (1982). The ethical crisis for cross-cultural counseling and therapy. *Professional Psychology, 13* (4), 492–500.

Ramirez, M. (1983). *Psychology of the Americans.* Elmsford, NY: Pergamon Press.

Ramirez, M. & Price-Williams, D. (1974). Cognitive styles in children: Two Mexican communities. *InterAmerican Journal of Psychology, 8,* 93–101.

Roland, A. (1988). *In search of self in India and Japan: Towards a cross-cultural psychology.* Princeton, NJ: Princeton University Press.

Rubel, A. (1966). *Across the tracks.* Austin: University of Texas Press.

Salcido, R. M. (1982). Use of service in Los Angeles County by undocumented families: Their perceptions of stress and sources of support. *California Sociologist, 5* (2), 119–131.

Siporin, M. (1982). Moral philosophy in social work today. *Social Service Review 56,* 516–38, as cited in R. Dolgoff & F. Loewenberg (Eds.). (1985). *Ethical decisions for social work practice.* Itasca, IL: F. E. Peacock.

Valle, R. and Mendoza, L. (1978). *The elder Latino.* San Diego, CA: Campanile.

Zuniga, Maria E. (1988). Clinical interventions with Chicanas. *Psychotherapy, 25,* 288–293.

Zuniga, Maria E. (1998). Families with Latino roots. In E. Lynch & M. Hanson (Eds.), *Developing cross-cultural competence: A guide for working with children and their families* (pp. 209–249). Baltimore, MD: Brooks.

CHAPTER 5

CRITICAL VALUES AND FIRST NATIONS PEOPLES

MICHAEL YELLOW BIRD

In the contiguous forty-eight United States and Alaska, many Indigenous Peoples are mistakenly called *Indians, American Indians,* or *Native Americans.* They are *not* Indians or American Indians because they are not from India. They are *not* Native Americans because Indigenous Peoples did not refer to lands as America until Europeans arrived and imposed this name. Thus, this chapter uses the terms *First Nations Peoples* and *Indigenous Peoples* to describe the original peoples of these lands (those mistakenly called American Indians and Alaska Natives). Although Native Hawaiians are also Indigenous Peoples whose struggles for political sovereignty and aboriginal rights are, in many respects, similar to those of First Nations Peoples on the mainland of the United States, this chapter focuses on those residing in the contiguous forty-eight United States and Alaska.

In this chapter, *Indian, American Indian,* or *Native American* are used only in direct quotes and are avoided because they are "colonized" and "inaccurate" names that oppress the identities of First Nations Peoples (Yellow Bird, 1999a). While *First Nations Peoples* and *Indigenous Peoples* are generic labels for more than 550 different tribal groups, they are introduced as empowering and accurate generalized descriptors. The terms are plural and capitalized to acknowledge the heterogeneity and political sovereignty of Indigenous Peoples.

The generic labels Indigenous Peoples prefer to be called varies. What is most respectful and appropriate is to refer to Indigenous Peoples by their tribal Nation or Indigenous affiliation. Often, this means using a name that each group has selected for itself from its own Indigenous language. This chapter discusses several key values of First Nations Peoples. The first part provides a brief definition of *Indigenous Peoples* and examines the effects of European American colonialism on the values of these groups. The second part concentrates on macro values critical to First Nations Peoples' empowerment and makes suggestions for culturally competent and justice-oriented social work practice. In this chapter, *culturally competent* refers to awareness, while *justice-oriented* refers to critical progressive actions.

WHO ARE INDIGENOUS PEOPLES?

Indigenous Peoples are diverse populations who reside on ancestral lands, share an ancestry with the original inhabitants of these lands, have distinct cultures and languages, and regard themselves as different from those who have colonized and now control their lands (Stamatopulou, 1994). Today, many Indigenous Peoples identify themselves according to affiliation in a band, nation, confederacy, tribe, or village. There is no typical group. Each has its own unique history, language, land, dress, food, sacred and secular ceremonies, worldviews, and social and political organization. Indigenous Peoples reside in different geographical regions in the United States: deserts, arctic and subarctic areas, mountains, plains, woodlands, everglades, and along rivers and oceans. The estimated population of Indigenous Peoples is 2.39 million (U.S. Census Bureau, 1999). In 1990, approximately 8.8 million claimed Indigenous ancestry (Passel, 1996). About 37 percent of Indigenous Peoples live on 279 reservations, in 223 Alaskan native villages, and on historic areas in Oklahoma (Snipp, 1996). The majority resides in off-reservation rural or urban areas.

Defining membership among First Nations is difficult. Each has its own requirements for recognizing members. Methods of identification include language, residence, cultural affiliation, recognition by a community, degree of "blood," genealogical lines of descent, and self-identification (Thornton, 1996). Many require members to have at least one-eighth Indigenous blood and others one-fourth to one-half. Some do not have a blood requirement rule and members only need to be able to document proof of ancestry. Thornton (1996) reported that twenty-one tribes had a blood requirement of more than one-fourth, 183 required one-fourth or less, and 98 had no minimum requirement. Most federal laws require that a person have one-fourth Indigenous blood to receive federal services and be considered First Nations (Pevar, 1992).

COLONIALISM AND FIRST NATIONS

Although Indigenous Peoples are diverse, they share a common history of subjugation under European American colonialism. *Colonialism* is the invasion by alien peoples of territories inhabited by peoples of a different race and culture and the establishment of political, social, intellectual, psychological, and economic control over that territory (Yellow Bird, 1999a). Under colonial rule, the colonizer appropriates, often through force or deception, the territory, resources, wealth, and power of the Indigenous Peoples. Simultaneously, Indigenous Peoples experience loss of life, wealth, culture, lands, and inherent sovereign rights. *Colonization* is the process phase of colonialism and refers to the methods that the colonizers use to establish control and domination.

European American colonizers have used different colonization methods to destroy the values of First Nations Peoples. One of the most common was forcibly taking First Nations children from their families and putting them in off-reservation boarding schools where they were taught that they were inferior to whites. Social workers, Christian missionaries, teachers, and government agents were the colonial vanguard of this assault. In boarding schools, children were subjected to harsh discipline when they were caught speaking their languages or expressing their values. In some instances, they were subjected to brutal punishment. A Salish elder, Henry Castle, who had attended a boarding school in British Columbia recalls:

> When his classmates were caught speaking their language one day at Coqualeetza school near Chilliwack they had their mouths pried open and sewing needles driven through their tongues into the bottom of their mouths by their caretakers (Crey, 1991, p. 153).

Teaching Indigenous children they were inferior to whites and punishing them because of their tribal values caused many to devalue their Indigenous identity. For example, Ralph Feather, a student at Carlisle Indian school in Carlisle, Pennsylvania during the late 1800s, wrote home saying, "I think of you all, but I don't like your Indian ways, because you don't know the good ways, also you don't know good many things" (Adams, 1995, p. 275). Children who did not attend off-reservation boarding schools were required to attend schools on the reservation. However, these environments were no better at respecting the children or their values.

Neocolonialism

Colonialism has not ended for Indigenous Peoples in the United States. Today, multinational corporations seeking control of Indigenous Peoples' natural resources and lands threaten their communities while the U.S. Congress, Secretary of the Department of the Interior, and the Bureau of Indian Affairs (BIA) administratively dominate the affairs of Indigenous Peoples. For instance, Congress maintains plenary power over Indigenous Peoples that is so complete that a simple Congressional act of legislation could terminate tribal governments, lands, and identity. The policies of the Secretary of the Department of the Interior and BIA often require tribal governments to seek permission for settling a tribal member's estate, building a road, starting an economic enterprise, or spending tribal monies.

Under neocolonialism, Indigenous Peoples' values and identity are still subjugated and controlled. For instance, some professional sports organizations use team names that refer to Indigenous Peoples in a stereotypical and racist manner. In football, the name of the professional team in Washington, DC is called the "Washington Redskins," even though *redskin* is an offensive label for First Nations Peoples (*Merriam-Webster Collegiate Dictionary*, 1992). The professional baseball team of Cleveland, Ohio, the "Cleveland Indians," has a team logo that is a red-faced, big-nosed, grotesquely grinning "Indian" with a single red eagle feather protruding from the back of his head. Eagle feathers are highly valued and considered very sacred to First Nations Peoples and, to many, the Cleveland Indians baseball team's logo is racist and sacrilegious.

Colonialism has produced various behaviors and feelings among Indigenous Peoples such as silence, avoidance, resentment, and resistance. Social workers must understand that it will be nearly impossible to practice culturally competent and justice-oriented social work with Indigenous Peoples without a clear understanding of the effects of past, present, and future colonialism.

VALUES AND FIRST NATIONS PEOPLES

According to Scheibe (1970) values are wishes, desires, goals, passions, and morals, and what is wanted, best, preferable, and what should be done. Stein (1985) suggests that "people not only use values to help them to decide among choices but also to help them constantly define who they are, whom they belong to, and who and what are to be regarded as outside" (p. 36). Studies of Indigenous Peoples' values have generally been anecdotal and drawn from small samples of different tribal groups. Much of what is known about the values of Indigenous Peoples emerged from ethnographic studies conducted by non-Indigenous Peoples at the turn of the century (Joe, 1989). Generally, case studies comparing value differences between Indigenous Peoples, and cross-cultural studies comparing the values of Indigenous and non-Indigenous Peoples, have been used to arrive at a general set of values of Indigenous Peoples (DuBray, 1993).

In the social work literature, much of the focus with respect to Indigenous Peoples' values has been on those relevant to micro practice situations. These values include, but are not limited to, noninterference or self-reliance (Good Tracks, 1973), respect for elders (Red Horse, 1980), present-time orientation, anonymity, and submission or nonconfrontation (DuBray, 1993; Joe, 1989). This chapter concentrates on several values relevant to macro practice situations and macro practice skills such as advocacy, consciousness-raising, and activism. However, the following values should not be construed as fixed or easily generalized to all Indigenous Peoples. What is valued among Indigenous Peoples varies a great deal.

The first set, primary values, are those that are fundamental to individual, family, clan, and tribal relationships. The second set, secondary values, are those that are forged, or sharpened, as a result of colonialism. The final set, emerging values, are those that are relevant to larger structural phenomenon, such as globalization, wherein First Nations Peoples in the United States are forming relationships with other Indigenous Peoples throughout the world due to a common history of colonization.

Primary Values

Identity as a Value.   The importance of ethnic identity varies among peoples in the United States. Indigenous Peoples are no exception. While some Indigenous Peoples have a deep sense of their tribal identity, others have been so forcefully colonized that they do not. However, for many, tribal identity is perhaps one of the most important of all primary values (Yellow Bird, 1999a). For instance, when

Indigenous Peoples meet one another, one of the most fundamental questions asked is, "What tribe are you?" This question is designed to understand who a person is in relation to an Indigenous group and what, if any, tribal connection exists between the person asking the question and the person answering.

A person's tribal identity is critical because it provides a connection to a principal cultural group that can give structure, meaning, direction, and purpose to one's life as it relates to specific tribal customs. Tribal identity provides a sense of belonging and tells individuals who they are, how they should behave, and to what they should aspire. Tribal identity creates a reality of attachment to a community and culture in which an individual can be validated, appreciated, and renewed. As a member of an Indigenous community, an individual can be involved in numerous public and private tribal events and ceremonies (Yellow Bird & Snipp, 1994). Some events are designed to help individuals strengthen their tribal identity. Tribal ceremonies, in which an individual receives a name that is connected to ancestors or reflects good deeds, help shape an individual's identity within his or her tribal community. Adoption into a specific tribal clan assists one to gain new clan relatives and an identity as a member of the clan.

Indigenous Peoples' identity has been under assault for hundreds of years under colonial rule. For example, in 1889, Commissioner of Indian Affairs Thomas Jefferson Morgan wrote the following policy statement to all who managed the education of Indigenous children:

> In all proper ways, teachers in the Indian schools should endeavor to appeal to the highest element of manhood and womanhood in their pupils, exciting in them an ambition after excellence in character and dignity of surroundings, and they should carefully avoid any unnecessary reference to the fact that they are Indians (Prucha, 1975, p. 181).

Today, the identities of Indigenous Peoples remain under threat. The "Indian" mascots of sports teams stereotype Indigenous Peoples' cultural identity. Federal budget cuts for tribal governments threaten Indigenous Peoples' political identity as sovereign nations. For instance, in 1994, Senator Slade Gorton, a Republican from Washington, proposed cutting $600 million dollars or 30 percent of the funding Indigenous Peoples would receive from Congress in 1995 (Slade Gorton vs. The Tribes, 1995). Finally, the individual tribal identities of First Nations Peoples are threatened because they are often unacknowledged and ignored by the U.S. public. For example, in a recent study of racial labels applied to Indigenous Peoples (Yellow Bird, 1999a), several of the First Nations participants in the study stated that Indigenous Peoples see the incredible differences among themselves. However, this diversity is not apparent to non-First Nations Peoples. For instance, one subject stated that, while non-First Nations students in his classes understand the difference between a Greek and Swede, they are totally lost when they are asked about the differences between a Tlingit and Kiowa or a Cherokee and Pequot.

To be culturally competent, social workers must respect tribal identity and learn about the diversity of Indigenous Peoples. Justice-oriented social work requires consciousness-raising about tribal diversity and respect for tribal identity. Justice-oriented social workers support Indigenous Peoples' efforts to protect identity that is under threat from sports teams and state and federal governments.

Spirituality.   Yellow Bird (1995), in reference to Sahnish (Arikara), says, "spirituality is the knowledge of, value for, and participation in our sacred ceremonies and traditions" (p. 66). For many First Nations Peoples, spiritual beliefs and practices have great value and have aided many to find meaning, consciousness, and wholeness in their lives. Often, Indigenous Peoples' spirituality is attained through long-established, organized First Nations or non-First Nations religion. At other times it arises from individual or group-oriented spiritual practices that may emerge from individual experiences, such as dreams, or a community crisis that brings people together. Sacred and secular tribal ceremonies have and continue to help Indigenous Peoples define and maintain their relationship with a creator and all that is living and alive in the Universe.

Sacred landscapes, rivers, forests, stories, songs, plants (medicines), dances, and symbols are often at the center of Indigenous spirituality and help First Nations Peoples find wholeness and renew their cultures. In past and present times, Indigenous Peoples have used spirituality to overcome despair and cope with the oppression brought on by forces outside their cultures. Many also use spirituality to celebrate who they are, what they know and believe, and the triumphs in life that they experience. For many, spiritual beliefs, ceremonies, and practices were, and remain, a major defense against European American colonization.

Indigenous Peoples' spirituality has continually been attacked and threatened under colonial rule. The ceremony called the Sun Dance, practiced by many plains tribes, was outlawed by federal authorities among the Sahnish, Hidatsa, and Mandan tribes in the early 1900s. Anyone guilty of participating in the Sun Dance had rations withheld, was jailed for a second offense, and jailed for ten days for practicing traditional medicine (Gilman and Schneider, 1987). Today, Indigenous Peoples' sacred beliefs and sites remain threatened. For instance, in northern Arizona there is an ongoing effort by the Hopi and Diné to prevent the U.S. Forest Service from converting San Francisco Peaks into a ski resort because this site is considered sacred by these two groups (Churchill, 1992).

Indigenous Peoples are also embroiled in efforts to repatriate the contents of ancestral burials and sacred and cultural patrimony from federal agencies, universities, museums, and private collectors. Often Indigenous Peoples' burial sites and their contents were routinely excavated without regard for their spiritual beliefs or respect for the dead. Sacred beliefs about the dead brought Indigenous Peoples together to work to pass federal legislation protecting their burial sites and to have their ancestors returned to them for reburial. The Museum Act of 1989 and the Native American Graves Protection and Repatriation Act of 1990 are two laws that help accomplish this repatriation.

To demonstrate cultural competence regarding the spiritual values of Indigenous Peoples, social workers must respect the rights of First Nations Peoples to express their spirituality as it relates to their cultural traditions. Justice-oriented social work requires strong advocacy for, and consciousness-raising about, the protection of Indigenous Peoples' sacred sites, cultural heritage, rivers, forests, stories, songs, plants (medicines), dances, and symbols.

Sharing and Generosity.   Sharing and generosity are important values among many First Nations Peoples. Helping others through the sharing of what one has, whether it is time, resources, or knowledge, is a way many groups reinforce their concern and appreciation for one another. These values help maintain healthy relationships and contribute to peace, harmony, and social justice among all tribal members. Among many tribes, generosity toward others is similar to making deposits in the social and moral bank of the tribal community. While most do not expect immediate returns for their goodwill toward others, many such deposits often return, to the giver, kind and generous treatment by those helped.

Many Indigenous Peoples often use "give-away" and "potlatch" ceremonies to share what they have. Give-away items often include food, clothing, blankets, money, and cookware and are equivalent to giving life to others (Pemina Yellow Bird, personal communication, July 10, 1999). For many, sharing and generosity are part of their original religious tribal teachings. Among the Sahnish, for instance, a holy being named Mother Corn taught them, "to provide for those who should be dependent upon them . . . to be generous and forbearing, to practise hospitality to strangers, to be kind to the poor . . . " (Gilmore, 1930, p. 108). In the past, the sharing and generosity of Indigenous Peoples were regarded as cultural defects and many attempts were made by whites to extinguish these values (Meyer, 1977). In one instance, a missionary working among the Mandan, Hidatsa, and Sahnish in the late 1800s declared, "They are a generous people and feel their responsibility toward their brother. But the mission work is gradually overcoming this" (Meyer, 1977, p. 128).

Today, sharing and generosity are important values among many First Nations Peoples. Culturally competent social workers will see these values as meaningful to Indigenous Peoples because they help form important bonds of caring and concern and represent important cultural strengths. Justice-oriented social workers understand that these values are important and will advocate for greater generosity and sharing among all peoples.

Language.   Language is critical to cultural expression because it is through language that unique cultural experience and meaning is shared and made relevant (Kelly, 1991). Since time immemorial, the tribal languages of Indigenous Peoples have enabled them to transmit their cultural stories, customs, beliefs, and values to contemporary and later generations. Language helps to identify speakers and listeners as individuals from unique tribal cultures and to establish relationships with those who share the same linguistic heritage. Tribal languages are central to cultural identity and form the fundamental means for the transmission and survival of their histories, religions, political institutions, beliefs and values (P.L. 101-477, Native American Languages Act, 1990).

The assaults by European American colonizers on tribal languages through government and Christian boarding schools have caused a declining ability by speakers to transmit this value to the next generations. Today, while there are about 155 First Nations languages spoken in the United States, 138 are classified as moribund, and most First Nations children grow up speaking English and only a few words of their Native language (Crawford, 1994). Culturally competent social workers will tune in to the trauma Indigenous Peoples experienced because of the attacks on their languages. Social workers will consider this history important when working with First Nations Peoples. Justice-oriented social workers will do more: They will raise the consciousness of others about this aspect of cultural genocide and proactively use their organizing and fund-raising skills to help Indigenous Peoples start language programs and create helping lexicons using the specific languages of their First Nations clients.

Secondary Values

Resistance and Rights.   Since the coming of Christopher Columbus, Indigenous Peoples have resisted European American colonialism. Indigenous Peoples did not willingly surrender their lands, water, timber, minerals, cultures, beliefs, and identities to colonizers. Nor did they surrender their aboriginal rights to fish, hunt, gather, and exist as sovereign nations. On the contrary, Indigenous Peoples have always vigorously resisted colonization, hoping that their aboriginal rights and sovereignty would someday be honored by those who invaded their lands. As early as the 1920s, Indigenous Peoples had approached the League of Nations to protest the racism and discrimination they faced in the United States (Human Rights, 1990). The League of Nations was created after World War I to encourage international cooperation to attain peace and security (Chamberlain, 1995). However, the United States never joined the League of Nations and condemned its activities.

While the history of the colonizer has, for generations, advanced the myth of "how the West was won," for many Indigenous Peoples the war is not yet over. Indeed, in *Peace, Power, Righteousness: An Indigenous Manifesto,* Taiaiake Alfred (1999) writes:

> Indigenous peoples today are seeking to transcend the history of pain and loss that began with the coming of Europeans into our world . . . Even as history's shadow lengthens to mark the passing of that brutal age, the Western compulsion to control remains strong. To preserve what is left of our cultures and lands is a constant fight . . . Thankfully, those who accept the colonization of their nations are a small minority. Most people continue to participate in, or at least support, the struggle to gain recognition and respect for their right to exist as peoples, unencumbered by demands, controls, and false identities imposed on them by others (p. xi).

Indigenous Peoples continue their resistance and voice their rights through tribal grassroots and government activism. Resistance is found in artwork, poetry, literature, academic essays, and revisionist histories telling Indigenous Peoples' side of European "discovery," "conquest," and "freedom." Indigenous rights and resistance have also entered the information age through numerous Websites on the Internet that contain discussions of powerful anticolonial rhetoric to children's stories describing First Nations cultures. For some, tribal economic development has become a major form of resistance. Initiatives such as tribal casinos create jobs on the reservation that allow tribal members to remain in their communities for employment. Casinos and other economic development strategies also fund language and culture programs, tribal colleges, and other cultural infrastructures.

Culturally competent social workers must be aware of Indigenous Peoples' resistance to colonization and their efforts to maintain their rights, and link these struggles to theories of resiliency and strengths. To counter colonialism, justice-oriented social workers will learn more about Indigenous Peoples' rights and resistance so they can actively raise the consciousness of others.

Land.   Land means life. Land insures the survival and well-being of Indigenous Peoples' cultures and, thus, has tremendous spiritual, cultural, and political significance. Because First Nations Peoples are the original inhabitants of the Americas, they have special cultural ties to these lands and histories predating all other groups. As the original residents, Indigenous Peoples have created ceremonies and maintained powerful and distinct spiritual and cultural beliefs that affirm their relationship to these lands. A common belief of First Nations Peoples is that the earth is their mother and they must maintain balance and harmony with their surroundings (Burger, 1990). One of the most quoted statements about Indigenous Peoples' relationship to the land comes from Chief Seattle (Seeathl) of the Suquamish Nation. His speech was made in 1854 to federal government officials who wanted to buy the lands of his people. The following is a brief excerpt:

> The Great Chief in Washington sends word that he wishes to buy our land . . . How can you buy or sell the sky, the warmth of the land? The idea is strange to us. If we do not own the freshness of the air and the sparkle of the water, how can you buy them? Every part of this earth is sacred to my people. Every shining pine needle, every sandy shore, every mist in the dark woods, every clearing, and all humming insects, are holy in the memory and experiences of my people . . . (Community Panel, Family and Children's Services, 1992, pp. 125–127).

To the European American colonizers land also means life. Churchill (1992) says, "Control of land and the resources within it has been the essential source of conflict between the Euroamerican settler population and indigenous nations" (p. 139). To build America, colonizers often illegally drove Indigenous Peoples off their lands using the force of their courts, warfare, or by breaking treaties they had made with Indigenous Peoples. Following the passage of the Indian Removal Act of 1830, thousands of Indigenous Peoples were removed from their traditional territories in the southeastern United States to lands west of the Mississippi River. The removal of the Cherokee from Georgia in 1838 is the most well-known forced removal. In 1828, the state of Georgia claimed jurisdiction over Cherokee land within their boundaries and declared Cherokee laws invalid. However, in 1832 the U.S. Supreme Court ruled that the State of Georgia had no legal jurisdiction over the Cherokee because they were a sovereign nation. Undaunted by the Supreme court's ruling, the state of Georgia, assisted by President Andrew Jackson, relentlessly tormented the Cherokee until they ceded their lands in 1838 (Thornton, 1987). Jackson cared little that thousands of Cherokee lost their lands, their homes, and died on the forced march to Oklahoma. Despite his genocidal removal policies toward Indigenous Peoples, he is memorialized on this nation's twenty-dollar bill.

The amount of lands illegally seized from Indigenous Peoples lands is outrageous. In 1500, Indigenous Peoples controlled billions of acres of land. By 1887, the land base of First Nations Peoples was down to 140 million acres and, by 1931, it had shrunk to less than 48 million acres (Olson and Wilson, 1986). Broken treaties and failures by the United States to ratify land agreements made with Indigenous Peoples resulted in Indigenous Peoples losing hundreds of millions of acres of lands. In 1980, "The federal government held in trust 52 million acres of Native American land" (Olson and Wilson, 1986, p. 209). However, struggles over the land between Indigenous Peoples and the United States are not over. The Lakota continue to assert their claims to the Black Hills in South Dakota, the Western Shoshone are asserting claims in Nevada, and, in New York, the Oneida and Seneca are seeking return of lands illegally seized.

The culturally competent social worker must not only respect Indigenous Peoples' value for the land, but must also support Indigenous Peoples' efforts to protect their lands from outside encroachment. Justice-oriented social work means social workers must vigorously advocate for returning lands to Indigenous Peoples that were illegally taken or resulted from broken treaties by federal or state governments.

Emerging Values

Indigenous Global Alliances.   An emerging value of Indigenous Peoples is their formation of global alliances to address corresponding problems brought on by past and present colonization. Such alliances are valued because they produce written resolutions of solidarity between Indigenous Peoples with respect to self-determination. According to Talal and Khan (1987),

> Indigenous Peoples' organizations are becoming increasingly active in gaining support and recognition by the world community. By demanding international access, they are challenging those traditional modes of international behaviour which contributed to domination and oppression that for so long have been their lot. Now, they are resisting as new assaults are carried out against them. They are struggling for survival as peoples, and they need the support of all those who believe in fundamental human rights (p. xii).

There are more than 1000 Indigenous Peoples' organizations worldwide (Burger, 1990). "Since 1975, the World Council of Indigenous Peoples (WCIP) has tried to unite indigenous peoples worldwide round a common programme" (p. 179). At the center of many Indigenous Peoples' alliances are concerns about environmental, biological, cultural, social, economic, land, and educational rights. For example, in May 1985, Indigenous Peoples from around the world gathered in Vancouver, British Columbia and formed the International Indigenous People's Education Association. Membership was open to all that believed the bridge to cultural survival and educational success lies in incorporating traditional values and beliefs with existing educational practices (World Indigenous Peoples Conference on Education, 1999). In 1987, over 1,500 people from seventeen different countries were associated with this alliance. By 1996, the number of people attending had grown to 6000.

Indigenous Peoples have formed numerous other international alliances. For instance, the Indigenous Women's Network (IWN) was created in 1985 to further the empowerment of Indigenous women, their families, communities, and Nations within the Americas and the Pacific Basin (The Indigenous Women's Network, n. d.). A recent Western Hemispheric alliance, the Indigenous Peoples Council Against Biopiracy (1998), was founded to protect Indigenous Peoples' biological resources, such as DNA, from exploitation. Finally, the National Congress of American Indians (1999), the oldest and largest Indigenous Peoples organization in the United States, and the Assembly of First Nations, the largest organization in Canada, recently created a Declaration of Kinship and Cooperation among the Indigenous Peoples and Nations of North America.

Indigenous Peoples' alliances have also been strengthened by their efforts to influence such organizations as the United Nations. Because of the international efforts of Indigenous Peoples to gain rights and recognition, the United Nations created a Working Group on Indigenous Populations that produced a Draft Declaration on the Rights of Indigenous People. The first paragraph reads:

> Indigenous peoples have the right to self-determination, in accordance with international law. By virtue of this right, they freely determine their relationship with the States in which they live, in a spirit of co-existence with other citizens, and freely pursue their economic, social, cultural and spiritual development in conditions of freedom and dignity (Suzuki & Knudtson, 1992, p. 251).

Individuals are also instrumental in building Indigenous alliances. In 1992, Rigoberta Menchú Tum, a Quiché woman from Guatemala, who was awarded the Nobel Prize for Peace, also became the United Nations Goodwill Ambassador for the 1993 International Year of the World's Indigenous People. In accepting her role, she commented on the unity of Indigenous Peoples:

> We believe in the wisdom of our elders and sages, from whom we have inherited strength and learned the art of speech. This has enabled us to reaffirm the validity of our thousand-year history and the justice of our struggles. In turn, this has provided the terrain in which, as indigenous peoples, we have in recent decades broken new ground. The result of this will be the honourable and peaceful renewal of contact between our cultures and the societies in which we live (United Nations, 1994, p. ii).

The formation of Indigenous Peoples' global alliances are critical values emerging from a common history of colonialism. Culturally competent social workers will recognize the need for such alliances. Justice-oriented social workers will help support the building of such alliances. They will also raise the consciousness of others, especially their governments, regarding the necessity for Indigenous Peoples to be free from colonial domination and to pursue global self-determination.

CONCLUSION

This chapter concentrated on values critical to Indigenous Peoples' empowerment, social justice, and self-determination. Several of the values are relevant to macro practice situations and require social work commitment at societal and global levels. At these levels, advocacy, activism, and consciousness-raising skills are essential. However, the above values should not be construed as fixed, most important, or easily generalized to all Indigenous Peoples. What is valued among Indigenous Peoples varies.

European American colonialism has damaging effects on many of the values of First Nations Peoples. Under colonial rule, Indigenous Peoples' values are often trivialized, assaulted, or ignored. Colonialism has produced silence, avoidance, resentment, and resistance and has not ended for First Nations Peoples. Indeed, in many respects, colonialism is clearly linked to many present social, economic, and political problems in Indigenous communities. If the mission of social work is truly about human well-being, social justice, and empowerment, social workers must critically confront the multiple dimensions and undemocratic realities of colonialism. If confrontation is spirited and intelligent, it will produce culturally competent social workers capable of using justice-oriented social work practices as antidotes to colonialism.

REFERENCES

Adams, D. (1995). *Education for extinction: American Indians and the boarding school experience, 1876–1928.* Lawrence, KS: University Press of Kansas.

Alfred, T. (1990). *Peace, power, righteousness: An Indigenous manifesto.* Don Mills, ON: Oxford University Press.

Burger, J. (1990). *The Gaia atlas of First Peoples.* New York: Anchor Books.

Chamberlain, W. (1995). The League of Nations. [On-line] Available: http://www.library.miami.edu/gov/League.html#Failures [1999, September].

Churchill, W. (1992). The Earth is Our Mother: Struggles for American Indian land and liberation in the contemporary United States. In M. Annette Jaimes (Ed.), *The state of Native America: Genocide, colonization, and resistance* (pp. 139–188). Boston, MA: South End Press.

Community Panel, Family and Children's Services. (1992). *Liberating our children, liberating our nations.* Legislative Review in British Columbia. Aboriginal Committee.

Crawford, J. (1994). Endangered Native American languages: What is to be done, and why? [On-line] Available: http://www.nceb.gwu.edu/miscpub/crawford [1999, August].

Crey, E. (1991). The children of tomorrow's great potlatch. In Doreen Jensen and Cheryl Brooks (Eds.), *In celebration of our survival: The First Nations of British Columbia* (pp. 150–158). Vancouver, B.C.: University of British Columbia Press.

DuBray, W. (1993). American Indian values. In Wynn DuBray (Ed.), *Mental health interventions with people of color* (pp. 33–59). St. Paul, MN: West.

Gilman, C. & Schneider, M. J. (1987). *The way to independence.* St Paul, MN: Minnesota Historical Society Press.

Gilmore, M. (1930). The Arikara Book of Genesis. *Papers of the Michigan Academy of Science, Arts and Letters XII,* 95–120.

Good Tracks, J. G. (1973). Native American non-interference. *Social Work, 18* (6), 30–35.

Human Rights. (1990). The Rights of Indigenous Peoples. Fact Sheet No. 9. Geneva, Switzerland: United Nations.

Indigenous Peoples Council Against Biopiracy. (1998). [On-line] Available: http://www.niec.net/ipcb/ [1999, September].

Indigenous Women's Network. (No date). [On-line] Available: http://www.honorearth.com/iwn/ [1999, September].

Joe, J. (1989). Values. In Edwin Gonzales-Santin & Alison Lewis (Eds.), *Collaboration: The key.* Office of American Indian Projects. Arizona State University, School of Social Work. Tempe, Arizona.

Kelly, P. (1991). The value of First Nations languages. In Doreen Jensen and Cheryl Brooks (Eds.), *In celebration of our survival: The First Nations of British Columbia.* Vancouver, B.C.: University of British Columbia Press.

Merriam-Webster's Collegiate Dictionary, 10th ed. (1992). Springfield, MA: Merriam-Webster.

Meyer, R. W. (1977). *The village Indians of the upper Missouri.* Lincoln, NE: University of Nebraska Press.

National Congress of American Indians. (No date). Available: http://www.ncai.org/[1999, September].

Olson, J. S. & Wilson, R. (1986). *Native Americans in the twentieth century.* Urbana, IL: University of Illinois.

Passel, J. S. (1996). The growing American Indian population, 1960–1990: Beyond demography. In Gary D. Sandefur, Ronald R. Rindfuss, & Barney Cohen (Eds.), *Changing numbers, changing needs: American Indian demography and public health* (pp. 79–102). Washington, DC: National Academy Press.

Pevar, S. (1992). *The rights of Indians and tribes: The basic ACLU guide to Indian and tribal rights,* 2nd ed. Carbondale and Edwardsville, IL: Southern Illinois University Press.

P.L. 101-477, Title I—Native American Languages Act, 1990. Available: http://www.ncbe.gwu.edu/miscpubs/stabilize/ii-policy/nala1990.htm [1999, August].

Prucha, Francis Paul. (1975). *Documents of United States Indian policy.* Lincoln, NE: University of Nebraska Press.

Red Horse, J. (1980). Family Structure and value orientation in American Indians. *Social Casework, 68* (10), 462–467.

Scheibe, K. E. (1970). *Beliefs and values.* New York: Free Press.

Slade Gorton vs. The tribes: Is tribal sovereignty in jeopardy? (1995). *Sovereign Nations, 10,* (1), 3–5.

Snipp, C. M. (1996). The size and distribution of the American Indian population: Fertility, mortality, migration, and residence. In Gary D. Sandefur, Ronald R. Rindfuss, & Barney Cohen (Eds.), *Changing numbers, changing needs: American Indian demography and public health* (pp. 17–52). Washington, DC: National Academy Press.

Stamatopoulou, E. (1994). Indigenous peoples and the United Nations: Human rights as a developing dynamic. *Human Rights Quarterly, 16,* 58–81.

Stein, H. F. (1985). Therapist and family values in a cultural context. *Counseling and Values, 30* (1), 35–46.

Suzuki, D. & Knudtson, P. (1992). *Wisdom of the elders: Sacred native stories of nature.* New York: Bantam.

Talal, H. B. & Khan, S. A. (1987). *Indigenous Peoples: A global quest for justice.* London: Zed Books.

Thornton, R. (1987). *American Indian holocaust and survival: A population history since 1492.* Norman, OK: University of Oklahoma Press.

Thornton, R. (1996). Tribal membership requirements and the demography of "old" and "new" Native Americans. In Gary D. Sandefur, Ronald R. Rindfuss, & Barney Cohen (Eds.), *Changing numbers, changing needs: American Indian demography and public health* (pp. 103–112). Washington, DC: National Academy Press.

United Nations. (1994). *Seeds of a new partnership: Indigenous Peoples and the United Nations.* New York: Author.

U.S. Census Bureau. (1999). Resident Population Estimates of the United States by Sex, Race, and Hispanic Origin. Population Estimation Program, Population Division. Washington, D.C.

World Indigenous Peoples Conference on Education. (1999). [On-Line]. Available: http://www.wipcehawaii.org/ [1999, August].

Yellow Bird, M. & Snipp, C. M. (1994). American Indian families. In Ronald L. Taylor (Ed.), *Minority families in the United States: A multicultural perspective.* Englewood Cliffs, NJ: Prentice-Hall.

Yellow Bird, M. J. (1995). Spirituality in First Nations story telling: A Sahnish-Hidatsa approach to narrative. *Reflections: Narratives of Professional Helping 1,* (4), 65–72.

Yellow Bird, M. J. (1999a). Indian, American Indian, and Native Americans: Counterfeit identities. *Winds of Change: A Magazine for American Indian Education and Opportunity, 14,* (1), 86.

Yellow Bird, M. J. (1999b). What we want to be called: Indigenous Peoples' Perspectives on racial and ethnic identity labels. *The American Indian Quarterly, 23,* (2), 1–21.

CHAPTER 6

VALUES AND ETHICS IN SOCIAL WORK PRACTICE WITH ASIAN AMERICANS: A SOUTH ASIAN MUSLIM CASE EXAMPLE

FARIYAL ROSS-SHERIFF

ALTAF HUSAIN

Values and ethics play a significant role in social work practice. In her 1910 presidential address to the National Conference of Charities and Corrections, Jane Addams laid the groundwork for a beginning discussion of ethics in the profession. In 1960, the National Association of Social Workers Delegate Assembly adopted a one-page code of ethics; the preamble counseled social work professionals to take responsibility and thus protect the community from unethical practices by individual social workers or social welfare organizations (NASW, 1960). Subsequently, the code has been amended or rewritten five times. The latest revision, carried out in 1996, contains twenty-seven pages with a preamble, statement of purpose, ethical principles for the profession's core values, and standards to guide practice. Two of the areas addressed in some depth are cultural competence and conflict of interest in family and group work (Congress, 1996). Over time, the social work Code of Ethics has been revised to be more comprehensive and sensitive to diverse United States populations, including Asian Americans. However, the code cannot guarantee ethical behaviors on the part of all practitioners, particularly when the practitioners may not be knowledgeable and educated for practice with diverse cultural groups.

As the population of the United States has diversified, and as Asian immigrants and refugees have increased in number, the need for culturally sensitive social work practitioners has also increased. Knowledge and awareness about Asian American and Pacific Islander groups in the United States has not kept pace with this increasing need.

Because ethics are rooted in values, it is necessary for practitioners to have knowledge and understanding of their clients' cultural values. Without these key ingredients, social workers are likely to face ethical dilemmas in their practice with this population. This chapter presents information on values and ethics in social work practice with Asian Americans. It is divided into four sections. The first section is on the array of Asian American worldviews and the resulting values. An overview of Asian American groups is presented with a focus on commonalties and differences in cultural values among them. The second section provides a discussion on ethics and ethical dilemmas. Next, the types of ethical dilemmas that social workers are likely to face in their work with Asian Americans are presented, accompanied by a case example and a discussion of whether such dilemmas are genuine or misconstrued. The chapter ends with guidelines for ethical practice with Asian Americans.

ASIAN AMERICANS AND THEIR VALUES

Several factors contribute to Asian American and Pacific Islander diversity. Among them are differences arising from the culture of the nation or area of origin, political beliefs, and economic status, as well as differences arising from period and experiences of migration to the United States. As the discussion below makes clear, their values reflect the richness inherent in diversity.

While not all Asian nationalities are represented in the United States, those that are exhibit considerable differences in culture, belief systems, and ethnicity. Starting in the mid to late 1800s, the Chinese, Japanese, and Filipinos were among the first groups to reach the United States in significant numbers. Following World War II, there was a dramatic increase in the number of Asians in the United States. According to the U.S. Census Bureau, in 1960 there were approximately one million people of Asian descent (Lee, 1996). In the 1960s, the term "Asian Pacific American" came into common usage to refer to anyone from the Asian continent or the Pacific Islands (Lee, 1996). Since then, the term *Asian American* has been prevalent in the literature and has referred to people from both the Asian continent and the Pacific Islands. This term, although convenient for counting the population, has resulted in generalizations about Asian Americans.

Most of the social work literature also succumbed to providing discussions about counseling or interventions with Asian American clients in general, without regard to their unique cultural, ethnic, or religious backgrounds (Ibrahim, Ohnishi, and Sandhu, 1997). Not only are the Asian American subgroups different from each other in these respects, but they have also come to the United States for very different reasons and at various times in U.S. history. Even a casual glance at the diversity of the subgroups tells us that "each Asian national group has its own distinctive cultural background, unique historical experiences, and reasons for immigration" (Sandhu, 1997, p. 8).

The Asian American Population

Today, there are some 10.4 million Asian Americans in the United States (U.S. Census Bureau, 1998). Their total population is predicted to reach approximately 23 million by the year 2030 (U.S. Census Bureau, 1996). From 1980 to 1990 alone, the total Asian American population increased by 107.8 percent (Sandhu, 1997). Social work practitioners and researchers must strive to understand both the subtle and obvious differences between Asian Americans of various backgrounds. Indeed, various researchers have estimated that the number of different nationalities therein may range from thirty to forty-three distinct ethnic groups (Lee, 1996; Sue and Sue, 1995). But exactly what makes them different? Religion? Language? Ethnicity? Or a combination of these factors?

National and Ethnic Diversity

As noted above, Asian Americans and their family members come from both the Asian continent and the Pacific Islands. Sue and Sue (1995) have divided this population into three major categories: Asian American (Asian Indians, Chinese Filipinos, Japanese, and Koreans), Southeast Asians (Cambodians, Laotians, and Vietnamese), and Pacific Islanders (Hawaiian, Guamanians, and Samoans). According to Sandhu (1997), there are five major Asian ethnic groups in the United States, namely the Chinese, Filipino, Japanese, Asian Indian, and Korean Americans. Sue and Sue list these same five ethnic groups (percent of total Asian American population in the United States: Chinese 23 percent, Filipino 19 percent, Japanese 12 percent, Asian Indian 11 percent, and Korean 11 percent) and also include the Vietnamese (11 percent of the total Asian American population in the United States). In addition to those listed above are distinct subgroups from South and Southeast Asia.

While the above discussion fairly portrays the major groups in the United States, a number of other groups and subgroups are still neglected. According to Ibrahim and associates (1997), within the South Asian population (the common term for people of the Indian subcontinent), there are further subgroups from Pakistan, India, Nepal, Tibet, Kashmir, Burma, Sri Lanka, Bangladesh, and Afghanistan, although the latter two are not mentioned by the authors. Within the literature on Southeast Asia, there is little or no mention of Indonesia, Malaysia, and Singapore. Central Asia also deserves attention as there are refugees and immigrants arriving in the United States, a result of the breakup of the Soviet Union.

Diversity in Language

Differences in language also contribute to the diversity of Asian Americans. Lee (1996) notes that there are over thirty-two different primary languages and many dialects within this population. Depending on the province of origin in China, a Chinese person may be fluent in Mandarin or Cantonese. While the official languages of India are Hindi and English, there are nearly twenty-two other languages spoken throughout the country. Of the fourteen Indian states, for example, a young doctor from the state of Maharashtra may be fluent only in Marathi or an engineer from the state of Kerala may be fluent only in Malyalam. In Pakistan, there are four provincial languages, namely Pushto, Punjabi, Sindhi and Baluchi, while the national language is Urdu (Ibrahim et al., 1997). While American-born Asians will most likely be fluent in English, the primary language at home may very well reflect their parents' national or ethnic origin.

Religion

Most of the world's major religions are represented in Asia. Various nations of South Asia alone, as Ibrahim and associates (1997) point out, have been influenced through their national history and their interaction with the people of the "Caucasus, the Turks, the Greeks, the Arabs, the Huns, and the British" (p. 37). Much of Asia has been exposed to influence from merchants, missionaries, and colonizing powers such as Britain, France, Netherlands, Portugal, and Spain. A major goal among many of these groups was proselytization for different Christian denominations. For example, the Vietnamese Americans are both Buddhist and Catholic, the latter being a result of the French occupation. Similarly, the Cambodians and Laotians believe in Brahmanism, which is derived from Hinduism and Buddhism. A significant majority of Korean and Filipino Americans follow the Christian faith. Lee (1996) notes that nearly 70 percent of Korean Americans are Protestant while Filipino Americans are mostly Catholic, owing to the past Spanish occupation of the Philippines. The Japanese identify with Shintoism, Buddhism (Zen sect), and Christianity, while the Chinese predominantly believe in Buddhism, ancestor worship, Islam, and also Christianity. It should be noted that the Hmong and the Mien identify with animistic beliefs and believe in supernatural causes (Lee, 1996).

Because religion is very much a part of the Asian identity, Asian Americans also tend to remain strong in their particular faith. Das and Kemp (1997) discuss the complexity of counseling South Asian Americans, due partly to the diverse religious backgrounds of the clients. While all major religions are also represented, a majority of the immigrants from Afghanistan, Bangladesh, Kashmir, and Pakistan are Muslims. There is considerable religious diversity within the Indians. A majority of the Indian immigrants are Hindus, although Buddhism, Christianity, Islam, Jainism, Judaism, and Sikhism are also represented.

RICHNESS IN DIVERSITY

Overall, the diverse Asian American population in the United States warrants the attention of both social work researchers and practitioners. Whether the client group is Asian American adolescents (Huang, 1994) or Asian American families (Lee, 1996), there are cultural, religious, and ethnic differences among Asian Americans that warrant further study. Sue and Sue (1995) note that there are differences within Asian American groups due to primary language, generational status, and acculturation. Due to the kaleidoscope of immigrants, Sandhu (1997) makes a strong assertion that "it is difficult if not impossible to generalize anything about Asian and Pacific Islander Americans" (p. 8). Ironically, embedded within the diversity among Asian Americans is a framework of values that allows for a degree of generalization.

Common values of Asian Americans are derived from their worldview and Eastern philosophical background. Lum (1999) states that, "values are beliefs about preferred choices that govern conduct, life decisions, and related normative action by individuals, families, groups and society" (p. 92). Furthermore, cultural values are "rooted in ethnic, religious, and generational beliefs, traditions, and practices which influence individual and social values" (p. 93). Given the diversity among Asian Americans, it becomes imperative for practitioners to appreciate the relationship between the values of this population and their worldview. Indeed, for Asian Americans, values stem directly from the worldview such that, as Ross-Sheriff (1992) notes, the worldview "determines how the individual thinks, behaves, makes decisions, analyzes events, and conducts social relationships" (p. 50). Practitioners cannot fully appreciate Asian Americans without first understanding their worldview, especially because migration tends to bring about changes in the worldview and its associated values. Mokuau and Matsuoka (1992) assert that "the formation of a worldview in a multicultural situation is complex in that the individual adopts and modifies cultural tradition to accommodate new forms of learning" (p. 68). Again, while the worldview is being transformed, Asian American values are also being affected.

Asian cultures "emphasize significant values such as family/kin responsibilities, obligations and filial piety, hierarchical order in carrying out responsibilities, sensitivity to the feelings of others, respect, loyalty, and righteousness" (Ross-Sheriff, 1992, p. 50). Asian families strive to uphold these values and, whenever differences arise, considerable attention is given to the value of saving face. Members also manage the interplay between shame and guilt to avoid upsetting harmonious relations within their families. Despite the widespread acceptance among Asian Americans of these same values, there are many factors adding to the complexity of their diversity. Therefore, it behooves the practitioner to account for certain factors such as the reason for immigration to the United States, the length of time since arrival in the United States, the degree of involvement of the family in its own ethnic community, the degree to which the family has retained its religious orientation, and, finally, the degree to which American-born children have internalized the values.

While a detailed analysis of these factors is beyond the scope of this chapter, it is necessary to make some brief remarks about their impact on the client–practitioner relationship. Following migration, both the client's culture of origin and the dominant culture work "either against each other or together to form and shape the new immigrant [client] into a participant in the culture of the United States" (Locke, 1992, p. 5). By paying attention to the factors mentioned above, the practitioner can avoid common pitfalls in assessing the Asian American client. First, she realizes that giving too much attention to the client as an individual will lead her to neglect the impact of the cultural group on the client. Second, she realizes that, should she give too much attention to the cultural group, she does so at the risk of stereotyping the client and, thus, denying the client her uniqueness.

The increasing diversity in the United States has created difficult situations for social work practitioners. With stronger efforts dedicated to the study of Asian Americans, it is hoped that, over time, social work practitioners and researchers will come to appreciate what Ibrahim and associates (1997) have termed, the "multi-dimensionality of the Asian American identity" (p. 34). While necessary, it is also not enough for practitioners to focus solely on the diversity of Asian Americans. Instead, as the following section makes clear, there are very real practice problems, which could be misconstrued as ethical problems if the practitioner is not equipped with knowledge and awareness of Asian American commonalties and the differences among subgroups.

ETHICS DEFINED

Linzer (1999)[1] defines *ethics* as actions that express those values which are society's normative standards of behavior, and ethical dilemmas "as a choice between two actions that are based on conflicting values" (p. 35). He further adds that, "both values are morally correct and professionally grounded but cannot be acted on together in the situation" (p. 38). Similarly, Blackburn (1996) defines *moral dilemmas* as "situations in which each possible course of action breeches some otherwise binding principle" (p. 250). In other words, moral dilemmas constitute a choice between two conflicting value systems. For example, in placing a Hmong child with a Buddhist religious background in a white Christian foster home, a social worker may feel that, while it may not be right, it may be the best course of action under circumstances of alleged child abuse. Consider an Afghan female adolescent of Muslim religious background who presents herself as distraught over her decision to pursue higher education. The practitioner may be faced with the dilemma of deciding to help her pursue the Western value of personal achievement against her family's values of early marriage and family building. The outcomes of such decisions may have grave implications for the clients and their families.

Based on personal values, level of knowledge, and understanding about the values of different Asian American groups, and understanding of the social work Code of Ethics, some social workers may feel caught in a lose–lose (no win) situation when making such decisions. There is a very important question that needs to be addressed specifically for those who may not have knowledge and understanding of the complexity of values held by Asian American clients: "Is the challenge facing them really an ethical dilemma?"

---

[1]For a discussion of ethics, morality, and professional ethics, refer to Linzer (1999) Chapter 4, pp. 33–46.

IS IT REALLY AN ETHICAL DILEMMA?

The difficult aspect of apparent ethical clashes in cross-cultural social work practice is whether the practitioner is actually facing a genuine dilemma. In common discourse, the word *dilemma* means nothing more than a difficult decision, a tough choice. However, the true meaning of the word is more specific, as discussed above. Although tough, a choice for a practitioner may not necessarily constitute a moral dilemma between the ethics of NASW and the Asian American client. Action on such a dilemma would not necessarily violate a binding principle. Constable (1989) has noted that practitioners must have a clear understanding of the distinction between practice problems and ethical problems. A practice problem becomes an ethical dilemma as a result of a "violation of a principle of practice" (p. 64). It follows, then, that the practice error must be corrected before attending to the ethical dilemma.

In addition, there are some choices that could be misconstrued as ethical dilemmas. It is important that the social worker distinguish between genuine (real) and apparent (perceived) dilemmas. Unlike a genuine ethical dilemma, in which the worker is confronted with choices in which all options lead to wrong action, in an apparent ethical dilemma there may be a right course of action, but difficult choices. For example, a social worker who does not have knowledge and understanding of Asian American values may have difficulty untangling the range of choices, one of which may be ethically correct. The following example provides guidelines for practice with Asian Americans that may assist practitioners in distinguishing between genuine and apparent ethical dilemmas and making responsible cross-cultural decisions.

A PAKISTANI FAMILY

Jamila, Karima, and Salma—ages eleven, fourteen, and fifteen—were referred to Ms. X, a school social worker, by their physical education teacher, who felt that the three sisters lived in a restrictive and "oppressive" home. They were expected to cover their bodies and were not allowed to wear shorts or clothing that "exposed" their bodies. They feared their father and believed they would be punished and restricted from participating in school-related extracurricular activities if they did not follow the culturally expected standards of dressing and behaviors.

During group sessions with the social worker, the girls were quiet and uncommunicative. During an individual session, fifteen-year-old Salma told Ms. X. about an altercation between the three siblings and their father when they had disobeyed his "orders" to come home before dark. They had been away with friends until midnight. As a result, their father had angrily threatened that he would lock them up, punish them, and bar their participation in any activities except formal schooling. The girls attempted to appeal to their mother on the basis that they no longer lived in Pakistan. They felt their parents were old-fashioned and did not understand why their parents would not give them the freedom that their peers in the United States had. While their mother cared for them and loved them, she did not understand them, either. After this incident, Salma and Karima planned to run away from home, despite knowing that their father would lock them up and punish them severely if he discovered their plans to run away. A Pakistani family well-known to the girls' family had just returned to Pakistan because the parents did not want their children to become Americanized. The girls suspected that their family might also return to Pakistan if they continued to stay out late and act like what their father referred to as "American girls."

Ms. X was startled when the girls related to her that their father had said, "I will kill you if you bring shame to our family by behaving this way." This comment confirmed Ms. X's fears that Muslim men would even resort to violence to preserve family honor. In addition, she did not realize that the girls were translating to her what he had said in Urdu, a language that they did not speak well. For example, in colloquial Urdu, *to beat, to kill,* and *to die,* are verbs derived from the same root word.

While gathering background information on the family, Ms. X learned that the girls' family was a Muslim family from Pakistan, where both of the parents had received a college education. The family had immigrated to the United States ten years earlier. To Ms. X, the father seemed authoritarian and did not welcome any intervention from the social worker in the family's life. Ms. X made an assessment that the girls' fears about their father's punitive nature were justified. After receiving repeated complaints from the three sisters about the increasing restrictions placed on them by their father, the school social worker initiated action to place them in foster care. Unable to understand completely the parents' worldview, and unwilling to overlook the right of her clients to self-determination, Ms. X concluded that she was facing a dilemma. Unfortunately, she was convinced that the girls' safety and welfare were endangered and they were placed in foster care.

Although Ms. X's claim that there is a dilemma may seem valid, it is wise to review whether her dilemma is genuine or merely apparent. In this case, Ms. X's ethical dilemma can be examined at two levels: first, cultural sensitivity versus family preservation, and, second, upholding the rights of the client. Further complicating the dilemma in Ms. X's mind was the factor that children are not accorded the right to self-determination until they are eighteen years of age. In particular, Ms. X's dilemma is complex and may be described as whether to:

> initiate an intervention with the family, while trying to be culturally sensitive, and preserve the family unit, or

> act on the girls' claim that they feared punitive action, that is, violence against them by their father, and place them in a foster home, thus upholding the rights of her clients by removing them from a potentially threatening environment.

The family was stunned that their daughters had been taken away from them. The father could not understand how the school social worker had concluded that the "safety and welfare" of the girls were endangered. The mother was overheard repeating several times that, no matter how bad the family situation was, foster care could neither be better nor a viable option for a Pakistani family. From her perspective, their family's name would be further disgraced if the girls were not quickly taken out of foster care and returned to them. The family appealed to the leadership of the *masjid* (house of worship) for their assistance in getting their girls back.

There are a few suggestions that may facilitate resolution of this scenario. To begin with, Ms. X must seek objective answers to some salient questions:

What are the sources of her information regarding this case? Are the girls the only source of her information?

Do the parents of the children know that they are seeing a counselor regularly?

Has she spoken to the parents at length about this issue?

Has she considered having a family meeting to examine all possible options with the father and mother?

How much does she know about the South Asian, specifically Pakistani, worldview?

What specific elements of the case give rise to her dilemma? Does it stem from her inability to come to terms with the Pakistani worldview as being different from her own U.S. worldview?

Would she perceive a dilemma if the situation were the same but the family was Amish American or Greek Orthodox?

How would the worker react if a similar case was referred to her but the children were born to Euro-American parents?

Has she identified any social work professionals who are familiar with the South Asian worldview, or are South Asians themselves, and could act as main counselors to the girls and the parents? Or, as consultants to her?

Intervention

Ms. X was contacted by the *masjid* leadership for reconsideration of the case. She realized that having the girls in the foster home was emotionally tormenting the parents and her decision was being questioned. After meeting with several community members, she came across an elderly Pakistani woman who gave her some critical insight into the case. She remarked that it was usual for parents in Pakistan to be overly concerned about saving face. With activities such as staying out late, mixing freely with boys, and disobeying their parents, the girls in this case could possibly bring shame to the family. Ms. X listened intently to the elderly woman. This idea of saving face had never crossed her mind. The woman continued to say that a common expression of anger among Pakistani fathers was that they would beat their children severely for having "blackened the family's face." She suggested that the social worker carefully explore previous history of abuse in the family. While the social worker should be concerned about such threats, it was not clear whether there had been any physical abuse in this family. Therefore, the social worker should have further explored this issue with both the girls and their parents and taken this threat seriously only after careful review. She reminded Ms. X that the girls did not speak Urdu well and may have relayed the expression out of context when they translated it into English. That is, they may have told Ms. X that their father threatened to kill them when his actual expression mentioned beating them. Finally, she told Ms. X that, while in the United States the teenagers could partake in activities such as dancing, dating, and staying out late, most Muslim families disapprove of these behaviors. Armed with this new information, Ms. X resolved to hold a meeting with the girls and their parents.

At first, the parents were furious and did not want to meet with Ms. X as they felt she had brought them shame in the community by breaking their family apart. Ms. X convinced the mother that the meeting might result in reuniting the family. The parents agreed and the girls were brought for the meeting. Ms. X was surprised at how emotional the reunion was for all the family members. Hesitant at first, even the father joined in and hugged his daughters and reassured them that everything would be all right.

Ms. X began to explain to the family that every member would have to cooperate in order to bring about resolution to the case. The parents would have to understand that their daughters were not engaging in harmful behavior because in U.S. culture these were considered age-appropriate behaviors. Ms. X added that the parents would need to spend more time explaining to their children what was age-appropriate in the Pakistani American culture. Similarly, the girls would have to understand that they did not have to feel pressured to conform to U.S. behaviors, especially if doing so strained family relations. Ms. X also pointed out to the girls that many U.S. families were also strict and not all families allowed their preteens and teenagers complete freedom. Through mutual consultation, the girls would do their best to communicate their desires with their parents and the parents would, in turn, exercise their judgment and allow for selective participation in extracurricular activities. In addition, Ms. X would work with the family for the rest of the academic year.

As the family listened, Ms. X could see from the relaxed look on their faces that the family was happy to be together again. When it was their turn to speak, their positive and forward-looking comments made her realize that they were ready to acknowledge and address the challenges that lay ahead. The most important point was that they were prepared to do so as a family.

Was this really an ethical dilemma or a practice problem? Lack of knowledge and understanding about the cultural background of the clients and misperceptions about Muslims led Ms. X to a situation that, in retrospect, could have been resolved with a more responsible cross-cultural decision. What initially seemed to be an ethical dilemma was, in reality, a set of problems that posed a difficult range of choices.

PRACTICE GUIDELINES FOR SOCIAL WORK WITH ASIAN AMERICANS

Merely acknowledging that diversity exists among Asian Americans will not in itself lead to more ethically responsive practice with this population. As noted above, thorough knowledge and awareness about the various subgroups in this diverse population are crucial if the practitioner is to distinguish between a genuine ethical dilemma and an apparent one. Similarly, with sufficient preparation, the practitioner is also likely to differentiate more accurately between a practice problem and an ethical problem.

Perhaps one of the biggest sources of potential dilemmas is a worker's insistence on identifying and empathizing only with those elements of the presenting problem that fit within his or her knowledge base, worldview, and values. This approach above all directs the worker to selectively listen to clients as they relate their problems. As in the example of the girls and Ms. X, a range of exchanges are likely:

> Words or deeds that initiate discomfort in the worker are dealt with as an unwelcome circumstance. Imagine the feelings of the worker dressed in her favorite knee-length skirt, listening to the girls as they tell her that their culture considers gym shorts immodest and that, in accordance with their religious duties, they will soon have to cover their heads.

> Questions and inquiries to the client are formulated in such a way as to elicit responses that substantiate the possible threat the worker feels towards his or her own worldview. For example, "How does that make you feel if you can't go out with your friends?" or what if the girls were asked, "You mean you've never dated a boy? You are all very pretty, I am sure some boys must have asked you out, haven't they?"

> Statements or expressions that are unfamiliar to the worker's worldview are met with nonverbal gestures such as leaning forward with a wide-eyed look as if to say "I can imagine your pain" or "That must be so tough" or "How awful!" To a client in search of affirmation, these are warm responses. However, an ironic side effect of this approach is that the client, deferring to the knowledgeable and skilled professional, begins to selectively relate only information that seems worthy of being further affirmed by the worker.

There are numerous points of importance that emerge from the case example presented here, and this discussion may be structured as being related to both assessment and cultural competence. First, extraordinary measures should be taken to keep the assessment phase as comprehensive as possible. The worker should be well prepared and recognize that critical information may become available at any point during the intervention. The actual assessment begins with the client's description of the presenting problem. The worker should note verbal and nonverbal gestures, taking note of everything as if it were the last meeting with the client. Both active listening and prompting require careful planning so that the worker does not interject personal biases or responses that reflect puzzlement or acceptance based on personal worldview.

As much as possible, the worker should try to involve significant others such as siblings, parents, or grandparents during assessment. Through multiple sources of information, the worker should build an evolving digest of cultural values, nuances, subtleties, and biases that are relevant to practice with this particular family. During assessment, the worker may encounter cultural values such as saving face and guilt and shame. Many Asian cultures emphasize saving face or preserving the dignity of the family. In a case where a family encourages saving face, the worker may find that members are unwilling to admit that a problem exists. The worker may not be able to elicit open and frank communication from family members during assessment if they are overemphasizing the value of saving face. In families where guilt and shame are emphasized, the worker may find that the member responsible for the presenting problem may be overcome with feelings of self-blame and intense guilt. In some ways, saving face and shame are related in that the ultimate concern is the preservation of the dignity and honor of the family. The worker must pay close attention to what extent the client is merely enacting culturally expected role behaviors and not actually expressing true feelings. In addition, the astute worker can begin to differentiate between the normative and practiced cultural and religious beliefs.

Second, the worker should strive to make sure everyone involved is familiar with the various cultures being discussed. One of the worker's goals is to move from only looking at the restrictive, punitive nature of the parents' behavior to a more comprehensive, culturally competent outlook. In doing so, the worker takes into consideration that, during the assessment and, indeed, throughout the intervention, there are three worldviews at work: (1) the children's cultural context, (2) the parents' worldview, and (3) the worker's worldview. While the first two are central to the case, the worker understands that knowledge of one's personal worldview and values are essential to the extent that the worker does not allow them to impinge on the final resolution of the case or to lead to a selective reading of the Code of Ethics. That is, it is quite possible that the final resolution may be diametrically opposed to the worker's own worldview and values.

In addition, for immigrant families the worker should try to juxtapose the children's cultural context with that of their parents to allow parents to come to terms with the reality that their view of what the children should believe is not necessarily what the children actually believe. It is entirely possible that coming to this realization will be emotionally difficult for both the children and the parents. One of the main challenges for the worker will be to facilitate the children's sharing of their beliefs with their parents. The worker must be prepared to help the parents as they discover, perhaps for the first time, that their children may not share their beliefs and values. It will also prove difficult for the worker to equip the parents with skills in cultural competence so that they may deal better with the cultural context of their children. Resolution may not be complete without the effective involvement of the extended family, the community, the *masjid*, or other community institutions.

Finally, an appreciation of the complex and comprehensive nature of Asian American diversity will remind the practitioner that there are many factors to be considered in order to avoid ethical dilemmas in practice with this population. First, practitioners must have a high degree of self-awareness so as to acknowledge their own feelings and attitudes towards racial and cultural diversity. Cross-cultural experiences in practice may have shaped a worker's outlook. This introspection will also allow practitioners to gauge to what extent their preconceived notions about race and culture impact their decision making in practice. Second, practitioners must realize that, regardless of their efforts to customize current assessment and intervention techniques to suit Asian Americans, there will remain biases from the dominant Euro-American worldview and its values. Guided by their zeal to assist the client, the practitioners may involuntarily impart notions of what is healthy and normal based on Euro-American standards. Third, practitioners must resist all urges to apply cultural models, lest they risk denying each individual or family their unique worldview. For too long, the literature has treated Asian Americans as if they were a homogeneous group. In response to that narrow approach, several cultural models have been developed that seek to further analyze Asian American diversity into distinct and identifiable parts. While the latter approach is a considerable improvement, the danger still exists that the practitioner will become prone to cognitive rigidity.

Overall, the common concern regarding work with Asian Americans is that the practitioner must recognize and plan to address the complex and multifaceted nature of their diversity. This high degree of sensitivity to the needs and values of the Asian American population will help practitioners better focus their energies on resolving practice problems and, should they genuinely arise, ethical dilemmas as well.

REFERENCES

Addams, Jane. (1910). The President's address: Charity and social justice. In A. Johnson (Ed.), *Proceedings of the national conference of charities and correction* (pp. 1–18). Fort Wayne, IN: Archer.

Blackburn, S. (1996). *The Oxford dictionary of philosophy.* Oxford: Oxford University Press.

Congress, E. P. (1996, February/March). What's new in the proposed 1996 Code of Ethics? *Currents, 5,* 5–6.

Constable, R. T. (1989). Relations and membership: Foundations for ethical thinking in social work. *Social Thought, 15* (3/4), 53–66.

Das, A. J. & Kemp, S. F. (1997). Between two worlds: Counseling South Asian Americans. *Journal of Multicultural Counseling and Development, 25* (1), 23–33.

Huang, L. N. (1994). An integrative approach to clinical assessment and intervention with Asian-American adolescents. *Journal of Clinical Child Psychology, 23* (1), 21–31.

Ibrahim, F., Ohnishi, H., & Sandhu, D. S. (1997). Asian American identity development: A culture specific model for South Asian Americans. *Journal of Multicultural Counseling and Development, 25* (1), 34–50.

Lee, E. (1996). Asian American families: An overview. In M. McGoldrick, J. Giordano, & J. K. Pearce (Eds.), *Ethnicity and family therapy,* 2nd ed. New York: Guildford.

Linzer, N. (1999). *Resolving ethical dilemmas in social work practice.* Boston, MA: Allyn and Bacon.

Locke, D. C. (1992). *Increasing multicultural understanding: A comprehensive model.* Newbury Park, CA: Sage.

Lum, D. (1999). *Culturally competent practice: A framework for growth and action.* Pacific Grove, CA: Brooks/Cole.

Mokuau, N. & Matsuoka, J. (1992). The appropriateness of personality theories for social work with Asian Americans. In S. M. Furuto, R. Biswas, D. K. Chung, K. Murase, & F. Ross-Sheriff (Eds.), *Social work practice with Asian Americans* (pp. 67–84). Newbury Park, CA: Sage.

National Association of Social Workers. (1960). Proposed Code of Ethics. *NASW News, 5* (2), 5.

Ross-Sheriff, F. (1992). Adaptation and integration into American society: Major issues affecting Asian Americans. In S. M. Furuto, R. Biswas, D. K. Chung, K. Murase, & F. Ross-Sheriff (Eds.), *Social work practice with Asian Americans* (pp. 45–63). Newbury Park, CA: Sage.

Sandhu, D. S. (1997). Psychocultural profiles of Asian and Pacific Islander Americans: Implications for counseling and psychotherapy. *Journal of Multicultural Counseling and Development. 25* (1), 7–22.

Sue, D., & Sue, D. M. (1995). Asian Americans. In N. Vacc, S. B. DeVaney, & J. Wittmer (Eds.), *Experiencing and counseling multicultural and diverse populations*. Bristol, PA: Accelerated Development.

U.S. Bureau of the Census (March 1996). *Resident population of the United States: Middle series projections, 2015–2030, by sex, race and Hispanic origin, with median age* [Online]. Available: http://www.census.gov/population/projections/nation/nsrh/nprh1530.txt.

U.S. Bureau of the Census. (March 1998). *The Asian and Pacific Islander population in the United States: Selected social characteristics of the population, by region and race* [Online]. Available: http://www.census.gov/population/socdemo/race/api98/table01.txt.

CHAPTER 7

COMPONENTS OF CULTURAL COMPETENCE: ATTITUDES, KNOWLEDGE, AND SKILLS

CHET M. OKAYAMA

SHARLENE B.C.L. FURUTO

JAMES EDMONDSON

Culture has a profound effect on the way we feel, think, and act. Culture initially determines what we value and believe, how we communicate, and the language(s) we use. Culture, thus, becomes the lens through which we all view, judge, and maneuver ourselves in the world (Gollnick & Chinn, 1994). There is not one aspect of human life that is not touched and altered by culture (Hall, 1976).

Cross-cultural competencies have been defined by categorizing them into the three dimensions of beliefs and attitudes, knowledge, and skills (Carney & Kahn, 1984; Sue et al., 1982). Lum (1999) described cultural competency as "the set of cultural awareness, knowledge acquisition, and skill development a social work practitioner must develop to work effectively with multicultural clients" (p. 3). In this chapter, we shall describe the attitudes, knowledge, and skills for cultural competence with multicultural clients such as First Nation Peoples, Latinos/Hispanics, African Americans, and Asians and Pacific Islanders.

ATTITUDES

Culturally competent attitudes evolve out of having an open mind and heart and a willingness to increase awareness about your own cultural identity and the cultures of others. Our earliest cultural learning involved generalized and judgmental thoughts ("good/bad" and "positive/negative" associations) about our own families and other people. Development of cultural competence necessitates going beyond our learned assumptions to deepen and broaden our attitudes and mindsets about the people and world we live in.

Self-awareness is the first step on the journey toward cultural competence (Harry, 1992). Varying degrees of acculturation may account for differences among people who come from the same cultural group. First generation immigrants would have a keen awareness of the cultural differences between the country they left and the country to which they moved. In the United States, individuals are often not aware that their own behaviors, habits, and customs are culturally based (Althen, 1988). According to Lynch and Hanson (1998), Anglo-Europeans who are part of the dominant or mainstream United States culture may have the least awareness of how their culture has influenced their behavior and interactions because Anglo-Europeans have predominated in the United States. The "melting pot" to which the United States aspired during the early waves of immigration resulted in a diminishing of immigrants' roots, which left many mainstream Americans feeling "cultureless." Hammond and Morrison (1996) suggest that one of the most common characteristics of mainstream Americans is their denial of any sort of collective culture.

Cultural competence in the 1990s has been presented as a "never-ending journey" that an individual explores, moving towards successful integration of personal awareness and professional cultural growth (Lum, 1999; Lynch & Hanson, 1998; Wehrly, 1995). There are a number of workshops and other training opportunities available that foster awareness of racism and prejudices and teach culturally competent skills. Materials such as family trees, ecomaps, cultural timelines, and other cultural development tools are also available to help guide your own cultural journey (Lynch & Hanson, 1998; Okayama, 1998).

An attitude of appreciation for and sensitivity towards the cultures of others develops as you gain deeper awareness and value of your own cultural heritage and identity (e.g., Baruth & Manning, 1991; Campinha-Bacote, 1994; Chan, 1990; Hanson & Lynch, 1995). A culturally sensitive social work practitioner acknowledges and understands how our learned prejudices and stereotypes, including racist attitudes and beliefs, have a direct effect on interactions with others.

A willingness to learn about cultural differences is another essential culturally competent attitude. Lynch and Hanson (1998) note that development of cross-cultural competence involves acknowledging and respecting cultural differences rather than minimizing them. Learning about differences and becoming more comfortable with variation leads to appreciation for cultural diversity and a new level of understanding and respect for the cultures of our clients.

Positive attitudes towards facing differences include a willingness to

- Listen and identify that which is different;
- Suspend habitual judgments, pay attention to the difference, face it, and engage in dialogue leading to a better understanding of differences;
- Explore, try out, and learn effective ways to work through misunderstandings and conflict based on differences;
- Sustain positive intentions and an attitude of mutual respect even when misunderstandings and unintended conflicts occur;

- Take risks in interactions: ask for clarification, admit ignorance, and reach out with understanding and forgiveness;
- Become aware of culturally influenced responses (For example, how do you react when someone says something that hurts at a deep and culturally based place? Anger? Avoidance? Rationalization? Helplessness? Blame? How can you move beyond that initial reaction to form a positive cultural bridge?);
- Share such hurt more directly with an attitude of openness towards cultural learning, forgiveness, resolution, and connection;
- Make efforts towards learning about and feeling more *comfortable* with differences (including differences in race, ethnicity, cultural values, religion, and other cultural differences); and
- Know and be open about your limitations in culturally sensitive circumstances. When appropriate, seek consultation with a cultural consultant or language translator or make a referral for services from a member of the client's own culture.

An attitude of respect for other worldviews is another essential component of cultural competence. The term *worldview* refers to your basic perceptions and understandings of the world (Ibrahim, 1985; Sue & Sue, 1990). Your worldview develops out of personal experience through interactions with members of your own culture (Wolcott, 1991). Social workers must respect other ways of thinking, feeling, and acting to promote the development of effective working relationships with multicultural clients.

Winkelman (1999) espouses the following attitudes for cultural competence: a positive attitude towards challenges; perseverance in the face of conflict, misunderstandings, and difficulties; tolerance of personal differences and ambiguities; and, lastly, nonjudgmental understanding of the validity of others' points of view. A commitment to make personal changes and effective adaptations are vital for cross-cultural adjustment and effectiveness.

The road toward cultural competence begins with open and willing cultural attitudes, leads to deeper self-awareness about your own cultural identity, winds around an eagerness to learn about other worldviews, and climbs towards true appreciation of and respect for differences. Lum (1999) adds that a willingness to interact with persons of different background and ideologies is needed for mutual understanding and a stronger sense of community. Cross-cultural interactions lead to new cultural knowledge and experiences, development of cross-cultural communication and intervention skills, and the development of lasting cross-cultural relationships.

KNOWLEDGE

Much has been written about the knowledge social workers need for effective cross-cultural competence. Several authors (Cox & Ephross, 1998; Furuto et al., 1992; Lynch and Hanson, 1998) believe that knowing and understanding one's own beliefs, stereotypes, and prejudices are basic to working well with cultural and ethnic groups. When the worker knows and understands the self, then he or she can better understand and work with the client on the micro, mezzo, and macro levels.

To carry out professional responsibilities, social workers should know (McPhatter 1997; Williams & Ellison, 1999) about the group's history, culture, traditions and customs, preferred language or primary dialect, values orientation, diversity and functioning of family structure, informal kinship care practices, religious and spiritual orientations, art, music, and folk or other healing practices. Social workers also need to know about the cultural group's social problems and issues, their neighborhood and community needs and resources (including ethnic resources such as churches and indigenous community-based programs), obstacles to change, and the dynamics of oppression, racism, sexism, and classism that defame culturally different clients. On a broader level, professionals need to know about the social welfare system, ethnic contributors to the system, and current issues plaguing diverse people in the social welfare system; social service interventions that incorporate alternative and culturally relevant theoretical and practice perspectives; and concepts related to strengths and resilience to explain behavior and approaches to intervention.

Lum (1999) espouses both the generalist and advanced levels of knowledge acquisition for culturally competent workers. Generalists should understand terms related to cultural diversity, knowledge of demographics of culturally diverse populations, development of a critical thinking perspective of cultural diversity, understanding the history of oppression and of social groups, knowledge of the strengths of people of color, and knowledge of culturally diverse values. Advanced level knowledge includes application of systems and psychosocial theory to practice with clients of color, knowledge of ethnicity, culture, minority identity, and social class theories, and mastery of social science theory.

Steward (1972) espouses the importance of knowing about the micro client by synthesizing the person's ethnicity, ethnic values, and ethnic behaviors. Social workers need to know about the ethnic person's activities, social relations, motivation, worldview, and self-perception by asking questions such as: How does this ethnic person approach the activity of achieving life goals? How does this ethnic person relate to others and define various roles? What is the achievement orientation of this ethnic person? What is this person's self-perception and worldview?

Bubis (1994) also suggests asking questions that not only help the worker better understand the ethnic client but also empower the client. Questions that follow indicate a collaborative worker gathering significant data that enhance the working relationship: Tell me about your concerns, How do you view these issues? What does this mean to you? What does this mean to your family? What does it mean to people important to you? Who do you go to for help? What do you recommend be done? Am I understanding you correctly? Knowing the answers to the above questions is critical to helping the ethnic person and should be included in social work practice frameworks.

Lum (2000) has developed a framework for social work practice with people of color. Fundamental are the contact, problem identification, assessment, intervention, and termination practice process stages and corresponding client-system practice issues, worker-system practice issues, and worker–client tasks. For example, social workers need to know about the following issues in the contact stage: communication barriers as a client-system practice issue, delivery of services as a worker-system practice issue, and nurturing as a worker–client task. Knowing about these issues will help the worker make a smooth transition to the problem identification stage and subsequent stages and then work through accompanying issues. This framework can be used with social work models for ethnic minority practice.

Bubis (1994) cites a number of models for cross-cultural practice, beginning with the dual perspective by Julia Norton, the cultural awareness approach by James Green, the ethnic sensitive practice by Devore and Schlesinger, the cross-cultural approach by Sue and Sue, the international cross-cultural approach by Kealey and Ruben, and the eclectic cross-cultural approach by Ramon Salcido. All of these approaches add to the growing knowledge base for social work theory.

While there are culture-centered systems theory (Bates and Harvey, 1975), cultural duality theory (Chestang, 1976), and cross-cultural relations theory (Bochner, 1982), Lum (2000) is one of the few to describe social work knowledge theory. He believes that social work knowledge theory includes theories of human behavior and practice, including systems theory and psychosocial theory, and that it needs to be analyzed on the micro, mezzo, and macro levels. Fundamental to culturally diverse knowledge theory are concepts such as ethnicity, which, according to DeVos (1982), can be categorized into four approaches: (1) ethnic or social behavior that ranges from organization to disorganization and produces social change; (2) patterns of social or ethnic functioning and deviancy in ethnic interactions; (3) focus on the self as the subjective experience of ethnic identity in terms of adaptation and maladaptation and changes in the life cycle or in social conditions; and (4) personality patterns in ethnic behavior that emphasize adjustment and maladjustment as well as psychosexual and cognitive development.

Social workers need knowledge specific to working effectively not only on the micro level but also on the mezzo and macro levels. Cox and Ephross (1998) propose these practice principles for group work: avoid having one of anything in a group; discuss with members the goals, purposes, and procedures for the group; allow time for discussion, questions, introductions, and consideration of issues; realize that, eventually, some members' feelings will be hurt, some will feel misunderstood, and some will be offended; minimize *naivete;* invest in the needs of the group-as-a-whole; be sharply aware of the importance of ethnic identities in groups and avoid stereotyping; celebrate diversity and help the groups do the same.

Cox and Ephross (1998) also discuss some variables when working with ethnic families such as language, speech norms, money, interethnic relations, the life cycle, work, job, career, illness, and medical treatment. Other important factors to know about and consider when working with ethnic families are religion, sex-role behaviors, education of children, family identity and obligations, the annual calendar, time, alcohol and other addictions, criminal behavior, and intimate partner relationships.

For a holistic approach, social workers need to have knowledge about ethnic communities. Cox and Ephross (1998) present a framework for practice with ethnic communities that includes gathering information regarding factors such as geography and population concentration; community problems, needs, and concerns; degree of homogeneity of the ethnic group; community resources (in businesses, ethnic organizations, and support networks); values, traditions, attitudes toward nonmembers; community leaders; degree of assertion or accommodation; and degree of visible ethnic links.

Social workers who learn about themselves and ethnic groups on the general and advanced levels can apply this knowledge to develop culturally competent skills on the micro, mezzo, and macro levels. This knowledge, along with the aforementioned attitudes and following skills, complete the components necessary for culturally competent practice.

SKILLS

Culturally competent social workers are able to integrate self-awareness and knowledge with practice skills throughout the process of service delivery to clients (Browne, Broderick, & Fong, 1993; Sue, Arredendo, & McDavis, 1992; Weaver, 1997). A social worker's intervention process includes the steps of planning, implementing, monitoring, evaluating, and terminating services. Culturally competent intervention incorporates culturally sensitive and culturally responsive skills at each step of service delivery.

General Practice Skills

Relationship building skills, such as effective listening, body language, and other ways of showing genuine interest and attentiveness, are fundamental for effective, culturally competent practice (Hogan-Garcia, 1999; Salcido, 1994). A major goal in development of cultural competency skills is to learn basic aspects of communication styles that are influenced by culture and language (Sue, 1992; Sue & Sue, 1990). Proxemics (the use of space in communication), kinesics (body movements and gestures), and paralanguage (vocal cues, volume of speech, when to speak and when not to speak) are critical components of cultural communication styles (Wehrly, 1995).

Awareness of different communication styles in *verbal and nonverbal interactions* and awareness of one's comfort level in these interactions are beginning steps toward development of advanced cross-cultural communication skills. Culturally skilled counselors are able to send and receive both verbal and nonverbal messages accurately and appropriately (Sue, Arredondo, & McDavis, 1992).

Our *use and interpretation of time and space* are dimensions determined by our personal cultures and their values (Okun, Fried, & Okun, 1999). Aspects of time and space that differ among cultures include past, present, and future orientation, polychronic and monochronic use of time (engagement in many tasks at once versus only one task undertaken at any given moment), activities and schedules, lateness and respect, and interpersonal space and boundaries. Social workers need to be skillful in using time and space when working with clients who have different perspectives about these aspects of communication.

Micro, Mezzo, and Macro Skills Levels

Culture and cross-cultural communication are dynamic in that they operate through us as individuals at the *micro level,* with unique family systems on the *mezzo level,* and within specific community and organizational contexts on the *macro level.*

Cross-cultural skills at the micro level include: (1) interviewing skills to accurately assess and overcome client resistance; (2) empathic communication skills such as the appropriate use of self-disclosure and use of a positive and open interactive style; (3) problem identification process skills; (4) assessment and intervention skills, including the establishment of mutually acceptable goals and formation of multi-level intervention strategies; and (5) termination skills (Lum & Lu, 1997). Weaver (1998) identified two groups of powerful skills based on a survey of First Nations Peoples: (1) *General skills,* including communication, problem solving, a strengths perspective, and the ability to truly empathize with indigenous people; and (2) *Containment skills,* involving patience, the ability to tolerate silence, and listening—all skills that require social workers to refrain from speaking—as opposed to skills that require more verbal activity (Shulman, 1992).

Working with families through *interpreters and translators* requires a special set of micro and mezzo level skills (Lynch & Hanson, 1998; Norton, 1978; Zastro, 1995). Acknowledgment of the need for an interpreter to manage communication across language and cultural systems, knowledge of interpretive approaches or styles, preparation for the interview, and debriefing of interview with an interpreter are the skills needed to form cultural bridges (Caple, Salcido, & di Cecco, 1995).

A social worker in the counselor or psychotherapist role may use *family therapy skills* to help clients improve functioning as a family unit. Sue, Arredondo, and McDavis (1992) recommend that counselors know about minority family structures, hierarchies, values, and beliefs as well as minority community characteristics and resources. For example, important cultural protocols are the appropriate ways to open, conduct, and end meetings. Working with the extended family as a system may be the culturally appropriate way to start working on a problem instead of immediately focusing on the individual client or nuclear family. Wehrly (1995) provides summaries of current literature that discuss therapy skills with families of specific cultural and ethnic groups.

Macro Skills

At the macro level, social workers may need to design social service programs in ethnic communities, develop services that are accessible, pragmatic, and positive, establish linkages with other social agencies, and conduct cultural skills development research (Lum and Lu, 1997). Nash (1999) describes how skills at the advanced macro level can be used to integrate cultural competence as a vital part of the strategic planning process for human service organizations and agencies. Macro skills include those used in organization and community work such as decision making, fund raising, grant writing, community awareness, ability to work as a trainer or facilitator of cross-cultural work, public relations, political activities, including lobbying and developing policies and procedures such as mission statements and goals incorporating cultural principles.

Mediation, negotiation, and conflict resolution skills include the ability to listen for and foster understanding in others, the ability to engage in and facilitate dialogue, and the ability to accurately communicate understanding when faced with differences. *Brainstorming* (Osborn, 1963) is an excellent technique for use with groups that are looking for ideas and possible ways to accomplish a common goal. Brainstorming can be useful in multicultural or cross-cultural groups because all ideas are accepted and members are encouraged to build on the ideas of others whenever possible. Brainstorming is a strengths-based approach with the opportunity for teamwork and community building through the process.

Skills in *public education and public relations* are generally not the focus of a social worker's background. However, the media has a powerful influence on public perception of human services and of cultural matters. Recent headlines have focused on racially and culturally based murders. These have included children killing other children. There is a very clear and compelling need for accurate and educational messages about cultural information to be communicated to the general public and children. Social workers need to develop competencies and skills in the public relations arena to help educate and make available information to the public. Public relations skills include familiarization with the rules of the media, familiarization with local (cultural) protocols, skills in writing news articles and public service announcements, designing community awareness materials, and finding and utilizing the community resources and people who can help with the actual publicity.

Fund-raising is a macro level skill that may also be a survival skill for agencies or groups that cannot get sufficient government help or are limited by the regulations and restrictions regarding expenditures. An extra benefit to successful fund-raising is that credibility is gained when the local people themselves support the program. Fund-raising also brings individual people together and allied relationships as well as community-based groups are built as people work towards a common cause.

Political activity and lobbying are other critical areas for many social workers. There is a growing acceptance in the social work profession of the need to understand the political process and to work with it (Zastrow, 1995). Social workers can effectively learn the skills of lobbying or influencing elected officials in their decisions regarding public policies and laws. The following principals are useful: (1) getting to know your legislators; (2) contacting legislators to approve of actions, to address concerns, and to make requests known; (3) treating people in public life with respect; (4) getting a bill passed into law; and (5) strategizing when your bill does not pass.

Computer skills, technical skills, and presentation skills such as assessment and use of Internet sites and the development of multimedia presentations already are essential skills that can help social workers to communicate effectively with people of all cultures and ages.

Allen and Naki (1988) suggest that the best way to ensure cultural competence in a program is to directly involve members of the community in the program design and implementation. Culturally competent workers are able to draw on community-based values, traditions, and customs and work with knowledgeable persons of and from the community in the development of focused interventions. The answers to questions about cultural competence may, indeed, lie within the people of each cultural group. Development of the skills to create a culturally safe environment, to empower culturally different people, then to work together to create pathways to common goals are approaches that will lead to effective and lasting outcomes for the people and communities with whom we work.

Cross-cultural skills development will remain an essential, ongoing part of the journey towards discovering new ways of knowing oneself and working effectively with others. The more we practice diversity competency skills, the sharper they become, and the more reflexively, spontaneously, and automatically we behave in a culturally competent manner. Ongoing sharpening of cross-cultural skills will enable us to build bridges with others.

CONCLUSION

Cultural competence is a dynamic attribute that helping professionals should value, develop, and share. Cultural competence has been presented as a changing and never-ending pathway that guides us towards an increasingly multi-ethnic future world. In this chapter, we have provided a general overview of culturally competent attitudes, knowledge, and skills needed for effective social work practice. Subsequent chapters will explore assessment, intervention, and evaluation with African Americans, Latinos, First Nations Peoples, and Asian Pacific Islanders in detail on the micro, mezzo, and macro levels.

Development of culturally competent knowledge and skills are essential but incomplete steps towards cross-cultural competence, for this is an area in which the head is less important than the heart. As Lynch and Hanson (1998) remind us: "After all the books have been read and the skills learned and practiced, the cross-cultural effectiveness of each of us will vary. And it will vary more by what we bring to the learning than by what we have learned" (p. 510). What may be most important is for social workers to maintain culturally competent attitudes as we continue to attain new knowledge and skills while building new relationships. Awareness, the valuing of all cultures, and a willingness to make changes are underlying attitudes that support everything that can be taught or learned. These attitudes and characteristics distinguish those individuals who can understand the journey ("talk the talk") from those who will actually take it. We have come full circle in this chapter as we reemphasize that sustaining culturally competent attitudes throughout our lifelong cultural journey is *the essential ingredient* as we "walk the walk" toward cultural competence in social work practice.

REFERENCES

Allen, M. & Naki, B. (1988). *Creating a culturally relevant environment.* Honolulu, HI: Institute for Family Enrichment.

Althen, G. (1988). *American ways—A guide for foreigners in the United States.* Yarmouth, ME: Intercultural Press.

Atkinson, D. R., Thompson, C. E., & Grant, S. K. (1993). A three-dimensional model for counseling racial/ethnic minorities. *The Counseling Psychologist, 21,* 257–277.

Baruth, L. G. & Manning, M. L. (1991). *Multicultural counseling and psychotherapy—A Lifespan perspective.* Upper Saddle River, NJ: Charles E. Merrill.

Bates, F. L. & Harvey, C. C. (1975). *The structure of social systems.* New York: Gardner.

Bochner, S. (1982). The social psychology of cross-cultural relations. In S. Bochner (Ed.), *Cultures in contact: Studies in cross-cultural interaction* (pp. 5–44). Oxford: Pergamon.

Browne, C., Broderick, A., & Fong, R. (1993). Lessons from the field: Social work practice with multicultural elders. *Educational Gerontology, 19,* 511–523.

Bubis, B. (1994). *Cultural connection: Cross-cultural competency training participant's guide.* A project of Eastern Los Angeles Regional Center for Developmental Disabilities and University of Southern California. A 1993–94 PDF Project sponsored by California State Department of Developmental Services/California State Council on Developmental Disabilities.

Campinha-Bacote, J. (1994). Cultural competence in psychiatric mental health nursing. *Mental Health Nursing, 29* (1), 1–8.

Caple, F. S., Salcido, R. M., & di Cecco, J. (1995). Engaging effectively with culturally diverse families and children. *Social Work in Education, 17,* 159–170.

Carney, C. G. & Kahn, K. B. (1984). Building competencies for effective cross-cultural counseling: A developmental view. *The Counseling Psychologist, 37,* 111–119.

Chan, S. (1990). Early intervention with culturally diverse families of infants and toddlers with disabilities. *Infants and Young Children, 3* (2), 78–87.

Chestang, L. (1976). Environmental influences on social functioning: The black experience. In P. San Juan Cafferty & L. Chestang (Eds.), *The diverse society: Implications for social policy* (pp. 59–74). Washington, DC: National Association of Social Workers.

Cox, C. B. & Ephross, P. H. (1998). *Ethnicity and social work practice.* Oxford: Oxford University Press.

DeVos, G. (1982). Ethnic pluralism: Conflict and accommodations. In G. DeVos & L. Romanucci-Ross (Eds.), *Ethnic identity: Cultural continuities and change* (pp. 5–41). Chicago: University of Chicago Press.

Furuto, S., Biswas, R., Chung, D., Murase, K., & Ross-Sheriff, F. (1992). *Social work practice with Asian Americans.* Newbury Park, CA: Sage.

Gollnick, Donna M. & Chinn, Philip C. (1994). *Multicultural education in a pluralistic society.* New York: Macmillan.

Hall, E. T. (1976). *Beyond culture.* Garden City, New York: Anchor.

Hammond, J. & Morrison, J. (1996). *The stuff Americans are made of.* New York: Macmillan.

Hanson, M. J. & Lynch, E. W. (1995). *Early intervention: Implementing child and family services for infants and toddlers who are at risk or disabled,* 2nd ed. Austin: Pro-Ed.

Harry, B. (1992). Developing cultural self-awareness: The first step in values clarification for early interventionists. *Topics in Early Childhood Special Education, 12,* 333–350.

Helms, J. E. & Richardson, T. Q. (1997). How "multiculturalism" obscures race and culture as differential aspects of counseling competency. In D. B. Pope-Davis & H. L. K. Coleman (Eds.),

Multicultural counseling competencies: Assessment, education and training, and supervision (pp. 60–79). Thousand Oaks, CA: Sage.

Hogan-Garcia, M. (1999). *The four skills of cultural diversity competence: A process for understanding and practice.* Belmont, CA: Wadsworth.

Ibrahim, F. A. (1985). Effective cross-cultural counseling and psychotherapy: A framework. *The Counseling Psychologist, 13,* 625–638.

Ivey, A. E. (1994). *Intentional interviewing and counseling: Facilitating client development in a multi-cultural society,* 3rd ed. Pacific Grove, CA: Brooks/Cole.

Losoncy, L. (1977). *Turning people on.* Englewood Cliffs, NJ: Prentice-Hall.

Lum, D. (1999). *Culturally competent practice: A framework for growth and action.* Pacific Grove, CA: Brookes/Cole.

Lum, D. (2000). *Social work practice and people of color: A process–stage approach,* 4th ed. Belmont, CA: Brooks/Cole.

Lum, D. & Lu, Y. E. (1997, March). Developing cultural competency within a culturally sensitive environment. Paper presented to the Council on Social Work Education annual program meeting, Chicago.

Lynch, E. W. & Hanson, M. J. (1998). *Developing cross-cultural competence: A guide for working with children and families.* Pacific Grove, CA: Brookes/Cole.

Matsumoto, D. (1996). *Culture and psychology.* Pacific Grove, CA: Brookes/Cole.

McPhatter, A. R. (January/February 1997). Cultural competence in child welfare: What is it? How do we achieve it? What happens without it? *Child Welfare, 76* (1), 255–278.

Mokuau, N. & Shimizu, D. (1991). In N. Mokuau (Ed.), *Handbook of social services for Asian and Pacific Islanders* (pp. 21–36). New York: Greenwood.

Nash, K. (1999). *Cultural competence: A guide for human service agencies.* Washington, DC: CWLA Press.

Norton, D. G. (1978). Incorporating content on minority groups into social work practice courses. In *The dual perspective.* New York: Council on Social Work Education.

Okayama, C. (1998). *A guide for establishing your multicultural identity.* Unpublished.

Okun, B. F., Fried, J., & Okun, M. L. (1999). *Understanding diversity: A learning-as-practice primer.* Pacific Grove, CA: Brookes/Cole.

Osborn, A. F. (1963). *Applied imagination: Principles and procedures of creative problem solving,* 3rd ed. New York: Scribner.

Salcido, R. (1994). In B. Bubis (Ed.), *Cultural connection: Cross-cultural competency training* (pp. 11–21). A Project of Eastern Los Angeles Regional Center and University of Southern California.

Shulman, L. (1992). *The skills of helping: Individuals, families, and groups.* Itasca, IL: F. E. Peacock.

Steward, E. C. (1972). American cultural patterns. La Grange Park, IL: Intercultural Network.

Sue, D. W. (1992). Culture-specific strategies in counseling: A conceptual framework. *Professional Psychology, 21,* 424–433.

Sue, D. W., Arredondo, P., & McDavis, R. J. (1992). Multicultural counseling competencies and standards: A call to the profession. *Journal of Counseling & Development, 70,* 477–486.

Sue, D. W., Bernier, J. E., Durran, A., Feinberg, L., Pederson, P., Smith, E. G., & Vasquez-Nuttall, E. (1982). Position paper: Cross-cultural counseling competencies. *The Counseling Psychologist, 10* (2), 45–52.

Sue, D. W. & Sue, D. (1990). *Counseling the culturally different: Theory and practice.* New York: Wiley.

Triandis, H. C. (1994). *Culture and social behavior.* New York: McGraw-Hill.

Weaver, H. N. (1997). The challenges of research in Native American communities: Incorporating principles of cultural competence. *Journal of Social Service Research, 23* (2), 1–15.

Weaver, H. N. (1998). Indigenous People and the Social Work Profession: Defining Culturally Competent Services. *Social Work, 44* (3), 217–225.

Wehrly, B. (1995). *Pathways to multicultural counseling competence: A developmental journey.* Pacific Grove, CA: Brookes/Cole.

Williams, E. & Ellison, F. (1999). Culturally informed social work practice with American Indian clients: Guidelines for non-Indian social workers. In Patricia L. Ewalt, E. Freeman, A.

Fortune, D. Poole, & S. Witkin (Eds.), *Multicultural issues in social work practice and research* (pp. 78–84). Washington, DC: National Association of Social Workers Press.

Wilson, L. & the Multi-Ethnic Training Project. (1982). *The skills of cultural competence.* University of Washington, School of Social Work.

Winkelman, M. (1999). *Ethnic sensitivity in social work.* Dubuque, IA: Eddie Bowers.

Wolcott, H. E. (1991). Propriospect and the acquisition of culture. *Anthropology and Educational Quarterly, 22,* 251–278.

Yetman, N. R. (Ed.). (1985). *Majority and minority: The dynamics of race and ethnicity in American life,* 4th ed. Boston: Allyn and Bacon.

Zastro, C. (1995). *The practice of social work.* Pacific Grove, CA: Brooks/Cole.

CHAPTER 8

STRENGTHS PERSPECTIVE INHERENT IN CULTURAL EMPOWERMENT: A TOOL FOR ASSESSMENT WITH AFRICAN AMERICAN INDIVIDUALS AND FAMILIES

KAREN L. WESTBROOKS

SAUNDRA H. STARKS

As the African American experience moves into the twenty-first century a new perspective on social work assessment for African American clients is needed. Traditional approaches have been less than successful in assessing and/or appreciating the strength and resilience that have survived despite oppression and a legacy of disenfranchisement. Paradigms that utilize dominant cultural values and fail to consider the social-historical or political context of the struggles and coping styles of African Americans are not effectively producing culturally competent social workers.

African Americans' feelings of caution, when seeking help, are understandable given the context of a documented history of being mis-assessed, misdiagnosed, mistreated and mishandled. Data drawn from the National Institute of Mental Health (Manderscheid & Sonnenchein, 1987) showed that on admission, African Americans were more frequently diagnosed with severe mental illness than were other ethnic or racial populations. Admissions of African Americans to state mental hospitals showed that 56 percent of these individuals received a primary diagnosis of schizophrenia, while only 38 percent of all individuals received a similar diagnosis. Flaskerud and Hu (1992) conclude that errors in diagnoses are the primary reason for this disproportionate rate of severe mental illness. Diagnosticians, unfamiliar with mental illness as manifested in populations of color, make these errors. With such a history, would you not be cautious?

According to Vargas and Koss-Chioino (in Karls & Wandrei, 1994, p. 159):

If social work is to be 'culturally responsive' to its clients, then understanding how the cultural contexts affect the expression of behaviors becomes an integral part of the assessment and intervention process.

The fact that social work is called to be "culturally responsive" might short-change the real possibilities for the development of skills and knowledge needed for cultural competence. The emphasis should not only be on understanding how cultural contexts affect expression of behaviors but also how expression of behaviors shapes culture. This perspective is shared by Logan, Freeman, and McRoy (1990) as well as Devore and Schlesinger (1996).

Assessment is defined in the social work dictionary as

the process of determining the nature, cause, progression, and prognosis of a problem and the personalities and situations involved therein; the social work function of acquiring an understanding of a problem, what causes it, and what can be changed to minimize or resolve it (Barker, 1999).

This bland "definition" of assessment limits the possible range of identified challenges and strengths. Indeed, culture is an integral part of everything we think, believe, suppose, value and do (Jackson & Meadows, 1991)! This chapter will discuss strengths and challenges for social workers and introduce a new model for the assessment of African American individuals and families.

DEMOGRAPHIC PROFILE OF AFRICAN AMERICANS

The term *African American* includes all black people of American and African descent as well as mixed race groups with African American blood. Any amount of black blood is still considered black in U.S. society. In 1997, people identifying as African American numbered approximately 33 million, or 12.6 percent of the population in the United States.

With regard to place of residence, income, and education, African Americans are non-surprisingly diverse. According to 1997 data from the U.S. Census Bureau, the top three counties for the highest numbers of African Americans were Cook County, (Chicago) Illinois with 1,369,633 (27.0 percent), Los Angeles County, California with 1,019,214 (representing 11.1 percent) and Kings County, New York with 924,862 (41.3 percent) (U.S. Bureau of the Census, 1998a). While Los Angeles is home to over one million African Americans, note that 11.1 is a slim percent of the overall population. This fact can shed some insight on "invisibility issues" with regard to recognition of needs for employment, housing and other basic necessities. While high numbers do not always ensure high percentage, high percentage does provide information about African Americans who have the experience of being the "majority race" in a given community. The top three counties for the highest percentage of African Americans are Baltimore City, Maryland with 65.4 (429,650), Orleans Parish, Louisiana with 63.7 (298,714), and Prince George's County, Maryland with 57.0 (438,970) (U.S. Bureau of the Census, 1998a).

According to 1997 American Housing Survey Data, over 18 million African Americans had incomes from wages and salaries and earned income from businesses, farms or ranches; 1.695 million were on welfare or Supplemental Security Income. Over five million African Americans (15 percent) have income less than $25,000 and are over-represented in service level positions. The median income for African Americans is $21,047 (U.S. Bureau of the Census, 1998b).

With regard to education, 1997 U.S. Census Data show that 76 percent of African Americans completed high school and 14.7 percent completed four years of college or more (U.S. Bureau of the Census, 1998c).

PROBLEMS AND ISSUES

In spite of civil rights gains, most African American families experience a myriad of inequities and discrimination in areas of housing, employment, education, health and welfare services. Institutionalized racism helps to maintain the disproportionate number of African Americans in the criminal justice system and hinders progress in the quality of life for many African Americans (Aquirre & Turner, 1995).

In addition, a myriad of inequities also exist in the practices that do not empower African American families due to a lack of knowledge, training, and experience. Even when a social worker is well-meaning, but not prepared for cultural competent practice, she too can become an agent of continued oppression. Such oppression is revealed in assumptions she may make in the assessment and intervention. If the assumptions have the impact of disempowering rather than empowering, a meaningful point of contact with the client will be lost. A disempowering assumption would lack the clarity of differentiating problematic or symptomatic behaviors from cultural norms and behaviors. An assessment that increases the client's experience of worthlessness and helplessness is an assessment that overlooks, devalues, disrespects, and dismisses what the client truly brings to the helping relationship and works to counter the empowerment mission of the social work profession. Therefore, while recognizing the sociopolitical context of the client challenge, the social worker is called to affirm the legitimacy of the client's struggle, embrace unconventional client strenghts, and seek to empower the client to function healthily in a life context.

CULTURAL STRENGTH OR VALUE

Relative to the struggles with racism and discrimination, African American individuals and families bring a diversity of strengths and resources to the assessment and social work practice setting. A survival structure exists that can be mobilized for empowerment.

Often consisting of relatives who are not blood related, African American families might include biracial, bisexual, and/or have a variety of functionally different structures. Terms such as kinship and fictive kin networks have been used to capture the concept of family (Martin and Martin, 1995). These terms describe families inclusive of many alternative structures.

STRENGTHS PERSPECTIVE INHERENT IN CULTURAL EMPOWERMENT (SPICE)

Because the Person-In-Environment (PIE) concept is considered best practice, and it is the major classification system for social functioning problems, PIE's role in assessment is our first point of challenge. PIE has been a progressive first step in social work practice because it quite appropriately directs attention to the contextual factors relative to assessment and intervention. Evidence of its merits are documented in core textbooks on basic skills of social work (Germain & Gitterman, 1980; Karls & Wandrei, 1994; Kirst-Ashman & Hull, 1993; Schulman, 1984).

However, PIE has not survived without criticism. Meyer and Mattaini (1998, p. 3) assert that

> the person-in-environment concept has governed practice since the work of Mary Richmond nearly a century ago and has been defined and redefined (Hamilton, 1951) over the years, its hyphenated structure has contributed to a continuing imbalance in emphasis on the person or the environment.

The term itself might suggest that the person and the environment are independent of each other; thus, a practitioner could readily choose to see case problems from one aspect or another.

It is our position, however, that cultural competence would require a reevaluation of the PIE assessment. Why? While PIE is an excellent tool for assessing the person in context, moving toward cultural competence would mean having a strengths perspective as an inherent part of cultural empowerment. A strengths perspective permits self-valuing as well as respect for the resources the client brings to the problem; therefore, in our model Person-in-Environment (PIE) becomes Strengths-Perspective-Inherent-in-Cultural-Empowerment (SPICE). Our SPICE model includes the basic guiding principles of empowerment-oriented social work practice while acknowledging cultural resources.

Our SPICE model is comprehensively contextual as it acknowledges the interaction of several cultural systems in which African American life takes place. Here the need is for a redefinition of assessment. The exciting possibilities of SPICE create new ways of thinking about client challenges and strengths.

SPICE—AN EMPOWERMENT PHILOSOPHY

In the social work profession, *empowerment* has been defined as a theoretical framework with specific behaviors, interventions, and outcomes (Gutierrez, 1990; Solomon, 1976). Components of this framework are directed toward helping individuals, families, and communities increase their personal, interpersonal, socioeconomic, and political strength and develop influence toward improving their circumstances (Barker, 1999). These components are deeply embedded in culture.

The core philosophy of SPICE is rooted in strengths and cultural empowerment, the guiding principles of social work practice. SPICE accents the roots of practice already established and leads the profession into the new millennium now equipped with an acronym that is a useful representation of the overall goals for cultural competence. As with any philosophy, there are possibilities for growth, movement, and direct action relative to the its tenets, beliefs, and values.

The purpose of SPICE is to provide the tools and a foundation for effectively helping both the client/family and the social worker successfully transform the effects of oppression into the response of empowerment. For most families oppression involves experiences of being dismissed, devalued, disregarded, and disempowered. On the other hand, empowerment involves experiences of validation that include being present, proud, pertinent, and powerful (see Table 8.1). SPICE offers the worker a way to help the client make the transition from the "stuckness" of the Ds to the empowerment of the Ps.

For those unfamiliar with the experience of the Ds, we offer this brief illustration. An African American social work intern is placed at a community agency. Her field supervisor has five such interns, one of whom, our trainee, is the only African American. The supervisor regards that trainee as "a token," thus dismissing her presence as a serious intern. Such a dismissal could result in the trainee devaluing her potential for becoming an effective practitioner. Secondly, during group discussion with all five interns, our trainee's possibly unique perspective may be regarded as "nonacademic" or "nonapplicable." To disregard her voice is a highly disempowering experience and affects not only the trainee but also the supervisory relationship. The purpose of the training is severely undermined and the trainee may exit that experience more damaged than confident. The positive

TABLE 8.1   Balancing Experiences of Racial Oppression

ACTIONS OF RACISM & OPPRESSION	ACTIONS OF RESILIENCE & STRENGTH
The 4 Ds:	*The 4 Ps:*
Dismiss	be Present
Devalue	be Proud
Disregard	be Pertinent
Disempower	be Powerful

results of Ps are obvious: Viewing the trainee as seriously present will contribute to her sense of pride, pertinence, and power!

A meaningful sense of presence, pride, pertinence, and power can be derived through spiritual life. In fact, recent perspectives have come to recognize spirituality as a form of functional diversity (Westbrooks, 1997).

Within the African American culture, spiritual life is one vehicle for "tapping into the Ps." For some African American families, spirituality is a core aspect of a multidimensional focus that includes individual, family, and community strengths, medical, social, and functional status, as well as family support. An emphasis on the spiritual life of a family rises above the functional or dysfunctional nature of a societal context and encourages us to consider an alternative, one that focuses on spirituality as one measure and standard for family values (Westbrooks, 1995).

Spirituality can be defined as a deeper connectedness that provides an energy source for empowerment, relevance, and life satisfaction (Starks, 1999). In the study of 148 African American women at midlife conducted by Starks, spirituality was found to be one of the major contributors to life satisfaction. Spirituality in this study was conceptualized as inclusive, holistic, personal, less structured, and different from traditional dominant culture religiosity.

For families who embrace spirituality, what goes on outside the family unit is also an appropriate focus of attention. A family's position in a social, economic, political, and spiritual environment affects its perspective of what is supportive and what is threatening. Families that are respected, validated, accepted, and seemingly protected from societal ills may not be aware of the external dynamics when such ills do not blatantly threaten family survival, identity, beliefs, and goals (Westbrooks, 1995).

One of the purposes of SPICE is to address the issue of positive identity formation as a step toward cultural empowerment. SPICE encourages us to listen to others without ignoring key aspects of their life reality. Some of you may be saying, "I don't ignore anyone." *Ignored* is mentioned here as one of the primary ways African Americans are dismissed, devalued, disregarded, and disempowered. Ignoring indicates making a judgment about the family based on *your* personal beliefs and values. You may say, "That is what we are supposed to do." Not so. When you make a judgment based on your own beliefs and values, you are essentially leaving the client out of the equation. The entire assessment becomes framed by what *you* know, believe, value, and hold true. That is precisely how the client gets ignored.

To validate presence, pride, pertinence, and power is to work within the *client's* own knowledge, beliefs, and values. All clients know something, believe something, and value something, whether or not it is readily apparent. It is important to acknowledge these beliefs and values early on. The SPICE assessment is intended to aid you in that process. Including the client in the assessment process helps validate that experience and builds a collaborative relationship. Gutierrez, Parsons, and Cox (1998) have encouraged empowering relationships with clients for almost a decade. Empowerment is possible when the social worker's actions affirm the client's identity and culture.

SPICE provides concrete tools for an empowering and culturally relevant assessment. Helping clients be present, proud, pertinent, and powerful would necessitate knowledge of the racist and oppressive environment in which they live. The skills needed to attain and maintain experiences that reinforce such empowerment is the SPICE of life. To live fully in a cultural context where identity is supported and strengths are recognized is a seemingly useful goal for a social worker in training. To maintain a strengths perspective is indeed challenging. SPICE provides an analysis, a "way in" for assessing African American individuals and families, as illustrated by the following case:

> **CASE EXAMPLE**
> Mr. Mack, a ninety-five-year-old African American resident of the Lynwood Long-Term Care Facility, has been restricted by the nursing staff from attending his regular weekly devotional service. The only family he has are his church friends, who continue to visit on a regular basis and provide support. This new restriction for him was precipitated by a fall that occurred during a Sunday morning devotional in the facility meeting room. The fall resulted in a bone fracture that has since completely healed. On this particular day, Mr. Mack was engaged in his usual singing, shouting, and testimonials, which always seemed to bring him such joy and peace. The facility's decision to place the restriction was also supported by his State Guardian, who had been appointed the previous year due to Mr. Mack's age and lack of relatives. Although Mr. Mack remains lucid and clear in his thinking, he has recently become despondent and more withdrawn and isolated in his behavior. He refuses to attend other activities that the facility offers. While ambulatory, he lately chooses to use a wheel chair. As the social worker of the center, your task is to reassess Mr. Mack.

Traditional versus SPICE Focus Using the Case Example

Seemingly, the traditional view is correct. While it is easy to view information at face value, it is more challenging to seriously consider a more helpful posture in the case of Mr. Mack. In the list of problems and strengths shown in Table 8.2, can you discern what may be the Ds (dismissed, devalued, disregarded, disempowered) that could be contributing to Mr. Mack's withdrawn, regressive, and uncooperative behavior? How was Mr. Mack dismissed? What was devalued? What was disregarded? How was Mr. Mack disempowered?

If these questions seem difficult to answer, you are not alone. It is always difficult to answer questions that do not fit our frame of reference. In the case of the ninety-five-year-old African American man, we are called to think according to the SPICE model. Note the difference it makes for Mr. Mack and us when we use the SPICE assessment model in this case. As you read, consider the opportunities and options now available to us using this new way of thinking while assessing the same information.

When Mr. Mack is viewed in context, we can see his withdrawn behavior as a natural response to loss. He has key losses in his life: weekly devotional service, decision making, support system, spiritual renewal, and surrogate family. In

TABLE 8.2   Comparison of Traditional Assessment and SPICE Assessment

THE CASE OF MR. MACK	
TRADITIONAL ASSESSMENT *Problems*	**SPICE ASSESSMENT** *Challenges*
1. Very elderly, fragile 2. No family, no support 3. Suffered fall, recovering from bone fracture 4. Despondent, depressed 5. Withdrawn 6. Regressive 7. Uncooperative, resistant	1. Loss of access to weekly devotional service 2. Loss of power over decision making 3. Loss of access to support system 4. Competing definitions of his identity 5. Loss of access to spiritual renewal and energy 6. Loss of access to "surrogate family" 7. Resurfacing of oppression issues 8. Addressing context in which he is being dismissed, devalued, disregarded, and disempowered
TRADITIONAL ASSESSMENT *Strengths*	**SPICE ASSESSMENT** *Strengths*
1. In a health care facility 2. Ambulatory 3. Lucid, clear thinking 4. Nurses and helping professionals	1. Has values and behaviors that can bring energy into his life 2. Has a support system 3. Oriented and engaged 4. Pride and dignity are his protection 5. Physically healthy at ninety-five, healed from broken bone 6. Ambulatory 7. Survivor

addition, his definition of self has been assaulted! He is in a system that views him as a frail old man needing protection. He views himself as a man who has been around long enough to demand respect. Mr. Mack has order in his life based on his beliefs and values. When a decision was made to restrict him from attending church service, naturally, some oppression issues began to resurface.

As a social worker, your main challenge would be to assess Mr. Mack's situation while addressing the context in which he was dismissed, devalued, disregarded, and disempowered. SPICE encourages us to use the client's own values and strengths as a first step towards empowerment. Mr. Mack (now despondent) already has values that can bring energy into his life. He already has the ability to be present, proud, pertinent, and powerful. These abilities are part of his strengths that can be actualized by viewing the case from Mr. Mack's perspective. At ninety-five years, he is physically present and still able to heal from a broken bone. He is a survivor who is oriented and engaged. The elements of his support system are so important to him that he views them as his surrogate family and they view his life as pertinent. Being proud and dignified is quite a strength for a man who has been around for almost a century! Recognizing his strengths helps to restore his sense of personal power.

COMPATIBILITY OF SPICE WITH ASPECTS OF AFRICAN AMERICAN CULTURE

SPICE, our proposed model of assessment for African American individuals and families, includes the basic guiding principles of empowerment-oriented social work practice. Because African Americans, in particular, have a history of being dismissed, devalued, disregarded, and disempowered, the assessment process needs to acknowledge how their resilience and strengths have risen above such experiences. Boyd-Franklin (1989) identified eight major strengths African American clients bring to the social work process: (1) extended family support, (2) centrality of spirituality or religion, (3) adaptability of family roles, (4) high value placed on children, (5) informal adoption, (6) cultural loyalty, (7) high priority on education, coupled with a strong work orientation, and (8) strong women.

Steps in the SPICE Assessment

The following suggestions are based on the SPICE philosophy and can be used to guide the assessment process:

- Identify the client systems or the focal system, including the ecology of the system;
- Establish a partnership with the client using suggested rapport-building tools for African Americans;
- Clearly articulate an understanding of the challenges/issues presented by the family by using reflection and active listening;
- Identify how the client system functions with other interacting systems (use of an EcoMap could be helpful);
- Clarify client strengths and validate client experiences;
- Identify goal-helping versus goal-hindering forces in the client's ecology;
- Use observation as well as questionnaires and/or other data-collecting tools;
- Engage the client in the development of action plans.

Factors to Always Consider in the Interview Process

The initial subjective content is important to the process. Hearing the story in the client's own words allows for culturally sensitive communication, clarification, and reflective content. What does the client think will happen or fears can happen? What is the client's future vision? What does the client say are his or her immediate needs? The value of starting where the client is still applies with African American individuals and families. We need to impart hope and the sincere desire to help and to see the problem or issue the way the client sees the problem or issue (Devore & Schlesinger, 1996).

Examples of Assessment Questions You Can Ask during Assessment

Because each situation and family is unique, it is important to be client-centered, remembering that the client is the expert regarding her or his situation. Until the client gives permission to do otherwise, always address African American clients as Ms., Mrs., or Mr. This indicates respect and promotes empowerment. The following are examples of appropriate questions to ask when assessing African American clients.

How can I be of help to you today?

Tell me what brings you here today?

In your own words, what do you see as difficulties?

What do you think or feel is working well for you now?

What in your life gives you a sense of strength?

How have you dealt with this experience in the past?

What do you think you need now to solve this problem/meet this challenge?

What role does your family play?

Tell me who in your environment provides support?

ECO-CULTURAL ASSESSMENT

Use the SPICE guide to develop your assessment based on the categories of information necessary to understand your client and develop an action plan with goals and objectives following the partnership model of empowerment.

Strengths
What is the focal system? Who are the identified clients? What is the status of the challenge? What are the current strengths? What is the client's perspective of what is working?

Perspectives
What are the goals of the client? How does the client envision the future? Internally and externally? Subjectively and objectively? Look at positive projections.

Inherent In
How does the client system define itself? What are its roles? Discuss gender, racial identity, income, education level, job/career, and family structure.

Cultural
What are the cultural antecedents? What are the client's racial and intergenerational experiences? How does the client present the problems?

Empowerment
What are the physical, emotional, economic, spiritual, familial, formal, and informal resources? What is the degree of energy going out of versus coming into the system?

Numerous challenges confront the social worker attempting to assess African American clients. The best practice would always have the social worker consider the context of the issues; however, with African American clients it is important to consider the cultural, sociopolitical, and generational contexts as well.

Preparation for conducting a culturally competent assessment involves starting with self-awareness, self-knowledge, and self-inventory. The inventory in Figure 8.1 can be used to develop a structured plan for acquiring the knowledge, skills, and experiences necessary for this process. Social work practice that has a

FIGURE 8.1   Cultural Competency Development Inventory

PERSONAL ASSETS (STRENGTHS)	PERSONAL CHALLENGES (LIABILITIES)
1.	1.
2.	2.
3.	3.
4.	4.
5.	5.

PAST EXPERIENCES WITH CULTURAL DIFFERENCES

Positive	*Negative*
_____	_____
_____	_____
_____	_____
_____	_____

GOALS TOWARD MASTERY OF SENSITIVITY, KNOWLEDGE, AND SKILLS

Short-Term	*Long-Term*
1.	1.
2.	2.
3.	3.
4.	4.
5.	5.

PLAN

1. _____
2. _____
3. _____
4. _____

Tables 8.3, 8.4, and 8.5 illustrate significant SPICE personal and professional challenges and recommendations for all social workers: Euro-American, African American, and all social workers of color (Asian Pacific Islander, African American, Latino American, and Native American). In each table the term *client* refers to African American individuals or families.

strong experiential base for cultural competency is vital to assessments with African American individuals and families.

CHALLENGES AND RECOMMENDATIONS: EURO-AMERICAN SOCIAL WORKERS

European American social workers-in-training, in order to work with African American clients, must have an initial awareness and understanding of what they bring to the practice setting in regard to assumptions, biases, limitations, and

TABLE 8.3   SPICE Assessment Challenges and Recommendations for Euro-American Social Workers

CHALLENGES	RECOMMENDATIONS
Having little or no firsthand experience with African American people	Supplementing academic training with experiential opportunities with African American people
Adopting a tentative, subservient, humble role	Adopting a role of willingness to learn and be led—a true student of the partnership model
Being "too impressed" with a client/family's ability	Responding genuinely to a client/family's ability
Using slang or talking "Black"	Using standard language and being comfortable with asking for clarification
Expecting to do an excellent assessment immediately	Expecting the assessment to take time (knowing that time is a very different construct across cultures)
Being anxious about perceived inadequacies of self	Taking an inventory of one's own challenges and strengths
Being afraid of clients who express anger	Allowing and validating appropriate expressions of anger from clients
Feeling like a failure when clients reject "help"	Respecting the client's right to reject "help"
Believing that, if race is not an issue for me, it's not an issue for the social worker–client relationship	Realizing that, even if I don't perceive race as an issue, my clients may
Trying to convince the client/family that you "understand"	Being comfortable with the client/family being the expert
Ignoring the dynamic of "nontrust" as a component of the legacy of oppression—Blaming the Victim (adapted from Boyd-Franklin, 1989)	Acknowledging the sociopolitical implications of the legacy of oppression for African American people

expectations. The strength of the SPICE model allows the trainee to (1) stretch beyond his or her assumptions, (2) identify both personal and professional challenges, (3) develop an experiential component that provides exposure, contextual understanding, a range of skills, and a renewed confidence in the ability to make assessments.

In our own training of Euro-American students for work with African American clients, we have found that, more often than not, students are eager, motivated, and have good intentions. While this eagerness is a positive expression of an effective service orientation, they must at some point deal with the sensitive issues encompassed in the legacies of white privilege and nontrust.

Expecting to have openness and nonbiased treatment from the client (because the worker feels totally unbiased or does not see race as an issue) is a mistake. As the worker, you are just one part of the partnership. All of us come to the profession with prejudices and stereotypes. It is virtually impossible to have been born and raised in the United States and not have certain prejudices and ethnocentric attitudes. Each person comes to the assessment with a history and legacy from past experiences. African Africans often come to the assessment with an additional legacy—oppression and abuse by the system—that needs to be factored into the context of the interaction.

Differences in expressiveness between the dominant culture and African American clients may leave the dominant culture social worker frightened at the intensity of ethnic expression. Anger, rage, and frustration, which are often part of the affective content of the session, become, too often, the focus, rather than the situation in which anger and rage make sense. Failing to validate these expressions of anger and frustration may halt the flow of information and block the productivity of the assessment.

The desire to understand needs to be conveyed via interaction with clients through communications such as "help me understand." Often this simple difference can move the process toward mutual trust and respect.

Challenges and Recommendations: African American Social Workers

While it may seem unnecessary that we have a section on challenges and recommendations for African American social workers, "shared race" does not preclude the need for specific training in the assessment of African American clients. Negating the differences within the ethnic group and the differences of education, acculturation levels, assimilation, income, and regional culture, the unprepared social worker would proceed rather presumptuously, adding confusion and further alienation to the process. It is vitally important to realize that your work will not necessarily be easier because you and your client are of the same race.

Boundary issues can also become a problem for African American social workers who work with African American clients. Becoming enmeshed in or overidentifying with the family can produce an assessment that lacks objectivity

TABLE 8.4   SPICE Assessment Challenges and Recommendations for African American Social Workers

CHALLENGES	RECOMMENDATIONS
Assuming that, because there is shared race, there is no need for a transition into the assessment process	Knowing that shared race can ease the transition into the assessment process, but it is also necessary to consciously apply social worker skills to build a relationship
Believing that clients will automatically trust you because you are African American	Knowing that, even if clients are less suspicious and guarded, trust is not automatic; trust has to be built
Expecting that you will automatically be assumed to be "real" because you are African American	Knowing that clients may expect something different from you on a personal level that will depend on you being "real"
Arriving at your own assessment without any real input from the client	Using input from the client to arrive at a meaningful assessment, thus building an effective partnership
Overidentifying with the client and losing objectivity	Understanding the temptation to overidentify and remaining steadfast in the role of social worker and not "friend"
Being perceived by the client as "less streetwise, less down and removed"	Understanding the client will have a perception of you "as something" and inviting them to let you know when it seems that you don't understand
Needing to prove to the client that you are "with them"	Having less to prove and more to offer
Encountering a projection of "self-hatred" that might come from a client believing an African American social worker is second-rate	Encountering projection of self-hatred and using it as an assessment tool
Encountering a projection of "being white" because you are a professional	Being grounded and clear in your own racial identity
Being anxious about perceived inadequacies of self	Being able to take an inventory of your own challenges and strengths
Blaming the victim	Seeing potential and inherent worth in each person

and limits the empowerment process for the client. For example, client X might remind you of your own uncle Joe. In this case, working through the assessment can create countertransferences that may be limiting and repressive or overly liberal. Either attitude presents challenges for African American social workers.

Perhaps the most critical understanding is the realization that being grounded and clear in your own racial identity will enhance the assessment process. If you are clear about who you are, you will be less likely to become involved in some of the challenges listed in Table 8.4, and more likely to search for an understanding of the presenting question before proceeding to assist with the development of an answer.

Challenges and Recommendations: All Social Workers of Color

For all social workers of color, including Asian Pacific Islanders, Native Americans, and Latino Americans who have little or no experience with or exposure to African American clients, similar pitfalls occur. A strong reliance on the myths and misconceptions portrayed in the media and through U.S. history leaves major gaps

TABLE 8.5   SPICE Assessment Challenges and Recommendations for All Social Workers of Color (Asian Pacific Islanders, Latino Americans, Native Americans, and African Americans)

CHALLENGES	RECOMMENDATIONS
Adopting dominant culture beliefs about all clients	Recognizing and utilizing different beliefs that families have about themselves
Having little or no exposure to clients	Supplementing academic training with exposure to African Americans
Ignoring the possible dynamics of cross-racial interventions involving different populations of color	Acknowledging the dynamics of cross-racial interventions within populations of color
Assuming that other people of color should be like you	Acknowledging the unique differences of individuals across cultures as well as within cultures
Assuming that the "meaning of things" is the same across populations of color	Respecting and valuing differences in the "meaning of things"
Blaming the victim	Seeing potential and believing in the worth and dignity of all people
Being anxious about perceived inadequacies	Being able to take an inventory of one's own challenges and strengths
Expecting nontrust on the part of your client	Recognizing preconceived attitudes that would hinder trust building
Assuming that hierarchical family relationships take priority over spousal relationships and friendship	Exploring the value and importance that the family itself gives to hierarchical spousal and friendship relationships

in awareness and promotes the influence and contamination of preconceived biases throughout the assessment process. Such gaps are totally incompatible with the SPICE model.

The literature on cross-racial interventions presents data supporting the dynamics possible among diverse people of color. Between the cultures and/or races animosities and rivalries often exist, having been fostered and nurtured by the dominant culture. Could this be designed to maintain dissention and separateness? Asian Americans are not set up as the "model minority" without repercussions and fallout. Native Americans, who have experienced the least political progress and advancement in this country, continue to struggle for equal rights and to maintain their native cultural rituals. People of color, and their many struggles, are similar within their own unique context.

Novice social workers, coming from a background of means, often have difficulty understanding the dynamics of abuse and oppression and the importance of the contextual variables that contribute to the overt behaviors and attitudes of African American clients. Blaming the victim compounds the experience of oppression and actually revictimizes the victim. African American clients, who have experienced incredible discrimination, injustice, and powerlessness, are greatly in need of the empowerment-based social work practice that Gutierrez (1990) proposes, the same basic philosophy that underlies the SPICE assessment.

It is only natural for all new social workers to experience some performance anxiety when engaged in assessment, regardless of race or ethnicity. Anxiety is a necessary element of learning and growing. Only when the level of anxiety is allowed to become dysfunctional does it impair the social worker and impede the assessment process. Expectations of perfection have no place in the training and development of culturally competent social workers. All students and trainees must accept and respect their starting place on the continuum of cultural competence and work from there. Use of the Cultural Competency Development Inventory (Figure 8.1) can be invaluable in the journey towards cultural competence in client assessment.

CONCLUSIONS

We hope you found this chapter useful, especially in reviewing a new assessment model for African American individuals and families. It is critical for African American clients to reconnect with their identity, worth, and value as they struggle with accessing formal helping services. The transition to becoming present, proud, pertinent, and powerful is possible with social workers who can genuinely validate and value the contribution that clients can make to the assessment process. Strength perspectives inherent in cultural empowerment (SPICE) are relevant not only in the assessment of African American clients but also as potentially powerful tools across diverse populations and clientele.

Our SPICE model suggests that an acknowledgment of strengths leads to cultural empowerment, cultural empowerment leads to achievement, and achievement leads to validation of strengths that leads to cultural empowerment. Empowerment needs to be attained, maintained, reinforced, and practiced. May you add a little *SPICE* to your training and practice as you acknowledge the gifts and strengths that you *and* your clients bring to the assessment process.

REFERENCES

Aguirre, A. & Turner, J. (1995). *American ethnicity: The dynamics and consequences of discrimination.* New York: McGraw-Hill.

Barker, R. L. (1999). *The social work dictionary, 4th Ed.* Washington, DC: National Association of Social Workers Press.

Boyd-Franklin, N. (1989). *Black families in therapy: A multisystems approach.* New York: Guildford.

Devore, W. & Schlesinger, E. G. (1996). *Ethnic-sensitive social work practice,* 4th ed. New York: MacMillan.

Flaskerud, J. H. & Hu, L. (1992). Relationship of ethnicity to psychiatric diagnosis. *Journal of Nervous and Mental Disease, 180* (5), 296–303.

Germain, C. & Gitterman, A. (1980). *Life model of social work practice.* New York: Columbia University Press.

Gitterman, A. (1996). *Life model of social work treatment: Interlocking theoretical approaches, 4th ed.* New York: Free Press.

Gutierrez, L. (1990). Working with women of color: An empowerment perspective. *Social Work, 35* (2), 149–153.

Gutierrez, L., Parsons, R. J. & Cox, E. O. (Eds.). (1998). *Empowerment in social work practice: A sourcebook.* Pacific Grove, CA: Brooks/Cole.

Hamilton, G. (1951). *Theory and practice of social casework.* New York: Columbia University Press.

Jackson, A. & Meadows, F. (1991). Getting to the bottom to reach the top. *Journal of Counseling & Development, 70,* 72–76.

Karls, J. M. & Wandrei, K. E. (1994). *Person-In-Environment system: The PIE system for classification for social functioning problems.* Washington, DC: National Association of Social Workers Press.

Kirst-Ashman, K. K. & Hull, G. H. (1993). *Understanding generalist practice.* Chicago: Nelson/Hall.

Logan, S., Freeman, E., & McRoy, R. (1990). *Social work with black families: A culturally specific perspective.* New York: Longman.

Manderscheid, R & Sonnenchein, M. A. (1987). National Institute of Mental Health Publications. United States Bureau of the Census (1996).

Martin, E. P. & Martin, J. M. (1995). *Social work and the black experience.* Washington, DC: National Association of Social Workers Press.

Meyer, C. H. & Mattaini M. A. (1998). The ecosystems perspective: Implications for practice. In M. A. Mattaini, C. T. Lowery, & C. H. Meyer (Eds.), *The Foundations of social work practice.* Washington, DC: National Association of Social Workers Press.

Starks, S. H. (1999). *African American women at midlife: The dance between spirituality and life satisfaction.* Unpublished manuscript. Louisville, KY: University of Louisville.

Schulman, L. (1984). *The skills of helping people and groups.* Chicago: F. E. Peacock.

Solomon, B. (1976). *Black empowerment: Social work in oppressed communities.* New York: Columbia University Press.

U.S. Bureau of the Census. (1995). Statistical abstract of the United States. Washington, DC: United States Department of Commerce.

U.S. Bureau of the Census. (1998a). *Where we live. Table of top 30 counties ranked by black population in 1997.* Constructed by Rincon & Associates. http://www.rinconassoc.com/black97i.htm

U.S. Bureau of the Census. (1998b). *What we earn.* detailed tables for occupied units with black householder. http://www.census.gov/hhes/www/housing/ahs/97cdtchrt/tab5-12.html

U.S. Bureau of the Census. (1998c). Our education. Percent of people 25 years old and over who have completed high school—selected years 1940 to 1998. http://www.census.gov/population/socdemo/education/tablea-02.txt

Vargas, L. A. & Koss-Chioino, J. D. (Eds.). (1992). *Working with culture.* San Francisco: Jossey-Bass.

Westbrooks, K. (1995). *Functional low-income families: Activating strengths.* New York: Vantage.

Westbrooks, K. (1997). Spirituality as a form of functional diversity: Activating unconventional strengths. *Journal of Family Social Work,* Vol 2(A), 77–87.

■ ■ ■ ■ ■

CHAPTER 9

CULTURALLY COMPETENT ASSESSMENTS OF AFRICAN AMERICAN COMMUNITIES AND ORGANIZATIONS

MAXWELL C. MANNING

Organization and community assessment in African American communities requires a broad, historical understanding of cultures with roots in Africa and the skills necessary to assess their needs. Because of the diversity within these communities, it is important to acknowledge that some people of African descent, e.g., Caribbeans, prefer the term *Black* or other references (Center for Mental Health Services, 1998). The author acknowledges these differences but uses *African American* as an inclusive term.

This chapter explores the importance of cultural competence and diversity when assessing African American communities and organizations, and will focus on the strengths and values of the African American community rather than its deficits and weaknesses. It views the African American community within the context of vertical and horizontal influences, the need for empowerment, and other ecological or environmental considerations.

SOCIODEMOGRAPHIC OVERVIEW

The African American community is a diverse and multidimensional community. There are many subgroups from countries in Africa and the Caribbean (U.S. Immigration and Naturalization Service, 1997), including people from Ethiopia, Haiti, Ghana, Nigeria, Jamaica, and Trinidad.

The African American (Black) population comprises 12.1 percent (30 million) of the total United States population (U.S. Bureau of the Census, 1991). The largest percent of this population is in urban cities like New York (2,102,512), Chicago (1,087,711), Detroit (777,916), Philadelphia (631,936), and Los Angeles (487,674) (U.S. Bureau of the Census, 1991). Of this population, available data indicate that, in 1997, Africans (52,889), Jamaicans (19,089), and Haitians (18,386) continue to immigrate in small numbers, particularly in Florida, New York, and New Jersey (U.S. Immigration and Naturalization Service, 1997).

CULTURAL VALUES AND BEHAVIORAL NORMS

Traditions, customs, and values play a significant role in the development of African American families, communities, and organizations (Hill, 1997; Pinderhughes, 1982). They are rooted in a rich African heritage, the influences of slavery, and other historical factors. Therefore, community assessments should incorporate techniques that measure the institutionalization of cultural traditions, customs, and values, and racial or reference identification. These techniques assess the level of commitment within community infrastructure, e.g., key institutions and leaders. If the institutional commitment is strong, they will reinforce affiliation, collectivity, spirituality, achievement, and a strong work ethic (Hill, 1997; Pinderhughes, 1982). These communities will have a sense of continuity and an ability to cope with a changing environment (Hill, 1997; Pinderhughes, 1982; Vargas & Koss-Chioino, 1992). For example, values like cooperation, sharing, and affiliation encourage African Americans to support one another and share resources (Hill, 1997; Pinderhughes, 1982).

African American values that emphasize a strong work orientation and achievement contribute both to the African community and larger society (Hill, 1997). African Americans have made significant contributions through inventions like the traffic light, air conditioner, and gas mask and their leaders, e.g., Colin Powell, Jesse Jackson, Pastor Reid, Apostle Montgomery, T. D. Jakes, and Congressmen Charles Rangel (Hill, 1997; Saleebey, 1992). The strong African American work ethic is reinforced in the family, which provides for its children and prepares them for the community workforce (Hill, 1997).

Spirituality and/or a strong religious orientation are very important values within the African American community and reinforce values like cooperation, sharing, and a strong work orientation (Hill, 1997; Pinderhughes, 1982; Schiele, 1996). The church, as an institution, reinforces cooperation, sharing, and work (Ellison, 1991, 1993). Church fellowship and activities become essential for nurturing and developing a positive sense of self, one's people, and the community. Through the religious community, African Americans continue to build educational institutions, provide for the poor, and share resources, e.g., Bethel Christian School (Bethel AME Church, Baltimore, MD), Nehemiah Housing Project (St. Paul Community Baptist Church, Brooklyn, New York), and Golden Rule Supermarket (Bible Way Church, Washington, DC) (Billingsley, 1992).

Worship of a divine or higher being is a core belief that drives the African American to participate in church. The church and the African American community are partners in traditions, customs, and values. Through participation in religious activities, African Americans are strengthened and their well-being is increased (Ellison, 1991, 1993; Hill, 1997; Pollner, 1989).

Affiliation and kinship bonds contribute to the unity within the African American community. Because African Americans feel historically connected, they may informally adopt unrelated children, support fictive kin, and share parenting responsibilities. The shared culture and history provide a basis for mutual understanding and drawing on common experiences. The racial identity and identification is a commonly shared experience by most African Americans.

Racial identity and identification are meaningful ways that African Americans express how they value their skin color, racial features, cultural heritage, and commitment to the community (Boyd-Franklin, 1989; Harvey, 1995; Hines & Boyd-Franklin, 1982). Several authors, Carter (1991), Cross (1991), Helms (1986, 1990), Helms & Parham (1985) and Parham (1993) have discussed the relationship between racial identity, self-esteem, and a commitment to the African American community. By assessing the importance of racial identification within a community and among its leaders, you can determine the level of positive self-esteem and commitment available for community change and development. African Americans with a strong racial identity or consciousness are more committed to community involvement (Cross, 1991; Gutiérrez, 1990).

Racial identity development is enhanced and increased when African Americans participate in cultural and community activities (Cross, 1991; Jackson & Sears, 1992; Manning, 1997). "Afrocentric replenishment" describes African customs, rituals and values like cooperation, sharing, and spirituality that reinforce their African heritage (Manning, 1997). For example, the rites of passage programs socialize and prepare African youth for adulthood and meaningful roles in their community. These programs transfer important African values to youth that encourage them to strengthen their communities and become future leaders (Harvey & Rauch, 1997). Afrocentric replenishment is essential for building strong and viable African American communities.

Therefore, the assessment of communities should determine the level of "Afrocentric replenishment" or reinforcement for values like collectivity, sharing, and spirituality. Once assessed, these communities can determine the strategies for increasing the emphasis on African American values and culture (Gutiérrez, 1990). As an empowerment strategy, Afrocentric replenishment is important for the survival of the African American people and community (Pinderhughes, 1989; Weaver, 1982). Empowerment strategies increase the African American's self-esteem, power relationship, and resources, i.e., finances, food, shelter (Gutiérrez, 1990, Pinderhughes, 1989; Weaver, 1982).

PROFILE OF SOCIAL WORK PROBLEMS

Assessing the African American community and its organizations should incorporate a consideration of the contextual influences of the larger and dominant white society (Reid, 1996). These contextual influences include sociopolitical and cultural factors (Lee, 1994). Sociopolitical factors like racism, oppression, and lack of resources impact the community members and their ability to function (Lee, 1994). Some members of the dominant society are insensitive to African American history and culture and, therefore, lack the cultural competence to facilitate change (Boyd-Franklin, 1989; Lee, 1994; Parham, 1993; Sue & Sue, 1990; Wilson; 1992). Therefore, cultural competence becomes central to any cross-cultural experience that involves a power transaction. Consequently, the power of African Americans is directly tied to economic and resource development with their communities and organizations.

Historically, African Americans have experienced less power than those in the dominant society. As a result, they tend to protect themselves from power brokers in the dominant culture, and analyzing the power dynamics becomes a critical survival skill. In cross-cultural experiences, the power differential between African Americans and the dominant culture becomes important for assessing any community or organization (Pinderhughes, 1989).

Lastly, the dominant society has historically described the problems of African Americans from a pathological and deficit perspective rather than looking at their strengths (Vargas & Koss-Chioino, 1992). Using this perspective, African American problems are seen as primarily internal with little emphasis on the external factors. This view of African Americans allows for "blaming the victim" and ignores the societal patterns of victimization. As a result, the focus becomes the "flawed character" of African Americans and its impact on their condition. This view ignores the impact of culture and sociopolitical factors. When the lack of resources and poverty is considered within a cultural and sociopolitical context, the larger society must acknowledge some responsibility for addressing the power inequities (Pinderhughes, 1989). Cultural competence is a first step toward acknowledging the need for change and recognizing the dominant culture's insensitivity toward difference (Cross, Bazron, Dennis, & Isaacs, 1989). Historically, this insensitivity is expressed by viewing difference as being less than or inferior (Cross, Bazron, Dennis, & Isaacs, 1989; Pinderhughes, 1989).

Cultural competence is a change in perspective that focuses on the strengths and abilities of all people to contribute to society (Parham, 1993; Pinderhughes, 1989). It also recognizes the need for an equal distribution of resources. Because many stakeholders want to maintain their power, they are not committed to cultural competence and social justice issues (Parham, 1993; Pinderhughes, 1989). As a result, it is difficult to develop the support to shift power and resources to the African American community (Parham, 1993). Cultural competence is important because it can facilitate the breakdown of cultural barriers, address issues of difference, validate the strengths of African Americans, and increase access to resources (Cross, Bazron, Dennis, & Isaacs, 1989; Parham, 1993). As result, the skills and talents of American Americans become available to benefit their own community and the larger society.

PRACTICE FOCUS: THEORETICAL APPROACH TO ASSESSMENT AND PRACTICE

A culturally competent assessment using the ecological perspective provides a framework to address sociopolitical factors while recognizing the cultural uniqueness of the African American population. This approach to assessing African American communities increases access to resources through the use of the empowerment and strength perspectives (Greene & Ephross, 1991; Muñoz & Sanchez, 1997). Empowerment and strength perspectives are utilized to assess the community's ability to empower African Americans and recognize their capacity (Greene & Ephross, 1991; Muñoz & Sanchez, 1997).

Generally, community practice explores the need for change by assessing the community's participation in such activities as social planning and social action (Kemp, 1995). Typically, when African Americans have limited participation in community activities, they have limited potential for meeting their needs and accessing resources.

From a culturally competent perspective, the community assessment should also focus on factors like diversity, cross-system and community resources, natural supports, and acceptable service modalities (Muñoz & Sanchez, 1997). Assessment should also consider the regional needs of the African American people (Muñoz & Sanchez, 1997). Often, because of historical, migration, and immigration factors, African American communities may have unique needs. These communities may have not only a mixture of Southern and Northern African Americans but also may include Africans, Caribbeans, and Haitians. Communities with more diversity have a need for more sensitivity to factors that limit their access to resources and power (Kemp, 1995).

Other important ecological factors are the impact of racism, acculturation, the urban environment, language and communication problems, sociopolitical influences, economics, inter- and intragroup conflict, and leadership (Isaacs, 1986). African American communities that have been impacted by historical racism may have an eroded infrastructure. These communities have fewer resources and more poverty. Similarly, housing patterns and suburban flight by whites has also contributed to crowded and poor urban communities. The poor economy and lack of employment in urban environments also contribute to a lack of resources and power (Isaacs, 1986).

The issue of language should be considered when assessing communities with Haitians, Caribbeans, or Africans. Many of these groups may have difficulty understanding the dominant culture's language and need services provided in their language. The struggle to acculturate may also impact these groups, as well as African Americans from lower socioeconomic groups.

Infighting between subgroups of African Americans may also limit their potential for exercising power and accessing resources. Because of an inability to unify, some African American communities may lack the ability to influence the sociopolitical environment, particularly when the sociopolitical environment is hostile and unresponsive to cultural issues.

COMMUNITY ASSESSMENT

From the perspective of cultural competence, the community environment can demonstrate policies that represent cultural destructiveness, cultural incapacity, cultural blindness, cultural pre-competence, cultural competence, and cultural proficiency (Cross, Bazron, Dennis, & Isaacs, 1989). The community should be assessed to determine its level of cultural competence on this continuum. In a culturally destructive environment, the community groups, networks, and organizations demonstrate attitudes and behaviors that are destructive, while cultural incapacity shows a lack of capacity to support and serve African Americans (Cross, Bazron, Dennis, & Isaacs, 1989). Culturally blind community groups, networks, and organizations seek to implement policies that are unbiased, while community groups, networks, and organizations at the pre-culturally competent level have reached a beginning level of awareness about the need for cultural competence training and approaches (Cross, Bazron, Dennis, & Isaacs, 1989). Both the cultural competence and cultural proficiency levels on the cultural competence continuum represent community groups, networks, and organizations that have demonstrated a level of competence and awareness of its needs (Cross, Bazron, Dennis, & Isaacs, 1989).

Any culturally competent assessment of the African American community should include assessing the use of empowerment activities like group consciousness, social networking, legislating policy, and utilizing social action and planning capacity within the community (Gutiérrez, 1990; Kemp, 1995). Those communities that exercise a limited use of these activities should plan and implement more of these strategies. These activities will increase infrastructure development in the African American community. Community strengths also contribute to the community's ability to exercise power and act collectively (Pinderhughes, 1989). For example, the African American's spiritual beliefs are demonstrated by a commitment to the church. As a result, the church community becomes a powerful organization within the community. As stated previously, churches like Bethel AME Church and St. Paul Community Baptist Church have provided educational and economic resources to the African American community.

When shifting to an empowerment and strength focus, professionals must recognize the power of African American communities and share the assessment responsibilities with its members (Office of Substance Abuse Prevention, 1991). The visions, talents, and expertise of the community must be included as a part of the assessment process. Community leadership can provide support, guidance, and direction to culturally competent assessment. Along with its leadership, the community should have maximum involvement in the decision-making process by participating on planning and service committees (Office of Substance Abuse Prevention, 1991).

Furthermore, professionals assessing African American communities are accountable to the community and should see its members as experts (Office of Substance Abuse Prevention, 1991). Most importantly, the diversity within the community must be considered throughout the assessment process. For example,

African American communities that have several subgroups, such as people from Jamaica, Haiti, or Africa, should include these community members in their assessment process.

ORGANIZATIONAL ASSESSMENT

To strengthen and empower communities, professionals must strengthen and empower organizations that support them. Organizations are strengthened and empowered when they improve their cultural competence (Family and Youth Services Bureau, 1994). The assessment of an organization's cultural competence is a significant step in that direction (Mason, 1994, 1995).

From a cultural competence perspective, the organization can also demonstrate policies that range from cultural destructiveness to cultural proficiency (Cross, Bazron, Dennis, & Isaacs, 1989). Once the level of cultural competence is determined, an assessment of the community strengths and resources must follow.

The culturally competent assessment of an organization should determine whether advisory committees and organizational leadership represent culturally diverse groups and seek feedback from the community (Family and Youth Services Bureau, 1994; Mason, 1994, 1995; Cross, Bazron, Dennis, & Isaacs, 1989). Professionals assessing an organization should also consider the extent to which it incorporates the internal and external perceptions from culturally diverse groups (Family and Youth Services Bureau, 1994). Demographic information should also be considered in a culturally competent assessment of any organization. Factors like the number of staff, the diversity of the staff, and their positions help in understanding the organization's commitment to increasing its cultural competence (Muñoz & Sanchez, 1997).

Other factors that should be considered in the assessment are whether the organization values diversity, conducts a self-assessment, acknowledges the dynamic of difference, institutionalizes cultural knowledge, and adapts to diversity (Cross, Bazron, Dennis, & Isaacs, 1989). In addition, the assessment should consider if the organization embraces values like the importance of culturally defined needs, the family as the primary point of intervention, the use of natural systems, and the idea that culture defines behavior (Cross, Bazron, Dennis, & Isaacs, 1989). The assessment of an organization should occur at the policy, administrative, practitioner, and consumer levels (Cross, Bazron, Dennis, & Isaacs, 1989).

Finally, the culturally competent assessment should employ methods that complement the culture of the community. Multiple methods, both quantitative and qualitative approaches, should be used in community assessments. These methods could also include the use of ethnographic interviewing, EcoMaps, and other approaches that focus on the strengths and competencies of the community. Similarly, community members should be involved in generation of data, analysis, and application of assessment tools (Kemp, 1995).

PRACTICE PRINCIPLES AND SKILLS

The culturally competent assessment of any community should include a six-stage implementation process: (1) culturally diverse professional participation, (2) community engagement, (3) community affiliation, (4) cooperative group effort, (5) community dissemination and feedback, and (6) community action (Manning & Rosario, 1991). These implementation stages utilize activities that reinforce values consistent with the African American culture (Hill, 1997; Pinderhughes, 1982; Vargas & Koss-Chioino, 1992).

In the *culturally diverse professional participation* stage, African American professionals and consultants are involved to give direction and guidance to the assessment process. They will assist in breaking down barriers and ensuring that culturally competent strategies are used in each step of the assessment process. African American professionals and consultants also bring a unique perspective to the assessment process. Their professional training, combined with their cultural experience, can facilitate a healthy collaboration between the community and professional assessors (Manning & Rosario, 1991).

The second stage, *community engagement,* occurs when the professional assessing the community establishes credibility and trust with its members (Manning & Rosario, 1991). Professionals would use the African American's focus on functional relationships to interface with community groups, community leaders, politicians, providers, and residents (Butler, 1992). It is very important that community members become acquainted and feel comfortable with the professionals conducting the assessment. Its members must believe that the professionals will not abuse the community and feel a sense of reciprocity. Too often, communities have been assessed without receiving any long-term benefits (Manning & Rosario, 1991).

During this stage, the professionals will emphasize the importance of involving families, informal social networks, community organizations, key informants, and other providers in the assessment process (Manning & Rosario, 1991). It is also important for the professionals to convey an interest in the community's agenda and needs. The professionals can contribute a great deal to community residents and organizations by providing technical assistance (Manning & Rosario, 1991).

During this stage, the professionals should also engage African American professionals working in the community. These professionals will be able to provide relevant information for the completion of a successful assessment process (Manning & Rosario, 1991).

The professionals will also identify the strengths of the community by exploring the existence of available resources with the community members. The strengths of the community will be used to assist in conducting the assessment (Manning & Rosario, 1991). For example, a community may have excellent resources in the faith community that can be utilized to assist in building a strong community infrastructure.

Once the engagement stage is complete and trust has been established, the professionals will conduct community forums to initiate the *affiliation* stage (Manning & Rosario, 1991). Community forums are used to educate the community about the assessment process while, at the same time, obtaining feedback. Experts are used to describe assessment methods, empowerment strategies, and advocacy approaches. The community participants, both residents and service providers, will be invited to contribute their experiences and ideas (Manning & Rosario, 1991). These community forums can also be used to establish stronger social networks and create community councils. Community council members will serve as a link to the community and provide feedback to the provider system (Manning & Rosario, 1991).

The community councils, based on the African American's value of cooperation and mutual aid, begin the *cooperative group effort* stage (Manning & Rosario, 1991). These community councils will meet regularly with professionals conducting the assessment and discuss in more detail various assessment methodologies. During the community council group process, community members will be reassured about issues related to reciprocity and a commitment to address their concerns (Manning & Rosario, 1991). If questionnaires are developed, the community council will provide feedback about their content.

Assessment implementation will also include the support of the community council by encouraging community members and providers to participate. Community council members will also contribute to the positive image of the professionals conducting the assessment and the possible benefits (Manning & Rosario, 1991).

Once results are collected, they are framed from a strength perspective. The *community dissemination* stage will consist of disseminating information to empower the community (Lee, 1994). The information should be used to advocate for additional services and programs (Kemp, 1995).

Finally, in the *community action* stage, the community councils can participate in social action activities that inform their legislators, influence local providers, and stimulate the development of collaborative proposals. Social action can also take the form of meeting with local, state, and federal government officials to discuss community needs (Lee, 1994). From these efforts, community councils can form permanent advocacy and policy organizations. These organizations can eventually play a significant role in building coalitions and establishing a permanent infrastructure.

The process of a culturally competent organizational assessment uses stages similar to the community assessment. Those stages should include: (1) involvement of culturally diverse professionals, (2) engagement, (3) affiliation, (4) cooperative group effect, (5) information dissemination, and (6) action (Manning & Rosario, 1991). The organizational assessment practice will be similar in nature to that of the culturally competent community assessment (Lee, 1994). The organization has some of the same sociopolitical influences and external factors as the community.

African American professionals need to be involved in the assessment process from beginning to end. As a part of the *culturally diverse professional participation* stage, their input needs to be taken seriously and they must play a substantial role in the implementation of the change process within the organization.

Stakeholders in the ecological system must be involved in the assessment process. Board members, community members, staff, and volunteers must play a role in helping to structure an effective assessment process. Their role is to assist the professionals assessing the organization in deciding on assessment tools and design. The involvement of representatives from the agency and the community is the beginning of the engagement stage (Manning and Rosario, 1991).

After community and organizational representatives participate in the *engagement* process, they can move on to the *affiliation and cooperative group effort* stage by creating more family and community involvement in the development of the organization (Manning & Rosario, 1991). During these stages, the professionals assessing the organization should involve families and service providers in the assessment process. These members of the community could participate in focus groups, serve on committees, and respond to surveys.

After the assessment data is collected, the providers, families, and other community members can participate by helping to disseminate the findings during the *feedback and dissemination* stage. In addition, they can assist with the development and an implementation plan for change during the *action* stage.

CASE VIGNETTE

A model assessment of African American and Latino communities was the Brooklyn Child and Adolescent Program. The Child Adolescent and System Service Program was a local program federally funded by the Center for Mental Health and sponsored by the New York State Office of Mental Health and the New York City Department of Mental Health, Mental Retardation and Alcoholism. The goal of the program was to provide culturally competent mental health services to children and adolescents in three community districts—Bushwick, Brownsville, and Bedford-Stuyvesant. Several strategies have been developed to provide services to children and adolescents, but these approaches needed to be modified to reach African American and Latino populations. In an effort to be culturally competent, the program focused on reaching out to the community and intimately involving its members in all aspects of developing community programs (Manning & Rosario, 1991).

The program initially focused on the engaging process. Community forums were conducted in each community district. The *culturally diverse professional participation* stage consisted of nationally known professionals making presentations on issues related to providing mental health services to culturally diverse populations. Dr. Lawrence Gary, of the Howard University School of Social Work, discussed issues related to the African American community, while Dr. Jaime Inclan, of the Roberto Clemente Family Guidance Center, spoke about the Latino community. In Dr. Gary's presentation, he discussed the strengths of the African American family and how considering them is important when designing service systems for children and adolescents. Dr. Inclan presented on the importance of community empowerment in the Latino community (Manning & Rosario, 1991). Both presenters reinforced the importance of affiliation, the *"community affiliation"* stage.

The community forums initiated the *cooperative group effort* stage by developing councils and further involvement of community residents and service providers. The council assisted with the development of an assessment strategy and helped with its implementation (Manning & Rosario, 1991). As a result, the community was directly involved in the assessment by expressing their "perceived need" through a survey.

Once the assessment was complete, the council helped with the dissemination of the findings during the *community feedback and dissemination* stage. They utilized the findings to advocate for additional services, which is a part of the action stage. Because of the culturally competent assessment, some providers received resources from local and state governments to improve their capacity to deliver services. As a result, these community providers participated in the development of a continuum of care for children and adolescents (Manning & Rosario, 1991).

Initially, the project focused on developing a continuum of mental health services for children and adolescents, but eventually broadened to construct a system of care that included all levels of social services. For example, the council was able to assess and address other social needs like substance abuse services, family day care, and teen pregnancy programs (Manning & Rosario, 1991).

Finally, these councils became a permanent part of the community infrastructure and continued to strengthen the community by advocating for an increase in social services. The council also became familiar with the community assessment process and how to use its findings for advocating for the community (Manning & Rosario, 1991).

CONCLUSION

Culturally competent assessments in the African American community must consider four elements: valuing diversity, dynamics of difference, institutionalization of cultural knowledge, and adaptation to diversity (Cross, Bazron, Dennis, & Isaacs, 1989). The communities and/or organizations must also be assessed using the cultural competence continuum. An assessment of the African American community must include an acknowledgment and respect for the predominance of culture in shaping behavior. Additionally, the assessment must consider the unique cultural values of African Americans, e.g., cooperation, sharing, spirituality, and past time (Pinderhughes, 1982). These values must also shape the community and organizational assessment process.

Finally, the assessment process should include the stages of community engagement, group cooperation, information dissemination, African American professional involvement, and the implementation of an advocacy plan. The culturally competent assessment process will stress community values, involvement, and empowerment (Manning & Rosario, 1991).

REFERENCES

Billingsley, A.(1992). *Climbing Jacob's ladder: The enduring legacy of African American families.* New York: Simon and Schuster.

Boyd-Franklin, N. (1989). *Black families in therapy: A multisystem approach.* New York: Guildford.

Butler, J. P. (1992). Of kindred minds: The ties that bind. In M. A. Orlandi, R. Weston, & L. G. Epstein (Eds.), *Cultural competence for evaluators: A guide for alcohol and other drug abuse prevention practitioners working in ethnic/racial communities* (DHHS Publication No. (ADM) 92-1884, pp. 23–54). Rockville, MD: U.S. Department of Health and Human Services.

Carter, R. T. (1991). Racial identity attitudes and psychological functioning. *Journal of Multicultural Counseling and Development, 19,* 105–113.

Cross, W. E. (1991). *Shades of black: Diversity in the African American identity.* Philadelphia, PA: Temple University Press.

Cross, T. L., Bazron, B. J., Dennis, K. W., & Isaacs, M. R. (1989). *Toward a culturally competent system of care: A monograph on effective services for minority children who are severely emotionally disturbed,* vol. 1. Washington, DC: CASSP Technical Assistance, Georgetown University Child Development Center

Ellison, C. G. (1991). Identification and separatism: Religious involvement and racial orientations among Black Americans. *Sociological Quarterly, 32,* 477–494.

Ellison, C. G. (1993). Religious involvement and self-perception among Black Americans. *Social Forces, 71,* 1027–1055.

Family and Youth Services Bureau, Administration on Children, Youth and Families, Administration for Children and Families, Department of Health and Human Services. (1994). *A guide to enhancing the cultural competence of runaway and homeless youth programs.* Silver Springs, MD: National Clearinghouse on Runaway and Homeless Youth.

Greene, R. R. & Ephross, P. H. (1991). *Human behavior and social work practice.* New York: Aldine-De Gruyter.

Gutiérrez, L. M. (1990, March). Working with women of color: An Empowerment Perspective. *Social Work,* Vol 35, 149–153.

Harvey, A. R. (1995, January). The issue of skin color in psychotherapy with African Americans. *Families in Society, 76,* 3–10.

Harvey, A. R. & Rauch, J. B. (1997, February). A comprehensive afrocentric rites of passages program for black male adolescents. *Health and Social Work,* Vol 22 (1), 30–37.

Helms, J. E. (1986). Expanding racial identity theory to cover the counseling process. *Journal of Counseling Psychology, 3,* 431–440.

Helms, J. E. (1990). *Black and white racial identity: theory, research and practice.* New York: Greenwood.

Helms, J. E. and Parham, T. A. (1985) Attitude of racial identity and self-esteem of Black students: An exploratory investigation. *Journal of College Student Personnel,* Vol 26 (1), 143–147.

Hernandez, R. & Sanchez, A.M. (1998). *Cultural competence standards in managed care mental health services for four underserved/underrepresented racial/ethnic groups.* Boulder, CO: Western Interstate Commission for Higher Education.

Hill, R. B. (1997). *Strengths of African American families: Twenty-five years later.* Washington, DC: R & B Publishers.

Hines, P. and Boyd-Franklin, N. (1982). Black families. In M. McGoldrick, J. K. Pearce, and J. Giordano (Eds.), *Ethnicity and family therapy* (pp. 84–107). New York: Guildford.

Isaacs, M. R. (1986). *Developing mental programs for minority youth and their families.* Washington, DC: Georgetown University Child Development Center.

Jackson, A. P. & Sears, S. J. (1992). Implications of an Afrocentric worldview in reducing stress for African American women. *Journal of Counseling and Development, 71,* 184–190.

Kemp, S. P. (1995). Practice in communities. In C. H. Meyer and M. A. Mattaini (Eds.), *The foundations of social work practice* (pp. 176–204). Washington, DC: National Association of Social Workers Press.

Lee, J. A. B. (1994). *The empowerment approach to social work practice.* New York: Columbia University Press.

Manning, M. (1997). The relationship between racial identity and self-esteem among African Americans. *Dissertation Abstracts International, 58* (09), p. 3723.

Manning, M. & Rosario, D. (1991). *Final report: Brooklyn child adolescent service systems program.* Washington, DC: Child and Family Support Program, Center for Mental Health Services.

Mason, J. L. (1994). Developing culturally competent organizations. *Focal Point: The Bulletin of the Research and Training Center on Family support and Children's Mental Health, 8* (2), 1–8.

Mason, J. L. (1995). *Cultural competence self-assessment questionnaire: A manual for users.* Multicultural Initiative Project. Portland, OR: Portland State University, Research and Training Center on Family Support and Children's Mental Health.

Muñoz, R. & Sanchez, A. M. (1997). *Developing culturally competent systems of care for state mental health services.* Baltimore, MD: Center for Mental Health Services and Boulder, CO: Western Interstate Commission for Higher Education.

Office of Substance Abuse Prevention. (1991). *OSAP Community Partnership Program Training Manual.* Washington, DC: U.S. Department of Health and Human Services.

Parham, T. A. (1993). *Psychological storms; the African American struggle for identity.* Chicago, IL: African American Images.

Pinderhughes, E. (1982, January). Family functioning of Afro-Americans. *Social Work,* Vol 1, 91–94.

Pinderhughes, E. (1989). *Understanding race, ethnicity, and power: The key to efficacy in clinical practice.* New York: Free Press.

Pollner, M. (1989). Divine relations, social relations and well-being. *Journal of Health and Social Behavior, 22,* 337–356.

Reid, W. J. (1996). Task-centered social work. In F. J. Turner (Ed.), *Social work treatment* (pp. 617–640). New York: Free Press.

Saleebey, D. (1992). *The strengths perspective in social work practice.* New York: Longman.

Schiele, J. H. (1996). Afrocentricity: Emerging paradigms in social work practice. *Social Work, 41* (3), 284–984.

Sue, D. W. and Sue, D. (1990). *Counseling the culturally different: Theory and practice.* New York: John Wiley & Sons.

U.S. Bureau of the Census. (1991). *1990 Census of the general population characteristics, United States.* 1990 CP-1-1. Washington, DC Population Division, U.S. Bureau of the Census.

U.S. Immigration and Naturalization Service. (1997). *1996 statistical yearbook of the immigration and naturalization services.* Washington, DC: Government Printing Office.

Vargas, L. A. & Koss-Chioino, J. D. (Eds.). (1992). *Working with culture: Psychotherapeutic intervention with ethnic minority children and adolescents.* San Francisco, CA: Jossey-Bass.

Weaver, D. R. (1982, February). Empowering treatment skills for helping black families. *Social Casework: The Journal of Contemporary Social Work,* Vol 63 (2), 100–105.

Wilson, A. M. (1992). *Awakening the natural genius of black children.* New York: Afrikan World Info-Systems.

CHAPTER 10

INDIVIDUAL AND FAMILY ASSESSMENT SKILLS WITH LATINO/HISPANIC AMERICANS

LIRIO K. NEGRONI-RODRIGUEZ

JULIO MORALES

This chapter delineates issues relevant to assessing Spanish-speaking Latinos/Hispanic American individuals and families, hereafter referred to as Latinos (Latinas when specifically referring to females), and discusses the skills needed by social work practitioners to facilitate an assessment process and product. The assessment skills proposed in this section are based on ecological, strength-oriented, and empowerment practice models. The use of an ecological, strength–empowerment assessment approach for working with Latinos is appropriate for the following reasons: (1) the approach offers a valuable frame for analyzing and understanding the socioeconomic and political realities of Latinos in the United States; (2) it is consonant with the correlation of Latino cultural values and behavioral norms; (3) it addresses the impact of oppression, stigma, and discrimination, a common experience among Latinos; and (4) it promotes the strengthening of individual self-esteem and family relationships.

SOCIODEMOGRAPHIC OVERVIEW

Latinos are usually associated with nineteen Spanish-speaking nations in the Caribbean and in Central and South America.[1] These nations share a history of colonization, similarities in their connection and adaptation to the Catholic church, in

---

[1]The nations are Cuba, the Dominican Republic, Puerto Rico, Costa Rica, El Salvador, Nicaragua, Panama, Guatemala, Honduras, Mexico, Bolivia, Paraguay, Uruguay, Ecuador, Venezuela, Colombia, Chile, Peru, and Argentina.

the dominance of the Spanish language, and in their ethnic and/or racial mixtures. As a result of the above, they also share similar cultural patterns.

Spanish-speaking Latino nations differ in geography, topography, specific customs, and racial and ethnic mixtures. For example, Argentina's population is overwhelmingly of European ancestry, and Puerto Rico is racially mixed. If pressed, some Puerto Ricans might identify as white, others as black, but most will say that they are *trigueño* (tan) like the color of *trigo* (wheat).

Puerto Rico was conquered by the United States and is a U.S. colony. Puerto Ricans are U.S. citizens and, like other U.S. citizens, are migrants, not immigrants. Cuba's population is also racially mixed and includes significant numbers of people of Jewish and Chinese ancestry. Cuba, like Puerto Rico, has had a history of U.S. occupation. The majority of Cubans in the United States immigrated, as refugees, after the Cuban revolution of 1959. Mexico, like most countries in Central America, has a population that is primarily mestizo, a mixture of Indian and European, although some Mexicans may identify as white and others as Indians. Mexican Americans have historically composed the largest of the Hispanic subgroups in the United States.

Approximately 31 million Hispanics live in the United States (U.S. Bureau of the Census, 1996). The census collects, analyzes, and disseminates information on five Hispanic subgroups. Mexicans, Puerto Ricans, and Cubans are distinct and identifiable subgroups. Latinos from Central and South America are combined into one category. Other Hispanics, the fifth category, are people who identify with more than one Hispanic group or who identify as Hispanic but not with any particular subgroup. In 1996, Mexican Americans comprised 63.4 percent of all Latinos living in the United States. Puerto Ricans comprised over 11 percent of Latinos living in the fifty states. This does not include the 4 million people living in Puerto Rico. Cubans comprised approximately 4 percent of U.S. Latinos, Central and South Americans 14.3 percent, and other Hispanics 7.3 percent of the Latinos in the fifty states (U.S. Bureau of the Census, 1996). Latinos live in all U.S. states and territories, and their numbers continue to increase dramatically.

The number of Latino children in the United States has surpassed the number of African American children (U.S. Census Bureau, quoted in *National Association of Social Workers News,* November 1998, p. 15). By the early part of the next decade, the United States will have more people of Latino heritage than people of African American heritage (U.S. Department of Commerce, 1996). Latinos will comprise 24 percent of the United States population by the year 2050. Despite their numbers, they, as a group, are invisible. For example, Latinos are dramatically underrepresented in mainstream television programs and in the media in general.

Latinos, as a group, are poorer than the nation's Asian, African American, or white populations.

> The poverty rate among Hispanic residents of the United States has surpassed that of blacks. Hispanic residents now constitute nearly 24 percent of the country's poor. . . . Of the poorest of the poor . . . 24 percent were Hispanics . . . income for

Hispanic households has dropped 14 percent since 1989 . . . while rising slightly for black ones (*New York Times,* January 30, 1997, p. 1).

The poverty rate of young children rose faster among Hispanic groups than among white or black children. Over the three years, the percentage of poor Hispanic children younger than 6 grew 54 percent, compared with a 30 percent rise among whites and 15 percent among blacks (*New York Times,* March 15, 1998, page 19).

Discussion of social, cultural, or economic characteristics of any group runs the risk of reinforcing stereotypes and may minimize individual uniqueness. We urge readers to be mindful of the above as they read the following section.

CULTURAL VALUES AND BEHAVIORAL NORMS

There are cultural, sociopolitical, historical, and racial differences among Latinos that highlight their uniqueness as ethnic groups. There are also cultural similarities. For example, Latinos share cultural values and behavioral norms, such as allocentrism, *respeto* (respect), *familismo* (familism), *confianza* (trust), *personalismo* (personalism), *machismo,* and *marianismo.* However, the persistence and strength of these values and norms vary. Allocentrism implies empathy and sacrifice on behalf of the interests of the group, and conformity to family and community expectations (Green, 1995).

Respeto signifies attention to the order assumed in interpersonal relations, and acknowledgment of the other's unique individuality (Díaz-Royo, 1983). The lack of respect (*falta de respeto*), rather than being a situational mistake, is viewed as a character defect. Respect is linked to *dignidad* (dignity) and includes ceremonial requisites based on age, gender, socioeconomic position, and contextual interactions, including behaviors related to property.

In traditional Latino cultures, young children are taught that behavior and boundary definitions stem from respect (Laureano & Poliandro, 1991). Respect demands that children: (1) remain silent when scolded or reprimanded and when adults speak or authority figures are talking in a group; (2) ask permission to speak (this varies depending on the situation and on the child's age); and (3) maintain certain nonverbal postures. Parents and the elderly must be respected and obeyed. Respect is shown by addressing people as *don* (sir) or *doña* (madam) followed by their first name and by using the formal *you* (*usted*).

Familismo refers to kinship relationships beyond the nuclear family, stressing family loyalty, interdependence over independence, affiliation over confrontation, and cooperation over competition (Ramos-Mackay, Comas-Díaz, & Rivera, L., 1988). *Familismo* fosters family responsibility. Individual needs are subordinated to family needs.

Confianza is dependent on *respeto,* is earned, and implies that "one's social self is placed in the realm of the other" (Díaz-Royo, 1983, p. 158). Trusting or giving trust precipitously implies lack of good judgment (Laureano & Poliandro, 1998). *Confianza* develops when there is perceived mutual respect and acceptance. *Per-*

sonalismo is "a culturally supported expectation of personalizing individual contact in important relationships" (Morales, 1995, p. 81).

Machismo sanctions male privilege and superiority and defines the man as provider, protector, and head of the household. Being *machista* denotes honor, dignity, and pride. *Marianismo,* after the Virgin Mary, values female spiritual sensitivity and self-sacrifice for the good of husband and children (Green, 1995). The mother and wife roles offer power to exercise authority in the home. However, women are also expected to be dependent on men. Because of strong traditional gender roles, heterosexism and homophobia are interconnected and women often are dichotomized as good and saintly or as sexually permissive (Morales, 1995).

Spiritual matters and religion are strong forces that shape Latinos' worldviews. Catholicism is predominant, but many Latinos show affiliation to other religions. Churches are a source of support and sometimes substitute for the extended family.

Latinos maintain a dual system of beliefs and practices concerning physical and mental problems—mainstream medical and psychotherapy approaches and traditional folk-oriented approaches (Falicov, 1998). Folk beliefs include *espiritismo* among Puerto Ricans, *curanderismo* among Mexicans and other Central and South Americans, and *santería* among Cuban Americans.

Espiritismo refers to the belief in spirits. Everyone is believed to have spirits of protection, and these can be increased by performing good deeds and decreasing evil. Latinos who ascribe to *espitirismo* believe that loved ones can be around in spirit after death and can lead one's life in times of difficulties. *Espiritistas* (spiritist healers) communicate with spirits and can be incarnated by them. Healing can take place with prescribed folk healing treatment.

Curanderismo, like *espiritismo,* is used to cure physical, emotional, and folk illnesses. *Curanderos/as* are healers who use a range of treatments, such as herbal remedies, inhalation, sweating, massage, incantations, and *limpieza* (a ritual cleansing). *Santería* combines African dieties with Catholic saints. The *santeros/as* are priests who function as healers, diviners and directors of rituals.

PROFILE OF SOCIAL WORK PROBLEMS AND ISSUES: THE INTERFACE OF CULTURE, POVERTY, AND PATHOLOGY

Among Latinos, poverty, migration or immigration, cultural transitions, invisibility, powerlessness, prejudice, and discrimination are similar and common experiences that represent potential risk factors for the development of health and mental health problems, family difficulties, and family violence.

Latino families tend to maintain much of their culture and values. However, traditional family dynamics and gender roles change with increased exposure to the dominant society. For example, Latino families may experience gender role reversals when the female works outside the home or obtains state financial support. This makes some Latino males feel marginalized and can create marital and family problems.

The individuation process, a salient therapeutic issue among Western practitioners, may proceed differently for those from Latino cultures (Vazquez, 1994). Values such as independence, individuality, and competition are usually not viewed as positive in Latino groups and may be accorded different levels of acceptance or rejection by individuals within Latino groups.

Presenting problems may be linked to cultural transitions as Latino clients encounter cultural dilemmas and adaptational impasses. Intergenerational conflicts, due to differences in rates of acculturation, are common. For example, a Latina grandmother may view her fourteen-year-old granddaughter's short skirts and makeup as inappropriate and may blame her daughter for not controlling the granddaughter.

An example of how acculturation impacts children and families is presented by Canino and Canino (1980), who call attention to aggression among Puerto Rican families who live in the States. While assertiveness, competitiveness, and independence are valued by non-Latino parents, they contradict *respeto* and other core values of Puerto Rican culture. Acculturated children may be perceived by their parents as *presentao,* that is, crossing the boundaries of respect and distance that govern behaviors in new relationships and in the presence of adults and older people. For some Latino adolescents, struggles between *respeto* and assertiveness lead to inner conflicts between self-effacement and expansiveness (Rendon, 1974).

A second example relates to traditional gender expectations. Latinas may be discouraged from demonstrating the level of assertiveness often associated with females from the dominant culture. This "lack of assertiveness" is congruent with Latino cultural norms but considered a weakness in the dominant culture. Due to minority status, many Latinas may feel forced to accommodate the expectations of the dominant society. Such accommodation can create conflicts with family and community networks.

A third example of how differences in cultural values introduce conflict illustrates how the imposition of dominant values leads to misinterpretation. It is not uncommon for Latino families to insist that their children, especially daughters, live at home until married. Furthermore, daughters are expected to take care of their parents. Such cultural tendencies, at times, have been labeled as examples of dependent or co-dependent behavior in the pathological sense (Vazquez, 1994).

Latino cultural patterns may cushion the alienation and problems that are often a function of racism and the environmental stressors and maladies identified earlier. Buriel (1984) found that third generation Mexican Americans displayed higher levels of personal and family maladjustment than first and second generations. Rejecting cultural traditions without replacing them with mainstream U.S. traditions can lead to maladjustments and deviance. Risk factors may adversely impact the development of new generations of Latinos in the United States. If Latino youngsters toss aside cultural patterns and identity without being accepted in the larger society, they may become more at risk.

Problems Encountered by Social Workers

Social work practitioners may face significant challenges when assessing the needs of Latino individuals and families. These include: (1) poor communication; (2) low service utilization; (3) poor client engagement in service provision; (4) poor relationship building; (5) low client retention; (6) lack of appropriate problems/needs definition; (7) lack of appropriate understanding of individual functioning and family dynamics; and (8) lack of effectiveness of helping approaches.

Assessing difficulties may stem from a lack of knowledge, understanding, or appreciation of previously discussed ethnocultural, socioeconomic, and political contexts, which are crucial in framing attitudes, behaviors, and needs. Difficulties with assessment can also happen when the practitioner is not well trained as a mental health helping professional.

PRACTICE FOCUS: ECOLOGICAL ASSESSMENT

Content and experiences that must be explored when assessing Latinos include migration, acculturation conflicts, and loss of cultural solutions, isolation, language barriers, discrimination, powerlessness, disempowerment, poverty, inequality, and the presence of stereotyping and bias.

Assessment of the Migration Experience

Migration or immigration experiences affect the ways people cope, adapt, and change. Such experiences can lead to opportunities and/or to psychological distress. The migration experience causes the uprooting of physical, cultural, and social meaning systems, and can lead to both psychological problems and family difficulties. Thus, they must be explored by practitioners.

Migration involves a series of events and developmental changes including pre-migration, migration itself, and encounters with cultural transitions following migration. Immigration is often a painful shared experience that impacts the immigrant, the relatives left behind, relatives who may have emigrated earlier and who wait in the new country, and the people of the new culture.

The social work practitioner, in assessing the migration experience, needs to ask many questions: How long has the individual or family been in the United States? Is the client a first, second, or third generation immigrant or migrant? Who migrated first and who was left behind? How was the individual or family received? Who is yet to be reunited? What were the reasons for the move to the new country? Are there any unfulfilled hopes and regrets? If so, what are those? What ordeals have been suffered? How well is the individual or family coping with the new language and new culture? Are some family members having more difficulties than others? If so, who and why?

Assessment of Level of Acculturation

Differences exist within specific Latino groups in terms of degree of acculturation and language. Some Latinos assimilate the dominant culture, losing or rejecting their original culture and identity. Others, to different degrees, blend or incorporate both cultures and alternate between them according to the social context. Still others, often first generation, maintain their traditional culture and cultural identity.

For the practitioner, it becomes crucial to understand how the client, and, in the case of a family, how each family member identifies culturally. The degree of acculturation may influence the types of problems Latinos face, the perceptions of the helping process, and the responses to that process.

Assessing compatibility between the individual's culture and the culture of the dominant culture is essential. The authors recommend Sue and Sue's (1990) conceptual framework for multicultural counseling.

Assessment of Social Class and Racism

Social class issues are missed because of a strong focus on culture. The practitioner must be careful not to attribute to cultural differences the negative impact of poverty and racial discrimination. It is important to explore the social status of the individual in the country of origin and the extent to which such status has changed in the United States.

Studies of class differences among Mexican Americans suggest that middle-class families are less patriarchal and relationships between spouses are more egalitarian than lower-income families (Longres, 1995b). There are numerous differences among Puerto Ricans including color, social class, religion, and time of migration.

The first waves of Cuban immigrants who came to the United States were middle- and upper-middle-class professionals. Some of them regained the professional status that they lost by immigrating to the United States. Others remained blue-collar workers in hotels and factories. The overall socioeconomic status of Cuban refugees, especially more recent immigrants, remains low and may be due to lack of English skills (Jiménez-Vazquez, 1995).

Assessment of Natural Support Systems

Latinos, in times of crisis, may seek traditional support systems and resources before accessing services. Nonkinship networks, embedded in the Latino culture and religious traditions, serve as sources of strength. For example, baptism and confirmation allow for new members, often close friends, to enter the family structure by becoming the childrens' *padrinos* (godfathers) and *madrinas* (godmothers). The godparents and the children's parents become *compadres/comadres* (co-parents). In traditional Latino cultures, *compadres* and *comadres* assume and are expected to look after their godchildren in times of need. In this way Latinos' definition of *familia* (family) is broadened to an extended family that includes friends and neighbors and enhances a sense of community. Longres (1995b) applies the term *fictive relatives* to people who achieve family member status.

Among Mexican Americans, three categories of support systems can be assessed: (1) natural support systems (group memberships); (2) link persons (a nongroup reciprocal relationship); and (3) kinship networks (Valle & Vega, 1980). Delgado and Humm-Delgado (1982) identify four support systems in Puerto Rican communities: (1) extended family; (2) folk healers; (3) religion; and (4) merchant and social clubs (grocery stores, botanical shops, marketplaces, hometown clubs, and barber/beauty shops). Folk healers and religious supports are discussed in the next section. Other forms of natural support systems, such as mutual aid and volunteer organizations, exist in different Latino groups and must also be explored.

The following questions may help assess the extensiveness and availability of support systems: What caused the client to seek formal help? Historically, what support systems has the client relied on (family, church, healer, friends)? What is the frequency and nature of the client's contact with support systems? Sometimes it may be advisable to contact support systems to obtain a perspective on their availability and willingness to help.

Assessment of Belief Systems and Mental Health Status

Because of religious and folk beliefs, many Latinos hold a different view of wellness, health, mental health, and physical and mental illness. Somatic complaints are common and are used to conceptualize mental health problems (Lecca, Quervalú, Nunes, & Gonzáles, 1998). They are commonly called *males naturales* (natural illnesses) and include *mal de ojo, susto,* or *espanto, empacho, nervios,* and *ataque de nervios. Mal de ojo* (evil eye) embodies the belief that someone can have power over another, and can impact the weaker person with his or her *vista fuerte* (strong vision) "robbing . . . their ability to act on their own accord" (Falicov, 1998, p. 133). *Susto* or *espanto* (fright) is a deep fear due to an experience a person witnesses. The person's physical and emotional reactions are seen as the result of the *susto.* It is like an acute reaction to trauma and can justify a passive sick role to control and avoid psychological stress. *Empacho* is a gastrointestinal minor infection that afflicts a person of any age, caused by both physiological and social factors.

Ataque de nervios is

> a culturally sanctioned response to acute stressful experiences, particularly relating to grief, threat and family conflict that occur at culturally appropriate times such as during funerals, at the scene of an accident, or during a family argument or fight (Guarnaccia, Canino, Rubio-Stipec, & Bravo, 1993, p. 158).

Manifested symptoms include trembling, heart palpitations, a sense of heat in the chest, faintness, seizurelike episodes, a sense of being out of control, attacks of crying, hyperventilation, and sudden bursts of verbal aggression.

Latinos use many folk and herbal remedies. This practice may influence compliance with medical prescription. Prayers, candles, saints, herbs, and other remedies used in traditional healing practices are sold in stores called *botánicas*.

Practitioners need to become familiar with these "culture-bound syndromes" and use them within the context of a biopsychosocial assessment. The fourth edition of the *Diagnostic Statistical Manual* (DSM) of the American Psychiatric Association (APA), an assessment tool that is used in the United States to identify psychopathology, has a section describing these and other culture-bound syndromes. The DSM IV also provides an outline for cultural formulation to supplement the multiaxial diagnostic assessment (APA, 1994). The authors also suggest that the reader examine the summary of cultural considerations for selected DSM IV diagnoses developed by Dr. Iván Quervalú (Lecca, Quervalú, Nunes, & Gonzéles, 1998).

Two additional factors may impede Latinos from seeking services: (1) their histories of being exploited and victimized by overt racism; and (2) the impersonality and bureaucratic nature of the systems. Negative experiences with the dominant culture and the government may dispose Latinos to approach helping agencies with skepticism, reluctance, and, at times, anger.

Due to language disparities and nonverbal gestures, there is a risk that practitioners may get a wrong impression of the client's problems and disposition to being served. For instance, short answers and a hesitancy to speak in English may occur in situations in which the client feels forced to speak English, but may feel shamed for not speaking it well. Discomfort about disclosing personal information to a stranger may also limit the client's involvement in the helping process.

Researchers have noticed that Latinos move their hands more often when thinking in Spanish and then translating into English (Lecca, Quervalú, Nunes, & Gonzéles, 1998). Such motor behavior should not be confused with anxiety, tension, and hyperactivity. The behavior could be a function of moving from one language to another.

The Spanish-speaking client with limited English language skills may have a lower speech rate and long silent pauses. Sometimes native language interferes with the second language and translations may result in unusual words. The practitioner may confuse situations like these with anxiety and illogical thinking. Even Latino clients with excellent English-speaking skills may use expressions that reflect Spanish-speaking environments.

There is a possibility for practitioners to assess patterns of nonverbal responses as depression. Such patterns may be a function of the client's efforts to give the practitioner what he or she thinks are the expected responses. Linguistic, cultural, and class differences raise issues about the validity of the questions and instruments used to assess areas of emotional functioning.

Assessment of Strengths and Empowerment

Cultural values that can be tapped into as strengths include the affective bonds among extended family members, traditional support and healing systems, and the levels of biculturalism and bilingualism. Furthermore, Latino hospitality, cooperation, and collective humanism enhance sharing feelings of fairness and justice (Morales, 1995). *Personalismo* and *respeto* facilitate building the helping process.

Empowering Latino clients may be more challenging when working with some Latinos who, out of respect, may view helping professionals as experts who define problems and indicate what needs to be done. Other clients may perceive seeking help as a sign of self and family weakness and failure. Practitioners need to consciously assess the ability to help Latino clients move from self-blaming and powerless views to being agents of change. Through this process, Latino clients will better use the knowledge and skills of practitioners and build a relationship of collaboration and partnership in problem-solving efforts.

An empowerment assessment reduces the risk of involuntarily intervening in ways that encourage Latino clients to adapt to unhealthy environments rather than empowering clients to change and/or leave such environments (Vazquez, 1994). Cowger (1994) suggests that practitioners: (1) give preeminence to the client's understanding of the facts, (2) believe the client, (3) discover what the client wants, (4) move the assessment toward personal and environmental strengths, (5) make assessment of strengths multidimensional, (6) use the assessment to discover uniqueness, (7) use language the client can understand, (8) make assessment a joint activity between worker and client, (9) reach a mutual agreement on the assessment, (10) avoid blame and blaming, (11) avoid cause-and-effect thinking, and (12) assess, do not diagnose.

Ecological Assessment

When Latinos interact with the dominant communities, value conflicts may emerge. Issues of gender, child-rearing, diet, identity, and age may surface. How the family manages such conflicts is crucial. Such conflicts may negatively impact the family's sense of self. Some family behaviors may be tied not to the culture but to the surrounding social institutions. For that reason, it is important to assess the nature of the family's use of those institutions and the nature of their interactions. The EcoMap (Longres, 1995a), the PIE Classification System (Karls & Wandrei, 1997), and the Culturagram (Congress, 1994) are useful tools that enhance the practitioner's understanding of the connections between the family and the environment.

PRINCIPLES OF PRACTICE AND ASSESSMENT SKILLS

Self-Awareness

Prior to meeting Latino clients, practitioners need some cognitive and affective preparation. Practitioners must have sound historical and theoretical perspectives of the client's culture and current socio-ecological environment (Delgado, 1998).

This may require self-study and actual involvement within the Latino community (Morales, 1995). Practitioners bring their cultural background, experiences, perceptions, and attitudes to their therapeutic encounters. Thus, assessing behaviors that differ from their own worldviews in the helping encounters is appropriate. While knowledge of cultural values, attitudes, and behaviors is crucial, practitioners must be careful not to overgeneralize and stereotype.

Practitioners face the challenges of identifying, understanding, and transcending differences between themselves and their clients. There is a level of anticipatory empathy that is required to acknowledge the cultural and socioeconomic issues that will be presented in the problem identification process. Tuning in to specific realities of the specific Latino ethnic group is crucial.

Effective Communication

Because linguistic patterns vary among Latinos, it is recommended that practitioners be bilingual. Although individual clients or family members may speak mostly English, there are high probabilities that Spanish is spoken among other family members. Practitioners should ask clients which language feels most comfortable, use the selected language, and, when necessary, ask for clarification of specific words and phrases to better understand concepts being discussed. When working with families in which parents speak mostly Spanish and children speak mostly English, practitioners, in respecting cultural values, should give priority to the parents' language and translate for the children. Do not assume that clients understand because they nod or say "yes, yes." It is important to observe, rephrase, and ask clients to briefly summarize what they understood. Practitioners should offer to answer any questions clients may have, even if they never take up the offer.

The use of interpreters is only recommended when the interpreter is linguistically competent, knowledgeable of the types of problems being assessed, and has a firm grasp of the cultural values and beliefs of the client's specific ethnic group. Issues of confidentiality must be addressed. Never use children as interpreters because it breaches confidentiality, creates conflictive role reversal, and may lead to adults withholding information they do not want the child to have. Effective communication always entails listening for and utilizing the strengths and expertise of the clients.

Development of Trust

The development of a relationship based on *confianza*, through the gradual development of a relationship based on *personalismo*, is crucial. Practitioners must be prepared to share of themselves and to participate, whenever possible, in cultural activities within the community and the client's family. Practitioners may be asked personal questions. This type of questioning, associated with *personalismo*, will transpire when a client feels sufficiently comfortable with the worker.

In situations in which clients experience distrust, the practitioner can help by: (1) paying close attention to generational differences; (2) avoiding language that might create feelings of alienation in non-English-speaking persons; (3) accepting hospitality and other offerings; (4) showing interest in clients' way of being; (5) providing empathic listening that fosters trust and rapport; and (6) showing appreciation for clients' survival and coping skills, ethnic and network resources, and situational accomplishments (Falicov, 1998).

Sue and Sue (1990) suggest engaging in respectful, warm, and mutual introductions, pronouncing names correctly, and giving a brief description of the agency and the services. If counseling, then give a brief description of what counseling is and the role of each participant. Have clients state, in their own words, the problems/needs as they see them. Use paraphrasing to summarize and to make sure the client knows that what is being said is understood. Have the client prioritize problems.

Latino clients may need to leave the first session with a feeling that it was useful and beneficial and with a sense that they gained something. Sometimes some direct guidance is very helpful if expected by the individual or family. Latino families find it difficult to openly discuss concerns about sex, including heterosexuality, bisexuality, and lesbian and gay issues. Conflicts in attitudes regarding sexual conduct and gay and lesbian relationships are common within and between generations. Homosexual conduct is strongly disapproved (Longres, 1995b). Laureano and Poliandro (1991) suggest that practitioners address these issues by asking clients permission to ask such types of questions, and by saying that, although the questions may feel too personal, the practitioner needs to ask them in order to provide better services.

CASE VIGNETTE

José Juan García-Rivera, a twelve-year-old Puerto Rican, was referred to the Latino Program of a child guidance clinic by a local school counselor. Behavior problems and poor academic performance were cited as the reason for the referral.

The García-Rivera family is composed of José Juan García Ortiz (Mr. G.), María de los Angeles Rivera de García (Mrs. G.), and their children, José Juan, Jr. (Jr.), age twelve, Ivette, age ten, and Taína, age six. The family moved from Puerto Rico two years ago. Both parents have Associate degrees and are employed in department stores.

The practitioner assigned to this case, Mrs. Socorro Betancourt Ayala (Mrs. B.), is a Puerto Rican woman who moved to the United States in 1985. This commonality facilitated the process of engaging the family, building a therapeutic relationship, and conducting the assessment. It also alerted Mrs. B. that she needed to consciously avoid projecting personal issues onto the family and overprotecting them by giving excessive attention to cultural factors and ignoring other issues that could be related to the presenting problems.

Mrs. B. conducted the interview in Spanish, the language of preference for the mother, addressed the son in English, and translated for both. Mrs. G. asked questions about Mrs. B.'s ethnicity, her time living in the United States, her time working in the agency, whether she had children and whether she was a doctor. Mrs. B. understood that these questions are typical, given the importance many Latinos/as place on the value of *personalismo* and the client's need for assessing the practitioner's credibility. This is an important matter in order for *confianza* to develop. Mrs. B. answered the questions with ease. She was also aware that Mrs. G. probably had expectations, concerns, fears, and wishes that corresponded to her views about getting professional help. Some of Mrs. G.'s apprehension could relate to cultural values, social class, and experiences with previous service providers. Mrs. B. wondered if this was Mrs. G.'s first experience with a formal mental health system.

Mrs. B. described the program's services and explained the clients' rights to confidentiality, the helping process, and what she anticipated would happen in that first meeting. Mrs. G. was given the opportunity to express her feelings and thoughts about receiving professional help.

To the question, "What brought you and your son to the Latino program?" Mrs. G. responded that they were there because the school had problems with her son. She claimed that her family had no problems and that her son was not crazy. Her statements revealed a dramatic difference between the referral source's perception of the problems and the clients' perception of a lack of problems. It also underscored Mrs. G.'s beliefs about seeking mental health services.

Mrs. B. focused on what was important to Mrs. G.: the school's approach to dealing with her son's perceived difficulties. She promoted the clients' active participation by inviting them to share their views about why the school felt that Jr. was having difficulties at school and the reasons for the school's referral to the Latino Program. Mrs. G. explained that Jr.'s situation at school had her "sufriendo de los nervios" and that she was considering seeing an "espiritista."

Mrs. B. validated Mrs. G. and Jr.'s views and their request to call a meeting at school. Such validation allowed Mrs. G. to be more receptive to examining other issues that could be related to her son's difficulties. As the clients provided more information, Mrs. B. noted that the family had recently lost their only support network, Mrs. G.'s brother. According to Mrs. G., Jr. had been very sad since his godparents and cousins left to Puerto Rico. Furthermore, the family faced economic needs and adjustment conflicts. Mrs. G. realized that there might be a correlation between family issues and the child's difficulties.

The following questions helped in the assessment and moved the focus from the child to the family: What does Mr. G. thinks of his son's situation? Will he join Mrs. G. and Jr. in future sessions? How have family members reacted to Jr.'s difficulties? Other than the school's referring him to the Latino Program, was there something else that was done by the parents, or the school, to help Jr.? What would other family members recommend to help Jr.? Is there anything else that the family may need to know or do in order to help Jr.? How could each family member support the school's efforts in helping Jr.? How are Ivette and Taína adjusting? Are there concerns about them?

Other issues that need to be assessed include: What can be done immediately? What are the socioeconomic conditions of this family? Is there racism, prejudice, and lack of cultural competence at school? How can the family develop a support network? How is the family coping with the new culture? Why does Jr. miss his "padrino's" family? How much are Mr. and Mrs. G. influenced by traditional gender roles? What are the strengths of this family? How can they use their strengths on their behalf?

CONCLUSIONS

To gain the credibility of the Latino client, it is important to show knowledge and foster respect, confidence, trust, and hope. This requires a genuinely caring attitude that discovers the abilities of the client, an understanding of what is unique and different, and an assessment of how such uniqueness and differences could be positive. Expectations for change must be compatible with the client's cultural values. The problems and needs should be conceptualized in a manner that is consistent with the client's belief system.

An assessment that follows an empowerment–strengths perspective will require that the practitioner tolerate ambiguity, form a trusting relationship, and start the process of identifying and working to develop the Latino individual/family strengths and social support networks in the agency and the natural community. Variations exist among different Latino groups that call for a careful assessment of the situation of individual Latino groups and the uniqueness of the individual client.

REFERENCES

American Psychiatric Association. (1994). *Diagnostic and statistical manual of mental disorders* 4th ed. Washington, DC: Author.

Buriel, R. (1984). Integration with traditional Mexican-American Culture and sociocultural adjustment. In J. L. Martinez, Jr. and R. H. Mendoza (Eds.), *Chicano Psychology.* Orlando, Florida: Academic Press.

Canino, I. A. & Canino, G. (1980). Impact of stress on the Puerto Rican family: Treatment considerations. *American Journal of Orthopsychiatry, 50* (3), 535–541.

Canino, I. A. & Spurlock, J. (1994). *Culturally diverse children and adolescents: Assessment, diagnosis, and treatment.* New York: Guildford.

Comas-Díaz, L. (1995). Puerto Ricans and sexual child abuse. In L. A. Fontes (Ed.), *Sexual abuse in nine North American cultures: Treatment and prevention* (pp. 31–66). California: Sage.

Congress, E. P. (1994). The use of culturagrams to assess and empower culturally diverse families (CEU Article #46). Washington, DC: National Association of Social Workers.

Cowger, C. D. (1994). Assessing client strengths: Clinical assessment for client empowerment. *Social Work, 39* (3), 262–268.

Delgado, M. (1998). *Social services in Latino communities: Research and strategies.* New York: The Haworth Press.

Delgado, M. & Humm-Delgado, D. (1982). Natural support systems: Source of strength in Hispanic communities. *Social Work, 27,* 83–89.

Díaz-Royo, A. (1983). Cultural themes in the enculturation of children from the Puerto Rican highlands. In R. J. Duncan, R. L. Ramírez, E. Seda-Bonilla, C. Buitrago-Ortíz, J. Wessman, M. Valdés-Pizzini, M. Morris, A. Díaz-Royo, & E. Jacob (Eds.), *Social research in Puerto Rico: Science, humanism and society* (pp. 149–165). Puerto Rico: InterAmerican University Press.

Falicov, C. J. (1998). *Latino families in therapy: A guide to multicultural practice.* New York: Guilford.

Green, J. W. (1995). Latino cultures and their continuity. In J. W. Green (Ed.), *Cultural awareness in the human services: A multi-ethnic approach.* Boston: Allyn and Bacon.

Guarnaccia, P. J., Canino, G., Rubio-Stipec, M., & Bravo, M. (1993). The prevalence of ataque de nervios in the Puerto Rico disaster study. *The Journal of Nervous and Mental Disease, 181* (3), 157–165.

Harper, K. V. & Lantz, J. (1996). *Cross-cultural practice: Social work with diverse populations.* IL: Lyceum.

Jiménez-Vazquez, R. (1995). Hispanics: Cubans. In *Encyclopedia of Social Work.* Washington, DC: National Association of Social Workers.

Karls, J. M. & Wandrei, K. E. (1997). Person-in-environment system. Washington, DC: National Association of Social Workers.

Laureano, M. & Poliandro, E. (1991). Understanding cultural values of Latino male alcoholics and their families: A culture sensitive model. In M. Laureano & E. Poliandro (Eds.), *Chemical dependency: Theoretical approaches and strategies* (pp. 137–155). New York: Haworth.

Lecca, P. J., Quervalú, I., Nunes, J. V., & Gonzéles, H. F. (1998). *Cultural competency in the health, social and human services.* New York: Garland.

Longres, J. F. (1995a). Hispanics: Overview. In *Encyclopedia of social work.* Washington, DC: National Association of Social Workers.

Longres, J. F. (1995b). *Human behavior in the social environment.* Ill: F. E. Peacock.

Morales, J. (1995). Community social work with Puerto Ricans in the United States. In F. Rivera and J. Erlich (Eds.), *Community organizing in a diverse society,* 2nd ed. Boston, MA: Allyn and Bacon.

National Association of Social Workers. *National Association of Social Workers News* (November 1998).

Ramos-McKay, J., Comas Diaz, L., Ruizra, L. (1988). Puerto Ricans. In L. Comas-Diaz and E. H. Griffith (Eds.), *Clinical guidelines in cross-cultural mental health* (pp. 204–232). New York: John Wiley.

Rendon, M. (1974). Transcultural aspects of Puerto Rican mental illness in New York. *International Journal of Social Psychiatry, 20,* pp. 18–24.

Sue D. W. & Sue, D. (1990). *Counseling the culturally different: Theory and practice.* New York: John Wiley & Sons.

U.S. Bureau of the Census. 1996. *The Hispanic population in the United States* (pp. 22–502). Washington, DC: Author.

U.S. Department of Commerce. (1996). *Population projections of the United States by age, sex, race, and Hispanic origin: 1995 to 2050* (Current population reports, pp. 25–1130). Bureau of the Census: Economic and Statistics Administration.

Valle, R. & Vega, W. (1980). *Hispanic natural support systems: Mental health promotion perspectives.* Sacramento, CA: State of California.

Vazquez, M. J. T. (1994). Latinas. In L. Comas-Díaz & B. Greene (Eds.), *Women of Color: Integrating ethnic gender identities in psychotherapy* (pp. 114–138). New York: Guilford.

CHAPTER 11

ASSESSMENT WITH LATINO/HISPANIC COMMUNITIES AND ORGANIZATIONS

GREGORY ACEVEDO

JULIO MORALES

In this chapter, we will discuss issues the practitioner needs to be mindful of when conducting assessments with Latino organizations and communities. The discussion begins by underscoring why it is important to tease apart the strands of "sameness" and "difference" between Hispanic groups, and the necessity to "disaggregate" information on the sociodemographic composition of Latinos. We then discuss the cultural and behavioral norms often associated with this population. A constellation of concerns, problems, and issues related to social work practice with Hispanics are profiled.

We then discuss theoretical approaches that serve as a foundation for the knowledge and skills necessary in the process of assessment with Latino organizations and communities: the ecological/person-in-environment, strengths, and empowerment perspectives.

The knowledge and skills needed to conduct these assessments are then outlined both as general aspects of any assessment, and as specific necessities in conducting assessments with Hispanic organizations and communities. Lastly, several cases are presented to illustrate how this knowledge and these skills are utilized.

A SOCIODEMOGRAPHIC OVERVIEW OF LATINOS

Latinos are not a monolithic group, "rather, they are a disparate collection of national origin groups with heterogeneous experiences of settlement, immigration, political participation, and economic incorporation into the United States" (Massey, 1993, p. 454).

What begins as statistical fiction created through a Census Bureau category is being shaped into an ethnic identity, an image that is refashioning the culture, politics, and identities of a people labeled *Hispanic*. Perhaps Latinos "are beginning to embrace the new and less precise categories of Hispanic or Latino so that they can be part of a larger and more influential group and thereby negotiate better terms of assimilation" (Fox, 1996, p. 241).

Yet, the term *Hispanic* continues to be a point of contestation. Some prefer *Latino* and *Latina*.[1] Aside from the etymological aspects of this debate, there is a crucial political aspect. The term *Latino* connotes a certain rebelliousness that some Hispanics appreciate. *Hispanic* seems too politically neutral for others. These debates are not likely to be resolved any time soon, and we will be using these terms interchangeably. In many ways, the fluidity of this compromise reflects the inherent "mosaic" quality of Hispanics as a people.

Clearly, the label *Hispanicity* covers a diverse set of peoples from a wide range of regions and nations. According to Graciela Castex (1994), some of the most important dimensions that comprise Hispanicity are *national origin and language, the complexity of racial ascription, the differences between self-ascription and ascription by others, and the role of immigration and citizenship status.*

These differences affect how Latinos choose to identify themselves, and much of this depends on context. This is what Felix Padilla calls "situational ethnic identity" (Padilla, 1985). At times, Hispanics may identify with nationality, race, or, at a broader level, as Latino or Hispanic. In the end, what matters most is the individual and community's ascription of themselves. And this ascription is likely to be fluid, temporal, and contextual.

It is important to note that Latinos are a mixture of both native-born and foreign-born individuals. The Caribbean, and Central and South America, have been some of the principal source-regions for U.S. immigration. Six of the top twenty countries of birth for U.S. immigrants between 1994–1997 are Latin American: Mexico is ranked first, Cuba sixth, the Dominican Republic seventh, El Salvador eighth, Colombia fourteenth, and Peru eighteenth (Immigration and Naturalization Service, 1999).

Citizenship status is important in determining access to services and resources. "Documented" and "undocumented" status affect mobility, employment, and legal rights. Disclosure of undocumented status may increase the fears, instabilities, and anxieties that come from the experience of migration itself.

While care must be given to understanding the distinctiveness and diversity among Hispanics, some generalizations can be made. Although the emphasis on difference is important, some consensus can be found around what common values and behavioral norms can be cautiously ascribed to people of Spanish-speaking origins.

LATINO CULTURAL VALUES AND BEHAVIORAL NORMS

According to Green (1995) and others, there is a case to be made for discussing generalized Hispanic American values and norms. However, it is important to keep in mind that these generalized values are not exclusive to Latinos. For example, what we call *machismo* is a pattern of gender- and sex-role behaviors that can also be seen in other racial and ethnic groups. The dynamics of machismo are probably not a pattern unique to Hispanics. It is more likely that *machismo* is the Latino "name" for a common theme that is cross-cultural. This being said, what are some the generalized values and norms associated with Hispanics?

Most obviously, there is a *commitment to using the Spanish language,* especially among first generation immigrants. Second generations tend to be bilingual, and future generations may connect to the Spanish language through such cultural expressions as music and food. Language is a critical aspect of ethnic identity.

Familism is the tendency to prize family matters above other institutions or activities, and to think of families in an extended sense, including kin and "fictive" kin. The system of *compadrazco,* grounded in relations of God-parenting, also creates and cements extended family networks. *Hijos de crianza,* or foster children, are generally treated equally as biological/"natural" children in the Latino family.

Personalism is a style in relations with others wherein individuals are judged in terms of their caring behavior with family and friends, and less on their formal roles or position; it is expressed in a strong personal commitment to others and warmth in relationships.

Respect for hierarchy and authority is important, especially in family relations and values, although authoritarianism outside the family is subject to challenge and negotiation.

Machismo refers to male dominance as an extension of hierarchy and authority. It is often discussed in terms of such negative behaviors as bravado, physical confrontation, womanizing and philandering, and alcohol abuse, although it is more appropriately associated with concepts of honor, trustworthiness, moral courage, and responsibility.

The complement of machismo is *marianismo* (derived from Christian worship of the Virgin Mary); it refers to the cultural tendency to see women as more spiritual than men. It is said to involve a "martyr complex" that emphasizes the woman's suffering and self-sacrifice for the sake of family members.

There are other generalized values that shape and define the character of relationships, and create the personalism that is cherished by Hispanics. *Confianza* is a sense of trust and connection that is necessary for relations to run more deeply than mere acquaintance. *Platicando* is an exchange, or dialogue, akin to "shooting the breeze" or "chatting"; this kind of conversation is necessary for personalismo and to establish confianza. *Dignidad* (dignity) and *respeto* (respect) are important in relations as well. Keeping a cordial, respectful, and dignified manner and comportment is critical, particularly in public. Understanding these generalized values and norms is crucial for social work practice, particularly in terms of building rapport and establishing trust.

In addition to these values and norms, Latinos can also draw strength from a vibrant *spirituality. Espiritismo* among Puerto Ricans, *Curanderismo* among Mexicans, and *Santeria* among Cubans, are all sets of folkways and beliefs that continue to be practiced by many. These practices involve such things as healing and protection from harmful forces; they do not supercede affiliation with major, traditional religious denominations and practices, but instead are syncretically integrated into them.

While not universally held or practiced within or among Hispanics for the most part, these generalized values and norms are part of the cultural patterns that hold Latino families, friendships, groups, and communities together. They can serve as sources of strength, stability, and resiliency that Hispanics demonstrate in coping with the concerns, problems, and issues that confront them in the United States today.

PROFILE OF SOCIAL WORK PROBLEMS AND ISSUES

An overall profile of social work problems and issues relevant to Latinos is Janus-faced. On the one hand, there is an aggregate, panethnic profile of Hispanics; on the other, there is a different "face," a constellation of economic and social outcomes that indicates a great deal of disparity in the well-being of the distinct Latinos groups.

In the aggregate profile, the median household income for Hispanics in the United States continued to fall until 1996, while those of (non-Latino) whites and (non-Hispanic) African Americans rebounded from the 1990–1991 recession and have increased since 1992. The poverty rate showed a similar trend. For both non-Latino whites and African Americans the poverty rate declined prior to that of Latinos. In 1997, the Hispanic American poverty rate for families was roughly 25 percent, compared to about 24 percent for African Americans and 8 percent for Whites (U.S. Bureau of the Census, 1998).

The gap between high school completion rates for African Americans and non-Latino whites has narrowed, but the gap between these two groups and Hispanics has increased. The percentage of Latinos with a high school diploma or higher was about 55 percent in 1997, compared to 75 percent for African Americans and 84 percent for whites (U.S. Bureau of the Census, 1998). The unemployment rate for Hispanics was 7.7 percent in 1997, compared to 10 percent for African Americans and 4.2 percent for whites (U.S. Bureau of the Census, 1998). These trends in Latino economic well-being are cause for concern. Somehow the climb up the ladder of economic mobility has stalled.

When statistics for Hispanics are disaggregated a sharp contrast appears between distinct subgroups. In 1997, the median household income was $35,616 for Cubans, $25,347 for Mexicans, $29,960 for Central and South Americans, and $23,646 for Puerto Ricans (U.S. Bureau of the Census, 1998). The profile becomes even more complex when we consider that "Central and South American" is in itself a categorical aggregate.

Overall, poverty immigration/migration, "documentation status," and the lack of substantial progress in educational attainment have powerful effects on the social and economic well-being of Latino communities.

Internal Cleavages

In addition to these stressors, there are internal social, political, and economic cleavages that affect Hispanic groups. There are political disputes that continue to ripple throughout and divide particular Latino communities. For example, the political status of Puerto Rico has had a destructive effect in Puerto Rican communities. Debates over how to deal with the political regime in Cuba have been a source of bitter disputes in Cuban communities. Recent or current civil conflicts in countries like Nicaragua, El Salvador, Guatemala, and Mexico have resulted in disruption and suffering for those communities.

There are also pronounced interethnic rivalries and disputes between the various Hispanic groups. Many of these conflicts stem from differences in their economic and social position, and their particular experiences of being incorporated into the United States.

There are also divisive problems that stem from internal oppressions in Latino communities. Gender relationships and sexism, sexual harassment, sexual assault, and domestic violence are pressing issues that affect Hispanics. The rights, treatment, and acceptance of gay, lesbian, bisexual, and transgender Latinos are also critical issues in these communities. A major downside of the generalized values and norms mentioned earlier, like machismo and certain religious beliefs, is that they may tend to support these oppressions.

Hispanics pose a wealth of contradictions, socially, economically, and politically. But Latinos also have a rich "hybrid" nature and a capacity for integration. They exhibit a spectrum of cultural diversity that "mixes" different races, ethnicities, traditions, beliefs, and passions. This hybridity is a tremendous cultural strength, and one well-suited to theoretical frameworks within social work that emphasize process, context, and transaction, such as the ecological, person-in-environment, strengths, and empowerment perspectives.

THEORETICAL FRAMEWORKS FOR CULTURALLY COMPETENT ASSESSMENT

The Ecological/Person-in-Environment Perspectives

The ecological perspective "emphasizes understanding people and their environment and the nature of their transactions" and focuses on processes of adaptation, the goodness of fit between people and their environments, as well as reciprocity, and mutuality. . . . [Analysis is turned toward] the interface between the individual (or group, family, or community) and the relevant environment" (*Dictionary of Social Work*, 1997).

Person-in-environment (PIE) is a system of classification and assessment that looks at problems as the outcomes of multiple factors within person–environment transactions. PIE emphasizes "client" (individual, group, family, or community) strengths in light of the stressors that have resulted in problems in living.

Both the ecological and PIE perspectives offer fruitful theoretical frameworks for assessing Hispanic communities and groups. The process and contextual orientation of these perspectives lends itself to understanding Latino hybridity and analyzing the constellation of problems that they face.

Migration, social and economic dislocation, and cultural transition are all changes and life transitions that are best understood conceptually in terms of environment, adaptation, transaction, goodness of fit, reciprocity, and mutuality. Viewed through the prism of strengths and coping, these problems seem less intransigent, insurmountable, and intra-individual.

The Strengths Perspective

By adopting a strengths perspective, generalized Hispanic values and norms can be seen as resources and strengths. Familism, personalism, confianza, dignidad, respeto, and spirituality are strengths that can be employed to resolve problems in living. Latino natural support systems and cultural resources can be drawn from, and the natural resiliency that comes from adapting to mobility and change should be understood. These are all valuable assets in efforts to promote growth and change to increase opportunity and well-being.

Aside from values and norms, the racial, ethnic, linguistic, and cultural diversity that characterizes Hispanic culture is in itself a strength that must be acknowledged and utilized. It reflects a powerful tendency toward syncretism that can offset countervailing tendencies toward conflict and division. It can be a resource to foster unity and build coalitions.

Empowerment [2]

Gutiérrez (1990) offers a succinct definition of *empowerment.* "Empowerment is a process of increasing personal, interpersonal, or political power so that individuals can take action to improve their life situations" (p. 149).

While the constellation of problems that Latinos experience is daunting, the resiliency that comes from coping with them can serve as the foundation on which to promote self-determination and empowerment. Hispanics who come to the attention of social workers generally have been the victims of oppressive forces of racism, colonialism, economic exploitation, and cultural domination. Internal oppression related to gender, sexual orientation, race, and class may have also contributed to problems and conflicts. These must be understood and addressed in the assessment of Latino organizations and communities.

ASSESSMENT WITH LATINO/HISPANIC COMMUNITIES AND ORGANIZATIONS

Knowledge and Skills for Assessment

Culturally competent assessment with Hispanic communities and organizations requires that practitioners know and practice a basic set of skills. This set of knowledge and skills falls into two dimensions: the *technical* and *cultural* requirements of assessment.

Technical knowledge and skills are the detailed methodological and procedural aspects of conducting assessments. Specific cultural knowledge and skills are also an aspect of assessment. Technical knowledge and skills of assessment are the capabilities practitioners use for identifying needs, defining problems, and, subsequently, measuring and prioritizing those needs/problems. Cultural knowledge and skills for assessment with Latino communities and organizations consist of the practitioner's understanding of the history of Hispanic national origin groups, the demographic profile of Latinos in the United States, and the cultural life of Hispanics, including their language and generalized values and norms.

Need Identification/Problem Definition

As Tropmann (1997) notes, needs may be normative, comparative, or felt. Normative needs are calibrated to an accepted standard or norm. Comparative need is gauged in comparison to other needs. Felt need is perceived need. Each of these needs may then become expressed need if they are articulated in some manner.

In this earliest stage of assessment, it is important for the practitioner to answer certain questions. How has the need or problem been articulated, defined, or identified? For example, was it through legislative action, protest, or organizational change? Who expressed the need? In this regard, the practitioner situates the articulated need in its political context, paying attention to dynamics of power.

Ensuring the involvement of stakeholders from as wide a range of views as possible, early in the process of need identification and problem definition, maximizes the potential for equitable influence over the articulation of needs.

Finally, the practitioner must know what the purpose is in conducting the assessment. Why has the community or organization charged someone to field this assessment? What are the desired and expected outcomes?

Measuring/Prioritizing Needs and Problems

Having understood how the need was identified and defined, the practitioner moves on to measure and prioritize the need. Measurement involves the adoption of quantitative or qualitative methods to ascertain the prevalence and intensity of the need (see Tropman, 1997). *Prevalence* is a measure of who is affected and how widespread the need is. *Intensity* is a measure of how pronounced or grave the need is. Quantitative measures include the use of social and economic indicators, survey methods, and techniques to elicit community responses. Qualitative measures include the use of focus groups, interviewing key informants, and participant observation.

Stakeholder Views

In their pursuit of a rigorous and appropriate assessment, the practitioner attempts to measure and prioritize needs or problems reliably and objectively. By enlisting the fullest level of participation across stakeholder groups, the assessment's validity is increased. The involvement of the clients, consumers, or individuals and groups whose needs are to be met is required. Representatives of the relevant organizational agents must be included, such as paid and volunteer staff, administrators, board members, and funding sources. The participation of sectors that make up the community context in which the need exists, and will be met is critical as well.

The inclusion of these various constituencies not only facilitates the stages of need identification, measurement, and prioritizing, it also begins to build the coalition and consensus that will result in successful outcomes for the recommendations that come from the assessment.

Developing Possible Alternatives

During the assessment, the practitioner must always keep an eye toward the future stages of the policy practice process. The recommendations that flow from the assessment should lead to successful implementation and evaluation. Assessments should be cost-effective and not overreaching. Recommendations should be posed as alternatives that are achievable and that lead to outcomes that can be evaluated. Assessments will more likely lead to successful outcomes when the practitioner understands clearly what the scope of the community or organization is, and what the overarching intent is for developing the alternatives that come from the assessment. This requires that the practitioner have a schema for defining the concept of community.

Defining Community in Community Practice

There are several essential elements that need to be included in any rigorous definition of *community*. These elements are also important for understanding the nature of organizations. First, a community is a collection of people with a particular social structure. There is also an affective component, the sense of belonging or the 'feeling' of community, as well as a territorial aspect, the community as a self-contained geographical area, or as tied to place.

All three of these elements define the character of community. Garvin and Tropman (1992) have defined *community* as being organized around a common location, activity, or belief. In their interpretation, location accounts for territoriality, activity reveals the structural nature of a community with respect to its purpose, and belief acknowledges the affective nature of community. However the practitioner conceptualizes community, having a clear idea of what kind of community is being assessed is necessary. Along with knowing what kind of community it is, the practitioner should also know what kind of intervention the assessment is leading towards (see Rothman, 1995).

Community Practice Interventions

The assessment process with communities and organizations leads to findings that will be translated into four general macro interventions: locality development, planning, social action, and administration. Locality development focuses on improving social and economic conditions in a community. Planning emphasizes technical solutions and process that can be utilized to solve social or organizational problems. Social action is geared towards organizing disenfranchised communities or groups to achieve goals that will empower and improve the social, economic, and political conditions in which they find themselves. Administration relates to solving problems within a particular organization.

While the general assessment process (need identification/problem identification, measurement/prioritizing, and developing possible alternatives) is the same for any of these desired ends, the practitioner must be clear about the ultimate intervention intended.

The assessment process will be structured by the intervention that is called for. For example, an assessment with a social action goal will need to be more sensitive to evaluating the political context than an administrative intervention might be, though it is a necessity in both. Planning and administration interventions may require an assessment to provide specific, quantitative results, more than might be needed for a social action intervention.

Analysis Skills and Assessment in Macro Practice

As part of their assessment skills the practitioner should be able to conduct discrete analyses of three factors: issues, communities, and organizations.

The analysis of issues can be conducted by gathering existing data and information on the topic, fielding surveys, holding public meetings and forums, or through individual and group interviews. Collecting relevant facts and figures through such sources as census data can help the practitioner objectify and describe particular issues. Culling newspaper editorials and articles on a given topic can also assist the practitioner in gauging the significance of issues. Being able to research issues will aid in identifying and defining needs and problems.

The practitioner should also be able to conduct a community analysis or profile. Through structured techniques like mapping, a community analysis should include:

- the background and setting of a community, including its history and geographical aspects;
- the community's demographic profile;
- the social and symbolic boundaries of the community, and how these shape the definition of in- and out-groups;
- the communications and transportation infrastructure of the community, including its media institutions, informal networks of exchanging information, and access to public and private modes of travel;
- the community's economic life, paying attention to both its productive capacity and patterns of consumption, including its labor–market conditions, access to credit, capital, and insurance, levels and types of entrepreneurship, and sources of public monies;

- the community's housing situation, including the quality and quantity of housing stock and its rates of homeownership;
- the governmental institutions, policies, and practices of the community, including its relationships to local, state, and federal government, political organizations, and institutions of public safety;
- the community's educational, artistic, and recreational institutions and resources, both public and private;
- the religious institutions of the community, including its particular denominations and interfaith relations;
- the community's health and social service institutions and resources, whether public, nonprofit, or private;
- the civic groups and associations of the community;
- the community's cultural traditions, fairs, feasts, parades, myths, and legends.

While this is not an exhaustive list, these are essential components of any community analysis.

Practitioners must also be able to conduct an analysis of organizations, institutions, or agencies. In general, any organizational analysis should include:

- a history of the organization;
- an understanding of its mission and purpose;
- a detailing of its structure and resources, including staffing, funding, and oversight;
- its community context, including the permeability of its boundaries;
- an understanding of the organization's power field, including the dynamics of power within the organization and the forces that impinge on it from without.

Analysis of an organization in this detail may be called for as part of a practitioner's assessment.

Cultural Knowledge and Skills for Culturally Competent Assessment with Latino Communities and Organizations

The technical knowldege and skills that we have detailed thus far are necessary in any competent community or organizational assessment. Assessment with Hispanic communities and organizations also requires specific cultural knowledge and culturally sensitive skills.

The practitioner fielding an assessment of a Latino community or agency should have knowledge of:

- the history of Hispanic groups in the United States, including their political development, both in the United States and in their nation of origin, the nature of class relations within their communities, their citizenship status and patterns of migration, as well as the political and economic policies that structured them;

- the demography of Latino groups in the United States, including their numbers, geographic locations and concentrations, and social and economic status;
- the cultural life of Hispanics in the United States, including Spanish language proficiency, an understanding of the similarity and differences between Latino groups, an appreciation for the complexity of the Hispanic identity and its dimensions of race, class, gender, and sexuality, and a familiarity with their generalized values and norms.

The knowledge the practitioner has of these aspects of Latino culture will help direct technical knowledge and skills toward culturally competent assessment with Hispanic communities and organizations.

Knowing the history and demography of Latinos will help practitioners understand better the particular circumstances of a Hispanic community, and will help guide their assessment. It will make them more knowledgeable about the special needs of the community they are working with. For example, they will know if the Latino community they are assessing has a substantial number of undocumented members with respect to citizenship status. This informs the practitioners' assessment by heightening their awareness of the special needs of this undocumented group. They will also be sensitive to the fact that gathering information may be more difficult, given a realistic fear of exposure to governmental authorities.

Proficiency in Spanish as well as English is important because it allows the practitioner to access information about the community in both languages.

Understanding the complexity of Hispanic identity is necessary so that practitioners can be sensitive to the racial and class diversity within the Latino community, and to the internal oppressions that relate to gender and sexuality.

Knowledge of generalized Hispanic values and norms will facilitate the practitioners' assessments with Latino communities and organizations. For example, Spanish language fluency is not merely an instrumental concern; addressing Hispanics in their preferred language is also a matter of respect. Practitioners should also be aware of the level of formality that is required in their use of Spanish. With certain groups, a street vernacular may be appropriate, while some groups may find this informal speech offensive. Much of this may have to do with class and gender differences and with religious values.

Working with the values of familism and *personalismo* is important for practitioners. Finding ways to invite Latinos to events as families will increase involvement. By involving children in planned activities, practitioners can increase parental involvement. This is why addressing day-care concerns is crucial to planning activities with Hispanic organizations and communities. Involving extended family, particularly the elderly, also increases participation.

In addition to these family-focused strategies, working with Latino personalismo is critical. Working with Hispanics generally requires a greater level of personal contact, and, usually, less formality. The "knocking on doors" kind of canvasing and home visitation that might be considered intrusive in some communities is more acceptable and appreciated in Latino neighborhoods.

Platicando, the kind of chatting that we mentioned earlier, is essential in contacts with Hispanics. Cultural expectations usually exceed the tightly bounded professional exchanges that are more typical outside the Latino community. A "cold" instrumental approach will not usually suffice; Hispanics expect a warmer, personal manner.

Understanding Latino values around hierarchy and authority is important for practitioners. Generally speaking, Hispanics have a deep respect for professionals and experts, and for governmental and religious authority. Though they certainly exercise their rights to challenge authority, Latinos may be more intimidated, at least initially, by authority figures. For example, they may be less likely to challenge school personnel and government authorities.

Religious leaders and institutions, from the more established denominations such as Catholicism to the storefront Pentecostal churches, can be instrumental in practitioner efforts within Hispanic communities. Tapping into this resource also draws on the strengths of Latino spirituality and religious commitment and practices.

Overall, understanding generalized Hispanic values and norms will facilitate assessments. These norms and values play a vital role in the community resources and cultural activities that practitioners might rely on in fielding their assessments.

Using Community Resources and Cultural Activities

Identifying the community's important formal and informal institutions, and its leadership, resources, and cultural activities, is a critical assessment skill. The practitioner should work with the established leadership and organizations in a given Latino community, and utilize resources that already exist.

Cultural activities are one important resource. For example, Cruz (1998) notes how the use of parades, festivals, and church groups was instrumental in the development of Hartford, Connecticut's earliest Puerto Rican community activists, organizations, and social service agencies.

Community-oriented Spanish language radio and television programs, local shops and market places, churches, and connections to schools and institutions of higher learning, all facilitate practitioners' efforts towards assessment with Latino communities and organizations.

We will now present some examples of assessments with Puerto Rican organizations and communities in Connecticut. These examples deal with two issues of great concern within the Puerto Rican community, education and AIDS. These assessments were conducted by faculty and students at the University of Connecticut School of Social Work (UCSSW).

CASE VIGNETTES

Example One
An M.S.W. student under the supervision of a UCSSW faculty member wanted to utilize the resources of her large Puerto Rican Pentecostal Church in Hartford, CT.

She hoped to organize strategies for making improvements within the church and the surrounding community.

In order to assess the interests and needs of the congregation, the student distributed questionnaires at church meetings and gatherings. She asked respondents to provide information about their needs and concerns. The results were shared with church members, along with recommendations on how to address the identified needs. As a result, literacy and English-as-a-second-language classes were formed, and workshops in leadership skills development, vocational training, resume writing, job interviewing skills, and public assistance eligibility were instituted.

The student's assessment efforts were helped by her participation in the activities of the church. She sang and played guitar at church services, mentored young church members, and actively involved church members in planning and conducting the workshops.

Example Two
In 1992, a UCSSW faculty member was hired by the Bridgeport school system in Bridgeport, CT to field a study on Puerto Rican school dropouts. A broad-based collaborative research team that included a significant representation from the Puerto Rican community was formed. They helped develop research instruments and conducted interviews with Puerto Rican youth and parents, as well as with teachers, administrators, social workers, and school staff. The questionnaires gathered information on community and school-related factors that contributed to the dropout problem. The results of the study were used to affect school policies, teacher training, and to develop a Puerto Rican studies curriculum.

Example Three
The Sheff v. O'Neill case was a landmark desegregation case on behalf of Hartford's public school children against the State of Connecticut. Over half of these students are Puerto Rican. In an effort to determine the awareness about the case in the Puerto Rican community, and to assess their knowledge and attitudes about desegregation policies, M.S.W. students, supervised by UCCSW faculty, interviewed Puerto Rican parents in Hartford, CT.

Respondents were interviewed in Hartford's El Mercado, a Puerto Rican shopping center in the heart of one of Hartford's largest Puerto Rican communities, and during parent–teacher organization meetings in two public schools. Interviews were conducted in either English or Spanish, and respondents were provided with definitions of terms such as *vouchers* and *magnet schools,* and other concepts regarding this policy issue. The findings from the study were publicized and made available to the community and the Hartford schools.

Example Four
Between 1986 and 1990, Puerto Rican students in the M. S. W. program at UCSSW interviewed Puerto Rican storeowners and employees of grocery stores, beauty parlors, or other businesses in Puerto Rican neighborhoods to assess their knowledge of AIDS. They were then given information on AIDS and asked to share it with their customers. The students also interviewed hundreds of Puerto Rican churchgoers after Sunday services. Again, these interviews were conducted in either Spanish or English. The information obtained from this assessment effort

was eventually brought to the attention of policymakers and AIDS activists and organizations.

These examples involving the assessment efforts of the UCSSW faculty and M. S. W. students illustrate the usefulness of practitioners having Spanish language fluency and utilizing bilingual assessment tools and methods. They demonstrate the importance of using formal and informal family-focused cultural activities and institutions such as schools, churches, and local shops. These examples also underscore the importance of "talking" with people in the Latino community. The assessment techniques were purposefully structured to maximize personal contact with community members in more informal settings, and to encourage interviewing that was conversational in character.

These example cases, and the substantive information on conducting technically and culturally competent assessments we presented earlier, can be integrated into a general checklist with which to assess an organization's overall sensitivity to Hispanics.

Assessing an Organization's Competence in Working with Latinos

The following is a list of questions that any organization working with Latino populations should be able to address:

- Does the organization know the racial and class composition, and national origins, of the local Hispanic community?
- Does the organization have working relationships with the community's social service agencies and community-based organizations?
- Does the organization have working relationships with the community's informal supports and natural helper networks?
- Does the organization have links to institutions of higher education, and to planners, chambers of commerce, and philanthropic groups that can provide accurate information on concerns and trends in the Latino community?
- Does the organization subscribe to Hispanic publications as another source of information?
- Does the organization do outreach to Latino churches, publishers, radio and television programs, social clubs and organizations, and local shops?
- Does the organization participate in the community's cultural, religious, and political events?
- Does the organization have an awareness of the cultural strengths and social problems of the community?
- Does the organization have Hispanic representation in staffing, both professional and paraprofessional, in management and administration, review committees, and on the board of directors and other policymaking bodies?
- Does the organization have brochures, publications, and materials available in Spanish?

- Does the organization have the empowerment of Latino communities, families, and individuals as part of its mission?
- Does the organization provide training in culturally sensitive practices with the Hispanic community?

CONCLUSION

Overall, we have discussed the importance of understanding the complexity of the Latino demographic and cultural reality in the United States for practitioners who conducts assessments with Hispanic organizations and communities. Possessing basic technical and cultural knowledge and skills to conduct these assessments is essential. Practitioners should be knowledgeable about the historical, political, social, and economic circumstances that most deeply affect Hispanic communities. They should have some fluency in the Spanish language and be skillful in working with generalized Latino values and norms. Practitioners must understand Hispanic racial and national origin diversity, as well as class, gender, and other differences that shape Latino identity. And practitioners should utilize Hispanic cultural institutions and resources in their work. Knowledge and skills in all these areas will be part of any accurate assessment with Latino organizations and communities.

REFERENCES

Castex, G. (1994). Providing services to Hispanic/Latino populations: Profiles in diversity. *Social Work, 39* (3), 288–296.

Cruz, J. E. (1998). *Identity and power: Puerto Rican politics & the challenge of ethnicity.* Philadelphia, PA: Temple University Press.

Dictionary of social work. (1997). Washington, DC: National Association of Social Workers Press.

Fox, G. (1996). *Hispanic nation: Culture, politics, and the constructing of identity.* Secaucus, NJ: Birch Lane Press.

Garvin, C. & Tropman, J. E. (1992). *Social work in contemporary society.* Englewood Cliffs, NJ: Prentice-Hall.

Green, J. W. (1995). *Cultural awareness in the human services: A multi-ethnic approach,* 2nd ed. Boston: Allyn & Bacon.

Gutiérrez, L. M. (1990). Working with women of color: An empowerment perspective. *Social Work, 35,* 149–154.

Massey, D. (1993). Latinos, poverty, and the underclass: A new agenda for research. *Hispanic Journal of Behavioral Sciences, 15* (4), 449–475.

Padilla, F. M. (1985). *Latino ethnic consciousness: The case of Mexican Americans and Puerto Ricans in Chicago.* Notre Dame, IN: University of Notre Dame Press.

Rothman, J. (1995). Approaches to community intervention. In Jack Rothman, John L. Erlich, & John E. Tropman (Eds.), *Strategies of community intervention,* 5th ed. (pp. 26–63). Itasca, IL: F. E. Peacock.

U.S. Bureau of the Census. *Statistical abstract of the United States,* (1998). Section one. Population. No. 51. Social and economic characteristics of the White and Black populations: 1990–1997, and No. 55. Social and economic characteristics of the Hispanic population: 1997. Washington, D.C.: U.S. Government Printing Office.

U.S. Department of Justice, Immigration and Naturalization Service, Office of Policy and Planning, Statistics Branch. *Annual report. Legal immigration: Fiscal year 1997*, (1999). Immigrants admitted by region and selected country of birth: Fiscal years 1994–1997, Table 2. Washington, DC: U.S. Government Printing Office.

Tropman, J. E. (1997) Community needs assessment. In *The encyclopedia of social work* (CD-Rom version). Washington, DC: National Association of Social Workers Press.

N O T E S

[1]*Latina* is the appropriate Spanish language term for a woman.

[2]For an insightful and critical discussion of empowerment, particularly with women of color, see the work of Gutierrez, L. M. (1990). Working with women of color: An empowerment perspective. *Social Work,* 35, 149–153, and Gutierrez, L. M. (1995). Understanding the empowerment process: Does consciousness make a difference? *Social Work Research, 19,* 229–237.

CHAPTER 12

CULTURALLY AND HISTORICALLY CONGRUENT CLINICAL SOCIAL WORK ASSESSMENT WITH NATIVE CLIENTS

MARIA YELLOW HORSE BRAVE HEART

Clinical social work assessment with Natives necessitates incorporation of cultural and historical perspectives. Culture informs definition of self, gender relationships, explanations of illness, symptom presentation, and response to the assessment interviewer. However, cultural assessment is complex; culture has been deleteriously impacted by a traumatic history to varying degrees among Natives. The extent of cultural reference must also be ascertained.

An emphasis on traditional Native culture is congruent with both strengths and empowerment perspectives. Indigenous concepts of strength and power are defined within the ecological framework of intimate relationships with the spirits and all of creation. This chapter will advance a Native-centric view integrating ecological, strengths, and empowerment perspectives. First, the traditional cultural context will be elaborated and advanced as a psychological milieu for manifest values, normative Native personality development, and indigenous explanations of empowerment. I continue with a description of historical trauma theory and its importance in assessment with Native clients. Next, the Diagnostic Statistical Manual (DSM IV) cultural formulation (American Psychiatric Association, 1994) will be applied to Natives. Additionally, common diagnoses and comorbidity will briefly be examined. Cultural sensitivity in the assessment proper will then be elucidated. The chapter will conclude with recommendations for assessment with Native clients.

SOCIODEMOGRAPHIC OVERVIEW OF THE LAKOTA: AN EXAMPLE OF ONE NATIVE CULTURE

Natives, also referred to as American Indians, are a diverse collective of indigenous nations. In this chapter, I describe Lakota culture, as this is the Native nation with which I am affiliated and within which I actively participate traditionally and spiritually. Native people have formed intertribal coalitions to cope with oppression and now often share common traits and experiences. An intertribal culture has emerged, particularly in urban areas. Further, many tribes hold similar beliefs despite diverse cultural manifestations.

The vast majority of the 100,441 people living in the Aberdeen Area Indian Health Service Population, including Rapid City and with the Dakota included, are Lakota/Dakota people (Aberdeen Area Population Release #34, 1999). For the Aberdeen Area Indian Health Services Unit, which includes all Lakaota reservations, the percent of people living below the poverty level is 49.6 whereas for all other races in the U.S. it is 13.1 percent (Indian Health Service, 1997). The median household income for the Aberdeen Area is $12,310, while it is $30,056 for all U.S. races (U.S. Census, 1991). Twenty six and a half percent of all males in the Aberdeen Area are unemployed, compared to 6.4 percent for all U.S. races (U.S. Census, 1991). The tuberculosis death rate for the Aberdeen Area is 6.0 compared to 0.4 for all U.S. races, and the suicide rate is 39.2 percent for the Lakota compared to 11.3 percent for all U.S. races (U.S. Census, 1991).

CULTURAL VALUES AND BEHAVIORAL NORMS OF THE LAKOTA

Traditional Cultural Perspectives: The Lakota Example

It is imperative that clinical social workers comprehend at least some of traditional Native culture. Notwithstanding the encroachment by the colonial European American mores, many Native people still embrace many indigenous values. Among the Lakota, we have seven laws (*Woope Sakowin*), including generosity, compassion, and humility. We value interdependence, respect for all of creation, and embrace principles of noninterference and tolerance. Our children are placed at the center of the Nation. Every decision we make is with the next seven generations in mind.

The Lakota collective ego ideal (Brave Heart, 1998) is an interdependent and generous person who places the good of the Nation before oneself, can manifest bravery and endure suffering for the good of others, embraces the sacredness of women and children, communicates with the spirit world, and has compassion for the animal world. Qualities include deliberation, humility, silence and observance, politeness, deference, respectful listening to all opinions without interrupting, and reserve in front of strangers. Complementary relationships between genders exist traditionally.

While modern Lakota espouse many traditional values, many Native clients will manifest varying degrees of these values as well as assimilation of European American deportment. One must not make assumptions that a Native person with a European American behavioral style does not internally identify with and embrace traditional Native values. With the influence of European values, such as male domination, many Native women and children have lost status as sacred beings and, in some families, have become victimized through domestic violence and child abuse. Each client must be viewed as a unique individual within the broader historical and cultural context.

Lakota Traditional Grief Experience: Problem and Resolution

Indigenous mourning resolution is distinct from European American grief. Among the Lakota, a loss of a relative is experienced as a loss of part of the self, exhibited by cutting the hair (Brave Heart, 1998). Decathexis (detachment) from the lost object, a part of the mourning resolution process (Pollock, 1989), is traditionally incomplete among the Lakota, who maintain an active relationship with ancestor spirits. Indigenous bereavement is compounded by massive group trauma, impairing normative grief. The extent and quality of losses limit time for culturally syntonic mourning resolution. Further, the legacy of federal prohibition of the practice of traditional Native spirituality mitigated bereavement in the natural communal milieu, resulting in unresolved grief across generations, manifested in various symptoms such as depression and self-destructive behavior (Brave Heart, 1998). The manifestation of generational trauma and unresolved grief is often diagnosed as unadulterated depression, post-traumatic stress disorder (PTSD), other anxiety disorders, and dependent personality disorders. Without incorporation of historical perspectives in assessing Native clients, treatment will not address the root causation and symptoms will most likely remain tenacious and chronic.

ASSESSING NATIVE CLIENTS USING EMPOWERMENT AND HISTORICAL TRAUMA THEORY

Traditional Lakota Concepts and Empowerment

In Lakota culture, all life dimensions are included in empowering an individual to function as an integral part of creation. Gaining or developing power, one definition of *empowerment* (Cox & Parsons, 1994), is viewed by the Lakota as securing help from the spiritual and natural world for a higher purpose than the individual self—to benefit the *Oyate* (Lakota Nation). The sense of self is developed in relation to the *Oyate*, the natural world, and all of creation. Empowerment practice facilitates influencing institutions affecting one's life (see Cox & Parsons,

1994). Historically, the Lakota invoked supernatural help to influence the natural world and life events. With such cataclysmic events as the 1890 Wounded Knee Massacre (see *Lakota Times,* 1990; McGregor, 1940/1987), genocide altered this capacity to affect life and the government-regulated environment. A return to traditional empowerment promises restoration of a sense of self and a healthy sphere of influence. Collective goals—a cornerstone of empowerment practice—can be fostered, based on the natural collectivity inherent in Lakota culture. Traditional Lakota culture can offer a model for egalitarian gender roles and relationships and provide protective factors against domestic violence and child abuse.

Historical Trauma Theory and Assessment with the Lakota

A *historical trauma response,* identified among the Lakota, is a constellation of features associated with massive cumulative group trauma across generations and within the current lifespan (Brave Heart, 1998, 1999a). This response is analogous to traits identified for Jewish Holocaust descendants (Danieli, 1998; Kestenberg, 1990). The historical trauma response includes characteristics such as anxiety, depression, self-destructive behavior, substance abuse, poor affect tolerance, survivor guilt, intrusive trauma imagery, identification with ancestral pain, fixation to trauma, somatic symptoms, and elevated mortality rates (Brave Heart, 1998, 1999a).

Historical trauma, the emotional and psychological injury intergenerationally, is the result of the genocide of Natives (see Legters, 1988; Stannard, 1992; Thornton, 1987) and ongoing oppression. The attending *historical unresolved grief* is the impaired mourning that emanates from generational trauma (Brave Heart, 1998). Historical trauma theory evolved from Lakota-centric qualitative and quantitative research, clinical experience, and observations among the Lakota (Brave Heart, 1998, 1999a, 1999b, 2000; Brave Heart-Jordan, 1995). It responded to the deficiency in PTSD nomenclature, which inadequately represents Native trauma and cultural influences on symptom presentation (Brave Heart, 1999a; Manson, Beals, O'Nell, Piasecki, Bechtold, Keane, & Jones, 1996; Robin, Chester, & Goldman, 1996). Manson and colleagues (1996) further posit that Natives have higher thresholds for clinical responses that would meet the PTSD criteria because of the pervasiveness of American Indian trauma. Congruent with these observations, historical trauma theory incorporates Native trauma across generations and in the lifespan. The concept of historical unresolved grief elucidates the character and prevalence of major and atypical depressions among Northern Plains tribes (Brave Heart, 1998, 1999a; Robin et al., 1996). Moreover, traditional manifestations of grief and the quality of indigenous mourning are incorporated in codifying historically unresolved bereavement.

One of the historically traumatic episodes in Native history is the "boarding school era" that began in 1879 (see Brave Heart & DeBruyn, 1998; Noriega, 1992; Tanner, 1982). Native children were forcibly removed under federal policy and placed in residential schools where they experienced physical and sexual abuse, incarceration, starvation, separation from family and tribal communities, sometimes for years at a time, and emotional deprivation. A large number of modern Native adults have descended from this legacy and have themselves survived their own negative boarding school experiences. What is now often deemed to be traditional behavior is frequently a trauma response feature passed across generations, i.e., stunted affect inherent in psychic numbing, expressly from boarding school abuse.

ASSESSING NATIVE CLIENTS IN PRACTICE

Utilizing the DSM IV and the Cultural Formulation

Clinical social workers employ the DSM IV (American Psychiatric Association, 1994). Common diagnoses for Natives include mood, anxiety, substance-induced, and substance abuse disorders (Duran & Yellow Horse-Davis, 1997). Shore, Manson, Bloom, Keepers, and Neligh (1987) found that chronic depression was common among a Northern Plains tribal culture area sample (which includes the Lakota). PTSD features were observed among Native samples, but the criteria were not fully met (Manson et al., 1996). Trauma response features delineated in the literature for Holocaust survivors and descendants, while not fully explicated under the PTSD criteria, fit clinical observations of the Lakota (Brave Heart, 1998, 1999b). The DSM IV cultural formulation, a beginning step in considering cultural factors, is examined here.

Cultural Identity of the Individual.   The cultural identity of the individual Native person must not be limited to "American Indian," but, rather, must incorporate the tribe/s from which the client descends or in which she or he is a member, as well as the tribal cultural reference group. For example, a person may be living among a tribe other than her or his own due to intermarriage, employment, and so on. It is important to examine the degree to which the individual identifies with the tribe of origin versus the tribe of reference. In urban areas, people often develop a pan-Indian identity that is more grounded in the tribal culture dominant in the region.

Identity involves the degree of full-blood Indian phenotype—skin color and features—as well as fluency in one's Native tongue, involvement in traditional culture, and assimilation of European American customs. Phenotype varies both between and within tribes and may be less important when combined with assessing the degree of identification and involvement in one's tribal community. It is important to understand the client's internalized self-representation and the extent to which that representation is traditional or assimilated.

Phenotype has been preliminarily examined as a contributing factor in traumatic experiences, with those more typically full-blooded at greater risk for traumatization related to oppression (Brave Heart, 1999a). In contrast, within the modern Native community, there is a resurgence of traditional identification, sometimes resulting in greater status for full-blood Indian phenotype. This can be a source of enhanced self- and group esteem, particularly when combined with traditional knowledge and language fluency. The clinical social worker should consider the extent of cultural affiliation and attend to tribe-specific versus pan-Indian identification, phenotype and internal identification, and conflicts between Christian religions and traditional spirituality. Indigenous language fluency is a complex identity issue. Unlike immigrant groups, Natives in boarding schools were often beaten for speaking Native vernacular, which consequently impaired the transfer of language across generations. Thus, lack of language fluency for Natives should not be construed as an indication of lower traditional cultural reference.

Finally, there are smaller cultural reference groups within each tribal community to which the clinical social worker should attend, such as gender, age, and sexual orientation. The idiosyncratic issues will be influenced by both traditional values and modern manifestations. For example, although sexual orientation was less stigmatized traditionally among the Lakota, stigma now exists as it does in the dominant culture.

Cultural Explanations of Illness. Indigenous interpretations of symptoms must be considered in assessment. "Bad medicine" or "being witched" may explain symptoms. Illness indicates a lack of balance and harmony with the natural world. Some tribes elaborate taboos which, if violated, can result in disease and require traditional ceremonies to restore functioning and harmony. There are extensive Native "disorders" excluded from the culture-bound syndromes glossary. Idiosyncratic explanations will also be offered when symptoms are "diagnosed" by a traditional healer.

Cultural Factors and the Psychosocial Environment. Examining the psychosocial cultural milieu requires indigenous interpretations of social stressors as well as social and spiritual supports. Among the Lakota, the extended kinship network or *tiospaye* (a collection of related families) provides extensive social support as well as obligations. A resurgence of adoption—the *Hunka* (making of relatives) ceremony binding the participants' spirits, traditionally considered more sacred than biological kinship—extends the *tiospaye*. The *tiospaye,* a potentially powerful support system, may provide alternative psychological resources if immediate kin are embroiled in dysfunctional patterns. Further, *Hunka* relatives may offer surrogate families for clients estranged from biological families. If the *tiospaye* (albeit biological or *Hunka*) embrace the *Woope Sakowin*—Seven Laws, they will participate in a reciprocal relationship within the Lakota Nation that incorporates generosity and respect. However, due to massive generational Native trauma, psychosocial problems now abound as well as an erosion of the *Woope Sakowin.* There is imbalance within the *tiospaye* system, with some members cleaving to the traditional mores while others are enmeshed in dysfunctional behavior. Consequently, many individuals are burdened with obligations and yet receive little support from the family. Psychosocial problems now include high mortality rates from alcohol-related deaths, suicide, and cardiovascular diseases (Brave Heart, 1999a; Indian Health Service, 1995) with grief reverberating throughout the large affiliated kinship network.

Socioeconomic hardships proliferate in Native communities due to high unemployment and poverty (Indian Health Service, 1995). Racism and discrimination, for both reservation and urban Indians, compound these psychosocial dilemmas. Fifty percent of Natives in the Aberdeen Area, including primarily Lakota and Dakota reservations, are living below the poverty level, compared with 13 percent for the general United States population (Indian Health Service, 1995). Interdependency and limited housing on many reservations result in multiple relatives living under one roof. On some reservations, all unmarried adult children must live with their parents.

Cultural Factors in the Clinical Relationship.   Cultural analysis requires examination of values and culturally grounded behaviors, issues of oppression and social status, language, the cultural significance of symptoms, varying cultural prescriptions for intimacy, and determining whether symptoms are pathological within the cultural context. Clinical social workers must maintain cognizance of the collective dominant cultural prototype for Natives in order to avoid its interference and potency in the assessment. The view of "the Indian" as savage and the aggregation of diverse indigenous inhabitants of the Americas into one homogenous group (Berkhoffer, 1978/1979) are racist constructs that permeate U.S. society. These constructs are embedded in the psyche of the general population and, therefore, may bias every interaction with Native clients.

Native values often conflict with European American mores. Native interdependency can be misconstrued as dependent personality characteristics rather than culturally sanctioned conduct. Traditional generosity often persists, even in dysfunctional situations such as enabling alcoholic relatives by financially supporting them. Commitment to family and community supersedes a modicum of self-care and is often placed before commitment to a non-Native employer. The consequent behavior may look like personality disordered characteristics when evaluated solely from European American paradigms.

Impairment on the Global Assessment of Functioning Scale on Axis V (American Psychiatric Association, 1994) might be impacted by the social realities. For Natives, problems in occupational, social, or educational sectors may result from cultural or sociopolitical conflicts with dominant institutions and the consequent "deficient" functioning should not be attributed to individual Native psychopathology. Impairment in mood or family relationships could erroneously be conjectured if indigenous affective reserve or interdependency is misconstrued as indicative of pathology.

In Native clients, spiritual manifestations might be misinterpreted as visual or auditory hallucinations as well as delusions, leading to misdiagnosis. Cultural informants can facilitate more accurate assessment as well as an examination of the total level of functioning of the client being assessed. Cultural informants can reveal if the person is seen in the community as spiritually gifted or pathological. The clinical social worker must examine the client's overall functioning within the cultural context, looking for patterns and confirmatory evidence from several domains in order to make an accurate assessment.

RUTH

Ruth is a thirty-two-year-old Lakota heterosexual single female who sought help with her seven-year-old niece, for whom she had been a part-time caretaker. Ruth suspected sexual abuse of the niece by the father, Ruth's brother. In the assessment interview, Ruth averted her eyes often and was reserved, but gradually made more direct eye contact and also manifested a fuller range of affect. On exploration, Ruth revealed her own symptoms of mild anxiety and depression, including some occasional insomnia. Ruth dated the onset of her symptoms to her disclosure—two months prior—about incest in her family and her own sexual abuse, at age seven, by an alcoholic stepfather. However, Ruth reported that she has always felt anxious and hypervigilant. Sexual abuse was rampant among Ruth's family. On her disclosure, which was precipitated by her wish to help her niece, the family ostracized Ruth.

Ruth's parents were boarding school survivors who had been sexually abused in the school. Ruth, a descendant of massacre survivors, divulged repetitive dreams about the atrocity. Further, Ruth recounted having infrequent visions of deceased ancestors and the massacre, both during and outside of ceremonies. Ruth's affect was appropriate. There was no evidence of a thought disorder.

The assessment indicated that Ruth had a high level of ego functioning, was drug- and alcohol-free, and had a solid work history. She manifested good object relationships and high-level defense mechanisms. Ruth was able to verbalize her feelings and had good insight and motivation for treatment. Ruth had some financial troubles because she was constantly giving money to alcoholic siblings and caretaking neglected nieces and nephews. Ruth manifested some PTSD symptomatology, including intrusive memories, anxiety, nightmares about both the abuse and the massacre, and unresolved grief, with the massacre being a core organizing psychic construct in her reality. Her anxiety was related to hypervigilance about the trauma as well as a reaction to her family who had wanted her to keep the incest a secret.

Ruth began thinking about moving to another Lakota reservation and living among her *Hunka* (traditional spiritually adopted) relatives whom she had met through recent involvement in traditional Lakota spirituality. However, Ruth felt ambivalent as she felt loyal to her biological relatives and had concerns about abandoning them. Contrary to Lakota tradition, Ruth's biological family was jealous of her *Hunka* relatives and did not support her involvement in traditional culture. Ruth felt used by her alcoholic family, who were ignorant about Lakota traditions. In addition to her loyalty to the biological family, Ruth also felt responsible to her new traditional relatives.

Possible diagnoses on Axis I included Adjustment Disorder with Mixed Anxiety and Depressed Mood as well as Anxiety Disorder Not Otherwise Specified, a way to account for the historical trauma-response features. The treatment plan included: (1) bolstering Ruth's relationship with her *Hunka* family, which would offer her emotional support, (2) reframing for Ruth that she could love and pray for her alcoholic family without remaining enmeshed with them and sacrificing herself, (3) presenting healthy alternatives to Ruth, such as caring for her nieces and nephews in the nurturing and healthy environment at the other nearby reservation with her *Hunka* relatives, and (4) supporting Ruth's commitment to traditional spirituality. Intervention around resolution of the historical trauma response, including the sexual abuse, was a longer-term therapeutic goal.

Ruth's manner of describing the presenting problem was a manifestation of Native cultural characteristics in that the focus was not on the self but on others' needs, i.e., her niece's. Ruth's avoidance of direct eye contact manifested traditional respect and her initial reserve could have been misinterpreted as an avoidant character style rather than traditional politeness. As she felt more comfortable and familiar with the Lakota clinician, she became quite candid and open. This would have taken a longer time with a non-Native interviewer. Without an understanding of traditional Lakota culture and the historical trauma response, the presence of visions could have been misinterpreted as hallucinations. The diagnosis had to be made in the context of Ruth's high level of ego functioning and good object relationships, manifested by successful employment on the reservation and a solid reputation as a well-liked and respected individual as well as her appropriate affect.

Another case example illustrates the importance of understanding traditional cultural mores and their impact on accurate assessment. Clinical outcome is influenced by proper culturally sensitive appraisal.

SARA

Sara was a six-year-old Lakota girl referred by a state social services agency for therapy and for help with determining whether she should be returned to her recovering alcoholic biological mother. The child welfare social workers felt that there was no bonding between the now sober biological mother and Sara, as they observed no expression of physical affection from the mother. The traditional Lakota reserve in front of strangers and outsiders resulted in the biological mother appearing stilted during the visitations. In a joint session with Sara and the biological mother, the Lakota clinician observed bonding manifested in overt displays of mutual affection, which the clinician was able to report, facilitating successful permanent reunification of Sara and her biological mother.

In contrast with Ruth's case, another client's visions did manifest psychotic features.

ROBERT

Robert, a twenty-seven-year-old recovering alcoholic with a history of violent behavior and poor object relationships, presented with avoidant eye contact and guardedness, and some paranoid ideation was evident. However, traditional spiritual practices seemed to help him not only to maintain sobriety, thereby limiting violent acting out, but also provided a context in which to contain his psychotic thinking and visual hallucinations. Spiritual interpretation of the content of his hallucinations brought his psychotic features into a more socially congruent context. His involvement in ceremonies also afforded him ego enhancement and a sense of mastery and competence. Due to his resistance to medication, the lack of command hallucinations (where one hears orders to kill oneself or others), the lack of danger to self or others, and the fact that he had been able to maintain sobriety for over one year with the help of ceremonies, he was not placed on psychotropic medication. The treatment plan included supporting his involvement in the spiritual traditions.

Comorbidity, Dual Diagnosis, and Common Disorders

Common diagnoses among a clinical sample of Natives include anxiety and mood disorders as well as substance-induced disorders (Duran & Yellow Horse-Davis, 1997). Dual diagnosis is common, with alcohol abuse or substance abuse disorders being the most prevalent. Dependent personality is the most common character pathology noted.

Depression and substance abuse are correlated with PTSD (Robin et al., 1996) with depression being the most common comorbid condition (Ursano, Grieger, & McCarroll, 1996). Atypical, chronic, and complicated depression is prevalent among Northern Plains Natives (Shore et al., 1987), suggesting unresolved grief and trauma response features, particularly the association with suicidal behavior (Brave Heart, 1998, 1999a). Other common diagnoses may include adjustment disorders and the V Codes, such as Spiritual Problem, Relationship Problem, and Problems Related to Abuse or Neglect (American Psychiatric Association, 1994). Because there is no diagnosis for historical trauma response, and Natives often do not meet the criteria fully for PTSD (Brave Heart, 1999a; Manson et al., 1996; Robin et al., 1996), one might consider using Anxiety Disorder Not Otherwise Specified, (NOS) because PTSD is classified under Anxiety Disorders. Further, Anxiety Disorder NOS can be used to indicate a disorder that is mixed with a mood disorder where the criteria for either is not fully met. Information about the historical trauma response could be included in the cultural formulation part of the assessment.

A psychodynamic formulation that could be incorporated into an assessment would include examination of common defense mechanisms, the level of emotional development, including the psychosocial stages of development, and levels of ego functioning. However, from a Native perspective, these theories may not be universal, applicable, and culturally congruent, despite Erikson's (1963) attempts to apply them to the Lakota within his Eurocentric framework. What is useful, nevertheless, is his concept of a collective ego ideal and his alluding to collective historical trauma (Erikson, 1959).

Because of indirect communication styles, the defense mechanisms of passive-aggressiveness and reaction formation may be observed. Defenses germane to trauma response features and grief, such as idealization of the past, as well as searching and pining behavior, should be noted. Obsessive-compulsiveness among more European-American acculturated Natives has been reported (Erikson, 1963). Sublimation can be observed among many Natives and is a healthy defense mechanism. Participation in traditional activities can sublimate longing for the past and facilitate grief resolution. Ability to delay gratification and impulse control—healthy ego functions—are evident in traditional Lakota ceremonies that require physical hardship, deprivation, sacrifice, commitment, such as fasting and endurance for a higher purpose, and transcendence. Altruism is another high-level defense observable in traditional Lakota values. Traditional culture and spirituality can facilitate healthy ego functioning and mastery of trauma as well as therapeutic intervention for PTSD (Silver & Wilson, 1988).

Cultural Sensitivity to Time and Nonverbal Communication

For Native clients, the initial assessment may take longer than it does with European American clients. Indirect styles of communication, values of noninterference and nonintrusiveness, polite reserve, and reticence about seeking help from European American institutions all foster hesitance in asking for help and revealing the presenting problem. It is not uncommon for Native clients to take several sessions to disclose emotionally laden material, thereby resulting in a protracted assessment. The style of verbalizing often involves recounting events or stories in a circular fashion rather than getting directly to the point. Non-Native clinicians may interpret this as tangential and circumstantial thinking or loosening associations, avoidance, or treatment resistance rather than a normative cultural style, which requires patience on the part of the interviewer. Allowing sufficient time for silence, even during the initial assessment is important, as many Natives are reflective and deliberate before speaking. In group settings, Native people may remain rather quiet and will often not repeat something that has already been said. This could be misinterpreted as passivity or resistance. Silence and humility can also be misidentified as ignorance. In reality, the innate intellectual capacity of the Lakota has been documented as well as the impact of trauma on decline in cognitive functioning (Erikson, 1963; Krystal, 1984; Macgregor, 1946/1975; Sack, Beiser, Clarke, & Redshirt, 1987). Lakota traditions include sophisticated abstract thought and conceptualizations as well as wisdom about the natural world. However, traditional humility may result in these intellectual gifts remaining hidden from non-Native interviewers.

In addition to variation in eye contact, cultural differences may exist in personal space and cross-gender interaction. Among some tribes, nonrelatives of the opposite sex may be kept at a comfortable emotional, physical, and psychological distance. For example, among the Lakota, an older traditional male will not speak directly to his mother-in-law but, rather, will address her through his wife and will avoid eye contact as a sign of respect. If there is an occasion to observe this in a family assessment interview, non-Natives might find the behavior peculiar and use this observation as evidence for a disengaged family system or attribute psychopathology to the male, his mother-in-law, or the wife.

Developing Rapport with the Native Client

One of the challenges in assessment with Native clients is developing rapport if the clinical social worker is from a different cultural background. In part, Native social workers from a different tribal community, unless viewed as traditional allies, may face some obstacles. Within intertribal communities, such as in a large urban area, traditional enemies may be assigned to work together. Even on some reservations, traditional enemies have been relocated to the same community by the government. When possible, these historical relationships should be considered in assigning cases. Varying degrees of acculturation or investment in traditional culture also create barriers. For instance, if there is a staunch Christian clinician who views traditional Native spirituality as superstition or even paganism, and she or he is assigned a traditionally oriented client, there is potential for cultural conflict and misdiagnosis. Intragroup prejudice can exist based on skin color and degree of traditional orientation. Social work values of acceptance of and respect for the client must be emphasized. However, despite these potential obstacles, there is the promise of some positive relationship formation because of the common racial bond between a Native social worker and Native client.

With non-Native clinicians, particularly European Americans, there is a greater impediment because of the negative historical legacy of genocide and persistent oppression of Natives. Trust issues are more magnified and, subsequently, the assessment process may take longer. There will be greater distance between the client and the worker, with more reserve and reticence on the part of many Native clients. Various Native clients may be hesitant to share information about traditional spiritual practices or phenomena and will most likely feel protective about this content. Therefore, there will often be incomplete and guarded disclosure of symptoms, problems, and family history. The dominant European-American style of direct communication is often experienced by the Native client as intrusive and rude. The clinician will have to listen closely for disguised requests from Natives with a more traditional indirect style. An example might be a client with a transportation problem who, rather than asking for a ride or a bus token, will simply quietly mention that their car does not work. This is intended to give the other person an opportunity to offer help without feeling pressure if asked directly. Also, rather than directly disagreeing with something, a client might be silent so as not to offend the clinician.

Disguised communication in stories, the use of metaphors, and talking in the displacement are common with Native clients. Native clients often respond indirectly to questions. An inappropriate or ill-timed question from the clinician will not be answered directly but, because politeness requires some response, the subject is changed or a story is told. However, the interviewer must listen closely as the response may initially appear irrelevant but may, in fact, be an answer to the question through the use of a metaphor in a story or recounting a personal experience or one that another individual has had. Indirect responses to a question may also involve talking in the displacement, that is, sharing something about another person—a neighbor or relative—that really represents the self.

CONCLUSION

This chapter underscored the incorporation of traditional cultural and historical perspectives in working with Natives in a clinical social work milieu. The diversity among Native clients was emphasized, while one specific tribal group was discussed, illustrating Native cultural complexity. Traditional Lakota empowerment was presented. The utilization of the DSM IV cultural formulation was applied to assessment with Native clients. Particular attention was paid to cultural and historical factors that impact accurate assessment of Native clients. Case examples were presented to demonstrate the complexity of an accurate, culturally congruent assessment. Comorbidity, dual diagnosis, and common disorders among Native clients were noted as well as cultural sensitivity in the assessment interview.

Culturally congruent and accurate assessment with Native clients may be protracted. The clinical social worker must often advocate with the broader mental health system to permit more time and sensitivity in assessment with Native clients. The historical legacy of genocide cannot be ignored and must be incorporated for successful appraisal of a Native client's clinical issues and appropriate development of a treatment plan that will empower the Native client.

REFERENCES

Aberdeen Area Population Release #34: Indian Health Service (Census) Population Estimates for Fiscal Years 1998–2007, February 1999.

American Psychiatric Association. (1994). *Diagnostic and statistical manual of mental disorders,* 4th ed. Washington, DC: Author.

Berkhofer, R. F., Jr. (1979). *The White man's Indian: Images of the American Indian from Columbus to the present.* New York: Vintage. (Original work published 1978.)

Brave Heart, M. Y. H. (1998). The return to the sacred path: Healing the historical trauma and historical unresolved grief response among the Lakota. *Smith College Studies in Social Work, 68* (3), pp. 287–305.

Brave Heart, M. Y. H. (1999a). *Oyate Ptayela:* Rebuilding the Lakota Nation through addressing historical trauma among Lakota parents. *Journal of Human Behavior in the Social Environment, 2* (1/2), pp. 109–126; and in Weaver, H. N. (Ed.), *Voices of First Nations People: Human services considerations* (pp. 109–126). New York: Haworth.

Brave Heart, M. Y. H. (1999b). Gender differences in the historical trauma response among the Lakota. *Journal of Health and Social Policy, 10* (4), pp. 1–21.

Brave Heart, M. Y. H. (2000). *Wakiksuyapi:* Carrying the historical trauma of the Lakota. *Tulane Studies in Social Welfare, 21–22,* 245–266.

Brave Heart, M. Y. H. & DeBruyn, L. M. (1998). The American Indian Holocaust: Healing historical unresolved grief. *American Indian and Alaska Native Mental Health Research, 8* (2), pp. 56–78.

Brave Heart-Jordan, M. Y. H. (1995). The return to the sacred path: Healing from historical trauma and historical unresolved grief among the Lakota. (Doctoral dissertation, Smith College School for Social Work, 1995). (Copyright by Author: reprints available through the Takini Network, P.O. Box 4138, Rapid City, SD 57709-4138)

BraveHeart-Jordan, M. & DeBruyn, L. M. (1995). So she may walk in balance: Integrating the impact of historical trauma in the treatment of Native American Indian women. In J.

Adleman & G. Enguidanos (Eds.), *Racism in the lives of women: Testimony, theory, and guides to anti-racist practice* (pp. 345–368). New York: Haworth.

Cox, E. O. & Parsons, R. J. (1994). *Empowerment-oriented social work practice with the elderly.* Belmont, CA: Brooks-Cole.

Danieli, Y. (Ed.). (1998). *International handbook of multigenerational legacies of trauma.* New York: Plenum.

Duran, E. & Yellow Horse-Davis, S. (1997). *Final Research Evaluation: Evaluation of Family and Child Guidance Clinic Hybrid Treatment Model;* Report to Indian Health Service.

Erikson, E. H. (1959). Identity and the life cycle [Monograph]. *Psychological Issues, 1* (1). New York: G. P. Putnam.

Erikson, E. H. (1963). *Childhood and Society* (Rev. ed.). New York: W. W. Norton.

Indian Health Service. (1995). *Regional differences in Indian health.* Washington, DC: U.S. Department of Health and Human Services.

Indian Health Service (1997). *Regional Differences in Indian Health.* Washington, D.C. U.S. Department of Health and Human Services.

Kestenberg, J. S. (1990). Survivor parents and their children. In M. S. Bergmann & M. E. Jucovy (Eds.), *Generations of the Holocaust* (pp. 83–102). New York: Columbia University Press. (Original work published 1982.)

Krystal, H. (1984). Integration and self-healing in posttraumatic states. In S. A. Luel & P. Marcus (Eds.), *Psychoanalytic reflections on the Holocaust: Selected essays* (pp. 113–134). New York: Holocaust Awareness Institute, Center for Judaic Studies, University of Denver (Colorado) and Ktav Publishing House.

Lakota Times (1990, December). Wounded Knee remembered. *Lakota Special Edition.*

Legters, L. H. (1988). The American genocide. *Policy Studies Journal, 16* (4), 768–777.

Macgregor, G. (1975). *Warriors without weapons: A study of the society and personality development of the Pine Ridge Sioux.* Chicago: University of Chicago Press. (Original work published 1946.)

McGregor, J. (1987). *The Wounded Knee Massacre: From the viewpoint of the Sioux.* Rapid City, SD: Fenske Printing. (Original work published 1940.)

Manson, S., Beals, J., O'Nell, T., Piasecki, J., Bechtold, D., Keane, E., & Jones, M. (1996). Wounded spirits, ailing hearts: PTSD and related disorders among American Indians. In A. J. Marsella, M. J. Friedman, E. T. Gerrity, & R. M. Scurfield (Eds.), *Ethnocultural aspects of Posttraumatic Stress Disorder* (pp. 255–283). Washington DC: American Psychological Association.

Noriega, J. (1992). American Indian education in the United States: Indoctrination for subordination to colonialism. In M. A. Jaimes (Ed.), *The state of Native America: Genocide, colonization, and resistance* (pp. 371–402). Boston: South End Press.

Pollock, G. H. (Ed.). (1989). *The mourning–liberation process, Vol. I.* Madison, CT: International Universities Press.

Robin, R. W., Chester, B., & Goldman, D. (1996). Cumulative trauma and PTSD in American Indian communities. In A. J. Marsella, M. J. Friedman, E. T. Gerrity & R. M. Scurfield (Eds.), *Ethnocultural aspects of Posttraumatic Stress Disorder* (pp. 239–253). Washington DC: American Psychological Association.

Sack, W. H., Beiser, M., Clarke, G., & Redshirt, R. (1987). The high achieving Sioux Indian child: Some preliminary findings from the Flower of Two Soils Project. *American Indian and Alaska Native Mental Health Research, 1* (1), 37–51.

Shore, J. H., Manson S. M., Bloom, J. D., Keepers, G., & Neligh, G. (1987). A pilot study of depression among American Indian patients with research diagnostic criteria. *American Indian and Alaska Native Mental Health Research, 1* (2), 4–15.

Silver, S. M. & Wilson, J. P. (1988). Native American healing and purification rituals for war stress. In John P. Wilson, Zev Harele, & Boaz Hahana (Eds.), *Human adaptation to extreme stress: From the Holocaust to Viet Nam* (pp. 337–355). New York: Plenum.

Stannard, D. (1992). *American Holocaust: Columbus and the conquest of the new world.* New York: Oxford University Press.

Tanner, H. (1982). *A history of all the dealings of the United States government with the Sioux.* Unpublished manuscript. Prepared for the Black Hills Land Claim by order of the United States

Supreme Court, on file at the D'Arcy McNickle Center for the History of the American Indian, Newberry Library, Chicago.

Thornton, R. (1987). *American Indian Holocaust and survival: A population history since 1492.* Norman, OK: University of Oklahoma Press.

U.S. Bureau of the Census. (1991). 1990 Census of the general population characteristics, United States. 1990 CP-1-1. Washington, D.C. Population Division. U.S. Bureau of the Census.

Ursano, R. J., Grieger, T. A., & McCarroll, J. E. (1996). Prevention of posttraumatic stress: Consultation, training, and early treatment. In B. A. van der Kolk, A. C. McFarlane, & L. Weisaeth (Eds.), *Traumatic stress: The effects of overwhelming experience on mind, body, and society* (pp. 441–462). New York: Guilford.

CHAPTER 13

ORGANIZATION AND COMMUNITY ASSESSMENT WITH FIRST NATIONS PEOPLE

HILARY N. WEAVER

This chapter has the challenging task of addressing issues relevant to assessment in First Nations communities and organizations. The terms *First Nations* and *Native American* refer to over 500 nations of indigenous people. These diverse groups have never shared a common language, religion, political structure, social structure, or culture (Weaver, 1998). This chapter will provide basic information on First Nations communities and organizations. However, in order to engage in culturally competent and effective work, it is imperative that social workers become familiar with the specific Native context in which they work.

In this chapter I present a sociodemographic overview and discuss cultural values and behavioral norms of First Nations people. Additional information on Native Americans is presented that focuses on an ecological or person-in-environment model, the strengths perspective, and the empowerment perspective, with an emphasis on assessing First Nations organizations and communities. Practice principles and skills are discussed and illustrated with a case example of a Native social service agency trying to improve services in a First Nations community.

SOCIODEMOGRAPHIC OVERVIEW

There were just under 2 million Native Americans in the United States in 1990 (U.S. Bureau of the Census, 1993). This is likely to be an undercount because some First Nations people do not consider themselves "Americans" and are resistant to being counted by a foreign government (Native American Leadership Commission on Health and AIDS, 1994; Weaver, 1998). Four Native nations have populations of over 100,000: the Cherokee of Oklahoma and the Southeast, the Navajo of the Southwest, the Anishnabeg (also known as Chippewa or Ojibwa) of the Midwest, and the Lakota/Dakota of the Northern Great Plains. Although these nations have land bases in the regions indicated, members of the nations can be found in various regions.

First Nations people are unique among groups in the United States in that our indigenous status reserves for us specific legal rights. Unlike other groups, we continue to exist as sovereign nations. Social workers must become familiar with the structure of the Native community where they work. This awareness may include an understanding of the type of government (e.g., a traditional system run by Chiefs, an elected government consisting of a Tribal President and Council). In other words, who has the authority to govern and authorize social projects? Although urban Native organizations and communities may not be bound by the same laws and policies as their reservation counterparts, they are often influenced by these structures. First Nations people in urban areas often maintain close ties to reservations and frequent movement between urban and reservation areas is common. Because of the strong sense of group membership, First Nations people in urban areas can often be considered a separate community even in neighborhoods that include people from other cultural groups.

Over two-thirds of Native Americans currently reside in urban areas (U.S. Bureau of the Census, 1993). In part, this is due to a U.S. policy in the 1950s that took First Nations people from reservations to urban areas in the hopes of increased employment opportunities (Bearskin & Spade, 1991). In urban areas, First Nations people from various nations often interact and intermarry, leading to a sense of pan-Indianness or a hybrid of First Nations cultures. In response to the needs of urban Native Americans, many Native communities developed their own social service and cultural organizations in the 1970s.

CULTURAL VALUES

The reader should approach this and any other general discussion of Native values with caution. By necessity, an overview chapter such as this one provides general information in order to meet the needs of readers who come from different regions and encounter different groups of First Nations people. Social workers must build on this foundation with information specific to the First Nations groups with which they work. The following discussion is meant to provide a general foundation of cultural information without minimizing the importance of diversity among and within Native communities.

Attachment to culture varies among and within First Nations communities. Some people hold tightly to their culture, beliefs, and language. These people are often termed "traditional." Others take on cultural characteristics of the dominant society and are considered more modern or "progressive." Some people are somewhere in-between or are traditional in some respects and progressive in others. Often U.S. policies forced assimilation of First Nations people, so many aspects of culture were taken away rather than given up willingly. For the century beginning after the Civil War, it was U.S. policy to take First Nations children from their homes and communities and send them to boarding schools, usually long distances from their homes, where they were socialized into the dominant society and taught to be farmers and servants (Hultgren & Molin, 1989). Children were beaten for speaking their languages or practicing any aspects of their cultures and religions (Brave Heart-Jordan & DeBruyn, 1995; Weaver & Yellow Horse Brave Heart, 1999). Despite this legacy of cultural loss and violence, Native cultures have not been eradicated.

Although First Nations people are culturally diverse, there are some important commonalities across Native nations. One such commonality is the importance of community. The emphasis on community and the well-being of the group is central. First Nations people often think of themselves primarily as members of groups (e.g., clans, communities, nations) rather than as individuals. This conceptualization is different from members of the dominant white society who tend to be more individualistic.

Most First Nations people have a sense of existing in a time continuum with both ancestors and children of the future having relevance for everyday life. This concept is often thought of in terms of seven generations. Our ancestors planned for the well-being of people who exist today and those of us who are alive now have a responsibility to insure the well-being of Native people and communities of the future. The concept of seven generations is commonly used in prevention programs targeting people at-risk (e.g., pregnant women who are drinking, teens who participate in unprotected sex) to emphasize the responsibility that we have to take care of ourselves today for the well-being of future generations (Moran, 1999).

Social workers must be aware of the long history of inappropriate actions by the U.S. government and its employees (including social workers) toward First Nations people. This history includes genocide, forced assimilation (cultural genocide), paternalism, and the deliberate creation of dependency through factors such as destruction of food supplies (Robbins, 1992). Many Native children have been taken away from their families and communities (Barsh, 1996; Mannes, 1995; U.S. Senate Select Committee on Indian Affairs, 1977, 1988; Weaver & White, 1999). For many First Nations people, as well as others, the image of a social worker that comes to mind is that of a child-snatcher. Additionally, the Indian Health Service, the largest employer of social workers in Native communities, while providing needed health care, is also associated with the involuntary sterilization of 42 percent of First Nations women of childbearing age in the 1960s and 1970s (Jaimes & Halsey, 1992). It should come as no surprise that many First Nations people are suspicious and distrustful of social workers and others associated with helping systems. Social workers must build trust with Native people before any work can be accomplished.

Respect and responsibility are key values in First Nations cultures. Every individual in the community is deserving of respect and, in turn, has responsibilities that must be fulfilled. The fact that community responsibilities tend to increase as people become adults has been credited when First Nations people, particularly men in their 30s and 40s, spontaneously stop heavy alcohol use without outside interventions or social programs (Leung, Kinzie, Boehnlein, & Shore, 1993; Maracle, 1993).

Community roles are often based on age. Elders are revered as wisdom keepers of the community. They have integral roles as teachers and provide moral guidance. Elders often have primary responsibilities during spiritual and ceremonial events and play significant roles in childrearing. They are typically treated with deference and their opinions valued. The current generation's responsibility to the coming generations begins with today's children. If not for them, there will be no future, no cultural continuity, and we will cease to exist as distinct communities.

In many First Nations cultures, women play important roles (Allen, 1986; Jaimes & Halsey, 1992; Kuhlmann, 1992). Some cultures, like the Seneca, are matrilineal and trace descent only through the mother. This has important implications for who can claim citizenship in a Native nation and have voting and land ownership rights. In some Native nations with traditional governments Chiefs function under the guidance of Clan Mothers. For example, among the Haudenosaunee (Iroquois confederacy), each clan (a large extended family system) receives guidance from a Clan Mother (an elderly woman who has responsibility for the well-being of members of the clan). Although not matrilineal, other cultures, such as the Lakota, hold women to be sacred. Women are closer to the Creator than men because we shed blood (menstrual cycle) and give life (birth).

An understanding of nonverbal behaviors is critical to effective work with First Nations communities and organizations. Nonverbal behavior is culturally determined and can often be misconstrued by people unfamiliar with the culture. While many forms of nonverbal communication are important, three significant ones are eye contact, handshakes, and use of silence. As with other cultural characteristics, this discussion of nonverbal behavior is a generalization that applies to many, but not all, First Nations people.

Many Native people will focus their eyes away from a speaker as a sign of respect. This is often misinterpreted by non-Natives as not listening or disrespect. Sometimes, children who do not make eye contact are assumed to be less intellectually capable than other children and are placed in remedial programs.

Likewise, a usual handshake with someone in the dominant society varies considerably from that typical among First Nations people. It is very common for First Nations people to offer a hand lightly as a greeting. The hand is offered gently and taken gently. Non-Natives may interpret this as a weak handshake, and possibly a gesture of insincerity, while Native people may interpret a strong handshake as being a sign of trying to dominate the interaction.

Silence is also commonly misunderstood. Social workers and other helping professionals often find silence to be anxiety-provoking and rush to fill it out of their own discomfort. First Nations people often take time to reflect before responding as a sign of respect to the speaker. Additionally, English is not the first language of some First Nations people who may translate the English they hear into their own language, formulate a reply, then translate the reply back into English before speaking.

Another commonly misunderstood value is noninterference. This value was clearly articulated in a classic article by social worker Jimm Good Tracks (1973). Out of respect for the choices and preferences of others, many First Nations people tend to be nondirective and use indirect communication. Generally, conversations are not interrupted and people are not asked to do favors, for this would be interference. Instead, people are likely to wait to be recognized before speaking and to communicate indirectly rather than making a request. In some instances, social workers have assumed that parents who value noninterference do not care about their children and this has led to charges of neglect. Rather than directly forbidding children to do something, some Native parents prefer to let children learn from their mistakes or offer guidance in forms such as storytelling. "There once was a little boy who liked to play too close to the hot stove . . . "

Another important value in many Native communities is generosity. Unlike the dominant society, where accumulation of possessions and wealth is considered a measure of success, for many First Nations people giving possessions away brings status. Some Native cultures have ceremonies such as a Potlatch or Give Away where possessions are given away to celebrate and honor someone, perhaps for receiving a name or graduating from college. This type of ceremony, particularly common among Native people of the Northwest, reinforces reciprocal obligations throughout the community. Native people are likely to share whatever we have with community members in need. Frequently, a social worker will identify a family without enough food or adequate winter clothing, mobilize resources to provide for them, and check back the next day only to find that, rather than using the resources within the household, the family distributed them to various relatives and community members who are also in need. This scenario often causes frustration for the social worker, who made an assumption that resources should be used within the nuclear family and may feel that his or her efforts were not appreciated.

The extended family is the norm in First Nations communities (Weaver & White, 1997). In Native communities that value the extended family and interdependence, the help and wisdom of in-laws are often appreciated and actively sought for activities like childrearing. It is not uncommon for adult children to live near parents, aunts, uncles, and other family members in an interdependent and supportive network. Pathological labels, such as *enmeshment* and *co-dependence,* are not relevant and are based on dominant society values of independence rather than Native values of interdependence.

While the values and behavioral norms discussed above apply to individual First Nations people, they are also relevant concepts when working with Native communities and organizations. The well-being of the community is often a primary value for all members.

SOCIAL ISSUES IN FIRST NATIONS COMMUNITIES AND ORGANIZATIONS

The challenges that face First Nations communities are legion. First Nations people are the poorest ethnic group in the United States and, in some reservation communities, there are still many households with no running water or electricity (U.S. Bureau of the Census, 1993). First Nations people suffer disproportionately with health problems such as diabetes and chronic otitis media (Parker, 1994; Weaver, 1999a; Wuest, 1991). The rate of HIV infection is increasing more quickly among First Nations people than any other group in the United States (Conway et al., 1992; Metler, Conway, & Stehr-Green, 1991). Alcohol and substance abuse have a major impact on some Native communities (Beauvais, 1992; Committee on Interior & Insular Affairs, 1992; Maracle, 1993; Moncher, Holden, & Trimble, 1990). Native suicide rates exceed the national norm (Angell, Kurz, & Gottfried, 1997), and violent crimes, including domestic violence, rape, and homicide, are problems on some reservations and in urban First Nations communities (Bachman, 1992).

It is far too easy to look at these statistics and assume that Native communities are mired in problems. While these problems should not be ignored or minimized, they must be assessed within the context in which they occur. Two other points are critical: (1) strengths exist in Native communities that have enabled them to survive in spite of many social problems, and (2) the problems cited above, while concerns in their own right, may also be symptoms of problems with deeper roots.

We need to begin by having First Nations people define the problems in our own communities. Too often, others have looked in from the outside and have made determinations about needs and problems. For example, many non-Natives have identified substance abuse as the primary problem in Native communities. While this is, indeed, a problem in some Native communities, it is not a problem in all communities, and rates of drinking vary from nation to nation (Beauvais & Trimble, 1992; Fleming, 1992; Young, 1992).

The roots of many social problems in First Nations communities can be traced to ongoing colonization. Although, initially, the British colonies and their successor, the United States, dealt with Native Nations as sovereign entities, throughout the centuries the United States gradually whittled away at this parity. Various laws and policies have attempted to destroy cultures, spirituality, languages, and communities through forced vocational education and forced conversion to Christianity in government and denominational boarding schools. Inherent sovereignty and treaty rights have been eroded through imposition of federal and state jurisdiction. The United States deliberately created dependency and, beginning with the Dawes Act in 1887, legally deemed full-blooded Native Americans (those without mixed ethnic heritage) to be incompetent to handle their own affairs (Robbins, 1992). Paternalistic helping bureaucracies infantalized First Nations people and deliberately undermined efforts at self-sufficiency. Is it any wonder that a myriad of social problems exist in our communities?

Native Nations face many challenges to their sovereignty and continued existence. In the 1950s the federal government instituted a termination policy that revoked all legal rights of and federal responsibilities toward certain Native Nations. Although termination is no longer a federal policy, other encroachments threaten sovereignty. In 1971 the Alaska Native Claims Settlement Act took away the indigenous status, nationhood, and sovereignty of the Native communities in Alaska and reorganized them into corporations with assets subject to devaluation and loss (Churchill & Morris, 1992; Robbins, 1992).

Today, many Native nations, faced with poverty and unemployment, opt to initiate casino gambling as a form of economic development. While, on the surface, this may appear lucrative for our communities, often, in order to set up a casino, a nation must sign a compact with a state, thus opening the door to state regulation and a further erosion of sovereignty.

One of the most destructive and least discussed problems in First Nations communities is the internalized oppression that results from colonization. We argue among ourselves about who is "Indian enough" based on skin color, language, blood quantity, politics, religion, place of residence, and a host of other factors. The boarding schools taught us that holding on to our cultures, languages, and religions was a "bad thing." Traditional people accused of wanting to "go back to the blanket" are seen as having an unrealistic hope of retreating from modern life. Those who value tradition sometimes see those who pursue education or seek success by dominant society standards as sellouts.

Day-to-day life is filled with negative messages and images of First Nations people. Aside from blatant stereotypical images of sports mascots, more insidious messages abound. It is common to hear phrases like "low man on the totem pole" and "the Natives are getting restless," yet few would stop to consider how these phrases reflect on First Nations people. Recently, a well-known social work professor was describing some activities in his program that the administration found inappropriate. As he phrased it, the administration felt they had "wandered off the reservation." What does such a phrase say about First Nations people? The speaker was completely oblivious to the impact of his words.

First Nations people often internalize these negative images and Native children often get mixed messages about what it means to be a First Nations person. Even in households that are strong in their culture, children are confronted with stereotypical television images of bloodthirsty heathens and noble savages. The future of our communities is threatened if our youth lose their culture and pride in being Native. Additionally, there are many First Nations people who believe we are predisposed to severe alcohol problems in spite of the fact that there is little if any empirical support for this belief (Maracle, 1993; May & Smith, 1988). Regardless of the truth, this is what we have been told about ourselves, and many of us believe it.

Anger often accompanies internalized oppression and we tend to fight among ourselves. Racist comments about "breeds" or "halfbreeds" are not uncommon. Questions regarding the legitimate leaders of Native communities have led to bombings and killings. As one First Nations man put it, "We keep shooting ourselves in the foot and we don't have much of a foot left."

Many social problems in our communities have roots in colonization, oppression, and internalized oppression. Until we are willing to look at these larger issues, we will only be putting bandages on festering wounds. This is not to say that it is not important to address problems such as poverty, violence, and substance abuse, but, in order to work on these issues, we must address their fundamental causes.

ASSESSING FIRST NATIONS ORGANIZATIONS AND COMMUNITIES

Ecological and Person-in-Environment Approaches

Mitakuye oyasin. This common Lakota phrase translates as "we are all related." An ecological perspective or person-in-environment framework is compatible with Native cultures that view all things in creation as related. People do not exist independently of other things, so it is natural for social workers to view clients within a context that includes a variety of people and systems. In order to do a complete assessment of a First Nations organization or community, it is important to examine the full context.

Although social work assessments usually focus on the social environment, it is also important to look at the land as an important factor. Many First Nations people have a strong attachment to place and even urban dwellers may frequently return to reservations where they have family and cultural connections. In many Native spiritual traditions, people are required to fulfill ceremonial obligations at specific places that may or may not be located on land still possessed by Native communities. Being away from and unable to access sacred geography can have an adverse impact on psychological well-being (Griffin-Pierce, 1997). First Nations people who attend college or seek employment outside their communities may experience a profound sense of isolation that goes far beyond homesickness (Lowery, 1997).

Many Native communities have been displaced from their traditional locations as European Americans sought their "Manifest Destiny" through a westward expansion across the continent. Dislocation and loss of environment have continued to be a threat in contemporary times. In spite of a 1794 treaty that guaranteed the United States would never claim Seneca land (the oldest treaty between the United States and a Native nation), the Army Corps of Engineers took over 10,000 acres of Allegheny reservation in New York State and flooded it as part of the Kinzua Dam project. In spite of a formal protest to President Kennedy in 1961 and a case that was appealed to the Supreme Court, the Seneca of Allegheny were left with only 2,300 acres on which to live (Clinton, Newton, & Price, 1991; Josephy, 1982). Likewise, in the 1980s and 1990s traditional Navajo people were ordered by the federal government to leave their homelands at Big Mountain on the Navajo reservation within the state of Arizona, supposedly as a peacekeeping effort between Navajo and Hopi communities. However, many observers believe this forced removal was due to the vast mineral wealth in the area (Churchill, 1993, 1994). Social workers must be cognizant of the significance of dislocation from environment for many First Nations people.

Unfortunately, First Nations communities are exposed to many instances of environmental racism. Toxic waste and environmental pollutants are common around many reservations. For example, when the Kerr-McGee corporation closed its Shiprock mining site on the Navajo reservation in the state of Arizona in 1980, the company left seventy-one acres of raw uranium tailings just sixty feet from the

San Juan river, the only significant source of surface water in the area (Churchill & LaDuke, 1992). Although many environmental problems exist, the extent and nature of these problems is often unknown or only partially known. Assessing the environment of First Nations organizations or communities can involve investigating these important issues.

At one time, all the land on the continent was in Native hands. Now only approximately 2.5 percent remains (Churchill & LaDuke, 1992). While some land was ceded legally (even though often under duress), other lands were seized illegally according to U.S. laws (Churchill, 1992). Many Native communities have pending land claims for return of lands taken illegally. While successful land claims may or may not result in the return of the land in question (cash settlements or returning other land are likely outcomes), this raises an important question about defining the relevant environment for First Nations communities.

Strengths Perspective

The many strengths that exist in First Nations communities are often overlooked by well-meaning outsiders who see only social problems and cultural loss. While the extent of cultural tradition that remains varies across Native nations as well as within those nations, much still exists of these cultures once targeted for annihilation. Cultures are not and have never been static; they change and grow over time. Although cultures change, their essential elements remain intact. Social workers must include the strengths of Native organizations and communities as a routine part of their assessments. Important strengths for social workers to consider include a group orientation, cultural continuity, wisdom of elders, and sovereignty.

The emphasis on the well-being of the group and community is clearly a strength in First Nations cultures. In a community where a family may be in need of food, clothing, or money for medical expenses, it is likely that other community members will come to their assistance without hesitation. The strong sense of interdependence leads to a strong support network.

Cultural continuity and traditions are also important strengths. People grounded in their cultures have a resilience that can help prevent or speed recovery from problems such as substance abuse (Oetting & Beauvais, 1991). Likewise, cultural traditions can provide a strong foundation for organizations and communities. Our cultures give us guidelines for living that have served us well for thousands of years.

One of the most important strengths that continues to exist in First Nations communities is the wisdom and guidance available from elders. From elders comes intergenerational transmission of cultural knowledge. While many Native adults went to boarding schools and may have lost pieces of their traditions, they still have much wisdom to offer. Elders teach and guide other community members. They have critical roles to play, such as raising children and teaching language, traditions, ceremonies, and cultural protocols. A social worker needs to consult with elders, and particularly Clan Mothers, when setting up a program in a First Nations community with a clan system. Their input is critical and they often act as gatekeepers.

Sovereignty is also a major strength. This formalized self-determination allows reservations to maintain their own governments, social welfare systems, laws, and so on. While reservations are bound by some federal laws and regulations, there are many choices that organizations or communities on reservations are free to make. Even urban organizations and communities sometimes may operate under different laws and policies than their non-Native counterparts. For instance, the Indian Child Welfare Act allows Native organizations to show preference to Native families in child welfare placements and gives full faith and credit to First Nation organizations that prefer to handle their own child welfare matters rather than utilizing a state system (Weaver & White, 1999). This would not be possible for children from other cultural or ethnic groups.

Rather than focusing on problems and cultural loss, social workers should approach their work with Native organizations and communities from a strengths perspective. Social workers can focus on what has been retained, including land, sovereignty, culture, language, and traditions. Many strengths continue to exist in spite of over 500 years of colonization and deliberate attempts at genocide, both physical and cultural. We are survivors who posses unique strengths, not victims.

Empowerment

Empowerment, a concept embraced by social workers during the last fifteen years, fits well when working with Native organizations and communities. Both empowerment and sovereignty are inherent, internal strengths. Neither empowerment nor sovereignty can be given by an outside entity; however, inappropriate U.S. social policies have encroached on sovereignty in ways that have been disempowering for First Nations people.

Native organizations have the power to advocate for their rights, beliefs, and values. They do not have to operate according to values of the dominant society. For example, Native organizations may have personnel policies and management guidelines that reflect the values and culture of their First Nations communities, rather than following common practices in the dominant society. Some nations continue their traditional forms of governance and have never accepted an elective system. Empowerment is an ongoing process and one that parallels the struggles of overcoming internalized oppression. Empowerment is critical for confronting the continuing impact of colonization.

While important, this type of empowerment is a very difficult process. Most First Nations organizations and communities are dependent on external funding, often from the federal government. This dependence on external funds makes total self-sufficiency unrealistic and puts limits on empowerment. Clearly, although there is much resentment against the federal government and its paternalistic bureaucracies, there is also considerable reluctance to "bite the hand that feeds us." Although funding often is guaranteed under treaties in exchange for land and other concessions, dependence on this funding is disempowering. This situation is likely to exist indefinitely.

The strength of women is empowering. As one common maxim states, "A nation can only be defeated when the hearts of its women are on the ground." Key roles that women play in Native organizations and communities are important for empowerment. Social workers must not overlook the significance of First Nation women in their assessments of Native organizations and communities.

Many First Nations youth and adults raised without their traditions, languages, and spirituality return and reclaim them and pass them on to their children. Language tapes are available in many Native languages and many Native organizations and communities offer language classes. Native people who left their communities decades or even generations ago now return in fulfillment of prophecies found in many First Nations cultures. Reclaiming culture, what is rightfully ours, is a tremendously empowering experience. Traditional values, far from being outmoded, can be a major source of strength in contemporary times. Valuing our elders, cultures, and traditions is also very empowering. Throughout First Nations communities many people have gone through and continue to go through an empowering process of reclaiming what is ours, spiritually, culturally, and through concrete means such as land claims.

SIGNIFICANT PRINCIPLES WHEN WORKING WITH ORGANIZATIONS AND COMMUNITIES

When assessing Native organizations and communities social workers should keep in mind the following principles:

1. Educate yourself about the specific First Nations cultural context in which you will conduct an assessment. Values and customs may vary among Native groups.

2. Always show respect for Native cultures and traditions. This includes respecting traditional forms of leadership and ways of being/doing.

3. Respect sovereignty and be willing to conduct an assessment within this context.

4. Offer assistance but don't impose your own values about what needs to be done or the best ways to do it.

5. Become known in the community. In this way you can build trust.

6. Demonstrate your values and genuineness. There is likely to be a period of testing before you are trusted enough to conduct an assessment.

Important Skills When Working with Organizations and Communities

Although a variety of practice skills are needed to effectively assess First Nations organizations and communities, five skills or values are particularly critical and will be highlighted here: (1) cultural assessment; (2) self-reflection; (3) social justice/decolonization; (4) listening, patience, humility; and, (5) working with traditional people and systems.

It is important to include a cultural dimension in your assessment. Culture guides priorities, beliefs, and the ways things are done in organizations and communities. Cultures vary across nations and levels of attachment to culture vary as well. Organizations have their own cultures that overlap with various Native cultural traditions to a greater or lesser degree. You may be working with a First Nations organization staffed by people with credentials recognized by the dominant society who provide services primarily according to the way they were socialized in their professional education. On the other hand, you may be working with an agency of people hired for their roles in the community and traditional values rather than professional credentials. Either way, you need to understand cultural factors relevant to the dynamics in the organization or community to do an accurate assessment.

The ability to be self-reflective is critical for culturally competent social work (Chau, 1992; Hardy & Laszloffy, 1992; McRae & Johnson, 1991; Ridley, Mendoza, & Kanitz, 1994; Van Soest, 1994; Weaver, 1999b). Social workers must reflect on their own beliefs and values and how they influence their assessments. For example, people raised in the United States are exposed to strong ideas about the value of democracy and are often led to believe that other forms of government are less desirable. A social worker in a Native community governed by hereditary Chiefs rather than an elected government may well have feelings and opinions about doing an assessment within such a system. Social workers must avoid imposing their own values on Native organizations and communities. This begins with the ability to honestly reflect on their own beliefs and feelings.

Social workers must value social justice, be able to recognize the ongoing impact of colonization, and possess skills in confronting oppression (Weaver, 1999b). Social workers need to become activists and use their skills to fight for social justice. Many Native communities are fighting against environmental racism (Churchill, 1993; Churchill & LaDuke, 1992), pursuing land claims (Churchill, 1992, 1993), fighting for water rights (Guerrero, 1992), struggling over the right to traditional forms of subsistence, such as fishing (Institute for Natural Progress, 1992), and fighting for freedom of religion (Deloria, 1992). The list of activist causes that Native organizations and communities are involved with goes on and on. An appropriate assessment provides an important foundation for activist work.

Listening, patience, and humility are key skills for conducting assessments in Native communities (Weaver, 1999c). Social workers must listen with patience and allow silence in interactions with First Nations people. They must be humble and willing to learn. It is not appropriate to approach a Native organization or community believing you have all the answers. You must work together respectfully to build a helping partnership.

Engaging in cross-cultural work can be challenging. First Nations organizations and communities with strong groundings in cultural traditions may have beliefs, values, and ways of doing things that differ from the dominant society. Additionally, it is important to know that not all First Nations people follow traditions and beliefs to the same extent. Indeed, it is common for friction to exist between Native organizations, between Native communities, and among individuals within those entities. Social workers should have some understanding of these frictions, have skills in assessing the situation, skills in working with people from various factions, and, at times, be a mediator.

CASE EXAMPLE

A case example of a First Nations organization and its efforts to assess the needs of an urban Native community will illustrate key concepts discussed here (Weaver, 1997, 1999c). The agency serves off-reservation Native people in a two-county area with an estimated population of 3,000 Native people. Approximately two-thirds of the population is concentrated in one city, with the remainder being in a smaller city. The population consists primarily of people from three to four interrelated nations. The area is surrounded by several reservations within a one- to two-hour drive, and travel between the reservations and urban areas is common.

Like many urban Native agencies, this organization was founded in the 1970s to serve the vocational needs of the First Nations community and now provides a variety of services including foster care, substance abuse assessment, elders programs, and youth services. In 1995, the agency contacted the author and asked her to develop a culturally congruent research design that would yield information for planning and enhancing services. In addition to collecting this information, one goal of the project was for the agency to reach out to the community to enhance communication and trust.

Initially, elders and other key community members were brought together to discuss the proposed project. The meeting included vocal community members who had previously expressed dissatisfaction with the agency. Through the meeting we were able to gain their support as well as their guidance. Because the level of trust between some community members and the agency was low, this was an important first step in getting the project off the ground.

Because of the importance placed on face-to-face interaction in First Nations cultures, the use of focus groups was the method of choice, and key individuals who could not attend groups were interviewed individually. Whenever possible, focus groups were conducted at preexisting meetings (e.g., parent groups from the First Nations magnet school, elders luncheon groups). Highly publicized, open community meetings were also held. In all, thirteen group and twenty-three individual interviews were conducted for a total sample of approximately one hundred people. All groups and interviews were guided by the following questions:

- What are the most pressing social needs of the Native community in this area?
- Which of these community needs are the most critical?
- What is currently being done about these needs?
- How familiar are you with services offered at the local Native social service agency?
- What should this agency be doing to address the needs that you identified above?

- Which of the programs at this agency are most helpful?
- Which of the programs offered at this agency are least helpful?

On some issues there was significant agreement, while on other issues community members' opinions varied. The respondents can generally be categorized into three groups: agency staff, agency clients, and community members not affiliated with the agency. Several themes emerged from the needs assessment, most notably the need to include culture as a foundation at all levels of programming and administration. On some issues, particularly what the agency should be doing about community needs, many different viewpoints were expressed. Some community members called for the agency to focus on providing cultural activities, such as beading, lacrosse events, and language classes, in addition to providing social services. Others emphasized the need to include culture as a critical dynamic in social services and administration of the agency. Public relations, communication, and outreach were also considered important.

Most comments on the agency focused on overarching issues related to service delivery rather than on specific programs. Clients were particularly concerned about the location of services. They desired more home visits and outreach. Staff expressed concern about the need for internal change related to professional issues and healing for themselves after difficult internal disputes. They stated that the agency and staff must be healthy and culturally grounded to serve the community well. The community at large wanted the agency to focus more on public relations, communication, and operating from a cultural base.

While different segments of the community offered different perspectives on what the agency should do to meet the needs in the community, all suggestions offered were compatible. In fact, all suggestions focused on different aspects of the same idea. Increased outreach to clients in the community, wellness within the agency, and improved communication and community relations were all based on a cultural foundation and grounded in the values of the First Nations community.

Community members invested time and energy in sharing their feelings and opinions in the hopes of improving agency services and the agency's relationship with the community. The agency now faces the challenge of responding to community members' voices. In order to strengthen the connection between the agency and the community it serves, the agency must respond with actions that demonstrate it values the opinions of community members.

At first glance, it may seem odd that an agency staffed by members of the First Nations community might be somewhat distanced from it and needed to refocus on integrating culture in its services and ways of operations. Because of past policies, such as the boarding schools, there are tremendous differences in the level of attachment to culture held by different Native people. Some know little of their traditional values and heritage. Additionally, the societal messages that many First Nations people receive devalue their culture and suggest that other values and ways of doing things are superior.

This case example illustrates the struggles of a Native organization attempting to deal with the effects of colonization and alienation from its own traditions. Social agencies are not a natural part of Native helping traditions. Such organizations face the challenge of blending the best of cultural traditions and Western helping methods in a manner that results in culturally congruent services and management practices.

CONCLUSION

Although the social work literature reflects a growing emphasis on cultural competence, usually the focus is on direct practice and encouraging social workers to be more culturally sensitive and self-reflective (McMahon & Allen-Meares, 1992). Rarely does the social work literature call for cultural competence in work with organizations or communities. Logically, it seems impossible for social workers to do culturally competent work if there is no support for cultural competence at the organizational level. We must pay attention to the context of our work.

This chapter has presented some general information and guidelines for culturally competent work in First Nations organizations and communities, illustrated with the struggles of one Native agency to be responsive to its community. In order to be truly culturally competent, social workers must move beyond general guidelines about First Nations people and tailor their work within a specific Native context. Once a social worker has determined the specific Native context, he or she must gather and apply information specific to that Native organization or community.

REFERENCES

Allen, P. G. (1986). *The Sacred Hoop: Recovering the feminine in American Indian traditions.* Boston: Beacon Press.

Angell, G. B., Kurz, B. J., & Gottfried, G. M. (1997). Suicide and North American Indians: A social constructivist perspective. *Journal of Multicultural Social Work, 6* (3/4), 1–25.

Bachman, R. (1992). *Death and violence on the reservation.* New York: Auburn House.

Barsh, R. L. (1996). The Indian Child Welfare Act of 1978: A critical analysis. In J. R. Wunder (Ed.), *Recent legal issues for American Indians, 1968 to the present* (pp. 219–268). New York: Garland.

Bearskin, B. & Spade, W. (1991). On relocation. In P. Nabokov (Ed.), *Native American testimony: A chronicle of Indian–White relations from prophecy to the present, 1492–1992* (pp. 348–351). New York: Viking.

Beauvais, F. (1992). The consequences of drug and alcohol use for Indian youth. *American Indian and Alaska Native Mental Health Research, 5* (1), 32–37.

Beauvais, F. & Trimble, J. E. (1992). The role of the researcher in evaluating American-Indian alcohol and other drug abuse. In M. A. Orlandi (Ed.), *Cultural competence for evaluators: A guide for alcohol and other drug abuse prevention practitioners working with ethnic/racial communities* (pp. 173–201). Rockville, MD: Office for Substance Abuse Prevention.

Brave Heart-Jordan, M. & DeBruyn, L. (1995). So she may walk in balance: Integrating the impact of historical trauma in the treatment of American Indian women. In *Racism in the lives of women: Testimony, theory, and guides to antiracist practice* (pp. 345–368). J. Adelman and G. Enguidanos (Eds.), New York: Haworth.

Chau, K. L. (1992). Educating for effective group work practice in multicultural environments of the 1990s. *Journal of Multicultural Social Work, 1* (4), 1–15.

Churchill, W. (1992). The earth is our mother: Struggles for American Indian land and liberation in the contemporary United States. In M. A. Jaimes (Ed.), *The state of Native America: Genocide, colonization, and resistance* (pp. 139–188). Boston: South End Press.

Churchill, W. (1993). *Struggle for the land: Indigenous resistance to genocide, ecocide, and expropriation in contemporary North America.* Monroe, ME: Common Courage Press.

Churchill, W. (1994). *Indians are us?: Culture and genocide in Native North America.* Monroe, ME: Common Courage Press.

Churchill, W. & LaDuke, W. (1992). Native North America: The political economy of radioactive colonialism. In M. A. Jaimes (Ed.), *The state of Native America: Genocide, colonization, and resistance* (pp. 241–266). Boston: South End Press.

Churchill, W. and Morris, G. T. (1992). Key Indian laws and cases. In M. A. Jaimes (Ed.), *The state of Native America: Genocide, colonization and resistance.* Boston: South End Press.

Clinton, R. N., Newton, H. J., & Price, M. E. (1991). *American Indian law: Cases and materials.* Charlottesville, VA: Michie.

Committee on Interior and Insular Affairs. (1992). *Indian Fetal Alcohol Syndrome Prevention and Treatment Act.* (Serial number 102-52). Washington, DC: U.S. Government Printing Office.

Conway, G. A., Ambrose, T. J., Chase, E., Hooper, E. Y., Helgerson, S. D., Johannes, P., Epstein, M. R., McRae, B. A., Munn, V. P., Keevama, L., Raymond, S. A., Schable, C. A., Satten, G. A., Petersen, L. R., Dondero, T. J. (1992). HIV infection in American Indians and Alaska Natives: Surveys in the Indian Health Service. *Journal of Acquired Immune Deficiency Syndromes, 5* (8), 803–809.

Deloria, V., Jr. (1992). Trouble in high places: Erosion of American Indian rights to religious freedom in the United States. In M. A. Jaimes (Ed.), *The state of Native America: Genocide, colonization, and resistance* (pp. 267–290). Boston: South End Press.

Fleming, C. (1992). American Indians and Alaska Natives: Changing societies past and present. In M. A. Orlandi (Ed.), *Cultural competence for evaluators: A guide for alcohol and other drug abuse prevention practitioners working with ethnic/racial communities* (pp. 147–171). Rockville, MD: Office for Substance Abuse Prevention.

Good Tracks, J. G. (1973). Native American non-interference. *Social Work, 18* (6), 30–34.

Griffin-Pierce, T. (1997). "When I am lonely the mountains call me": The impact of sacred geography on Navajo psychological well being. *American Indian and Alaska Native Mental Health Research, 7* (3), 1–10.

Guerrero, M. (1992). American Indian water rights: The blood of life in Native North America. In M. A. Jaimes (Ed.), *The state of Native America: Genocide, colonization, and resistance* (pp. 189–216). Boston: South End Press.

Hardy, K. V. & Laszloffy, T. A. (1992). Training racially sensitive family therapists: Context, content, and contact. *Families in Society: The Journal of Contemporary Human Services, 73* (6), 364–370.

Hultgren, M. L. & Molin, P. F. (1989). *To lead and to serve: American Indian education at Hampton Institute, 1878–1923.* Virginia Beach, VA: Virginia Foundation for the Humanities and Public Policy.

Institute for Natural Progress. (1992). In usual and accustomed places: Contemporary American Indian fishing rights struggles. In M. A. Jaimes (Ed.), *The state of Native America: Genocide, colonization, and resistance* (pp. 217–240). Boston: South End Press.

Jaimes, M. A. & Halsey, T. (1992). American Indian women: At the center of indigenous resistance in contemporary North America. In M. A. Jaimes (Ed.), *The state of Native America: Genocide, colonization, and resistance* (pp. 311–344). Boston: South End Press.

Josephy, A. M., Jr. (1982). *Now that the buffalo's gone: A study of today's American Indians.* New York: Knopf.

Kuhlmann, A. (1992). American Indian women of the plains and northern woodlands. *Mid-American Review of Sociology, 16* (1), 1–28.

Leung, P. K., Kinzie, J. D., Boehnlein, J. K., & Shore, J. H. (1993). A prospective study of the natural course of alcoholism in a Native American village. *Journal of Studies on Alcohol, 54* (6), 733–738.

Lowery, C. T. (1997). Hearing the messages: Integrating Pueblo philosophy into academic life. *Journal of American Indian Education, 36* (2), 1–8.

Mannes, M. (1995). Factors and events leading to the passage of the Indian Child Welfare Act. *Child Welfare, 74* (1), 264–282.

Maracle, B. (1993). *Crazywater: Native voices on addiction and recovery.* Toronto: Penguin.

May, P. A. & Smith, M. B. (1988). Some Navajo Indian opinions about alcohol abuse and prohibition: A survey and recommendations for policy. *Journal of Studies on Alcohol, 49,* 324–334.

McMahon, A. & Allen-Meares, P. (1992). Is social work racist? A content analysis of recent literature. *Social Work, 37* (6), 533–539.

McRae, M. B. & Johnson, S. D., Jr. (1991). Toward training for competence in multicultural counselor education. *Journal of Counseling and Development, 70* (1), 131–135.

Metler, R., Conway, G. A., & Stehr-Green, J. (1991). AIDS surveillance among American Indians and Alaska Natives. *American Journal of Public Health, 81* (11), 1469–1471.

Moncher, M. S., Holden, G. W., & Trimble, J. E. (1990). Substance abuse among Native-American youth. *Journal of Consulting and Clinical Psychology, 58* (4), 408–415.

Moran, J. R. (1999). Preventing alcohol use among urban American Indian youth: The Seventh Generation Program. In H. N. Weaver (Ed.), *Voices of First Nations People: Human service considerations* (pp. 51–67). New York: Haworth.

Native American Leadership Commission on Health and AIDS. (1994). *A Native American leadership response to HIV and AIDS.* New York: American Indian Community House.

Oetting, E. R. & Beauvais, F. (1991). Orthogonal cultural identification theory: The cultural identification of minority adolescents. *International Journal of the Addictions, 25* (5A & 6A), 655–685.

Parker, J. G. (1994). The lived experience of Native Americans with diabetes within a transcultural nursing perspective. *Journal of Transcultural Nursing, 6* (1), 5–11.

Ridley, C. R., Mendoza, D. W., & Kanitz, B. E. (1994). Multicultural training: Reexamination, operationalization, and integration. *The Counseling Psychologist, 22* (2), 227–289.

Robbins, R. L. (1992). Self-determination and subordination: The past, present, and future of American Indian governance. In M. A. Jaimes (Ed.), *The state of Native America: Genocide, colonization, and resistance* (pp. 87–121). Boston: South End Press.

U.S. Bureau of the Census. (1993). *We the First Americans.* Washington, DC: U.S. Department of Commerce, Economics and Statistics Administration.

U.S. Senate Select Committee on Indian Affairs, Ninety-fifth Congress. (1977). *Indian Child Welfare Act of 1977: To Establish Standards for the Placement of Indian Children in Foster or Adoptive Homes, to Prevent the Breakup of Indian Families, and for Other Purposes.* Washington, DC: U.S. Government Printing Office.

U.S. Senate Select Committee on Indian Affairs, One Hundredth Congress. (1988). *To Amend the Indian Child Welfare Act* Washington, DC: U.S. Government Printing Office.

Van Soest, D. (1994). Social work education for multicultural practice and social justice advocacy: A field study of how students experience the learning process. *Journal of Multicultural Social Work, 3* (1), 17–28.

Weaver, H. N. (1997). *Assessing the needs of the urban Native American community: Erie and Niagara Counties, NY.* Buffalo, NY: Native American Community Services of Erie and Niagara Counties.

Weaver, H. N. (1998). Indigenous people in a multicultural society: Unique issues for human services. *Social Work, 43* (3), 203–211.

Weaver, H. N. (1999a). Health concerns for Native American youth: A culturally grounded approach to health promotion. *Journal of Human Behavior in the Social Environment, 2* (1/2), 127–143.

Weaver, H. N. (1999b). Indigenous people and the social work profession: Defining culturally competent services. *Social Work, 44* (3), 217–225.

Weaver, H. N. (1999c). Assessing the needs of Native American communities: A Northeastern example. *Evaluation and Program Planning: An International Journal, 22* (2), 155–161.

Weaver, H. N. & White, B. J. (1997). The Native American family circle: Roots of resiliency. *Journal of Family Social Work, 2* (1), 67–79.

Weaver, H. N. & White, B. J. (1999). Protecting the future of indigenous children and nations: An examination of the Indian Child Welfare Act. *Journal of Health and Social Policy, 10* (4), 35–50.

Weaver, H. N. & Yellow Horse Brave Heart, M. (1999). Examining two facets of American Indian identity: Exposure to other cultures and the influence of historical trauma. *Journal of Human Behavior in the Social Environment, 2* (1/2), 19–33.

Wuest, J. (1991). Harmonizing: A North American Indian approach to management of middle ear disease with transcultural nursing implications. *Journal of Transcultural Nursing, 3* (1), 5–14.

Young, T. J. (1992). Substance abuse among Native American youth. In G. W. Lawson & A. W. Lawson (Eds.), *Adolescent substance abuse: Etiology, treatment, and prevention* (pp. 381–390). Gaithersburg, MD: Aspen.

CHAPTER 14

CULTURALLY COMPETENT ASSESSMENT OF CAMBODIAN AMERICAN SURVIVORS OF THE KILLING FIELDS: A TOOL FOR SOCIAL JUSTICE

PAULA T. TANEMURA MORELLI

Social work practice has historically recognized assessment as a powerful tool for understanding nuances of the human condition and engaging the client-system in a collaborative process of determining and implementing appropriate interventions. The assessment process examines a client's problems within the context of a "multi-causal interacting framework" (Vigilante & Mailick, 1987 in Meyer, 1993, p. 3). As an ongoing process, assessment involves several interrelated tasks, which include identifying, specifying, and clarifying problems, describing characteristics of clients, their needs, strengths, resources, environments, and situations, and interpreting and integrating the data collected in order to select the foci of outcomes (Nay, 1979 in Gambrill, 1997; Hepworth, Rooney, & Larsen, 1997). Meyer (1993) describes assessment as a " . . . generic process applicable to all problems, to all practice modalities with individuals, families and groups, to all temporal frameworks of brief, episodic and open-ended treatment, and to all clients of any description," developed with the use of an organizing framework to understand the meaning of case situations.

Assessment can be an equally powerful tool for social justice. Social workers, often the primary professionals to assess clients in need of services, have the authority to define problems in relation to particular health beliefs, determine or make recommendations for culturally appropriate interventions, facilitate access to care, and support healing and recovery. These functions are especially crucial to our culturally diverse clients, who rely on professionals to protect them from subtle forms of systemic oppression.

As Western social work practitioners, we champion practice theories that contextualize our clients via ecological, strengths, and empowerment perspectives, confident that, in doing so, we support social justice. In cross-cultural practice, however, we often fail to fully assess, advocate for, and facilitate culturally appropriate interventions and services that have a greater potential for meeting the clients' needs. This, in part, stems from the fact that culturally sensitive assessment and interventions, which recognize differences in health beliefs, spiritual traditions, and healing practices, are often at odds with Western biomedical theory, practice, and treatment, diagnostic classification systems, and sanctioned health care benefits.

Western biomedicine maintains central authority over health care in this country, endorsing specific practices of healing, treatment, and associated care. A major assumption of the Western biomedical model is the arbitrary separation of mind and body in the evaluation of functioning and treatment of an individual. This assumption is in direct opposition to traditional Asian models of health, which tend to view an individual's well-being as a function of the balance between body and mind. Moreover, mental health in Asian conceptualizations of well-being, unlike Western models, cannot be separated from bodily health or spiritual well-being. It is of vital importance that the assessment process capture the relationships between health beliefs, attributions, and logically related interventions among cultural minorities and that those relationships be better understood by those involved in the delivery of health and mental health services in diverse communities. Without such knowledge, societal efforts to provide needed assistance are doomed to failure and will contribute further to nativist sentiments, which blame victims for their distress and stigmatize communities for their presumed deficiencies.

Another paradigm from which to view certain problems encountered in transcultural practice and healing is to examine what Hall (1977) refers to as the *continuum of contexting* within cultures. Cultures in which people are deeply involved with one another, where information is widely shared and commonly understood, and relatively simple messages convey deep meanings are considered to be "high context" (Hall, 1977); such cultures are " . . . rooted in the past, slow to change and highly stable," and may become " . . . overwhelmed by mechanical systems and lose their integrity" (Hall, 1977). In contrast, low-context cultures are characterized by relatively shallow involvement between people, high individualization, the need for large amounts of detailed information, alienation and fragmentation. Understanding the nature (high–low) of contexting within a culture is important in determining what is important to the individual and community, i.e., what is attended to or not attended to. The point to be emphasized is that understanding a culture's contexting is critical to understanding the adjustment difficulties and conflict that are inevitable when members of high-context cultures must adapt to the cultural milieu and practices of a low-context host society. High-context patterns, such as expecting service providers to intuit what is ailing the high-context client, are frustrated by Western health and mental health practices that are based on frank client self-disclosure. Moreover, high-context individuals may assume, consistent with their high-context experiences, that service providers will understand the complex interconnections involved in the client's attributions of his or her difficulties. Only in a few instances can a high degree of ethnographic expertise be relied on to reach deeper cultural understandings. It is far more likely that the client's constructions will remain a mystery to those practitioners unprepared to ask for such information, and likely to be discounted by those who do seek the client's own accounts of their suffering.

In conducting assessments, for example, the symptoms or complaints of Cambodian refugees are rarely assessed within the context of their cultural meaning systems, and few attempts are made to provide or advocate for culturally appropriate services. Moreover, Western service providers are often unaware of the geopolitical history or U.S. political and military involvement that contributed to Cambodians' refugee status, and, therefore, are unaware of our moral obligation to these individuals. Culturally competent assessment of Cambodian refugees should take into account their cultural identity, meaning systems, explanations of illness, possible within-family explanations (Kleinman, 1992), and the historic geopolitical context of their plight in order to provide client-centered, culturally appropriate, and optimally effective interventions. The National Association of Social Workers Code of Ethics stresses that social workers "have a knowledge base of their clients' cultures and be able to show competence in the provision of services that are sensitive to clients' cultures and to differences between people and cultural groups" (NASW, 1996, p. 9).

The purpose of this chapter is to provide practitioners with a cultural knowledge base to aid in the assessment of Cambodian survivors of the "Killing Fields." Four areas are addressed toward that end. First, a brief discussion of the historic events that precipitated Cambodians' exodus from their homeland, the nature of their trauma and suffering, and clinical studies of their mental health status and Western treatment efficacy provide the assessor with important contextual information. Second, a discussion of Cambodian spiritual values and beliefs, health beliefs about the causes of health and illness, and meanings attributed to pain and suffering offer the assessor a knowledge base of possible meaning systems utilized by Cambodians. Third, the case history of a Cambodian American survivor of the Killing Fields who received treatment within the Western system of health care reveals the kind of difficulties Cambodians experience within the Western health care system. Finally, five areas to improve assessment practice are suggested when working with Cambodian American survivors of the Killing Fields and other cross-cultural refugee groups.

CAMBODIAN AMERICANS: SOCIODEMOGRAPHICS AND ISSUES OF HEALTH STATUS

Prior to 1992, the National Center for Health Statistics (NCHS) recognized Chinese, Japanese, Hawaiian, Filipino, and other Asian/Pacific Island cultures. Beginning in 1992, the NCHS expanded the categories to include Vietnamese, Asian

Indians, Koreans, Samoans, Guamanians, and remaining A/PI, which included Southeast Asians (Spector, 1996). By 1995, the U.S. Department of Health and Human Services defined A/PI as persons, " . . . having origins in any of the original peoples of the Far East, Southeast Asia, the Indian subcontinent or the Pacific Islands." This shift in recognized A/PI categories was influenced by the influx of over 670,000 refugees from Southeast Asia (U.S. Committee for Refugees, 1996) at the close of the Second Indochinese War (Vietnam War). The major groups represented in the exodus were Vietnamese, Lao Highlanders, Lao Lowlanders, and Khmer, the culturally and numerically dominant indigenous ethnic group of the geographic area known as Cambodia (the term *Cambodians* includes Khmer, Vietnamese, Chinese, Cham-lays, and other minority groups making their home in Cambodia). It has been projected that, by the year 2000, over a million Cambodian, Lao, and Vietnamese will be residing in the United States (D'Avanzo, 1997).

Like the Laotians and Vietnamese, Cambodian refugees suffered extreme trauma, having experienced the bombing of their homes and villages, the arbitrary and preventable deaths of family members, being orphaned, tortured, raped, witnessing mass killings, brutal robberies, experiencing disease and illness without medical care, starvation, torturous escape through mine-infested jungles or by inadequate sea vessels, and serious injury, such as amputation as the result of land-mine encounters. Over 600,000 Cambodian refugees sought asylum at the Thailand border after 1979, fleeing not only the ravages of war within their country, but also the horrors of genocide. Under the leadership of Pol Pot, the Khmer Rouge directed the mass murder and torture of intellectuals, professionals, people from urban backgrounds, Buddhist monks, Chinese ethnics (Albin & Hood, 1990), and members of the preceding Lon Nol regime. These "New People" were identified via their physical appearance, actions, deeds, words, and language, and any other form of association with Western imperialism. Those that survived endured starvation, forced separation from family, the murder of loved ones, torture, chronic illness, and constant fear.

Cambodians in the United States

Approximately 150,000 Cambodian refugees who fled Pol Pot's "Killing Fields" were subsequently resettled in the United States. Due to extreme difficulties in coping with survival demands and assimilating the traumatic experiences associated with the war, escape, and transcultural resettlement, Cambodian refugees are at extremely high risk for emotional dysfunction. In a study of psychiatric diagnoses among Hmong, Laotian, Cambodian, and Vietnamese refugees, Kroll and others (1989) found that 73.3 percent of the 404 participants in the study were diagnosed with a major depressive episode according to DSM criteria. The second most frequent diagnosis was post-traumatic stress disorder (PTSD), occurring at a rate of 13.3 percent, and often diagnosed in combination with depression. Cambodian refugees were reported with the highest rate of diagnosed PTSD among Southeast Asian refugees. In a random sample of fifty male and female Cambodian refugees selected from 500 Cambodian refugees resettled between 1983 and 1985, who had departed from their homes in Cambodia an average of 9.9 years ago, and had been living in the United States for an average of 5.4 years, Carlson and Rosser-Hogan (1993) found the rates of PTSD (86%), depression (80%), anxiety levels (78%), and dissociation (mean score 37.1) extremely high. These Cambodian refugees continued to suffer mental distress without seeking mental health treatment.

Among those that did seek treatment, the effectiveness of Western biomedical psychiatry in treating severely traumatized Southeast Asian refugees has been found to be limited (Cheung 1993; Kinzie, et al., 1987; Kinzie 1989; Morris, Silove, & Manicava Sagar, 1993). Psychodynamic interpretation and insight-oriented psychotherapy appear to be of little use to Southeast Asian refugees (Nguyen, 1984 cited in Cheung, 1993), who expect more concrete, i.e., physical or social, forms of intervention. Moreover, the Southeast Asian patient's attributional beliefs are often in conflict with the basic tenets of Western assessment and treatment. In Cheung's case study (1993) of Cambodian patients diagnosed with depression and post-traumatic stress disorder, the patient's belief in karma was cited as the "main stumbling block" or source of resistance to psychotherapy. It is unfortunate that the patient's beliefs were conceptualized as an obstacle rather than as an avenue to understanding the patient's worldview, which could have aided in treatment. Discounting of patient accounts is common in current health sciences practice and provides one major example of how different systems of cultural attributions and meanings collide in the context of cross-cultural assessment and service provision. Missing from our approach to facilitating the healing (the mitigation or alleviation of pain and suffering) is a strong need to explore, examine, and accept differing worldviews and cultural meaning systems.

CAMBODIAN MEANING SYSTEMS AND CULTURAL VALUES

Spirituality: Theravada Buddhism

Theravada Buddhism, the national religion of Cambodia, is practiced with a blend of elements from Hinduism (although not recognized as such in daily custom) and the traditional, indigenous folk religion. Theravada Buddhism has been the primary influence on Khmer behavior and belief since the fourteen century (Aronson, 1987; Frye, 1993). Buddhist practices became fused with earlier forms of animism and subsequently with Islam and Christianity (Chandler, 1972; Ebihara, 1968; Frye 1993). In her study of Cambodian life in the Village of Svay, Ebihara (1968) observed that, for the ordinary Khmer villager, the traditions from these religious sources were conceived of as part of a single religious system in which different aspects are called on at distinct, appropriate times.

Buddhist teachings submit Four Noble Truths: life is suffering; suffering is caused by desire; suffering can be eliminated by eliminating desire; to eliminate desire one must follow the eight fold path of: right understanding, right purpose, right speech, right vocation, right effort, right thinking and right meditation (Aronson, 1987). Through these teachings the individual is held responsible for his or her actions and the resulting good or bad consequences.

The Cambodian weltanschauung and beliefs about health and illness have evolved in large part from Cambodian interpretations of Buddhist principles. These principles include the law of karma, in which the individual's present good or bad actions affect his or her well-being in future incarnations. Thus, a child's congenital defect, such as being born without a hand, could be explained by accumulated sin from a previous life, or the child's mother having committed a sin (Aronson, 1987).

Spirits and the Supernatural

Cambodians often practice Buddhism alongside animism, sorcery, magic, and elements of Brahminism. In certain instances, supernatural forces/spirits are thought to be responsible for misfortune, accidents, certain bodily illness, and insanity (Aronson, 1987). These spirits are considered to act in both good and bad ways, and, if not properly respected and propitiated, may cause illness. Of the large number of spirits recognized by Khmer, particular spirits are considered to be more critical to health than others.

Neak Tha, Preay, and *Ab,* for example, are spirits identified with matters of personal health and well-being. One or two *Neak Tha* guardian spirits protect each community or social group, but not their individual members. *Neak Tha* is conceptualized as the spirit of an old man or grandfather, usually benevolent, but easily angered and vengeful. *Neak Tha* may live in a tree, forest, mountain, river, or rice paddy. If a *Neak Tha* is not properly worshipped, illness and misfortune will result. *Neak Tha* are thought to cause abdominal pain, vomiting, high fever, constipation, nightmares, inappropriate laughing and crying, and sudden death from cardiac arrest or trauma (Aronson, 1987; Frye, 1993). *Preay* and *Ab* are ancestral spirits and spirits of those who have suffered untimely deaths and are believed to affect an individual's health. *Preay* are demon spirits that can scare people to death, and cause high fevers, sleeplessness, and weight loss. *Ab* are witch spirits that cause illness to all individuals with whom they come in contact.

Spirits of stillborn children, women in labor, and those who experienced untimely deaths that did not permit necessary Buddhist funeral rituals are considered to be especially dangerous (Aronson, 1987). Evil spirits are thought to rise from slowly decaying bodies, hence the strict observance of cremation (Zadronzny, 1955 cited in Boehnlein, 1987). Immoral behavior is also thought to cause ancestral spirits to haunt a family (Duncan, 1987; Frye, 1986; Frye, 1993; Kemp, 1985; Marcucci, 1986; Martin, 1983).

Spirit invasion as an explanation for bodily illness and severe emotional distress is neither understood nor accepted by Western health-care providers. Because they cannot be "scientifically" proven, such occurrences may be thought of as cultural artifacts, or the conversion of emotional distress into physical complaints, as in somatic complaints. However, for the Cambodian, the use of spirit invasion in explanations of illness provides the sufferer with greater latitude for explaining the often unexplainable and more avenues to healing.

Khmer Beliefs about Natural Causes of Health and Illness

The health beliefs and practices of Cambodians living in the United States are no longer entirely traditional (Aronson, 1987). However, traditional beliefs and practices continue to influence Cambodian help-seeking behavior in response to illness. Cambodians do not have a single, dominant perspective on health and illness such as the Western biomedical model. Disease is believed to result from of a state of imbalance caused by the natural or supernatural environment. The existence of vital organs is recognized, but their functions are not understood in Western medical terms. Metaphysical and supernatural forces such as "offended spirits, moral transgressions, diet or behavior-induced humoral imbalances and sorcery . . . " are deemed responsible for health status (Aronson, 1987).

Equilibrium is the core principle of health within the traditional Cambodian belief system (Frye, 1993), which is directly related to the Buddhist and Daoist teachings of taking the "middle road." The balance of food intake, emotional states, interpersonal relations, pace of work and rest, and interaction with the environment are all understood to contribute to an individual's well-being. A "hot" or overactive physiological state is exacerbated by culturally defined "hot" foods (meat, salt, alcohol, and spicy food). And a "cold" or weak physiological state is exacerbated by "cold" foods (fruits, vegetables). In traditional practice, oppositional food treatment is used to bring the body back into balance.

Environmental winds can be a source of imbalance and illness. The body is thought to be in disequilibrium when the individual experiences deep states of anger, grief, or overwork, resulting in what is described as "wind illness" (Frye, 1993). In a mild state, wind illness may take the form of a headache, and would be treated with dermabrasive therapy, such as *khyal* (coin rubbing), skin pinching, or moxibustion. These techniques bring "bad wind" to the surface of the body for excretion (Frye, 1993; Kemp, 1985; Marcucci, 1986).

Kchall koo, for example, is a life-threatening form of wind illness in which bad wind has become "frozen wind" as a result of extreme exhaustion, emotional distress, or spirit possession. The *kchall koo*-afflicted person may become immobilized. Treatment includes emergency acupuncture, family members praying, chanting, and physically holding the sick person to impede the process of immobilization (Duncan, 1987; Frye, 1993).

Khmer Meanings of Pain and Suffering

Critical to a deeper understanding of Cambodian constructions of trauma and healing is the knowledge that the Khmer concept of pain and its expression in suffering is significantly different from Western beliefs and forms. In the Khmer culture, the concept of pain extends beyond pain as an indication of illness. It is part of a larger process of suffering and healing, which continually contributes to their kinship and familial solidarity and reciprocity, and ethnic identity maintenance (Marcucci, 1994).

Although the Khmer acknowledge scientific explanations of pain, such knowledge is not separated from the spiritual aspects of pain derived from Buddhism. The values and practices of Theravada Buddhism contribute to the Khmer formulation of the meaning of pain, and also constitute a core element of Khmer identity. In the Khmer belief system, " . . . life itself is the essence of suffering" (Robinson & Johnson, 1982, cited in Marcucci, 1994, p. 130). Through the syncretic use of both Buddhism and folk religion, Khmer are able to explain the transcendental questions of existence and take responsibility for coping with more immediate problems (Ebihara, 1968, p. 442; Marcucci, 1994).

Ordinary imbalances of "wind" may be treated by pinching, cupping, and coining. In the Khmer health belief system, it is critical that treatment be directed to the cause, or causes of affliction, if the individual is to be healed (Marcucci, 1994). These causal factors may include social, psychological, supernatural, or magical conditions. Khmer distinguish the degree of an individual's suffering by the type of affliction and the type of treatment.

The sharing of pain is part of the Khmer socialization process and is important to developing one's identity within a group. This collective sharing of pain, " . . . distinguishes Khmer identity and provides meaning to their existence" (Marcucci, 1994). The skillful assessor must take time to understand Cambodian clients' health beliefs through the use of translators, cultural brokers in the community, such as Cambodian social workers, health professionals and other helping professionals, in order to articulate their needs and advocate accordingly.

Emotional Stress and Behavior

Western medical providers find that emotionally distressed Cambodian refugees commonly present with somatic complaints, such as many forms of physical pain (headaches, abdominal pain, chest pain, etc.) and sleep disturbance (Cheung, 1993; Kroll et al., 1989). Somatization may be thought of as an alternative form of communication in which the individual's expression of emotional suffering is translated into physical suffering.

In some traditional Asian cultures, somatization is thought to occur because of several factors. The first of these is the tendency to minimize or often ignore the symptoms of trauma because of guilt and shame (Cheung, 1993). The Buddhist belief that suffering is an expected part of life and that expression of dissatisfaction or strong display of affect are incongruent with these tenets is considered another factor contributing to somatization (Cheung, 1993; Seanglim, 1991). The display of strong and uncontrolled emotions is considered pathological (Landerman & Esterik, 1988 cited in Cheung, 1993), thus predisposing the individual to suppress emotional distress, which may be somatized. Within this high-context culture, somatization provides a nonverbal signal that enables family members to respond to the suffer's affliction. According to Cheung (1993), Cambodians and other

Southeast Asians associate the concept of "madness" with all psychiatric conditions, the sole treatment for which is long-term confinement in a rudimentary psychiatric institution.

Koucharang (thinking too much), an apparently culture-bound syndrome indicating severe stress, is identified by complaints of headaches, somatic complaints of chest pain, palpitations and shortness of breath, excess sleeping, and withdrawal (Frye & D'Avanzo, 1994). In Frye and D'Avanzo's (1994) comparison study of Cambodians in Massachusetts and California, the primary cause of *koucharang* was attributed to memories associated with the Khmer Rouge, precipitated by nightmares or flashbacks of the Killing Fields. Cambodians describe management of *koucharang* as involving respect for cultural taboos and the use of certain coping strategies. Avoidance of alcohol, drugs, and sad thoughts are the three most important proscriptions to observe in dealing with *koucharang*. When a family member afflicted by *koucharang* becomes emotionally or physically violent, the primary management strategies used are to verbally discourage sad thoughts and not leave the individual alone. The afflicted individual similarly uses the coping strategies of avoidance of sad thoughts and being alone. However, suicide is a considered option, and other coping behaviors might include alcohol and substance abuse to control stress and spousal abuse.

These traditional beliefs form an important context for understanding Cambodian conceptualizations of illness. However, adherence to their beliefs, intensity of distress and symptomatology may vary by age, gender, and generational differences (Frye, 1993). Thus, the preceding cultural knowledge base, albeit limited in scope and depth, and subject to within-group differences, provides the assessor with a foundation for gathering data to develop a viable assessment and client-centered interventions.

The following case history provides examples of the cross-cultural barriers that one Cambodian survivor of the Killing Fields encountered in her quest for healing within the Western health care system.

THE CONTINUOUS SEARCH FOR HEALING: A CASE HISTORY

The following case history from a study of the social networks and health-seeking efforts of Cambodian Americans describes the trauma and suffering of a survivor of the Killing Fields and her search for healing. Sophiap's narrative reveals the adversity endured within the Western health-care system and some glaring gaps between what she needed and what the system offered. Her story strongly suggests that assessment practice that included a basic understanding of Cambodian cultural meaning systems could have enabled the practitioner to better advocate for Sophiap throughout the health service system and prevented the systemic abuse and oppression she suffered.

Sophiap's Story

Sophiap was born in 1965 to a farming family in the province of Kompong Speu. Her father died several months after she was born, leaving her mother to raise and support their seven children. Sophiap was the sixth of seven children. Her eldest sister, Sokha, was followed by four brothers. The seventh child was a female. Her third brother died of illness some time in the early 1970s. Following that period, the family was unable to make a living in farming due to a drought, and they moved to Svay Sisophon.

In 1975, the Khmer Rouge evacuated the entire family from Svay Sisophon. During the evacuation Sophiap's mother became ill. She worried about the home they used to live in, and, without medication, she became increasingly sick and died. Shortly after that, Sophiap's three brothers were taken away by the Khmer Rouge; she has never seen two of them since that time. At that time Sophiap was nine years old, her eldest sister, Sokha, possibly eighteen or nineteen years of age, and the youngest sister, perhaps seven or eight years old. Sophiap was separated from her sisters and sent to a work camp. Eventually, her youngest sister was separated from Sokha and placed in a koma (a group for children under ten years of age).

Over a four-year period under Pol Pot and another six years in the refugee camps, Sophiap endured forced separation from her family, beatings, starvation, forced labor, reeducation, her own attempted murder, being shot and wounded, and the tragic death of her oldest sister, Sokha. She witnessed mass killings and the daily deaths of individuals by starvation or murder.

After six years in the camps, Sophiap and her remaining family members (a niece, an older brother, and his wife) were finally resettled in the United States in December 1985. She was twenty years old, with much of her childhood lost. Having faced and survived extreme physical and emotional injury, Sophiap has been continuously ill since 1987.

Sophiap's Suffering

Sophiap spoke no English when she arrived in Washington state. Her family was sponsored by a Cambodian family, who provided them with enough money for a deposit and a month of rent. Church groups donated beds, blankets, and food, but, unable to communicate in English, the family often sat staring at the Americans. She began English-as-a-second-language classes and vocational training, but says, "I fell ill and I haven't been able to do anything since." Sophiap describes her initial suffering this way:

> I could not pinpoint it, like headaches and dizziness. And inside, my physical body was not well, my hands and my legs started shaking. So my sponsor advised me to go to the doctor. They checked my blood and everything else but could not find anything. So in June 1987, they looked and said I had a bladder infection. I no longer had the energy that I used to have . . . I became very thin, 98 pounds. Like walking around, I could hardly do that. I got thinner and thinner, not knowing the reason why. I kept going to the doctor, they said I wasn't sick, but I kept losing pounds. They gave me TB test and stuff like that.
>
> . . . So I kept getting sick until 1990. One day in 1990, I was not able to get out of bed, I could no longer walk, I kept on having pain, starting in 1987. Whatever I ate hurt me, I could not eat a lot. So the doctor said I had an ulcer, the doctor in Beaverton. So in a week I was put to sleep twice, they gave me shots then they inserted a tube down my throat to my stomach.

After continuing to experience extreme pain in her stomach area, she was brought by a friend to the emergency room and an X-ray was taken. Sophiap states she was diagnosed with gallstones and was operated on in December 1990. Her experience in the hospital left her somewhat confused, as she recalled.

> I was a bit disappointed, because when they explained, they only talked about removing gallstones, but then they also removed the gallbladder. When I was in surgery, I didn't have a Khmer translator . . . [I] understood some and not some, because according to what I understood, it was not the removal of gallbladder, but just the stones.
>
> . . . I have had a change of heart [about doctors], but I never mention it. And ever since the time of the operation up until now, inside of my body is not well. When I'm exhausted, I'm just so totally exhausted . . . without energy.

Although the gall bladder operation relieved the acute pain, Sophiap continued to experience bodily pain and other symptoms. Her heart beat irregularly, her hands and feet shook, she could not sleep, and she experienced pain all over her body. She was prescribed more than fifty different kinds of medication since 1987, but their effects are not long-lasting and she struggles with how to deal with the pain.

> . . . Those medications, you can't say they don't help, when I take them they help, when I stop, it hurts again and that's how it's been. That's why I say, how long am I going to live if I keep getting sick like this. If not this, it's that. When it hurts bad, I think in my thoughts that I do not want to live.

From the Western psychiatric standpoint, Sophiap has the classic symptoms of post-traumatic stress disorder. Throughout the course of her six interviews, Sophiap described reexperiencing traumatic events through auditory and visual flashbacks, emotional numbing through dissociation, and increased physiological arousal. This is part of what she describes:

> It is like for those four or five years my brain was totally attached to that [Pol Pot era] without forgetting at all you know, for those four or five years. . . . Like yesterday, going to class, like there was a suffering within me, there was a problem, I was unhappy. And when the teacher spoke to me. . . . I stared at his face. I stared just like that, but I had no idea what he was asking, I blanked out for that moment . . . because my brain was thinking about other stories, it's I wasn't focused on him, but I heard him . . . everybody in the whole class laughed so hard. I kept staring at him when he questioned me, I snapped out of it only when he called my name, but I had no idea what he was lecturing on, I was thinking about who knows where, my brain went to Cambodia actually. . . .
>
> Sometimes I keep thinking about my first sister [Sokha] that I often talk about, the one that died, I keep recalling it as if it's right in front of my eyes, how she was dying, whatever took place then, I keep seeing it exactly like that . . .
>
> Sometimes I dream that I dig through dead bodies, sometimes there are sixty of them in a bunker. I would keep on digging, searching for my sister that was killed at the bottom of the ditch, sobbing, when I wake up, my tears stream down my face as if I was truly crying. I sweat as if I was really working.

Sophiap's psychiatrist confirmed a diagnosis of post-traumatic stress disorder; however, her internist's response negates these findings. In this passage she shares how the internist discounts her suffering:

> I ask my doctor why am I so sick, I'm sick constantly. The doctor then answered that he cannot detect it, but my ailment cannot kill me, it cannot kill me like cancer and stuff. That's how he answered me. And so I responded that the ailment cannot kill me, that may be true, but it can hurt me and make it hard for me to live . . .
>
> For me, I might have hope with the ACRS (Asian Counseling and Referral Service) counselor, but with my regular doctor, I have no hope. He has thrown quite a bit of unpleasant words at me. He said, "You're sick, but you're not sick every day and you should be able to work."

The robotic procedures of the welfare system and workers' apparent lack of knowledge about Cambodians' refugee status or post-traumatic stress disorder caused Sophiap needless suffering. She described her interaction with the welfare system this way:

> Welfare calls me to see them almost everyday. If they don't call, they send letters. They keep threatening to cut off assistance for this and that constantly, and that stirs up my mind so much . . .
>
> Last month, welfare wrote to me to go to work and stuff, they are cutting me off from welfare. And another thing, the doctor doesn't help me very much. So I'm having such a hard time, I worried so much in the last couple of days, that I got sick again.

Physicians' conflicting views of Sophiap's illness, complicated by welfare policy, which would not validate the special circumstances of her illness or accept moral responsibility to aid these individuals, continually, thwarted Sophiap's attempts to heal and exacerbated her illness.

ASSESSMENT PRACTICE PRINCIPLES

Assessment practices that purposefully seek to understand how survivors of torture and extreme stress conceptualize their suffering are essential to determining the combination of healing and treatment practices that will facilitate the individual's healing processes. Differing normative definitions of illness and suffering within societies not only are linked to differing systems of intervention, but also may ultimately determine the appropriateness and effectiveness of treatment. Thus, a societal group in which illness is " . . . defined and caused by anatomical and physiological alterations will focus on these physical characteristics . . . in seeking prevention or cure" (Hahn, 1995, p. 19). In such a society, the system of medical evaluation does not ordinarily consider the individual capable of self-diagnosis and will often not listen to the attributions or complaints of the afflicted person. By contrast, a society that defines illness through " . . . human experience and caused by human interactions—physiological as well as social—may attend more to its social organization and the understandings of its patients in addressing prevention and cure" (Hahn, 1995, p. 19).

Studies of Cambodian American refugees have found that they prefer services that are accessible, the provision of language translators, and sensitivity to their cultural needs and background (Frye, 1990; Morelli, 1996). Five areas to improve cross-cultural assessment practice may be gleaned from Sophiap's narrative. The first of these is the necessity for trained, competent language translators. These translators need a sound understanding of the differences in cultural beliefs and values regarding family, social customs, and health care between the host and immigrating culture. Translators need to have basic knowledge of the Western concept of PTSD as well as an understanding of how PTSD symptoms may be understood in the Cambodian culture.

Second, social workers who work with Cambodian refugees need to be informed about their sociocultural traditions, health care, and spiritual beliefs, as well as any other pertinent information mediating their functioning for the purpose of not only informing the assessment process, but, equally importantly to educate interdisciplinary professionals who work with this population. A sound understanding of the refugee's cultural and personal background provides the basis for a deeper understanding of the client's situation, and, thus, a more informed basis for multilevel coordinated, efficacious intervention and service planning.

Third, in matters of health care with Asian refugees, Western service providers need to be open to collaboration and consultation with family elders, trusted family friends, or respected community leaders. Conferring in this way with elders and other trusted, respected individuals provides a more comprehensive picture of events, chronology, and family history, and offers the refugee the collective assurance of the family network.

Fourth, social work practitioners working with refugees should have a working knowledge of the symptoms and dynamics of post-traumatic stress disorder, current treatment modalities, and the prognosis, from both Western and culture-specific perspectives. Such an understanding would aid service providers in advocating for services on behalf of refugees while educating interdisciplinary colleagues about their unique situation and needs.

Finally, culturally competent assessment practices should include awareness of policies and geopolitical histories that may have contributed to power imbalances and, in turn, civil unrest. Without these macro level perspectives, practitioners are not simply less effective in intervention, research, and policymaking efforts, they become purveyors of guileful forms of oppression.

Conclusion

Assessment processes that bring to awareness clients' cultural health beliefs, traditional health practices, spiritual values, geopolitical history, and other culture-specific factors have greater potential to effect culturally appropriate interventions and, equally importantly, mediate social justice for our clients. When the cultural context in which the survivor has lived, reasoned, adjusted, and found meaning is cut away, the individual's identity in relation to that culture is also discounted. This decontextualization, ultimately, perpetuates cultural oppression and reduces the chances for accurate assessment as well as creative avenues to healing. Culturally competent assessments that are based in clients' cultural context and conducted from a strengths perspective have a greater likelihood of contributing to the healing process by enabling Cambodian refugees to receive the care and treatment congruent with their health beliefs.

REFERENCES

Albin, D. A. & Hood, M. (1990). *The cambodian agony.* Armonk: M. E. Sharpe.

Aronson, L. (1987, February). Traditional Cambodian health beliefs and practices: Understanding Cambodian traditions will facilitate their care in a Western setting. *Rhode Island Medical Journal, 70,* 73–78.

Boehnlein, J. K. (1987). Clinical relevance of grief and mourning among Cambodian refugees. *Social Science and Medicine, 25* (7), 765–772.

Carlson, E. & Rosser-Hogan, R. (1993). Mental health status of Cambodian refugees ten years after leaving their homes. *American Journal of Orthopsychiatry, 63* (2), 223–231.

Chandler, D. P. (1992). *A history of Cambodia.* Boulder, CO: Westview.

Cheung, P. (1993). Somatisation as a presentation in depression and posttraumatic stress disorder among Cambodian refugees. *Australian and New Zealand Journal of Psychiatry, 27* (3), 422–428.

D'Avanzo, C. (1997). Southeast Asians: Asian-Pacific Americans at risk for substance misuse. *Substance Use and Misuse, 32* (7–8), 829–848.

Duncan, J. (1987). *Cambodian refugee use of indigenous and Western healers to prevent or slleviate mental illness.* Unpublished Dissertation, University of Washington, Seattle.

Ebihara, M. M. (1968). *Svay, a Khmer village in Cambodia.* New York: Columbia University Press.

Frye, B. A. (1990). The process of health care decision making among Cambodian immigrant women. *International Quarterly of Community Health Education, 10* (2), 113–124.

Frye, B. A. (1993). Health care decision making among Cambodian refugee women. In S. Bair (Ed.), *Wings of gauze: Women of color and the experience of health and illness* (pp. 93–108). Detroit: Wayne State University Press.

Frye, B. A. & D'Avanzo, C. D. (1994). Cultural themes in family stress and violence among Cambodian refugee women in the inner city. *Advances in Nursing Science, 16* (3), 64–77.

Gambrill, E. (1997). *Social work practice: A citical thinker's guide.* New York: Oxford University Press.

Hahn, R. A. (1995). *Sickness and healing: An anthropological perspective.* New Haven: Yale University Press.

Hall, E. T. (1977). *Beyond culture.* Garden City, NY: Anchor.

Hepworth, D. H., Rooney, R. H., & Larsen, J. A. (1997). *Direct social work practice.* Pacific Grove, CA: Brooks Cole.

Kinzie, J. D. (1989). Therapeutic approaches to traumatized Cambodian refugees. *Journal of Traumatic Stress, 2* (1), 75–91.

Kinzie, J. D., Leung, P., Boehnlein, J. K., & Fleck, J. (1987). Antidepressant blood levels in Southeast Asians: clinical and cultural implications. *Journal of Nervous and Mental Disease, 175* (8), 480–485.

Kroll, J., Habenicht, M., MacKenzie, T., Yang, M., Chan, S., Vang, T., Nguyen, T., Ly, M., Phommassouvanh, B., Nguyen, H., Vang, V., Souvannasoth, L., & Cabugao, R. (1989). Depression and posttraumatic stress disorder in Southeast Asian refugees. *American Journal of Psychiatry, 146* (12), 1592–1597.

Kuo, J. & Porter, K. (1998). *Health status of Asian Americans: United States, 1992–1994. Advance data from vital and health statistics* (p. 298). Hyattsville: National Center for Health Statistics.

Marcucci, J. (1994). Sharing the pain: Critical values and behaviors. In M. M. Ebihara, C. A. Mortland, & J. Ledgerwood (Eds.), *Cambodian culture since 1975: Homeland and exile* (pp. 129–140). Ithaca, NY: Cornell Press.

Meyer, C. H. (1993). *Assessment in social work practice.* New York: Columbia University Press.

Morelli, P. T. (1996). *Trauma and healing: The construction of meaning among survivors of the Cambodian Holocaust.* Unpublished Dissertation, University of Washington, Seattle.

Morris, P., Silove, D., & Manicavasagar, V. (1993). Variations in the therapeutic interventions for Cambodian and Chilean refugee survivors of torture and trauma: A pilot study. *Australian and New Zealand Journal of Psychiatry, 23* (3), 429–435.

National Association of Social Workers. (1996). *Code of ethics.* Washington, DC: Author.

Seanglein, B. (1991). *The warrior heritage: a psychological perspective of Cambodian trauma.* El Cerrito, CA: The Author.

Spector, R. E. (1996). *Cultural diversity in health and illness,* (4th ed.) Stamford: Appleton and Lange.

U.S. Committee for Refugees. (1996). 1995 statistical issue. *Refugee Reports, 16* (12), 1–13.

The author gratefully acknowledges the participants of the Cambodian American Health-Seeking and Social Networks Project and The National Research Center on Asian American Mental Health for their support of this work.

CHAPTER 15

ASSESSMENT OF ASIAN AMERICAN/PACIFIC ISLANDER ORGANIZATIONS AND COMMUNITIES

JULIAN CHUN-CHUNG CHOW

As U.S. society has increasingly become culturally diverse, there is concern that social work must be practiced in a culturally competent manner. The term *cultural competency* has generally referred to "the set of knowledge and skills that a social worker must develop in order to be effective with multicultural clients" (Lum, 1999, p. 3). Although different cultural competence practice models have been introduced, cultural awareness, knowledge acquisition, and skill development are the major tasks for social workers to comprehend if cultural competence practices are to be effective (Devore & Schlesinger, 1999; Diller, 1999; Green, 1999; Lecca, Quervalu, Nunes, & Gonzales, 1998; Lum, 1999).

Within the generalist practice framework, cultural competence must be realized throughout the helping process. It should begin from the early planning of engagement and assessment to the implementation of intervention and evaluation. Successful intervention is based on adequate assessment of a situation in which practice occurred (Kirst-Ashman & Hull, 1999). As such, a culturally competent assessment can be seen as one of the most critical stages in social work practice.

It is important to recognize that individuals do not exist in a vacuum. Assessment, therefore, must be conducted across practice levels: practitioner, agency, and community (Miley, O'Melia, & DuBois, 1998). While assessment conducted at the micro level targets the individuals' strengths, resources, and capacity to resolve their difficulties, assessment at the macro levels aims at both the organization and community aspects of individuals' lives. At the organizational level, culturally competent assessment examines the agency's context of social work practice. Of particular interest are two issues: First, the extent to which the organization environment supports culturally competent practice, and, second, the responsiveness of service delivery to multicultural groups. At the community level, assessment is conducted to evaluate the impact of the larger social and political context on the aggregated needs of the individuals (Greene & McGuire, 1998). This chapter focuses on the assessment of organization and community in the Asian Americans/Pacific Islanders (AAPI) population.

THE MYTHS OF COMMUNITY PRACTICE: PROBLEMS IN ASSESSING AAPI POPULATIONS

In order to conduct culturally competent assessment adequately, it is first necessary to address the myth of community practice within the AAPI context (Chow, 1998).

The Myth of "Lump Sum"

The first myth to be challenged is that all AAPI are alike, ignoring the diverse geographic and cultural backgrounds, immigration histories, or generation differences within these groups. For example, the term *Asian Americans and Pacific Islanders* actually refers to a multiethnic group of two large categories of Asian Americans and Pacific Islander Americans, lumping more than thirty distinct ethnic groups together. In a community as diverse as the AAPI, we must recognize the diversity within and between various ethnic groups, while, at the same time, not losing sight of the similarities among these groups in terms of the discrimination, prejudice, and oppression that they experience in this country.

The Myth of "Dim Sum"

People who hold this assumption, which focuses solely on the uniqueness of each ethnic/cultural group, believe that each group has its own perspective and only those who belong to the same group can understand one another. But this exclusive view ignores the larger forces that affect all minority groups, and further pits ethnic groups against one another. In a multiracial society, all members of ethnic minority groups, in fact, share a common fate. For example, California's Proposition 187, in 1994, which denied public assistance to undocumented immigrants, was first carefully orchestrated as the "solution" to prevent illegal Mexican migrants from entering the United States (Gibbs, 1999). Indeed, a significant proportion of minorities voted in favor of the issue. Unfortunately, such an anti-immigrant, anti-foreigner sentiment has gradually emerged into an antiaffirmative action, antisocial spending campaign from which all people of color suffer.

The Myth of "Zero Sum"

The "zero sum" myth is based on the assumption that someone's gains are someone else's losses. It promotes the belief that resources for human services are limited and only the most "needy" groups can be served. Groups try to outdo each other by portraying themselves as having the most severe problems and, thus, deserving of the most aid. Different racial and ethnic groups are fighting, oftentimes against each other, for the same piece of the pie, which is already too small to begin with. The zero sum myth has become a control mechanism to direct one's attention to maintaining the existing pie, rather than making the pie bigger. The consequences of a zero sum strategy are clearly seen in the recent movement of block grants for human services. With a set dollar amount, different groups have to justify their needs in order to obtain funding. Once again, the dominant groups are better able to demonstrate need and are thus more likely to receive support. Consequently, tension rises between the smaller and the dominant groups, further creating resentment and fragmentation within the AAPI communities (Espiritu, 1992).

The myths of lump sum, dim sum, and zero sum are often intertwined to create a distorted view of multicultural community practice. Due to cultural differences and a lack of communication, misunderstandings between and within the AAPI and other ethnic minority communities are likely to happen. For example, Gibbs (1999) warns that the AAPI group is being played against other ethnic groups for their visible "success" in recent years. Culturally competent social work practice must develop strategies to dispel these myths so that accurate assessment is conducted and appropriate intervention can be implemented. This is particularly important when working with a group as diverse as the AAPI population. Without recognizing these myths, practitioners are likely to base their assessment on faulty assumptions, and, thus, draw mistaken conclusions about the community's service needs. As a result, we may sabotage efforts to provide appropriate interventions and obtain desirable outcomes.

SOCIODEMOGRAPHIC OVERVIEW

Culturally competent assessment should begin with a better understanding of the varied composition of the target population. The AAPI community comprises ethnic groups from various geographic areas in Asia, the Pacific Rim, and the Pacific Basins. Geographically, Asian Americans include groups that originated from East Asia (e.g., Chinese, Japanese, Korean), Southeast Asia (e.g., Cambodian, Hmong, Laotian, Vietnamese, Filipino, Thai), the Indian subcontinent or South Asia (e.g., Indian, Pakistani, Nepalese), whereas Pacific Islander Americans include people who originated in the Pacific that can be grouped in three categories: Polynesians (e.g., Hawaiians, Tongans, Samoans, Tahitians), Micronesians (e.g., Guamanian, people from Marshall Islands, Kiribati, Federated States of Micronesia), and Melanesians (e.g., Fijian, people from the Solomons, Papua New Guinea, Vanatu).

AAPIs were the fastest growing ethnic minority group in the 1980s. The Census Bureau reported that the AAPI population in 1990 was 7.3 million, an increase of 95 percent from 3.4 million in 1980, and has continued to grow in the 1990s. The number of AAPIs was projected to be 10.7 million in April 1999, an increase of 46.6

percent from 1990, compared to a 9.7 percent increase of the overall population during the same period of time.

AAPIs are geographically concentrated in certain portions of the country. In 1990, 55 percent of the AAPI lived in the West, compared to 22 percent of the overall population. Five states, California, New York, Hawaii, Texas, and Illinois, housed more than 60 percent of the AAPI population. Almost all AAPI (94%) lived in the metropolitan areas and a large proportion (44.7%) resided inside central cities, making them the most urbanized group among all racial ethnic groups in the United States. Overall, about 63 percent of the AAPIs were born outside of the United States. However, there are tremendous variations within groups. For example, only 13 percent of Pacific Islander Americans were foreign-born, and over 70 percent of Japanese Americans were born in this country (many are third- and fourth-generation Americans). A higher proportion of the people from Southeast Asia was born in other countries. The majority (over 75%) of the Vietnamese, Cambodian, Laotian, and Hmong in the United States came since 1975, after the passage of the Indochina Migration and Refugee Assistance Act. Immigrants could become U.S. citizens through naturalization. AAPI immigrants are more likely to become naturalized citizens than are Europeans. Naturalization rates among immigrants from Asian countries have historically been above the national average.

A large proportion of AAPIs was raised with a second language other than English. About two-thirds of AAPI persons five years old and over spoke an Asian or Pacific Island language at home. About half (55.6%) of AAPIs reported that they did not speak English "very well." The proportion was highest among the Southeast Asians, who were the most recently arrived and whose primary language is not English. Interestingly, still over one-third of the Filipinos and Asian Indians reported that they did not speak English very well, even though English is commonly used in these countries.

Perhaps socioeconomic status is one of the most midunderstood statistics for the AAPI population. There is a stereotypical perception that AAPI is a "model minority" because of its economic success and high education attainment. What is being overlooked is the fact that 14 percent of Asian Americans and 17 percent of Pacific Islanders lived in poverty in 1989, both above the national average of 13 percent. The poverty rate for the Homng was 64 percent, and 43 percent for the Cambodians. The model minority image simply does not apply to many AAPI populations.

The selected demographic highlights above point out the diverse nature of the AAPI population. It is particularly important, therefore, to emphasize that the term *Asian American Pacific Islander* is not homogeneous and distinctions must be recognized when working with this population.

VALUES AND NORMS

The importance of understanding the role of cultural values on organization and community assessment cannot be overstated. The value system of AAPI cultures presents a different worldview from the dominant U.S. culture. Such a difference directly influences the way AAPIs perceive the existing service delivery system. The extent to which services match the cultural values determines the appropriateness of it. For example, AAPIs place a high value on harmony in relationships. For many AAPIs, mutual dependency, instead of individual independence, is the ultimate achievement (Chung, 1992; Lee, 1998). The cultural values of filial piety, modesty, respect for authority, and communal responsibility, all reflect the underlying philosophical principle of pursuing and maintaining a harmonious relationship in one's life. Ideally, a mutually dependent relationship should first be created in one's own family, then followed by the extended family, including the kinship and the clan network, and, finally, in the community. As a result, AAPI often put family interests above individual interests. Therefore, the dynamic interaction among individual, family, organization, and community must be carefully assessed for the AAPI population.

The diversity among AAPIs makes it difficult to identify a set of cultural values or norms that can be generalized to the entire population. For example, while it is generally believed that AAPIs are influenced by the religious beliefs of Confucianism and Buddhism, Filipinos are often Catholic and Koreans are most likely Christian. It is important, then, to keep in mind the differences within as well as across the AAPI population (Lecca, et al., 1998; Uba, 1994). We will now consider some of the practice implications for assessment at the organization level.

ORGANIZATION ASSESSMENT: PRACTICE PRINCIPLES AND SKILLS

Cultural competence assessment in organizational settings addresses the agency context in which services take place. The central question is whether the agency and the services it provides are responsive to the needs of the AAPI population. Social workers must be sensitive to the overall climate of service delivery in the organization. For many ethnic groups, it has been suggested that a culturally familiar background (e.g., folk music, ethnic posters, receptionists who speak their languages) for service delivery would reduce the barriers to service use (Cross, Bazron, Dennis, & Issacs, 1989; Dana, Behn, & Gonwa, 1992). As AAPIs have repeatedly been found to underuse social services across settings (Lee, 1997; Mokuau, 1991; Yamashiro & Matsuoka, 1997; Zane, Takeuchi, & Young, 1994), it is important for the agency to create a welcoming and inviting environment for AAPIs when services are provided.

For the purpose of this discussion, service agencies include both mainstream and AAPI-specific agencies. Generally speaking, mainstream agencies refer to those human and social services agencies that provide services to the general population in the community. AAPI-specific agencies are those agencies that target AAPIs as their primary service population. There is no reason to assume that mainstream agencies cannot be culturally competent; likewise, it is not necessary that an ethnic-specific agency will automatically be culturally competent. Cultural competence, therefore, should be seen as a means, rather than an end. It is a process that service providers ought to pursue in order to improve their service delivery. Among social workers, culturally competent practice must occur in both types of agency settings.

Three categories of information can be used to assess the level of cultural competence in an organizational setting: the user, the service, and the agency profile.

The User Profile

The first question to address is "who uses services?" When working with a group as diverse as the AAPI, it is important not only to know who the users are but also to differentiate their ethnicities. In addition, special attention should be given to family structure, immigration history, socioeconomic status, languages, and literacy of the individuals.

Ideally, the user profile should reflect the population of different groups in the community. This is particularly important because the composition of the AAPI population is changing rapidly. The Hmong population, for example, has increased 1,631 percent between 1980 and 1990. Service providers should be sensitive to the issue of representation when reviewing their user profile. If a disparity among different groups is noticed—for example, if current users are underrepresentative (or overrepresentative) of certain subgroups—it is necessary to further determine the reasons behind such patterns.

The Service Profile

The service profile examines the extent to which the agency's services reach the AAPI population and what kinds of services are used. By collecting information, such as the existing service inventory, the ways these services are provided, and the patterns of service use, possible barriers to service can be identified, and, eventually, removed. The following factors should be examined in a service profile analysis:

Accessibility.   Accessibility is concerned with the question of whether the agency's services are easily and openly accessible to the AAPI population. Accessibility can be physical or psychological. Studies have indicated that the geographic location of services is an important factor for service use by AAPI populations (Chow, 1999; Mokuau & Shimizu, 1991). When services are located in the immediate neighborhood where AAPIs reside, the likelihood of use increases (Iglehart & Becerra, 1995). Accessibility, however, should also be assessed psychologically. For example, an agency will be perceived as psychologically accessible when people feel safe about the surrounding areas of the agency.

Availability.   The types of services available to the AAPI populations need to be assessed carefully. The concern, however, must go beyond simply asking if a particular service is provided (e.g., child care or family counseling). Rather, the question is whether culturally and linguistically competent services are available. The availability of linguistically proficient services is especially important for the recent immigrants. Even if a broad array of services exists in an agency, recent immigrants are not likely to use them due to their limited English-speaking capacity. Services, therefore, must be available in the languages that the AAPI groups use.

Appropriateness.   Perhaps the question of whether the services are appropriate to the AAPI population is the most crucial one. However, there is no consensus around how to define *appropriateness.* Nonetheless, analyzing the patterns of service use by different AAPI groups may provide some evidence. For example, if, when compared to other ethnic groups, AAPI mental health service consumers repeatedly have a higher premature termination rate, that is, early dropout from services before termination, one would argue that the AAPI consumers might not have received the appropriate services (Uba, 1994). Appropriate services should fit into the cultural context of the community they serve (Aponte & Morrow, 1995; Uba & Sue, 1991; Yamashiro & Matsuoka, 1997). For example, a multiservice, one-stop neighborhood center is considered a culturally appropriate approach for Chinese immigrant communities in the United States (Chow, 1999).

Service Outcome.   Another important indicator is the service outcome for the AAPI users who receive services. Analyzing how long a desired effect has lasted could assess service outcome. For example, to find out the service outcome of a job-training program for a group of recent Southeast Asian refugees, it would be important to know what proportion of them have remained employed after an extended period of time. In addition, while client satisfaction surveys are common outcome measures, the survey instrument selected should be properly designed to assess levels of cultural and linguistic competence of services providers.

The Agency Profile

Services are delivered in an agency setting. It is important to know to what degree and in what ways the agency is supportive of culturally competent practice. Mason, Benjamin, and Lewis (1996) point out that the commitment of an agency to cultural competence can best be observed at the policymaking level. The organizational culture should be one in which culturally competent practice is encouraged and implemented throughout the agency, rather than being isolated or marginalized in a few units (Fong & Gibbs, 1995). A culturally competent agency will prepare its entire work force with the necessary policies, procedures, staffing, and environment, such that services and programs can be delivered in a culturally appropriate manner.

Policies and Procedures.   There should be written policies and procedures regarding cultural competence practices in the organization. Miley and her colleagues (1998) point out that organizational policy guides an agency's operations in the areas of human resources, program evaluation, and service eligibility. All policies and procedures should aim at providing and promoting an environment for delivering culturally competent services that are appropriate to the AAPI community.

Leadership Development.   The extent to which the agency is committed to the AAPI population can be seen at the leadership level. For example, the ethnic composition of the board of directors and administrative and managerial staff should reflect the ethnic groups in the community. Within the AAPI community, many social service agencies are directed by Chinese, Japanese, or Korean Americans because they have a longer history in professional services. Leadership development and capacity building for the newer groups, such as Filipinos and Southeast Asians, must be encouraged.

Human Resources and Staff Development.   One common frustration among many AAPI social workers is that, in many agencies, only a few bicultural or bilingual direct caregivers are hired, and they are usually isolated in certain departments (Fong & Gibbs, 1995). Therefore, it is crucial that a diverse work force be recruited at all levels: managerial, administrative, professional, and clerical. While active recruitment is a necessary first step, another critical element is retention. Staff turnover rate for the AAPI employees should be low in a culturally competent agency. Ongoing staff development and training should be provided to insure that the most qualified and knowledgeable staff at the agency implements culturally appropriate services.

Agency Networks.   A culturally competent agency must go beyond its own field of practice by developing multiple networks, both to receive referrals from and to make referrals to other sources (Miley, O'Melia, & Dubois, 1998). A strong organizational network can be seen as a power base for community organizing and empowerment purposes (Gutierrez, GlenMaye, & Delois, 1995; Rivera & Erlich, 1998). It is particularly important for the agencies to recognize the many possible resources that exist within the AAPI community. Despite the more traditional social and human service providers, an AAPI culturally appropriate network should include many formal as well as informal resources. Some examples are the community leaders from civil organizations, self-help groups, religious organizations (e.g., churches in the Korean and Filipino communities and temples in the Thai and Vietnamese communities), surname or clan organizations in the Chinese communities, ethnic or language-specific media, and a variety of advocacy groups that one can find locally.

COMMUNITY ASSESSMENT: IDENTIFYING PROBLEMS AND POTENTIAL FOR CHANGE

The ecological framework in generalist social work practice recognizes the importance of community in shaping the well-being of an individual's daily life. As with other communities (Netting, Kettner, & McMurtry, 1998), the different ethnic AAPI communities can be defined in terms of geographic areas (e.g., Chinatown, Korean Town, Little Toyko), religion (e.g., Buddhism, Hindism, Muslim, Catholic, Christian), immigration history (e.g., foreign-born, U.S.-born), and many other possible means. The purpose of conducting a community assessment is to better under-stand the characteristics of the target population so that appropriate intervention can be developed and delivered.

Assessing Community Needs.   With the increasing number of AAPIs in cities all across the United States, social service agencies serving AAPI communities dis-covered that new needs and demands have emerged. This is particularly impor-tant for those community agencies that historically served a single ethnic population such as Chinese, Japanese, or Korean Americans. With the changing demographic and ethnic composition of the AAPI population, the demand for new services has made existing agencies realize that they must be prepared for the influx of a newer population. Even within the same ethnic group, there are sub-group differences. For example, there has been a recent increase in the number of immigrants from the People's Republic of China, the majority of whom came from rural areas and do not speak Mandarin, but a local dialect such as Shanshainese or Fujanese. Thus, agencies must seek ways to meet the new needs of the changing AAPI population. One commonly used method to identify needs is to conduct a community needs assessment. Throughout the 1980s, several comprehensive com-munity needs assessments were conducted in areas where large numbers of AAPIs resided.

In response to the growing number of AAPIs in Los Angeles, the United Way conducted a comprehensive needs assessment of ten AAPI groups (Cambodian, Chinese, Japanese, Korean, Lao, Filipino, Samoan, Thai, Tongan, Vietnamese) in 1988. The purpose was to determine the human service needs for the ethnic-specific as well as the overall AAPI community. As anticipated, there were considerable variations in terms of service priorities for different ethnic groups. For example, while social adjustment and employment have been identified as the top priority needs for emerging AAPI groups such as the Southeast Asian and Filipino, some other groups expressed community empowerment and advocacy as the major con-cerns. Despite the inter-group differences, six service needs were identified in two priority groupings for the overall AAPI community: The highest priority group includes the needs of community resource development and advocacy, mental health and health services, and elderly services. The secondary priority group includes services for the youth, family services, and employment and language education (United Way of Los Angeles, 1988).

During the 1980s, the AAPI population increased by more than 210,000 in New York, New Jersey, and Connecticut. As a result of the influx of the AAPI population, a needs assessment study was conducted in 1989 by the United Way of Tri-State. Seven AAPI groups, including Chinese, Filipino, Korean, Japanese, Indochinese (Vietnamese, Laotians, and Cambodians), and other AAPIs (Hawaiians, Samoans, Eurasians, and other Southeast Asians) were studied. A number of priority needs, particularly focusing on language difficulties and lack of opportunities, such as English proficiency, bilingual education, business and employment, affordable housing, child care, family services, and health care, were identified (United Way of Tri-State, 1989).

Another comprehensive community needs assessment was conducted in 1992 by the Asian Community Center of Sacramento Valley in California. The study population included eleven AAPI groups: Cambodian, Chinese-Vietnamese, Hmong, Iu Mien, Lao, Vietnamese, Chinese, Filipino, Japanese, Korean, Pacific Islander. Like the Los Angeles study, different ethnic groups prioritized different needs. More importantly, generation differences in service needs were clearly demonstrated by the immigrant and the U.S.-born respondents. The first-generation AAPI immigrant groups are most concerned with their basic daily living problems. Issues such as language difficulties, jobs, housing, health care, and social services are crucial for their adjustment to the new society. On the other hand, the U.S.-born groups are more concerned with societal and community needs. Issues such as cultural activity and employment opportunity are top on their list. Both groups, however, share common concerns for crime and education (Asian Community Center of Sacramento Valley, 1992).

The irony is that service needs are largely differentiated by generations. Therefore, a culturally competent community needs assessment must be aware of the internal differences and not overgeneralize its findings to other populations. In this way, appropriate services can then be planned to meet the articulated needs. For the first-generation immigrant population, immediate individual needs for settlement and adjustment are the most important concern. Social services, such as English as a second language, job training and employment, affordable housing, and health care are usually ranked as priorities. However, getting access to these services in the community has become another important issue that needs to be addressed. The needs of the U.S.-born generation are mainly focused on the well-being of the AAPI community as a whole. Participation in the larger society on issues such as improving the conditions of school and education, equal opportunity for jobs and employment, political advocacy on civil rights and coalition building are commonly identified.

The difference in the needs of the two generations is not surprising and can be understood as existing along a continuum. While meeting individual needs for the immigrant generation represents a first step in coping with life in the new environment, eventually the community must work together to pursue the collective good. The concerns of the U.S.-born AAPIs on larger societal issues reflects such an effort. Outreach to other ethnic communities and coalition building must become part of the community building effort.

Assessing Community Strengths. Community needs assessment has traditionally focused on problems; equally important for community building and empowerment, however, is assessing strengths in the community (Gutierrez, Parsons, & Cox, 1998; Saleebey, 1997). A community strengths assessment aims to identify both the existing and potential resources, which, in turn, could be used for capacity building and development purposes (Kretzmann & McKnight, 1993). A strengths assessment focuses on partnership and collaboration, and efforts are made to enhance relationships and connections that are formed in the community.

Building capacity for the community to prevent and resolve problems is the premise of the strengths assessment. Glickman & Servon (1998) point out that successful community development should help the community to build capacities in five areas.

Resources

The community should have the capacity to attract and receive resources for improving the well-being of the AAPI community. Resource development should be multifaceted, including not only those for human and social services but also for economic development, such as investments and assets in the community.

Organizational

Capacities for both the public and private institutional basis of the community should be enhanced. In addition to the more traditional social agencies that provide services to the community—health care, housing, and recreation—other key institutions such as banks, police, libraries, schools, and churches are only a few examples of the organizational capacity that should have developed in the community.

Programmatic

The capacity to provide a comprehensive system of care over the life span should be developed in the community. For the AAPI community, early preventive program development for children, youth, adults, and elderly are important because AAPI are less likely to use treatment methods of intervention. In addition, programs should be tailored to the particular needs expressed by different AAPI generations.

Network

The capacity to improve the overall well-being of the AAPI community would be enhanced when coalitions are built successfully with other ethnic minority communities. Inter- and intra-agency outreach and collaboration should occur both inside and outside the AAPI community.

Political

The capacity to exercise political power to influence and to leverage constructive change in the AAPI community should be realized. With active political participation through advocacy and election, the U.S. political establishment will have to pay closer attention to the needs of the AAPI community.

CASE STUDY

Mary and Tom are school social workers in a junior high school in an inner city school district on the East Coast. It is a neighborhood school where most children walk or ride their bikes to school. Over the years, the community where the school is located has gone through many changes. Formerly a blue-collar neighborhood with the majority of its residents from eastern European ethnic groups, it is now mostly AAPI-, Latino, and African American. Although the demographic composition of the student body has changed gradually over time, one noticeable change is the influx of recent AAPI immigrants with diverse backgrounds. Many of the AAPI children do not speak English when they first attend school, although the majority of them successfully master the language in a short period of time. There are also a sizable number of AAPI students who were born in the United States, and English is their first language. Despite the fact that both groups come from immigrant families, the two groups tend to play with their own peers.

Although it is generally believed that AAPI children excel in school, Mary and Tom soon found out that some AAPI students do well academically, but many others are struggling. Also, there has been an increasing number of AAPI students referred to the school social work office over the last two years. The situation worsened when the school district cut back on bilingual education, so resources are inadequate to accommodate the many new needs of the AAPI students.

In addition to the concern of academic achievement, Mary and Tom are aware of the problem of latchkey AAPI children; many AAPI students simply stay at school, while others hang out on the playground until very late. They have also noticed that many children under ten years of age stay home by themselves after school, and some are even responsible for the care of younger siblings.

When Mary and Tom shared their concern with the teachers, it was further discovered that many parents worked long hours and did not get home until late in the evening. As a result, parental involvement in school activities is low. Most parents of latch-key children did not attend parent conferences; those who did had to rely on the children for translation, creating an awful situation, particularly when the teachers try to discuss some of the concerns that they have regarding the children.

Mary and Tom have decided that something should be done for these latchkey children. By using the organization and community assessment framework provided in this chapter, discuss and develop a plan to assess the readiness of the organization and the community to serve these AAPI students.

REFERENCES

Aponte, J. & Morrow, C. (1995). Community approaches with ethnic groups. In J. Aponte, R. Rivers, & J. Wohl (Eds.), *Psychological interventions and cultural diversity* (pp. 128–144). Boston, MA: Allyn & Bacon.

Asian Community Center of Sacramento Valley. (1992). *Needs assessment of the Asian/Pacific Islander community in Sacramento County.* Sacramento: Author.

Chow, J. (1998). Reaction to "Multicultural social work education—A perspective on community practice" by Felix Rivera. Paper presented at the Multicultural social work education in the 21st century, December 4–5, 1998, Ann Arbor, MI.

Chow, J. (1999). Multiservice centers in Chinese American immigrant communities: Practice principles and challenges. *Social Work, 44,* 70–81.

Chung, D. (1992). Asian cultural commonalities: A comparison with mainstream American culture. In S. Furuto, R. Biswas, D. Chung, K. Murase, F. Ross-Sheriff (Eds.), *Social work practice with Asian Americans* (pp. 27–44). Newbury Park, CA: Sage.

Cross, T., Bazron, B., Dennis, K., & Issacs, M. (1989). *Toward a culturally competent system of care.* Washington, DC: Georgetown University Child Development Center.

Dana, R., Behn, J., & Gonwa, T. (1992). A checklist for the examination of cultural competence in social service agencies. *Research in Social Work Practice, 2,* 220–233.

Devore, W. & Schlesinger, E. (1999). *Ethnic-sensitive social work practice,* 5th ed. Boston, MA: Allyn & Bacon.

Diller, J. (1999). *Cultural diversity: A primer for the human services.* Belmont, CA: Wadsworth.

Espiritu, Y. (1992). *Asian American panethnicity.* Philadelphia, PA: Temple University Press.

Fong, L. & Gibbs, J. (1995). Facilitating services to multicultural communities in a dominant culture setting: An organizational perspective. *Administration in Social Work, 19* (2), pp. 1–24.

Gibbs, J. (1999). The California crucible: Towards a new paradigm of race and ethnic relations. *Journal of Multicultural Social Work, 7,* 1–18.

Glickman, N. & Servon, L. (1998). More than bricks and sticks: Five components of community development corporation capacity. *Housing Policy Debate, 9,* 497–540.

Green, J. (1999). *Cultural awareness in the human services: A multi-ethnic approach,* 3rd ed. Boston, MA: Allyn & Bacon.

Greene, R. & McGuire, L. (1998). Ecological perspective: Meeting the challenge of practice with diverse populations. In R. Greene & M. Watkins (Eds.), *Serving diverse constituencies: Applying the ecological perspective.* Hawthorne, NY: Aldine De Gruyter.

Gutierrez, L., GlenMaye, L., & DeLois, K. (1995). The organizational context of empowerment practice: Implications for social work administration. *Social Work, 40,* 249–258.

Gutierrez, L., Parsons, R., & Cox, E. (Eds.). (1998). *Empowerment in social work practice: A sourcebook.* Pacific Grove, CA: Brooks/Cole.

Iglehart, A. & Becerra, R. (1995). *Social services and the ethnic community.* Boston, MA: Allyn and Bacon.

Kirst-Ashman, K. & Hull, G., Jr. (1999). *Understanding generalist practice,* 2nd ed. Chicago: Nelson Hall.

Kretzmann, J. & McKnight, J. (1993). *Building communities from the inside out: A path toward finding and mobilizing a community's assets.* Evanston, IL: Center for Urban Affairs and Policy Research, Northwestern University.

Lecca, P., Quervalu, I., Nunes, J., & Gonzales, H. (1998). *Cultural competency in health, social, & human services.* New York: Garland.

Lee, E. (Ed.). (1997). *Working with Asian Americans: A guide for clinicians.* New York: Guilford.

Lee, P. (1998). Organizing in the Chinese American community: Issues, strategies, and alternatives. In F. Rivera & J. Erlich (Eds.), *Community organizing in a diverse society,* (3rd ed.), (pp. 117–145). Boston, MA: Allyn & Bacon.

Lum, D. (1999). *Culturally competent practice: A framework for growth and action.* Pacific Grove, CA: Brooks/Cole.

Mason, J., Benjamin, M., & Lewis, S. (1996). The cultural competence model: Implications for child and family mental health services. In C. Heflinger & C. Nixon (Eds.), *Families and the mental health system for children and adolescents* (pp. 165–190). Thousand Oaks, CA: Sage.

Miley, K., O'Melia, M., & DuBois, B. (1998). *Generalist social work practice: An empowerment approach.* Boston, MA: Allyn & Bacon.

Mokuau, N. (Ed.). (1991). *Handbook of social services for Asian and Pacific Islanders.* New York: Greenwood Press.

Mokuau, N. & Shimizu, D. (1991). Conceptual framework for social services for Asian and Pacific Islander Americans. In N. Mokuau (Ed.), *Handbook of social services for Asian and Pacific Islanders* (pp. 21–36). New York: Greenwood Press.

Netting, F., Kettner, P., & McMurtry, S. (1998). *Social work macro practice,* 2nd ed. New York: Longman.

Rivera, F. & Erlich, J. (Eds.). (1998). *Community organizing in a diverse society,* 3rd ed. Boston, MA: Allyn & Bacon.

Saleebey, D. (Ed.). (1997). *The strengths perspective in social work practice,* 2nd ed. White Plains, NY: Longman.

Uba, L. (1994). *Asian Americans: Personality patterns, identity, and mental health.* New York: Guilford.

Uba, L. & Sue, S. (1991). Nature and scope of services for Asian and Pacific Islander Americans. In N. Mokuau (Ed.), *Handbook of social services for Asian and Pacific Islanders* (pp. 3–20). New York: Greenwood Press.

United Way of Los Angeles. (1988). *United Way Asian Pacific needs assessment technical report.* Los Angeles: Author.

United Way of Tri-State. (1989). *Outlook: The growing Asian presence in the Tri-State region.* New York: Author.

Yamashiro, G. & Matsuoka, J. (1997). Help-seeking among Asian and Pacific Americans: A multi-perspective analysis. *Social Work, 42,* 176–186.

Zane, N., Takeuchi, D., & Young, K. (Eds.). (1994). *Confronting critical health issues of Asian and Pacific Islander Americans.* Thousand Oaks, CA: Sage.

CHAPTER 16

INDIVIDUAL AND FAMILY INTERVENTION SKILLS WITH AFRICAN AMERICANS: AN AFRICENTRIC APPROACH

AMINIFU R. HARVEY

We are a Black Gold Mine. And the key that unlocks the door to these vast riches is the knowledge of who we are—I mean who we really are.

—Tony Brown

This chapter focuses on social work interventions with African Americans. For the purpose of this chapter, African Americans are defined as persons whose ancestry originated on the continent of Africa, are at least the second generation living in the United States, and define themselves as being Colored/Negro/Black or African American. There are a few exceptions to this definition. Some persons from the diaspora are first generation in the United States, but consider themselves African American by acculturation. There are persons of African descent who are the second generation in the United States, but who refuse to define themselves as African Americans. When I refer to Black people in this chapter, I mean people who fit the criteria I have established, no matter what their skin color may be. When referring to African American culture, I am constructing it on a historical continuum, from being kidnapped from the continent of Africa to present-day existence in the United States.

The information in this chapter is based on over thirty years of social work practice with African Americans. The majority of the people I have provided services to have been African Americans who can at least trace their ancestry back to slavery, although a considerable number have been from the Caribbean, South America, Central America, and the continent of Africa. The author acknowledges that there are various ethnic groups that compose the African diaspora. Yet, there are essential elements of an African worldview that are common to all ethnic groups that have roots in African culture (Mbiti, 1969), allowing for some commonality in social work interventions.

Social work recognizes the importance of culture and ethnicity in social work practice (Atkinson, Morten, & Sue, 1993; Devore & Schlesinger, 1996; Green, 1982; Winkelman, 1999). Within this cultural approach to social work services, some social work scholars have focused specifically on the relationship of African American culture and the delivery of social work services to African Americans (Martin & Martin, 1985, 1995; Jackson & Brisset-Chapman, 1999; See, 1998). Social work scholars, e.g., Carlton-LaNey (1999), Harvey & Rauch (1997), and Schiele (1994), have begun to develop an Africentered philosophical and theoretical approach to the delivery of services to African Americans. Some social work scholars have even developed practice models (Gregory & Phillips, 1999; Harvey & Coleman 1999; Poitier, Niliwaambieni & Rowe, 1999) of Africentered social work. This chapter is a further development of the Africentered philosophical and theoretical paradigm and practice models for providing culturally competent services to African Americans.

SOCIODEMOGRAPHIC OVERVIEW

The client base from which I worked and developed this Africancentered approach is probably representative of the general population of the people of African descent in the United States of America. My client base was the metropolitan Washington, D.C. area, which included the city of Washington, D.C. and the surrounding areas of Virginia and Maryland. Clients came for individual, couples, or family therapy and to participate in at-risk prevention programs for African American males ranging in age from twelve to nineteen years. Some clients were self-referred while others were referred from various social welfare, juvenile justice, and educational institutions.

CULTURAL VALUES AND BEHAVIORAL NORMS

At least as far back as ancient Kemet (called *Egypt* by Europeans), people of African descent directed their lives by a value system (Budge, 1967) that laid the foundation for humanistic existence based on a belief in the spirituality of humans (T'Shaka, 1995). Traditional African philosophy is epitomized in the 42 Confessions/Declarations of Innocence (42 Principals of MAAT), which the ancient Kemetians employed as directives for their behavior (Budge, 1967; Karenga, 1990).

In the introduction to *The Husia: Sacred Wisdom of Ancient Egypt* (Karenga, 1984), Jacob H. Carruthers writes that the people of the Nile Valley had a tradition of holy or sacred writings that governed their daily life. Adams (1994) contends that MAAT's Seven Cardinal Virtues—order, balance, harmony, compassion (some scholars call this righteousness: Karenga, 1984; T'Shaka, 1995), reciprocity, justice, and truth—provide the philosophical foundation for Kemetian culture. The Virtues and the Declarations were the guidelines for an ethical way of life for the individual, family, and the entire society. The essence of African culture is rooted in a spiritual relationship with human beings and nature (Some, 1998), the development of moral human beings having the obligation to live in harmony and cooperation with each other to enhance the welfare of the community.

Hill (1971) conducted a national study to determine the social factors that held Black family units together in African American society. His research produced five strengths (this was a significant movement from a deficit model to a strengths perspective in Black family analysis): a strong achievement orientation, a strong work orientation, flexible family roles, strong kinship bonds, and a strong religious orientation. Hill's work is significant to social work because it provides documented African American norms, providing the framework by which social workers can evaluate a person's cultural integration and design culturally appropriate interventions.

Boykins and Toms (1985) have specified nine interrelated, but distinct, dimensions of expression in African Americans. The significance of these dimensions of African American expression to social work is that they explain the way that African Americans relate to and interact with the world. They provide the dimensions to understanding of African American behavior and provide the concepts on which to establish the content of Africentric interventions.

- Spirituality—conducting one's life as though its essence were vitalistic rather than mechanistic, and as though transcending forces significantly govern the lives of people;
- Harmony—placing a premium on versatility and placing an emphasis on wholeness rather than discreteness;
- Movement—approaching life rhythmically, particularly as expressed through the patterned, interwoven mosaic of music, movement, and percussiveness;
- Verve—psychological affinity for variability and intensity of stimulation, particularly stimulation emanating from the movement complex;
- Affect—a premium placed on emotional sensibilities and expressiveness;
- Communalism—sensitivity to the interdependence of people and the notion that group concerns transcend individual strivings;
- Expressive Individualism—a premium attached to the cultivation of distinctiveness, spontaneity, and uniqueness of self-expression;
- Orality—a special emphasis on oral and aural modes of communication, especially the use of the spoken word to convey deep textural meanings not possible through the written word;
- Social Time Perspective—a commitment to time as a social phenomenon much more than a concoction objectively drawn through clocks, calendars, and other inanimate markers (p. 41).

PROFILE OF SOCIAL WORK PROBLEMS AND ISSUES

People of African descent face many social-psycho-educational problems. There are many symptoms of these problems, but from an Africentered perceptive the etiology of the problems is a lack of cultural knowledge, appreciation, and identification (Evans, 1995). Therefore, the reverse is probably true: The more knowledge, appreciation, and identification one has with African American culture, the fewer problems one should have, and the more effective one should be in dealing with them.

Racism presents barriers to a healthy life and exacerbates the problems of living for people of African descent (Evans, 1995; Nobles, 1997). Racism functions to inculcate negative views of their Africaness among African Americans, to such a degree that they psychologically disempower themselves and place people of white ancestry in positions of superiority. For example, it is not uncommon to hear African American children saying, "Getting As in school is a white thing," or that certain activities, such as playing tennis, golf, and whitewater rafting, are white activities. Thank God for the Williams Sisters and Tiger Woods!

Many African Americans have internalized negative views, myths, and stereotypes to such an extent that they are overwhelmed by the perceived power of white supremacy. They become engaged in nonself-enhancing behaviors, becoming destructive to themselves and others. I term this phenomenon as an "alienation from one's African American self," and it is characteristic of persons who engage in black-on-black crimes, bright students who perform poorly academically, and persons who are embarrassed by the color of the skin or physiology and of their African heritage. These are people who would innately employ Boykins' and Toms' (1985) nine dimensions of African American expressiveness, but are embarrassed to do so. Because of this denial of self, they sometimes seek psychological refuge in drugs, alcohol, withdrawal from society or aberrant behaviors. Many are enraged from being alienated from their African self, but they have no idea of the cause of their rage. They so fear the destructive power of their rage that they self-medicate or create their own world in which they are in control (schizophrenia).

A problem that African Americans experience is trying to determine their place and role in white society. What they are trying to ascertain is when to act white in order "to get over" because they recognize that many African American behavioral patterns, such as dress and hairstyles, will be looked down on. African Americans also have to figure out "to what degree do I interact in white society and how much of my Black self do I disclose and to whom?" Finally, African Americans struggle to figure out which cultural norms to adhere to: Eurocentric or Africentric. It is not uncommon to experience some members of a family valuing and participating in a more Eurocentric way of life while other members value and participate in a more Africentric way of life. In the struggle to find their cultural comfort, many members of the same family participate in different religious sects, which often creates family disruption and conflict. This phenomenon of family diversity is dramatized in Lorraine Hansberry's play *Raisin in the Sun*. In this play, a Black family struggles to determine whether integration is better than separation, how to overcome the denigration of the African American male, and, finally, struggle to discover and appreciate their African roots, while simultaneously respecting their African American selves.

There are African Americans who overidentify with street culture, and it becomes normative in African American culture. This phenomenon is especially acted out in adolescence; prostitutes act as the model for dress, defiance replaces respect, violent confrontation replaces cooperation, and personal greed replaces community sharing. During the developmental process, African Americans have three different groups of issues to work through: issues of adolescent development that are common to all adolescents, such as sexual identification, issues connected with being an oppressed minority, and, thirdly, issues related to being a person of African descent.

Racism has created a struggle in the African American community to define itself and appreciate its diversity. Part of this struggle concerns the issues of skin color and hair texture (Harvey, 1995). Even in today's society African Americans are given preference and defined as intelligent and acceptable based on the color of their skin. The lighter you are the more acceptable you are to white society. The darker you are the more violent and dangerous and less intelligent you are supposed to be. Historically, straight hair, lightness of skin, and sharp facial features have been the norm of beauty in U.S. society. I have heard children tease other children about being too dark or too light.

U.S. culture values material acquisition and the individual accumulation of material objects more than spiritual development, communal sharing, and humanistic behavior. As a result, many African Americans have also begun to conceptualize the world as only a material phenomenon (Harvey, in press), which means that nothing, not even humans, has any intrinsic value. Therefore, any behavior that allows you to acquire material wealth is okay as long as you do not get caught. Thus, young people increasingly define their self-worth by whether they have the latest designer shoes and clothes, and a computer, TV, DVD, sound system, or phone in their room. So serious is this material consciousness that it has become okay to kill another Black person in order to take their designer clothes, sneakers, and money. The youth call this "getting paid."

THEORETICAL APPROACH TO PRACTICE

The theoretical approach employed in working with African American individuals and families is an Africentric theoretical and practice orientation. It is important to note that Africentric theory and practice is an outgrowth of a continuum of the Black perspective developed by such scholars as Hill (1971), Martin and Martin (1985), and Solomon (1976). African scholars such as Harvey (in press) Myers, (1988), Nobles, (1982), Phillips (1996), and Schiele, (1994) have defined three assumptions about human beings that form the basis of an African-centered paradigm. Schiele concludes that these are the basis for an African-centered social work paradigm: (1) individual identity is a collective identity, (2) the spiritual component of a human being is the essence of human existence, and (3) the affective approach to knowledge is epistemologically valid. Four resulting concepts from this African-centered paradigm are: (1) humanism is developed and defined through and within the interactions and relationships of the group, (2) all decisions must be made to benefit the group, (3) the main task of the human being is not the possession of material things but the development of a way of life that is Creatorlike and enhances the interrelatedness of all the universe, and (4) humans have the capacity to intuit knowledge. This theory is based on the belief that the Creative Force exists in all things and that there is a harmony and rhythm to the world. The question that the client must answer is, "Why was I born at this particular time, at this particular place, to this particular racial ethnic group, and to this particular family under these particular circumstances?" One of the essential premises of this theory is that our task here is to become more Godlike in order to enhance the well-being of all God's creations and to assist others in alleviating their misery. Thus, the more one has been blessed with, the more one has an obligation to share with others to enhance their physical, psychological, material, emotional, and spiritual well-being. Being oppressive, abusive, and neglectful are counteractive to our purpose and throw the community (universe) out of order.

Underlying this theoretical approach is a number of basic assumptions: (1) Most African American problems are due to a lack of knowledge and appreciation for African American culture; (2) white supremacy employs racism to destroy African American culture, including an African sense of family and community; (3) the solution rests in "whmy msw" that is the reawaking of the African memory or the teachings of the African Ancients (Hilliard, 1997); (4) the Creative Force does not create what is ugly or bad or negative; (5) every person is born with a creative genius and has a unique contribution to make to the world; (6) the social worker's task is to assist people in discovering their path in life; and (7) the social worker is to assist the client in developing and maintaining a balance between mind, body, and spirit and between the material and spiritual.

PRACTICE FOCUS: INTERVENTION

The Africenteric theoretical and practice approach has many similarities with the three central social work approaches to practice: the ecological model, with an emphasis on person-in-environment, the strengths perspective, and empowerment. Saleebey (1997) incorporates the ecological and empowerment perspectives in the lexicon of the strengths model, laying out six terms of the model that, in theory and practice, are congruent with the Africentric approach:

> Empowerment—to empower is the intent to assist individuals, groups, families, and communities to discover and use the resources and tools within and around them and to seize some control over their lives and the decisions that are critical to their lives. (In the Africentric paradigm, empowerment is accomplished by the

social worker assisting clients in gaining cultural knowledge, appreciation, and identity. This is accomplished by employing various interventions that will be described later in this chapter.)

Membership—to be without membership is to be alienated, to be at risk for marginalization and oppression. (The group interventions are designed to provide a community to the clients.)

Resilience—refusal to cheerfully accept one's difficult and traumatic life experiences, or naïvely discount life's pains; rather, to bear up in spite of these ordeals. (The knowledge of history provides models by which individuals and families learn to overcome obstacles to their self-fulfillment.)

Healing and Wholeness—Healing implies both wholeness and the inborn facility of the body and mind to regenerate and resist when faced with disorder, disease, and disruption. Healing also requires a beneficial relationship between the individual and the larger social and physical environment. We have a native wisdom (intuition) about what is right for us and what we should do when confronted with organismic or environmental challenges. (This is the ecological perspective. The task is to assist clients to respect their own community and learn how to build the community so that it is conducive to the healthy development of its members.)

Dialogue and Collaboration—Humans can only come into being through a creative and emergent relationship with others. Without such transactions, there can be no discovery and testing of one's powers, no knowledge, and no heightening of one's awareness and internal strengths. In dialogue, we confirm the importance of others and begin to heal the rift between self, other, and institution. (This is accomplished through social group work interventions.)

Suspension of Disbelief—There are many representations of the "real" world (pp. 8–11). (Various interventions that enhance and reinforce African American culture are employed to instill respect and appreciation for African American culture.)

Following in the tradition of ancient Africans, Karenga (1965) recognized the need to develop a value system for African Americans in order to assist them in addressing the root cause of social problems in the African American community. Karenga developed the Nguzo Saba (Seven Principles) as guidelines for constructive behavior. In Africentered social work, the Nguzo Saba can be employed as a value system to foster an Africentric worldview (Brookins & Robinson, 1995). The Nguzo Saba are as follows:

Umoja	*Unity*—To strive and maintain unity in the family, community, nation, and race.
Kujichagulia	*Self Determination*—To define ourselves, name ourselves, and speak for ourselves instead of being defined and spoken for by others.
Ujima	*Collective Work and Responsibility*—To build and maintain our community together and to make our brothers' and sisters' problems our problems and to solve them together.
Ujamaa	*Cooperative Economics*—To build and own stores, shops, and other businesses and to profit from them.

Nia	*Purpose*—To make as our collective vocation the building and developing of our community in order to restore our people to their traditional greatness.
Kuumba	*Creativity*—To do always as much as we can, in the way we can, in order to restore our people to their traditional greatness.
Imani	*Faith*—To believe in our parents, our teachers, our leaders, our people, and ourselves, and the righteousness and victory of our struggle.

Harvey (1997), addressing the qualities needed to develop the internal character of the person in order to adhere to the Nguzo Saba, developed the following Principles of Afro-centricism (RIPSO):

7 Rs: Responsibility, Reciprocity, Respect, Realness, Restraint, Reason, and Reconciliation;

3 Is: Interconnectedness, Interdependence, and Inclusivity;

3 Ps: Participation, Patience, and Perseverance;

3 Ss: Sharing, Sacrifice, and Spirituality;

3 Others: Cooperation, Discipline, and Unconditional Love with Discipline (p. 165).

The author realizes that the Principles of Afro-centricism (RIPSO) probably need to be defined within an Africentric paradigm, but for the purpose of working with clients I have let the client employ his or her definition of each principle in relationship to their own circumstances. Each client does have to define these Principles in relationship to the liberation (self-determination) of African people and how he or she will employ each principle in personal development in order to enhance the self-determination of African people or in relationship to the implementation of Nguzo Saba.

MEZZO LEVEL

From an African spiritualistic perspective, one of the tasks of the social worker is to reinforce community through ritual and ceremony (Some, 1993). This is accomplished through social work group activities. For Manns (1981) heritage-reminding, a type of symbolic validation, is an important intervention when working with African Americans. From an Africentric perspective, one means of implementing this intervention is what traditional Africans call the "pouring of libation." All group sessions open with pouring of libation. This is the pouring of water into a plant, which symbolizes the nurturing of the earth, the relationship between the dead and the living, and the calling of the names of historical and personal ancestors. The ritual brings all the participants together as a small community. It ritualizes the opening and sanctifies the setting as a sacred place where only respectful behaviors are allowed. The Ancestral Transformation Activity involves reminding the individual of his or her racial background through role-modeling significant personalities in black history or of positive personal ancestors. In this activity the participant assumes the qualities of a famous ancestor. He or she is then faced with a life situation and must role-play how the ancestor would handle the situation. After the role-play, it is reinforced that the person can carry the spirit of the ancestor with them. By calling on the ancestors, African and African American history is learned, it allows a time for mourning and moaning of historical and personal ancestors (Martin & Martin, 1995), and it reinforces the importance of culture and demonstrates the relationship between African American and African culture. All sessions are closed with a reading from a holy text of the participants' choice, from a book of affirmations, or with each participant providing words of encouragement.

RETREATS

Retreats are interventions that provide the opportunity to bring the participants together in a community gathering. There are family-based retreats, youth retreats, and individual adult retreats. The common elements of retreats include the opening ritual of pouring libation. Tie-dying is a ritual incorporated into the retreats as an ice-breaker. This is the point at which different participants have the opportunity to interact with members of other families, assisting each other in the accomplishment of a task. They mix the dye, assist each other in tying the cloth, cutting the string, and hanging the cloth to dry. On the final day of the retreat, the cloth is untied and, like magic, the white cloth is transformed into many beautiful colors and designs, just like the African American community. It is a ritual that is fun and, on family retreats, provides the opportunity for children and parents to interact in a non-parent–child function. This exercise is symbolic of transformation and the synergy of bringing together various divergent elements to form a new creation. The exercise provides the impetus for group discussions on the variation of skin tones, ethnic groups, and lifestyles in the African American community. The tie-dyed cloth also acts as a memento of the occasion and, when viewed, will bring back pleasant memories and sensations.

As a part of the retreats, participants participate in "naming ceremonies." This activity is designed to reconnect the participants with their culture by replacing their slave European names with their true heritage names. Participants are given an African name symbolic of their personality. After choosing the name, a ritual of transformation, involving the entire group, is conducted, bestowing the name on the participant. The inherent meaning of the name acts as a reminder and an empowerment to the individual to fulfill his or her path in life.

The retreats provide the opportunity to reduce the psycho-social-educational barriers between staff and clients. Many of the participants, having less formal education, lower incomes, and living in resource-deficient areas of the city, will consider the staff to be "bourgeoisie." The prolonged informal and self-disclosing nature of the retreats help to bridge the social barriers between staff and participants, resulting in enhanced rapport and connectedness. Thus, the knowledge, skills, and views of the staff are validated, and are respected by the participants.

FAMILY ENHANCEMENT AND EMPOWERMENT DINNERS

The family enhancement and empowerment component is a multifamily and community activity. All adult members of families are invited by mailed invitations and telephone calls to attend. It is open to the public, with special invitations to referring agencies, the sponsoring organization's advisory board, its board of directors and any other organization affiliated with the sponsoring organization. The sessions each meet once a month with a buffet dinner. The family enhancement each session focuses on issues of parenting and family bonding. There is usually a topic, with a cartoon serial representative of the topic that is passed out to all participants to provide some humor to the meeting. Staff and participants will role-play scenarios in order to enhance participants' repertoire of appropriate response. After the role-plays the situation will be processed with all in attendance having input. Participants are encouraged not to ignore their intuition about their children's friends and situations that they or other family members might be encountering.

The objective of the empowerment activity is to empower parents through group support and community activities to act as advocates on behalf of their children and families and to be proactive in their communities. Speakers are invited to give presentations on such topics as advocating for your child in school, knowing who to contact in the school system to get action, getting the city to respond to maintaining your neighborhood, and ridding your apartment building of drugs. These dinners are not only informative, but they also provide a respite for families and demonstrate to parents that they are valued and appreciated.

PRINCIPLES OF PRACTICE

An Africentric approach to practice emphasizes the following principles of practice:

- To assist people in learning to discriminate and to be appropriate in their behaviors;
- To foster a sense of excellence, which consists of developing their Creative genius;
- To develop the uniqueness of the person in relationship to the development of the African community;
- For the social worker to understand that change occurs through the quality of the relationship the social worker has with the client based on this axiology of human-to-human relationships. Thus, the clients must tell their story;
- The worker must validate the client. For example, it is important for the worker to reinforce how difficult it is to be a cultural person in a racist society;
- The more participatory the interaction, the quicker and more intrinsic the transformation. For change to be intrinsic and long-lasting, it must take place on the cognitive, emotional, behavioral, and spiritual levels. It is important

that, if we are working with behaviors, people must practice the new behaviors, and role-playing is an excellent technique;

- The worker needs to be in harmony with the client, not in conflict, and must emotionally connect with the client through validation;
- Racism and the lack of knowledge, understanding, and appreciation of African culture are key factors in the psycho-social issues faced by people of African descent;
- The reclamation of African culture is key to the survival and positive existence of people of African descent and is a healing phenomenon (Hilliard, 1997).

PRACTICE SKILLS

Social workers should employ participatory interventions. They should discuss positive aspects of African American culture and behavior patterns and discuss their functionalism for Black people in the United States and explain how not employing them can create problems.

As well, they should recognize different cultural behavioral patterns and respect these differences rather than try to impose Eurocentric behavioral patterns on the clients.

Social workers should use Good Speech, what the ancient Africans of Kemet called "Medew Nefer" (Carruthers, 1990). Carruthers defines *Good Speech* as the articulation of thoughtful speech informed by reflection, reason, truth, tradition, and experience. They should also inculcate the use of proverbs as Good Speech and as a method of teaching the wisdom of the Ancestors. Proverbs help people to identify actions for specific situations and to be critical thinkers. Metaphors are also Good Speech and allow for a more circumscribed and indirect method of communication that is congruent with an African traditional style of communication. This style is less confrontative, so the client is more inclined to hear because there is less of a tendency to be defensive. Analogies are also a form of Good Speech as they employ a reference with which the client is familiar in order to assist the client in understanding and internalizing the message.

In establishing a relationship workers must initially rely on a personal approach to validate themselves as being competent to assist the client rather than "I am capable because I have a degree." This usually means that workers must appropriately self-disclose.

It is important for workers to recognize the strengths and efforts that the clients have made in coping and surviving in a racist society and validate them for these efforts. This includes allowing the opportunity for the client to tell and demonstrate their story. This is important because orality and movement are dimensions of the expressiveness of African American culture.

Interventions should be structured to include spiritually-oriented rituals and ceremonies that enhance the interaction between all participants, including the social worker. These interventions should include music and food as replications of the signs of welcome to the participants.

Finally, the social worker must be authentic and be able to demonstrate her or his knowledge and appreciation of the African American continuum.

SAPPHIRE SYNDROME

The Sapphire Syndrome is a phenomenon that I found common with many African American women. It is an image that has been historically fostered of African American women. The syndrome began as the Aunt Jemima stereotype of the overweight, extremely black-skinned woman who speaks slowly, in broken English, and is excessively psychologically and physically strong, devoted to the plantation mistress, and in no need of physical or psychological nurturing. This image was updated in the middle of the twentieth century. She is now, metaphorically, Kingfish's wife from the old radio and TV show *Amos and Andy.* In this role she is the big, strong woman who is constantly belittling Kingfish (portrayed as a skimming buffoon lawyer) in front of his friends.

Many African American women sought assistance because they were strong and self-determined. When they assumed these positions, there was a tendency for them to be labeled as "Sapphire," that is, castrating women who were insensitive to the needs of their man and in no need of care or attention, not even from their family. Clinically, the paradox is that these women are sapphires, strong, beautiful, and valuable jewels, needing to be treated with care and cherished.

Usually these women came to treatment with symptoms of depression. There was also an aspect of confusion and loneliness and feelings of being degraded. As a treatment intervention, we reviewed the stereotypes of Black women, and these women began to understand how racism was employed by white supremacists to create feelings of inadequacy. This was accomplished by juxtaposing the standard of womanhood as being a petite, delicate, white-skinned, passive woman, always submitting to her man. As part of the treatment, women would be shown books depicting these images and requested to see movies like *Gone with the Wind.* This helped them to understand the systematic attempt to create the internalized inferiority that led to their depression. The second part of treatment was directed at empowerment by providing a traditional view of the woman's role in African culture. For example, women controlled the marketplace (Sudarkasa, 1981) and kept the proceeds; they also chose the tribal king.

Another intervention was to review the life histories of such women as Harriet Tubman, Sojourner Truth, Rosa Parks, and Barbara Jordan. These examples helped women to define womanhood from their own cultural perspective. It was important to shown visual images of the variation in body type, color, and hair texture in order to nullify a white standard of beauty as being appropriate for women of African descent. Without exception, all of these women were spiritually oriented, so that the concept of spirituality was appropriate in the healing process. Each woman was asked if God makes mistakes, to which they all invariably answered no. This was helpful to them in understanding that people created the concept of ugly. Once they were able to define their reason for being, they were able to recognize they were doing God's work and, thus, were able to be resilient in their life when attacked.

HANDYMAN SYNDROME

In my practice I have seen a number of well-educated male clients who were supporting themselves by working at such menial jobs as handymen and taxicab drivers. There are a few who stand out in my mind. One case in particular was a middle-aged, very fair-skinned African American male who had attended a prestigious Black college and obtained a degree in architecture. When he came to see me he was working as a handyman, doing odd jobs such as painting and carpentry. He stated that his problems started when he was commissioned as an officer in the United States Army. He was so fair-skinned that the white officers thought he was white and would engage in derogatory conversations in front of him about African Americans. But the Black soldiers knew he was Black and solicited assistance from him concerning racial issues they were encountering. He wanted to take a stance on their behalf, but his wife told him not to because it would jeopardize his career. He found himself facing one of what I call the Paradoxes of Blackness (Harvey & Rauch, 1997). The dilemma was so overwhelming for him that he was hospitalized for depression and eventually received a medical discharge. His wife divorced him and he had difficulty maintaining employment in his profession. He began to use his architectural skills in working on handyman jobs, barely earning enough money to support himself. He came for services because he felt depressed and stated, " I do not fit in and feel misdirected." The client participated in all the interventions previously described. He eventually began to participate in community activities, volunteering to teach youth basic home-repair skills and regularly participating in community-based spiritual activities. At a later meeting, he stated that he found service to the community rewarding and that he could now appreciate the African American race as having all the colors of the rainbow. He also began to establish a clientele and accumulate a small savings.

In many cases the men were exhibiting symptoms of depression. Most of the men thought they were failures and were personally responsible for not being successful and living up to the "American dream." The depression was really anger turned inward. They actually were afraid that, if they allowed their anger to manifest itself, they would be out of control. The men were fearful that they would either destroy themselves or someone else or both. They questioned their ability to get along with others and blamed themselves for all their problems. The treatment was to allow them to be angry, assist them in recognizing the racism they each faced, and help them to recognize their strengths and how to maximize these strengths in their lives and to appreciate their God-given skin complexion and natural talents. In working on the anger, for those who identified themselves as being Christian, we read the story of Jesus and his justified anger with the money changers in the

Temple. This intervention allowed the client to understand that it is okay, and, at times, healthy to be angry, especially when we follow the anger with appropriate action.

CONCLUSION

When providing interventions to African American individuals and families it is critical to understand and be knowledgeable of the African American cultural continuum, that is, the traditional ways that Africans on the continent related to the world based on their worldview prior to Arab and European invasions. Also, the worker must have knowledge of the means by which kidnapped Africans adapted to oppression in order to survive but still maintained residues of their traditional cultural heritage. From an Africentric perspective, African American culture is the starting point for the provision of services and the intent is to assist the person and family in being accepting of their Africanness and engaging in behaviors that are in the best interest of the group, not the individual. This also means that normative behavior is not based on a European perspective but on an African cultural perspective.

I advocate providing services from an Africentric perspective. From this perspective, the etiology of psychosocial issues confronting African Americans are caused by racism—white supremacy, which intentionally tries to destroy the self-determination of African American people. The resilience of the race rests in the development of an identification and acceptance of an African American culture based on knowledge of their African American heritage, and the promotion of behaviors, thoughts, and emotions that foster the liberation of African people from oppression and repression—that is, to be antiracist, antisexist, and antiexploitative. The worker's task is to implement interventions that include traditional rituals and ceremonies that enhance the development of a race conscious, competent, and capable people and family units.

An Africentric approach encourages African Americans to rely on the cultural thought and behaviors of their Ancestors and apply it to their daily lives. The intent of an Africentric approach to providing interventions to individuals and families is to empower African Americans to be self-determined.

REFERENCES

Adams, H. H., III. (1994). *MA'AT: Return to virtue—return to self* [Monograph].

Atkinson, D. R., Morten, G., & Sue, D. W. (Eds.). (1993). *Counseling American minorities: A cross-cultural perspective,* 4th ed. Madison, WI: Brown Benchmark.

Boykins, A. W. & Toms, F. D. (1985). Black child socialization: A conceptual framework. In H. P. McAdoo & J. L. McAdoo (Eds.), *Black children: Social, educational, and parental environments.* Beverly Hills, CA: Sage.

Brookins, C. C. & Robinson, T. L. (1995). Rites of passage as resistance to oppression. *The Western Journal of Black Studies, 19* (3), 172–180.

Budge, E. A. W. (1967). *The Egyptian Book of the Dead: The papyrus of Ani.* New York: Dover.

Carlton-LaNey, I. (1999). African American social work: Pioneers' response to need. *Social Work, 44,* 311–321.

Carruthers, J. H. (1990). Divine speech: The foundation of divine wisdom. In M. Karenga (Ed.), Reconstructing Kemetic culture: Papers, perspectives, projects. Los Angeles; University of Sankore Press.

Devore, W. & Schlesinger, E. G. (Eds.). (1996). *Ethnic-sensitive: Social work practice,* 4th ed. Boston, MA: Allyn & Bacon.

Evans, E. (1995). The relationship of childrearing practices to chaos and changes in the African American Family. In S. M. Moore (Ed.), *African presence in the Americas* (pp. 279–312). Trenton, NJ: African World Press.

Green, J. W. (1982). *Cultural awareness in the human services.* Englewood Cliffs: NJ: Prentice-Hall.

Gregory, S. D. & Phillips, F. B. (1999). "Of mind, body, and spirit": Therapeutic foster care—An innovative approach to healing from an NTU perspective. In S. Jackson & S. Brissett-Chapman (Eds.), *Child welfare perspectives: Serving African American children* (pp. 125–140). New Brunswick, NJ: Transaction.

Harvey, A. R. (1995). The issue of skin color in psychotherapy with African Americans. *Families in Society: The Journal of Contemporary Human Services, 76* (1), 3–10.

Harvey, A. R. (1997). Group work with African American youth in the criminal justice system: A culturally competent model. In G. L. Grief & P. H. Ephross (Eds.), *Group work with populations at risk* (pp. 160–174). New York: Oxford University Press.

Harvey, A. R. (In press). A general paradigm of African-centered social work: A social work paradigm shift in the struggle for the liberation of African people. *The Annals of African-centered Psychology.*

Harvey, A. R. & Coleman, A. A. (1999). An Afrocentric program for African American males in the juvenile justice system. In S. Jackson & S. Brissett-Chapman (Eds.), *Child welfare perspectives: Serving African American children* (pp. 193–207). New Brunswick, NJ: Transaction.

Harvey, A. R. & Rauch, J. B. (1997). A comprehensive rites of passage program for Black male adolescents. *Health and Social Work, 22* (1), 30–37.

Hill, R. (1971). *Strengths of black families.* New York: Emerson-Hall.

Hilliard, A. S. (1997). *The reawaking of the African mind.* Gainesville, FL: Makare.

Jackson, S. & Brissett-Chapman, S. (1999). *Child welfare perspectives: Serving African American children.* New Brunswick, NJ: Transaction.

Karenga, M. (1965). *Kwanzaa: Origins, concepts, and practice.* Los Angeles: Kawaida.

Karenga, M. (1984). Selections from the husia: Sacred wisdom of ancient Egypt. Los Angeles: Kawaida.

Karenga, M. (1990). The book of the coming forth by day: The ethics of the declaration of innocence. Los Angeles: University of Sankore Press.

Manns, W. (1981). Support systems of significant others in Black families. In H. P. McAdoo (Ed.), *Black families* (pp. 238–251). Beverly Hills, CA: Sage.

Martin, J. M. & Martin, E. P. (1985). *The helping tradition in the Black family and community.* Washington, DC: National Association of Social Workers.

Martin, J. M. & Martin, E. P. (1995). *Social work and the Black experience.* Washington, DC: National Association of Social Workers.

Mbiti, J. S. (1969). *African religions and philosophies.* New York: Praeger.

Myers, L. J. (1988). *Understanding an Afocentric world view: Introduction to an optimal psychology.* Dubuque, IA: Kendall/Hunt.

Nobles, W. W. (1997). African American family life. In H. P. McAdoo (Ed.), *Black families* (pp. 83–93). Beverly Hills: Sage.

Nobles, W. W. (1982). The reclamation of culture and the right to reconciliation: An Afro-centric perspective on developing and implementing programs for the mentally retarded offender. In A. R. Harvey & T. L. Carr (Eds.), *The Black mentally retarded offender: A holistic approach to prevention and habilitation* (pp. 39–61). New York: United Church of Christ Commission for Racial Justice.

Phillips, F. B. (1996). NTU psychotherapy: Principles and processes. In D. Ajani ya Azibo (Ed.), *African psychology in historical perspective and related commentary.* Trenton, NJ: African World Press.

Poitier, P. L., Niliwaambieni, M., & Rowe, C. L. (1999). A rite of passage approach designed to preserve the families of substance-abusing African American women. In S. Jackson & S. Brissett-Chapman (Eds.), *Child welfare perspectives: Serving African American children* (pp. 169–191). New Brunswick, NJ: Transaction.

Saleebey, D. (1997). *The strengths perspective in social work practice,* 2nd ed. New York: Longman.

Schiele, J. H. (1994). Afroncentricity as an alternative world view for equality. *Journal of Progressive Human Services, 5* (1), 5–25.

See, L. A. (Ed.). (1998). *Human behavior in the social environment from an African American perspective.* New York: Haworth.

Solomon, B. (1976). *Black empowerment: Social work in oppressed communities.* New York: Columbia University Press.

Some, M. P. (1993). Ritual: Power, healing and community. Portland, OR: Swan/Raven.

Some, M. P. (1998). The healing wisdom of Africa: Finding life purpose through nature, ritual and community. New York: Tarcher/Putnam.

Sudarkasa, N. (1981). Interpreting the African heritage in Afro-American family organization. In H. P. McAdoo (Ed.), *Black families* (pp. 37–53). Beverly Hills: Sage.

T' Shaka, O. (1995). Return to the African mother principle of male and female equality, vol.1. Oakland: Pan African Publishers and Distributors.

Winkelman, M. (1999). *Ethnic sensitivity in social work.* Dubuque, IA: Eddie Bower.

CHAPTER 17

A HEURISTIC PERSPECTIVE OF STRENGTHS WHEN INTERVENING WITH AN AFRICAN AMERICAN COMMUNITY

ALFRIEDA DALY

This chapter begins by defining major groups of those who fall under the general rubric of African Americans with a brief overview of how these groups merged into the present mix. This descriptive demographic portrait of African Americans is followed by a presentation of cultural values and behavioral norms. Various perspectives and relevant frameworks that affect and effect issues in the African American community are addressed. The premise of this chapter is that the strengths and intelligence of African Americans are clearly evident in their accomplishments, contributions, and survival strategies employed as they negotiated pervasively harsh realities during their sojourn in the United States. The focus throughout this chapter is on intervention principles and skills with African American communities and organizations.

SOCIODEMOGRAPHIC OVERVIEW

While African Americans are not homogeneous, the complexity of in-group differences is rarely addressed in the literature. It may be more accurate to refer to them as *Africans in America* because this term conveys the notion of entry into the United States from various routes. It also implies variation in cultural expectations and experiences, as core aspects vary. An advantage of understanding the complexity of various interacting components of African American culture is that it contradicts stereotypes of members of this group. These differences can be crucial for effective interventions when working with African American communities and organizations.

Three major groups of Africans in America are identified here. The largest of these are those of African ancestry in the United States prior to the Emancipation Proclamation of 1861. The next largest presence are those of African Caribbean ancestry, e.g., immigrants of former European colonies of the West Indies (Allen, 1997; Healey, 1995; Parillo, 1996). Jamaicans are reported to be the largest group of non-Hispanic migrants from the Caribbean Islands, while the largest groups of immigrants from the Caribbean are from Cuba and the Dominican Republic (Allen, 1996; Parrillo, 1996). Haitian immigration to the United States began in the 1950s. Since the 1970s, about 300,000 people have fled the brutal Haitian government (Parrillo, 1996; Stepnik & Portes, 1986).

Recent immigrants from countries of the African continent (e.g., Nigeria, Ethiopia) are the third largest group. African immigrants from the continent were all but nonexistent prior to passage of the 1965 Immigration Law, which made it easier for non-Europeans to migrate to the States. Three percent (or 151,101) of the total population of legal immigrants who came between 1991 and 1994 are from the continent of Africa (English & Ross-Sheriff, 1998). Nigerians and Ghanaians are the largest groups of these immigrants (Healey, 1995). Many African immigrants came because of the effects of war, military dictatorship, intolerance, and famine. As with Haitians, many arrived with limited economic assets or social networks awaiting them (English & Ross-Sheriff, 1998; See, 1998a).

Cultural differences suggest that *African American* is an ethnic designation, not racial (Washington, 1993). Thus, African and Caribbean immigrants to the States are not ethnic African Americans. They are, however, significant actors in the African Diaspora and, therefore, are appropriately included here (Healey, 1996). Africans in America have demonstrated their ability to work together toward mutual goals and to address common threats without regard to their origin or route here. In this regard, all become African American.

Twenty-six percent of African American families are reported as having incomes below $10,000, but 42 percent have incomes between $25,000 and $50,000. This is compared with 8 percent of white families earning less than $10,000 and 69 percent who earn $25,000 or more (O'Hare, et al., 1991). Some of this disparity is explained by the large number of single-headed households. O'Hare and his colleagues suggest that the embeddedness of unacknowledged racism is a more powerful explanatory variable. The increase in income and assets is explained largely by a threefold increase in African American college graduates who earn a median income that is 93 percent of what whites earn (O'Hare, et al., 1991). Unfortunately, African American wealth and accumulation of assets continue to lag behind that of whites (Cose, 1999; Miller, 1999).

Despite the 1857 Dred Scott Supreme Court decisions affirming Africans in American as property, there is ample evidence that many were prodigious in accomplishments in science, engineering, oratory, entrepreneurship, and the arts (Asante & Abarry, 1996; Butler, 1991; Johnson & Smith, 1998; Kitano, 1991).

African American scholars in the social sciences and humanities have been prodigious in the production of knowledge about African cultural heritage and the African American experience (Asante & Abarry, 1996; Billingsley, 1968; Boyd-Franklin, 1989; Chestang, 1976; Collins, 1990, 1998; Daly, 1994; Hill, 1971; McAdoo, 1981; Norton, 1978; See, 1998a, 1998b; Schiele, 1998a, 1998b; Solomon, 1976). Post-modernism has shaped the deconstruction of many negative images and led to more contextualized understanding and analyses of this community's issues (Collins, 1990, 1998; Daly, 1998; Rothenberg, 1990; Washington & McCarley, 1998). At the same time, empirical data, such as the work of Crane (1994), deconstructs persistent myths of the intellectual inferiority of African Americans.

CULTURAL VALUES AND BEHAVIORAL NORMS

Traces of African culture and codes of conduct are present among Africans in America regardless of the point and time of entry into the United States. Similarities in cultural values among Africans in America include mutual sharing and responsibility for the well-being of others, sharing familial relations with fictive kin, and recognition of the dignity of all people regardless of their station in life (Daly, 1994; Schiele, 1998a). Social class is differentiated largely by lifestyle rather than an economic hegemony (Healey, 1996; Wilkerson, 1995). The following incident illustrates the universality of understanding the code of helping and support.

> Three female graduate students, an African American woman from the Southeast, another African American woman from the West Coast, and a white student from Connecticut had an automobile collision while on spring break in rural Canada. Their car could not be driven away, so the police offered to take them to the nearby city where they could find lodging. The African American from the Southeast suggested they be dropped off at the airport. Immediately, the West Coast student agreed while the white woman from Connecticut was baffled. The two African American women explained that one of the skycaps would help them out. One of the skycaps, a person of Caribbean descent, immediately took all three women under his care and, when he was off duty, escorted them to a motel near the center of the city. He saw that they were registered before he left, and refused any compensation for his time.

PROFILE OF SOCIAL WORK PROBLEMS AND ISSUES

Powerful environmental factors impact and contextualize social problems and issues in the African American community. Unanticipated consequences of environmentally driven actions can be costly for this community, for example, public and social policies. The public policy arena, an environmentally driven factor, illustrates potential effects on shaping and attenuating the life experiences of

African Americans. Public policies often exacerbate rather than resolve problems in the African American community. Public policies, which address issues of concern in the African American community, are rarely shaped by attention to understanding cultural differences. Awareness of cultural differences by the dominant group tends to be expressed as a need to retain the structures of the social hegemony as is. Carter and Quereshi (1995) define *culture* as a "learned system of meaning and behavior that is passed from one generation to the next." Culture shapes perceptions and interpretation of the environment, and these processes affect attitude, behaviors, and structures (Carter and Quereshi, 1995; Daly, 1998; Daly, et al., 1995; Turner, 1991). Several significant events during this decade of the national saga illustrate polarizing differences between the dominant culture and African Americans, e.g., the South Los Angeles implosion of 1992, the O. J. Simpson verdict of 1995.

A consequence of the global dominance of a European hegemony is that people of color are not often equitable benefactors of policies established to address social issues (Davis, 1993; English & Ross-Sheriff, 1998; Kozol, 1991, 1996; McCann & Selsky, 1984; Rothenberg, 1990). As resources become scarcer and issues that disproportionately affect groups at the lower end of the social hegemony appear unresolvable, a process called "social triage" emerges (McCann & Selsky, 1984). This involves the preservation and allocation of scarce resources for those perceived as best able to utilize them well. This is accomplished through social policies that legitimize the process to achieve appropriate goals. For example, inner city schools receive far less educational funding in contrast to the generous funding for many suburban schools (Kozol, 1991; Suarez, 1999). Likewise public funding for housing deteriorated until inner cities were comparable to war zones during World War II (Dubrow & Garbino, 1989). Other illustrations of this social triage can be found in public transportation policy and the placement of toxic waste dumps in African American communities.

Social policy has a direct and indirect role in shaping the environment, accessing resources, and decision making for target systems. As such, social policy is a significant factor in shaping the milieu into which people are born (Davis, 1993; Kozol, 1991, 1996; Krivo, et al., 1998; Suarez, 1999). It is crucial that policies that affect people of color be sensitive to the racial and ethnic contexts in which they have significant impact. Embedded racial attitudes and defenses of the dominant culture should be of equal concern.

African Americans are frequently portrayed in the media and public spheres by a negative and pejorative view of who they are and what they are about. This feeds stigmatized perceptions that have been socially constructed since the sixteenth century (Milloy, 1999; Thomas, 1997). These perceptions and beliefs affect major institutions, policies, and social processes that construct access to health care, adequate education, and resources.

The research of Zhang and Snowden (1999), who examined the ethnic ratio of several DSM-III mental disorders among whites and ethnic groups of color in the Los Angeles area, offers a more nuanced example. They found significant variances of diagnoses for several mental disorders among Hispanics, Asians, and African Americans. Interestingly, these investigators found similar rates of schizophrenia among African Americans and whites that is at variance with the commonly held belief that African Americans have higher rates of schizophrenia than whites. The authors suggest that this higher rate was the result of misdiagnosing affective disorders as schizophrenia. These research findings tend to corroborate others that suggest that depression in African Americans may manifest itself differently than in whites. Misdiagnosis of depression may contribute to the high death rates among young African American males (Molock, et al., 1994; Schiele, 1998a and b; Tolleson, 1997; Washington & McCarley, 1998). Such findings suggest an essential need for social work to emphasize skills in critical thinking and analyses of theoretical assumptions used in interventions with African American communities.

Another very sensitive issue for the African American community has to do with a range of gender issues. While there are factors that have shaped male–female relations very differently than in the dominant culture, the focus here is on a dilemma unique to African American women, the problem of single parenthood. This problem is shaped historically and through public policies that not only do not address critical needs of these women but contribute directly to problems that precipitate the large incidence of single parenthood of these women (Collins, 1998; Franklin, 1997; Gary & Leashore, 1982, Guttentag & Secord, 1983). The literature is replete with references to the problems of single-female heads of African American households. What is extremely rare is reference or scholarly interest in the ratio of African American women to African American men or to policies that exacerbate this problem.

Guttentag and Secord (1983) pointed to an imbalance in the ratio of marriageable Black men and Black women in the early 1980s. Furthermore, this imbalance has been increasing since the 1950s, at which time the ratio was comparable to that between white men and women of marriageable years. As of 1970, there were 30 percent less marriageable Black men in the pool than for marriageable Black women (1983, p. 201). The ratio has widened since then for reasons that can be directly attributed to social public policies, market forces, and economic realities. Discourse by policymakers focuses mostly on a lack of values rather than biological and procreative realities.

PRACTICE FOCUS: INTERVENTION

African Americans have a rich history in organizing, community development, and founding organizations to meet needs and to stimulate progress toward equity in access to opportunity and full participation in society (Butler, 1991; Carlton-La'Ney, 1997, 1999; Healey, 1995; Iglehart & Becarra, 1995). Sojourner Truth, Frederick Douglas, and Booker T. Washington are known for their roles in the abolitionist movement, which advocated against holding slaves. Charlotte Hawkins Brown, Mary McCloud Bethune, and others founded educational institutions, some of which are now among the Historically Black Colleges and Universities

(HBCU) (McCluskey, 1997). Elizabeth Ross Haynes illustrates another arena of achievement of African Americans in institution building as she addresses the needs of orphans in her community (Carlton-La'Ney, 1997). Ida B. Wells and Mary Church Terrell, contemporaries of Jane Addams, both developed settlements and affected policy development (Iglehart & Becarra, 1995).

Presently, a growing middle class has organized various new coalitions and the like through which they "give back" to the community. A United Black Community Fund supports both educational enrichment activities and social and agency needs in New Jersey. African American sororities and fraternities, with chapters in historically black colleges, as well as many others, have historically focused on organizational goals that address evolving needs in the community. This rich history of organizing to provide mutual aid and to achieve mutual goals for their community suggests that African Americans have traditionally seen macro-level interventions as empowerment strategies for their own.

DEFINING LEVEL OF PRACTICE

Social work intervention at the community and organizational level is complex and multifaceted as it must be able to handle competing ideologies and values that are inevitable in a mobile and diverse society. Although community is traditionally thought of as "place," an alternative view is that geographic territory is not essential for community to exist (Fellin, 1993; Iglehart & Becarra, 1995; Longres, 1995; Schriver, 1998). Community members, who have shared experiences that shaped their worldviews, share similar interests, concerns, and preferences. This does not suggest a lack of diversity within the community, as many indices reveal the existence of a significant range in areas such as education level, locality, and socioeconomic status. The concept of community encompasses the notion of within differences, such as values and political positions (Netting, Kettner, & McMurty, 1993).

Organizations can also be defined as systems of purposive, goal-oriented activity that involve two or more people in specified and interdependent activities for the purpose of achieving a goal. Organizations are the principal mechanism by which a highly differentiated society gets things done, particularly those things that are beyond the reach of one person (Netting, et al., 1993). Thus, macropractice involves both communities and organizations.

THEORETICAL APPROACHES TO PRACTICE

Communities, organizations, institutions, and institutional arrangements all interact within a particular social system in patterned ways to form the social system itself. Interaction between components of a system (i.e., individuals, groups, institutions, events, and attitudes) forms a social environment that has some relationship to an encompassing context or the larger surrounding environment (Martin & O'Conner, 1989).

Ecological/Person-in-Environment Theory

While some argue about differences and similarities between social systems and ecological perspectives (Longres, 1995; Martin & O'Connor, 1989), Schriver (1998) points out that both help bridge the gap between traditional theoretical paradigms and the newer or alternative paradigms for addressing populations that have experienced oppression. Both focus on the interconnectedness of various components (system parts; e.g., leadership, policies, funding sources) and behavioral interactions between them and the social environment. In other words, the ecological perspective concerns itself with collective behaviors in the context of interdependence with larger institutions and social systems with which they interact dynamically.

In African American communities, lifestyle is generally more significant than economic level. Racial and ethnic group membership may provide less information than location of origin or religious affiliation as identity issues are varied and, in these dynamic times, often in transition (Simmons, 1990). For these reasons, age becomes a valuable demographic factor when working with African American communities and organizations. The racial environmental context that was prevalent during the adolescent and early adult years of a majority in a focal system can be invaluable in understanding and crafting effective community interventions. This is important for equipping non-African Americans to understand nuanced behavioral responses and reactions.

One of the strengths of the person-in-environment perspective is that it enables professionals to focus on linkages between the target system, communities or organizations in this instance, and the environmental sectors with which it interfaces, e.g., the education system, municipal services, and so forth. This approach allows the identification of problems at system boundaries. In the case of African American communities and agencies, this can point out problems of equity in service.

Strengths Perspective

One way to undo negative learning about African Americans is through use of the strengths perspective. This perspective focuses on the strengths of clients in a target system and problem areas are deemphasized while intervention strategies that utilize strengths are implemented (Longres, 1995; Schriver, 1998). A rationale is that social workers must encourage the engagement of the communities and agencies in the helping process. This approach is appropriate in a postmodern world as it engages client systems in positive reconstruction which challenges negative views.

Cowger (1998) questions the strengths perspective for two reasons: (1) the theory does not adequately address the problems of social service structures that are driven by a market economy and its need to exercise social control, and (2) the tendency toward clientelism, which leads to dependency in patron versus client relationships, the opposite of the intent. In order to overcome these problems, Cowger (1998) suggests the profession should focus on restructuring "power" roles, and policies that generate the implementation of more action strategies.

Empowerment

The strengths perspective is related to the empowerment movement. Longress (1995, p. 536) succinctly describes empowerment as a process for increasing a community or organization's (sic) interpersonal or political power. Those in situations of limited power can then take action to improve their life situation. Schriver (1998, p. 27) concurs when he focuses on Gutierrez's work, which defines *empowerment* as "the perception of power from various, even infinite sources, that can be generated through social interactions." Ultimately, at the macrolevel, empowerment is the process of recognizing and utilizing social power to bring about social change and transformation.

Principles of MacroLevel Practice

The first principle is self-awareness. This is a core principle in any social work intervention. The greater the social distance between the social worker and target system, the greater the need for honest self-appraisal of personal attitudes. Honesty about potential areas that may be conflictual, personal styles, and preferences that may raise barriers to diversity need to be explored. Most importantly, sources of pride, unearned privileges, and fears need to be identified. It is important to look at corporate practices and policies of the agency providing services to uncover similar sources of negative attitudes and barriers. African American social workers are also vulnerable to unconscious and hostile attitudes that may need to be uncovered and examined (Simmons, 1990). Finally, there are materials for guidance in self-examination for unrecognized potential conflictual areas such as Abramson's (1996) exercise for examining one's values.

A second principle involves preparation for a system in which mixed-race/ethnic identity issues are potentially inflammable (Mayadas, Elliot, & Ramanathan, 1999; Simmons, 1990; Taylor, 1997). Mixed-race and ethnic identity issues surface more frequently as African Americans search their roots and intermarry. Awareness of the need for special sensitivity to potential behavioral responses as well as words that can be misinterpreted are important. Economic frustrations and politics can also engender inflammatory responses within the community. No professionals would want to contribute to the exacerbation of such negative events because they were not informed about historical perspectives that shaped present attitudes and positions.

A third principle is the inclusion of the target system in the change process. A community group, agency, and any organizational system should be fully engaged in the process of developing macrolevel interventions. Professionals can encourage and facilitate client participation by asking for their ideas early, providing opportunities to give feedback in multiple ways, acknowledging potential usefulness of input given, and sharing tasks, such as information gathering, to be completed for subsequent meetings.

Critical thinking in macropractice is essential for problem definition and strategy development. The analytic phase of problem solving and intervention strategizing should be dynamic, involving much exchange, recasting and reformulating plans as the process evolves. Understanding assumptions of the theoretical framework may be a concern, as well as obtaining input from as broad a base as appropriate to the situation. When a problem is identified and defined and an intervention implementation strategy agreed on, commitment to carrying it out is the next step. This commitment to the intervention planned should be shared by both the professionals and the target system in order to achieve effective outcomes.

If these prior stages have gone well, there should be sufficient energy among target system members and professional staff to carry out a planned intervention. Desired outcomes should be defined and articulated in language understood by both the social worker and the client system. All parties concerned will have some notion of the process through which the project is anticipated to go in order to reach the desired outcomes. An important part of the critical thinking and planning stage should address alternatives to unanticipated outcomes or contingencies. Finally, some monitoring or evaluation of strategy and intervention to obtain appropriate feedback should be in place. The system should provide objective data that will indicate how well the intervention performs as well as areas where adaptation is indicated. Be prepared to alter the initial plan if the data received indicates a need for change.

Practice Skills for African American Communities and Organizations

A crucial beginning skill in planning an intervention with African American communities and organizations is multicultural competency. A critical part of this is the development of communication skills for multicultural situations. One basic technique is to have the receiver in a communication dyad repeat what his or her perceptions are of decisions, and so on. If there is incongruence in understanding or perception between the two, this can be clarified. Beckett and colleagues (1997) have developed a two-stage process model to guide practitioners in preparing effective communications in multicultural situations. The model addresses the need to identify and appreciate differences in values and stereotyping as well as the acquisition of recovery skills when mistakes are made.

A second critical area when working with African American communities and organizations involves skills needed to work effectively with the community leadership. While leadership is generally a multifaceted dimension, social distance and political realities can complicate consensus around leadership factors in an infinite number of ways. African American leadership frequently emerges out of an indigenous democratic process that may be relatively informal, but it is clearly understood within the community. This natural selection of leadership is thwarted externally by those who desire to work with leadership with whom they are comfortable. This siphons energy and focus from progressive leadership processes, which can result in attenuating a free flow of positive ideas, creativity, and social action initiatives from the community.

The dialectic positions of M. L. King and Malcolm X illustrate two very different but effective use of skills and strategies in bringing social change. These two individuals also illustrate the significant influence of the encompassing environment on African American leadership. A problem with African American leadership is that it is often exercised in hostile circumstances that require strong skills in coping with political realities. Additionally, those perceived as current African American leaders may have been created externally rather than from indigenous processes. For example, as the 1990 decade ends, conservative African Americans are overrepresented in the media. Clearly, many conservative positions are embraced by many African Americans, but these are usually not indicative of political affiliation. The clear disservice to the African American community of overrepresentation of political conservatism impacts policy, funding, and the accuracy of perceptions, facts, and needs of the community.

One final area where skills are needed is when working with the church. The African American church has traditionally been involved in community outreach and social movements. Presently, many argue that grassroots and faith-based groups are the natural answer to fill the void left by welfare reform. Two models for churches interfacing with community are utilized presently. The first is some form of coalition with service organizations in a community or catchment area; the second is a collaboration between a church and some government auspice in a free-enterprise zone (Rogers & Ronshiem, 1998; Williams et al., 1999). The political arrangements that must be negotiated with a complexly intense task environment with competing constituencies and alliances can be overwhelming (e.g., federal and state agencies, gaining access and meeting standards of various statutory requirements, hiring staff in environments that are driven by timelines, different protocols, etc.). Each component can take on a life of its own so that the project consumes more energy than the church may find feasible. Additionally, the focal community may find the benefits that accrue to be too expensive.

In contrast, a coalition with area agencies may be more efficacious by virtue of the cooperating organizations' ability to engage in parallel processes or a pattern of isomorphism (Rogers & Ronsheim, 1998, pp. 107–108). This encourages trust and cooperation between participating agencies, in addition to avoiding the external pressures of externally driven statutory requirements and organizational complexity. This suggests more adaptability to the needs of the sponsoring agencies and institutions as well as to the evolving needs of the communities served.

CASE EXAMPLE

Recently, the federal government earmarked an area on the outskirts of Harmony as a new location for nuclear waste materials. Not many of the residents of Harmony were aware of this action until one of the local ministers brought it up in his Sunday sermon. People began to discuss this and became upset that once again Harmony was targeted as a dumping ground.

The residents began to organize under the auspices of their ministers with the help of a macropractitioner who was approached by the local ministers' council. Using the ecological approach, they helped to link members of the congregation with parents and youth in the schools, county government representatives, and other constituents. One of the key principles followed by leaders and residents was that of inclusion of the target system. This community group made a concerted effort to remain open to all opinions and include as many residents as possible throughout the intervention process of developing a plan and a contingency plan, implementing strategies and tactics, fundraising to meet expenses, forming coalitions, and so on. Skills of participants were recognized, news media were informed of issues from the community's perspective, and representatives at the state and federal levels were made aware of the growing political awareness and strengths of the community. These activities led to a satisfactory resolution and a more isolated location was sought for depositing the nuclear waste.

CONCLUSION

The terrain of African American communities is dynamic and evolving. This requires social work professionals to acquire modalities and frameworks that can adapt to new knowledge as they emerge, challenge stereotyping schema that may operate unconsciously, and be prepared to adapt interventions to new challenges. As an example, some tactics and strategies of communities and organizational practice are driven by views on poverty and its effects on problems and behavior in this community, tactics and strategies are based on assumptions unsupported by emerging empirical evidence (Figueira-McConough, 1995; Krivo, et al., 1998). Krivo and colleagues (1998) studied a confluence of factors, including demographics and race, regarding the concentration of poverty in relatively isolated pockets in the Northeast and Midwest. They found structural characteristics linked to planning and policy associated with causal factors for poverty for Blacks and Hispanics, but not for whites. Such findings suggest a need to focus on social action strategies as well as community development (Fellin, 1993; Iglehart & Becarra, 1995; Longres, 1995).

Forces within and external to the African American community and the dominant culture continually interact in ways that produce behavior (Davis, 1993; Prigoff, 1999). Social work should monitor government policies that do not encourage political and economic empowerment within the community and educate community members to increase their analytical skills in identifying policies that have deleterious effects for the community. As the larger environment rapidly moves towards globalization, it is imperative that the African American community be educated about the economic and social impact on them. Many urban areas are strongly affected by political and economic events already (Mayadas, et al., 1999). Clearly, there is a critical need for community advocates to address problems regarding the endangerment of Black men and single parenthood issues in the African American community.

Interventions with communities and organizations with African Americans should always focus on process with an awareness that desired outcomes may have to be revised to accommodate evolving information, new knowledge, and contingencies. So much has been mislearned and misapplied with communities of color. Newer research methodologies are providing empirical bases for refining these techniques all the time. Interventions should be designed with data collection in mind so that knowledge development is enhanced. Macro-level research, both qualitative and quantitative, should be encouraged as a basis for developing more efficacious models of intervention with African Americans.

REFERENCES

Abramson, M. (1996). Reflections on knowing oneself ethically: Toward a working framework for social work practice. *Families in Society, 77,* 195–202.

Allen, J. A. (1997). African Americans: Caribbean. In *Encyclopedia of social work,* (3rd ed.). Washington, DC: National Association of Social Workers Press.

Asante, M. K. & Abarry, A. S. (1996). African intellectual heritage: A book of sources. Philadelphia: Temple University Press.

Beckett, J. O., Dungee-Anderson, D., Coy, L., & Daly, A. (1997). African Americans and multicultural interventions. *Smith College Studies in Social Work, 67* (3), 540–563.

Billingsley, A. (1968). Black families in white America. Englewood Cliffs, NJ: Prentice-Hall.

Boyd-Franklin, N. (1989). Black families in therapy: A multisystems approach. New York: Guilford.

Butler, J. S. (1991). *Entrepreneurship and self-help among Black Americans: A reconsideration of race and economics.* Albany, NY: State University of New York.

Carlton-La'Ney, I. (1997). Elizabeth Ross Haynes: An African American reformer and womanist, 1908–1940. *Social Work, 42* (6), 570–583.

Carlton-La'Ney, I. (1999). African American social work pioneers' response to need. *Social Work, 44* (4), 311–321.

Carter, R. T. & Quereshi, A. (1995). A topology of philosophical assumptions in multicultural counseling and training. In J. G. Pontevotta, L. A. Suzuki, & C. M. Alexander (Eds.), *Handbook of multicultural counseling* (pp. 239–262). Thousand Oaks, CA: Sage.

Chestang, L. (1976). Environmental influences on social functioning: The Black experience. In P. Cafferty & L. Chestang (Eds.), *The diverse society: Implications for social policy* (pp. 59–74). Washington, DC: National Association of Social Workers Press.

Collins, P. H. (1990). Black feminist thought: Knowledge, consciousness, and the politics of empowerment. New York: Rutledge, Chapman & Hall.

Collins, P. H. (1998). Fighting words: Black women and the research for justice. Minneapolis, MN: University of Minnesota Press.

Cose, E. (1999, June 7). The good news about Black America. *Newsweek, 233,* 28–40.

Cowger, C. D. (1998). Clientelism and clientification: Impediments to strengths based social work practice. *Journal of Sociology and Social Welfare, 25* (1), 25–37.

Crane, J. (1994). Exploding the myth of scientific support for the theory of black intellectual inferiority. *Journal of Black Psychology, 20* (2), 189–209.

Daly, A. (1994). African American and white managers: A comparison in one agency. *Journal of Community Practice, 1* (1), 57–79.

Daly, A. (Ed.). (1998). Workplace diversity: Issues and perspectives. Washington, DC: National Association of Social Workers Press.

Daly, A., Jennings, J., Beckett, J., & Leashore, R. B. (1995). Effective coping strategies of African Americans. *Social Work, 40* (1), 240–248.

Davis, E. (1993). Social policy, psychosocial development and minorities. In Y. I. Song & E. C. Kim (Eds.), *American mosaic: Selected readings on America's multicultural heritage* (pp. 101–114). Englewood Cliffs, NJ: Prentice-Hall.

Dubrow, N. F. & Garbino, J. (1989). Living in the war zone: Mothers and young children in a housing development. *Child Welfare, 69,* 3–20.

English, R. A. & Ross-Sheriff, F. (1998). Diversity and challenges of new immigrants in the changing workplace. In A. Daly (Ed.), *Workplace diversity: Issues and perspectives* (pp. 21–35). Washington, DC: NASH Press.

Fellin, P. (1993). Reformulation of the context of community based care. *Journal of Social Work and Sociology, 20* (2), 57–67.

Figueira-McConough, J. (1995). Community organization and the underclass: Exploring new practice directions. *Social Service Review, 59,* 57–85.

Franklin, D. L. (1997). Insuring inequality: *The structural transformation of the African American family.* New York: Oxford University Press.

Gary, L. & Leashore, R. B. (1982). High risk status of black men. *Social Work, 27* (1), 54–58.

Guttentag, M. & Secord, P. F. (1983). Too many women? The sex ratio question. Beverly Hills: Sage.

Healey, J. F. (1995). *Race, ethnicity, gender, and class: The sociology of group conflict and change.* Thousand Oaks, CA: Pine Forge Press.

Hill, R. (1971). *Strengths of Black Families.* New York: Emerson Hall Press.

Iglehart, A. P. & Becarra, R. H. (1995). *Social services and the ethnic community.* Boston: Allyn & Bacon.

Johnson, C. & Smith, P. (1998). *Africans in America: America's journey through slavery.* New York: Harcourt-Brace.

Kitano, H. L. (1991). *Race Relations.* Englewood Cliffs, NJ: Prentice-Hall.

Kozol, J. (1991). *Savage inequalities: Children in America's schools.* New York: Random House.

Kozol, J. (1996). *Amazing grace: The lives of children and the conscience of a nation.* New York: Harper Collins.

Krivo, L. J., Peterson, R. D., Russ, H., & Reynolds, J. R. (1998). Race, segregation, and the concentration of disadvantage: 1980–1990. *Social Problems, 45* (1), 61–79.

Longress, J. F. (1995). *Human behavior in the social environment.* Itasca, IL: F. E. Peacock.

Martin, P. Y. & O'Connor, M. (1989). *The social environment: Open systems applications.* New York: Longman.

Mayadas, N., Elliot, D., & Ramanathan, C. S. (1999). A global model of ethnic diversity conflict: Implications for social work with populations at risk. In C. S. Ramanathan & R. J. Link (Eds.), *All our futures: Social work practice in a global era* (pp. 138–155). Belmont, CA: Brooks-Cole.

McAdoo, H. P. (Ed.). (1981). *Black families.* Beverly Hills: Sage.

McCann, J. E. & Selsky, W. J. (1984). Hyperturbulence and the emergence of Type-5 environments. *Academy of Management Review, 9* (7), 461–470.

McCluskey, A. (1997). "We specialize in the wholly impossible": Black women school founders and their mission. *Signs: The Journal of Women in Culture and Society, 22,* 403–426.

Miller, D. W. (1999, March 19). A ghetto childhood inspires the research of a Yale sociologist. *Chronicle of Higher Education,* vol XLV, A15–A16.

Milloy, C. (1999). A look at tragedy in Black and White. *Washington Post,* May 2, C1.

Molock, S. D., Kimbrough, R., Lacy, M. B., McClure, K. P., & Williams, S. (1994). Suicidal behavior among African American college students: A preliminary study. *Journal of the Black Psychologist, 20* (2), 234–251.

Netting, F. E., Kettner, P. M., & McMurty, S. L. (1993). *Social work macro-practice.* New York: Longman.

Norton, D. J. (1978). *The dual perspective: The inclusion of ethnic minority content in the social work curriculum.* New York: Council on Social Work Education.

O'Hare, W. O., Pollard, K. M., Mann, T. L., & Kent, M. M. (1991). African Americans in the 1990s. *Population Bulletin, 46* (1), pp. 2–38.

Parrillo, V. N. (1996). *Diversity in America.* Thousand Oaks, CA: Pine Forge.

Prigoff, A. (1999). Global social and economic justice issues. In C. S. Ramanathan & R. J. Link (Eds.), *All our futures: Social work practice in a global era* (pp. 156–173). Belmont, CA: Brooks/Cole.

Rogers, B. W. & Ronsheim, D. (1998). Interfacing African American churches with agencies and institutions: An expanding continuum of care with partial answers to welfare reform. *Journal of Sociology and Social Welfare, 25* (1), 105–120.

Rothenberg, P. (1990). The construction, deconstruction and reconstruction of difference. *Hypatia, 5* (1), 42–57.

Schiele, J. H. (1998a). The Afrocentric paradigm and workplace diversity. In A. Daly (Ed.), *Workplace diversity: Issues and perspectives* (pp. 341–353). Washington, DC: NASH Press.

Schiele, J. H. (1998b). Cultural alignment, African American male youths, and violent crimes. In L. See (Ed.), *Human behavior in the social environment from an African American perspective* (pp. 165–182). New York: Haworth.

Schriver, J. M. (1998). Human behavior and the social environment: Shifting paradigms in essential knowledge for social practice. Boston, MA: Allyn & Bacon.

See, L. A. (1998a). Diversity in the workplace: Issues and concerns of African and Asians. In A. Daly (Ed.), *Workplace diversity: Issues and perspectives* (pp. 354–373). Washington, DC: NASH Press.

See, L. A. (Ed.). (1998b). *Human behavior in the social environment from an African American perspective.* New York: Haworth.

Simmons, L. (1990). *Black America: Still searching for identity. The Crisis, 160* (4), 22–28.

Solomon, B. B. (1976). *Black empowerment: Social work in oppressed communities.* New York: Columbia University Press.

Stepnik, A. & Portes, A. (1986). Flights of despair: A profile of recent Haitian refugees in South Florida. *International Migration Review, 20,* 329–350.

Suarez, R. (1999). *The old neighborhood: What we lost in the great migration: 1966–1999.* New York: Free Press.

Taylor, R. L. (1997). The changing meaning of race in the social sciences: Implications for social work practice. *Smith College Studies in Social Work, 67* (3), 277–298.

Thomas, H. (1997). *The slave trade: The story of the Atlantic slave trade: 1440–1870.* New York: Touchstone.

Tolleson, J. (1997). Death and transformation: The reparative power of violence in the lives of young Black inner-city gang members. *Smith College Studies in Social Work, 67* (3), 415–431.

Turner, R. J. (1991). Affirming consciousness: The afrocentric perspective. In J. E. Everett, S. S. Chipungu, & B. Leashore (Eds.), *Child welfare: An Afrocentric perspective* (pp. 36–37). New Brunswick, NJ: Rutgers University Press.

Washington, J. (1993). Black or African American: What's in a name? In Y. I. Song & E. C. Kim *American mosaic: Selected readings on America's multicultural heritage* (pp. 57–64). Englewood Cliffs, NJ: Prentice-Hall.

Washington, R. O. & McCarley, L.D. (1998). A postmodern perspective on Black suicides in the United States. In L. See (Ed.), *Human behavior in the social environment from an African American perspective* (pp. 225–242). New York: Haworth.

Williams, D. R., Griffith, E. H., Young J. L., Collins, C., & Dodson, J. (1999). Structure and provision of services in Black churches in New Haven, Connecticut. *Cultural Diversity and Ethnic Minority Psychology, 5* (2), 118–133.

Wilkerson, I. (1995). Middleclass Blacks try to grip a ladder while lending a hand. In P. S. Rothenberg (Ed.), *Race, class and gender in the United States: An integrated study,* 3rd ed (pp. 155–162). New York: St Martin's Press.

Zhang, A. Y. & Snowden, L. R. (1999). Ethnic characteristics of mental disorders in five U.S. communities. *Cultural Diversity and Ethnic Minorities, 5* (2), 134–146.

CHAPTER 18

INTERVENTION WITH MEXICAN AMERICAN FAMILIES

FERNANDO GALAN

Scholars in social work education and social work professionals in hospitals, schools, and nonprofit organizations have been faced with challenging issues about how to address the psychosocial needs of Mexican American individuals and families. The impact of the acculturation process of newer generations caused by increasing levels of formal education among Mexican Americans and economic realities have created a new challenge regarding what it means to be culturally competent with this group.

We have expanded our knowledge base and much of it has remained descriptive without sufficient guidance on what to do beyond the assessment process. Too little practice evaluation that explores, explains, and evaluates approaches on how to effectively intervene with families in the problem solving and problem resolution process remains a major challenge (Holtzman, 1995). We continue to observe that so-called laundry-list approaches to working with ethnic minority groups limit our understanding of newer family dynamics. Because the acculturation process has introduced so much cognitive content for families to consider, social workers need to understand this and how to use it. This is particularly important because the field has moved from building cultural awareness and cultural sensitivity to analyzing issues of practice competence. Working with families without a knowledge base of treatment approaches that address acculturation dynamics may limit our cultural competence.

What we hope to introduce is a discussion of the emerging concepts and terms of processes of culture change and discuss the significance in how to choose and implement interventions with Mexican Americans. Social workers who do not have a base knowledge of culture, acculturation, cultural conflict, cultural destructiveness, cultural incapacity, cultural blindness, cultural pre-competence, cultural competence, and cultural proficiency may fall short in using a culturally competent system of care.

SOCIODEMOGRAPHIC OVERVIEW

Various counts and analyses of the culturally diverse population in the United States conducted in the decade of the nineties reflected various patterns, among them a major influx of immigrants, refugees, and undocumented workers into the United States. Many came from Asia, Central America, and Eastern Europe. The five most populous states with Hispanics included Texas, California, Florida, New York, and Illinois, home for many Mexican Americans, Cuban Americans, Puerto Rican Americans, and other Spanish-language dominant groups.

In 1978, groups of color constituted 20 percent of the population of the United States and Hispanics were 6 percent. Today, Hispanics represent one of the largest growing groups, and the Census 2000 promises to reveal the major changes in immigration and birth rates that are already known by state. California has conducted research profiles indicating that the youth population of Hispanics continues to increase. The number of Hispanics in the population has increased significantly because of the younger age and higher fertility rate of these groups, as well as due to legal and illegal immigration. With the "mother country" of Mexico immediately to the south, and the problem of unstable markets in Central and South American countries, Hispanic populations along the United States–Mexico border have continued to grow.

Changes in the migration patterns have affected the geographic location of Hispanics, who have shifted their geographic areas of residence. While many Hispanics have always moved in search of better employment and social conditions, the three states that have seen massive growths in Hispanic populations are California, Texas, and Florida. It is becoming increasingly clear that the southern United States is heavily populated by large groups of Hispanics.

With respect to income levels, there has been great variation. While many Hispanic families have entered the ranks of the middle and upper-middle economic classes, many newly arrived immigrants and native displaced workers continue to fill the categories of the poor, single mothers, and elderly. The Hispanic median family income has not increased substantially in the last twenty years despite the fact that more Hispanics enter college. Retention and graduation rates continue to lag behind the general population. The increase in single-mother units and in adults without employment due to displacement has contributed to the proportion of persons below the poverty level, especially in areas along the United States–Mexico border.

In addition to lower incomes, Hispanics struggle with employment options due to language barriers. Many new immigrants do not speak English and must learn the language in order to advance in positions that require it. Those who are bilingual appear to continue to be at an advantage, but the number of Hispanics who do not speak Spanish may signal the effects of third and fourth generations and influences of the acculturation process.

No discussion of the Hispanic population is complete without a word about terminology. While the term *Hispanic* continues to be used as an umbrella term by many, it does not necessarily enjoy nationwide approval or acceptance. The Spanish-language population uses a variety of terms, such as *Latino*, *Spanish*, and others. Regional geographic differences and differences within the subgroups of the population produce terms that are varied and make accurate demographic profiles a challenge. Within the umbrella term of *Hispanic* may be Mexican Americans, who may or may not use that term; some may use *Chicano* or *Mexicano* or other terms more reflective of where they live. Other groups, such as Puerto Ricans, Cuban Americans, may also have different ethnic terms. For the purposes of our discussion, we will use *Latino* or *Mexican American* interchangeably to denote practice observations predominantly along the southern section of the United States for native and succeeding generations, as well as for families that predominantly migrate from Mexico.

CULTURAL VALUES AND BEHAVIORAL NORMS

Practice knowledge developed from social work with Mexican American client systems suggests that the adherence to traditional cultural beliefs and subsequent behavioral norms appear to be directly linked to established family social functioning. Earlier literature on social work practice with Mexican Americans emphasized that workers needed to be aware of the differences and be culturally sensitive to those differences (Lum,1999). Many social workers found that their client loads, however, seemed more uniform than diverse. This may have been attributed to the fact that many earlier Mexican Americans who used services were primarily immigrants, first- or second-generation families whose cultural orientation was more traditional. The focus in the literature appeared to emphasize that social workers needed to understand the importance of the Spanish language, the values of the reference group, the role of natural support systems, immigrant status issues, economic stresses associated with poverty, and so on. Earlier generations of Mexican American families, however, had children and the offspring were biculturally socialized with two competing systems of family and community.

Earlier understandings of how to work with Mexican Americans began to be questioned because their application did not seem to address the needs of newer groups of acculturated Mexican Americans. Cultural competence suggests that any system of care for Mexican Americans must recognize that it is a predominantly bilingual/bicultural group and that the dynamics inherent within the culture are challenged by new issues of stress, coping, and adaptation. Many Mexican American clients must learn the skills to navigate between two dominant systems of values, each with its own language, and two sets of behavioral norms, often in conflict with each other. Additionally, social workers need to understand the dynamics inherent when cultures intersect with each other and introduce a myriad of issues around cognitive content and language.

Behavioral norms become more difficult to assess and work with because they are more often influenced by the level of acculturation in the family system. Unquestioned loyalty to traditional beliefs about behavior is sometimes challenged by the power of the social situation and whose beliefs are being used to determine what is appropriate and what not.

While the Mexican American family still represents the primary system of support and nurturing, more and more family members experiment with contemporary beliefs and modern behaviors. This can disrupt the traditional family, which may be threatened by these changes. How one conducts an assessment of the internal dynamics operating in the family, and how a bilingual/bicultural status creates a unique set of mental health issues are important pieces of knowledge to have prior to intervention.

Because individuals and families make different behavioral choices based on which values are being adhered to and which not, the dynamics of the social context need to be acknowledged, accepted, and adjusted to. One of the most important issues in intervention is determining what the family wants to preserve and who in the family wants to exercise social control in managing change.

Galan (1978) introduced a multidimensional transactional model that built on earlier linear explanations of the acculturation process. He posited that an individual who adopted community beliefs and behaviors in order to accommodate and adapt did not necessarily have to reject traditional worldviews, but simply incorporate the understanding that different social situations may call for different levels of adherence to beliefs to promote adaptation. The theory suggests that, in order to understand dynamics that can occur within and among Mexican American individuals and families, one needs to examine the social context. Social situations can produce multiple collisions in beliefs and behavioral choices. Conflicts with beliefs and behavioral dissonance can surface when individual members attempt to address whether traditional family rules or community expectations will be followed. The issue is whether decisions about behavior are perceived and interpreted as rejection of family beliefs.

ISSUES OF INTERVENTION

When issues that cause stress and tension are apparent, cognitive treatment approaches appear to be very helpful in intervention. While there is a large number of studies that supports the efficacy of cognitive methods, few outcome studies are available to determine their comparative efficacy with Mexican American families. However, those of us who have been practicing with Mexican Americans using cognitive treatment methods are encouraged, because the methods can be used to demonstrate and illustrate the respect so needed for cultural competence.

Helping individuals and families determine what is in their best self-interest is an important element of how to use cognitive treatment methods. Ultimately, families struggle with looking at behaviors in families and which beliefs will be reinforced as a result. Individual family members who are interested in preserving traditional beliefs of family functioning may clash with other family members who are more interested in behaviors that reflect contemporary beliefs. Family disruption is sometimes caused by what an individual family member does because communication has not occurred about what the behavior means to others in the family. Additionally, part of reestablishing cohesion among relations relates to the amount of flexibility that exists in a family, which allows individual members to act in certain ways without threatening family stability.

Issues of social control usually surface among family members who want to preserve the way of the family. The process of acculturation requires that beliefs be questioned. Do I act the way my parents want me to or do I act the way I want to? Earlier generations in the same family may insist that traditional beliefs be honored; later generations may want more flexibility. Beliefs adopted by different individuals in families may represent a rejection of tradition and an adherence to the English language, English institutions, and the norms of the dominant group. Different members of the same family may have different views, based on their level of adherence to, or separation from, original beliefs about family functioning.

Because each individual family member may be at a different level of acculturation, some members may be very traditional and others may be more assimilated. Additionally, some may be marginal and others may be transitional, unsure of what they believe. Others may have bicultural, acculturated views that allow them to function more flexibly because they have more coping skills. The amount of acculturation stress present in a family situation becomes important knowledge to have to assist the helping and problem-solving process.

Intervention Using Cognitive Concepts

Granvold (1995, pp. 526) discusses several cognitive treatment features that may lend themselves to a better understanding of intervention applicable in the treatment of Mexican American families who are experiencing acculturation stress. We have selectively chosen to discuss what he calls idiosyncratic subjective experience, collaborative effort, the education model, the Socratic method, and constructivism.

Idiosyncratic Subjective Experience.   Granvold (1995, pp. 526) points out that people find personal/unique meanings in life experiences (including emotions) and that these contribute to beliefs that represent the client's reality. Intervention is the process of addressing an issue presented by the individual or family that requires resolution. After an assessment that includes not only demographics, the client's description of the problem, the expectations of the social worker, and the goals the family has for resolution, the social worker needs to enter the family communication network and ask a series of critical questions (Brisbane & Womble, 1992). Subsequently, it is important to know the perceptual patterns and the beliefs being used to understand particular life events or behaviors. Projective techniques ask clients to project their meanings onto art renderings or clay sculptures they make. This creates sufficient distance from the actual life event and may help the client to express emotions tied to the meanings he or she has attributed to those life events or behaviors. This is especially helpful if a past traumatic experience surfaces. Intervention that helps to illuminate for the family the problems in communication that prevent them from resolving their own matters then and now is culturally competent practice because it allows the individual or family to bring forth their own meanings and cognitive appraisals. It may or may not be helpful to use bilingual members of a family as cotherapists because some clients may prefer to explain something using a Spanish phrase or word that may not be known by an English-speaking therapist.

Education Model. Granvold (1995, p. 526) also discusses the importance of client instruction before the impact of generation status became apparent; many Mexican American families were monolingual, using only the Spanish language. Later generations either are monolingual in English or quite fluent in both languages. The fact that members of a family may have different levels of bilingual fluency may signal that the worker may need to learn content in the Spanish language relevant to the treatment process (Granvold, 1995). For example, information on cultural change processes and the dynamics of acculturation have been found to be very helpful in providing a common understanding of cognitive processes for family members never before understood or discussed. Helping families have a common language base can aid the communication process.

Cognitive intervention appears to be effective in working with Mexican American families because methods are culturally sensitive and can be applied to individual members who are at different levels of acculturation. What is at issue is not always necessarily language, per se, but the need to help the family uncover the meaning of language terms or behaviors. What is important about language is that so many meanings of behaviors are actually encoded in Spanish words and mannerisms. In that sense, the worker needs to know what linguistic implications and idiosyncratic factors are being brought into play.

The Socratic Method. Adequate family social functioning in a bilingual/bicultural Mexican American family is a goal of intervention that requires of the social worker an understanding of how to bring clarity to a situation that may not have ever been examined fully by all family members.

Granvold states that the use of "Socratic questioning or guided discovery leads the client in a process of self discovery and reasoning." It helps to disclose critical cognitive data. The social worker, acting chiefly as a probing facilitator, serves to enhance the type of intra-family communication that helps the family view the "problem" away from culture and more toward generation, belief, or economic class differences. The beliefs and behavioral norms that often come into question in a family have to do with whether the family system is flexible and permeable and allows for multiple and different beliefs among its members.

The Socratic method helps the client focus definitions of the problem and gives the social worker insight as to how the client perceives, processes information, and problem-solves. It exposes what the client believes. As Granvold (1994b) explains, it also exposes the client's tolerance of stress and allows for irrational beliefs to be challenged as part of problem solving. What I have seen is that progressive questioning helps the client become more active in treatment and helps equalize the relationship between worker and client.

Constructivism.   Constructivism's assertion "that humans actively create and construe their personal and social realities" (Mahoney, 1988) is an important feature of cognitive intervention because social workers can learn with their clients how reality is being shaped by the events that occur, have occurred, and are currently occurring. The manner in which the client is ordering his or her life becomes apparent in the therapeutic relationship, especially when it is viewed as a lifelong process (Duran & Duran, 1995).

The effective helping relationship that is culturally appropriate is the one that is based on the social worker's being both humane and efficient, in applying ethical principles, such as acceptance, respect, empathy, immediacy, and practicing technique principles, such as individualization, partialization, and self-determination. The helping relationship is also built on an appreciation for human diversity and support for the values of pluralism. Multiple individual and family orientations around race, religion, geography, sexual orientation, the intrinsic worth of people, and of their individualization in understanding differences and treating each family member equally are additional factors.

Cognitive Intervention

Hollon and Beck (1986) discussed cognitive interventions as "those approaches that attempt to modify existing or anticipated disorders by virtue of altering cognitions or cognitive processes." According to Hollon and Beck, cognitive interventions use basic mechanisms of therapeutic change. These include: (1) *rational analyses,* "which involve procedures of disconfirmation and reconceptualization," a procedure used successfully with Mexican Americans when the worker is also skilled at using the Socratic method; (2) *logical-empirical assessment,* which focuses on the "systematic analysis of evidence that confirms or refutes the client's cognition." This does not appear to be a central concern for Mexican American families who are trying to preserve traditional cultural beliefs; and (3) *repetition or practice,* which emphasizes practice and the persistent exposure of faulty cognitions. Helping individuals focus on particular life events or behaviors, analyze them from the standpoint of what internalized beliefs were used to evaluate the event, what emotional state was experienced at the time, and bringing the entire social situation to the present for rational analysis, seems to work well with Mexican Americans using cognitive restructuring as the basic intervention method.

We have found that the relationship between cognition and affect plays an important role in intervention because many Mexican Americans place a high premium on the expressions of emotions surrounding life events. Culturally, there is greater permission to associate particular emotional states with life events. Szabo (1987) has noted, in clinical cases with postpartum mothers in Houston, that a negative life event may actually "lock in" an emotion that, until cleared and expressed, can become the basis for which continual symptoms of stress and tension reoccur. Research conducted by Galan and Guerra (1999) found that survivors of violence, some of whom were Mexican American, who had witnessed an execution of an inmate who committed a family homicide, came to peace intellectually, but appeared to have difficulties with emotions associated with such life events because of an unwillingness or inability to address those issues. This, in turn, appeared to keep the event and its emotional effects from dissipating. While many family social functioning problems originate from perceived and actual conflicts in beliefs and/or emotional states, some members of Mexican American families may find fault with socialization processes brought by exposure and subsequent adoption of community beliefs that emphasize only logic.

The concept of bicultural socialization in Mexican American families suggests that a dynamic process may be occurring at all times and that, while beliefs and behaviors may appear to be in conflict with each other, mastery of both cultures can be achieved (deAnda, 1984). *Bicultural conflict* "occurs when an individual's family values or beliefs are different from those of society at large; there is a high degree of incongruence or contrast between family values and societal values" (Galan, 1992, p. 236). *Bicultural tension,* in contrast, "occurs when an individual's available coping skills are based on only one cultural or family value system: either that of the family or that of society. Social functioning of a family member is often a major challenge when the individual is not able to use his or her coping skills in *both* the family and in the community, which is what bicultural identity requires.

Because Mexican American families are at different levels of acculturation, younger members may have or want more permission or greater flexibility to express contemporary beliefs that are not part of the family system. Individuals in families who are able to "integrate positive qualities of their culture of origin and contemporary community culture achieve bicultural competency" and develop an ability to enhance their social functioning in the family and in the community because of a widened coping repertoire. Many challenges for individuals and families have to do with the fact that bilingual/bicultural clients are not culturally deprived, but are, instead, culturally oversupplied with beliefs from two major cultures, one English language-based and the other Spanish language-based. This means that they have cultural belief and behavioral norm systems to consider in choosing what to do in any social situation.

The social worker needs to be able to understand that effective interventions must incorporate knowledge of acculturation dynamics. It is important to know how far from a traditional belief system the individual is. Because bicultural socialization is a dynamic process, and much of what causes disruption and discomfort is centered around the meanings of behaviors, effective intervention with Mexican Americans emphasizes on bilingual communication.

Multiple meanings about an individual member's behavior are often at the crux of a family issue. For example, a Mexican American family was asked to plan a simple weekend vacation for the parents and their adult children with their children at an island resort. As the family members talked with each other, the older son took a leadership role and suggested possibilities of where they could stay. Some discussion ensued, and it appeared as if all were in consensus about a decision for the entire family to rent a three-bedroom condominium. Mom decidedly took on a withdrawal stance and seemed not to like the idea because she felt that two units might be better for privacy. She was offended that she had not been asked first for her opinion because of "who she was" as the parent who "should be respected." The issue had nothing to do with privacy; it was about respecting her position in the family. The adult children acknowleged that she had not been asked, but they also stated that they wanted one unit to save money because they were going to pay for the condominium rental. The mom became infuriated that money was the major consideration and decided that she didn't want to go. In exploring this in a family session, she felt that way because she perceived that her traditional "control tower" role in the family was compromised and not respected by her children. Her sense of control and power came into question through the actions of her children, which she interpreted as being disrespectful. When her adult children talked honestly about their own motivations and explained that their actions were strictly based on financial considerations, it seemed to resolve the misunderstanding, but situations like this can escalate if there is not clarity.

When one considers the fact that, in some social situations involving Mexican Americans, two languages are often used interchangeably in conversation, it raises the possibilities that the words themselves can be misunderstood or perceived to be barriers in communication. Later generations of Mexican Americans may not speak Spanish fluently, and their use of English may cause some parents to wonder if their language of origin will disappear, as will any symbolic meaning that comes with that.

Practice Principles and Skills Related to Bilingual/Bicultural Intervention

Intervention with bilingual/bicultural clients that is culturally competent seeks to achieve a balance in value–behavior congruence. Clients need to know that they have been guided through a process of examination of their beliefs and the perceived beliefs of their own reference group in the community. They need to understand that the options in behavior choices have been examined, and that their meanings have been analyzed for their potential benefits and consequences. The capacity to engage in critical thinking about reality contributes to a greater sense of mastery and illustrates how social workers can use cultural knowledge in a competent way. Using cultural knowledge is key to cultural competence in social work practice. A capacity for examination of self in relation to culture and an assessment of where one is as a professional culturally is important in cultural competence.

Knowing the content of perceived cultural beliefs is necessary to help establish a foundation for understanding what the client brings to the helping relationship. In intervention, however, the emphasis is on what we call the "processing of cultural beliefs," defined as helping the client know how to weigh cultural information and how to prioritize with respect to choosing appropriate behavior in order to maintain integrity in one's belief and behavior nexus. Applying critical thinking and cognitive concepts to the identification of a source of discomfort, an analysis of beliefs and the relative level of importance to the client, an analysis of the social situation that requires action, and an analysis of the options in behavior choices are part of intervention. It involves knowing how to establish an alliance with the client and knowing how to use oneself as a facilitator to help the client or family navigate through the multiple competing interests that present themselves when one tries to maintain cultural congruence between what one believes and what one does.

Culturally competent social work engages in a questioning dialogue or social construction with the client to help question reality and determine what it is she or he wants to do. Rather than presenting alternatives for action, the culturally competent social worker remains detached from the client's cultural content. Instead, the worker engages in a process of asking deeper and more probing questions to help the client gain more and more awareness of her or his own cognitive appraisals.

The goal of a culturally competent relationship is helping each family member achieve internal consistency among values, behaviors, and identity within a given social context. This cultural identity integration is a measure of healthy family social functioning, where each family member can openly or appropriately discuss what is going on in his or her life and how events challenge his or her view of the world, him- or herself, and relationships with others.

Because bicultural socialization involves two distinct sets of beliefs and behaviors from family and from community cultures, as these beliefs become fully internalized, they become a resource on which individuals can draw. The bilingual/bicultural member in the Mexican American family expands her or his coping repertoire and the ability to be more culturally adaptive. As a result of supportive communication in the family, a dual identification process that calls into question competing values and behaviors may enhance the social functioning of all in the group.

CASE VIGNETTE

Alejandro is a thirty-eight-year-old Mexican American male born in Laredo, Texas. He went to a border elementary and high school, played football, was regarded as smart and quiet. After he went to the community college for a couple of years, he enlisted in the Navy and completed his basic training in Long Beach, California. He describes himself as a businessman. He is the oldest of five children of two living parents. After his completion of service, he chose to move to Los Angeles, changed his name to Alex Soares, changed the last letter of his last name from "z" to "s," and took up residence in the inner city district. He invested in and fixed an apartment complex with a partner named Josh, an Anglo-Saxon male from Santa Barbara. At twenty-eight, Alex "discovered" that he was a gay male after having entered into several relationships with men. He committed himself to a man named Aaron, thirty-five, an Anglo-Saxon male, and they moved in together as partners. They lived together for ten years and became good friends with Josh, Trey, and Rosie, mutual friends.

His life with Aaron was comfortable until he received a call from Nina, his sister in Laredo. She and Alex were very close for many years as brother and sister and she wanted him to come to Laredo for her wedding. She called, and he initially said no. She said she was hurt, and he was finally convinced to come. When Alex tried to explain to Nina that his business concerns in Los Angeles prevented him from coming without hardship, Nina could not believe Alex would choose business over family concerns. Alex committed. Alex discussed the family event with Aaron and explained that he needed to go to Laredo. Aaron wanted to make the trip with him, but Alex said no. Aaron could not understand why Alex would not want him to go and assumed that it was because Alex was gay and he didn't want his family to know. Alex insisted that it had nothing to do with that, but Aaron was not persuaded. The day of the trip, Alex began to perspire and feel his heart pounding. He felt dizzy and light-headed; his hands began to shake, and he felt he was choking. At the ticket counter, the agent asked him if was alright because he was shaking.

At the Laredo airport, he was greeted by his Mom and Dad, Nina, Laura, Tony, and other family members. He criticized Laura for wearing too much makeup and said that she should not be so loud in her dress. They all looked at him and wondered why he was so critical. Then he did not speak Spanish in the car, and criticized Nina for listening to a Spanish language station.

At the wedding reception, Alex could not speak with Cuka, who had been the family housekeeper since he was a child. Cuka joked that Alex couldn't speak Spanish anymore and he felt uncomfortable. Aunt Rosa and "Guela," the grandmother, tried to reconnect with Alex, but he could not relate very well with them and he left. He went to the reception hall bathroom and snorted a line of cocaine, returned to the reception, and drank beer while listening to the mariachi band. He met up with his high school best friend, Rudy, whom he had not seen in over ten years. Rudy joked with Alex and Alex criticized him for working at a local hamburger restaurant, despite the fact that Rudy was a district manager. Rudy punched Alex in the arm and told him to stop being such a jerk. They both left the reception and went cruising in Rudy's truck. Rudy took out a marijuana cigarette and started smoking. Alex joined him. They stopped on a private road, snorted cocaine, and talked. As the conversation got deeper, the sun was setting and Alex became more critical of Rudy and told him that he couldn't believe he hadn't changed much. Rudy became angry and asked Alex what had happened to him and why was he so uptight with his own family? He told Alex that he was different and that he had forgotten who he was. Alex became paranoid and began to perspire; his right hand began to shake. Alex knew on some level that he could not stay any longer, so he changed his flight ticket and returned to Los Angeles three days ahead of schedule. His mother was very disappointed, and Alex told her that he had to return to business matters.

A number of issues are evident in this example—class, sexual orientation, cultural beliefs, and family relationships—affected by the levels of acculturation in the family. The kind of diagnostic activity that examines how these issues contribute to the difficulties in the client's social functioning may facilitate the therapeutic movement during the period of intervention.

Using a projective technique and the Socratic method, the client needs to be able to discuss what is going on inside of him and how he feels about it. A projective technique might include the expression of a no-word part of himself, an artistic doodle on a notepad or a sculptured piece of clay, for example. In this way, the client can displace thoughts and feelings that may be difficult to express directly onto the object or drawing. The use of the Socratic method becomes very important because the practitioner needs to ask leading questions of the client to help him make full use of the tool. Asking questions like, "What is going on in this draw-ing?" or "Where is the most energy in this clay figure?" and using various gestalt techniques can help the client express what is going on. Other questions may focus on where in time and space the person felt powerless, such as, "When in time did you feel you lost your power to make statements or decisions for yourself?" "Did you have that power yesterday?" "Did you have that power last year?" "Did you have that power two years ago?" Using this backchaining method (Galan, 1992) to find the time and space when the client felt he lost his power is important. Deter-mining what happened then and what decisions were made regarding self, others, or life may aid in helping the client discover where he might have gotten "stuck" in an old belief or judgment that governs his life today.

The exploration of those old beliefs and the accompanying emotions taken on in a social situation of perceived powerlessness may help the client realize how her or his present thinking is faulty. Releasing those beliefs and accompanying emo-tions can have important cathartic effects. This kind of intervention may help the client face the implications and consequences of her or his current thoughts, feel-ings, and behaviors. The social worker can help the client express any hostility, anxiety, or guilt that was associated with role conflict and confusion. Intervention discussions may lead the client to redefine her or his self-concept and to examine what has happened to create an lack of integrity in self.

In my example, the client needs help in looking at what is going on and whose beliefs contributed to the difficulties he had with his family. The worker can help him undertake changes in his role. The client may gain considerable emo-tional insight about the conflicts that he is experiencing with his family.

By redefining the social situations that have caused stress, the worker can help the client meet needs and restructure social roles with the family on a more complementary basis. Initially, it is important to establish communication between the client's thinking and subsequently, with the members of the family who want to understand. The social worker must employ the techniques of clarification, interpretation, and confrontation in order to help the client with problem solving. Probing the client and facilitating a dialogue in the client between what he chose to believe then and what he chooses to believe today may set up an empowering sit-uation in which the client can exercise control over his life. In successful applica-tion, issues of identity may also surface for review and resolution, as in the case study.

The individual in the family situation has a series of issues that require care-ful examination to help the client return to a level of integrity and balance between who he is and what he says and does. The process of helping the client regain his personal power and improve his functioning in the family may be facilitated by forming an alliance with the client, restructuring communication in the family, and employing various structural family therapy principles to produce insight. Often, older family members perceive loss of control or outright conflict between con-temporary and traditional beliefs about how one should live. The release of emo-tions can also be useful for family members and can be facilitated through various affective processes. Ultimately, a resolution that can occur for Alex may have more to do with helping him address his own personal issues. Variations in the beliefs and behaviors that occur among family members do not necessarily have to mean that something is wrong and that there is a disruption of personal functioning or family unity.

CONCLUSION

The skills that the social worker needs to develop in order to be culturally competent are multiple, and primarily involve communication, facilitation, alliance building, confrontation, analysis, and, most importantly, the skill of synthesis, helping the client see how multiple elements are involved in the difficulty in family social functioning. In the same manner, individuals can come to understand that their beliefs often determine their behavior and that social functioning can be enhanced by ensuring that personal power and personal integrity are reestablished and maintained. The social construction of a therapeutic relationship between client and social worker may help to promote a continuous examination of the reality of the client. Such emphasis on the process of helping and a trust in that process may help social workers develop respect in our work with those who seek our help.

REFERENCES

Brisbane, F. L. & Womble, M. (1992). *Working with African Americans: A Professional's Handbook.* Chicago, Illinois: Human Resources Development Institute.

De Anda, Diane D. Bicultural socialization: Factors affecting the minority experience. *Social Work, 29,* 101–107.

Duran, E. & Duran, B. (1995). *Native American postcolonial psychology.* Albany: State University of New York Press.

Galan, F. 1985. Traditional values about family behavior: The case of the Chicano client. *Social Thought.*

Galan, F. J., and Robbins, S. P. (1998). *Theories of assimilation, acculturation, and bicultural socialization.* In S. P. Robbins, P. Chatterjee, & E. R. Canda, *Contemporary human behavior theory: A critical perspective for social work.* Boston: Allyn and Bacon, pp. 119–150.

Galan, F. & Guerra, D. (1999). Initial results from research on victims who witness an execution, Unpublished notes.

Granvold, D. (1994). Concepts and methods of congitive treatment. In D. K. Granvold (ed.) *Cognitive and behavioral treatment: Methods and applications.* Pacific Grove, California: Brooks/Cole.

Granvold, D. (1995). Cognitive treatment. *Encyclopedia of social work.* Washington, D.C.: National Association of Social Workers, pp. 525–534.

Hollon, S. D., & Beck, A. T. (1986). Cognitive and cognitive behavioral therapies. In S. Garfield and A. E. Bergin (Eds) *Handbook of psychotherapy and behavior change.* New York: John Wiley and sons.

Holtzman, W. H. (Ed.) (1995). Psychiatric assessment of Mexican-origin populations: Proceedings of the ninth Robert Lee Sutherland seminar in mental health. Austin, Texas: Hogg Foundation for Mental Health, the University of Texas.

Lum, D. (1999). *Culturally competent practice: A framework for growth and action*. Belmont, California: Brooks/Cole.

Mahoney, M. (1988). The cognitive sciences and psychotherapy: Patterns in a developing relationship. In K. S. Dobson (Ed.) *Handbook of cognitive therapies* New York: Guilford, pp. 357–386.

Szabo, E. (1987). Lecture training notes on wholistic therapeutic intervention. Houston, Texas: Hermann Hospital.

CHAPTER 19

ORGANIZATIONS AND COMMUNITY INTERVENTION SKILLS WITH HISPANIC AMERICANS

MARIA PUIG

In a first-ever national poll of 2,011 U.S. voters sponsored by the Ford Foundation's Campus Diversity Initiative, the majority of respondents supported diversity courses and programs and recognized the educational advantages of a diverse campus and curriculum (*Diversity Digest*, 1998). This poll reflects the prevalent campus opinion that this nation's growing diversity and the global economy make it more important than ever to understand people who are different from ourselves. Diversity education, according to those polled, helps students learn critical skills, including communicating with those of differing backgrounds, teamwork, and problem solving (*Diversity Digest*, 1998). Nowhere is the need to learn these skills greater than among social workers responsible for carrying out planned change to meet the needs of diverse groups of people, communities, and organizations. And nowhere are these skills more necessary than among practitioners serving Hispanics or Latinos. As noted in a recent report by the U.S. Department of Health and Human Services (1994), there is no one Hispanic or Latino culture. Rather, "country of origin, recency of immigration, and geographical location in the United States contribute to the cultural diversity within the Hispanic population." It is also clear that idiomatic differences of the Spanish language increase Hispanic's cultural diversity.

Americans of Hispanic or Latino descent constitute one of the fastest growing segments of the United States's population. It is estimated that 62 percent of Hispanics in the United States were born in this country, with persons of Mexican heritage making up over 60 percent of all Latinos, Central and South Americans approximately 14 percent, Puerto Ricans another 12 percent, and Cubans, 5 percent (*Current Population Survey*, 1994). Based on the Current Population Survey conducted by the U.S. Bureau of the Census (1994), Hispanics numbered about 26.6 million and made up over 10 percent of the nation's nearly 260 million population.

There are several reasons for the rapid increase in the Hispanic population, including a natural increase (the difference between births and deaths) and substantial immigration from Mexico, Central and South America, and the Caribbean. Census officials predict that the Hispanic population will multiply well into the twenty-first century (U.S. Bureau of the Census, 1990) due to the continued instability and economic difficulties that plague many Latin American countries. Other factors include the people's desire to migrate to achieve family reunification, the anticipation of financial opportunities, and the chance for an improved life. This increase should alert all social workers to the important problems experienced by this population, and to be more mindful of the need for more intensive and culturally sensitive macro interventions that address the core causes of problems caused by the "browning" of the United States.

SOCIODEMOGRAPHIC OVERVIEW

The 1990 Census reported that 22,354,059 persons classified themselves as being of Hispanic origin, a 53 percent increase since 1980. The term *Hispanic* is used by the Census as an ethnic, not a racial designation because Hispanics can be White, Black, Asian, and indigenous. Similarly, the term *Latino* is used interchangeably with *Hispanic*, even though the preferred referent will change according to region, locale, and nationality. It should also be noted that many Hispanics choose to identify themselves by their own "national" identity, such as Cubans or Nicaraguans.

A general descriptive profile of Hispanics living in the United States indicates that they are likely to be young (a median age of 26 years), and to have proportionately more children and fewer elderly than the rest of the nation's population (*Current Population Survey,* 1994). Ethnically, Hispanics are a diverse group, geographically clustered in about ten states, with California being home to approximately 7.7 million Latinos, or 34 percent of the nation's total Hispanic population (*Current Population Survey,* 1994). Other states that have a large concentration of Hispanics include New York, New Jersey, Florida, Illinois, Texas, Arizona, and New Mexico. The majority of Hispanics in the United States, or about 87 percent, lives in large urban cities such as Miami, Los Angeles, San Francisco, Chicago, Houston, Galveston, Dallas, and San Antonio.

An examination of critical socioeconomic indicators, such as education, employment, and income, provides a demographic overview of this group. It must be acknowledged, however, that these are averages and that, among Hispanics, like other ethnic groups, variability exists.

> **Education.**   Despite some recent gains in high school graduation rates, Hispanics continue to lag educationally, particularly in higher education. Only 6 percent of Hispanics reported having a Bachelor's degree in 1994, in comparison to 21 percent of non-Hispanics (*Current Population Survey,* 1994).

Employment.   Hispanic unemployment is nearly twice that of non-Hispanics, with the exception of Cubans, who may be more likely than other Latinos to be self-employed (*Current Population Survey,* 1994). Gender appears to have had very little effect on the types of jobs Hispanics hold, as compared to non-Hispanics, as both males and females are more likely to be engaged in low-paying, less stable, and more hazardous occupations.

Income.   Hispanic families were found to be more than twice as likely as non-Hispanic white families to be living below the poverty level. Hispanic families have three times the poverty rate of non-Hispanic white families, ranging from a high of over 35 percent among Puerto Rican families to a low of 17 percent among Cuban families. Consequently, Hispanic children are more than twice as likely to be living in poverty, with four in ten living below the federal poverty level as compared with about one in eight of nonwhite children (*Current Population Survey,* 1994).

Language.   Among Hispanics, nearly 32 million persons, five years and older, speak a language other than English at home (Census of Population and Housing, 1990). This is approximately 14 percent of the population in the United States, with Spanish being the most common language spoken.

CULTURAL VALUES AND BEHAVIORAL NORMS

The notion of self-identity is rooted in a person's culture, the manner in which individuals come to understand their world, its order and expectations, as grounded on commonly shared beliefs, values, behaviors, attitudes, norms, and language. Ho (1995) conceptualizes *culture* as a set of **internalized influences** that "operate within the individual that shape (not determine) the personality formation and various aspects of psychological functioning" (p. 5). Culture, then, is the organized grouping of knowledge and experiences and, because most people are enculturated into one or more cultures, the manner in which they behave depends on environmental and individual circumstances. This explanation of culture is particularly appropriate for Hispanics because they have become a part of the dominant culture in the United States through observation, practice, and education. Nonetheless, most Hispanics maintain and impart to their children sufficient cultural traits, including language, values, norms, traditions, celebrations, rituals, and other group-specific attributes, demanding that notice be given to each subgroup's characteristics. The diversity among Hispanic groups, however, makes it impossible to generalize about cultural values and behavioral norms. In spite of these inter- and intra-group similarities, practitioners are cautioned not to use shortcuts for learning and understanding the singularity of each Hispanic subgroup or person. Generalizations about any group should be treated as hypotheses to be tested with each individual.

Marin and Marin (1991), through their culturally sensitive research protocols with Hispanics, have identified eleven values which, they propose, can be generalizable to most Latinos: (1) familialism, (2) a commitment to the Spanish language, (3) personalism, (4) the recognition that individualism embodies the uniqueness of a person's personality, (5) respect, (6) the concept of *machismo*, (7) a sense of fatalism,

(8) group orientation or *simpatia,* (9) collectivism, (10) a more contact-oriented culture, and (11) a more flexible view of time. The following is a brief, explanatory discussion of three values that are most important when working with Hispanic groups, communities, and organizations.

The value of familialism, or the belief that the family is paramount, continues to be of great importance to most Hispanics. Included in this concept of family are not only relatives or blood relations, but fictive kins—non-blood relatives who are integrated and accepted into the family unit. Organizationally, Hispanics tend to view colleagues and professional associates as more than just coworkers. Oftentimes, the people with whom Hispanics work become part of this broadly based family network.

The commitment to the Spanish language, as a cultural value, is another highly regarded belief. It is through language that people learn to shape their experiences, predetermine observations, and interpret events. For Hispanics, the Spanish language, laden with literal and analogic (hidden or underlying) meanings, is an extension of their identity.

The value of personalism (*personalismo*) is associated with how people relate to and with one another. The Hispanic cultural norm is that one should be affable or charming (*simpatico*); to be otherwise makes one *"un mal educado,"* lacking in social graces. The value of personalism entails knowing when and how to relate to others, regardless of their gender or social position, and to have a strong personal commitment to one's family, friends, and people in general. This is particularly true in organizations, where Hispanics easily move between maintaining their roles as professionals to that of personal friends who are entitled to provide advice on almost any topic or situation.

Hispanics generally are comfortable with issues concerning personal distance, touch, and body/facial gestures. Hispanics will use their hands and facial expressions to communicate their thoughts and feelings. These mannerisms are part of the culture's communication style and serve to convey the passion for whatever topic is being discussed. Likewise, Hispanics touch each other; it is not unusual to see two men hug, or women exchange kisses. However, because the value of *respeto* is also part of these dynamics, Hispanics are socialized into knowing when and whom to touch and when touching is appropriate. In an organizational setting, it is not unusual to see this type of physical contact among coworkers.

An understanding of the cultural values, behavioral norms, and the causes and effects of the demographic changes among Hispanics will promote self-awareness and greater recognition of the "dynamics of difference" (Cross, et al., 1989), so necessary for the culturally competent adaptation of professional social work practice skills.

PROFILE OF SOCIAL WORK PROBLEMS AND ISSUES

What, then, are the implications of understanding cultural norms for social work practice with Hispanics? A primary purpose of this question is to sensitize practitioners to the difficult macro-practice issues and problems facing Hispanics in the

United States. Macro-practice, though often dichotomized as a separate field of professional practice, is simply an extension of the profession's commitment and responsibility to address social problems at all levels. While the majority of cross-cultural social work texts focus on how to work with individuals, families, and groups, most do not address how to set in motion culturally appropriate macro-level interventions to deal with the social conditions that create, or contribute, to the personal problems faced by clients.

Many individuals encounter personal problems such as poverty, domestic violence, and homelessness. When thousands of people, living in rural, urban, and ethnic communities, face these same problems, they are no longer personal. They are social problems. These problems increasingly affect more and more ethnic populations due to policies and practices that do not take into account other issues that people of color have to deal with, including prejudice, racism, and institutional discrimination. Merton and Nisbet (1966) have concluded that social problems, in comparison to personal problems, have the following characteristics:

1. The problem must have social causation rather than be an issue of individual behavior.
2. It must affect a large number of people.
3. It must be judged by an influential number of people to be undesirable.
4. It must be collectively solvable by the community rather than by individual action.

When social problems are viewed as menacing the culture and values of a group of people, social workers should attempt to correct the situation through collective action. The need to intervene at the macro-level requires that social workers know the history of the people affected and the history of the problem, including the role that society played in its creation, for example, the issues of racism and discrimination among Cuban refugees who came to the United States during the 1980 Mariel boatlift.

Unlike other groups of Cuban refugees who had emigrated prior to 1980, *Marielitos,* as this wave of refugees became known, were not met with open arms by the community-at-large. By early June, 1980, the Mariel boatlift had turned into a major domestic and international political crisis for the United States, when more than 80,000 Cubans had arrived in Key West, Florida. By the time the boatlift ended in September 1980, more than 125,000 Cubans had emigrated to this country.

This boatlift was allegedly overrepresented by criminals, prostitutes, and people who had been incarcerated or institutionalized in Cuba. In retrospect, follow-up studies confirmed that approximately 10 percent of this population had, in fact, been incarcerated in Cuba (Clark, Lasaga, & Reque, 1981). When the public learned about these "social undesirables," *Marielitos* became the objects of widespread hostility, resentment, and discrimination by both non-Hispanic whites as well as other Hispanics. Even Cuban Americans, who had previously provided support, were apprehensive about associating with these refugees for fear of being tainted by their disreputable image.

One of the reasons most often cited to explain why this wave of Cubans was treated so differently was race (Clark, Lasaga, & Reque, 1981). Unlike Cubans from the 1960s and 1970s, the Mariel boatlift consisted of approximately 30 to 40 percent single, Black males, with limited education and job skills, who lacked familial support in this country. Other factors that contributed to their disenfranchisement and rejection encompassed the social and economic conditions of the time, such as unemployment, inflation, and the residual effects from the Viet Nam War and the economic policies of the 1970s.

In an attempt to ameliorate the situation and to tidy its image, the Cuban community rallied to help these refugees integrate into society. The Cuban community realized that these problems were unjustly affecting a large number of people, many of whom were not the cause of the discontent. Civic, business, educational, and political leaders publicly denounced the treatment of the refugees and pledged jobs, found sponsors, and established educational centers so that *Marielitos* could learn English. Money was donated to help defray the cost of resettlement. Community leaders also made sure that refugees who committed crimes were treated fairly when facing the judicial system. As the Cuban community assumed responsibility for the Mariel refugees and publicly condemned their treatment, discriminatory and racist incidents diminished. Almost twenty years later, it can be said that despite the initial maltreatment, most Mariel refugees have adjusted and survived the stressful process of migration and resettlement.

THEORETICAL APPROACHES TO PRACTICE

Payne (1991) said it best when he wrote that "social work theory is created within social work, out of an interaction with social work practice . . . " (p. 9). In other words, social work involves the recognition that what we do as practitioners is very much guided by the social context in which we practice. The "social context" of which we speak is determined by the client's and practitioner's culture, including the client's situation, the worker's agency, and the organization in which the practice occurs.

Much of what happens in practice is based on a model of prepared and repeated interactions between social workers and clients so that there is a sense of structure to these encounters. These structures are referred to as approaches, perspectives, or models of practice; occasionally, they are even called "theoretical frameworks." The three approaches selected for this chapter are examples of practice models that connect and represent the union of theory and practice.

THE ECOLOGICAL/PERSON-IN-ENVIRONMENT APPROACH

Coming out of systems theory (von Bertanlanffy, 1971), the ecological or "life model" approach to practice (Germain & Gitterman, 1980) sees people as constantly adapting to their environment through reciprocal adaptation. All living systems, including human beings, must try to maintain a good fit with their environment. When this fit is not achieved, human beings experience stress, which results in an unbalance between the person(s) and their environment. Clients come to social workers for help to achieve or reestablish this fit. Often, though, the lack of reciprocal adaptation between clients and their environments are causes of social problems. The assessment of the problem and resulting interventions must, therefore, include the community and organizations that make up the clients' environment.

From a macro perspective, the ecological model requires that clients' social and physical environments—including political, economic, and social structures—be assessed to determine how these systems contribute to and affect their ability to achieve a good fit. Oftentimes, some of the problems experienced by clients result from deplorable community conditions and from unresponsive organizations that fail to react to these situations. Using the ecological/person-in-environment approach to practice, social workers must advocate, mediate, and organize to change the various systems in the environment. However, social workers must also provide or facilitate the provision of ancillary social and psychological services many clients need. In macro-practice, the key to the ecological/person-in-environment approach is the recognition that problems are not linear in nature. On the contrary, most problems are the result of the interfacing of systems and their shared boundaries.

THE STRENGTHS PERSPECTIVE

The idea that all people have strengths (value, power, and capacity) has been widely accepted in social work practice. It is, however, a striking change from the days when social work had adopted a medical model and clients were regarded as "sick" people who needed to be cured. The strengths perspective in practice proposes that everything social workers do on behalf of and in collaboration with clients must be based on the investigation and utilization of clients' strengths and resources to help them achieve their goals (Saleebey, 1997). Furthermore, the strengths perspective affirms that having a "problem" is not really *the* problem. The focus of this approach is on the processes by which individuals, groups, and communities transcend difficulties through people knowing what they want and mobilizing resources. At the heart of this practice perspective lies the recognition that all clients have the innate ability to change because, as human beings, everyone has possibilities.

The strengths perspective is suitable for cross-cultural social work practice because it acknowledges that culture is an influential passageway for exploration and transformation. It is also powerful because it incorporates the notion of collaboration between clients and practitioners and that, jointly, they are purposeful agents of change (Saleebey, 1997).

The strengths perspective further recognizes that people and communities are resilient, even those from divergent cultures. As such, they have the capacity to rebound from difficulty and misfortune. In cross-cultural practice, social workers must recognize and acknowledge the adversity people of color have had to endure and how, through individual strengths, as well as that provided by their cultures, communities, and organizations, disenfranchised groups have learned to overcome many obstacles. The strengths perspective, rather than focusing on what has gone wrong, exhorts the principles that individuals, families, groups, communities, and organizations will develop and flourish when given positive options to apply their knowledge and skills.

EMPOWERMENT

Empowerment, or the use of specific strategies to reduce, eliminate, combat, and reverse negative valuations by powerful groups (Solomon, 1976), is a practice approach that employs political action to promote social change. This practice approach focuses on the merging of both casework and social action through advocacy, strategic planning, choice, evaluation, and outcomes measurement to achieve personal transformation and interdependence. Empowerment emphasizes the building of capacity among individuals to eliminate the negative valuations people, particularly members of ethnic groups and other minorities, receive. In effect, such individuals or groups experience power absence rather than power failure (Payne, 1997).

Based on the work of Solomon (1976), empowerment advocates with the belief that disenfranchised groups must address the issues of power and power relationships in order to promote social and economic change. Underpinning this practice approach is the notion that clients are unique, and that they must take charge of their personal lives in order to have choices that provide more control over their present situation. When empowerment is used as an approach to practice, social workers are required to pay attention to the dynamics of personal or individual power and social power as it relates to the client's environment, and the relationship between the two.

Empowerment-based practice is designed to have clients examine their base of power and the distribution and access to societal resources that promote the development of individual strengths and capacities (Solomon, 1976). Closely associated with the principles of the strengths perspective in social work practice, empowerment uses the client's personal competencies as a foundation to foster the belief that individuals have the knowledge and skills necessary to solve their personal, structural, and environmental problems. As individuals learn to trust and believe in themselves and their capabilities, self-empowerment occurs. This, then, allows individuals to deal with the multiplicity of issues affecting their lives.

These three social work practice approaches attempt to be responsive to the ethnic reality. The culturally competent practitioner, however, must still adapt these principles to ensure congruence with the cultural norms of the group, community, or organization with which he or she is working. These are practice principles that, when used appropriately, can guide and enhance social work practice methods across all cultures and peoples.

LEVELS OF PRACTICE: MICRO, MEZZO, AND MACRO

Social work practice can be divided into levels of practice such as micro, mezzo, and macro. Micro social work involves the provision of direct services or interventions that target the individual, family, or group and the presenting problem. Mezzo-practice consists of looking beyond the individual, family, or group and examining how communities, organizations, and other, more formal groups impact individuals and the problem(s). At the macro-level, the individual and the problem are seen in the broadest context so that social workers examine the "big picture" in order to solve social problems and initiate social change at all levels.

The three levels of practice can be conceptualized as a more integrated approach to assist society in finding solutions to social, economic, political, and structural problems. However, because social problems are complex, they generally encompass all three levels of practice. This requires that practitioners have the skills and competencies necessary to intervene, simultaneously or in combination, at the micro-, mezzo-, and macro-levels. This tri-level intervention approach can best be described as having the ability to see the total ecosystem and the individual trees.

PRINCIPLES OF PRACTICE

Whether intervening at the micro-, mezzo-, or macro-level, there are general principles that apply to all three. The adaptation and utilization of these principles in cross-cultural practice situations is the concern for all social workers. The following are basic principles that should be incorporated into all levels of cross-cultural social work macro-practice.

Principle 1: Build a knowledge base about the people, their community, and organizations.
Recognize that what may seem different, conflicting, or inconsequential to you is commonplace, rational, and consistent to the community. Spend time talking to residents in a Cuban community like "Little Havana," and allow the people and the community to educate you.

Principle 2: Assess the ethnic reality.
Learn from your personal encounters with the people living in ethnic communities. For example, access information that will teach you about the group, its population size, migration history, socioeconomic base, political power, religious practices, and general norms. These factors are nothing more than operationalized illustrations of a people's ethnic environment.

Principle 3: Acknowledge that you may be evaluating the group's culture in terms of your own values and norms.
Making assumptions may cause you to make costly mistakes by simplistic misinterpretation of events, explanations, cultural rituals, and norms. For example, the

manner in which many people presumed that all Marielitos were criminals or mentally ill is an example of a simplistic misinterpretation of a cross-cultural event.

Principle 4: Recognize the dynamics of ethnicity, culture, agency, and organizational environment relationships.

Culture affects the way in which people interact with their communities and organizations. Understand that, for Hispanics, the survival of their communities and organizations depends on the group's ability to learn and adapt to changing environmental contingencies.

Principle 5: Understand community and organizational structures.

Hispanics are group-oriented and often rely on both informal and formal sources of authority to initiate change and exert influence. The options for social action in many Hispanic communities depend on the collaboration and coalitions that are built around specific problems. For example, when the Cuban community enlisted the support of the Archdiocese of Miami to establish schools for the Guantanamo refugees, a powerful coalition was established, capable of addressing the refugees' education problem.

Principle 6: Assess duration and urgency.

Practitioners should examine the factors and conditions that cause major problems in ethnic communities in terms of the length of time the problem has existed and the extent to which it is considered threatening to the community's survival. For the Cuban community, allowing the "indefinite" detainment of refugees in Guantanamo was a longstanding problem affected by the ongoing status of United States/Cuba relations. It was also a threat to the community's established ability to resettle the refugees.

Principle 7: Assess the community's acculturation level.

Acculturation should be a central variable in community assessments. Dana (1993) suggests that practitioners keep in mind how acculturation affects clients' or communities' view and reaction to situations and how practitioners, then, evaluate and interpret these responses.

Principle 8: Professional boundaries may need to be "relaxed" when working with clients, communities, and organizations whose culture may not follow the same standards.

Social work practice students are taught not to cross that fine line between their professional and personal selves. Even seasoned social workers occasionally question whether they have "done the right thing." When working with Hispanics, it is not unusual for people to demonstrate their caring and respect by inviting you to share a meal or a *cafesito* (a small demitasse of espresso). These displays of public affection are nothing more than expressions of cultural norms associated with friendship and acceptance.

PRACTICE SKILLS

In relation to the practice principles presented here, it is necessary to discuss the corresponding skills. Skills that are basic to practice should include the following capacities:

The ability to communicate:

Communication does not just involve words. When working with Hispanics, practitioners should remember that subtle cultural and linguistic complexities may influence both parties' ability to listen and provide adequate feedback. Hispanics tend to talk quickly and are expressive in their conversations. They may even talk loudly and gesture with their hands. Any communication should take into consideration the underlying significances of messages, as practitioners have to rely on their ability to decode between the literal and analogic meanings in these cross-cultural exchanges.

The ability to convey regard:

This skill is the capability to give, receive, and maintain respect for clients and their communities by acknowledging that there are "differences." By admitting the obvious, social workers connect and relate to clients and adapt their practice to meet the specific needs of differing clients.

The ability to be "theoretically flexible" in practice:

Research during the past ten years (Draguns, 1981; Kim & Berry, 1993; Sue & Sue, 1990) points to the fact that most theories and practice assumptions have been built around white European culture and values. Practitioners who insist on using theoretical frameworks that represent the dominant culture's values do nothing more than reinforce the subordinate position to which most ethnic people and their cultures have been relegated. Cross-cultural practice is all about looking for and acknowledging that there are options in the ways people perceive and interact in and with the world.

The ability to think outside of the box:

Social workers must be able to problem-solve and to see issues from various levels and points of views. The more complex the problem, the more layers practitioners have to examine. Thinking outside of the box is essential to helping people meet their needs, particularly when working with ethnic communities whose resources and power are scarce to begin with.

The ability to use idiosyncratic credits:

Social workers who have achieved a certain level of expertise often are allowed to bend or break the rules with few repercussions for these actions. Use the idiosyncratic credits you have rightfully earned to promote and enhance macro efforts on behalf of ethnic clients and their communities. An example of how to use these skills is presented in the following case vignette.

CASE VIGNETTE

Background

In the summer of 1994, the existence of *balseros,* Cubans who left their homeland in makeshift rafts, became the focus of national and international political and media attention. Unlike previous waves of Cuban refugees, the balseros were not granted immediate entry into the United States. Instead, they were subject to the "policy of interdiction," which allowed U.S. Navy and Coast Guard vessels to intercept the balseros at sea and take them to camps located at the U.S. military bases in Guantanamo or Panama (U.S. Seventh Coast Guard District, *Cuban Rescue Statistics,* 1995). At that time, interdiction was seen as a politically acceptable solution for addressing the latest U.S. refugee crisis. Eventually, more than 34,000 Cuban refugees were detained in Guantanamo, including 2,833 accompanied children under the age of seventeen, and sixty-eight unaccompanied minors (U.S. Seventh Coast Guard District, *Cuban Rescue Statistics,* 1995).

The Community Responds

In an attempt to address the physical, mental, and emotional health of the refugees, the Cuban community in Miami organized a plan by which the refugees, particularly the children, could be brought to the United States at little, or no cost, to taxpayers. The U.S. Justice Department had made it very clear that any resettlement effort would not be funded by the government. Financial responsibility for the refugees had to be assumed by the Cuban community.

Organizers, or the "Ad Hoc Committee for Family Reunification," included social workers, doctors, lawyers, educators, businessmen, and community leaders. "Ad Hoc" members were responsible for developing a resettlement plan that became known as "Operation Angel." This plan was formulated under the auspices of the U.S. Justice Department and followed the policies set forth by the Refugee Act of 1980.

"Operation Angel": A Community Intervention Approach

The services identified as most critical to the resettlement effort included legal sponsorship, education, employment, health care, and transportation from Guantanamo to the United States. Social workers experienced in community practice led the effort by using a methodical, problem-solving approach to carry out the resettlement plan.

Implementation of Services

Every Guantanamo refugee had to have a sponsor to be paroled out of Guantanamo. Being a sponsor required the signing of an affidavit of support, whereby the sponsor made a commitment to financially support the refugee until that person was capable of supporting him- or herself. Sponsorship included the provision of housing, food, clothing, and employment.

Almost every Cuban refugee in Guantanamo had family in the United States who were willing and financially able to assume this responsibility. Committee members used volunteers to locate refugees' family members and to ascertain their ability to become sponsors. Families who did not meet the financial guidelines for sponsorship had to find a cosponsor for the refugee. Once it was determined that a refugee could be sponsored by his or her family, social workers and other volunteers assisted the families with the completion of the required paperwork. Refugees who did not have family in the United States were taken care of through the "Adopt-A-Rafter" program, and through monies they earned once employed.

Transportation
The provision of transportation from Guantanamo to the United States was another condition the U.S. Justice Department wanted addressed by the Ad Hoc Committee, because Federal monies were not to be used for this service. As a result, committee members worked with "Brothers to the Rescue," a volunteer group made up of Cuban pilots (and other pilots as well) who agreed to fly the refugees for free. In addition, major commercial carriers also donated their planes and pilots and contributed many hours to help transport the refugees. In the end, neither federal nor state funds were used for this portion of the resettlement plan.

Health Care
Many refugees, particularly the elderly and children, required medical and mental health services. The costs for the provision of these services had to be borne by the community and had to be outlined and justified in the resettlement plan. The Ad Hoc Committee turned to members of the medical, insurance, and mental health professions to help develop a functional plan. Medical doctors agreed to provide free or low-cost medical services; Cuban doctors who owned and/or were affiliated with HMOs agreed to become medical care providers. Similarly, mental health professionals also agreed to do the same, recognizing the necessity to meet the emotional and psychological needs of this population. Ad Hoc Committee members, with assistance from representatives from various insurance companies, developed contractual agreements to ensure that these services were made available to the refugees for a one-year period. Sponsors were also required to provide health insurance coverage for the refugees for whom they had legally become responsible. This was done to reduce the use of public funds for health services. It must be noted, however, that many refugees without sponsors or those with major medical problems were given services by county-run agencies such as Jackson Memorial Hospital.

Education
For these newly arrived refugees, education, particularly the ability to learn English, became the means by which they would achieve self-sufficiency. But state, county, and federal officials were concerned with the overcrowding of public schools and the overwhelming impact the refugees would have on an already overburdened public school system.

The Ad Hoc Committee, in partnership with the Archdiocese of Miami and a coalition of private lay schools, established temporary schools where Cuban children and adults could learn English. Over $45,000.00 was raised to fund these educational centers. The monies raised paid for certified teachers and aides as well as school supplies. The educational centers were located in parish halls that the Catholic Archdiocese very generously donated towards this effort. The intent behind the centers was to establish a stable environment in which the refugees could learn English while adjusting to their new environment.

Employment
To stimulate the refugees' chances for employment, the Ad Hoc Committee, along with staff from a well-known and respected social services agency located in the heart of Little Havana, developed a job/employment training network using the

vast number of Hispanic-owned and -operated businesses in the Cuban community. Businesses were canvassed by agency staff, and the Hispanic media were used to encourage the business sector to commit to this effort.

As the network was established, business owners were asked either to provide on-the-job training or hire at least one adult refugee. The goal was to have as many refugees as possible gainfully employed or enrolled in training that would eventually turn into an employment opportunity for the individual. A year after arriving in the United States, approximately 40 percent of the Guantanamo refugees were employed (Puig, 1996).

Implications

"Operation Angel" provides a community-based, resettlement framework that may be of benefit to other practitioners working with refugee populations. "Operation Angel" purposely attempted to address the stressors most often found to cause anxiety and tension among refugees, including the lack of housing, employment, and inability to speak the language. These factors are also interrelated with other influences that affect refugee resettlement efforts, including the breakdown of family ties, cultural change, and the abrupt change in the environment (Berry & Annis, 1974).

Another lesson learned during "Operation Angel" was the recognition that Cuban balseros, as a group, had special characteristics that had not been found among earlier waves of Cuban refugees. This required the acknowledgment that, even though the balseros were Cuban, their "culture" and value structure had changed during the past thirty years. Any resettlement effort had to operate from this premise, and interventions had to take into account the particulars of this group of Cuban refugees. From a practice perspective, it clearly proved, once again, the need to provide interventions that were congruent to the balseros' "culture," while maintaining a sense of "fit" with the values and cultural structure of South Florida's Cuban community.

Because Cubans are present-oriented, the resettlement efforts contained in "Operation Angel" had to take advantage of the crisis in Guantanamo and use the crisis to stir the Cuban community into action. Furthermore, because the balseros had experienced high levels of environmental and psychological pressures—the voyage at sea, their internment in Guantanamo, and their inability to enter the United States—the resettlement plan purposely set out to create a sense of interdependence and interconnectedness between the balseros and the Cuban community at large. This sense of interconnectedness helped to secure community support and ease the intergenerational, political, and cultural tensions among and between each preceding wave of Cuban refugees.

Most important to the resettlement effort was the appreciation that the balseros' families exerted the greatest influence over these individuals. By working with the families, Ad Hoc members were able to facilitate the balseros' integration into the community. "Operation Angel" had, as one of its cornerstones, the belief that the family was the most important system to draw on. Establishing a strong link with the refugees' families was critical, not only because they were the source of sponsorship and entry into the community, but because families validated the refugees' preference for maintaining known cultural and structural relation patterns.

CONCLUSION

This chapter attempts to provide information on social work practice issues that are necessary to understand and master when working with Hispanic or Latino populations. The starting focus was to point out the importance of macro-level practice. However, an attempt was also made to elucidate practice principles applicable to all levels of social work practice. The primary focus of this chapter was to illustrate how cultural commonalities and diversity among human beings, even those who belong to the same ethnic group, may be used to demonstrate an acceptance of the person or community seeking professional help. By first focusing on the strengths of the Hispanic culture, and on the resources that Latino individuals, families, and communities possess, social workers can traverse the complexities of cross-cultural practice. In the end, cross-cultural competency is all about facing, rather than overlooking, the real challenges that ethnic clients and communities bring to social work practice.

REFERENCES

Berry, J. W. & Annis, R. C. (1974). *Ethnic psychology: Research and practice with immigrants, refugees, native peoples, ethnic groups and sojourners.* Amsterdam and Berwyn, PA: Swets & Zeitlinger.

Clark, J. M., Lasaga, J. L., & Reque, R. S. (1981). *The Mariel exodus: An assessment and prospects.* Council for Inter-American Security. A Special Report. Washington, D.C.

Cross, T. L., Bazron, B. J., Dennis, K. W., & Isaacs, M. R. (1989). *Towards a culturally competent system of care.* Washington, DC: Georgetown University Child Development Center.

Census of Population and Housing. (1994). *We, the American Hispanic. Current Population Survey,* CPC-L-96.

National poll reveals strong public support for diversity in higher education. (Fall, 1998). *Diversity Digest,* pp. 4–5.

Dana, R. H. (1993). *Multicultural assessment perspectives for professional psychology.* Boston: Allyn and Bacon.

Draguns, J. (1981). *Dilemmas and choices in cross-cultural counseling: The universal versus the culturally distinct.* In P. B. Pedersen, J. G. Draguns, W. L. Lonner, & J. E. Trimble (Eds.), *Counseling across cultures* (pp. 3–22). Honolulu: University of Hawaii Press.

Germain, C. B. & Gitterman, A. (1980). *The life model of social work practice.* New York: Columbia University Press.

Ho, D. (1995). Internalized culture, cultocentrism and transcendence. *The Counseling Psychologist, 23*(1), 4–24.

Kim, U. & Berry, J. W. (1993). *Indigenous psychologies.* Newbury Park, CA: Sage.

Marin, G. & Marin, B. (1991). *Research with Hispanic populations.* Newbury Park, CA: Sage.

Merton, R. K. & Nesbitt, R. (1966). *Contemporary social problems,* 2nd ed. New York: Harcourt Brace.

Payne, M. (1991). *Modern social work theory: A critical introduction.* Chicago, IL: Lyceum Books Inc.

Payne, M. (1997). *Modern social work theory: A critical introduction.* 2nd ed. Chicago, IL: Lyceum.

Puig, M. E. (1996). The adultification of Cuban refugee children from the Guantanamo wave: Sociocultural implications for social work practice. Unpublished research study report. Colorado State University.

Saleeby, D. (1997). *The strengths perspective in social work practice.* New York: Longman.

Solomon, B. B. (1976). *Black empowerment: Social work in oppressed communities.* New York: Columbia University Press.

Sue, S. W. & Sue, D. (1990). *Counseling the culturally different: Theory and practice,* 2nd ed. New York: Wiley.

U.S. Bureau of the Census. (1994). Characteristics of the population. General population characteristics. Part 1. United States Summary.

U.S. Department of Health and Human Services. (1994). Population projections of the United States by age, sex, race, and Hispanic origin: 1991 to 2050.

U.S. Seventh Coast Guard District. (1995). *Cuban Rescue Statistics.*

von Bertanlanffy, L. (1971). *General systems theory: Foundations, development, application.* London: Allen Lane.

CHAPTER 20

CULTURALLY AND HISTORICALLY CONGRUENT CLINICAL SOCIAL WORK INTERVENTIONS WITH NATIVE CLIENTS

MARIA YELLOW HORSE BRAVE HEART

Like assessments, interventions with Native clients should incorporate historical and cultural perspectives. This chapter builds on Chapter 12 and extends the paradigm to interventions with Natives incorporating empowerment and strengths perspectives. Issues for working with Native individuals and families and group historical trauma interventions are elucidated. Illustrations of interventions with Lakota clients are offered as practice examples. However, despite some generalizability to other tribal cultures, the uniqueness of each Native culture must be respected and practice must be modified accordingly.

DEMOGRAPHICS, CULTURAL VALUES, AND SOCIAL PROBLEMS

Please refer to the sections in Chapter 12, "Sociodemographics and Overview of the Lakota: An Example of One Native Culture," for demographic information; "Traditional Cultural Perspectives: The Lakota Example" for cultural values information; and "Lakota Traditional Grief Experience: Problem and Resolution," for information regarding this particular social problem.

INDIVIDUAL CLINICAL PRACTICE
WITH NATIVE CLIENTS

Empowering Native historical and cultural perspectives can be incorporated into stages of individual practice interventions including the beginning phase, transference and countertransference, the development of a therapeutic alliance and working through, and termination. Individual empowerment practice is based on (1) having egalitarian relationships with clients, (2) viewing the client as an expert in her or his culture, (3) valuing the client's culture, and (4) consciousness-raising and examination of external sociopolitical forces that impinge on a client's life circumstances while, simultaneously, attending to emotional or intrapsychic issues (Cox & Parsons, 1994). Acknowledging the inherent wisdom of indigenous therapeutic techniques is consistent with an empowerment perspective. Traditionally, Natives utilize a variety of methods for healing mental, emotional, spiritual, and physical turmoil. Interventions are formulated after diagnosing the problem through diverse rituals. Indigenous grief and trauma healing practices facilitate healthy, culturally congruent mourning resolution. Healing ceremonies involve extended kinship networks, thereby fostering integration and social support for the client, congruent with empowerment strategies (see Cox & Parsons, 1994).

With the impact of genocide and spiritual oppression, the practice of Native healing has diminished across generations. Although many Native people still participate in or have resumed practicing traditional ceremonies, others are fearful, ignorant of, resistant to, or conflicted about indigenous rituals. Consequently, some Native clients are more comfortable with European-American intervention models and might resist a clinical social worker's efforts to facilitate incorporation of traditional healing. However, Natives steeped in traditional culture and spirituality may be resistant to seeking help from a clinical social worker. Plausibly, many Natives are somewhere along this continuum.

Just as assessment may take longer with Native clients, the beginning stage of treatment may be prolonged and complicated by culture and historical trauma (see Chapter 12). Developing trust may be protracted for Natives working with European-American clinicians who represent oppressors and the perpetrators of genocide. Unlike the heritage of social work's evolvement from the "friendly visitor," social work with Natives emanates from the War Department, once home to the Bureau of Indian Affairs, which is now responsible for social services and progenitor of Indian Health Service under which mental health services are provided. Clinical social workers must attend to subtle content influenced by this historical legacy.

THE BEGINNING STAGE IN INDIVIDUAL
CLINICAL PRACTICE

The same principles described in Chapter 12 should be applied in the beginning phase of the intervention and, periodically, throughout the course of clinical practice. These include attending to timing, nonverbal communication, culturally congruent verbal communication styles, developing rapport with the client, and incorporating traditional cultural and historical perspectives. Techniques that focus on narratives in therapy are highly relevant to Native communication styles, to empowerment practice with individual clients (see Cox & Parsons, 1994), and therapeutic methods with trauma survivors (van der Kolk, McFarlane, & Weisaeth, 1996).

Silence can be powerful and comfortable for Native clients. Gentle exploration that encourages clients to tell their story as well as attentive and patient listening is required. Mirroring techniques, whereby the clinician responds in kind to the client, are helpful. For example, if a client averts her or his eyes, the clinician can facilitate more comfort by not staring and by also averting her or his gaze more often. The clinical social worker also needs to develop comfort with more indirect communication styles, permitting time for stories and metaphors. The social worker will have to adapt to each client as an individual. Some Native clients—usually more assimilated to the dominant European American culture—will be assertive, maintain a great deal of direct eye contact, and request more directive interventions. The clinical social worker can then behave in a way similar to that used while working with non-Native clients and still maintain cognizance of the historical legacy and complex cultural issues. The social worker should be prepared to alter her or his intervention style when manifestations of more traditional Native communication patterns occur during a session.

As members of a massively traumatized population, Natives may manifest identification with the aggressor or internalized oppression (Brave Heart & DeBruyn, 1998). This could be enacted in sessions in numerous ways: (1) self-deprecation, (2) idealization of the European American clinician and culture or of an assimilated Native clinician, (3) conflicts about Native phenotype (skin color and features), (4) emulation of the European American or a European American-oriented Native clinician, (5) devaluation of Native culture, and (6) defense mechanisms such as denial, reaction formation, or displacement of aggressive impulses to other Natives. In the beginning phase, these issues should be noted, but overt intervention in response to these manifestations should be reserved for the working-through phase. Because these defenses are unconscious and emotionally laden, exploration and intervention should be reserved for a later time when more trust is established and the client's ego strength is bolstered. However, attention to these phenomena, which are influenced by the broader sociopolitical context, is consistent with empowerment practice through consciousness-raising (Cox & Parsons, 1994).

As a traumatized population, Natives can benefit from the trauma treatment paradigm used when working with other trauma survivors. Techniques for working with post-traumatic stress disorder (PTSD) (van der Kolk, McFarlane, & Weisaeth, 1996) may be highly effective for intervention with Native clients in general. Despite some literature on PTSD among Native people (Manson, et al., 1996), historical trauma has received minimal attention with a few exceptions (Robin, Chester, & Goldman, 1996). Instead, the symptoms of the historical trauma response (Brave Heart, 1998) are embedded in literature on suicidal behavior, substance abuse, symptoms among boarding school children, or in Eurocentric early personality studies (Erikson, 1963; Macgregor, 1946/1975).

In the beginning phase, generational and current lifespan history of boarding school attendance should be explored. Questions can facilitate consciousness-raising about external historical and political factors. Details about the nature of these traumatic boarding school experiences should be postponed until an assessment of ego strength is made, as one would with any emotionally laden and traumatic content. The clinical social worker must maintain a delicate balance here. Progressive communication and narratives about boarding schools should not be discouraged if the client is introducing the material. However, the clinician must simultaneously facilitate containment of powerful affects and attend to timing so that a client will not become overwhelmed, fearful, and leave therapy.

As appropriate, facilitating client involvement in traditional interventions imparts a sense of mastery of the trauma and offers emotional containment (Brave Heart, 1998; Silver & Wilson, 1988). PTSD, alcohol and drug abuse, and mental health treatment programs also have contacts with spiritual leaders who provide purification ceremonies for Native clients (see Duran & Yellow Horse-Davis, 1997).

Gender issues need to be noted in the beginning phase. Cross-gender relationships may present difficulty for some traditionally oriented clients and clients who have been sexually abused or battered by the opposite sex. Trust issues and cultural mores surrounding interactions across genders must be considered. In rural settings, a clinical social worker might be the only available mental health professional in a geographically broad area. Therefore, the clinical social worker will have to develop particularly sensitive and competent behaviors in order to engage a client that otherwise might maintain a great deal of social distance.

The best course of action with a traditionally oriented Native client, particularly an elder, of a different gender from the clinician is to silently and unobtrusively observe the client's behavior, be very respectful and proceed slowly, and use mirroring, i.e., averting one's eyes as the client might. Engaging in conversation about nonthreatening material is helpful, and even offering coffee to the client, modifying classical psychodynamic parameters, will put that person at ease. Flexibility with time is essential, allowing a client the space for narratives and storytelling; listening with a "third ear" for the meaning behind the metaphors is crucial. For example, in response to a clinician's question, a Native client may relate a fable, tell a joke, or detail an account of a relative's experience that may, initially, seem unrelated to the question. This is often a disguised communication congruent with traditional Native etiquette.

Indirect communication is preferred for these early stages, particularly with more traditional clients who might come to see the clinical social worker as someone with whom they enjoy "visiting." They may also need the flexibility of being able to "drop by" unannounced and the clinician will need to make every effort to be available. This is challenging if one works in a setting with scheduled appointments. The social worker should make some personal contact with the client, communicate a desire to visit, and ask the client to wait if one is in session with another client. The clinician can attempt to schedule an appointment but the more traditional Native client will be more likely to miss that appointment because something else interferes and will "drop in" again. This will require patience and understanding from the social worker, who must always communicate pleasure at seeing the client, emotional availability, and openness. Over time, some clients do learn to keep appointments, but breaking appointments must not be viewed nor interpreted like a classical resistance to therapy. The fluidity of time in traditional Native culture, the importance of relationships and interpersonal interactions, and the fact that the mental health clinic setting is modeled on a dominant cultural paradigm must be considered.

Therapy across sexual orientation can also be challenging. The gay, lesbian, or transsexual Native client, while traditionally more accepted in some Native cultures, now faces stigma because of the dominant societal forces. These clients may be more open than in the dominant European American culture if the tribal culture is traditionally more accepting. Clinical social workers must be careful to consider the traditional tribal culture in working with gay, lesbian, and transsexual clients and not pathologize behavior that is culturally congruent. Some stigma may still have been attached to homosexuality or transsexuality in traditional Lakota culture. However, there were cultural explanations of the origin of transsexuality and socially prescribed functional roles in society. For example, a *winkte* (a transsexual who may or may not have been gay) would perform naming ceremonies in the tribe (names traditionally have been given to newborns, adolescents, or adults at times of transition or to honor specific accomplishments, and with adoptions).

In summary, the beginning phase may be prolonged for a Native client. This phase requires cultural sensitivity and competence, nonintrusiveness, and establishing trust through honesty and sensitive use of mirroring techniques. Patience is dictated as well as the capacity for silent observation and comfort with indirect styles of communication. Adaptability and flexibility are also required in order to be proficient with the shift between more European-American communication styles and more traditional Native manners often manifested by the same client.

TRANSFERENCE AND COUNTERTRANSFERENCE

Transference is displacement and reenactment, in the clinical relationship, of emotional issues, fantasies, and conflicts with early parental figures (Greenson, 1967; Hepworth & Larson, 1993). This unconscious phenomenon is a necessary and inevitable component of individual clinical social work practice; theoretically, working through it leads to healing. The nature of an ongoing relationship in which a clinical social worker listens to a client's life story, without judgment, heightens the emotional significance of the therapist in the client's life and calls forth earlier significant relationships, particularly the parental figures. Contrary to popular thought, dependency is not deliberately fostered, but until the transference is worked through, the clinical relationship holds a great deal of significance for the client. Moreover, transference can still take place in the egalitarian relationship fostered by the empowerment-oriented clinician as it is based on emotional significance rather than power differences.

The clinician's feelings and reactions in response to the transference is countertransference (Freud, 1910; Greenson, 1967; Hepworth & Larson, 1993). This can be the feelings that the early parental figures had toward the client, which are unconsciously induced, the feelings the client has about the self, or the feelings that the client is needing to induce in another for emotional growth to occur.

Both transference and countertransference may be positive, negative, or ambivalent. Both are impacted by culture and the histories of the individuals in the clinical relationship. The collective European American representation of Natives as a "savage" and pagan homogenous race (see Chapter 12) influences clinical interactions between Natives and non-Natives. Recognition of its potency and effect will facilitate its management in therapy. A clinical empowerment perspective adopts an accurate view of Natives as the First Nations of this continent and as sovereigns, the only ethnic group in this country with whom the government has treaties. In order to embrace this empowering view, European American clinical social workers must face the fact that they are descendants or relatives of colonizers and invaders of this land. The consequent guilt, resentment, victim-blaming, and rationalization that may emerge must be worked through so that it does not interfere with clinical social work practice with Natives. This might be deemed a collective historical countertransference resistance, which will compound any individual idiosyncratic countertransference that normally occurs in therapy. There is also the propensity for Native clients to develop a collective negative transference towards European American clinicians. This can be appropriately managed by noting its existence and validating the feelings of the client.

Managing transference and countertransference and working towards their resolution are major components of clinical practice. Culture is a significant part of this process. Devereaux (1951) analyzed a professional Plains Indian woman who exhibited European-American acculturation. However, in the transference reaction, she manifested traditional values and demeanor, which created a treatment impasse. With the help of Native colleagues who provided the information facilitating his intervention, Devereaux informed the client that she was responding to him like a traditional woman wrapped in a courting blanket (couples would wrap themselves in a blanket to provide some privacy while in full view of older relative chaperones); this interpretation resolved the treatment impasse and progressive communication continued. In essence, even the most overtly assimilated Natives may still harbor traditional beliefs and behaviors that can impact the therapeutic relationship. Caution must be taken when making such traditional interpretations, because they could be experienced as racist and stereotypical. Like Devereaux, non-Native clinicians need to develop a relationship with Native consultants from the tribal culture of the client.

Idealization in the transference of a European American or European American-oriented Native clinician might be misinterpreted as a positive transference, while in reality it might be identification with the aggressor or internalized oppression. One should attend to subtle self-deprecating or disparaging comments, particularly with cultural themes or references to phenotype. Discernment of in-group disparaging jokes from true self-hate is required. Alertness to manifestations of internalized oppression and appropriate intervention are opportunities to utilize empowerment consciousness-raising strategies.

DEVELOPING A THERAPEUTIC ALLIANCE AND WORKING THROUGH THE PHASE

Once rapport is established with a client (see Chapter 12), more intimacy will develop. Native clients often begin to see the clinical social worker as a trusted individual, regardless of that person's race. At this point, the Native client will be open, candid, often humorous, warm, and may extend certain privileges reserved for close friends and relatives. The social worker may be invited to traditional social functions and even to ceremonies. This presents a challenge for the psychodynamically oriented clinician who has classically been trained to limit contact outside of the formal therapy session. In Native communities, particularly rural and reservation areas, this formality and these rigid boundaries are not possible or desirable to maintain. One can still be professional and attend powwows, community dinners, and even ceremonies if invited. Accepting such invitations actually facilitates a greater therapeutic alliance. If the clinical social worker's own spiritual beliefs prohibit attendance at ceremonies, this must be delicately communicated to the client, with recognition that this could create irreparable damage in the relationship.

Another issue is maintaining professional neutrality while participating in a purification ceremony. One can pray for the client and other participants but reserve personal prayers for one's own spiritual functions. For Native clinicians, this boundary may be more fluid because of both traditional values and expectations from Native clients that the Native social worker would actively participate in a ceremony and might inadvertently disclose personal information through verbalized prayers. Further, there are no secrets that can escape the "moccasin telegraph," so Native social workers must learn to be comfortable with fluid professional boundaries. Non-Native social workers who remain in a Native community on a long-term basis will begin to become acculturated to Native ways and may find themselves in a position akin to a Native clinician, with fluid boundaries becoming more comfortable.

A component of the therapeutic alliance is the client's development and manifestation of an observing ego, defined as the capacity to observe one's behavior with some objectivity, and akin to insight. An observing ego is evident in the client's relating content of the sessions to behavior as well as remembering and referencing material from previous sessions (Greenson, 1967). Once rapport and sufficient trust have been established, Native clients are typically proficient at utilizing an observing ego, often commenting on behavior with humor and through anecdotal information or narratives. The clinical social worker must attend to indirect communication of those self-observations.

The Working-Through Phase

During the working-through phase, content emerges including dreams, resistance, and catharsis. Dreams also begin to incorporate session content and the clinician. This is evidence of the therapeutic alliance, transference, and working through in which repressed material becomes conscious. However, some Natives are reticent about sharing dreams, except with a spiritual interpreter, if they feel that telling a dream could lessen its spiritual power. Others may share dreams, but may wait until after they have disclosed the dream in a ceremony.

Dream content may include cultural manifestations, which could be misinterpreted. For example, dreams of bodily flying are sometimes interpreted as grandiose fantasies suggestive of some core narcissistic disorder. However, in Native cultures such dreams are often spiritually significant. The clinical social worker must be careful not to misconstrue such dream content and erroneously assume psychopathology.

Cathartic release of affect during the working-through phase and the lifting of repressions, so that emotionally charged memories become conscious, can both lead to fear among clients and discomfort for clinicians. One must be careful not to leave clients feeling overwhelmed by emotions. The therapy must provide an emotional container so that the client feels safe and competent to handle the affect that emerges. Timing is important, ending sessions with a debriefing period when the clinician imparts hope and confidence that the client can handle the emotions that emerge.

During this process, acting out might develop and, sometimes, depressed clients become greater suicidal risks. In addition to assessing lethality and initiating suicide prevention activities about which a clinical social worker must be aware, reinforcing drug- and alcohol-free states is helpful here as Native suicide is often substance abuse-related (Claymore, 1988; May, 1973). Traditional culture can foster a norm for a clean and sober lifestyle. The clinician may need to advocate for the client with family and community members, assisting the client in identifying resources to strengthen drug- and alcohol-free social support networks. A clinical social worker may need to attend support groups with clients in the beginning of this process or organize meetings, consistent with empowerment approaches.

It is natural for all clients to consciously and unconsciously resist emotional discomfort to some degree. Handling this type of resistance requires persistent but sensitive management by the clinical social worker. Traditional ceremonies provide safe affective containers for clients as well as facilitating cathartic release of emotions (Brave Heart-Jordan, 1995; Silver & Wilson, 1988). Promoting the availability of ceremonies for clients is important. In an urban area, this may be more challenging and non-Native social workers must depend on Native contacts to make such arrangements. Although family members should help a Native client with ceremonies, in families in which the Native client may be isolated in his or her openness to traditional healing, the clinical social worker may need to assist the client in identifying resources for arranging a ceremony.

As elaborated in Chapter 12, it is critical that the legacy of genocide and oppression be included in assessment and intervention for Natives. First, an assessment of the presence and degree of historical trauma features must be conducted (see Chapter 12). Both traumatic history and culture impact symptom presentation and treatment interventions. The following case illustrates the presence of historical trauma over three generations as well as cultural factors for a Lakota boy diagnosed with gender-identity disorder.

> **INCORPORATING HISTORICAL TRAUMA THEORY AND CULTURE IN THERAPY: CASE VIGNETTE OF JOEL**
>
> Joel is an eleven-year-old attractive full-blood, dark-skinned Lakota male with short dyed blonde hair and glasses. He presented with exaggerated feminine behavior and associated almost exclusively with female peers. Joel was referred because of poor grades, problematic behavior, and pregnancy fantasies. Joel would attend late-night alcoholic parties. In a histrionic, effeminate style, Joel boasted about his precocious escapades and attempted to impress the clinician with his cognizance of the latest reservation scandal.
>
> Joel avoided discussing his past history, particularly his neglectful alcoholic mother, whose current whereabouts was a mystery. He was being cared for by his overwhelmed, but well-meaning grandmother, Mrs. A., who was a boarding school survivor. Joel had been sexually abused at the age of nine by a gang of older boys at a boarding school two years ago. After that, Mrs. A. brought Joel home to attend a reservation day school.
>
> Taught that she needed to abandon her Lakota culture, language, and spirituality through strappings at boarding school, Mrs. A. embraced Catholicism and consulted with the local priest, who was advising her to send Joel to a Catholic boarding school to "straighten him out." However, Mrs. A.'s Lakota belief system still presented itself with some tenacity and she wondered if Joel could be a *winkte* [a transsexual].

Joel exemplifies the complexity of a case of gender-identity disorder within the Lakota cultural context and the generational transfer of the historical trauma response among the Lakota. Joel's symptoms included the trauma response features of anxiety, impulsivity, substance abuse, self-destructive behavior, and a legacy of boarding school experience incorporating sexual abuse (see Irwin & Roll, 1995). Although Joel's lifespan trauma mirrors many children raised in multiproblem families, in which abandonment, multiple placements, and alcohol abuse are present, superimposed is the generational boarding school trauma. Further, there is the confusing and ambivalent familial relationship with a Christian denomination, undermining traditional values and practices that could serve as a protective factor or a stress inoculator.

Gender-identity disorder may appear as a result of the sexual abuse, abandonment, and emotional unavailability of the mother, self-hatred, and generational trauma (Coates, 1992; Coates, Friedman, & Wolfe, 1991). Joel's boarding school experiences and his mother's alcoholism and abandonment are consistent with these findings. However, Joel's "disorder" manifests some internalized oppressive reactions in his dyed blonde hair, symbolizing a wish to be Caucasian. Joel may be a *winkte,* suggesting the need to examine symptoms in light of traditional Lakota culture. Examining Joel's gender-identity "disorder" from a Lakota perspective, a traditional ceremony may have reduced stigma for him and provided a more socially acceptable outlet for Joel's developing transsexualism and his probable homosexuality.

MEDICATION MANAGEMENT ISSUES AND CULTURE

Some Natives are suspicious of "white man's medicine" due to the historical legacy of genocide. Further, there is an absence of mind- or mood-altering substances in most indigenous cultures. Therefore, medication management will most likely be challenging with Native clients. This author advocates use of psychotropic medication only when it is clear that biologically based mood and anxiety disorders exist and cannot be managed through other means, including therapy, support groups, and traditional ceremonies. Many Native people manage such disorders without medication and without suicidal risk if there are sufficient therapeutic and community resources (see Chapter 12). However, if medication is needed, a clinical social worker could enlist the help of traditional spiritual leaders and coordinate with them to facilitate client acceptance of the medication and empower its effectiveness.

Two brief examples illustrate some of these issues. A Lakota woman had been diagnosed as a schizophrenic, had been hospitalized, and was placed on antipsychotic medication. She sought the help of a traditional healer who performed a ceremony for her and gave her a spiritual interpretation to explain her symptoms. After the ceremony, the woman stopped taking her medication and has remained symptom-free with no signs of psychosis.

After the death of his mother, a Lakota male began to experience suicidal impulses for which Indian Health Service staff prescribed antidepressants. The precipitating factor was described; immediately after the funeral, a friend had a premature traditional ceremony to mark the end of his mourning period in a misguided effort to be helpful. After that ceremony, the bereaved individual was unable to cry and felt that he had needed the longer traditional mourning period. He sought the help of a traditional healer and it was interpreted that his mother's spirit was feeling so bad about his emotional pain, and her alcoholic neglect of him as a child, that her spirit was returning for him. This resulted in his suicidal impulses; he was responding to his mother's spirit calling him. After the ceremony, the client was again able to mourn; his mother's spirit had been asked, during the ceremony, to leave him alone to complete his time on Earth. All suicidal ideation disappeared without the help of antidepressants. This Lakota male has remained free of suicidal ideation.

TERMINATION

From a traditional cultural perspective, there is no way to say good-bye in many Native languages because it is believed that spiritual contact may continue beyond the physical reality. A clinical social worker should leave the door open for a client who otherwise could go through the normal termination process, to return if needed. For many Native people, the degree of interpersonal attachments is stronger than in the European American culture. Termination may magnify earlier loss issues to a greater degree than in the general client population. For the Lakota, suicidal behavior is often associated with the loss or threat of loss of a relationship (May, 1973). Therefore, the clinical social worker must also attend to suicidal risk factors at this phase of therapy. Connecting clients with ongoing support networks, a goal of empowerment practice, will effect an easier termination.

CLINICAL SOCIAL WORK PRACTICE WITH NATIVE FAMILIES

While there are a multitude of family therapy models, there are some general principles that merit consideration before applying any model to intervention with Native families. Empowerment perspectives foster egalitarian relationships with families, view the family as the expert, link the family with external social supports, and raise consciousness about political forces that may impinge on optimal family functioning. For Native families, this requires an examination of historical trauma and linkages, as feasible and appropriate, with traditional cultural resources. Incorporating extended family kinship networks is congruent with both traditional ceremonies and empowerment practice, where there is communal support. Intergenerational transfer of trauma should be examined, with attention to the impact of genocide.

Some challenges to conducting family therapy include indigenous communication patterns and taboos. For example, among the Lakota, there has been strict regulation of cross-gender interaction patterns between siblings and a male with his mother-in-law, both of which limit direct verbal communication. Physical affection may not be overtly expressed in front of outsiders, particularly non-Natives (see case example in Chapter 12). Where family members sit may have less to do with alliances and more to do with cultural prescriptions; to sculpt a family in a therapy session (asking clients to sit next to specific family members) or to require a client to directly address another family member verbally and with direct eye contact may be asking a Native family to violate taboos and tolerate too much discomfort by departing from traditional behaviors. Consequently, many Native adults might feel more comfortable with individual or peer group interventions. Younger adult Native clients, often more bicultural, may be comfortable with various modes of family treatment. In working with children and families, the clinician needs flexibility rather than being invested in a particular modality or theory.

Extended kinship networks and Native family relationships can be confusing for non-Native clinicians. Relationships are defined differently, and are more extensive and more intimate than in the European American community. Maternal aunts and paternal uncles as well as grandparents, in addition to the biological parents, are often considered and addressed as "mother" or "father." Further, traditional Native adoptions extend the size of families, so one may have several sets of parents and siblings. First and second cousins might be considered siblings and fifth cousins as close relatives, in contrast to relationships in the general population. Clan or band relationships are important ways of relating and identifying oneself. When inviting a Native family into a session, clinicians must be inclusive and prepared to involve large numbers of individuals. The social worker must also recognize that a Native client has numerous obligations and responsibilities to relatives. Caution is in order so as not to label a Native family as enmeshed when the family is simply following traditional cultural behaviors.

Finally, intergenerational boarding school trauma and internalized oppression are important factors for integration in treatment. In family sessions, alliances might be observable based on phenotype. For example, darker, full-blood, more traditionally oriented family members might be ostracized or devalued by lighter, mixed-blood, more European American-assimilated family members. Attention to these types of alliances provides opportunities for empowerment practice through identifying the role of internalized oppression.

CLINICAL SOCIAL WORK GROUP PRACTICE: HISTORICAL TRAUMA INTERVENTIONS AMONG THE LAKOTA

The focus of historical trauma intervention is ameliorating the cumulative trauma response through a brief intensive psycho-educational group experience (Brave Heart, 1998, 1999). Intervention goals include imparting a sense of mastery and control (van der Kolk, McFarlane, & Weisaeth, 1996) in spite of oppression and cumulative historical traumatization within a safe traditional context. Necessary for effective treatment, participants are exposed to historical traumatic memories as well as occasions for cognitive integration. Small- and large-group processing provide opportunities for verbalization of traumatic experiences, thereby reducing psychic numbing. Traditional Lakota culture and ceremonies are integrated throughout the intervention. Ceremonies have been observed as having a curative effect on PTSD (Silver & Wilson, 1988) and also serve as an emotional container and a vehicle for increased reconnection to positive Lakota values and a pre-traumatic Lakota past (Brave Heart, 1998; Brave Heart-Jordan, 1995).

Increased affect tolerance from mastery of trauma, serving as a protective factor against depression and other psychiatric disorders, is an intervention outcome. The incorporation of traditional spirituality and culture enhance protective factors against the development or exacerbation of PTSD (Silver & Wilson, 1988). Sharing trauma and grief affects in a traditional context provides cathartic relief and participants affirm the utility of historical trauma response theory in facilitating a healing process. There is a reduction of these affects over time, during and after the intervention, as well as significant changes in concepts, such as more positive self-representation and group identification (Brave Heart, 1998; Brave Heart-Jordan, 1995). Historical trauma interventions have been incorporated in a parenting curriculum among the Lakota (Brave Heart, 1999). Although more research is warranted, preliminary findings suggest that historical trauma interventions are experienced as helpful in the healing process and result in at least short-term amelioration of trauma response features.

Further development of group, as well as individual and family, empowerment intervention is the aim of the *Takini* (Survivor) Network, a collective of Lakota traditional spiritual leaders and service providers, formed in 1992 to address healing from our historical trauma. The Takini Network is conducting research, community education, and community healing aimed at validating Native historical trauma and providing forums for Native people to begin to confront the traumatic past.

CONCLUSION

Traumatic Native history has been subjugated. The general population lacks awareness and sensitivity to our genocide. Germane to healing, validation of the trauma and giving testimony through narratives suggest that acknowledgment of our trauma is crucial for liberating us from the effects of our historical legacy. Clinical social work practice can facilitate this process through culturally sensitive and culturally congruent interventions that are grounded in empowerment practice with Native individuals, families, and groups. Spiritual and cultural empowerment, through interventions conducted by the Takini Network, promise to deliver healing to Native people so that we can claim who we are and reclaim our past, *hecel lena oyate kin nipi kte* (so that our people may live!).

REFERENCES

Brave Heart, M. Y. H. (1998). The return to the sacred path: Healing the historical trauma and historical unresolved grief response among the Lakota. *Smith College Studies in Social Work, 68* (3), 287–305.

Brave Heart, M. Y. H. (1999). *Oyate Ptayela:* Rebuilding the Lakota Nation through addressing historical trauma among Lakota parents. *Journal of Human Behavior in the Social Environment, 2* (1/2), 109–126; and in Weaver, H. N. (Ed.), *Voices of First Nations People: Human services considerations* (pp. 109–126). New York: Haworth.

Brave Heart, M. Y. H. & DeBruyn, L. M. (1998). The American Indian Holocaust: Healing historical unresolved grief. *American Indian and Alaska Native Mental Health Research, 8*(2), 56–78.

Brave Heart-Jordan, M. Y. H. (1995). The return to the sacred path: Healing from historical trauma and historical unresolved grief among the Lakota. (Doctoral dissertation, Smith College

School for Social Work, 1995). (Copyright by Author: reprints available through the Takini Network, P.O. Box 4138 Rapid City, SD 57709-4138.)

Claymore, B. (1988). A public health approach to suicide attempts on a Sioux reservation. *American Indian and Alaska Native Mental Health Research, 1* (3), 19–24.

Coates, S. (1992). The etiology of boyhood gender identity disorder: An integrative model. In J. W. Barron, M. N. Eagle, D. L. Wolitzky (Eds.), *Interface of psychoanalysis and psychology* (pp. 245–265). Washington, DC: American Psychological Association.

Coates, S., Friedman, R. C., & Wolfe, S. (1991). The etiology of boyhood gender identity disorder: A model for integrating psychodynamics, temperament and development. *Psychoanalytic Dialogues: A Journal of Relational Perspectives, 1,* 341–383.

Cox, E. O. & Parsons, R. J. (1994). *Empowerment-oriented social work practice with the elderly.* Belmont, CA: Brooks-Cole.

Devereux, G. (1951). Three technical problems in the psychotherapy of Plains Indian patients. *American Journal of Psychotherapy, 5,* 411–423.

Duran, E. & Yellow Horse-Davis, S. (1997). *Final research evaluation report—Evaluation of family and child guidance clinic hybrid treatment model.* Report to Indian Health Service.

Erikson, E. H. (1963). *Childhood and Society,* rev. ed. New York: W. W. Norton.

Freud, S. (1910). The future prospects of psychoanalytic therapy. In *The standard edition, 11,* (pp. 141–151). London: Hogarth.

Greenson, R. R. (1967). *The technique and practice of psychoanalysis.* New York: International Universities Press.

Hepworth, D. H. & Larson, J. A. (1993). *Direct social work practice: Theory and skills,* 4th ed. Pacific Grove, CA: Brooks/Cole.

Irwin, M. H. & Roll, S. (1995). The psychological impact of sexual abuse of Native American boarding-school children. *Journal of the American Academy of Psychoanalysis, 23* (3), 461–473.

Macgregor, G. (1975). *Warriors without weapons: A study of the society and personality development of the Pine Ridge Sioux.* Chicago: University of Chicago Press (original work published 1946).

Manson, S., Beals, J., O'Nell, T., Piasecki, J., Bechtold, D., Keane, E., & Jones, M. (1996). Wounded spirits, ailing hearts: PTSD and related disorders among American Indians. In A. J. Marsella, M. J. Friedman, E. T. Gerrity, & R. M. Scurfield (Eds.), *Ethnocultural aspects of posttraumatic stress disorder* (pp. 255–283). Washington DC: American Psychological Association.

May, P. (1973). *Suicide and suicide attempts on the Pine Ridge Reservation.* Pine Ridge, SD: PHS Community Mental Health Program.

Robin, R. W., Chester, B., & Goldman, D. (1996). Cumulative trauma and PTSD in American Indian communities. In A. J. Marsella, M. J. Friedman, E. T. Gerrity, & R. M. Scurfield (Eds.), *Ethnocultural aspects of posstraumatic stress disorder* (pp. 239–253). Washington, DC: American Psychological Association.

Silver, S. M. & Wilson, J. P. (1988). Native American healing and purification rituals for war stress. In John P. Wilson, Zev Harele, & Boaz Hahana (Eds.), *Human adaptation to extreme stress: From the Holocaust to Viet Nam* (pp. 337–355). New York: Plenum.

van der Kolk, B. A., McFarlane, A. C., & Weisaeth, L. Eds. (1996). *Traumatic stress: The effects of overwhelming experience on mind, body, and society.* New York: Guilford.

CHAPTER 21

ORGANIZATION AND COMMUNITY INTERVENTION WITH AMERICAN INDIAN TRIBAL COMMUNITIES

EDDIE F. BROWN

BETHNEY N. GUNDERSEN

Tribal communities enter the twenty-first century facing the most profound challenges and opportunities of the last one hundred years. Although confronted with devastating social and economic conditions, landmark legislation passed within the last twenty-five years has dramatically changed the federal government's approach toward working with American Indian communities. These legislative efforts toward greater Indian self-determination and tribal self-governance have given new hope for the survival and empowerment of tribal communities. This chapter represents an up-to-date description of American Indian tribal communities, including a framework for the study of communities, theoretical approaches to practice, and a community development model for empowerment of tribal communities.

SOCIODEMOGRAPHIC CHARACTERISTICS

There are 557 federally recognized tribes[1] in the Unites States, consisting of 1.2 million enrolled tribal members (Russell, 1997). These tribal groups maintain a special political relationship with the federal government based on treaty, executive order, or congressional legislation. Through this legal relationship, tribes reserved acres of land, along with the rights to the water, resources, and wildlife for their own use. These lands and resources are held in trust by the federal government, which is legally obligated to preserve and protect the lands and resources from being exploited by states or private interests (O'Brien, 1989).

Federally recognized tribes occupy approximately 55 million acres of land in the lower forty-eight states and 40 million acres in Alaska (Russell, 1997). These lands are referred to as "Indian Country," and are subject to tribal laws and customs as well as federal law. The geographic size of these tribal communities varies greatly. Navajo tribal lands are the largest, covering more than 14 million acres. The majority of tribal lands are small, with only ten tribes occupying tribal lands greater than one million acres (Russell, 1997).

Tribal communities residing on these lands come in a variety of sizes and are referred to by a variety of names: tribal nations and Indian reservations can consist of up to several hundred thousand members, while pueblos, rancherias, and colonies are considerably smaller. The Cherokees of Oklahoma make up the largest tribe, with 308,000 members.

SOCIAL PROBLEMS AND ISSUES IN AMERICAN INDIAN TRIBAL COMMUNITIES

American Indian tribal communities are described as having the highest unemployment, poverty, and disease rates of any community within the United States (Cooper, 1996). Of the total potential labor force within federally recognized tribal communities, 49 percent were unemployed in 1995 (U.S. Department of the Interior, 1995). Fifty-one percent of American Indians living in tribal communities lived below the poverty level, compared to 13 percent of the total U.S. population (Sandefur & Liebler, 1996). Alcoholism is four-and-a-half times that of the U.S. population (U.S. Department of Health and Human Services, 1994). American Indian adolescents are four times more likely than are non-Indians to attempt suicide (Russell, 1997). The rate of tuberculosis and diabetes is seven times greater for tribal members compared with the non-Indian population (Russell, 1997). "If social health statistics provide a reliable barometer of a group's well-being, Indians are at the very bottom of the ladder in American society" (Cooper, 1996, p. 604).

A FRAMEWORK FOR THE STUDY AND ANALYSIS OF TRIBAL COMMUNITIES BASED ON CULTURAL VALUES

American Indians living on reservations typically identify themselves with their tribal community and corresponding cultural values. This is not to say that the family and individual are not important to American Indians, but that they are valued in the context of their relationship to the tribe. As social workers prepare to practice in tribal communities, they must understand how community is defined and how to apply this definition to American Indians within the context of their values. In this section, we will draw from work by Roland Warren (1963) to create a systems framework to understand and interpret the concept of community and how it relates to Indian Country.

Warren (1963) describes communities as "that combination of social units and systems that perform the major social functions having locality relevance" (p. 9). The two main components of a community are common social interests and geographical proximity. Both of these components must be present in some form in order to have a community system. A tribal community, for the purpose of this discussion, is described as a social system with specified geographical boundaries, a written constitution, specified membership requirements, written rules and regulations, and specified procedures for choosing leaders. Examples of tribal communities include all federally recognized Indian reservations, Oklahoma Indian communities, California rancherias, New Mexico pueblos, Nevada colonies, and Alaska Native villages. Within this systems framework, Warren (1963) identifies five major locality relevant functions that must be carried out such that a community can provide for the day-to-day needs of its members. These functions include production–distribution–consumption, socialization, social control, social participation, and mutual support, all of which are valued by tribal communities.

The major social function of production–distribution–consumption relates to the tribal community's ability to provide access to goods and services within the community. This function's focus is on the structures that determine the extent to which tribal members are able to work, shop, and purchase those items necessary for daily living within the boundaries of their community. Cohen (1960a) suggests that the more the tribal community controls these economic and social units, the greater the possibility of creating economic enterprises in which all tribal members can participate and benefit.

Socialization "involves a process by which society . . . transmits prevailing knowledge, social values, and behavior patterns to individual members" (Warren, 1963, p. 10). American Indian family members continue to play a major role in providing for the socialization of their tribal members. The school system, however, which has played a major role in the forced assimilation of American Indian children, continues to be a principal institution to carry out this social function. Therefore, the greater the control and participation of tribal community members within the Bureau of Indian Affairs and state public school systems, the greater the assurance of an educational curriculum that addresses the preservation of tribal history, social values, culture and language.

Social control is how a community enforces norms of behavior on its members (Warren, 1963). Typically, local governmental institutions have discharged this function through the passage of laws and ordinances. Local police and court systems ensure that the laws and ordinances are enforced. Within tribal communities, these functions, along with other municipal responsibilities designed to protect and to provide for the well-being of tribal members, have historically been performed by the federal government through the local agencies of the Bureau of Indian Affairs. The gradual transfer of these municipal functions to tribal governments has resulted in greater local autonomy and tribal self-determination.

Another aspect of social control relates to the tribal community's responsibility to protect its members from outside threats from surrounding non-Indian communities, state governments, and congressional actions. American Indian history is rife with broken treaties, massacres, land steals, and general dehumanization of American Indians. Tribal communities must be prepared to defend the sovereign rights of their members from the outside federal and international justice systems.

The function of social participation is to encourage participation of community members in a variety of organizations and events (Warren, 1963). This is reflected in Cohen's analysis of the need for tribal communities to provide recreational activities such as community dances, ceremonies, sports, and festivities. According to Cohen (1960a, p. 225), tribal control and support of these activities does more to ensure a strong inter-tribal psychological identification "than many activities of government that political theorists may consider more essential."

The last major locality function a community carries out, mutual support, involves the participation of community members in caring and helping activities, such as "care in time of sickness, exchange of labor, or helping a local family in economic distress" (Warren, 1963, p. 11). While extended family members play an important role in carrying out this social function, tribal community members (similar to the experience of other citizens) have experienced a gradual shift of this function to outside federal and state health and welfare agencies. For instance, state governments, the Indian Health Service, and the Bureau of Indian Affairs currently share the responsibility for the provision of health and welfare resources and services to tribal communities. Tribal input, participation, and eventual contracting of these resources and services by tribal government is essential to ensure relevant, culturally sensitive services to tribal members.

The five locality relevant functions described here help to define the tribal community in terms of the functions it performs. Social workers practicing in American Indian communities should be aware of the importance and value of these functions and how the social work profession can work with the community to maintain tribal control over the five functions. In the next section we describe the theoretical approaches to practice that achieve the goal of tribal control over locality relevant functions.

THEORETICAL APPROACHES TO PRACTICE WITH AMERICAN INDIAN TRIBAL COMMUNITIES

Ecological Approach

In applying an ecological perspective to a tribal community system, the focus should be on the administration and interaction of the social units and delivery systems developed to carry out the locality relevant functions (Hepworth, Rooney, & Larsen, 1997). While these social units and delivery systems all have locality relevance, in that they are structured specifically for American Indians within geographic proximity, tribal community responsibility and control of these social units and systems will vary depending on the flexibility of federal legislation, availability of resources, and the tribal government's readiness to develop its own local delivery systems and administrative structures.

Fellin (1995) states that, in order to understand a locality-based system, the social work professional needs to have a thorough grasp of the health and welfare services delivery system of a community, including knowledge about the agencies and organizations (social units) that make up the various fields of service. Furthermore, knowledge about the community's politics, economics, and educational and religious institutions is needed because the major community functions identified by Warren are carried out through these systems. Therefore, to work with American Indians, social workers must understand how U.S. policies have sought to disempower tribal communities through the destruction of tribally controlled social units.

Social workers who are aware of American Indian political history can play an important role in empowering tribal communities through the reinforcement of tribal self-determination policies and the development of strong tribally controlled social service and economic development social units. This does not imply that tribal communities must eliminate the funding patterns established by the federal trust responsibility, but suggests that these outside federal resources will be much more effective if the tribal communities are able to determine for themselves how best to use them. Social workers must understand and keep in mind the following three points concerning the tribal/federal/state relationships that serve as the basis for tribal empowerment:

- The United States Constitution gives authority in all Indian Affairs to the federal government and none to state, county, or city governments (National Congress of American Indians, 1999).
- The United States clearly recognizes the governmental status of Indian tribes and, by law, has created a unique federal relationship with tribal communities known as the Federal Trust Responsibility. This is one of the most important doctrines of Federal Indian law. It is a legally enforceable obligation of the United States to protect tribal self-determination, tribal lands, assets, resources, and treaty rights (National Congress of American Indians, 1999).
- Federally recognized Indian tribes, as governmental entities, have the power to determine their form of government, impose requirements for tribal membership, make their own civil and criminal laws, and operate their own governmental activities, including all municipal services pertaining to the well-being of their citizens (e.g., health care, social services, education, law enforcement, and judicial systems). Therefore, all federal, state, and local governments deal with Indian tribes as governments and not as special interest groups (National Congress of American Indians, 1999).

Strengths-Based Approach

The strengths-based approach utilizes the existing assets and capabilities of the tribe to enable the community to address community concerns and problems from within (Saleebey, 1992). The strengths-based approach must begin with knowledge of federal Indian law and policies, as described above. This knowledge is especially critical when social workers enable tribal communities to negotiate with outside state and local governments. A common error on the part of professional social workers is, unknowingly, weakening tribal government powers by agreeing to accept state social service or health care standards rather than building on the tribal community's strengths by encouraging the development of tribal standards. There is a tendency for tribal social workers to agree to externally imposed standards in order to obtain much-needed state and local resources.

Knowledge of federal Indian law and policies is the starting point for facilitating a strengths-based approach to community practice in tribal communities, but a social worker must also adopt a new perspective regarding American Indian tribal communities. For most Americans, names like *Indian, reservation,* or "Pine Ridge, South Dakota" bring to mind perspectives that are overwhelmingly negative: Tribal communities are destined to be poor and economic development in the tribal community will never succeed; tribal governments are incapable of effectively managing their social service and health-care delivery systems; tribal community members are not capable of organizing to effectively address the social and economic conditions affecting their communities. These perspectives are based on the false notion that tribal communities are deficient in many ways and that they are incapable of addressing their deficiencies.

In today's world of Indian self-determination, a paradigm shift has taken place in how we view and work with tribal communities. As professional social workers, we must pull away from those problem-oriented attitudes and old paradigms that have dictated the way outside agencies and organizations have historically dealt with tribal communities. The new paradigm focuses on a strengths-based approach in which tribal communities are viewed as the asset through which effective community development can occur. Only by ridding ourselves of the negative and problem-oriented notions and attitudes is it possible to envision the true potential of American Indian communities.

If we want tribal communities to respond positively to their challenges and opportunities, we must empower them to use their strengths and assets to move beyond the disparaging social and economic conditions they face daily and see the realistic reasons for hope. We can no longer afford to view tribal communities as the problem. They are, in truth, the solution. Social workers need to focus on the development of policies and activities based on the strengths, skills, and assets of American Indian people and their communities. An example of a strengths-based approach follows.

On August 27, 1976, the Indian Child Welfare Act was introduced. The bill was a response to the tribal community's concern about the disproportionately large number of Indian children who were being removed from their families and placed in non-Indian substitute care and adoptive settings (Plantz, Hubbell, Barrett, & Dobrec, 1988).

Tribal communities believed that the only way to alleviate this problem was to remove sole authority for the protection of Indian children and the delivery of child welfare services from the State. The proposed alternative was to build on the existing strengths of tribal governments to meet the needs of Indian children and families through the development of the tribal governmental infrastructures (Mannes, 1995). By doing so, the tribal community would begin utilizing the strengths and assets found within their community to begin to address a community problem. This strengths-based approach was a radical shift away from the traditional problem-oriented response of placing Indian children in off-reservation, non-Indian foster care settings.

The bill immediately generated controversy within the social service and child welfare professional community. State social service agencies, child welfare and adoption organizations, and even outside religious groups rose up in opposition to the bill. Armed with old prejudices and outdated perceptions of Indian communities, they questioned the ability of tribal governments to responsibly address the welfare needs of Indian children. Horror stories were generated by outside organizations, which would no longer have free reign in the removal and adoption of Indian children. They presented exaggerated scenarios in which Indian children would languish in tribal foster systems and be left unprotected because of tribes' inability or unwillingness to work with state agencies and child welfare organizations.

Nonetheless, given the administration and congressional support for the concept of Indian self-determination, and the strong support and involvement of tribal leaders and parents, community social workers, and a handful of outside legal advocates, the Indian Child Welfare Act became law on November 8, 1978. This legislation ushered in a new era for the rights of tribal governments to care for the well-being of their most precious resource—their children.

It must be noted that, in response to the debate and concerns raised by outside agencies concerning the competency of tribal governments to administer their own child welfare services, a 1988 Status Report on the implementation of the Indian Child Welfare Act stated that tribal programs are "doing a very creditable job of following standards of good casework practice and achieving family-based permanency for out-of-home children. This is particularly noteworthy in light of the inadequate and unstable federal funding arrangements under which they must work" (Plantz, Hubbell, Barrett, and Dobrec, 1998, p. 9). The successful results of this bill demonstrate that the strengths-based approach is a very effective way to address issues found in tribal communities.

Empowerment Approach

The empowerment approach focuses on the transfer of power from outside authorities to the tribe. Tribal communities "are in a transition that began with independence, moved to paternalism, and is now moving toward self-determination and control" (O'Brien, 1989, p. 294). Since the passage of the 1975 Indian Self-Determination Act, tribal communities have experienced a major effort on behalf of the U.S. government to have tribal governments take over the direct administration of federal programs serving tribal communities. Tribal communities are, therefore, under tremendous pressure to develop the necessary social units and systems to effectively provide for the social, economic, and educational needs of their tribal members. This is no easy task after 200 years of legislative and administrative attempts to eliminate tribal communities and their horizontal social units and systems. Early research findings indicate that successful tribal communities that have broken the vertical patterns of institutional dependency have done so "in a two step process of first asserting and taking control of their own sovereignty and second, backing that up by building their own institutions of government" (Cooper, 1996, p. 620).

INTERWEAVING APPROACHES TO THE DEVELOPMENT OF TRIBAL COMMUNITIES

The focus of community practice with tribal communities must involve a strong community development approach that empowers tribal communities through a "process designed to create conditions of economic and social progress for the whole community with its active participation and fullest possible reliance on the community's initiative" (Rothman, 1995, p. 28).

The purpose of community development is to utilize the strengths of the community and to build the capacity of the community through the achievement of the following three goals. First, problem solving must come from within the community. Therefore, community development should promote greater involvement and participation of community-elected officials, service providers, and community members in addressing the social welfare and health needs of the community. Second, community development should strengthen the horizontal relationships and interactions of community health and social service systems through tribal control and operation of local programs. Third, tribal communities must be able to exercise the full extent of their tribal sovereign powers and authority in the development of tribal health and welfare systems, regulations, standards, and practices.

Under our proposed model of community development, the professional social worker, working through existing tribal community structures, achieves these goals by possessing capacity-building skills in the areas of locality development, social planning, and social action (Rothman, 1995). Although each of these approaches is a distinct intervention strategy, community practice within tribal communities requires expertise in using and interweaving all three approaches.

Locality Development

Locality development seeks to strengthen relationships among members of the community through building solidarity and competence (Cnaan and Rothman, 1995). Locality development requires skills in organizing and guiding community groups, group consensus building, and strengthening local participation and leadership. The social worker should act as a facilitator in bringing community members together to discuss community problems important to all. The social worker does not act as the leader of the discussion, but rather develops local leadership by encouraging participation among all members and seeking consensus. The focus of locality development is on building the group's ability to make decisions that members can agree on and enact together. The social worker builds the capacity for tribal group members to explore felt needs, determine desired goals, and take appropriate action.

There are four points a social worker should be mindful of when promoting locality development. First, locality development is a process through which awareness of a problem emerges. A problem in an American Indian community may persist without members actively engaging in discussion about it. Once members are brought together to specifically address their concerns, awareness of the problem grows, and action can ensue. Therefore, the social worker's role is to create consciousness and awareness among tribal members. Second, locality development must include a broad cross-section of community members that incorporates the views of various tribal factions. Third, locality development should build local self-determination and honor the tribal culture by allowing the members to decide what the eventual solution to the problem is and how fast they want to move towards that goal. Fourth, locality development should not become dependent on the expertise of the social worker. Instead, the social worker should empower the residents to gain the capacity to solve their problems internally (Cnann and Rothman, 1995).

Social Planning

Social planning requires rational, future-oriented decision-making skills (Rothman and Zald, 1995). The goal of social planing is to anticipate future needs and develop programs accordingly. Therefore, social planning requires community diagnosis, information and data collection, data analysis, and evaluation.

However, unlike the more elitist role of "expert" planner, the role of the social worker in our model is also to serve as a teacher and enabler in empowering tribal members to become social planners themselves. This is achieved by allowing tribal members to become personally involved through direct participation in fact gathering, analysis of information, and making decisions on the most appropriate course of action.

The answer to appropriate social planning lies with the tribal members. Social planning is also used to create social and political control among tribal members. It helps members to maintain power, reach consensus, build networks, and justify their decisions (Rothman and Zald, 1995).

Social Action

In terms of community development, social action involves moving tribal community groups to action based on their agreement for change. It is a tribally administered approach to social action. It identifies and focuses on those areas of disagreement between the tribal community and outside institutional policies and administrative attitudes that unjustly limit health and welfare resources and services to tribal members. Social action challenges the structures that exclude, oppress, and disempower tribal communities (Fisher, 1995).

The social action model requires skills in organizing community members to take action through confrontation, negotiation, and resolution. The role of the social worker is to empower community groups to act on behalf of their interest in confronting outside power structures (e.g., federal, state, and local governments, health and welfare organizations, and economic development interests). Empowerment is achieved through confrontation and negotiation to ensure the development of locally controlled and administered social welfare and health care systems, including the development of tribal government regulations, standards, and practices.

A social worker, using social action as a community development approach, needs to build strong groups of members organized to address their concerns through conflict and action. The members should be taught how to challenge prevailing ideologies that, in any way, hinder or oppress their communities. From this point, tribal communities can then begin to transform those internal or external institutional systems that oppress them and create a society that is more responsive to the needs of American Indian communities.

Example of Community Intervention for Tribal Administration of TANF.   Organization and community practice within tribal communities require professional social workers to be knowledgeable of the historical and political emergence of today's tribal communities, to have confidence in tribal members' ability to self-govern, and to have the skill to readily select the most appropriate intervention method for the task at hand (Rothman, 1995). The Personal Responsibility and Work Opportunity Reconciliation Act of 1996 (PRWORA)[2] provides an example of how social workers must combine all three of the above attributes. Social workers should work with tribal communities to enable them to exercise the full extent of their sovereign powers in planning for the administration of Temporary Assistance to Needy Families (TANF).

Under Title I, Section 412 of PRWORA, tribal communities can apply for a Tribal Family Assistance Grant to administer their own TANF services. Tribal communities have been slow to take advantage of this opportunity due to concerns related to the lack of administrative start-up costs, potential loss of state matching funds, stringent federal reporting requirements, and strict eligibility time limits and work requirements. Professional social workers can play an important role in assisting tribal administrations and legislative councils to sift through these concerns, implement a plan of action, and engage the state and federal governments in negotiation to ensure the flexibility and funding needed for the tribal administration of TANF services.

The application of a locality development intervention mode is needed in the initial stage of tribal community discussion. The community social worker should work closely with the tribal administration in organizing a tribal TANF work group to address the challenges, opportunities, and concerns posed by PRWORA. The work group should consist of a tribal representative from all TANF-related services (e.g., tribal employment and training, social services, child care, mental health, adult education, and welfare recipient advocates).

There are several purposes of the work group: First, acquire an overall working knowledge of the legislation, with specific understanding of Title I; second, identify and discuss tribal concerns related to the administration and delivery of TANF services; third, develop a course of action to determine the feasibility for the tribal administration of TANF services. The social worker role would consist of facilitating group discussion across TANF issues and opportunities, educating group members on PRWORA legislation, and building group consensus toward a plan of action.

In order for the tribal work group to determine the feasibility of administering its own TANF services, it must have information about the existing tribal and state program social units and delivery systems. The application of a social planning mode is required in this effort, along with the necessary supporting role of the social worker. Information on education and training services, potential for job creation, and social support services to assist tribal recipients in the transition from welfare to work are examples of the kinds of information that need to be collected by the various work group representatives.

The budgeted amount of tribal and state funds needs to be identified for 1994 Aid to Families with Dependent Children (AFDC) caseload levels, as well as the current TANF caseload in the tribal community. The amount of federal funds to be allocated to the tribal community for the delivery of TANF services is based on the total cost for the delivery of state AFDC services to tribal community residents in 1994. This amount is taken from the state federal allocation by the U.S. Department of Health and Human Services and directly allocated to the tribe.

The social worker role is to serve as a teacher and enabler in assisting work group members in fact gathering, analysis of caseload data and budget sheets, and in using this information to justify their decision regarding the most appropriate course of action to take in the administration of TANF services. The collection and analysis of data by the work group members, rather than total reliance on outside planning and research consultants, help tribal members maintain power and build internal administrative and planning networks.

The collection of state data, determination of federal allocation amounts, and planning for the coordination of outside delivered services require extensive tribal negotiations with both state and federal representatives. The potential for conflict and disagreement between the negotiating parties will vary among the tribes, states, and federal agencies, depending on their historical relationships and the extent to which outside governmental agencies have attempted to control tribal resources and programs.

Preparing the work group for negotiation with state and federal officials requires a social action mode of intervention. The work group must be prepared to confront the outside agencies on behalf of the tribal community's interest to ensure its fair share of resources, flexibility to design its TANF service delivery systems, and the authority to develop its own standards to meet the economic and social needs of its members. More specifically, at the tribal/state level, there is the need to negotiate with state officials for the provision of state matching funds based on tribal members' rights as state citizens.[3]

The social worker's role entails preparing the work group representatives with the information and data necessary for presenting a strong case on their behalf. An understanding of the tribal community's and members' rights and the process for appealing state or federal decisions under this legislation is critical. Work group members should also be prepared to show how tribal/state cooperation and coordination would benefit state and federal interests.

Professional social workers working within tribal communities must therefore possess the knowledge, attitudes, and skills necessary to increase the tribal members' abilities in problem solving to effectively respond to the welfare and health needs of their communities. The social worker's ability to readily diagnose the tribal work group's needs and to interweave the appropriate modes of intervention and worker roles will allow tribes to carefully examine their concerns and potential benefits in regard to the administration of TANF services. This, in turn, will assist them to arrive at well-reasoned judgments and negotiated agreements for the administration of TANF services.

CONCLUSION

Perhaps the most important practice skill a social worker must have to effectively work with American Indian communities is to become firmly rooted within the community. By becoming part of the tribal community, a social worker can begin to understand how the community operates. This knowledge facilitates an understanding of the strengths found within the American Indian community. The social worker can then begin to empower the community to draw and build on its assets to enable the community itself to address the problems and issues that are perceived by the community members.

Social workers who master this skill will soon realize that the American Indian community has a vibrant culture, strong family commitments, and a sense of perseverance and self-determination. These attributes have not been lost, despite hundreds of years of oppression and destruction. We are now beginning an era when policymakers have finally realized the importance of recognizing and cultivating the strong leadership and determination found within the American Indian community. Social workers have an important role to play in this new era through their ability to respect and empower communities to build on their internal strengths.

REFERENCES

Cnaan, R. A. and Rothman, J. (1995). Locality development and the building of community. In J. Rothman, J. L. Erlich, & J. E. Tropman (Eds.), *Strategies of community intervention* (pp. 327–340). Itaska, IL: F. E. Peacock.

Cohen, F. S. (1960a). How long will Indian constitutions last? In L. K. Cohen (Ed.), *The legal conscience: Selected papers of Felix S. Cohen* (pp. 222–229). New Haven, CT: Yale University Press.

Cohen, F. S. (1960b). Indian Self-Government. In L. K. Cohen (Ed.), *The legal conscience: Selected papers of Felix S. Cohen* (pp. 305–314). New Haven, CT: Yale University Press.

Cooper, M. (1996). Native America's future: The issues. *The Congressional Quarterly Researcher, 6* (26), 601–624.

Fellin, P. (1995). Understanding American communities. In J. Rothman, J. L. Erlich, & J. E. Tropman (Eds.), *Strategies of community intervention* (pp. 114–128). Itaska, IL: F. E. Peacock.

Fisher, R. (1995). Social action community organization: Proliferation, persistence, roots, and prospects. In J. Rothman, J. L. Erlich, & J. E. Tropman (Eds.), *Strategies of community intervention* (pp. 327–340). Itaska, IL: F. E. Peacock.

Hepworth, D. H., Rooney, R. H., & Larsen, J. (1997). *Direct social work practice: Theory and skills.* Boston, MA: Brooks/Cole.

Mannes, M. (1995). Factors and events leading to the passage of the Indian Child Welfare Act. *Child Welfare, 74* (1), 264–282.

National Congress of American Indians. (1999). *An Introduction to Indian Nations in the United States.* Washington DC: National Congress of American Indians.

O'Brien, S. (1989). *American Indian tribal governments.* Norman, OK and London: University of Oklahoma Press.

Plantz, M. C., Hubbell, R., Barrett, B. J., & Dobrec, A. (1988). *Indian child welfare: A status report.* Washington DC: Center for Scientific Review.

Rothman, J. (1995). Approaches to community intervention. In J. Rothman, J. L. Erlich, & J. E. Tropman (Eds.), *Strategies of community intervention* (pp. 26–63). Itaska, IL: F. E. Peacock.

Rothman, J. & Zald, M. N. (1995). Planning and policy practice. In J. Rothman, J. L. Erlich, & J. E. Tropman (Eds.), *Strategies of community intervention* (pp. 327–340). Itaska, IL: F. E. Peacock.

Russell, G. (1997). *American Indian facts of life: A profile of today's tribes and reservations.* Phoenix, AZ: Russell.

Saleebey, D. (Ed.). (1992). *The strengths perspective in social work practice.* New York: Longman.

Sandefur, G. D. & Liebler, C. A. (1996). The demography of American Indian families. In G. D. Sandefur, R. R. Rindfuss, & B. Cohen (Eds.), *Changing numbers, changing needs: American Indian demography and public health.* Washington DC: National Academy Press.

U.S. Department of Health and Human Services. (1994). Trends in Indian Health. U.S. Department of Health and Human Services: Indian Health Services.

U.S. Department of the Interior. (1995). Indian Service Population and Labor Force Estimates. U.S. Department of the Interior: Bureau of Indian Affairs.

Warren, R. L. (1963). *The community in America.* Chicago: Rand McNally.

ENDNOTES

1. A federally recognized tribe is any Indian tribe, band, nation, rancheria, pueblo, colony, or community that is recognized by the United States government as eligible for the special programs and services provided by the Secretary of the Interior to Indians because of their status as Indians (Russell, 1997).

2. PRWORA consists of nine major titles, three of which specifically address the needs of tribal communities: Title I, Block grants to tribes for TANF administration; Title III, grants to tribes to develop their own child support enforcement programs; and Title VI, funds for tribal

communities to further develop tribal child care services. For the purpose of this illustration, focus will be primarily on Title I.

3. Although states are required to provide state matching funds for the administration of their TANF services, states are not required to provide matching funds for tribally administered TANF services within their state boundaries. It is dependent on the tribal community's ability to negotiate with state representatives for the provision of the state match. Without state match, tribes lose a minimum of one third of the 1994 costs for the delivery of public assistance to tribal member residents.

CHAPTER 22

INDIVIDUAL AND FAMILY INTERVENTION SKILLS WITH ASIAN AND PACIFIC ISLAND AMERICAN LESBIANS AND GAY MEN

VALLI KALEI KANUHA

While the social work profession has long been associated with the major social movements in the United States, Mallon (1998b) suggests that "social work's history with gay men and lesbians can best be described as an ambivalent relationship" (p. 7). The Delegate Assembly of the National Association of Social Workers (NASW) adopted a statement of commitment to gay and lesbian issues in 1977, but it was not until 1992 that the Council on Social Work Education formally required the study of lesbians and gay men as part of the core social work curriculum (Mallon, 1998b). And, while social work texts concerned with gay men and lesbians have expanded considerably in the past two decades (Appleby & Anastas, 1998; Hidalgo, 1995; Hidalgo, Peterson, & Woodman, 1985; Laird & Green, 1996; Longres, 1996; Mallon, 1998a; Shernoff, 1996; Tully, 1996), in a recent review of the four major social work journals from 1964 to 1993, less than 1 percent of almost 6,000 articles addressed lesbian or gay issues (Mallon, 1998b). However, there is a particular paucity of social work literature regarding practice with lesbians and gay men of Asian and Pacific Island American (A/PIA) heritage.

SOCIODEMOGRAPHICS

Due to many and complex factors, it is almost impossible to establish a demographic profile of lesbians and gay men in the United States. First, it is both theoretically and behaviorally difficult to delineate the parameters of human sexuality to encompass more than just sexual behavior or conduct, i.e., do we measure the prevalence of homosexuality (or heterosexuality, for that matter) by the kinds and frequency of sexual contact between two persons, or is one "counted" as gay or lesbian only if he or she is in a long-term, monogamous relationship with another man or woman? Second, due to the deeply stigmatizing nature of any deviation from heterosexuality, most lesbians, gay men, and bisexual persons do not acknowledge or reveal their sexual identities to others and, often, deny it to themselves. Therefore, measurement and social psychological issues confound any attempt to depict the true population of lesbians and gay men in the United States, regardless of their racial or ethnic background.

The pioneering work on human sexuality was conducted by Alfred Kinsey and his associates in the early 1950s (Kinsey, Pomeroy, & Martin, 1948; Kinsey, Pomeroy, Martin, & Gebhard, 1953). Kinsey established a linear framework of human sexuality, suggesting that 10 percent of the population is almost exclusively homosexual based on self-reports of sexual behavior. However, Kinsey's research has often been criticized due to its reliance not only on self-reports by predominantly white male samples, but its primary focus on sexual conduct without consideration of contextual factors, such as psychological commitment or other practices associated with gay life (gay social support, engagement in gay activities) (DeCecco & Parker, 1995; Gonsiorek & Weinrich, 1991). More recently, in a survey by Laumann, Gagnon, Michael and Michaels (1994), 8.6 percent of women and 10.1 percent of men reported same-sex sexual desire, conduct, or affiliation with lesbian/gay/bisexual identity. However, when asked if they considered themselves to be lesbian, gay, or bisexual, only 2.8 percent of men and 1.4 percent of women claimed to be predominantly nonheterosexual as part of their identities.

An integral part of the difficulty not only in identifying but describing gay and lesbian populations is *homophobia*, a term commonly used to describe negative beliefs, attitudes, and behaviors with regard to homosexuals, homosexuality, and anyone perceived to be gay or lesbian (Appleby & Anastas, 1998; Pharr, 1988). The consequences of heterosexism and homophobia include the fact that many gay men and lesbians are denied employment and/or promotion in the workplace, or, specifically in the U.S. armed forces, are threatened with discharge (Anderson & Smith, 1993; Badgett, 1996; Diamant, 1993; Woods, 1993). In addition, hate speech and violence against lesbians and towards gay men are well-documented, and include all forms of psychological and physical abuse including homicide (Appleby & Anastas, 1998; Herek, 1991; Herek & Berrill, 1992). These deeply prejudicial attitudes and behaviors subsequently result in lesbians and gay men concealing their lives and experiences from others, making it nearly impossible to accurately depict this population.

In summary, because there are no empirical or universal criteria by which to measure "who" is gay or lesbian, combined with societal heterosexism and homophobia that keep many lesbians and gay men "in the closet," any prevalence or descriptive data on this group is limited.

CULTURAL VALUES AND NORMS OF
A/PIA GAY MEN AND LESBIANS

Due to the importance of family loyalty, "saving face," and other cultural values that are integral parts of many Asian and Pacific Island communities (Mokuau, 1991; Sue & Wagner, 1973; Uba, 1995), social workers who work at the individual or family levels with A/PIA gay men and lesbians must be sensitive to the myriad ways this population balances cultural aspects of A/PIA family life while also learning to know themselves as gay and lesbian persons. For social work practitioners working with A/PIA gay men and lesbians, helping these clients learn the skills to maintain communal connections to their A/PIA history and culture (through family and community life), while also affirming their sexual and intimate personal selves, is, perhaps, the most significant consideration for individual or family-level interventions. As the following section suggests, the most salient work for A/PIA gay men and lesbians is in understanding, accepting, and adapting to the unique yet tension-filled aspects of being both A/PIA *and* gay or lesbian.

Same-Sex and Same-Gender
Identities in A/PIA Cultures

Most Asian and Pacific Island cultures have documented the centuries-old existence of same-sex behavior and relationships. In the Phillippines, *bakla* refers to a man who assumes a female gender role and sometimes same-sex roles and behaviors, similar to the *mahu* in Native Hawaiian or Kanaka Maoli (indigenous people of Hawai'i) culture (Manalansan, 1994; Souza, 1976; Wong, Chang, Ross, & Mayer, 1998). The early journals of Captain Cook's voyages to Hawai'i cite the importance of *"ai'kane,* who were male consorts of the male ruling class of Kanaka Maoli' " (Morris, 1990). Same-sex roles and practices are also traced to the *fa'afafine* in Samoa and the Tongan *fakaleti* (Hall & Kauanui, 1996), and have also been reported in Korea, Japan, and China (Choi, Salazar, Lew, & Coates, 1995; Leong, 1996; Lim-Hing, 1994; Liu & Chan, 1996; Wong, et al., 1998).

For Asian and Pacific Island peoples who have either been colonized in their own homelands (such as Hawai'i or Samoa) or have emigrated to the United States, it is suggested that the influence of Western religiosity, social norms, and acculturation/assimilation patterns have significantly altered once-acceptable variations in values and practices regarding sexuality (Dynes & Donaldson, 1992; Hall & Kauanui, 1996; Kanuha, 1997). While there have always been lesbians and gay men (albeit often closeted) across every A/PIA community, most A/PIA persons perceive homosexuality as a "white" phenomenon (Hom, 1996; Takagi, 1996; Wat, 1996). And, from the contemporary and more mainstream, predominantly white gay and lesbian movement, a longstanding belief is that A/PIA and people of color are more homophobic than Caucasians, although this has never been documented (Ayala & Diaz, in press; Chan & Liu, 1996; Leong, 1996).

Valuing the Family versus the Individual

Perhaps the most oft-cited stressor that exists for many A/PIA gay men and lesbians is balancing adherence to A/PIA values and beliefs regarding the centrality of one's family of origin while developing an autonomous, personal identity as lesbian or gay. Wong and associates (1998) suggest that "a stronger value (is) placed on loyalty to family roles than on the expression of one's own sexual desires." As one Pacific Island gay man states, "My parents accept me, but they don't accept me. As long as I don't talk about 'it' we get along" (Kanuha, 1999). In studies of A/PIA gay and bisexual men in Hawai'i, participants report that their families of origin (parents, siblings, aunts, uncles, grandparents) were important social supports but were also the source of greatest internal conflict with regard to being gay or lesbian (Kanuha, 1997; Kanuha, 1999; Souza, 1976). As a result, many A/PIA men and women in these and other studies state that they are reluctant to either disclose or nondiscretely enact their homosexuality for fear of losing the connection to family members (Chan, 1997; Chan & Liu, 1996; Liu & Chan, 1996). The responsibility to one's family is particularly gendered for gay men of Chinese descent who are considered "bad sons" if they have not found a suitable female companion in a timely fashion, and also if they do not produce offspring (Wong et al., 1998).

Knowing Oneself through White
Gay/Lesbian Norms and Practices

Chan (1997) reported that A/PIA gay men and lesbians express difficulty developing a stable sense of gay or lesbian identity because the organized lesbian and gay movement in the United States is predominantly white. Asian and Pacific Island lesbians and gay men from Hawai'i consistently reported that they were socialized to believe that only white people were homosexual, and, particularly among A/PIA gay men, that Caucasian gay men were more intelligent and physically attractive (Kanuha, 1997; Kanuha, 1999). Due to sexist role expectations and depictions of Asian women as submissive, exotic commodities of men, the Asian woman is often constructed as heterosexual in society-at-large and in A/PIA communities. The following account by Ann Yuri Uyeda describes the confusion and anxiety associated with being both Asian or Pacific Island *and* lesbian:

> When it came to my own 'coming out' I stayed in the closet for a long time, knowing the truth about my sexuality but never speaking it because I just didn't think there *were* any queer Asian Americans—while I knew gay men and lesbians, everyone was White. My fear was that I didn't know what it would be like to be an Asian lesbian (Uyeda, 1994, p. 111).

In summary, social work practitioners who provide culturally competent interventions at the individual or family levels with A/PIA gay men or lesbians must be cognizant that the cultural norms, values, practices, and traditions of this population reflect a complexity of race/ethnicity and sexuality, as well as age, gender, class, and other factors. While there are well-documented reports of diverse sexual and gender practices in many A/PIA cultures, the effect of societal homo-phobia in contemporary U.S. life has resulted in repression or rejection of A/PIA lesbians and gay men in their own A/PIA communities. Social work practitioners should become knowledgeable of the indigenous sexual and gender traditions that impact their work with A/PIA gay men, lesbians, and their families.

Working with A/PIA gay men and lesbians to develop a healthy sense of self requires that social workers appreciate deeply important A/PIA cultural norms that valorize family and communal life. At the same time, practitioners must assist A/PIA clients to enact a gay or lesbian sexual identity, which is often constructed in the context of a gay/lesbian movement predominated by Caucasian Americans. These multiple and conflicting loyalties and processes are significant clinical aspects of either individual or family-level interventions with this population.

THEORETICAL APPROACHES TO WORKING WITH A/PIA GAY MEN AND LESBIANS AS INDIVIDUALS AND IN FAMILIES

Three prominent theoretical frameworks that inform social work practice are: the *ecological* model, the *strengths* perspective, and *empowerment.* In this section, each framework will be reviewed briefly, followed by a discussion of the application of the framework to individual and family-level interventions with Asian and Pacific Island American lesbians and gay men.

Ecological

The ecological model of social work practice posits a series of interconnected social and systems domains that influence the development of an individual in society. Compton and Galaway (1989), Hepworth and Larsen (1993), and Meyer (1983, 1988) are some of its primary proponents. Several considerations are implied in an ecological approach to social work practice with individual gay men and lesbians of Asian or Pacific Island descent: Historical messages about homosexuality, the institutionalization of gender and heterosexuality, and specific norms and tradi-tions in A/PIA cultures are a few examples of the ecological domains that help clients understand the interconnections in their lives. For family-level interven-tions using the ecological framework: The importance of family life, especially for more traditionally socialized Asian and Pacific Island lesbians and gay men, can-not be overstated. A/PIA clients—whether gay or heterosexual—universally report that their families are among their most significant social supports.

Strengths

Saleebey (1997) is the primary social work scholar to posit what he calls the frame-work known as the *strengths* perspective. The strengths perspective argues that all client groups "must be understood and assessed in the light of their capacities, competencies, knowledge, survival skills, visions, possibilities and hopes, however dashed and distorted these may have become because of oppression, discrimination, trauma, illness or abuse" (p. 17).

Working from the strengths perspective with individual A/PIA lesbians and gay men includes the following:

- While acknowledging the social stigma attached to homosexual behavior and identity, clients should be encouraged to view sexuality as a joyful and integral part of human life.
- Many A/PIA cultures have certain values and norms that reject homosexuality; however, Asian and Pacific Island cultures also tolerate diverse sexual and gender practices. A strengths perspective assists clients in learning to accept the rich diversity and sometimes contradictory traditions of their A/PIA cultures.
- Clients that are A/PIA *and* gay must not have to choose between their race/ethnicity, sexuality, or any other parts of the self that are significant to them. Social work's strengths perspective affirms the dynamic, lived experience of all aspects of human life.
- While "passing" as heterosexual is commonplace for many A/PIA lesbians and gay men, a strengths approach would suggest that passing is not necessarily shame-based or due to internalized homophobia, but perhaps a protective strategy employed to resist societal discrimination (Kanuha, 1997). This alternative analysis of passing appreciates how lesbians and gay men "have managed to survive, given their circumstances" (Saleebey, 1997, p. 17).

For A/PIA families dealing with coming out issues or adjusting to the "news" of a gay or lesbian family member, the strengths perspective might include these approaches:

- There are conflicts and struggles within most A/PIA persons who are also gay or lesbian due to intense loyalties to family and self. Deciding to affirm a lesbian or gay identity, but moreso coming out to one's family, must be viewed as a strength.
- The importance of balance in A/PIA cultures enhances the family's ability to regain equilibrium when coping with a gay and lesbian family member.

Empowerment

The theory and practice of *empowerment* in social work are implicitly linked to both the ecological and strengths perspectives. Nagda offers this working definition of empowerment:

Empowerment refers to both a process and outcome whereby persons, especially those who belong to a stigmatized social category, develop a sense of personal or collective power, increase skills in the exercise of influence and performance of valued social roles. It suggests both individual determination over one's life and democratic participation in the life of one's community (Nagda, 1996).

Applying empowerment theory to individual practice with A/PIA lesbians and gay men should include the following:

- The ability to affirm oneself as gay or lesbian, and, as a person of Asian or Pacific Island descent, occurs through joining with like others. The process of building social support networks not only builds self-esteem in an oppressive social environment but facilitates community-building for social change.
- Coming out and other acts of empowerment must be culturally compatible with the important beliefs and values of A/PIA traditions, while also acknowledging one's right to love someone of the same sex.
- By increasing their visibility and dignity as gay *and* Asian/Pacific Island persons, clients can serve as role models to empower others in their communities who are not able, willing, or prepared to come out due to the pervasive nature of societal homophobia and heterosexism in the United States and other A/PI countries.

Employing empowerment theory to family level interventions with A/PIA gay men and lesbians should incorporate the following:

- There are social networks for parents, friends, and other support people of gay men and lesbians throughout the United States, such as Parents and Friends of Lesbians and Gays (PFLAG), where Asian and Pacific Island families can gain support and serve as role models for other families in A/PIA communities.
- Gay and lesbian A/PIA parents can also join others in collective action to affirm and protect the rights of gay men and lesbians and their families.

PRACTICE PRINCIPLES

There are four fundamental practice principles that form the basis for interventions with Asian and Pacific Island Americans who are also gay or lesbian.

1. Social workers must understand and acknowledge the pervasive condemnation of homosexuality that exists in society-at-large as well as in many Asian and Pacific Island communities in the United States, in spite of significant changes in social policies and practices.

2. The dual tension of being A/PIA *and* gay is frequently mentioned as the primary life challenge and source of distress for A/PIA gay men and lesbians. The prevalence and importance of this inherent conflict cannot be underestimated in social work interventions with individuals or families.

3. Many Asian and Pacific Island cultures include beliefs and practices that recognize homosexuals, bisexuals, and transgendered persons. These traditions must be contextualized in social work practice with individuals and families dealing with A/PIA gay and lesbian issues.

4. "Coming out" as gay or lesbian is not a one-time affair, but an ongoing, life-long process. Social work practice with A/PIA gay men and lesbians must always consider the complex factors that affect revealing or concealing one's sexuality with others, and help clients assess the impact of same on themselves, their families, and their various communities.

PRACTICE SKILLS

The social work practice skills that are used in working at the individual and family levels with A/PIA lesbians and gay men build on an overview of cultural values and beliefs, social work theories and frameworks (ecological, strengths and empowerment), and principles for practice. Many of these practice skills, as they apply to the general population of lesbians and gay men, are discussed more fully in Appleby (1998), Mallon (1998b), Hidalgo (1995), and Longres (1996).

Working with Individuals

- Accept that human sexuality is at best dynamic and diverse. There is not necessarily a stable set of sexual behaviors or "best" sexual identity that individuals will maintain throughout their lifetimes.
- Do not expect that a masculine, virile Tongan man is necessarily heterosexual. Likewise, do not assume that a Vietnamese female who fits the social stereotype of the demure, exotic woman is not a lesbian.
- Learn all you can about the history of lesbian and gay life in the United States. Learn about the norms, values, beliefs and practices that are specific to the Asian or Pacific Island populations you work with. Remember to make links between the relevant concepts of gay/lesbian culture and A/PIA culture, as well as to gender, class, age, ability, and other client factors.
- Critically analyze whether the information you've obtained about gay and lesbian communities are normed predominantly on white gay men and lesbians, and whether or not information on A/PIA populations makes mention of the unique needs of its lesbian and gay members.
- Until we live in a world without heterosexism and homophobia, help clients learn to accept and manage the social stigma associated with homosexuality.
- Assume that every A/PIA client who is dealing with his or her sexuality, whether or not they are gay, may also be conflicted in part by their racial/ethnic beliefs and traditions.
- Take public advocacy positions on behalf of gay and lesbian rights. It is much easier to support Asian and Pacific Islander issues, such as Hawaiian sover-

eignty or protecting welfare benefits for Asian immigrants, than to advocate for guarantees that same-sex partners have legal benefits that are equivalent to those enjoyed by heterosexual couples.

Working with Families

- Most A/PIA lesbians and gay men, and probably more so their families, are very reluctant to seek professional assistance for issues related to sexuality for fear of "losing face." Practitioners must "start where the client is at," expecting that the therapeutic process can help restore stability in A/PIA families.

- A/PIA lesbians and gay men are also parents with their children. It is just as difficult for them to protect themselves and their children from homophobic discrimination as for heterosexual parents to deal with the effects of having gay or lesbian children.

- Social workers should consider the specific burdens of societal racism, combined with A/PIA heterosexual cultural traditions, in their understanding of family life for A/PIA gay men, lesbians, and their families.

- A/PIA families of lesbians and gay men are likely to feel shame, humiliation, anger, and fear of being "discovered" with a gay child. Some families may react by rejecting or, perhaps, disowning their children. Most A/PIA cultures do not believe in permanently severing ties with their family members (Mokuau, 1991), and, in fact, most reports confirm that A/PIA families may not enthusiastically accept their gay children but still love and support them (Duvauchelle, Kauanui, Loelani, & Thompson, 1994; Hom, 1996).

- Clinicians should focus on family interventions that foster accurate information about sexuality and homosexuality in particular, and help parents and gay/lesbian children to be sensitive and tolerant with each other as they address these challenging issues.

CASE VIGNETTE

Kimi is twenty-five years old, the only daughter of middle-class parents, a Chinese-American mother and Japanese American father born and raised in San Francisco. Kimi is a third-generation American, as both sets of grandparents were immigrants to the United States. While her parents are very acculturated to U.S. ways, they retain some of the cultural values associated with their respective ethnic origins.

Kimi always had male and female friends, but she also had "crushes" on some of her girlfriends and female teachers. As she entered puberty, Kimi felt disinterested in most boys her age. When Kimi was in her senior year of high school, she started spending more time with Cass, another seventeen-year-old Caucasian girl from a working-class family. Kimi began having sexual feelings and thoughts about Cass, which scared and confused her. Kimi had never met a lesbian, although she knew about homosexuality through the popular media and living in the Bay Area.

Kimi and Cass eventually had a sexual encounter that was exciting, fulfilling, and scary for Kimi. Her feelings of fear were almost solely related to her Chinese-Japanese background and her relationship with her parents. Kimi believed that, if her parents found out, they would be angry, disappointed, and ashamed. The more her parents questioned her about her lack of boyfriends and dates, the more Kimi withdrew into lies and distancing herself from them. The accompanying tension of maintaining a secret affair from everyone close to her led Kimi to bouts of depression that she began to manage with occasional alcohol and pot use.

On graduation from high school, Kimi decided to attend college away from her parents where she became very active in gay and lesbian groups on campus, began to "come out" with close friends at school, and, after almost three years, decided to tell her parents about being a lesbian.

When Kimi told her parents, they reacted almost as she had imagined during her years contemplating this moment. They cried and asked what they had done wrong, and how Kimi could disappoint them by deciding to be "like that." They wondered if it was the "bad influence" of Cass, her "white friend" that caused this to occur. They said it was against all their teachings and everything they believed in, and that her behavior was an insult to her ancestors. Finally, her mother said it was only "white devils" that were homosexual and that Asian people did not have such behaviors in their culture. Kimi and her parents have been estranged since she came out to them, about two months. She would like to keep working this out with them, but they have asked for no contact right now.

Case Analysis
Kimi's family background, and particularly her parents' socioeconomic class, indicates to some extent their level of acculturation and subsequent cultural belief systems about being second-generation Asian Americans.

The fact that Kimi's first sexual and affectionate relationship was with a girl who was working class and Caucasian, both at odds with Kimi's class and race status, may have compounded her parents' disappointment and resultant inability to accept her lesbian identity. Similar to most accounts about A/PIA parents of gay and lesbian children (Chan & Liu, 1996; Hom, 1996), Kimi's parents reacted to her coming out with self-blame, anger, disappointment, and, specific to Kimi's Chinese heritage, attributed her lesbian identity to "white devils."

In this case vignette, the implications for social work practice include:

- At the individual level, helping Kimi express her own feelings about her parents' reactions to her "coming out" should be a first step in the intervention. Kimi might also need help being patient about the process that her parents may have to go through in understanding her sexuality, including the fact that they might never fully accept her. Kimi might also want to talk about the impact of homophobia and sexuality on her history of depression, alcoholism, and social adjustment.
- At the family level, Kimi's parents should be allowed to express their feelings of disappointment or shame about the situation, including expressions of loss that their daughter is not "who she was supposed to be." It might also help to give them accurate facts about homosexuality, gay and lesbian life, and the

reality of A/PIA lesbians in the A/PIA community, as well as resources or contact persons on A/PIA and gay/lesbian issues.

CONCLUSION

The life histories of Jane and Al Nakatani (Fumia, 1997), a Japanese-American couple, both born and raised in Hawai'i in the early 1940s, are a fitting conclusion to this chapter on Asian and Pacific Island gay men and lesbians in the United States.

Alexander and Jane Nakatani were second-generation Japanese Americans who were socialized in the "American way" to succeed socially and academically. As Al recalls after receiving his first poor grade in college:

> I knew how important it was to keep shame from visiting our family. It was important to all the families I knew. As children, we understood without ever talking about it. I think they live in the walls of every Japanese house (Fumia, 1997, p. 38).

Al and Jane eventually married and had three sons, two of whom were gay. As Jane recounts:

> I was brought up in an environment where gays were thought to be disgusting, and we had absolutely no connection with them or even the idea of them. They were unnameable. And yet I knew gays were out there, and I was afraid . . . It was all very clear and unchallenged: Some people were to be avoided (Fumia, 1997, p. 40).

Over less than a ten-year period, all three Nakatani children would be dead, one from a shooting and two from AIDS.

The Nakatanis' story is a poignant example of the complex and important themes discussed in this chapter. As Asian Americans, both Al and Jane were acculturated to adopt middle-class U.S. norms while retaining aspects of their Asian culture, including those Japanese American values of respect for and not bringing shame to the family. They were also taught by their own and mainstream U.S. cultures to disdain homosexuality, lesbians, and gay men, and believed that this lifestyle would "disrupt" the balance in their Asian American family life.

The loss of their two gay sons to AIDS transformed the Nakatanis from a "typical" Asian American couple into social activists, who now work on behalf of HIV/AIDS, and gay/lesbian and human rights. As Al Nakatani, who also happens to be a career social worker summarizes:

> Ultimately my family's story is not about AIDS or homosexuality, but about what happens to all of us when a child is denigrated, whether it be because of race, gender, sexual orientation, size, or shape—the reason doesn't matter, and the damage is the same (Fumia, 1997, p. 313).

Social work practitioners who provide individual and family interventions with A/PIA lesbians, gay men, and their families need to develop culturally competent knowledge and skills that will enable them to heal and prevent the damage resulting from denigration of this vulnerable population.

REFERENCES

Anderson, C. W. & Smith, H. R. (1993). Stigma and honor: Gay, lesbian, and bisexual people in the U.S. military. In L. Diamant (Ed.), *Homosexual issues in the workplace* (pp. 65–89). Washington, DC: Taylor and Francis.

Appleby, G. A. & Anastas, J. W. (1998). *Not just a passing phase: Social work with gay, lesbian, and bisexual people.* New York: Columbia University Press.

Ayala, G. & Diaz, R. (In press). Racism, poverty, and other truths about sex: Race, class and HIV risk among Latino men. *Journal of Homosexuality.*

Badgett, M. V. L. (1996). Employment and sexual orientation: Disclosure and discrimination in the workplace. *Journal of Gay and Lesbian Social Services, 4* (4), 29–52.

Chan, C. S. (1997). Don't ask, don't tell, don't know: The formation of a homosexual identity and sexual expression among Asian American lesbians. In B. Greene (Ed.), *Ethnic and cultural diversity among lesbians and gay men* (pp. 240–248). Thousand Oaks, CA: Sage.

Chan, C. S. & Liu, P. (1996). Lesbian, gay, and bisexual Asian Americans and their families. In J. Laird & R. J. Green (Eds.), *Lesbians and gays in couples and families: A handbook for therapists* (pp. 137–152). San Francisco: Jossey-Bass.

Choi, K. H., Salazar, N., Lew, S., & Coates, T. J. (1995). AIDS risk, dual identity, and community response among gay Asian and Pacific Islander men in San Francisco. In G. M. Herek & B. Greene (Eds.), *AIDS, identity, and community: The HIV epidemic and lesbians and gay men* (pp. 115–134). Thousand Oaks, CA: Sage.

Compton, B. R. & Galaway, B. (1989). *Social work processes.* Belmont, CA: Wadsworth.

DeCecco, J. P. & Parker, D. A. (1995). The biology of homosexuality: Sexual orientation or sexual preference? In J. P. DeCecco & D. A. Parker (Eds.), *Sex, cells, and same-sex desire: The biology of sexual preference* (pp. 1–27). New York: Harrington Press.

Diamant, L. (Ed.). (1993). *Homosexual issues in the workplace.* Washington, DC: Taylor and Francis.

Duvauchelle, Z., Kauanui, J. K., Loelani, M., & Thompson, D. (1994). Tita talk: A cross-talk with Zelie Duvauchelle, J. Kehaulani Kauanui, Leolani M., Desiree Thompson. In S. Lim-Hing (Ed.), *The very inside: An anthology of writing by Asian and Pacific Islander lesbian and bisexual women* (pp. 85–108). Toronto, Canada: Sister Vision Press.

Dynes, W. S. & Donaldson, S. (Eds.). (1992). *Asian homosexualities.* New York: Garland.

Fumia, M. (1997). *Honor thy family: One family's journey to wholeness.* Berkeley: Conari Press.

Gonsiorek, J. C. & Weinrich, J. D. (1991). The definition and scope of sexual orientation. In J. C. Gonsiorek & J. D. Weinrich (Eds.), *Homosexuality: Research implications for public policy* (pp. 1–12). Newbury Park, CA: Sage.

Hall, L. K. C. & Kauanui, J. K. (1996). Same-sex sexuality in Pacific literature. In R. Leong (Ed.), *Asian American sexualities: Dimensions of the gay and lesbian experience* (pp. 113–118). New York: Routledge.

Hepworth, D. H. & Larsen, J. (1993). *Direct social work practice: Theory and skills.* Pacific Grove, CA: Brooks/Cole.

Herek, G. M. (1991). Stigma, prejudice and violence against lesbians and gay men. In J. C. Gonsiorek & J. D. Weinrich (Eds.), *Homosexuality: Research implications for public policy* (pp. 60–79). Newbury Park, CA: Sage.

Herek, G. M. & Berrill, K. T. (Eds.). (1992). *Hate crimes: Confronting violence against lesbians and gay men.* Newbury Park, CA: Sage.

Hidalgo, H. H. (1995). Lesbians of color: Social and human services. *Journal of Gay and Lesbian Social Services, 3* (2).

Hidalgo, H., Peterson, T. L., & Woodman, N. J. (Eds.). (1985). *Lesbian and gay issues: A resource manual for social workers.* Silver Spring, MD: National Association of Social Workers.

Hom, A. (1996). Stories from the homefront: Perspectives of Asian American parents with lesbian daughters and gay sons. In R. Leong (Ed.), *Asian American sexualities: Dimensions of the gay and lesbian experience* (pp. 38–49). New York: Routledge.

Kanuha, V. (1997). *Stigma, identity and passing: How lesbians and gay men of color construct and manage stigmatized identity in social interaction.* Unpublished doctoral dissertation, Order No. 9819258, University of Washington, Seattle.

Kanuha, V. K. (1999). *A needs assessment study of Asian and Pacific Island gay and bisexual men and HIV risk in Hawai'i.* Honolulu: Hawaii Department of Health, STD/AIDS Branch.

Kinsey, A. C., Pomeroy, W. B., & Martin, C. E. (1948). *Sexual behavior in the human male.* Philadelphia: Saunders.

Kinsey, A. C., Pomeroy, W. B., Martin, C. E., & Gebhard, P. H. (1953). *Sexual behavior in the human female.* Philadelphia: Saunders.

Laird, J. & Green, R. J. (Eds.). (1996). *Lesbians and gays in couples and families: A handbook for therapists.* San Francisco: Jossey-Bass.

Laumann, E. O., Gagnon, J. H., Michael, R. T., & Michaels, S. (1994). *The social organization of sexuality: Sexual practices in the United States.* Chicago: University of Chicago Press.

Leong, R. (Ed.). (1996). *Asian American sexualities: Dimensions of the gay and lesbian experience.* New York: Routledge.

Lim-Hing, S. (Ed.). (1994). *The very inside: An anthology of writing by Asian and Pacific Islander lesbian and bisexual women.* Toronto, Canada: Sister Vision Press.

Liu, P. & Chan, C. S. (1996). Lesbian, gay and bisexual Asian Americans and their families. In J. Laird & R. J. Green (Eds.), *Lesbians and gays in couples and families: A handbook for therapists* (pp. 137–152). San Francisco: Jossey-Bass.

Longres, J. F. (Ed.). (1996). *Men of color: A context for service for homosexually active men.* Binghamton, NY: Haworth.

Mallon, G. P. (Ed.). (1998a). *Foundations of social work practice with lesbian and gay persons.* Binghamton, NY: Harrington Park.

Mallon, G. P. (1998b). Knowledge for practice with gay and lesbian persons. In G. P. Mallon (Ed.), *Foundations of social work practice with lesbian and gay persons* (pp. 1–30). Binghamton, NY: Harrington Park.

Manalansan, M. F. (1994). Searching for community: Filipino gay men in New York City. *Amerasia Journal, 20,* 59–73.

Meyer, C. H. (Ed.). (1983). *Clinical social work in the eco-systems perspective.* New York: Columbia University Press.

Meyer, C. H. (Ed.). (1988). *The eco-systems perspective.* New York: Brunner/Mazel.

Mokuau, N. (Ed.). (1991). *Handbook of social services for Asian and Pacific Islanders.* Westport, CT: Greenwood.

Morris, R. J. (1990). Aikane: Accounts of Hawaiian same-sex relationships in the journals of Captain Cook's third voyage (1776–80). *Journal of Homosexuality, 19* (4), 21–54.

Nagda, B. R. (1996, February 19). *Empowerment of agency-based social workers: Similarities and differences between African American and White workers.* Paper presented at the Colloquium, University of Washington, School of Social Work, Seattle, WA.

Pharr, S. (1988). *Homophobia: A weapon of sexism.* Inverness, CA: Chardon Press.

Saleebey, D. (1996). The strengths perspective in social work practice: Extensions and cautions. *Social Work, 41* (3), 296–305.

Saleebey, D. (Ed.). (1997). *The strengths perspective in social work practice.* New York: Longman.

Shernoff, M. (Ed.). (1996). *Human services for gay people: Clinical and community practice.* New York: Harrington Park.

Souza, G. A. (1976). *The mahu as seen by mahu and nonmahu Hawaiian males.* Unpublished Master's thesis, University of Hawaii, Honolulu.

Sue, S. & Wagner, N. (Eds.). (1973). *Asian Americans: Psychological perspectives.* Palo Alto: Science and Behavior Books.

Takagi, D. Y. (1996). Maiden voyage: Excursion into sexuality and identity politics in Asian America. In R. Leong (Ed.), *Asian American sexualities: Dimensions of the gay and lesbian experience* (pp. 21–35). New York: Routledge.

Tully, C. (Ed.). (1996). *Lesbian social services: Research issues.* New York: Harrington Park.

Uba, L. (1995). *Asian Americans: Personality patterns, identity, and mental health.* New York: Guilford.

Uyeda, A. Y. (1994). All at once, all together: One Asian American lesbian's account of the 1989 Asian Pacific Lesbian Network Retreat. In S. Lim-Hing (Ed.), *The very inside: An anthology of writing by Asian and Pacific Islander lesbian and bisexual women* (pp. 109–122). Toronto, Canada: Sister Vision Press.

Wat, E. C. (1996). Preserving the paradox: Stories from a *gay-loh.* In R. Leong (Ed.), *Asian American sexualities: Dimensions of the gay and lesbian experience* (pp. 71–80). New York: Routledge.

Wong, F. Y., Chang, C. L., Ross, M., & Mayer, K. H. (1998). Sexualities as social roles among Asian- and Pacific Islander American gay, lesbian, bisexual, and transgender individuals: Implications for community-based health education and prevention. *Journal of the Gay and Lesbian Medical Association, 2* (4), 157–166.

Woods, J. D. (1993). *The corporate closet: The professional lives of gay men and lesbians in America.* New York: Free Press.

CHAPTER 23

INTERVENTIONS WITH KĀNAKA MAOLI, CHAMORRO, AND SAMOAN COMMUNITIES

SHARLENE B. C. L. FURUTO

RONALD JOHN SAN NICOLAS

GWENDOLYN E. KIM

LOIA M. FIAUI

This chapter describes three communities, the *Kānaka Maoli*/Hawaiian community in Hawaii, the Chamorro community in Guam, and the Samoan community in Hawaii. Each community is described by an author who resides in that community. Issues are presented and principles and practice skills for working with each community are described. A comparative analysis is made of the three communities, with closing remarks centered on social justice with these Pacific Island communities.

WORKING WITH THE *KĀNAKA MAOLI*/ HAWAIIAN COMMUNITY

As indigenous and "minority" populations in Western societies struggle against negative labeling and stereotyping, a basic assumption that must be understood is the destructive process that occurs as one culture asserts hegemony over another. *Kānaka maoli* (indigenous people of *ka pae'aina* or Hawai'i) have experienced this systematic process prior to and since the illegal overthrow of the Hawaiian government by the United States in 1893 (Blaisdell & Mokuau, 1991). We need to understand this destructive domination process and the people's history and culture to work effectively with *Kānaka maoli* communities.

Costly Western-oriented programs are not relevant to *Kānaka maoli* communities as they mirror the dominant system from which the problems emanate, rather than looking to the community for their inherent strengths (Kingsley, McNeely, & Gibson, 1997). Another basic contradiction exists in that a community-driven program can become so successful in challenging the status quo that it could endanger future funding. This part of the chapter will discuss characteristics of successful programs in native communities—community-based, community-driven, and culturally competent—in the hope that these programs can be replicated and funded.

Sociodemographic Overview, Problems, and Issues

The population of *ka pae'aina* according to the 1995 U.S. Census was estimated at 1.186 million, of whom a low estimate of 210,000 are believed to be *Kānaka maoli*. The pre-Western contact population is estimated at 1 million and, almost one hundred years later, in 1876, had decreased to 40,000 due to lack of immunity to introduced contagious diseases (Blaisdell & Mokuau, 1991). *Kānaka maoli* today make up 36.5 percent of all people in prison and are overrepresented there and on public assistance rolls (Office of Hawaiian Affairs, 1998).

In the mid-1800s, *Kānaka maoli* had one of the highest literacy rates in the world in their own language, as "formal literacy became almost universal" (Reinecke, 1969). Following the imposition of English and the devaluation of native language and culture, 30 percent of native adults presently are identified with the greatest literacy needs (Omnitrak, 1989). Accurate knowledge of history creates a context for understanding the downward spiral in social indicators, creating fertile ground for the current sovereignty movement.

Values and Behavioral Norms

Kānaka maoli culture is antithetical in many ways to Western culture. It highly esteems the *'ohana* (extended family), which oftentimes lives together under one roof. The *'ohana* is the root of one's identity and basic to forming interrelationships with others. Private land ownership is in direct conflict with the traditional concept that one never "owns" the land, as we are all only caretakers.

A treasured value is *lōkahi*, living in harmony with others and the environment. This value is manifested by preferring to share rather than save, helping others before focusing on oneself, and working collectively as a team member rather than competitively and individualistically.

Another value of *Kānaka maoli* is pride in the culture. *Kānaka maoli* have increasingly become educated in their own language. Importantly, they can now go to original documents and translate history, describing the full impact of colonial devastation rather than accepting the Western version (Kame'eleihiwa, 1992).

Macro Interventions

After working for a number of years in *Kānaka maoli* communities, I have concluded that successful programs have the three Cs: community-based, community-driven, and culturally competent along vertical and horizontal dimensions. *Community-based* is having staff hired from the community, and the program is located in the community it serves. *Community-driven* means that people from that community are involved in making key decisions about the structure and content of the program, such as "who, what, where and how." *Culturally competent* is having staff with a deep understanding of the people and place, an understanding reflected in program content, policies, procedures, and the living character of the program.

Nā Kamalei (Precious Children): An Early Education Program.   In mid-1995 our rural Oahu community of approximately 20,000 was shaken by the decision of our funding source, a large private educational trust, to discontinue a number of programs that directly affected our area. One such program, a traveling preschool program for two- and three-year-olds accompanied by parents, ran twice a week for two hours a day. What subsequently occurred was the formation of a successful new program that demonstrated the three Cs based on a holistic, ecological approach.

   1. A *community-driven process* occurred immediately in a meeting sponsored by our agency, where concern was expressed. An action committee of volunteers and staff organized a petition drive and secured a meeting with a key Trustee to present their case. Realizing they were unsuccessful in convincing the powers-that-be to reconsider, community members resolved to do it themselves. After numerous community meetings garnering a broad base of both vertical and horizontal support, they began with a volunteer teacher, a site, donated equipment, and eight families. Three years later, there is a maximum enrollment of twenty-five families (approximately thirty-five children), a waiting list that never goes below thirty-five, native teachers who have earned certification via the program, and a strong parent/community board and council. Parent education and leadership development are built into the program. Future plans include expansion, independent nonprofit status, and documentation of the culturally competent curriculum. Resource experts are consistently consulted, but they come to the table as equal partners and do not drive or shape the vision.

   2. A *program is community-based* if its staff is from the community and its site office is located there, making it easily accessible by car and public transportation. Who knows best what is needed than the very people the program targets? The lead teacher sought was someone with teaching skills as a highly respected *kapa* (a maker of cloth from tree bark), chanter, and hula instructor. A conscious attempt was made to seek those already regarded by the community as native healers and helpers. A strong program of staff development and leadership training was provided. The underlying assumption is that it is easier to teach educational concepts and skills to committed cultural practitioners than to instill commitment and teach cultural competence.

      Critical here is that these training opportunities do not train out of staff those very characteristics that made them most effective in the first place. Otherwise, a terrible process can occur of training cultural sensitivity and competence out of the grassroots native practitioner as the system "professionalizes" them (Moss &

Wightman, 1993). For example, emphasizing Western clock time rather than task completion and maintaining professional distance are both undervalued by the *Kānaka maoli* community. Respected *kupuna* (elder) Malia Craver said that *"aloha kekahi i kekahi"* (that we love one another), is most important and how is this done at a "distance"?

3. *Culturally competent practice* is at first perceived in an almost instinctual way—one feels it. Everything comes together in a certain way. This is how *Nā Kamalei* feels. Interactions reflect extended *'ohana.* Everyone takes responsibility for the children. It is difficult to tell staff from parents and volunteers. Learning and play stations are not individually or nuclear family-focused. *Lōkahi* and teamwork are emphasized. Interactions are organic, not linear or hierarchical.

One day a fisherman may visit to demonstrate net-throwing, another day an auntie may come to teach weaving of tree fronds. Native language, chants, and instruments are utilized. Pride in culture, historic strengths and skills are reflected in every aspect of the program. Contextual paradigms of thinking are *of* the people, not *at* the people.

The importance of making connections with each other is demonstrated as people are joined as friends, and honor is bestowed when help is given at deeper levels and one becomes viewed as a member of the extended family. A hierarchical professional relationship and distance are not relevant; rather, different skills and abilities are to be appreciated and shared as resources in respectful ways.

Community people come with experiential cultural competence. As leaders and designers of this program, experience is then raised to a higher level in identifying what works, what doesn't, and how so much of the Western curriculum does not connect with the children. Comparative critical analysis then occurs, rather than just passive acceptance or passive resistance, and there is true ownership. Practice and experience move to the realm of theory and consciousness and foster cultural competence and excellence.

Strengths, Empowerment, and Ecological Approaches

As can be seen in the above community example, the strengths perspective and ecological theory are applicable when working with *Kānaka maoli.* They are the most sensitive to their needs and solutions, and have the collective knowledge, creativity, and wisdom to develop, implement, and evaluate programs. Powerful systems that touch the lives of native people are all too often represented by faces not of their ethnicity. The joy and relief of greeting another islander, knowing that so much need not be explained or justified, is deep. On the other hand, as a nonnative, born and raised here in a rural area, surrounded by cultural practices, I have almost always been greeted and welcomed with *aloha,* as I, too, continue my journey of learning. In those rare instances when I have experienced rejection and hostility, my understanding of history and the present-day situation help to keep balance and understand that the hostility is not directed at me as an individual.

Coming from an oral tradition, verbal skills are highly prized and demonstrated by shared storytelling rather than the assertive verbalization valued in Western society. The aggressive debate format is seen as arrogant and intrusive. Sincerity and humility are highly valued as a demonstration of respect and the willingness to continually learn from one another. Knowledge and skills are readily shared when someone is approached with genuine respect, but his or her initial reaction may be wary and self-protective due to past negative experiences. For the beginning practitioner, it is best to talk less and listen more. What you do and say will be closely observed. You will be judged by your work and actions. Given an opportunity to speak, choose your words carefully and make your most important point. The relevant sharing of self and use of allegory or metaphor are good if you have the skill. Skill can only be built by preparation, practice, and the courage to try.

Kānaka maoli, long acutely aware of their environment, adapt readily to the ecological theory and all its related components. They are an inclusive people and their present-day wariness is based on a history of hurt. They have a history of intense political involvement and participate actively in their local and broader communities.

Practice Skills and Practice Principles

Two basic skills—verbal and nonverbal communication—can be perplexing and detract from working in the community. Macro practitioners must be aware of allegorical and metaphorical communication, realizing that comments, seemingly unrelated, are actually significant. For example, committee members might be trying to decide whether to partner with another group to create a stronger coalition. As they discuss the pros and cons, someone may interject, "Last night I had a bad dream. My family went on a hike. While crossing a stream, it suddenly rose, sweeping some of us down. I was hanging onto the roots of a tree. I woke up in a sweat." This could well be the speaker's attempt to express that the plan is not sitting well with her, but she doesn't want to be direct and offend or hurt anyone. Macro practitioners must recognize such indirect communication as related to the topic. Relating the dream might not be rejection, only an observation that the timing might not be good.

The role of food as part of protocol should also be addressed. Food connects people, and it is traditional to mark the beginning and end of endeavors with food. Most generic macro-practice methods and skills apply and should be done within the cultural context.

Conclusions

Being community-based, community-driven, and culturally competent characterize successful initiatives that have great potential for sustainability. It is important that programs with these characteristics be supported and replicated.

Our profession has a proud history, born of social movements and based on a strong belief in social justice and dignity. When we study history, communities, and cultures, we realize the only direction forward is to base ourselves there, develop truly humane alternatives, and commit to change at the macro-level.

ÁFÁMAOLEK: COLLABORATIVE SOCIAL WORK PRACTICE WITH CHAMORROS IN GUAM

The Chamorro communities from Guam and the Mariana Islands are best described as extensions of the family system and kinship groups. For Chamorros, *áfámaolek* (collaboration) is a core cultural value that promotes a sense of harmony and interdependence among all individuals. It is important for social workers engaged in community practice with Chamorro communities to appreciate this value, because it describes the worldview of the people of the Mariana Islands.

Sociodemographic Overview

Guam, where the United States' day begins, describes the unincorporated territory farthest west of the United States. The Organic Act of Guam, passed into law by the United States Congress in 1950, naturalized the indigenous population as U.S. citizens and created the term *Guamanian* to distinguish and identify the residents of Guam. The island's indigenous and largest ethnic group is the Chamorro people (see Table 23.1). The name *Chamorro,* used interchangeably with *Guamanian,* is a racial, ethnic, and cultural term describing the people of the Mariana Islands.

TABLE 23.1   Ethnic Composition of Guam's Total Population

TOTAL POPULATION	133,152	
Ethnic Origin	*Total*	*Percentage*
Chamorro	49,935	37.5%
Filipino	30,043	22.5%
Caucasian	19,160	14.3%
Korean	3,391	2.9%
African American	3,158	2.4%
Japanese	2,244	1.7%
Chinese	1,959	1.5%
Chuukese	1,919	1.4%
Paluan	1,858	1.4%
Other Micronesian Islanders	1,095	1.0%
*Carolinian		
*Kosraean		
*Marshallese		
*Pohnpeian		
*Yapese		
Other Ethnic Groups	17,850	13.4%
Total	132,616	100%

Source: 1990 U.S. Census

Cultural Values and Behavioral Norms

There are unique cultural values and behavioral norms that describe the Chamorro people in Guam and the Mariana Islands. For example, honor and respect for one's own family and relatives is a paramount value for Chamorros. The social status of Chamorros and Asian Pacific Islanders is determined by an individual's immediate and extended family. For Chamorros, *y familia* (the family) is the basic nurturing and socializing force that maintains and enforces social mores, values, and beliefs. Concern for one's own family is expressed in honor, respect, and the sacrifices one is willing to endure for parents, children, the elderly, and the disabled. Mutual cooperation and the maintenance of harmony are equally important values for Chamorros. For Chamorros, collaboration or cooperation is an important value for relating to one's family and community on the basis of trust, respect, and a sense of obligation toward each other. This value emphasizes fostering interdependence based on reciprocity.

Profiles of Social Problems and Issues

Over the past eighty years, the population in Guam grew rapidly, saw considerable shift in its ethnic composition, and noted significant cultural changes from its traditions. These changes occurred gradually and cannot be compared to the rapid modernization or Americanization of the Island following World War II. Prior to the turn of the century, the Chamorro way of life was propelled from an agrarian, extended family system to an individualistic and capitalistic society. Agriculture was replaced by a dependency on the importation of all its food and goods at expensive prices. Guam's transition to a Western way of life was accomplished within a fifty-year period. While Guam's cultural heterogeneity is shifting, social tensions have also increased. As a result, problems such as high rates of substance abuse, violent crimes, homicide, and suicide may be partially attributed to the cultural transitions and demographic changes the island and its people face.

Social Work Practice Focus

Theoretically, the collaborative approach is fundamental to social work practice and emphasizes client self-determination (Biestek & Gehrig, 1978), consideration of the person-in-environment fit (Germain, 1979), the reinforcement of client strengths (Saleebey, 1997), the building of client competencies (Maluccio, 1981), and the understanding of reciprocal interactions between the client groups and the practitioner (Petr, 1988). In social work practice, collaboration is described as the process of working together with client groups in such a way that the client's needs are given due consideration (Hatfield, 1994). This is a departure from traditional hierarchical relationships in which the social worker assumes the expert role, retaining the balance of the power while clients play a passive role. In a collaborative approach, power is shared. This means that the social worker and clients work together in defining the problem, share in the decision-making process, and maintain shared responsibilities.

The following discusses the intervention principles that are culturally relevant to social work practice with Chamorro communities.

Developing Professional Cooperation and Community Teamwork.   *Áfámaolek* is important when working with the Chamorro community. Collaborative practice with Chamorros requires that the social worker become proactive in nurturing cooperation while, at the same time, remembering that, even under the best circumstances, building community teamwork can be challenging. The social worker must be committed to creating and reinforcing cooperative behavior.

Empowerment.   *Aturisa* (empowerment) is an important aspect of collaborative practice with Chamorros. Guiterrez (1990) describes empowerment as a process of increasing personal, interpersonal, or political power so that individuals take action to improve their life situations. The primary role of the social worker is to assist the client to develop a sense of control and power.

Recognition of Strengths.   Equally important to the empowerment process is *y kualidát taotao*, the recognition of client strengths. Building on strengths is based on the assumption in social work practice that clients possess the abilities to better their life situation. Because this perspective views clients as the true experts regarding their situations, the social worker's role is that of a facilitator or consultant (Sheafor, Horejsi, Horejsi, 1994). While the social worker does bring professional expertise to the working relationship, the social worker is not necessarily the sole expert. In essence, the social worker and client are viewed as complementary resources in facilitating change.

Instilling in Clients and Their Families a Vision of Hope to Learn and Grow.   An important intervention in social work practice is instilling in clients a vision of *dishea* (hope) to learn and grow from their life difficulties. In community practice, the social worker can offer new perspectives and use techniques that lend encouragement and assist client groups to achieve their desired aspirations in life.

> **CASE VIGNETTE**
>
> During the early 1980s, the Guam Department of Mental Health and Substance Abuse helped to facilitate the establishment of a local nonprofit community organization for families of the seriously mentally ill. The Guam Alliance for Mental Health, Incorporated (GAMHI) was organized with the same goals and objectives as the National Alliance for the Mentally Ill (NAMI).
>
> Unfortunately, GAMHI became defunct apparently due to the stigma and lack of interest experienced by families. Over the past two years, mental health social workers have attempted to reorganize the dormant organization at the grassroots level by focusing on the development of a collaborative relationship with clients and families.
>
> A primary goal of the community organization efforts was for the mental health social workers to help empower Chamorro families of the seriously mentally ill to recognize their potential to improve their life situations regardless of the difficulties they experienced. The interventions used to reorganize the GAMHI, focused

on building and fostering the strengths and positive attributes of all the individuals involved. This process also generated a team-building approach consistent with the Chamorro value of *áfámaolek.* Equally important, the interventions were directed toward helping clients and their families view the role of the mental health social workers as consultants who possessed the skills and knowledge necessary to help them address their collective needs and aspirations.

While there remains more work ahead for the organization, the GAMHI is now poised to carry out its mission of educating the public about mental illness and advocating for the improved quality of mental health in the community. The challenge for mental health social workers in Guam is to continue developing and fostering collaborative relationships with Chamorro client groups.

Conclusion

The concept of collaboration is central to the long-standing professional commitment of social work to client self-determination (Sullivan, 1992). Applied to community practice, collaboration requires that the worker and client groups define the area of interest and establish a set of measurable and achievable goals to guide the process of change. Community organization that is empowerment-based emphasizes the active participation of clients in the change process. This requires a team-building effort to help client groups view themselves as causal agents in achieving solutions and accomplishing their aspirations in life.

Embedded in a collaborative approach with Chamorros are several key principles that include the development of professional cooperation and community teamwork, empowerment, recognition of strengths, and instilling in clients a vision of hope to learn and grow from their life experiences. The collaborative approach is congruent with the principles and assumptions found in social work and applicable to practice with Chamorro communities in Guam.

WORKING WITH THE SAMOAN COMMUNITY

The purpose of this part of this chapter is to present an overview of the Samoan community, with a focus on intervention using the ecological, strengths, and empowerment approaches. I will conclude with a discussion of principles and skills that would be well-received by the Samoan community and end with a vignette of Kuhio Park Terrace, a low-income housing complex which is also a Samoan community.

SOCIODEMOGRAPHIC OVERVIEW AND PROBLEMS IN THE SAMOAN COMMUNITY

Samoans entered the United States particularly in the 1950s when the U.S. military base at Pago Pago, American Samoa closed and Samoan servicemen and their families moved to Hawaii. Today, approximately 63,000 Samoans live in the United

States, most of whom are from American Samoa (U.S. Census, 1998). Fifty percent of the Samoans live in California and 24 percent live in Hawaii (U.S. Bureau of the Census, 1998). Samoan families are large with several generations living in the same dwelling, and about 52 or 53 percent of Samoans in Hawaii live in public housing (Fiaui, 1999).

Samoans frequently have a difficult time making the transition from an agrarian village to the technologically advanced lifestyle of a complex society with values sometimes the opposite of those "back home." As a result, Samoans are disproportionately overrepresented in prison, public housing, and as family violence perpetrators, while being underrepresented in professional positions and on university campuses.

While 10 percent of all public school students in Hawaii were suspended in the 1997–1998 academic year, 17 percent of all Samoan students were suspended— the second highest rate of all ethnic students suspended (LeMahieu, unpublished report). Samoan youth decisively lead all other ethnic youth groups in Hawaii by being overrepresented in juvenile arrests and Family Court cases, relative to their proportion in the general youth population (Kassebaum, 1995).

American Samoans experience serious problems in obtaining jobs, with unemployment rates as high as 80 percent among young adult Samoans in Los Angeles and Seattle (Northwest Regional Educational Laboratory Division of Evaluation, Research and Assessment, 1983). The employed are oftentimes in service-related areas (Fiaui, 1999). In terms of health, Samoans at all ages and of both sexes are considerably heavier than most U.S. males (McPherson, et al., 1978).

Samoan Cultural Values and Behavioral Norms: Start and/or Resolve Problems

Several classic, highly treasured Samoan values can both help and keep this marginalized group from poverty as well as advancement in society. For example, Samoans value the *aiga* (the entire family), and, while this value strengthens the family back home, it can be a limitation in the United States, where four "visiting" adult cousins can stay for six months without helping with expenses. Meanwhile, in an effort to keep harmony—another value highly esteemed—in the family and to fulfill expectations, the result can be delinquent utility bills.

Samoans value their *matai* (chief/extended family head), donating several hundred dollars regularly and frequently at his request for extended family expenses such as funerals, weddings, medical bills, travel, and so forth. While this contributory custom, called *fa'a lavelave,* helps some family members financially, it also strains the already small income of other family members.

Most Samoans attend church weekly and are strongly influenced by their *faife'au* (minister). Unfortunately, membership in these Samoan-speaking churches also keeps many Samoans from networking with powerful non-Samoans and using non-Samoan resources in the community.

Samoans respect the vertical position of power, whereby the *matai* (chief) tells the *aiga* (extended family heads) what to do and they, in turn, direct their family members. Major decisions have traditionally been made by the *matai,* keeping married men from making decisions at home. At work, supervisors may view Samoan personnel waiting to be told what to do as "lacking initiative, indecisive, lazy" and, therefore, not qualified for pay raises.

Intervention with the Samoan Community

Clearly the Samoan community is having a difficult time surviving today. Social workers need to be trained in social work to understand the collective, hierarchical leadership nature of Samoan *matai* (chief) and *faife'au* (minister) and how to use these cultural strengths to work conjointly with them on the micro-, mezzo-, and macrolevels. In so doing, we will foster macro social work practice according to the *fa'a Samoa* (the Samoan way) and work more effectively with the Samoan community.

Using the Ecological, Strengths, and Empowerment Approaches with the Samoan Community.   The social worker can successfully use all three approaches when working with the Samoan community. The Samoan community may include the following influential leadership components: *matai* council, church *faife'au,* public housing tenant association officers, local Samoan association officials, educated Samoans, and well-known Samoan athletes or singers who live in or near the Samoan community, visiting Samoans who may be well-connected back home, Samoan radio or TV program personalities, editors of Samoan newspapers, Samoan parent leaders who promote education for their children in the schools, and so on.

Social workers need to identify the strengths of the Samoan community: first, a decision-making structure already in place with community members ready to follow; second, an intense ethnic pride that can energize fund-raising, training, or health projects; third, a strong, organized religious system that can immediately and regularly communicate with nearly the entire Samoan community; fourth, a close-knit community bonded by blood, marriage, religion, and/or ethnicity; fifth, deep respect for the community leaders, *faife'au,* and elders; sixth, a vibrant mutual assistance bond between extended family members; and, seventh, the way in which service to family, friends, and community is highly revered.

The leadership infrastructure is already organized in the Samoan community, allowing the macro social worker to focus on empowering the local Samoan leadership to learn the U.S. system, organize, and meet their needs. The Samoan indigenous leadership, and the *faife'au,* take their roles and status seriously and actively lead the community, and their constituents readily follow.

Practice Principles and Skills When Working with the Samoan Community. The locality development model does not seem to fit well with the hierarchical power structure of the Samoan community nor does the social planning model, because a macro level practitioner would be intrusive in the Samoan community. The social action model is inconsistent with the more harmony-oriented behavioral norm of the Samoan people.

Perhaps the best model to use when working with the Samoan community follows the ecological, strengths, and empowerment approaches: Become familiar with the history of the Samoan people back home and in their new community; learn the customs of the people in their community; start from the top down by first getting to know many matai *faife'au,* Samoan association officers, educated, and well-known Samoans; bring gifts of food when meeting with select matai and *faife'au* for the first time; ask how you can participate and help; discuss problems from the Samoan perspective; meet with others and *faife'au* individually and collectively for them to reach consensus in assessment and development of a plan of action; await the *matai* and *faife'au* announcement of the plans to their constituents for their support; be a shadow facilitator while helping them implement the plan within the community; allow community leaders to evaluate and terminate the project and their relationship with you.

Social work practitioners with the Samoan community may need to be passive and await instructions from the leaders in following customary procedures. In addition, the following macro skills are also useful: lobbying, grant writing, and teaching the leadership to lobby and apply for grants. While many Samoan leaders are accustomed to the political process back home, few are involved in the U.S. political arena. Grant writing is a new phenomenon to the Samoan community, and a valuable source of external funds.

CASE VIGNETTE: KUHIO PARK TERRACE: A PUBLIC HOUSING SAMOAN COMMUNITY
Kuhio Park Terrace (KPT) is a high-rise public housing project in Honolulu. Because approximately 63 percent of the tenants are of Samoan ethnicity (Mageo Aga, 1999), in many ways KPT is a disadvantaged Samoan community. It is appropriate to bring the concept of school to the housing project/community because Samoans value education and refrain from "outside" services. The macro practitioner should get approval from the adult education principal to bring trained personnel and Samoan cultural specialists to KPT to teach English as a Second Language, assimilation and adjustment learning experiences, vocational English, and also U.S. and Samoan culture.

The macro practitioner should be in touch with the *Matai* Council at the housing project, the church *faife'au* who live at KPT (or whose members reside there), and leaders of the KPT Tenants Association. In advance, the macro-practitioner should identify the most highly respected elder of those invited to the meeting to ask if he wants the "school." All suggestions and comments the elder makes should be used to indicate the macro practitioner's respect for the leader and acceptance of the *fa'a Samoa* (Samoan way). After the planning meeting for the leaders, a full meal should follow. The older, highly respected elder should be invited to facilitate discussion and decision making among the leaders.

Decisions the leaders make can be communicated to the Samoan community over the pulpit by the *faife'au* when he makes announcements to his congregation. Other Samoan leaders use Samoan radio and TV programs, and Samoan newspapers. Many older Samoans depend on radio programs such as Samoa Malo Ua

Maua, Inc. in Hawaii, which is appreciated for its free public-service announcements, food basket donations (valued at $75,000 a year), and a lot of of free clothing.

Conclusion

Samoans in the United States are struggling as they enter the new millenium. As human service workers become more aware of their worldviews, reality, and strengths, we will be better able to further empower them. The Samoan community is particularly fortified and ready for macro practitioners because Samoan communities already have well-functioning decision-making and communication structures. A culturally competent model for macro practice that highlights the strengths, empowerment, and ecological approaches by collaborating with the *Matai* Council and *faife'au* should be used for best results. This model differs considerably from the three classic community development models. The many strengths of the existing *matai* and church structures of the Samoan community should be used to enhance their lifestyle.

ANALYZING *KĀNAKA MAOLI*, CHAMORRO, AND SAMOAN COMMUNITIES

This section contrasts the three Pacific Island communities by looking at their similarities, differences, and areas in which macro social workers can perhaps best support them.

Kānaka maoli, Chamorro, and Samoan communities have many similarities, several of which will be mentioned. First, all three communities are compatible with the ecological approach. The communities, while varying from the more structured Samoan and Chamorro communities with their *faifeau, matai,* and village mayors to the more loosely organized Hawaiian community, all have extended relationships with their immediate and greater environment (schools, local to federal governments, *matai* council, ethnic organizations, community associations, etc.). A second way in which all three communities are similar is that they all firmly value the extended family and community and strive for harmonious interactions. Distance by miles and by relationship do not keep extended family members at an emotional or social distance; for example, a "second cousin twice removed" or a *hanai* (a relative or person adopted in the traditional Kānaka maoli system) is family and accorded due respect. Individuals try to resolve conflict in a harmonious manner. In addition, *Kānaka maoli,* Chamorros, and Samoans living in their ethnic communities are proud to reside there with their distinct cultural and ethnic uniqueness and try to resolve issues harmoniously.

Two other situations impact disadvantaged Pacific Islanders in terms of social work practice. The U.S. government illegally took over Hawaii in 1898 and Guam after World War II and has neither returned the land back to Kānaka maoli and Chamorros nor compensated them for the continued use. Not owning land on a small island has resulted in serious economic and accompanying social problems to the indigenous peoples. In the Christian realm, Samoans and Chamorros have a high sense of religiosity, with approximately 92 percent of the Chamarros and a clear majority of the Samoans attending church.

Macro practice with *Kānaka maoli*, Chamorros, and Samoans has some distinct differences in terms of social worker roles and strategies. Kānaka maoli in Hawaii prefer the social service program planner to be a facilitator, mediator, and sensitive to being a leader and follower as appropriate. Macro-practitioners should base their efforts on facilitating community-based, community-driven, and culturally competent programs. Word-of-mouth from family to family seems to be the best way for inter-community communication regarding social programs.

Chamorros in Guam prefer the macro-practitioner to share the power and authority with the indigenous leaders. Appropriate roles for the social worker include being a collaborator, facilitator, enabler, and consultant. Chamorros prefer that the social worker work with the community through the immediate and extended family in mutual cooperation. A macro practitioner who recognizes and facilitates the community strengths while instilling hope would be welcomed.

The Samoan community, with its well-defined hierarchical structure through the *matai* and church systems, prefers the social worker to play a secondary role. Usually the *matai* or *faife'au* knows the community issues and has an idea of how to address them. They oftentimes have in mind how they want to use the social worker. On the other hand, in many communities the social worker can proactively align with the *matai* and *faife'au* to collaborate or lead in resolving community issues. The macro-practitioner should keep in mind the significance of culture and religion and use both in the plan of action. For example, the *faife'au* can facilitate communication by making announcements from the pulpit and advertising a fund-raising activity that will feature Samoan food, dances, and music.

Where Is Social Justice?

The social work profession has been making commendable advances in working with diverse communities. We have gone from ignoring ethnic groups to working with them in a culturally competent manner to currently recognizing the need to advocate and assure social justice for them.

Social justice for the Chamorros and *Kānaka maoli* means that their land will be returned to them or that they will be fairly compensated. White and ethnic social workers alike need to stand together with the Chamorros and *Kānaka maoli* and regain the lost land by actively organizing, petitioning, demonstrating, lobbying, fund-raising, forming coalitions, networking, attending committee meetings, brainstorming—in short, whatever it takes.

Samoans in the United States and American Samoa are U.S. nationals and as such can vote in state and federal elections and qualify for civil service jobs only if they give up their American Samoan citizenship and become naturalized U.S. citizens. This is a dilemma for many, particularly in respect to property ownership in American Samoa. Culturally competent social workers encourage Samoans to register and vote for those who share their perspectives while justice-oriented social workers help Samoans become naturalized U.S. citizens, run for office, and author bills that reflect the needs of their people.

Practitioners truly committed to the profession of social work are also compelled to work actively on an issue that will ensure social justice for others in the community.

REFERENCES

Biestek, F. P. & Gehrig, C. G. (1978). *Client-self determination in social work: A fifty-year history.* Chicago: University of Chicago Press.

Blaisdell, Kekuni & Mokuau, Noreen. (1991). Kānaka Maoli, indigenous Hawaiians. In N. Mokuau (Ed.), In *Handbook of social services for Asians and Pacific Islanders* (pp. 131–154). Westport, CT: Greenwood.

Fiaui, Loia. (1999). Faa Samoa 2000 Committee and Council of Samoan Churches of Hawaii, Honolulu, Hawaii. Unpublished data.

Germain, C. B. (1979). Ecology and social work. In C. B. Germain (Ed.), *Social work practice: People and environments* (pp. 1–22). New York: Columbia University Press.

Gutierrez, L. M. (1990). Working with women of color: An empowerment perspective. *Social Work, 35* (2), 149–153.

Hatfield, A. B. (1994). The family's role in caregiving and service delivery. In H. P. Lefley & M. Wasow (Eds.), *Helping families cope with mental illness* (pp. 65–78). City, State: Harwood Academic.

Hawaii Statewide Literacy Assessment. (1989). Presented to Governor's Office of Children and youth by Omnitrack Research and Marketing Group, Inc., Honolulu, Hawaii.

Kame'eleihiwa, Lilikala. (1992). *Native land and foreign desires.* Honolulu, HI: Bishop Museum Press.

Kassebaum, Gene. (1995, March). *Identifying disproportionate representation of ethnic groups in Hawaii's juvenile justice system: Phase one.* Honolulu: Center for Youth Research, Social Science Research Institute, University of Hawaii at Manoa.

Kingsley, Thomas G., McNeely, Joseph B., & Gibson, James O. (1997). *Community building coming of age: Development Training Institute and Urban Institute, Inc.* Washington, DC: Publisher.

LeMahieu, Paul. (1999, August). State of Hawaii Department of Education unpublished data given to the Health Department.

Luce, Pat & Mamak, Alex. (n.d.). *Samoan Americans in employment and training.* National Office of Samoan Affairs, 1855 Folsom Street, San Francisco, California 94103.

Mageo Aga, Simeamativa. Personal communication, June 22, 1999.

Maluccio, A. N. (1981). Competence-oriented social work practice: An ecological approach. In A. Maluccio (Ed.), *Promoting competence in clients: A new/old approach in social work practice.* New York: Free Press.

McPherson, Cluny, Shore, Bradd, & Franco, Robert. Eds. (1978, September). *New Neighbors . . . Islanders in Adaptation.* Center for South Pacific Studies, University of California, Santa Cruz.

Moss, Barbara & Wightman, Barbara. (1993, August/September). From use of skills to use of self: Professional development through training to enhance relationships. *Zero to Three* Washington, DC: National Center for Infants, Toddlers and Families.

Native Hawaiian data book. (1998). Office of Hawaiian Affairs, Honolulu, Hawaii.

Northwest Regional Educational Laboratory Division of Evaluation, Research and Assessment. (May 6, 1983). *Technical Proposal for (Part 2) Study of Unemployment, Poverty, and Training Needs of American Samoans.* Portland, Oregon.

Petr, C. G. (1988). The social worker–client relationship: A general systems perspective. *Social Casework, 69,* 620–626.

Reinecke, John. (1969). *Language and dialect in Hawaii*. Honolulu, HI: University of Hawaii Press.

Saleebey, D. A. (1997). *The strengths perspective in social work practice*, 2nd ed. New York: Longman.

Sheafor, B. W., Horejsi, C. R., & Horejsi, G. A. (1994). *Techniques and guidelines for social work practice*, 3rd ed. Boston: Allyn & Bacon.

Sullivan, W. P. (1992). Reclaiming the community: The strengths perspective and deinstitutionalization. *Social Work, 37*, 204–209.

U.S. Bureau of the Census. (1998). *Statistical abstract of the United States: 1998*. Washington, DC: U.S. Government Printing Office.

U.S. Bureau of the Census. (1995). *Statistical abstract of the United States: 1995*. Washington, DC: U.S. Government Printing Office.

U.S. Bureau of the Census. (1990). *Statistical abstract of the United States: 1990*. Washington, DC: U.S. Government Printing Office.

CHAPTER 24

EVALUATION SKILLS WITH AFRICAN AMERICAN INDIVIDUALS AND FAMILIES: THREE APPROACHES

EDDIE DAVIS

The professional social worker must be skilled in the delivery of intervention and skilled at evaluating the effectiveness of the intervention(s) used. "Evaluation is directed towards measuring the results (dependent variables) of . . . interventions, and the nature of the interventions themselves (the independent variables), with a research design that allows the outcome to be measured in the change process . . ." in a summative way (Compton & Galaway, 1999, p. 457). For intervention with African Americans, this process may be complicated by social work's Eurocentric framework. Such complications occur because, as Schriver (1998) notes:

> The traditional and dominant paradigm is inordinately influenced by, and its content controlled by, white persons of European descent. What this has come to mean is that all persons, both white and nonwhite, have come to be judged or evaluated in virtually all areas of life according to standards that reflect the values, attitudes, experiences, and historical perspectives of white persons, specifically white persons of European descent (p. 64).

Therefore, special efforts must be made in designing interventions and in evaluating their effectiveness with African American individuals and families. Each social worker must pay close attention to the African American client's birth, process of development, and current existence within mainstream U.S. society.

African Americans are "buffeted by overpowering forces in the society at large that are beyond their control" (Massaquoi, 1993, p. 30). On a daily basis they struggle to keep from being sucked into the "black hole" of Eurocentric U.S. mainstream culture. To lose that struggle means the loss of psychosocial identity. Everything that is uniquely African American then becomes defined as "deviant or pathological" by Euro-American standards. Skinner (1971) made the point that "a culture, like a species, is selected by its adaptation to an environment; to the extent that it helps its members to get what they need and avoid what is dangerous, it helps them to survive and transmit the culture" (p. 123).

SOCIODEMOGRAPHIC OVERVIEW

The African American that the mass media present does not exist. African Americans are as diverse as any other U.S. ethnic group. Reid (1976) states that the image of *"the African American"* is further distorted by research that is considered to be legitimate. She argues that "white studies tend to focus on the pathology of the black family, and on low-income families, equating poverty with racial inferiority" (p. 44). African Americans make up approximately 13 percent of the population of the United States, and "nationally, African American families, which comprise more than 30 million people, have a combined annual income exceeding $300 billion" (Carter, 1997, p. 532). But they are not all cut from the same bolt of cloth. For example, there are African American families that do not have the slave history and legacy in their genealogy, and there are African American families whose history is derived from indentured servitude. African American families are at every socioeconomic stratum of the United States. "The Black family is not a monolithic unit about which we can make definitive statements. Instead, it is a type of social organization whose form changes from social class to social class, region to region, country to country, and culture to culture" (Staples, 1971, p. 3). Each African American family in the United States is a unique and complex phenomenon because each has had its own experiences in a society that is, at best, ambivalent about its existence on a U. S. Constitutional par with non-African American families. *The African American family* referred to in the mass media is a unique product of survival in the United States. For example, among the slaves, "marriage, for them, was denied any standing in law" (Elkins, 1971, p. 14). The African American family survived that legacy and flowered despite the persistence of oppression, exploitation, and denigration (Davis, 1993).

CULTURAL VALUES AND BEHAVIORAL NORMS

African American culture has strongly held traditional values with roots and strengths anchored in African heritage and solidified through the subjugation of slavery. That history forced all African American social and economic classes to share a common geographical residential community. Such conditions blurred class distinctions typical of mainstream America. Mainly, it was a condition that fostered development of a stronger sense of unity among social and economic classes of African Americans that exist today.

That cultural context, and the close relationships within it, were the prime sources of affirming personal identity and providing psychological support. Moral development, spirituality, achievement incentives, pride, and a sense of personal security were derived from family, culture, and community working together. Within the secure protection of the segregated African American community, a number of emerging family forms and behavior patterns were accepted, supported, and valued. Billingsley (1968) identified these family forms as nuclear, extended, and augmented families (pp. 16–21).[1] In all these forms,

> African Americans ascribe primacy to family relationships, particularly with regard to dependent members such as children and elders; revere ancestors; possess deep spiritual values; invest in their communities; value education; and depend on the formal and informal counsel of elders (Akoto, 1992; Billingsley, 1992; Madhubuti, 1990 cited in Carter, 1997, p. 532).

With the advent of the Civil Rights Movement in the late 1950s, and subsequent passage of antiapartheid legislation by the U. S. Congress, many affluent and middle-class African Americans moved out of segregated communities. In doing so, many traditional values of African Americans have been undermined, derided, questioned, and dismissed as not being viable in the instrumental market society of the United States.

The class-diverse and racially segregated African American community was the source of individual and familial consistency; however, access to previously closed residential communities, new job opportunities, and unexplored social outlets have undermined many of the traditional values that previously gave strength, nurtured psychological health, and *governed* social behavior for its members.

PROFILE OF SOCIAL WORK EDUCATION PROBLEM

The 1996 Council on Social Work Education Curriculum Policy Statement, B6.6 and M6.8, state that "the curriculum must provide content *about* people of color, women, and gay and lesbian persons. Such content must emphasize the impact of discrimination, economic deprivation, and oppression upon these groups" (p. 101 & 140). Proctor and Davis (1994) note that "(k)nowledge of the cultural nuances of a people depends on meaningful personal interactions. Thus, cross-racial professional interactions are hampered by the pervasiveness of segregation and separation in society" (p. 315). As a result, students leave social work programs and schools of social work without a working knowledge of the histories, cultures, family structures, life chances, or understanding the perception of what is real for ethnic Americans of color (Davis, 1993).

PRACTICE FOCUS: EVALUATION

Evaluation with African Americans includes an understanding of the social, economic, psychological, and political context in which they survive. In other words, "this evaluation should include the perceptions of the practitioner and of the (individual) family" (Hanna & Brown, 1999, p. 263).

The skilled use of summative evaluation with African American clients must take the facts of race and racism into account. The by-products of these forces—suspicion, anxiety, suppressed anger and rage, and questioning of any social worker's competence—may relate more to survival tools than personal or familial pathology.

The ecological perspective works well and is effective with African American clients when the social worker is knowledgeable of conditions the African American experiences on a day-to-day basis. The strengths perspective begins from the premise that the client already possesses strengths. The social worker must then be prepared to modify the Eurocentric intervention framework, learned in social work education, to incorporate a strengths view of the African American client. The empowerment perspective begins from the premise that each individual or family possesses the potential power and resources but lacks the necessary attributes to operationalize them. It relies on the social worker's skills and readiness to act as a guide and facilitator of "empowering" clients rather than controlling or infantilizing them as "needing" the social worker's help.

THEORETICAL APPROACH TO PRACTICE

Ecological/Person-In-Environment

The ecological perspective is an outgrowth of the psychosocial approach developed by Florence Hollis in 1964. Hollis's model "has consistently recognized the importance of *internal psychological processes,* external social and physical conditions, and the interplay among them" (Woods & Hollis, 1990, p. 27). The ecological perspective focuses on the "goodness of fit" between client and environment. Hollis's psychosocial model *includes the sum* of the exchange between person and environment that encompasses the psychodynamic processes stimulated by their interaction. This factor takes into account the client's individual and reference group histories.

Use of the ecological perspective to evaluate the outcome of intervention with African American clients needs to be based on several considerations. First, the course of intervention must have been one mutually agreed on by client and worker: a collaboration. This requires a skill in collaboration based on knowledge of the client's ecological background. This also acknowledges that, frequently, "the definitions of problems, goals, and solutions can differ among cultural groups and among social workers" (Lee & Greene, 1999, p. 22). In this way the social worker moves "away from a hierarchical position ("Do what I want you to do") and into a collaborative position ("Teach me what is important for me to know about you")" (Hanna & Brown, 1995, p. 103). Knowing the client's ecological background, the social worker not only has a different perspective from which to evaluate the effectiveness of intervention, but gains an ally to do so.

Second, the social worker needs to be keenly aware of, and willing to candidly discuss, racial, class, cultural, and/or religious differences between him- or herself and the client. This requires both sensitivity and skill and also aids the social worker in developing a culturally based, client-identified baseline against which to evaluate and understand outcomes of intervention.

Third, along with understanding African American ecology, and developing sensitivity to important differences, the social worker must skillfully project his or her unqualified respect for the client and the problem or issue that moved the client to seek professional help. These are minimal qualitative skills that must be brought to the table when using social work's ecological perspective to evaluate the effectiveness of social work intervention with African American clients.

The Strengths Perspective

Use of the strengths perspective to evaluate the outcome of intervention with African Americans requires the social worker to alter his or her framework for evaluating behaviors that vary or differ from the behavior of Eurocentric mainstream society. Saleebey (1992) makes the argument that undergirds this perspective when he notes that:

> The strengths perspective does not require the helper to blithely ignore a client's concerns, problems, illnesses, and conflicts. It demands, instead, that they be understood in a larger context of individual and communal resources and possibilities. At the least, the strengths perspective obligates workers to understand that, however downtrodden or sick, individuals have survived (and in some cases even thrived). They have taken steps, summoned up resources, and coped (pp. 172–173).

Because each African American client has inherent strengths on which to draw in the helping situation, the evaluation of intervention effectiveness with African American clients should include the use of such resources.

A major indicator of African American strength lies in their ability to compete in mainstream culture and in the African American community concurrently. That strength requires paying close attention to reality in both worlds. For the social worker, it requires the skills of discernment, understanding, and respect for the meaning of the behavior being observed.

The strengths perspective, used in conjunction with other models, such as the ecological perspective, the problem-solving model, and the empowerment perspective, is a powerful tool for evaluating the outcome of intervention with African American clients. It permits the social worker to take into account the impact of structural discrimination in the United States (e.g., African American lifestyles and family structures) from a strengths perspective. Racism and other forms of institutionalized discrimination produce patterns of African American behavior that often deviate from the Euro-American ideal of human behavior in the social environment.

The strengths perspective, like the Freudian, neo-Freudian, and other theories of human development and behavior, is generally consistent with the basic tenets of capitalism (Kriegman & Knight, 1988), which is fundamentally a system of exploitation. This contextual backdrop is extremely influential in *African American reality*. It cannot be overlooked or underestimated in evaluating the outcome of intervention with African Americans; therefore, a social worker *must* possess a knowledge of oppressed minorities in an exploitive economic system.

The strengths perspective intake and assessment necessarily lead first to identifying the problem *as perceived by the client* (and the etiology of the problem *as the client experienced it*). It is from those basic data that the client's strengths are identified and an intervention plan is made. Overall goals and specific objectives of intervention are determined, and a baseline for evaluation is established. Once these steps have been completed, the social worker should identify in collaboration with the client, where he or she envisions going with the problem.

For the social worker, two responses may be elicited: (1) a beginning view of the client's *reality*, and (2) a premise for developing mutual trust between client and worker. The second point, identifying the type of outcome the client is hoping for (as opposed to the social worker's prognosis) indicates that the client's wishes are respected. It also says to the client that there is the possibility of achieving the goal. Framing the third point as a question to the client extends an invitation to the African American to take the initiative in this delicate situation.

Use of the strengths perspective to evaluate the outcome of intervention with African Americans requires the social worker to know and do something important to African Americans: get to know the client as a unique person whose uniqueness is compounded by the existential fact of the African American experience. There needs to be a willingness to enter the client's frame of reference and understand the meaning of the world *as the client sees and experiences it*. This is important because "there are aspects that the client may not be able to conceptualize, but is not free to give up or replace, and these aspects—however idiosyncratic their form—bear the stamp of his home group's culture" (LeVine, 1973, p. 19). Above all else, the social worker must have great awareness and intimate knowledge of him- or herself *prior to* venturing into the complex world of African American individuals or families.

To successfully intervene with African Americans and their families, the social worker must have the skills to understand the dynamic nature of relationships among family members as a reaction to oppression. Family organization and individual lifestyles are always relative responses to the dominant society.

Empowerment

By itself, the empowerment concept simply means the instilling of confidence, will, and a sense of personal authority in one to act on his or her own behalf at a given time, and in given circumstances. It is a process that "requires respect for what people already know and can do, strengthening the person's sense of integrity in health care, and teaching problem-*posing* as well as problem-*solving* skills" (Savo, 1983, p. 19). Woodside and McClam (1998) refer to empowerment as an *activity*, but describe it as a phenomenon when they write that "[a]ssertiveness promotes the self-confidence and self-respect that supports empowerment" (p. 320). Gutierrez, Parsons, and Cox (1998) begin by describing empowerment as a process and conclude by saying that it is both a process and an outcome (p. 19). Cox and Parsons (1994) note that "[t]wo closely related assumptions are basic to the empowerment oriented practice model . . . (1) *all* human beings are potentially competent, even in extremely challenging situations . . ., [and] (2) *all* human beings are subject to various degrees of powerlessness" (p. 17).

The basic evaluation skills influential in social work were developed in relation to the dominant U.S. culture. That baseline population is predominantly Euro-referenced white Americans. Given that fact, social work models and perspectives need to be adjusted for evaluation of African Americans. For example, the simple strategy of reframing a problem as a barrier needing an alternate problem-solving approach, instead of framing the problem as personal pathology, is a technique often used by social workers to engender a sense of self-empowerment. However, such reframing may not be effective with African American individuals and families whose experiences of discrimination and oppression have taught them that structures in society (institutional and personal racism) will act to block alternate paths to success for them.

The task of surviving in a hostile environment saps the energy of African Americans and engenders a sense of powerlessness throughout the community. Therefore, attempts to empower such clients through education, or simply provide information so that they can negotiate the system for themselves, may be viewed as insincere. Their suspicions and doubts about the fairness of human service systems contribute to the African American client's sense of powerlessness. Evaluating the outcome of intervention with African Americans from the the empowerment perspective may be complicated by differential social experiences, family constellations, and economic circumstances in which they survive.

A significant factor in evaluating the outcome of intervention with African Americans from the empowerment perspective rests with understanding, and being sensitive to, the historical and current ways in which human service systems engage the client. From the outset, elements of outcome evaluation must be inextricably linked to specific assessment data gathered from the initial interview and assessment process including through the skilled use of tools such as the intake interview, a genogram, and in-depth social history.

Early in the client relationship, the social worker needs to develop an understanding of how this *individual or family system* works. Such information can be gathered by exploring with the client past patterns of problem solving; discovering or uncovering the overt and covert channels of communication, cooperation, and coalitions between family members; and conducting a guided self-examination of the individual or family to uncover ways in which each member *owns*, and benefits from a piece of the problem that initially led the family to seek help. Thus, the worker can establish a baseline of the African American family or individual against which to evaluate the outcome of intervention based on the empowerment perspective.

PRINCIPLES OF PRACTICE

The overriding principle of social work practice is to begin where the client is. This principle suggests that the professional social worker should always be able to measure where the intervention began and where it ended. In order to honor this first principle of social work practice, the social worker must be *able and willing* to acknowledge, respect, and take into account the fact that "discrimination (disadvantaging) against African Americans is evident in all sectors of social, political, and economic life" (Karger & Stoesz, 1998, p. 81). To begin where the African American client is means to be knowledgeable of, and sensitive to, the nature and extent of the burden of discrimination—historically and currently.

The principles underlying the currently vogue "single-subject" research design recommend a method for the social worker to develop a culturally sensitive baseline with African American clients while measuring the effectiveness of the intervention's outcome.

PRACTICE SKILLS

Outcome evaluation is an integral part of social work practice. Its construction is based in the intake assessment, and its effectiveness is proved or disproved at the culmination of the helping relationship. Effective intervention requires a broad knowledge of African American culture, history, and conditions of survival. This knowledge must be skillfully integrated with sensitivity and timing during the intervention process.

The skillful use of knowledge, sensitivity, and timing is crucial in developing trust with African American individuals and families because there is a natural wariness of the system that, historically, has oppressed the client and a wariness of the social worker who is representative of that system. Also, there is a natural tendency for people in the United States to keep private as much as possible.

The skills needed to evaluate effectiveness of intervention with African Americans are the same skills used with any non-African American. However, as noted above, special attention must be given to the unique African American experience in the United States, including sensitivity to the history and continued oppression of and discrimination against African Americans and their reality factors:

1. Discrimination and oppression on the basis of race continue to be a reality.
2. The dominant social work paradigm does not encompass African Americans.
3. African American culture, values, and lifestyles are equally as viable as those of the mainstream culture.
4. African American culture, values, and lifestyles are derived from African cultures but are uniquely American—not foreign alien, or deviant.
5. A social worker must have self-knowledge and a deep, abiding respect for self and people who are different.

The recognition and employment of the above realities as fundamental parts of ones social work practice with African American individuals and families represent a beginning development of skills critical to evaluating the effectiveness of social work intervention with African American individuals and families.

CASE VIGNETTE

Renee M. is a forty-year-old African American woman who has been married for sixteen years. At the time of the interview, she was separated from her husband and living with her mother—taking care of her mother in her own home—while her husband was living in their home. She stated that her mother's two-flat house is quite run-down, and she has had to do a lot of work since moving in. Ms. M. was referred to The Community Mental Health Center (TCMHC) by a friend. She telephoned for an evaluation appointment about 9:30 A. M. on December 10, 1996. She was given an intake appointment for 11:30 A. M. that same day. In the initial telephone contact, Ms. M. stated that she was depressed and anxious. She complained of not being able to sleep at night and a loss of appetite. She stated that the symptoms began just about one-and-one-half weeks earlier (Thanksgiving weekend) when she almost passed out at work.

During intake Ms. M. was in a very depressed and weepy state. She reported experiencing frightening and anxious feelings in her stomach. She also stated that she was very depressed and believed that she had been depressed, off and on, her whole life. Shortly after this statement, Ms. M. requested a referral for medication and an appointment with a psychiatrist. She stated that she had visited another doctor two days before, and he had prescribed Dalmaine for sleep; however, she did not feel that that medication worked as well as Dardin. She informed the worker that she normally kept sleeping pills in her medicine cabinet and used them about two or three times per year.

When asked about other things going on in her life, Ms. M. stated that she enjoyed her work and wanted to get back to work to prevent becoming more depressed. That statement contradicted the complaint of being physically exhausted. She currently is involved with one full-time and two part-time jobs, enrolled in two courses at a local university, and cares for her eighty-year-old mother, who suffers from Parkinson's Disease.

Ms. M. said that she had not wanted to get married but got pressured into it by friends who kept talking about what a perfect couple they were. She described her husband as being chronically pessimistic and said that he is always talking about suicide. She stated that he always looks at the gloomy side of things.

At various points in the interview, Ms. M. expressed suicidal ideation of her own, saying, "I don't see the purpose of life and never did," and "I didn't believe that I would live past twenty-one; my two roommates from Howard University are dead." She expressed the feeling that everyone takes advantage of her. She stated that she had considered suicide on several occasions. When asked how she might do it she said that she'd probably overdose.

In gathering additional history, it was learned that Ms. M. is the youngest of two female siblings. Her sister, who is ten years older, lives in Tucson, Arizona. Her father died after spending one-and-one-half years in a nursing home. She stated that her mother "just sits there with the house dark and gloomy waiting to die." When asked about her relationship with her father she described him as "a very dynamic person who was president of a paper union—and treated his family like dirt." She stated that he was "a terrible person." His job required him to travel frequently. Things were so miserable when he was home that she once asked her mother to leave him. She stated that she told several people that she hated him because of his verbal abuse. He refused to provide the necessary funds for her to attend Howard University. She had to work her way through college. She stated simply that, "I wound up caring for him when he was old." She also informed the worker that she cried at her father's funeral because he was so pitiful at death: "He paid for his life." She said that her mother did not visit him while he was in the nursing home, nor did she "shed a tear" at the funeral. The daughter who lives in Tucson did not attend the funeral.

In a much lowered voice, almost under her breath, Ms. M. said that she has always had problems with men; however, she hastened to say that she has more male than female friends, but they are different from her husband. By way of example, she said that, at one point in her life, "a man held me at gun point," and tried to force her into his car, "but I didn't do it and got away." She added that a week later she left church because the minister "made a play" for her.

In this case, it is clear that dysfunctioning is occurring, and that a variety of factors are operating at several different levels. For example, there are individual identity development issues that are complicated by cultural value issues and compounded by situational life problems. The *ecological perspective* might seek to discover the elements of the environment this person is in. What is the interplay between person-in-environment that is causing the imbalance in this person's life? What elements should be changed that would help restore balanced functioning for the client? The focus is on the person-in-situation. The cultural value issues emerge when the client implies a sense of obligation to "take care" of a father whom she feared, hated, or felt had betrayed her throughout her life. Situationally, she also returned *home* to take care of her aging and ailing mother as a reprise or refuge from an ailing and failing marriage. She has boxed herself in with commitments that overextend her personal resources: three jobs, school, marriage, and parental care.

The *strengths perspective* might observe that this person obviously possesses a great deal of strengths to successfully get to this point in life. What are they and how have they served her in the past? What are the characteristics of strength this client demonstrates in her pursuit of a college education without the financial support of her parents? How has she survived in a questionable marriage for sixteen years? What made it possible for her to be able to return and take care of an ailing father, whom she either feared or hated or both, and still be able to shed tears at his funeral? Finally, after her older sister's abdication of familial responsibility, the client, in the midst of marital strife, returned *home* to care for her aging and ailing mother. Clearly individual strength is evident: strength of identity, strength of character, strength of African American cultural values, and strength of determination to achieve and succeed.

The *empowerment perspective* would proceed along an affirmative path with this client. The issue then becomes, what are the resources available to the client?

What are the components of the client's foundation that she can build on and that will *empower* her to act on her own behalf with confidence? There are additional questions: First, how can this client be encouraged to accept herself as a worthy individual, independently of valuation by others? Second, how can she be moved to identify and accept herself and her achievements as evidence of strengths? Third, how can this client be guided to discover that, from these strengths and resources, she can act on her own behalf without guilt?

CONCLUSION

The evaluation skills needed to be effective with African American clients require social workers to develop intimate knowledge of African American *reality*, a reality that varies from mainstream Eurocentric reality. Therefore, different evaluation skills, knowledge, and sensitivities are required.

The use of the ecological perspective, the strengths perspective, or the empowerment perspective in evaluation with African American clients requires skills at several levels: (1) skill in the use of the *perspective of choice;* (2) skill in intake, process, and outcome evaluation; (3) knowledge of, and sensitivity to, African American "*reality.*" The social worker must be able to empathize with the client's view of the problem from an informed and sincere premise. Lastly, the social worker must be skilled in evaluating internal and external client resources to judge what is reasonable to expect in the way of change in the client.

The **ecological perspective** requires a working knowledge of the systems engaged by the client, an understanding of barriers confronted in that environment, and *the usual problem-solving methods* of the client and his or her reference group. The **strengths perspective** requires the skill of being able to interpret and reframe behavior, ideation, and defenses presented by clients in a way that defines them as strengths, not pathologies. Use of the **empowerment perspective** requires the social worker to confront the raw issues of power and powerlessness. It requires an understanding of *the African American's sense of personal power* and ability or will to act in the face of institutional power. In conjunction with this last matter, race is critical.

ENDNOTE

[1]The nuclear family and the extended family both take three forms: incipient, simple, and attenuated. The augmented family has "unrelated individuals living with them as roomers, boarders, lodgers, or other relatively long-term guests" (Billingsley, 1968, p. 21).

REFERENCES

Billingsley, A. (1968). *Black families in white America.* Englewood Cliffs, NJ: Prentice-Hall.
Carter, C. S. (1997, September/October). Using African-centered principles in family–reservation services. *Families in Society, 78 (5),* 531–538.

Compton, B. R. & Galaway, B. (1999). *Social work processes,* 6th ed. Pacific Grove, CA: Brooks/Cole.

Cox, E. O. & Parsons, R. J. (1994). *Empowerment-oriented social work practice with the elderly.* Pacific Grove, CA: Brooks/Cole Publishing Company.

Davis, E. (1993). Social policy, psychosocial development, and minorities. In E. Kim & Y. I. Song (Eds.), *American mosaic: Selected readings on America's multicultural heritage* (pp. 101–114). Englewood Cliffs, NJ: Prentice-Hall.

Davis, E. (1993). Racial denigration: Neglected problems of African Americans. Paper presented at the Thirty-ninth Annual Program Meeting of the Council on Social Work Education. New York.

Elkins, S. M. (1971). Slavery in capitalist and noncapitalist cultures. In R. Staples (Ed.), *The black family: Essays and studies* (pp. 13–16). Belmont, CA: Wadsworth.

Gutierrez, L. M., Parsons, R. J., and Cox, E. O. (1998). *Empowerment in social work practice: A sourcebook.* Pacific Grove, CA: Brooks/Cole.

Hanna, S. M. & Brown, J. H. (1995). *The practice of family therapy: Key elements across models.* Pacific Grove, CA: Brooks/Cole.

Hanna, S. M. & Brown, J. H. (1999). *The practice of family therapy: Key elements across models.* 2nd Ed. Pacific Grove, CA: Brooks/Cole.

Karger, H. J. & Stoesz, D. (1998). *American social welfare policy: A pluralist approach,* 3rd Ed. New York: Longman.

Kriegman, D. & Knight, C. (1988, Fall). Social evolution, psychoanalysis, and human nature. *Social Policy,* 49–55.

Lee, M. & Greene, G. J. (1999). A social constructivist framework for integrating cross-cultural issues in teaching clinical social work. *Journal of Social Work Education,* Vol. *35 (1),* 21–37.

LeVine, R. A. (1973). *Culture, behavior, and personality: An introduction to the comparative study of psychosocial adaptation.* Chicago: Aldine.

Massaquoi, H. J. (1993, August). The black family nobody knows. In *Ebony, 47, (10),* 28–31.

Proctor, E. K. & Davis, L. E. (1994). The challenge of racial difference: Skills for clinical practice. *Social Work,* Vol *39 (3),* 314–323.

Reid, S. (1976). White ideology and black mental health. In S. Reid, (Ed.) *Black perspectives and the helping professions: A reader* (pp. 40–69). New York: University Press of America.

Saleebey, D. (1992). Ed. *The strengths perspective in social work practice.* New York: Longman.

Savo, C. (1983, Summer). Self-care and empowerment: A case study. *Social policy, 14 (1),* & 19.

Schriver, J. M. (1998). *Human behavior and the social environment,* 2nd ed. Boston, MA: Allyn & Bacon.

Skinner, B. F. (1971). *Beyond freedom and dignity.* New York: Bantam.

Smalley, R. E. (1967). *Theory of social work practice.* New York: Columbia University Press.

Staples, R. (1971). Ed. *The black family: Essays and studies.* Belmont, CA: Wadsworth.

Woods, M. E. & Hollis, F. (1990). *Casework: A psychosocial therapy,* New York: McGraw-Hill.

Woodside, M. & McClam, T. (1998). *Generalist case management: A method of human services delivery.* Pacific Grove, CA: Brooks/Cole.

CHAPTER 25

EVALUATION SKILLS WITH AFRICAN AMERICAN ORGANIZATIONS AND COMMUNITIES

DARLENE GRANT

As African American organizations and communities continue to experience social and economic problems that impinge on their growth and development and test the limits of their endurance, social work practitioners, educators, and researchers will need to be increasingly cross-culturally competent and armed with effective evaluation strategies. Ethnic-sensitive social work practice with African Americans involves an emphasis on and valuing of their unique worldview, distinctive history, strengths, and efforts towards self-determination. This emphasis includes the implementation of organizational and community practice and evaluation focused on building alliances to balance power relationships, acknowledging organizational and community members' unique identities and contributions, identifying, studying, and analyzing needs, and subsequently proposing culturally congruent solutions (Netting, Kettner, & McMurtry, 1998; Wambach & Van Soest, 1997).

For example, after establishing an alliance with the neighborhood association, a social work community organizer, accompanied by a community mentor, might conduct a door-to-door survey of the incidence rate of disease in a low-income inner-city African American community in which an outdated electrical power plant has contaminated the environment for decades. Survey results might suggest a lack of knowledge about disease rates, a general sense of hopelessness, and a lack of cohesion among residents regarding their power to effect change.

Following the survey, a panel of experts familiar with the evolution of African American communities is consulted to evaluate the effectiveness and validity of this community survey and subsequent efforts to petition for the plant's closure. The panel of experts cautions the evaluator to be mindful of potential bias or misinterpretation of the results. They felt the evaluator could assume that concern with disease, and the related goal of getting rid of the power plant, are real priorities of the community when, in reality, the community is preoccupied with high levels of unemployment, school dropouts, drug addiction, crime, and violence. The evaluator had defined the problem prior to understanding the history and dynamics of the people making up the community in relation to the broader socioeconomic environment.

This broader socioeconomic context includes a history of racism and oppression, marginalization and economic exploitation, political domination, psychosocial stress, and the development of various coping mechanisms to insure survival. Culturally specific coping mechanisms can range from the development of extensive support systems to the use of alcohol and/or other drugs to anesthetize or escape the pain and frustrations of life.

This hypothetical evaluation might be refocused to include an "empowerment" formulation of community change as discussed by Solomon (1976), suggesting that the helper/helpee partnership goals include knowledge and skill exchange between the community and the social worker, development of a collaborative problem-solving effort, and strategy development based on a view of the "power structure" as multipolar with areas vulnerable to the community's influence. This relationship provides a model for how the African American organization and/or community will later work with the city council, power plant authorities, and other players with vested interests on one side or the other of the issues.

In pursuing the development of culturally competent evaluation skills, it is important to focus on: (1) the historical context of the group, the Afrocentric perspectives of kinship, systems of collaboration and networks, sociopolitical organizations, socialization, economy, conflict, and religion (Billingsley & Morrison-Rodriguez, 1998; Martin & Martin, 1985; Secret, Jordan, & Ford, 1999; Wambach & Van Soest, 1997); (2) contemporary issues and debates inside and outside the African American community that impact organizational and community dynamics; and (3) the acquisition of interpersonal and research skills grounded in strengths and empowerment perspectives. These three themes form the underlying framework of the discussion in this chapter.

An *Afrocentric perspective* is defined as one that places people of African descent at the center of understanding and intervention. This perspective highlights African beliefs, values, and mores that have survived the Diaspora and years of slavery and oppression in North and South America and the Caribbean (Bigelow, 1995; Hamilton & Hamilton, 1992; Horne, 1994; McAuley, 1998; McPherson et al., 1971; Warfield-Coppock, 1995, 1996).

This chapter is organized into four main parts: an overview of the history and sociodemographics of African Americans, their cultural values, and a profile of problems and issues they encounter in organizations and communities; a conceptual framework for Afrocentric evaluation is described and two types of evaluation strategies that social workers typically consider—evaluation as monitoring intervention and performance and evaluation as examining needs and outcome; an empowerment philosophy of social work evaluation of African American organizations and communities; and, finally, theory is translated into concrete evaluation practice skills and illustrated with a case vignette.

HISTORY AND SOCIODEMOGRAPHIC OVERVIEW

An estimated 270 million people live in the United States: Whites compose about 70 percent of the population, African Americans and Latinos about 12 percent each, Asians about 3.3 percent, and Native Americans 0.8 percent (Russell, 1996). More specifically, there are an estimated 32 to 35 million African Americans in the North American population today, a group that is projected to grow to around 45 million by the year 2020 (Asante, 1991; Bigelow, 1995; Horne, 1994; Russell, 1996).

These numbers do not, however, distinguish between African Americans, African Caribbeans, Africans from the other Americas, and African immigrants from Africa. Given intra-group diversity and our limited understanding of it in this context, Gray (1995) reports the following general U.S. demographics:

- The median age of the Black population is six years younger than that of the white population, with Black women living longer than Black men.
- Most Blacks live in large metropolitan areas.
- More Black women than Black men have completed college.
- Blacks are unemployed at more than twice the rate of whites; however, more Black women are employed than white women, and the proportion of employed Black women is higher than employed Black men.
- The median income of Black families in 1990 was only 83 percent of the median income of comparable white families.
- The number of Black female-headed households increased from 1980 to 1990.
- The number of professional Blacks increased from 1980 to 1990 (p. 78).

History

Africans were brought to the Americas and the West Indies (Caribbean) in the early sixteenth century when West African slaves were sold to the Portuguese and Spanish for sugar plantation work. However, the first Africans were brought to the United States as indentured servants (Asante, 1991; Bigelow, 1995; Horne, 1994). In actuality, the system of slave-based plantations began in the Caribbean (Green, 1998). In the next two hundred years, an estimated 10 to 12 million Africans, predominantly from western Africa, were captured, imported, and sold as slaves in the New World (Bigelow, 1995).

By the time of the Emancipation Proclamation in 1863, there were 4.5 million people of African descent in the United States, including the Yoruba, Wolof, Mandingo, Hausa, Asante, Fante, Edo, Fulani, Serer, Luba, Angola, Congo, Ibo, Ibibio, Ijaw, and Sherbro tribes. African Americans in the United States have since intermarried with Native Americans, particularly Creek, Choctaw, Cherokee, and

Pawnee, as well as with Europeans from various ethnic backgrounds (Asante, 1991).

African Americans of West Indian descent or West Indian immigrants in the United States, however, have a cultural identity that is different from that of African Americans whose descent is more limited to Africa and North America (Green, 1998). Slavery in the West Indies ended a full generation earlier than it did in the United States, with the number of people of African descent at that time greatly outnumbering whites. This resulted in socioeconomic independence and a system of self-governance that African Americans in the United States never experienced. Further, the cultural identity of African Americans of West Indian descent follows a British standard while maintaining a strong long-distance kinship network with their island of origin. In comparison to African Americans whose descent is more limited to Africa and North America, West Indian cultural distinctions extend to greater emphasis placed on island-based Christianity (with aspects from African religious creeds), the acquisition of property, herbal medicines and folk healers, and the privacy of family life (Gopaul-McNicol, 1993; Green, 1998).

Through the late 1800s and early 1900s, the Black population in the United States, regardless of its cultural roots, was largely subjected to racial hatred, discrimination, political and economic injustice, inequity, and human rights abuses (Bigelow, 1995). The mass migration of Blacks to the North that began in 1920, peaked around World War II, and ended after the decrease in manufacturing jobs in the 1960s and 1970s, was in part due to these abuses (Bigelow, 1995).

The court-ordered elimination of segregation in schools in 1954, and the subsequent passage of federal civil and voting rights bills in 1964 and 1965, highlight gains achieved in the African American civil rights movement. The struggle in the 1970s, 1980s, and 1990s focused more on antidiscrimination, affirmative action, and economic advancement. The fact remains, however, that full equality of opportunity for African Americans continues to be an unrealized goal.

The history of the oppression and resilience of African Americans is important to understanding many of this population's values, norms, and advances as well as problems.

AFRICAN AMERICAN VALUES, ORGANIZATIONAL, AND COMMUNITY NORMS

Long-lasting exclusion from and disparate treatment of African Americans within public services, such as orphanages, schools, hospitals, and other city, state, and federal facilities, resulted in the development of a familial and community self-help network that addressed the needs of African Americans of all ages from long before the Civil War until today (Grant, 1999; McAuley, 1998). African American churches, for example, organized as early as the colonial period, have historically functioned as institutions for social relations, leadership training, and the development of political agendas. Ministers placed themselves between the white system and the church membership, teaching the membership how to resist cultural, physical, economic, spiritual, and political domination, prejudice, and oppression (Asante, 1991).

Some African American survival tactics have taken on traditionally European American characteristics including petitions, lawsuits, and organized protests (Bigelow, 1995). Other tactics have their bases in African cultural heritage, including "the formation and utilization of mutual aid societies; independent Black churches; lodges and fraternal organizations; and educational and cultural institutions designed to fight Black oppression" (Bigelow, 1995, p. 20), as well as educate, uplift, and empower African Americans. Green (1998) adds to this list, "indigenous forms of assistance, senior citizen services, day care, credit unions, housing developments, and education in survival skills" (p. 201). Organizations such as the Urban League, National Association for the Advancement of Colored People, and the Southern Christian Leadership Conference, as well as the Black Panthers Party evolved out of church and spiritual leadership, each employing strategies with roots in African American self-help and activism philosophies.

It is logical, then, to view African American organizations and communities as being guided by patterns of assumptions, expectations, customs, and needs that develop out of the history of the people. Although subtly evidenced today, the history of the evaluation of African American organizations and communities is based on a traditionally "deficiency-oriented" framework that extends back to slavery. In places such as the infamous Moynihan report (1965), deficit-based evaluation practices have resulted in assessments of African American people, organizations, and communities as a tangle of pathology. In publications such as the *Bell Curve* (Hernstein & Murray, 1995), evaluation findings focus on African American functioning based on cultural deprivation, multiple-problem families, and broken homes, and further suggest that members of this group are intellectually inferior, with an inherent predisposition to underachievement.

PROFILE OF PROBLEMS AND ISSUES ENCOUNTERED BY/IN AFRICAN AMERICAN ORGANIZATIONS AND COMMUNITIES

African American organizations are defined as collectives made up predominantly, but not necessarily solely, of African American individuals gathered together to provide services to and for African American individuals, families, and groups whose specific goals include education, human services, business and finances, leisure, community care, religious, and other services (Holland, 1995; Netting, Kettner, & McMurtry, 1998). African American Communities are broadly defined to include geographical, spacial, and territorial communities in which the predominant number of members are of African descent, as well as nongeographically based functional, relational, and associational communities of African American affiliation (Netting, Kettner, & McMurtry, 1998).

In examining African American cultural values and organizational and community norms, we must also consider the broader Eurocentric context in which they function. Warfield-Coppock (1995) argues that the more *enculturated* the African American organization—the more it is "a blend of the Eurocentric organization with some influences of Black culture. . . . using [Eurocentric] methods and strategies for success" (p. 41), the more confused it is and the more it uses practices that damage Blacks' self-concept. Warfield-Coppock further proposes that the enculturated African American organization has lost its African-centered frame of reference or subordinated it to a Eurocentric one that is grounded in individuality, competition, oppressive authority, material gain, lack of trust among members, and an internalization of oppressive and negative stereotypic beliefs about African Americans, particularly those who are poor, dependent, and disenfranchised.

If we extend Warfield-Coppock's proposition to its logical end, traditional Eurocentric dynamics are counter to the African-based values of harmony and cooperation. Thus, an important and culturally competent approach to evaluation would involve measuring the degree and extent to which such organizations have taken on Eurocentric ways of thinking, being, and doing, and then interjecting more Afrocentric ways of thinking, being, and doing and, subsequently, evaluating the results of this recommended intervention.

We should avoid blaming or condemning the enculturated African American organization or community for its survival strategies. Practices of placing blame result in pathologizing the normal responses of African Americans to oppression and racism, and the internalization of the idea that the Eurocentric model of organizations and communities works best in our society. Neither should we "denigrate" Euro-Americans for the values and cultural base on which their organizations and communities work. In each instance, blame or denigration is counterproductive to efforts to be informed and more effective regarding what African American culture is and implementation of culturally relevant social work practice and evaluation.

Profile of Social Work Problems and Issues

Social work's commitment to a *strengths and empowerment perspective* recognizes the context, resources, and opportunities that, along with a people's culture and history, shapes individuals, organizations, and communities. Evaluators are encouraged to use environmental context and evaluation results to explode stereotypes, accomplish more effective and sensitive evaluation, and develop a more informed picture of African American organizational and community structure and functioning. Poverty, undereducation, inferior medical treatment, and stress are all factors suggested to have strong negative impact on community stability.

For example, social work evaluators might be called on to evaluate and design intervention to address low rates of access or utilization of health services among the African American elderly, redlining by banks and lending institutions that result in low rates of home ownership, or the subsequent low level of business investment in predominantly African American communities. Evaluation might also focus on low-income African American communities impacted by the presence of low-wage industries that no other community wants, including garbage dumps, drug rehab centers, prisons, half-way houses, hospitals for the mentally ill, and recycling centers. Other problems requiring evaluation include community decline via infrastructure decay, the zoning of large portions of communities for nonresidential use, obsolescence of services, drug dealing, deinstitutionalization, white flight, gentrification, the complacency of city councils, shifting federal and state funding priorities, and redrawn congressional districts that impact representation.

African American organizations and communities may manifest problems that can be tied to the lack of available skilled and unskilled jobs paying a living wage, family dissolution, declining marriage rates and increasing out-of-wedlock birth rates, addiction and exploitation, high rates of incarceration of African American men, homelessness, high rates of poverty, and high rates of violent crime.

EVALUATION AS MONITORING IMPLEMENTATION AND PERFORMANCE, NEEDS, AND OUTCOME

Evaluation strategies grounded in the Afrocentric and ecological frameworks are crucial to continued funding and the economic viability of African American organizations and communities. A commitment to this theoretical overlay is the primary way for a reasonable chance for their sustainability and success. Rubin and Babbie (1996) discuss two types of evaluation strategies that social workers typically consider: (1) outcome evaluation in which the degree of goal attainment is examined, and (2) needs evaluation, with subsequent monitoring of how organizations and communities plan and implement new programs.

Macro level social work practice is the focus of these evaluation strategies. *Macro practice* is "professionally guided intervention designed to bring about planned change in organizations and communities" (Netting, Kettner, & McMurtry, 1998, p. 3). This definition can be extended to include small groups and the policy arena (DiNitto, 1995; Jansson, 1998; McNeece, 1997).

In 1994, for example, President Clinton and Vice President Gore designated seventy-two urban areas and thirty-three rural communities as Empowerment Zones or Enterprise Communities scheduled to collectively receive more than $1.5 billion in performance grants and more than $2.5 billion in tax incentives (DiNitto, 1995). The legislative creation of Empowerment Zones to stimulate urban inner-city and rural African American community, economic, and human development by creating jobs and business opportunities is one example of macro level intervention. To achieve Empowerment Zone and Enterprise Community goals, tax incentives are provided. Other incentives include performance grants and loans, and support to people looking for work including job training, child care, and transportation.

The two types of social work evaluation strategies employed in this example might focus on (1) evaluating the socioeconomic and cultural needs of a large inner-city African American community and, subsequently, monitoring how the community comes up with a plan to utilize Empowerment Zone funding, and (2) the impact or outcome of Enterprise Community funding on community goals of decreased levels of school dropouts and increased levels of employment and business investments in that African American community. At the same time, these evaluation approaches include aforementioned partnership development, histori-cal cultural analysis, feedback from the African American community, each of its collaborative partners, and the funder.

Ecological/Person-In-Environment

"Ecological systems theory posits that individuals are engaged in constant trans-actions with other human beings and with other systems in the environment and that these various persons and systems reciprocally influence each other" (Hep-worth, Rooney, & Larsen, 1997, p. 3). This theory is important when conducting evaluations as it emphasizes inter- and intra-group uniqueness across all individ-uals, families, organizations, and communities.

Further, people are considered actors on and reactors to their environments, thereby contributing to how organizations and communities that they are a part of are organized, supported, or boycotted. Effective evaluation of the African American organization or com-munity, then, must involve consideration of uniqueness and the reciprocal impact of indi-viduals, organizations, and communities on each other.

Billingsley and Morrison-Rodriguez (1998) suggest that "the challenge for social workers is to understand how the social systems of African American com-munities function in order to mobilize various components of those systems to reverse the disturbing decline in the quality of Black family life" (pp. 33–34). It seems logical, given the history reviewed in this chapter, that evaluation must include an analysis of all of the forces impinging on the various facets of organiza-tions and communities and the impact of those forces on success, sustenance, and effectiveness. These components/facets of organizations and communities might include size, leadership structure, leadership quality, political savvy, membership and resource base, technical assistance, access to information, and funding sources (Billingsley & Morrison-Rodriguez, 1998).

The Strengths and Empowerment Perspective

Cowger (1994) extends the empowerment perspective to include the assumption that

> resources and opportunity for that empowerment are available. Social justice, involving the distribution of society's resources, is directly related to client social empowerment and, therefore, simultaneously to personal empowerment (p. 263).

The "ideal" of empowerment suggests that people reach their optimal development when able to be in charge of their own destiny, to develop and maintain positive individual and group identity, inter- and intra-relational harmony and actualization in environments (family, organizations, and communities) within a context that offers equality in access to resources and opportunities within the larger socioeconomic system.

Social workers often use the concept of empowerment as something they can do for or give African Americans. The premise of empowerment as something we give to our clients is a deficit view of the client including a belief that the problem is inherent in the individual, organization, or community, that the social worker knows what's best, can find the answers, and that all the client needs to do is follow the worker's prescriptions for change to feel and function better.

The converse suggests that culturally sensitive evaluation focuses on giving African American clients control over defining their presenting problems and subsequent solutions, when, historically, African American organizations and communities have been challenged by a society in which they get few resources and fewer opportunities to use their skills to develop, coordinate, and administer essential services. Empowerment evaluation efforts grounded in the principle of African American self-determination, then, advocates for a more equitable distribution of political, economic, and social choices available to these organizations and communities. Empowerment evaluation should maintain a commitment to equity and justice (Cowger, 1994).

For example, in the late 1800s there were up to thirty predominantly African American populated, owned, and governed communities in Oklahoma. Between 1940 and 1970 that number declined to twelve, due in part to white controlled "external economic structure and governmental resources, [which] weaken the towns' economic arrangements and limit the development of their infrastructures forcing the Black towns to pay for [or establish] their own schools, limiting road improvements, and openly withholding funds from the communities" (McAuley, 1998, p. 446).

Accusations of "separatism," "reverse discrimination," "anti-White sentiment," being "non-American," and "not being able to get over slavery and move on," often follow today's efforts to attain African American empowerment. The culturally sensitive evaluator is encouraged to be aware of these reactions. Three goals of empowerment evaluation in this context are to help the African American organization or community (1) gain the skills necessary to make important decisions, (2) develop skills necessary to taking socioeconomic control in accessing resources and opportunities, and (3) educate the broader society regarding African American history and its importance to the well-being and strength of the United States.

In sum, evaluators work in partnership with African American organizations and communities following a process of empowering the client to: (1) recognize and define the problems, (2) assess obstacles to problem resolution, and (3) develop goals for change (Cowger, 1994).

Ethics and Principles of Macro Practice

Evaluation is a political endeavor involving program supporters and opponents. Individuals, organizations, and communities have vested interests and agendas that help or hinder evaluation design or implementation (Rubin & Babbie, 1996). There is also pressure on the evaluator to end up with positive findings that make the organization and/or community look good so that funding is continued or increased. For example, findings of an African American community evaluation might affect how the city planning commission zones property in that community. Zoning decisions dictate which companies are permitted to establish themselves within that community, subsequently affecting housing, jobs, programs, and investments.

Ethical dilemmas come into play when evaluation procedures, findings, data analysis, and subsequent conclusions drawn are: (1) inattentive to the psychosocial, cultural, and economic history and needs of the organization or community, or (2) dictated by those with vested interest against the client's advancement and empowerment. Evaluation research results may be utilized to uplift, tear down, or ignore the needs and achievements of the African American organization or community.

Whatever the case, the evaluator makes ethical decisions at all levels of the evaluation process, from who defines the problem, the type of research design used, how variables are defined and measures selected, who is included in the study population and who is not, the degree of observance of confidentiality of individuals in the evaluation, how data is collected, to how the results are presented. "Duty to warn" the entity being evaluated, then, becomes a primary issue critical to evaluation, particularly in cases where findings are "negative" or rather opposite to what the client expected or wanted (Loewenberg & Dolgoff, 1996).

In sum, the National Association of Social Workers Codes of Ethics (1993) prescribes the ethical behavior of social workers, including that of providing evaluation services to African American organizations and communities. The evaluator is ethically responsible to:

- make the client's interests her or his primary interest,
- avoid an exploitive relationship with the client,
- avoid condoning any form of discrimination, and
- seek the counsel of colleagues or withdraw services when either action is in the client's best interest.

PRACTICE FOCUS: EVALUATION

Evaluation is defined as the extent to which we can answer the question of whether an organization or community is effective in reaching its goals (Rubin & Babbie, 1996; York, 1997). Evaluation, in the context of this discussion, focuses on how effective African American organizations and communities are at reaching education, human services, business and finances, leisure, community care, religious, and other services goals.

York (1997) emphasizes the need for evidence that there was an "intervention" with a group of people in order for evaluation research to occur. When "community care," for example, is the African American organization's goal, relevant evaluation questions would include: Does participation in an all African American community-based halfway house enhance the recovery experience of drug-addicted African American men? Does growing up in an African American community instill greater self-esteem in African American children? In answering such questions, the evaluator might compare participation in an all African American halfway house to living in a multicultural halfway house or predominantly white halfway house, or the impact of living in an African American community to that of living in another type of community.

A three-pronged conceptual framework is recommended to guide the evaluation of African American organizations and communities. This conceptualization provides a guide to the development of culturally sensitive evaluation.

First, develop a thorough knowledge of the problems faced by the organization and/or community, and relevant historical incidents that help define the problems (Netting, Kettner, & McMurtry 1998). Second, develop an understanding of African American people and how they are affected by the problems. This includes analysis of race, age, gender, role expectations, level of education, socioeconomic status, and other key population variables, as well as power dynamics across micro, mezzo, and macro systems in the organizations and communities. This should also include examination of the theoretical perspectives that inform the analysis of data gathered for the evaluation (Netting, Kettner, & McMurtry 1998). Third, define and understand the broader context in which the organization and communities function including city, state and federal politics, funding imperatives, and their history in relations with African Americans (DiNitto, 1995).

For example, during a town hall-style community focus group the evaluator uses the empowerment framework approach of permitting the community to define the problem, assess barriers and obstacles, and develop possible solutions. Residents of a predominantly African American community might note that the lack of affordable quality child care and jobs that pay a living wage to the parents of young children are key problems for their community. Coalitions, cooperatives, quality, seamless systems of care, child-care fee supplements, safety, and so forth may be issues that arise as the focus group participants move towards discussing possible resolutions to the problems.

The above evaluation model is variously summarized in the literature. Rubin and Babbie (1996) and York (1997), for example, provide overviews of evaluative research that include the following recommended phases:

1. Problem Formulation
2. Developing Research Design and Methodology
3. Analyzing Data
4. Drawing Conclusions

TRANSLATING THEORY INTO
MACRO PRACTICE EVALUATION

Social workers committed to a strengths perspective of evaluation approach clients as (1) competent, (2) having a historical and cultural base that is relevant to current functioning, organization, and operations, (3) able to recognize and define their problem and their strengths, (4) able to assess obstacles to problem resolution and functioning at the highest level possible, (5) and, in partnership with the social worker, able to develop goals for change (Cowger, 1994; McAuley, 1998). The hypothetical case of East Grantsville provides a case in point.

CASE VIGNETTE

Residents of East Grantsville, a small, economically impoverished, predominantly African American community including a small number of low-income Mexican American residents located on the east side of a large, predominantly white, fictitious city in the southwest, say that when they deal with the police, they want to interact with officers they can trust, officers who will respect and listen to them before jumping to the worst conclusion about them. They also want city police officers to be held accountable if they overstep their bounds. Many residents report that individuals in their community receive poor treatment from police, ranging from unwarranted stops, slow response times, and disrespectful language, to being treated as suspects when reporting crimes. The police, on the other hand, say they try to treat residents all over the city equally but realize there is room for improvement in some areas.

The catalyst that resulted in an evaluation of the relationship between East Grantsville residents and the city police, and the subsequent development of a culturally sensitive intervention strategy, was the death of a young African American male who was beaten by police at a garbage dump site. The police claimed necessary force was used on the vagrant who (1) fit the description of someone who had recently robbed a local convenience store, and who (2) picked up a tree limb and began swinging it threateningly at the officers on the scene. Community leaders claimed that unnecessary force was used in the same way that it was generally used by members of the police force on young African American males in that community, and that the police had a system of "profiling" young African American males such that a majority of these males were suspected of one crime or another. Community members alleged that all African American males fitting the basic description of being tall, of medium build, close-shaven, having short to no hair, one or more earrings, and wearing baggy clothing with visible insignias, were at risk of harassment by the local police.

An evaluation by handpicked consultants headed by a social worker was commissioned by the city council to supply the police department and city council information from residents that would help guide the department in its efforts to forge better relations with East Grantsville residents.

The social work evaluator entering into this evaluation agreement should immediately note the vested interests of the police department and city council to have an evaluation report that finds moderate to minimal malfeasance, racism, or cultural biases and prejudices on the part of the police department. Further, the evaluation team would immediately require a view of the historical development and functioning of the African American community within the Euro-American city and as a microcosm.

Methodologically qualitative data collection would dominate the evaluation effort. Questions could be posed to various subgroups and individuals from all segments of this society including community members, indigenous helpers and organizations, the city council, the planning commission, the business community, and the state legislature, using focus group, narrative, and survey methods of data collection. What is the history of the East Grantsville community? How did the community evolve? Who are the leaders? What is the power structure based on? What does the indigenous helping system look like? What is the degree of access to and/or utilization of public and private social and medical services not funded or run by indigenous people? What are the real and/or imagined barriers to adequate housing, drug addiction treatment, schools, jobs, and so on, in the East Grantsville community? What are the dominant problems and strengths in the community?

A "town hall" forum might be utilized to pull together as many of the community members, police, schools, community business, mental health treatment, social work, and other helping professionals to discuss the above questions. In her or his capacity as a "partner" and change agent with the community in the evaluation process, the evaluator may also establish a working relationship with a known community leader who can act as guide and consultant providing entree and insight into the culture.

CONCLUSIONS AND IMPLICATIONS FOR CULTURALLY COMPETENT EVALUATION OF AFRICAN AMERICAN ORGANIZATIONS AND COMMUNITIES

The literature suggests that the functioning and success of African American organizations and communities is historically grounded and understandable. The evaluator must take time to cull critical information from organization and community members themselves. Implications of the ecological, empowerment, and Afro-centric models for developing evaluation skills with African American organizations and communities surface throughout this chapter, suggesting that thorough knowledge and history, an understanding of the impact of oppression and racism, and an understanding of the broader context are critical to this process. Evaluation must proceed ethically and in partnership with the stakeholders for a balance between the use of both Afrocentric and Euro-American models of evaluating and understanding the world.

REFERENCES

Asante, M. K. (1991). African Americans. In T. J. O'Leary & D. Levinson (Vol. Eds.), *Encyclopedia of world cultures,* Vol. 1 (pp. 10–13). Boston, Mass: G. K. Hall.

Bigelow, B. C. (1995). African Americans. In J. Galens, A. Sheets, & R. V. Young (Vol. Eds.), *Gale encyclopedia of multicultural America,* Vol. 1 (pp. 16–42). Detroit, MI: Gale Research.

Billingsley, A. & Morrison-Rodriguez, B. (1998). The black family in the 21st century and the church as an action system: A macro perspective. In L. A. See (Ed.), *Human behavior in the social environment from an African American perspective,* (pp. 31–49). New York: Haworth.

Cowger, C. D. (1994). Assessing client strengths: Clinical assessment for client empowerment. *Social Work, 39* (3), 262–268.

DiNitto, D. M. (1995). *Social welfare: Politics and public policy,* 4th ed. Boston, MA: Allyn & Bacon.

Gopaul-McNicol, S. A. (1993). *Working with West Indian families.* New York: Guilford.

Grant, D. (1999). Effective therapeutic approaches with ethnic families. In C. Franklin & C. Jordan (Eds.), *Family practice: Brief systems methods for social work* (pp. 259–297). Pacific Grove, CA: Brooks/Cole.

Gray, M. (1995). African Americans. In J. Philleo & F. L. Brisbane (Eds.), *Cultural competence for social workers* (pp. 69–101). Rockville, MD: CSAP/SAMHSA.

Green, J. W. (1998). *Cultural awareness in the human services: A multi-ethnic approach.* Boston, MA: Allyn & Bacon.

Hamilton, D. C. & Hamilton, C. V. (1992). The dual agenda of African American organizations since the New Deal: Social welfare policies and civil rights. *Political Science Quarterly, 107* (3), 435–452.

Hepworth, D. H., Rooney, R. H., & Larsen, J. A. (1997). *Direct social work practice: Theory and skills,* 5th ed. Pacific Grove, CA: Brooks/Cole.

Hernstein, R. J. & Murray, C. A. (1995). *The bell curve: Intelligence and class structure in American life.* New York: Free Press.

Holland, T. P. (1995). Organizations: Context for social services delivery. In *Encyclopedia of social work,* 19th ed., Vol. 2 (pp. 1787–1794). Washington, DC: National Association of Social Workers Press.

Horne, G. (1994). African American population—diversity within. In S. Auerbach (Vol. Ed.), *Encyclopedia of multiculturalism,* Vol. 1 (pp. 45–48). New Bellmore, NY: Marshall Cavendish.

Jansson, B. S. (1998). *Becoming an effective policy advocate: From policy practice to social justice,* 3rd ed. Pacific Grove, CA: Brooks/Cole.

Loewenberg, F. M. & Dolgoff, R. (1996). *Ethical decisions for social work practice,* 5th Ed. Itasca, IL: F. E. Peacock.

Martin, J. M. & Martin, E. P. (1985). *The helping tradition in the black family and community.* Washington, DC: National Association of Social Workers Press.

McAuley, W. J. (1998). Historical and contextual correlates of parallel services for elders in African American communities. *The Gerontologist, 38* (4), 445–455.

McNeece, C. A. (1997). Future directions in justice system policy and practice. In C. A. McNeece and A. R. Roberts (Eds.), *Policy and practice in the justice system* (pp. 263–269). Chicago, IL: Nelson-Hall.

McPherson, J. M., Holland, L. B., Banner, J. M., Jr., Weiss, N. J., & Bell, M. D. (1971). *Blacks in America.* Garden City, NY: Doubleday.

Moynihan, D. P. (1965). *The Negro family: The case for national action.* Washington, DC: Department of Labor.

National Association of Social Workers (1993). *Code of ethics.* Washington, DC: Author.

Netting, F. E., Kettner, P. M., & McMurtry, S. L. (1998). *Social Work Macro Practice,* 2nd ed. Menlo Park, CA: Longman.

Rubin, A. & Babbie, E. (1996). *Research methods for social work,* 3rd ed. Pacific Grove, CA: Brooks/Cole.

Russell, C. (1996). *The official guide to racial and ethnic diversity: Asians, Blacks, Hispanics, Native Americans, and Whites.* Ithaca, NY: New Strategist.

Secret, M., Jordan, A., & Ford, J. (1999). Empowerment evaluation as a social work strategy. *Health and Social Work, 24* (2), 120–127.

Solomon, B. B. (1976). *Black empowerment: Social work in oppressed communities.* New York: Columbia University Press.

Wambach, K. & Van Soest, D. (1997). Oppression. *1997 supplement: Encyclopedia of social work,* 19th ed. (pp. 243–252). Washington, DC: National Association of Social Workers Press.

Warfield-Coppock, N. (1995). Toward a theory of Afrocentric organizations. *Journal of Black Psychology, 21* (1), 30–48.

Warfield-Coppock, N. (1996). Empirical measurement of the Black organization form an Afrocentric perspective. In R. L. Jones (Ed.), *Handbook of tests and measurements for Black populations,* Vol. 2 (pp. 519–531). Hampton, VA: Cobb & Henry.

York, R. O. (1997). *Building basic competencies in social work research: An experiential approach.* Boston, MA: Allyn & Bacon.

CHAPTER 26

SOCIAL WORK EVALUATION WITH MEXICAN AMERICANS

ROBERTO F. VILLA

La Fe de la Gente (the people's faith/spirituality) is a theoretical framework developed to address issues of culture, traditions, values, religion and spirituality among Mexican Americans. This framework highlights the importance of indigenous coping strategies used in their everyday life. Although *Fe* is a person-specific approach, it does encompass the family, group, and community. It provides a systemic approach to social work practice and evaluation. Even though based on research of Mexican Americans, it can be used with other Latino groups.

Social work practice and evaluation with Latinos must take into account issues of diversity that exist among Mexicanos, Chicanos, Mexican Americans, Cubans, Cuban Americans, Puerto Ricans, and other people of Spanish-speaking Central and South America (Castex, 1994; Gallegos, 1991; Villa, 1994, 1999). All of these groups have been subsumed under the label *Hispanic,* but it is not readily accepted by all. *Latinos* is another term used to identify this ethnic group and is the preferred term for use here.

Social work evaluation with Latinos involves a two-way exchange of ideas, feelings, beliefs, and values that are not always readily apparent. Evaluation begins with the social worker's own value system as a necessary first step to assess and accept who he or she is and what he or she brings to the relationship (Devore & Schlesinger, 1999).

Latinos are a complex and diverse population that merits appropriate evaluation techniques. Evaluations should adopt a three-pronged approach that evaluates personal strengths, environmental strengths, and the interactions between both. In other words, social work evaluation with Latinos needs to consider personal and environmental strengths simultaneously so that interactional effects become part of an in-depth approach. It is this interaction that produces coping strategies such as *La Fe de la Gente,* a critical aspect of the Latino worldview.

One important similarity across Latino groups is their *Fe* (faith/spirituality). Within *Fe* are located important indicators of a person's personal and environmental strengths. *La Fe de la Gente* posits that people use their faith or spirituality to cope with problems (Bullis, 1996; Carson, 1989; Sheridan, Bullis, Adcock, Berlin, & Miller, 1992; Villa, 1994).

Problems as solutions are defined and solved within an ethnocentric perspective. Latinos use their history, culture, tradition, and values to examine and solve problems. Language is the mortar that binds or holds the Latino worldview together (Villa & Jaime, 1993). It is through language that meaning is gained and behavior ritualized. Thus, solutions or strategies are symbols that direct action toward culturally defined solutions. These solutions arise out of the personal strengths that are inherent in people.

The strengths perspective as used in this model refers to *La Fe de la Gente* (Villa & Jaime, 1993; Villa, 1994). Spirituality is a measure of a person's inner strengths that is used on a daily basis to cope with life and the problems and stressors that may arise. *Fe,* as defined here, encompasses the history, values, traditions, and *movidas* (strategies) (Ramos, 1979) people use to survive. The two-dimensional character of this model evaluates personal and environmental strengths in an objective and subjective manner (Villa, 1994).

Objectively, on the horizontal dimension (*la vida*, life), the worker evaluates environmental resources such as family, informal support networks, community, religious and agency services available to the person. On the subjective, or vertical dimension (*La Fe*), the worker evaluates the person's inner sources of strength (Villa, 1994) such as faith, hope, and love (Carson, 1989).

The empowerment function of this framework allows the worker to highlight the person's strengths within his or her own value system. One empowers people by using their spirituality to lead them to self-discovery. *Fe* is a powerful concept in that *con Fe todo es posible* (with faith/spirituality, everything is possible). To empower people is to help them realize they have the strengths necessary to initiate appropriate action.

DEMOGRAPHIC PROFILE

The literature on Mexican Americans is vast and as varied as the people subsumed under the label *Hispanic.* There are some differences among Hispanics that can be accounted for by regional, ethnic, and hereditary influences. These differences are especially salient in contrasting Mexicans with Cubans, Puerto Ricans, and Spaniards in their language, food, traditions, and religious beliefs. All of these differences must be accounted for when applying evaluative techniques (Castex, 1994; Gutierrez, 1995).

In 1994, approximately 26.4 million Latino Americans were living in the continental United States. Of these, 64 percent were Mexican American, 13 percent were from Central and South America and the Caribbean, 11 percent were Puerto Rican, 5 percent were Cuban, and 7 percent were classified as "other." Latino

Americans live in every part of the United States, but are more heavily concentrated in Arizona, California, Colorado, Florida, Illinois, New Mexico, New York, Texas, and Puerto Rico (http://www.inet.ed.gov/pubs/faultline/who.html, 1998).

Mexican Americans comprise the largest segment of the Latino population. Although a majority live in urban areas, there are three agricultural migrant streams that flow from north to south across the country at least twice a year (http://www.inet.ed.gov/pubs/faultline/who.html, 1998).

Beginning in the 1600s, Mexicanos were the first Americans to homestead the southwest and, literally, built the cities of Los Angeles, San Diego, Tucson, Albuquerque, Dallas, and San Antonio. Mexican American workers participated in the 1800s massive industrial expansion in the Midwest by building the railroad systems and steel mills. Few, if any, Mexican American families received formal education and, when they did begin to attend public schools, they faced discrimination due to language, socioeconomic status, and cultural barriers (http://www.inet.ed.gov/pubs/faultline/who.html, 1998).

CULTURAL VALUES AND BEHAVIORAL NORMS

Language constitutes the single most important characteristic in maintaining a separate ethnic identity. It has gained importance more as a symbol that provides cohesion and unity to the group rather than its actual use or the proficiency of all group members (Sotomayor, 1977). The values, traditions, and beliefs of the people are uniquely communicated through the use of language. For people of Mexican heritage, Spanish has been the vehicle by which spiritual and religious coping concepts are expressed. Phrases such as *Adios* or *Vaya con Dios* and *Mi casa es su casa* are widely recognized, even by non-Spanish speakers (Villa & Jaime, 1993). The underlying dimension being referred to is commonly placed within the interactional processes of spirituality and is uniquely communicated through the [Spanish] language (Berger & Luckmann, 1996; Rosow, 1967).

LA FE DE LA GENTE

The concept of *Fe* incorporates varying degrees of faith, spirituality, hope, love cultural values, and beliefs. *Fe* is the spiritual realm of human existence that makes each person a unique human being. *Fe* is a holistic approach to life. *Fe* can be conceptualized as a continuum of behaviors and beliefs that begin with conception and continues through the *batismo* (baptismal ceremony), *el día de los muertos* (day of the dead). *Fe* includes the sharing of food and drink to celebrate a birth as well as a death (Villa, 1994). *Fe* is the healing force that a *curandero* (healer) uses to invoke divine will or intervention in curing the sick. Both the curandero and the sick person must have *Fe* for the cure to work (Knowlton, 1971).

Fe is a concept that bridges the realm between daily life and one's spiritual dimension. It includes relevant cultural values and beliefs such as: (1) *Lo que Dios manda* (God's will be done); (2) *La vida es prestada* (life is on loan); (3) *Si Dios nos presta vida* (If God lends us life); (4) *Dios sabe lo que hace* (God knows what he/she does); (5) *Respeto* (respect); and (6) *El deber de los hijos* (filial responsibility). *Fe* implies a continuous interactional process with *Dios* or whatever supreme value guides the individual's life (Villa & Jaime, 1993; Villa, 1994).

Fe is central to all aspect of life. The spiritual dimension involves the sense of identity and purpose that translates into cultural values. These shared values are what define a particular culture or people. Each individual maintains his or her unique set of values within her or his spirituality or *Fe*. This *Fe* then serves to direct behavior within the immediate family and the larger society (Villa, 1994, 1999).

PROFILE OF SOCIAL WORK PROBLEMS AND ISSUES

With the signing of the Treaty of Guadalupe Hidalgo on February 2, 1848, Mexicans in the Southwest were given an opportunity to declare citizenship with Mexico or the United States. Mexicans who decided to stay in the United States became citizens with certain rights and privileges guaranteed by the Treaty of Guadalupe Hidalgo (Acuna, 1988; Barrera, 1979; Martinez & Vasquez, 1974).

As with most treaties signed by the United States with indigenous peoples, those rights and privileges were soon rescinded. From that day forth, most people of Mexican heritage have developed an attitude of distrust toward the U.S. government and those whom they perceive as its agents. Most dealings with government and officials have reinforced these feelings of mistrust that form the basis for lack of access to social services (Acuna, 1998; Barrera, 1979; Martinez & Vasquez, 1974).

Those in the helping professions, such as social work, need to acknowledge the historical oppression and discrimination (Gutierrez, 1995; Proctor & Davis, 1994; Van Voorhis, 1998) suffered by people of Mexican heritage. This structural discrimination has resulted in the evolution of coping strategies that rely on the tenets of magic, faith, and fatalism. All or some of these concepts are to be found in *La Fe de la Gente*.

This evaluative framework is based on a spirituality framework developed by Carson (1998) and, as used here, by Villa (1994). *Fe*, as used here, goes beyond its literal translation, which means faith; the word embodies a way of life that is part magic, part religion, but, mostly, spirituality (Villa, 1994).

The Indicators of *Fe* Scale was administered to a nonprobability purposive sample (N = 143) of Mexican heritage elders (mean age = 72) in El Paso, Texas in an effort to explore perceptions of culture, values, traditions, and *Fe*. The total possible score on this scale is 60 and respondents, on the average, scored 52.16, with a standard deviation of 10.94 (Villa, 1994).

Trujillo (1998) used this same scale with a younger sample (N = 45) in Rio Chiquito, New Mexico and obtained similar results. The mean age for this sample was 46 and the average score on the Indicators of *Fe* Scale was 55.84. Although this was a small nonprobability purposive sample, the replication of Villa's study adds to the evidence for the need to further explore *Fe* within the Latino culture. Again, this scale does not measure spirituality, but uses indicators of *Fe* developed from a critical review of the literature and extensive field work.

PRACTICE FOCUS

A critical understanding of *La Fe* framework (Villa, 1994) will assist the social worker in attaining competence in applying a culturally appropriate evaluation method (Van Voorhis, 1998). This research-based evaluation method incorporates a two-dimensional approach that will highlight personal and environmental strengths. The two factor dimensions being referenced are from the 1994 study by Villa in which Factor Analysis, a statistical analysis test used to reduce number of variables, resulted in two factors or dimensions.

The first factor contained a total of eleven variables. Variables in this factor were related to the vertical dimension of spirituality and is labeled *La Fe*. There was evidence of a dimension oriented toward God or a supreme being. The variables loaded on this dimension are that, in order to have *Fe*, it is necessary to believe: (1) in a Supreme Being, (2) in Jesus Christ, (3) that *Fe* can help with life's problems, (4) that *Fe* is personal between you and God, (5) that our life is in the Hands of God, (6) in the goodness of others, (7) that *Fe* is necessary in order to have good mental and physical health, (8) that there is a real purpose to life, (9) that God, and not man, cures, (10) in eternal life, (11) and that all people are good and/or God's children.

As can be seen by the variables that loaded on this dimension, there seems to be evidence of a continuous process with what supreme value guides an individual's life. For example, Mexican Americans usually will place their fate in God's hands when faced with adversity. *Dios que me ayude:* "God will help me". It is critical to understand the importance placed on *el destino* (destiny) and *lo que Dios manda* (what God sends) or fate. Feelings of faith, hope, and love are all concepts, which define spirituality and are critical aspects of coping.

The second, or horizontal, dimension, is named *La Vida*, or Life, contains four variables. These suggest that, in order to have *Fe*, it is necessary to believe: (1) that *Fe* is part of the Mexican culture, (2) that our family will care for one another, (3) in *La Virgin de Guadalupe*, and (4) in the goodness of all people. On the horizontal dimension the indications are that we are all God's children and should care for one another (Carson, 1989). Environmental or social conditions are also located within this dimension.

Social conditions encompass socioeconomic status, social support (*la familia*) and access to services (Link & Phelan, 1995). Also located in this dimension are racism, discrimination, oppression, and poverty, all of which can and do have negative effects on quality of life.

Typically, this is where social support systems are located and used. The importance here is to remember the informal networks of support that people use everyday, may not be readily apparent to the outsider. The concept of *el vecino*—the neighbor—is much more than what it translates to. It is a person for whom you have respect and *Fe* that they will help in times of need, because they also have the same respect for you. A person who has *Fe* believes or hopes that things will work out for him or her in due time. People who feel loved will be more disposed to use *Fe* and empower themselves to take action.

Fe within the Mexican American community is central to all aspects of life. The spiritual dimension involves a sense of identity and purpose that translates into cultural values and norms. These shared values are what define a particular people's culture. To share the same culture does not necessarily mean sharing the same concept of spirituality or religious beliefs. Each individual maintains a unique set of values within his or her specific definition of *Fe*. This *Fe* serves to direct behavior within the immediate family and the larger society. The individual's ability to remain integrated within his or her *Fe* is paramount to perceived life quality (Villa, 1994). *Con Fe todo es posible*—with *Fe* everything is possible—is an example of how Mexican Americans perceive their *Fe*.

Environmental factors such as poverty, segregation, structural racism, discrimination, and oppression all have an important role in how a person constructs his or her reality and must be acknowledged. These factors are an inherent part of a people's history and are transmitted through language, which acts as the mortar that cements a person's culture and holds their ethnic identity intact. Here, Spanish, the language of birth and of choice, is important both as a symbol of unity and as an expression of an ethnic identity.

Through interactions within la familia, language, culture, traditions, and *Fe* are transmitted to the next generation. It is *la familia's* responsibility to socialize children in the traditional manner of conduct that embodies *respeto* (respect) for elders and their role in the family and society. It is within *la familia* that children learn who they are and where they come from. A sense of *orgullo* (pride) and to be *humilde* or humble are part of this training.

In the conceptual framework described here, equal value is given to indigenous (Azteca) and European influences on the religious practices and cultural traditions that are part of *Fe* and the Mexican American heritage. It is posited that these influences are still in place today. Most would agree that Latinos are a complex and proud people. This can only be understood from a historical perspective such as the one presented here. No one would deny the importance of language in promoting a separate ethnic identity. Language is the mortar that holds together the building blocks of a people's ideology. The building blocks of concern here are the Aztec and European cultures and religions and their influence on *Fe* (Villa, 1994). It is the blending or mixing of these cultures that produced what has come to be known as the *mestizo* or person of mixed blood who is referred to here as Mexican American.

DISCUSSION OF THE MODEL

Evaluation of social work practice with Mexican Americans necessarily begins with *conocimiento* (knowledge/understanding) of their history, culture, and traditions. This can be accomplished through the use of *La Fe* framework. As stated earlier, social workers need to be bilingual and bicultural in order to gain *la confianza* (the confidence) of the people. This framework emphasizes the importance of understanding how people of Mexican heritage view their place in the world. Social workers who comprehend the importance of this framework will have studied it before entering the field or attempting an evaluation.

A critical aspect of social work practice is the point of contact. For example, is the contact person male or female, is it the mother, father, or child? If the worker and the contact person are of the opposite sex, then caution needs to be exercised, particularly if the contact is male and the worker female.

Latino males do not readily accept outsiders into their personal inner self. This is based on the need to remain complete and untouched by outside influences such as therapy. And, if they do, they may pull a *movida* (strategy) to make the worker believe they are cooperating when in fact they are pulling the wool over his or her eyes (Ramos, 1979). Males appear to scrutinize the worker's motives for asking personal information they believe can and will be used against them. This defense mechanism is widely used within the Latino culture to keep others out of his or her innermost self.

Phase one is to conduct evaluations in the home to further assess the person's cultural heritage. This strategy has two purposes: First, it provides the opportunity to assess the environment in which the person lives (horizontal/*la vida* dimension); second, it shifts the locus of control back to the person and away from the social worker in an informal environment. This provides an opportunity for initiating the preferred mode of conducting daily affairs, *la platica* (polite, informal, mutually rewarding conversation).

This phase is the most critical in that it provides the worker with opportunities to acknowledge respeto for the person and to evaluate his or her language preference. At no time should the social worker assume that, because a person is of Mexican descent, he or she prefers to communicate in Spanish. In some cases it would be derogatory to assume that a person speaks or prefers Spanish. Depending on experience with racism, discrimination, and immigration, the opposite might be true.

Phase two is to apply *La Fe* framework in evaluating the person along the vertical and horizontal dimensions described. As in the problem-solving process, the first step is to identify the nature of the problem or problems, whether they can be resolved, or how they can be resolved (McMahon, 1996). In other words, does the person see the same issue as a problem, or is it the worker's training that becomes the problem? The problem could be one associated with poverty and the lack of access to equitable services. Is the problem located in the vertical or horizontal dimension, or is the problem related to the interactions of social conditions (poverty, familial, illness, citizenship status) with spiritual needs (lose of hope, feelings of abandonment, loss of faith)? *No tengo fe* is an indicator of loss of faith, but why is there this sense of loss? Could it be that the family is absent, or perhaps present but not attending to the person? Or sometimes the presence of the family could be the source of the problem. These situations challenge the worker's cultural competence and his or her spirituality.

The second step is to evaluate the person's strengths along the vertical and horizontal dimensions. On the vertical dimension, evaluation is concerned with a person's inner strengths or *Fe*. The concern is with feelings of self-worth, happiness, hope, love, and *una vida buena y sana* (a good and healthy life). Feelings of *lo que Dios manda* (God's will be done), *sí Dios me presta vida* (if God loans me life), and *Dios sabe lo que hace* (God knows what he/she is doing) are expressed along this dimension.

Evaluation that takes place on the vertical dimension is correlated with spiritual strengths. In this part of the evaluation, the social worker and the person are assessing the spiritual and/or personal strengths that can be brought into play. Does this person have a strong sense of *Fe* that could be used to cope with the stress brought about by perceived circumstances? As with poverty, it is not the fact that a person is poor, but their perception and experience of poverty that impacts quality of life. If people see themselves in hopeless poverty, then despair and hopelessness could begin to manifest themselves and weaken their sense of *Fe*. But if they see themselves as living a simple, humble life, then their *Fe* is strong and they have the courage and dignity to deal with life stressors such as poverty.

Evaluation along the horizontal dimension requires assessment of strengths associated with family, community, and religion. *La vida* (life) presents the social worker with assets and/or deficits related to the environment. Social conditions impact quality of life in that they produce stress (Link & Phelan, 1995). For example, if a person is living in poverty, such factors as access to health/mental health services, full employment, adequate housing, and an equitable education can be severely limited. However, if the family is present and providing assistance, then the person or family has access to a very dynamic source of strength to help them cope with stress.

Once the source of stress or problems has been identified and prioritized, the next step is to evaluate potential for change (McMahon, 1996). In this step of the process, the worker and the person look for possible solutions to the problems in order of priority. Priority sets the stage for addressing problems based on their feasibility for successful resolution.

Gender differences are more salient in the evaluation of the Latino male worldview. *La mascara del hombre* (the mask men wear) (Paz, 1986) is a *movida* or strategy (Ramos, 1979) used to keep outsiders from accessing or getting close to the [spiritual] self. To let someone get too close, or reveal too much, would be to *rajarse* (give-up, quit, or crack) and to lose face (Paz, 1986). Most Latino males will not readily participate in the social work process without the necessary steps of *conocimiento, respeto, dignidad,* and *platica.* This becomes even more problematic for female social workers, unless they acknowledge and respect the Latino male perspective. One way around this would be to use the third-person form of communication in which one does not speak about the individual directly, for example, "I hear some of your friends and neighbors are experiencing problems with their employer?" In this manner the person is not threatened by revealing too much and will be more willing to cooperate. Of course the key here is to exercise patience.

In a pilot program, Hart (1998) used *Fe* to empower young men to see themselves in the developmental stages of fathering and to lead them to self-discovery.

Metaphorically, the development of fatherhood in Joseph in his fathering of Jesus parallels and taps into the strengths of *La Fe* for young men (Hart & Hareide, 1999). The goal was to help young Latino males acknowledge, accept, and participate in their child's life (Hart, 1998).

This is, by far, the best way to engage Latino males in the social work process. A direct approach may act as a barrier, whereas an indirect approach would be less threatening and more acceptable. In other words, caution must be used in every phase of the relationship process.

THEORETICAL APPROACH TO PRACTICE

La Fe de la Gente model can be used by the culturally competent social worker at the micro-, mezzo-, or macro-level, depending on level of expertise. The micro-level is the hardest to comprehend and to evaluate and is, therefore, the focus of this chapter. At the personal level, the social worker has to be equipped with culturally syntonic skills in order to succeed. The necessary skills are a critical understanding of the language, ability to apply *La Fe* framework, ability to carry out la platica interview, and to do all these things within a multicultural perspective.

The most important skill in the social worker's repertoire is cultural competence. This includes the ability to apply a multicultural perspective to the evaluation of the individuals, their environment, and the position they occupy in the social structure. Success depends on the worker's active listening skills. A good listener will follow the person's cues and body language and determine how to proceed with the platica. Most Latinos will talk around issues instead of the Western method of speaking directly.

Bilingual competence is a necessary part of the social worker's skills. Without at least a conversational level of language skills, the worker must rely on third-party interpreters who may confuse the translations and interfere with the *personalismo* (personal) aspect of the interview. Not all spoken Spanish is the same, and some words can have different meanings, depending on the social context and ethnicity, which makes a multicultural approach to interventions or assessments even more necessary.

PRACTICE PRINCIPLES, SKILLS, AND METHODS: PLATICA NARRATIVE

Evaluation in social work practice begins with assessment and continues through the evaluation of outcomes. The worker needs to assess and evaluate the person, situation, and environment simultaneously. They are separate factors, but, taken together, they provide a more complete evaluation.

En platicando se establese el conocimiento (it is through conversing that understanding is established). Language has its beginnings in face-to-face conversations between actors (Berger & Luckman, 1996). It is through the language of everyday life that reality is objectified. In the case of social work, *la platica* becomes the focal point of the intervention. It is through this interactional process that the worker comes to *conocer* (know) the person and vice versa. The social worker has to understand the language of the Latino if a deeper understanding of that reality is to be reached.

Social workers should be cognizant of the diversity that exists among Latinos and should use caution when applying labels. The best strategy is to let self-identification emerge from *la platica* and not from the worker's vocabulary. The use of a particular label will give the appearance of objectivity to the subjective nature of the meanings ascribed to the labels (Berger & Luckman, 1996). In other words, if the term *Chicano* is used by a particular person, then the task becomes one of discovering why this is the preferred term.

In order to set the stage for the process of *la platica* (polite, mutually rewarding, informal conversation) and to progress naturally, whenever possible visit individuals in their homes. This shifts the locus of control to them, which, in turn, makes them feel more comfortable in discussing personal issues. *Personalismo* is a term that conveys the importance of personalizing the social work process. This process of relating to a person in a personal way is characteristic of Latinos, who adhere to accepted cultural values and patterns for interaction (Devore & Schlesinger, 1999).

Once a relationship has been established, it is important to let individuals initiate the topics of *la platica* and to become an active participant in the social scene being played out (Berger & Luckman, 1996). A good way to do this is let them reminisce about their lives. Latinos love to *platicar* (talk) about life and how they survived because it presents an opportunity to remember past failures as well as accomplishments. The key is to concentrate on what is being said and focus on the positive aspects of failure and how it helps strengthen *La Fe.*

Latinos have a tendency to belittle or downplay their accomplishments because *no hay que ser orgulloso* (one need not be arrogant), *pero siempre ser humilde* (but to always be humble). Being humble is to accept one's position in life, not as permanent, but within the context of one's *Fe.* Humility symbolizes one's *crianza* (upbringing), which dictates that one should not be arrogant at the expense of making others feel they are inferior. This is extremely important in that the social worker should not be so arrogant as to impose his or her worldview on the person who is seeking *ayuda* (help).

During *la platica,* pay close attention to issues surrounding significant life events such as the death of a loved one, divorce, absence of family, unemployment, ill health, anger, loss of dignity, or a loss of *Fe.* Social factors exert a tremendous amount of stress on Latinos because they are usually tied to a lack of opportunities, which, in turn, leads to a sense of loss or hopelessness. This loss can manifest itself through destructive behaviors that are often exhibited through substance abuse, anger, violence, and neglect.

If a person is remorseful, angry with self or God, he or she may vocalize anguish by such phrases as *no hay Dios* (there is no God), *Dios me ha abandonado* (God has abandoned me), *Dios me quito la razón de vivir* (God took my reason for living), or *me quiero murir* (I want to die). All are expressions of spiritual distress or need. Caution must be used to allow individuals the time to compose themselves and to talk about their losses. *Paciencia* is very necessary at this juncture of the interview. To rush the person would be disrespectful.

Issues of *vergüensa* (shame) are very real and alive to persons of Mexican heritage, and are especially salient in males. It is important to note that these issues may be self-disclosed during *la platica*. Individuals may denigrate themselves through such phrases as *no valgo nada* (I'm not worth nothing), *soy borracho* (I'm a drunk), *no sirvo para nada* (I'm a good for nothing), all of which indicate feelings of low self-esteem and loss of *Fe*.

CASE VIGNETTE

Señora X (Mrs. X) is an eighty-five-year-old woman who lives in one of the many *colonias* (barrios) situated in El Paso, Texas along the United States–Mexico border. *Colonias* are unicorporated parts of El Paso that lack most utilities such as water, sewerage, electricity, and the like. In visiting a colonia, the first thing one notices is the quality of housing most people live in. As in the Mexican tradition, the typical dwelling begins as a small one-room shack, usually constructed out of other people's discards. But as you drive up to the house, you notice rose bushes and trees growing in the yards. The planting of roses is in honor of *La Virgin de Guadalupe* (Virgin of Guadalupe), and the trees represent the belief that we are part of the land and, therefore, tied to it.

You meet Señora X at the door to her home in *la colonia.* You are there because her ten-year-old grandson, Roberto, has been missing school and falling behind in his studies. Roberto has been absent from school each Monday and Friday for the past month. The school has been unsuccessful in contacting his parents, who are part of the migrant farmworker stream that follows crop harvesting throughout the United States.

Señora X is eighty-five years old and does not speak or understand English. During *la platica,* the worker mentions that numerous letters have been sent to her by the school and she has not responded. Señora X gets up and brings the unopened letters to you and states that she doesn't know how to read in English or Spanish. She knows the letters are important because of their appearance, but her grandson is too young to read them to her and she is too embarrassed to ask her neighbors. You take the letters and read them to her in Spanish as she prefers and she gets really apprehensive and starts to utter in Spanish, *"Hay Dios mio, que he hecho?"* (Dear God, what have I done?) After serveral minutes you manage to calm her down and tell her you will help her resolve this problem.

As *la platica* resumes, you find out that her grandson has a job working after school for a man who collects and sells junk. Her grandson is paid $1.75 per hour in cash for helping collect junk. The man needs Roberto on Friday through Monday afternoons, so Roberto misses school in order to work. Señora X is unaware that her grandson is missing school in order to work.

During the visit you mention to Señora X that there are government programs to help people in need. Señora X replies, *"Dios nos da todo lo que necesitamos. Hay otra gente que en realidad necesita ayuda. ¡Yo no! No hay vergüensa en hacer pobre. ¡Dios sabe lo que hace!"* (God gives us what we need. There are other people who really need help. I don't! There is no shame in being poor. God knows what he/she is doing).

La Señora's family sends what money they can, but it is not enough, so Roberto, having been raised in the traditional way, takes it on himself to provide for his own and his grandmother's needs. Roberto's parents know how important an education is and had left Roberto behind so that he could continue his schooling and take care of his grandmother.

Señora X has been ill lately and has been going to a *curandera* (natural healer) who has been taking care of her without charge. But Señora X is very tradtional and reciprocates for her care by giving gifts of food. The herbs the *curandera* prescribes cost money and Señora X has a lot of *Fe* in their ability to cure, so she takes money from her small budget to pay for them.

Roberto's parents send Señora X $300.00 a month for her and Roberto to live on. This money is used to make the payments on their home, utilities, and food. Roberto works to provide money for the rest of their needs, such as herbs, clothing, school supplies, and such. Roberto is very smart and wants to go to school, but knows that his grandmother needs his help. Putting his needs second, he assumes the role of provider in the traditional way and knows what he is doing is right.

So, in ending *la platica,* you thank Señora X for her time and assure her that you will help her in any way you can. Knowing that the people of the *colonias* are suspicious of government and its promises, you reassure her that you will keep in touch and will investigate what you can do for her neighbor, also. *Dios te bendiga por todo y vuelve* (God bless you for everything and come back).

CONCLUSION

Social work evaluation with individuals and families of Mexican descent is a process that needs to begin with comprehension of that which makes them unique, their *Fe.* The worldview that evolved out of the bloody conquest of indigenous peoples of the Americas is embedded in two worlds. These worlds collided and one was conquered. The conquered people survived using a mestizo philosophy as the basis for their sense of *Fe.*

The importance of *Fe* as a coping resource and strategy is modeled in the vignette described earlier. Señora X relies on her *Fe* to explain her situation in life and to accept what life, or, in this case, *Dios* provided. She does not dwell on her poverty; instead she acknowledges that there are people who live in worse poverty than she. To be poor is not the issue, but perceiving her situation as being *lo que Dios manda* (what God sends) and providing all that she needs. Her strength is in her *Fe* and in this way she copes with little material wealth.

Although the family is not with her, they are with her in her *Fe.* She is secure in the fact that, if they could, they would be with her. But she also has *Fe* that, if she really needs them, they would not hesitate to rush to her side. *"Con Fe todo es posible"* as so many people of Mexican heritage say.

In the traditional sense, she has the support of the community in everyday life. Her *Fe* encompasses the community as part of her extended family and they provide help when it is needed. In this communal lifestyle, a person doesn't have to ask for help in times of need; the community is there and readily provides assistance.

This chapter provides a link between theory and practice through the use of a model that is grounded in the Mexican American culture and traditions. It is intended to assist the worker in all aspects of social work practice with Latinos. The model is broad enough to be used with most minority groups if the worker is culturally competent.

REFERENCES

Acuna, R. (1988). *Occupied America: A history of Chicanos,* 3rd ed., New York: Harper & Row.

Anderson, N. B. & Armstead, C. A. (1995). Toward understanding the association of socioeconomic status and health: A new challenge for biopsychosocial approach. *Psychosomatic Medicine, 57,* 213–225.

Barrera, M. (1979). *Race and class in the Southwest: A theory of racial inequality.* South Bend, IN: University of Notre Dame Press.

Bullis, R. K. (1996). *Spirituality in social work practice.* Washington, DC: Taylor & Francis.

Carson, V. B. (Ed.) (1989). *Spiritual dimensions of nursing practice.* Philadelphia: W. B. Saunders.

Castex, G. M. (1994). Providing services to Hispanic/Latino populations: Profiles in diversity. *Social Work, 39,* 288–296.

Devore, W. & Schlesinger, E. G. (1999). *Ethnic-sensitive social work practice,* 3rd ed., Boston, MA: Allyn & Bacon.

Gallego, J. S. (1991). Culturally relevant services for Hispanic elderly. In M. Sotomayor & A. Garcia (Eds.), *Empowering Hispanic families: A critical issue for the '90s* (pp. 173–190). Milwaukee, Wisconsin: Family Service America.

Gutierrez, L. M. (1995). Understanding the empowerment process: Does consciousness make a difference? *Social Work Research, 19,* 229–237.

Hart, J. L. (1998). *Becoming a father: The real work of a man's soul.* Deerfield Beach, FL: Health Communications.

Hart, J. L. & Hareide, B. (1999). *World fathering: Fathering in groups in Norway and Hispanic fathers in Northern New Mexico and the Southwest.* Paper presented at the Eighth European Groupwork Symposium, London, 18–20, August 1999.

Internet. http://inet.ed.gov/pubs/faultline/who.html, 1998.

Jennings, G. (1980). *Aztec: A novel.* New York: Atheneum.

Knowlton, C. S. (1971). Cultural factors in the non-delivery of medical services to southwestern Mexican Americans. In M. L. Riedesel (Ed.), *Health related problems in arid lands* (contribution 14 of the Committee on Desert and Arid Zone Research Symposium) (pp. 59–71). Paper presented at the 47th annual meeting of the Southwestern and Rocky Mountain Division of the American Association for the Advancement of Science. Tempe, AZ.

Link, B. G. & Phelan, J. (1995). Social conditions as fundamental causes of disease. *Journal of Health and Social Behavior,* (Extra Issue), 80–94.

Martinez, E. S. & Vasquez, E. L. (1974). *Viva la raza! The struggle of the Mexican-American people.* New York: Doubleday.

McMahon, M. O. (1996). *The general method of social work practice: A generalist perspective,* 3rd ed., Boston, MA: Allyn & Bacon.

Paz, O. (1986). Mascaras Mexicanas. In C. M. Montross & E. L. Levine. *Vistas del mundo hispano: A literary reader.* New York: Charles Scribner's Sons.

Proctor, E. K. & Davis, L. E. (1994). The challenge of racial difference: Skills for clinical practice. *Social Work, 39,* 317–323.

Ramos, R. (1979). Movidas: The methodological and theoretical relevance of interactional strategies. *Studies in Symbolic Interaction, 2,* 141–165.

Rosow, I. (1967). *Social integration of the aged.* New York: Free Press.

Sheridan, M. J., Bullis, R. K., Adcock, C. R., Berlin, S. D., & Miller, P. C. (1992). Practitioner's personal and professional attitudes and behaviors toward religion and spirituality: Issues for education and practice. *Journal of Social Work Education, 28,* 190–203.

Sotomayor, M. (1977). Language, culture, and ethnicity in developing self-concept. *Social Casework, 58,* 195–203.

Villa, R. F. & Jaime, A. (1993). *La fe de la gente.* In M. Sotomayor & A. Garcia (Eds.), *Elderly Latinos: Issues and solutions for the 21st century* (pp. 129–142). Washington, DC: The National Hispanic Council on Aging.

Villa, R. F. (1994). *Religion and Fe as correlates of the preceived life satisfaction of older persons of Mexican heritage.* Unpublished doctoral dissertation, University of Utah Graduate School of Social Work.

Villa, R. F. (1999). *La fe y la familia.* In M. Sotomayor & A. Garcia (Eds.), *La familia: Traditions and realities* (pp.107–121). Washington, DC: The National Hispanic Council on Aging.

Van Voorhis, R. M. (1998). Culturally relevant practice: a framework for teaching psychosocial dynamics of oppression. *Journal of Social Work Education, 34,* 121–133.

CHAPTER 27

PROGRAM EVALUATION IN HEALTH AND HUMAN SERVICE AGENCIES SERVING LATINO COMMUNITIES

EDGAR COLON

There are approximately 17 million Latinos in the United States. At current rates of growth, it is projected that the Latino population will be the largest ethnic group and comprise 15 percent of the U.S. population by the year 2020 (Carasquillo, 1991).

The Latino population in the United States is a diverse community whose sociopolitical history is characterized by political struggle and economic and educational accomplishment. It is a U.S. community of considerable diversity of culture, race, ethnic and national origin. It is a community on the forefront of significant demographic change and sociopolitical growth as we enter the twenty-first century (U.S. Bureau of the Census, 1991).

SOCIODEMOGRAPHICS

The Latino population is an aggregation of several subgroups: Mexicans, Puerto Ricans, Cubans, Central and South Americans, and Dominicans. At present, Mexican Americans are the largest group. The second largest group is that of people from Central and South America. The Puerto Rican subgroup is the third largest group. Cubans make up one of the smallest population groups at approximately 6 percent of all Latinos. Dominicans are also a rapidly growing Latino subgroup, making up approximately 2 percent of the U.S. Latino population, at more than 2 million people (Novas, 1994).

It is important to recognize the nature of intra-group heterogeneity in relation to this population. In some contexts, the term *Hispanics* includes Spaniards, Portuguese, and Brazilians. However, because the term was not used as an ethnic label until the 1970s, many members of the group do not accept it. The cultural tenacity exhibited by Latinos in this country demonstrates the fact that Latinos do not abandon their traditions and assimilate, but selectively use their cultural background to define a sense of identity (Keefe, 1992). Thus, it is not uncommon to find reference to terms such as *Latino* or *La Raza* (literally, "the race") as the preferred ethnic labels in many communities. Similarly, there is diversity of opinion about which label is most appropriate within each subgroup.

Hispanic is not a term coined by the people it identifies. Its general familiarity is the result of a decision by the U.S. government's Office of the Management and Budget in 1978. This decision was made to help census takers who needed a term for whites (and others) who claimed some degree of Spanish language and/or cultural affiliation.

On the other hand, the term *Latino* is one coined by the people it is meant to identify (Facundo, 1995). For the Latino person, the use of this term provides both the advantage of a linguistic association and a geographic referent. Viewed in this context, the term *Latino* would appear to be the more historically and geopolitically accurate term to describe and identify populations of Caribbean and Latin American origin living in the United States (Bonilla-Santiago, 1993). The term *Latino* will be used throughout the chapter to refer to members of the Latino population.

The purpose of this chapter is to describe program evaluation practice issues that influence the evaluator's ability to effectively conduct program development and program outcome studies in health and human service agencies serving Latino communities. It begins with a brief sociodemographic profile of the Latino community in the United States, followed by an overview of Latino health and mental health beliefs and values. A section on the ecological perspective and program evaluation is also provided. The final section includes a case illustration that incorporates important evaluation practice principles.

LATINO HEALTH AND MENTAL HEALTH VALUES AND BELIEFS

Several research studies found that Latinos hold a dual approach to seeking physical and mental health care (De La Cancela & McDowell, 1992). Latino health beliefs and knowledge derive from a combination of sources: medieval Spanish traditions, indigenous Indian magical health beliefs, elements of Western health traditions, and biomedical knowledge (Le Vine & Padilla, 1980). The recent research literature reports that the Latino community across the Latino subgroups still maintains many of these belief systems. However, the studies also suggest that Latinos, particularly those individuals who are acculturated, tend to integrate Western beliefs in health and illness alongside folk medicine beliefs and practices. In examining Latino folk beliefs and views toward illness, it is evident that informal social groups play a prominent role (Perez, 1993; Rodriguez, 1989).

In relation to the completion of program evaluations in Latino communities, the evaluator's failure to understand how Latino clients gain strength form their nontraditional beliefs and values is partially due to the societal norm of cultural blindness (Morales & Sheafor, 1995). The program evaluator's lack of understanding of Latino health and mental health beliefs seriously affects the collection of relevant program data and the development of research methodology. The program evaluator must therefore act on his or her understanding of these values and beliefs by placing all Latino clients in their cultural and community contexts.

AN ECOLOGICAL PERSPECTIVE FOR PROGRAM EVALUATION

The ecological model of practice recognizes that transactions between the individual and the environment are products of all these domains and levels and are thus, complex and disruptive of the usual adaptive balance or goodness of fit, which often results in stress. This approach to practice emphasizes the adaptive, evolutionary view of human beings in constant interaction with all elements of their environment (Morales & Sheafor, 1995). At each systemic level, Latinos are engaged in a set of reciprocal exchanges, both adaptive and maladaptive, with their environment, which influences their ability to interact in a mutually responsive manner in search of a goodness of fit. A central issue to be addressed by the evaluator involves whether the program services targeted for Latinos have achieved the intended program results.

Moreover, as the evaluator attempts to address this and other related issues, he or she must collaborate with Latino clients, adopting a professional posture that recognizes the fact that there may be untapped reserves of mental, physical, and emotional resources that can be called on to help conduct the evaluation tasks. The Latino client's perception of his or her health and human service program needs, as well as the agency worker's and administrator's of these perceptions, is complex and variable (Marin & Marin, 1990). All Latino persons do not necessarily experience particular program services or administrative processes in the same way or as either negative or positive (Lenrow, 1978). The organization and delivery of program services must also consider the impact of Latino race and ethnicity on how to effectively evaluate health and human services. This concept suggests, within an ecological perspective, multiple definitions and various degrees of relevance to agency service providers.

In this regard, it is important to recognize that, among Latinos, ethnicity represents a sense of personhood, a psychological and social identity involving commonality and loyalty to race, religion, nationality, and ancestry. In sum, Latino health and mental values and beliefs serve as protective factors for the members of Latino subgroups as they attempt to meet their physical health, mental health, and related human service needs within their environments (Vega, 1990). The challenge for the program evaluator is to better understand the life transitions, environmental pressures, and the interpersonal processes that are unique to the Latino community.

The knowledge, values, and skills proposed in this framework only serve as a foundation for cultural intervention with Latinos. Indeed, culturally competent practice is a personal and professional matter, one that requires each professional to embrace the concept of cultural diversity and to develop a framework that reflects his or her level of experience, comfort, and familiarity. In this framework, the ecological perspective is suggested as one approach that is considered uniquely suited for practice with Latinos. Latino health and mental beliefs and values influence the nature of social interactions not only between individuals but also between Latino individuals, community systems, and social organizations. Therefore, the role of the program evaluator in the Latino community requires:

less involvement with oppressive institutional practices;

greater provision of accountable services in which Latino cultural norms and values are acknowledged;

stronger support of informal natural and spiritual network relationships; and

effective targeted identification of collaboration sources for working with the Latino family.

The following section describes a nine-step approach to program evaluation that takes into consideration the influence of Latino health and mental health beliefs and values.

PRACTICE PRINCIPLES AND SKILLS IN PROGRAM PLANNING AND IMPLEMENTATION

STEP 1: THE PREPARATION OF A WRITTEN PROPOSAL

When beginning a program evaluation, the first step is to complete a proposal that outlines the steps that will be undertaken. It is important to begin by addressing the following questions:

1. What are the program goals and objectives that are congruent with the beliefs, values, and special interests of the Latino community?

2. Who, from the Latino community, must be involved in the identification of program strategies and objectives?

3. What strategies must be undertaken to ensure that the design of program processes and outcome evaluation measures is consistent with a culturally appropriate response to the social programming needs of the Latino community?

4. What is the social makeup and employment status of the Latino community in general, and of potential program participants in particular?

5. What is the level of political knowledge and involvement in the Latino community?

6. Who are the identifiable Latino community leaders?

7. What are the quality and status of social and educational services available to the Latino community?

Most program evaluations begin in one of three ways. Program personnel themselves may initiate the evaluation or seek to have an evaluation team conduct one; the funding agency or central management may require an evaluation of a sponsored or planned program; or, an internal evaluation department might suggest that the organization would benefit from the evaluation of a particular phase of its activities.

As the preparation of the written proposal will require the support of all the individuals who will be involved in the evaluation process, it is of critical importance that the evaluator identify the stakeholders. The program evaluator must seek to involve as many stakeholders as possible in the early stage of evaluation planning. Stakeholders are individuals who are involved in the program, who derive some or all of their income from the program, whose future status or career might be affected by the quality of the program, or who are the clients or recipients of the services of the program.

The important questions that must be asked of Latino stakeholders include the following:

1. Who wants the evaluation?
2. What type of evaluation is desired?
3. Why is the evaluation desired?
4. When is the evaluation desired?

Based on the answers to these and other questions, evaluators can understand what issues must be addressed and make certain decisions before the collection of data begins. They also need to learn about the goals and mechanics of the program, about key stakeholders who sponsor the program, about the program personnel, and about people who may resist the evaluation of the program.

After obtaining this information, evaluators must decide whether an evaluation can be done. If the program is planned in a way that permits evaluation, then a decision needs to be made as to whether it should be done immediately, whether it should be done in the way it is proposed, or whether it should be done at all. Once the evaluator has prepared the written proposal and obtained the approval of the stakeholders, he or she will need to conduct a literature review to elucidate the issues raised during the initial engagement period. Many of the program-related issues raised during this period will need to be further studied by researching the past experience of similar programs attempting to address the health and human service needs of Latinos. One example of a program issue is the conflict that may arise when attempting to evaluate a mental health program that, although originally designed within a Western model, has evolved to include the involvement of folk healers and other members of Latino natural support systems. The evaluator will need to research the available literature on the use of indigenous providers in the delivery of mental health services.

STEP 2: THE COMPLETION OF A LITERATURE REVIEW

Once all the published research has been collected, evaluators should proceed to collect community-generated information and institutional archival data relative to the prevailing needs of the Latino community. Such information can be obtained directly from persons who live or work in the community itself. Institutional information can be obtained from existing city, county, state and agencies. Whether such information is community-generated or institutional, there are two important challenges to overcome.

The first challenge is that, although there are communities that have been well summarized in the literature describing the Latino culture (e.g., the Spanish language, Catholicism, family orientation, and respect for elders and persons in authority), many of these cultural attributes are continually undergoing modification as a result of acculturation. The second challenge is that the evaluator must understand and appreciate intra-group variability as well as inter-group diversity.

STEP 3: THE IDENTIFICATION AND SELECTION OF A RESEARCH METHODOLOGY

As there may be several challenges for the evaluator, given the lack of valid and reliable data for assessing risks and social programming needs within the Latino population, the evaluator may wish to develop his or her own questionnaires and surveys. However, he or she must keep in mind that, to maximize the utility and generalizability of the information gathered, the reliability and validity of the instruments will need to be established, in particular, the content and face validity of the instruments. In addition, the evaluator should determine whether standardized instruments have been validated with a Latino population.

The program evaluation issues raised when attempting to address this research question can be the source of considerable confusion, frustration, and doubt. Program evaluators and community leaders must therefore establish a common understanding with respect to the analytical dimensions for establishing an evaluation protocol. Most importantly, program evaluators must understand the influence of Latino norms and values that need to be addressed when designing and implementing a comprehensive evaluation process for community-based Latino agencies. Even more potentially troublesome, however, are the pitfalls inherent in trying to determine who is involved in the first place. These program evaluation issues must, therefore, be addressed prior to identifying the evaluation agenda. These dimensions, which may be thought of as analytical perspectives for establishing an evaluation protocol, are often thought of by the evaluators as being grounded in scientific rigor, and, therefore, objective. It is this impression that is often at the heart of a communication breakdown, which may adversely affect the data collection process.

STEP 4: THE SELECTION OF A RESEARCH MODEL

A number of different approaches to evaluation are available (process, outcome, program monitoring) to guide the planning and implementation of program evaluations. At times, disagreements over the best way to carry out an evaluation have been based on different assumptions about what is the best, or even the proper way to evaluate a program. The specific evaluation research questions being addressed by an evaluation or the unique aspects of the program setting often suggest which model will be most useful. When attempting to select a research model for an evaluation of program services delivered to Latinos, it is crucial for evaluators and stakeholders to avoid selecting a model before thoroughly analyzing the setting and the uniqueness of the client population. In this regard, Zambrana (1991) suggests that the evaluator must remember that values such as impartiality, rationality, empirical knowledge, and ethics committed to the dignity of the individual and public welfare are Western concepts that, although not foreign to Latinos, may not be important to their perceptions of program services.

STEP 5: THE COLLECTION OF DATA

The importance of including program information relative to cultural considerations in the evaluation of human service organizations responsible for the delivery of health and human services in Latino communities is of critical importance. The program evaluator must identify culturally relevant contextual factors that influence or enhance data gathering, program development, and program evaluation processes. The utilization of such information increases the probability of obtaining positive results in program evaluation efforts.

The program evaluator formulates questions of what, where, and when, relative to the evaluation, he or she will approach the task on the basis of his or her own beliefs and expectations. Therefore, the ability of a client and evaluator to agree on an evaluation depends, in part, on the concerns and attitudes they bring with them when they meet to discuss an evaluation. An important question that informs this dialogue is: What are the barriers that must be overcome when the rhetoric of evaluation confronts the rhetoric of culture? The following questions are useful for the development of a data-collection approach that comes out of that dialogue.

1. What are the available formal and informal sources for data that can provide a cultural lens for understanding the social needs of the Latino community?

2. What are the agency indicators that may suggest that the agency staff and administrators may be experiencing cultural blindness relative to the social needs of the Latino community?

3. What input is required to modify existing questionnaire or survey instruments to ensure greater validity and reliability, given the needs of the Latino community?

The program evaluator working within a Latino community-based agency, or one serving a largely Latino population, must identify and collect evaluation data that will lead to the development of an action strategy that will produce a comprehensive evaluation process. The gathering of evaluative information may present major challenges to the evaluator, such as:

> the *limited or negative experiences* that Latinos may have had with social service agencies identified in one form or another with mainstream America;

> the *past negative experiences* that certain Latino communities have had with government agencies or social scientists, who, to obtain desired information, have promised that the information would result in benefits to the community, but have been quick to renege on such promises once the information was obtained, or may even have used the information to the detriment of the community;

> general *mistrust of any impersonal agency* that might seek information that the individuals are not accustomed to giving or are fearful of sharing with anyone (e.g., legal status in the country or politically motivated atrocities they may have experienced in their country of origin).

STEP 6: CONDUCTING THE SURVEY RESEARCH

Evaluators may find that the use of service provider surveys or a review of available archival data may prove useful for obtaining baseline data. Although this level of information is oftentimes not adequate for conducting a comprehensive evaluation, evaluators may than work in close collaboration with program staff to identify or develop the most culturally and educationally appropriate need-assessment instruments that can be used to gather the desired data. If more extensive and statistically reliable data is needed, then the use of select standardized questionnaires and surveys may prove useful. The following issues should be considered when using the following approaches to do survey research.

1. Telephone Interview

The telephone interview, as a data gathering approach, presents similar challenges to those inherent in using personal/household interviews. Oftentimes the evaluator may find that Latino individuals are distrustful and fearful of providing information in a personal interview; these feelings will quite likely be intensified when respondents are asked to provide such information on the telephone. It is also important, as described in relation to the use of the personal interview, that the evaluator maintain a high level of personal comfort and establish rapport. The best approach is to engage in friendly conversation to allay any fears and or concerns. It is also of paramount importance that the purpose of the call be fully explained; in particular, an explanation of how the information provided is to be used is essential.

2. Mail Surveys

From a cost-effective perspective, there is no question that mail surveys facilitate and expedite information gathering. However, the low response rate often associated with mail surveys tends to dissuade many evaluators from using this approach. It should be noted that this approach is also plagued with challenges similar to those described for the personal and telephone interview methods.

3. Personal/Household Interviews

A major challenge associated with the use of the personal interview is the overall lack of familiarity that certain Latino subgroups may have with this rather obtrusive research method. Standard interviewing methods are derived from European cultural models, which assume that direct questioning is the most effective way to find out what one wants to know. It is quite likely that these methods may not be as culturally appropriate and effective when used with Latino subgroups, which are more traditional in nature. To overcome this challenge, evaluators should consider training interviewers to gather such information indirectly, such as within the context of friendly conversation. In addition, evaluators should consider hiring data collectors who are recognized, trusted, and respected members of the Latino community.

In this author's experience, the most effective way of overcoming the challenges of conducting surveys in Latino communities requires asking community leaders to alert the targeted Latino community of the forthcoming survey. In addition, the signature of such leaders should appear on the cover and explanatory letters that accompany the surveys. Lastly, as the evaluators may not know the language preference of the receiver, it is essential that both Spanish and English versions be used.

STEP 7: THE COMPLETION OF AN ANALYSIS OF THE SURVEY DATA

The analysis of survey data is also a complicated issue, involving the technical question of what makes a good measure of the research criteria selected by the evaluators and the stakeholders to evaluate the Latino program-related process and outcome experience. Given the nature of the ambivalent racial and ethnic identification among Latino groups, the conflict in selecting accurate measures is great. In this regard, the evaluator is reminded that, given the strong association with cultural values of group membership and the maintenance of warm, intimate personal relationships, the Latino struggles concurrently with self-rejecting tendencies and positive feelings about group membership. From a mental health perspective, the emotional turmoil that results may lead to love and hate feelings about being Latino. For example, a Latino may refuse to speak Spanish, or identify as a Catholic, or marry within the group. However, the same individual may have strong preferences for Latino foods, prefer living in a Latino neighborhood, and become involved in Latino civil rights activities. Therefore, when analyzing evaluation survey data, the evaluator must carefully consider the cultural complexity that must be accounted for when attempting to identify relevant program evaluation measures.

STEP: 8 THE DEVELOPMENT OF PROCESS AND PROGRAM OUTCOME RECOMMENDATIONS

When engaged in conducting a process or outcome evaluation, the evaluator must understand and appreciate intra-group variability as much as inter-group diversity. When attempting to collect this critical information, the evaluator is cautioned to seek out further information from knowledgeable sources (Latino leaders in targeted communities, research literature, etc.).

The evaluator must, therefore, gather data from many sources, from both the agency archives and the community, to develop an in-depth understanding and appreciation of the cultural knowledge about Latinos required to formulate relevant and appropriate questions, hypotheses, and procedures that are more in line with the insider's view. The evaluator must also seek to create a community support strategy to overcome the major challenges that may influence the collection of critical program data. The evaluator must carefully consider the types of research approaches used for the data collection when working toward the evaluation of policies and programs aimed at addressing the social needs of Latinos. Evaluators should develop an approach for gathering desired information through the use of indirect or unobtrusive methods.

Lastly, the evaluator should develop a collaborative relationship with the agency administrators and staff working in Latino communities. They may very well serve as cultural guides and mentors, and help to empower Latino clients through the process of participating in the research activities involved in process and outcome evaluation. The client may then be helpful to the evaluator in appreciating the influence of selected demographic, sociological, and psychological variables that must be carefully considered when evaluating social programs earmarked for Latinos.

STEP 9: THE PREPARATION OF THE EVALUATION REPORTS: INTERPRETING AND COMMUNICATING FINDINGS

Evaluators must take an active role to ensure that positive program and outcome results are effectively communicated to members of the Latino community. To this end, evaluators should use the medium that is most effective in delivering information to the community; in most cases, this would probably not be a professional journal. Providing such information to people in the community could raise the hope and expectation that the community can empower itself.

Evaluators must be also be willing to provide, to any and all educational and social agencies that serve the Latino community, detailed information on the activities and strategies that led to the positive outcomes. This information would enable such agencies to replicate the successful activities and, in so doing, maximize the benefits that can accrue to the Latino community. Lastly, evaluators should meet with community advisors for their expertise regarding any and all sociocultural variables that need to be considered in viewing the outcome results realistically.

CASE EXAMPLE: THE UPPER MANHATTAN TENANTS COUNCIL LATINO YOUTH DEVELOPMENT PROGRAM

As an evaluator, this author was asked to conduct a program evaluation of a Latino Youth Development Program. This program is among the human service programs offered by the Upper Manhattan Tenants Council. From the initial inception of my work at the agency, I was faced with many of the challenges to program evaluation described earlier. I will describe difficult issues I faced when attempting to complete step one. As I was preparing the written proposal for the evaluation, I was asked to conduct a need assessment of twenty-five sixteen-to twenty-year-old males who had completed a substance abuse prevention and education group work program. The goal of the six sessions group work program was to provide the participants with information about substance abuse and how to decide whether to begin or continue the use or abuse of substances. I chose to conduct focus groups as a data-collection approach.

As I conducted the focus groups, I was quite surprised by the level of hostility that emerged among the focus group participants. It was evident to me that the hostility had also been occurring during the group sessions. As I conducted further focus groups, I came to better understand the reason for the hostile feelings among the group participants. It seems that the group of fifteen included four Puerto Ricans, two Cubans, three Dominicans, three South Americans, and three Mexicans. In addition, the racial makeup of the group was quite varied. The group racial composition consisted of two light-skinned individuals and five dark-skinned males; the rest were varied shades of brown. Before I was able to continue with the need assessment, I had to address the issue of racial and ethnic identity conflict within the group.

As an evaluator, I learned a valuable lesson about racial and ethnic identity as exhibited among the Latino population, which truly reflects the rainbow spectrum of physical characteristics and racial makeup. I further came to appreciate the fact that, given this reality, the inner dynamics of ethnic identity for many Latinos may lead to ambivalent identification with ethnic group membership. Moreover, inner conflicts in ethnic identity may ultimately find expression in some form of overt behavior. As I worked with young men in my evaluation study, I found that, for those individuals holding a negative sense of self-identification, aspects of their ethnic self were either actively rejected or disowned.

From this experience I came to adopt many important practice principles that I believe are important for conducting evaluation in health and human service agencies serving Latino communities. I share the following principles with you.

PRACTICE PRINCIPLES

1. The program evaluator need must recognize the need for building consensus regarding terminology when providing effective program evaluation services to Latino community-based organizations. As there is such a diverse range of ethnic

identifiers among Latinos, it is important that evaluators adopt terminology that recognizes this diversity of self-identification.

2. The program evaluator must appreciate the extent and nature of changing Latino value systems and worldviews. The incorporation of his or her under-standing of these aspects of Latino culture will assist in the process of need assessment and the development of an evaluation methodology.

3. Program evaluators should involve Latino individuals in every aspect of the cross-cultural evaluation process, including program planning and implementation, whether they are formally trained in evaluation or not. Equipped with appropriate training, such individuals will be in a position to make outstanding contributions.

4. Program evaluators are strongly advised to interpret any information with a great deal of caution and should examine other sources of data. These sources may include observational or archival data as well as that obtained from opinion leaders in the Latino community that substantiates and validates their interpretations.

5. The program evaluator should give serious consideration to establishing a Latino Affairs Advisory Board made up of persons from the Latino community who can provide guidance and feedback in relation to the content, length, language, and cultural appropriateness of the questionnaire or survey.

CONCLUSION

It is clear that, as we enter the twenty-first century, Latino communities are emerging as highly complex social collectivities. Ethnicity, nationality, levels of acculturation, generation, socioeconomic status, race, legality of residence, and language differences are the obvious differences. These characteristics influence the way in which health and human services can be optimally evaluated and delivered, and challenge the program evaluator to develop culturally competent approaches that incorporate an understanding of Latino health and mental health beliefs and values.

To meet this challenge, program evaluations must demonstrate a firm understanding of the interaction of these characteristics, all of which impact on program outcomes. These factors ultimately influence the Latino target populations served in relation to the patterns of utilization of human services and the organizational structure of the health and human service agencies providing services in the community.

Lastly, the principles and skill approaches in this chapter suggest a starting point. They are not an end in themselves, but a guide for a cultural learning process that will promote and inform the program evaluator's continuous learning and maintenance of a firm commitment to the valuing of Latino diversity in it's many forms and structures. As culturally competent practice evolves in the social work profession, program evaluators must respond with new and creative approaches to program evaluation with renewed cultural awareness and sensitivity to the social programming needs of the Latino community into the twenty-first century.

REFERENCES

Abad, V., Ramos., J. & Boyce, E. (1974). A model for delivery of mental health services to Spanish speaking minorities. *American Journal of Orthopsychiatry, 44* (4), 584–595.

Bonilla-Santiago, G. (1993). *Breaking ground and barriers: Hispanic women developing effective leadership.* San Diego. CA; Marin.

Carrasquillo, A. L. (1991). *Hispanic children and youth in the United States: A resource guide.* New York: Garland.

De La Cancela, V. & McDowell, A. (1992). AIDS: Health care intervention models for communities of color. *Journal of Multicultural Social Work, 2,* 107–109.

Facundo, A. (1995). Sensitive mental health services for low income Puerto Rican families. In Marta Sotomayor, (ed.), *Empowering Hispanic families: a critical issue for the 90's.* Milwaukee, WI: Family Service of America.

Garcia-Preto, N. (1990). Hispanic mothers. In *Ethnicity and mothers* (Special issue). *Journal of Feminist Family Therapy, 2* (2), 1–65.

Green J. W. (1999). *Cultural awareness in the human services.* Englewood Cliffs, NJ: Prentice-Hall.

Hayes-Bautista, D. & Chapa, J. (1978). Chicano patients and medical practitioners: A sociology of knowledge paradigm of lay professional interaction. *Medical Anthropology, 2* 47–62.

Keefe, S. E. (1992). Ethnic identity: The domain of perceptions and attachments to ethnic groups and cultures. *Human Organization, 51,* 35–43.

Lenrow, P. (1978). Dilemmas of professional helping: Continuities and discontinuities with folk healing roles. In L. Wispe (Ed.), *Altruism, sympathy and helping: Psychological and sociological principles. Hispanic Journal of Behavioral Sciences, 4,* 315–329.

Leslie, L., & Leitch, M. L. (1989). A demographic profile of recent immigrants: clinical and service implications. *Hispanic Journal of Behavioral Sciences, 4,* 315–329.

Le Vine, P. S., & Padilla, A. M. (1980). *Crossing cultures in therapy: Pluralistic counseling for the Hispanic.* Monterey, CA: Brooks/Cole.

Marin, B. V. & Marin, G. (1990). Effects of acculturation on knowledge of AIDS and HIV among Hispanics. *Journal of Hispanic Behavioral Sciences, 12* (2), 110–121.

Molina, C. (1983). Family health promotion: Conceptual framework for "La Salud" and "El Bienestar" in Latino communities. *In S. Andrade, (Ed.), Latino families in the United States* (pp. 135–144). New York: Planned Parenthood Federation of America.

Morales, A. & Sheafor, W. B. (1995). *Social work; A profession of many faces,* 9th edition. Boston: Allyn & Bacon.

Novas, H. (1994). *Everything you need to know about Latino history.* New York: Plume/Penguin.

Perez, S. M. (1993). *Moving from the margins: Puerto Rican young men and family poverty.* Washington, DC: National Council of La Raza.

Rodriguez, C. E. (1989). *Puerto Ricans: Born in the U.S.A.* Winchester, MA: Unwin Hyman.

U.S. Bureau of the Census. (1991). 1990 population data (on-line statistical data) M. Pees (Ed.). Washington, DC: Bureau of the Census. November 7.

Vega, W. A. (1990). Hispanic families in the 1980's: A decade of research. *Journal of Marriage and the Family, 52,* 1015–1024.

Zambrana, R. E. (1991). Ethnic differences in the substance use patterns of low-income pregnant women. *Family Community Health, 13,* 1–11.

CHAPTER 28

DEVELOPING CULTURALLY SENSITIVE PRACTICE EVALUATION SKILLS WITH NATIVE AMERICAN INDIVIDUALS AND FAMILIES

DORIE J. GILBERT

CYNTHIA FRANKLIN

Like other marginalized groups, Native Americans[1] have endured a long history of oppression, disenfranchisement, and cultural misunderstanding in the United States. The social work literature emphasizes the need for social workers to be knowledgeable about the ways in which sociocultural factors impact disenfranchised groups and to transform this knowledge into skills that produce effective interventions (Blount, Thyer, & Frye, 1992; Devote & Schlesinger, 1996; Pinderhughes, 1989; Van Voorhis, 1998). Previous chapters in this book have covered culturally sensitive assessment and intervention skills with American Indians. This chapter focuses on evaluation of practice interventions with individuals and families to determine the extent to which an intervention achieved its objectives. Practice evaluation skills provide tools to determine the efficacy of our culturally sensitive interventions.

This chapter begins with an overview of the American Indian sociodemographic, cultural, and psychosocial issues. Next, we discuss theoretical approaches to practice evaluation that incorporate ecological issues, clients' strengths, and empowerment. A guide to direct practice evaluation is presented within the framework of seven evaluation skills and relevant cultural considerations. Finally, a case study is presented to illustrate the application of practice evaluation skills to American Indian clients.

HISTORICAL AND SOCIODEMOGRAPHIC OVERVIEW

Prior to the arrival of Columbus in 1492, approximately 15 million indigenous people lived on the continent, representing about 300 separate tribal groups that were enormously diverse with many distinct cultures, social organizations, technologies, economies, and over 300 distinct languages (Davis, 1994; Mohawk, 1992; Sale, 1990). The arrival of Europeans forever altered the existence of the native peoples. On contact, Europeans set in motion a series of exploitations that included genocide, colonization, disease, alcohol, religious conversion, and forced assimilation. Much of the exploitation was justified by a belief that the Indians were savages, and, at first encounter, even the question of whether or not Indians were human was raised (McGrane, 1989; Todorov, 1984). After three centuries of contact with Europeans, the American Indian population and their land had dwindled drastically, and their cultures, languages, and religions had been severely disrupted (McDonnell, 1991; Snipp, 1989).

Today, American Indians number just over 2 million, less than 1 percent of the U.S. population, but they are one of the fastest growing groups within the United States due to increased birthrates, decreased infant mortality rates, and a greater willingness to report American Indian ancestry (McLemore & Romo, 1998). Yet, American Indians remain one of the most disadvantaged groups in the United States. Fully 30 percent of America Indians are poor (Russell, 1998). Over half of American Indians, 53.7 percent, are part of metropolitan communities, while 46.3 percent are living in nonmetropolitan areas (Russell, 1998).

CULTURAL VALUES AND BEHAVIORAL NORMS

Understanding cultural values and behavioral norms is essential to developing practice evaluation skills. There can be a fine line, however, between describing the cultural norms and behaviors of a group and stereotyping, and the intent here is to avoid overgeneralization. Gross (1995) notes that the professional literature can perpetuate the notion that "true Indianess is traditional and fixed," which ignores the complexities of modern and postmodern approaches to social problems in American Indian communities (p. 209). While it is important to know the historical and collective experiences of American Indians, social workers must individually evaluate each client's values and behavioral patterns. In assessing a client's cultural orientation, practitioners should consider the intersecting intragroup differences such as race/ethnicity, age, sexual orientation, gender, and class. Other factors, such as appearance, religion, community, education, geographic origin, biracial identity, and the extent to which a person's identity is defined around race or ethnicity, add further complexity to defining cultural orientations (Gilbert, 1997).

Although American Indians represent a great many people with different cultural backgrounds, those who follow or have been exposed to traditional practices may share some common cultural values and behavioral norms (Broken Nose, 1992; Ho, 1987; Weaver & White, 1997). Weaver and White (1997) describe values and norms associated with traditional native culture, including, but not limited to:

- a deep respect for people, especially elders
- generosity and sharing beyond the family unit
- a collective identity strongly linked to family, clan, and nation
- cooperativeness among people while valuing individual responsibility
- harmony with nature and a continuous, rather than linear worldview
- noninterference, particularly the reluctance to interfere in someone else's life
- religion or spirituality may play an important role in development and rites of passage

This knowledge helps to place clients' experiences in a cultural context that can lead to empowerment rather than marginalization. For example, Indian children in mainstream school environments may have difficulties that reflect value conflicts rather than deficits of the child. Nel (1994) notes that the reinforcement of Eurocentric values in the classroom, such as competition and individualism, conflict with the values of generosity, sharing, and cooperativeness that characterize some traditional American Indian children.

American Indians are predominantly urban, and the extent to which this translates into a majority culture ideology varies greatly. Some urban Indians, for instance, may have had little contact with traditional tribal customs and may be acculturated into mainstream ideas and norms and may, as a result, find native values and behaviors alien (Franklin, Waukechon, & Larney, 1995). Younger Indians who live in cities attain higher average levels of education and move toward assimilation in education, occupations, income, health, and marriage (McLemore & Romo, 1998).

For many American Indians, a bicultural identity reflects fluid transitions from one environment to another. While the dichotomous presentation of mainstream versus native values and norms may imply that, once acculturated, Indians replace their identity with a Eurocentric one, American Indians can be simultaneously highly acculturated and tribally or ethnically identified (Choney, Berryhill-Paapke, & Robbins, 1995; Weaver, 1996). For some urban Indians, identities are tied to their metropolitan communities and a pan-Indian ideology in which they are assimilated, in part, but maintain strong tribal identity (Liebow, 1989). In a study of 310 urban American Indian adults, Walters (1999, p. 177) found that:

> native peoples have survived by taking the best of both worlds, integrating them, maintaining and transforming native cultures, and ultimately, buffering against negative colonization process through the internalization of positive identity attitudes and the externalization of negative dominant group attitudes.

PROBLEMS ADDRESSED BY SOCIAL
WORK PRACTITIONERS

There is, no doubt, great resilience among American Indians, but individuals and families within the group also experience serious social problems. Similarly to other historically oppressed groups, American Indians may not seek out services due to a lack of trust in the dominant culture's solutions and/or culturally insensitive services (Lum, 1992; Sue & Sue, 1990). Many of the problems presented by American Indians are no different from those of the majority population; however, poverty and racial/ethnic inequality often underlie and exacerbate their problems. The average family income of American Indians is $21,619, compared with a national average of more than $35,000 (Statistical Abstract of the United States, 1997). Thus, their experiences with inequality cannot be disconnected from the types of problems that cause them to seek help.

The most often referenced social problem among American Indians is alcoholism, so much so that the literature may perpetuate the stereotype of the "drunken Indian" (Thompson, Walker, & Silk-Walker, 1993). Unfortunately, Indians themselves may internalize this image of themselves (May & Smith, 1988). While American Indians, in general, are four times as likely to die of alcoholism than the general population (Snipp, 1989), patterns of chemical dependency vary greatly among this group. The medical and social patterns of chemical dependency are linked to high rates of cirrhosis, automobile accidents, homicide, delinquency, and other problems (Armstrong, Guilfoyle, & Melton, 1996; Thompson et al., 1993).

Suicide, for example, is linked to depression, psychosis, and other mental disorders, in addition to substance abuse, which has been reported in over 75 percent of suicides among American Indians (May & Van Winkle, 1993; Thompson et al., 1993). Indian teenagers are four times as likely to attempt suicide as other teens (May & Van Winkle, 1993). Bechtold (1994) notes two culture-specific determinants of suicide among American Indian youth. First, difficulties may arise in cultural identity formation for youth who are not part of Native traditions or fully assimilated into the dominant culture. Second, separation and the individuation necessary to establish oneself as an autonomous adult may be difficult to achieve because of unemployment and economic deprivation.

Another concern is the issue of internalized oppression or internalized negative attitudes about oneself based on stereotypes promulgated by dominant group members. In studying urban American Indians, Walters (1999) found that members of this group can hold "very negative attitudes about oneself as an Indian and toward Indians as a group, yet still, behaviorally, maintain customs and norms that reflect identification with Indian culture" (p. 175). Identity conflict that results from self-hate or an absence of connection to one's culture can have devastating consequences on an individual's psyche (Bachman, 1992; Pinderhughes, 1989). Thus, the development of positive identity, self-esteem, and cultural appreciation is an important prevention strategy among native people. Fortunately, American Indians are experiencing a resurgence of ethnic identity and culture revitalization within reservations and urban communities (Nagel, 1996).

PRACTICE EVALUATION

Practice evaluation is a type of evaluative research whereby the social work practitioner determines the extent to which an intervention achieved its objectives.
Evaluation of practice occurs on any of the three intervention levels: micro (individuals), mezzo (families and groups), and macro (communities and organizations). We discuss practice evaluation at the micro-level with American Indian
clients.

Evaluation is a component of micro-practice in the same way as assessment
and intervention, and it makes sense that the growing body of literature on culturally competent assessment and interventions should be applied to the third practice component: evaluation. Unfortunately, there is a tendency to separate practice
evaluation from assessment and intervention. This is due to several often-cited
barriers to practice evaluation, such as time constraints, research design, measurement difficulties, and the objection that evaluation is too "scientific" (Staudt, 1997).
Staudt argues, however, that these barriers are pseudoissues because they ignore
the fact that evaluation is inextricably tied to assessment and intervention. Indeed,
failure to evaluate one's practice may be unethical (Bloom & Orme, 1993).

THEORETICAL APPROACHES TO PRACTICE
EVALUATION WITH AMERICAN INDIANS

Theories that guide practice, and our evaluation of that practice, should meet two
criteria: (1) the theory should be valid, and (2) it should be appropriate for the particular case (LeCroy, 1992). Theoretical foundations for evaluating American
Indian clients must be grounded in the native culture of individuals and communities for whom the intervention is targeted and should incorporate nonmajority
values in explaining behavior and problem-solving strategies. Three theoretical
perspectives that guide effective practice evaluation with American Indians are:
ecological or person-in-environment, clients' strengths, and empowerment. These
theoretical perspectives have been discussed and illustrated throughout this book.
Here we summarize how the major tenets of these perspectives relate to evaluation
skills with American Indian clients.

The Person-in-Environment Perspective

The basic premise of this perspective is that individuals are involved in transactions with other systems (family, peers, organizations, community, etc.) within
their environment and that these various systems influence each other (Germain,
1991). Further, "individuals are perceived as a system composed of biological, psychological, and emotional dimensions" (Jordan & Franklin, 1995, p. 5), all of which
should be assessed to determine clients' strengths and deficits as they interact with
external systems. Systems can be looked at in terms of different layers of the environment, each of which has risks (direct threat to or absence of opportunities for

healthy development) and opportunities that are often assessed using ecomaps (Garbarino, 1982).

For Native Americans, potential environmental influences include: tribal chiefs and elders, extended families, spiritual leaders, tribal laws, the Bureau of Indian Affairs (BIA), societal prejudice, and economic challenges. Central to this perspective is the notion that human beings are not only impacted by their environment, but also can take an active role in influencing this environment. This idea dovetails with social work's focus on self-determination and social justice. It implies that our work with American Indians and other disenfranchised groups should include advocacy and the encouragement of clients to engage in social change at all levels.

Strengths Perspective

In describing the basic principle of the strengths perspective, Saleebey (1996) states that, "All must be seen in the light of their capacities, talents, competencies, possibilities, visions, values, and hopes, however dashed and distorted these may have become through circumstance, oppression, and trauma" (p. 297). From this standpoint, evaluation plans are collaborative efforts in which practitioners focus on clients' strengths, positive goals, and small successes. When evaluative studies are grounded in a strengths perspective, social workers should be able to identify clients' strengths, even when these do not match the values or norms of the majority culture. For instance, Eurocentric values of individualism and competition, central themes of many dominant theoretical perspectives, directly conflict with values of cooperation and collaboration that American Indian and other populations may hold. Cultural traditions are important strengths to consider in selecting evaluation designs. For example, because extended-family life is a source of pride, security, identity, and protection against outside threat (Ho, 1987; Weaver & White, 1997), practitioners may use extended family as a source of evaluation and utilize instruments that reflect increases in family functioning.

Empowerment

Dubois and Miley (1996) delineate three common elements that characterize the empowerment process: focusing on strengths, working collaboratively, and linking personal and political power. In essence, the "clients should be involved both in their own change process from defining their situation to determining goals, selecting their course of action and evaluating the results" (p. 27). If evaluation is based on an empowerment framework, practitioners should evaluate whether or not personal and socioeconomic power for the individual and family were increased. In order to evaluate whether our interventions are empowering clients, Van Voorhis (1998, p. 129) urges practitioners to evaluate four components of empowerment. She recommends that practitioners evaluate the extent to which they helped the client in: (1) claiming a positive identity, (2) developing, mutually empathic relationships, (3) mobilizing resources and power to respond to oppression, and (4) increasing proactive behavior as a member of one or more oppressed groups who seek change.

PRINCIPLES OF PRACTICE EVALUATION

Elsewhere in this book, you have read about appropriate assessments and therapeutic approaches with American Indians. If we utilize culturally sensitive assessments and therapeutic approaches and our interventions are effective, we should be able to document this success using evaluation tools and outcome measures. If our interventions are not effective, it is even more crucial that we know and alter interventions to more effectively serve the client. Effective practice evaluation with American Indian clients requires the integration of evaluative research skills and critical thinking skills to ensure that culturally specific considerations are made in each step of the process.

SUMMARY OF PRACTICE EVALUATION
SKILLS WITH AMERICAN INDIANS

Next, we present a seven-step guide to developing practice evaluation skills with American Indians. For each skill, we discuss how to integrate native cultural aspects.

STEP 1: ESTABLISHING A TRUSTING RELATIONSHIP

Evaluation must take place within a context of trust and respect for the client. Although this applies to all clients, American Indian clients may be hesitant to trust social workers or researchers, particularly those outside of their community, based on negative images or experiences (Weaver, 1997). Practitioners must have self-awareness about their own cultural orientation, sufficient knowledge about or affiliation with the client's community, and a sound assessment of the client's cultural orientation before determining how best to establish trust. The trusting relationship is crucial to ensure that clients feel comfortable providing the type of input necessary for the evaluation process. Paniagua (1994) suggests planning to collect data on the client gradually and warns against collecting a large amount of information before a trusting relationship is established. Dana (1998) states that American Indian clients want to know that the practitioner is proficient in helping to solve problems and is culturally competent. Establishing a cooperative evaluation process is also important, and, to do so, the practitioner may need to gain acceptance with significant others in the client's environment, such as tribal leaders or community gatekeepers whom the client respects and looks to for guidance (Mihesuah, 1993). As part of a collaborative helping relationship it is important for the practitioner to communicate to the client the benefits of practice evaluation and to engage the client in the evaluation process.

STEP 2: CONCEPTUALIZING PROBLEMS, GOALS, AND OBJECTIVES

Being specific about problems is a crucial link between assessment, intervention, and evaluation. In addition, problems, goals, and objectives should be conceptualized within the aforementioned theoretical frameworks, in that problems should not be deficit-based, but focused on strengths of both the client and the environment (Cowger, 1994). As noted earlier, many problems presented by American Indian clients are linked to a long history of economic and sociopolitical inequalities. Van Voorhis (1998) recommends that problem definition with marginalized clients should include an assessment of psychosocial effects of oppression and ways in which clients have experienced alienation.

Extensive knowledge about clients and their environments is required to ensure culturally grounded conceptualizations. In conceptualizing physical or mental health-related problems, practitioners working with Native Americans should ascertain the effects of folk beliefs (spirits, hexes, or other unseen events). Practitioners may include an evaluation of culture-related syndromes, such as "ghost sickness," a weakness or dizziness resulting from the action of witches and evil forces (Dana, 1998). When working with American Indian families, it is also important to integrate the norm of interdependence of family members, group consensus, and the family's place in the broader community system (Weaver, 1997).

Goals and objectives should be formulated with the client's involvement and only after considering the client's strengths, resources and sources of personal power, and the client's primary pattern of coping (Germain, 1991). Goals are statements about what the client and relevant others desire as the final outcome of the intervention; objectives are the intermediate steps necessary to achieve the ultimate goals.

STEP 3: ESTABLISHING BEHAVIORAL DEFINITIONS AND SELECTING MEASURES

Once major concerns are conceptualized, behavioral definitions of the problems are used to establish what will be measured. Bloom, Fisher, & Orme (1999, pp. 73–76) provide a six-part guideline for "going from the vague to the specific" in setting targets of intervention: clarity, countability, verifying sources, avoiding abstractions, determining whether the target measured should be increasing or decreasing, and measurability. For example, for a client who reports feeling "down and blue," a practitioner might conceptualize the problem as depression and operationally define this by a particular score on a depression scale. With Native American clients, levels of acculturation and potential language barriers must be explored before behaviorally defining problems and setting targets for intervention. Consider, for a moment, a practitioner working with a school-aged Indian child to increase self-esteem, and who chooses the classroom as an observational setting to test the intervention. The practitioner might be inclined to measure increased self-esteem by such indices as "shows assertiveness," "speaks up in class," and "expresses pride in accomplishments." While these indicators reflect mainstream associations with positive self-esteem, they are in conflict with native values such as indirect communication and shared praise with family and community versus a focus on personal accomplishments.

Before selecting measures, practitioners must determine the level of acculturation (Dana, 1993, 1998) and cultural orientation of clients. Standardized measures, while consistent, accurate, and representative of the construct being measured, do not address the issue of cultural bias. An instrument may have high levels of reliability and validity and yet define a construct in such a way that it reflects and reinforces cultural stereotypes (Jordan & Franklin, 1995). Although some standardized measures have proven to be culturally relevant for American Indians, there are valid concerns about cultural bias in measurement tools used with Native Americans and other ethnic minority groups. Highly biased instruments include clinical interviews, such as the mental status examination, trait measures, and self-report psychopathology measures (Paniagua, 1994). The least biased approaches involve direct behavioral observations, self-monitoring (clients' own records of thoughts, behaviors, feelings, etc.). and self-report individualized rating scales, which can accurately capture the client's interpretations and beliefs about behavior (Paniagua, 1994). If standardized measures are used, aspects of the measure that capture strengths, positive coping strategies, and resiliences of the client should be highlighted (Berg, 1994; Berg and DeJong, 1996; Franklin, 1996; Franklin & Jordan, 1999).

STEP 4: FORMULATING AN OUTCOME MEASUREMENT STRATEGY

Concurrent to selecting the best measurement instruments, practitioners are collaborating with the client about a practice evaluation plan and measurement strategy. Paniagua (1994) notes the importance of including American Indian extended families and others as deemed appropriate to be sources of support as well as to provide measurement sources, obtrusively or unobtrusively. Because measurement strategies often involve cooperation from multiple sources, it is crucial to be certain that the client and others are committed to the intervention and evaluation process. For each target goal, a decision is made about "who will do what, to what extent, and under what conditions" (Bloom, Fisher, & Orme, 1999, p. 80). Practitioners can empower American Indian clients by accepting the client's view of reality and the capacity for clients and extended family or community to participate in data collection, such as individualized rating scales or logs.

STEP 5: SELECTING AN EVALUATION DESIGN

Several models of practice evaluation exist, including the often-cited single-subject designs. We discuss single-subject designs and the incorporation of qualitative components in the evaluation design. For disenfranchised populations, Wambach and Van Soest (1997) note that, while qualitative research methods provide contextualized information, the power of quantitative methods must also be preserved. Thus, practice evaluation designs utilizing both quantitative and qualitative methodologies are recommended.

Single-Subject Designs
Evaluative single-subject designs employ repeated measurements of the target behavior or dependent variable for a single subject. The advantage of the single-subject designs is that they allow us to examine whether the client progresses based on measures taken before and after the intervention is implemented. The most common single-subject design is the AB design. The baseline period, denoted by A, is defined as the period of time prior to initiation of the intervention. Data is collected on the dependent variable during the baseline period. After an intervention is introduced, the dependent variable is measured on a continuous basis during the intervention period, denoted by B. The analysis involves examining the trend of the problem (i.e., better, worse, sporadic, or stable) that was underway during the baseline and comparing it to the trend that takes place during the intervention phase. The efficacy of the intervention is determined by whether the pattern of data during the treatment period is significantly better than the pattern that would have been predicted by the baseline trend.

Qualitative Evaluation Techniques

Qualitative methods, such as interviewing, journal logs, narrative storytelling, can be content-analyzed and incorporated into quantitative practice evaluation designs. Content analysis of the client's verbal communications provides a way of listening to and interpreting a client's account of events and can provide a viable way to monitor the progress of therapy (Viney, 1993). Qualitative methods can help identify important changes in the client's environment that may have coincided with changes in quantitative data and can also be useful in determining whether the intervention or some other variable produced change in target problems (Rubin & Babbie, 1998).

STEP 6: ANALYSIS AND REPORTING

The practitioner should analyze the results of the intervention and engage the client in reflecting on the intervention outcomes. Visually examining the data for trends can, in many cases, help determine whether the intervention goals were achieved. When there is any doubt after visually examining the data, more rigorous analyses are required, including descriptive statistics (i.e., computing means, modes, ranges) or tests of statistical significance to determine if there is a systematic difference in the target between baseline and intervention phases (Bloom, Fisher, & Orme, 1999). The details of analyses are beyond the scope of this chapter; however, other texts cover this topic in detail (Bloom, Fisher, & Orme, 1999; Rubin & Babbie, 1998).

STEP 7: EVALUATING EMPOWERMENT GOALS

American Indians continue to suffer societal oppression and, to the extent possible, social workers should evaluate their own commitment to social justice with this population. By incorporating Van Voorhis's (1998) four empowerment goals into their evaluation plan, practitioners can explore whether they helped clients to increase personal and political power.

CASE STUDY

Sue is eighteen years old, one-fourth Kickapoo Indian, and, for the past two years, has lived with her mother in an urban city about 300 miles away from the reservation where Sue grew up. Sue and her mother travel back and forth to the reservation often to visit Sue's four older siblings and extended family. Three months ago, Sue witnessed her boyfriend's fatal car accident. Both Sue and her boyfriend had been active Indian Pow Wow dancers, and had participated in the cultural activities. After her boyfriend's death, Sue stopped participating in cultural activities and began avoiding the reservation and Indian people. Sue's teachers reported that Sue suddenly stopped completing her school assignments a month ago and appears to have lost interest in school. Sue's mother described her as becoming "haunted by the death of her boyfriend."

Presenting Problems

Sue was referred to a school social worker, Mary, who collaborated with the American Indian Education Program (AIEP) in Sue's school district. Mary worked slowly at building rapport and helped Sue construct an ecomap to identify the many systems in Sue's life and the harmonious or nonharmonious nature of each relationship. Sue expressed concern about extended family members who were using inhalants and said that her boyfriend had been "high" on the night of the car crash.

Sue described dreams and images of the night of her boyfriend's death and stated that she felt "haunted" and was confused about what to do with her life. Mary told Sue that social workers sometimes call the dreams that she is experiencing "flashbacks." Mary explored Sue's comfort level with the term *flashback* as opposed to another way of speaking like *dream* or *haunting,* for example. Sue said she liked the word *flashback* and wanted to know what people do to get them to stop. Sue also indicated a desire to resume her cultural involvement but her exposure to the inhalant use on the reservation made her feel confused about what it meant to be Indian. She did not want to be a drug user but felt that was part of being Indian for a lot of people she knew. Sue also wanted to improve her ability to complete her school assignments but the flashbacks "got in the way." Sue also wanted her mother to be involved with the counseling.

Simultaneously with the assessment and intervention planning, Mary began to devise an evaluation plan. Mary asked Sue to talk more about the flashbacks (i.e., how long they had been occurring, how many times a day, what time of the day they happened, etc.). Sue recalled the details about the flashbacks from when they started, about a month earlier when she overheard a classmate saying something about "drunken Indians." Mary and Sue discussed how the negative thoughts and feelings associated with the flashbacks were related to her identity conflict. Sue could not recall exact details about the missed homework but gave Mary permission to obtain this information from her teachers.

Mary and Sue worked together to identify Sue's biggest concerns, goals, and objectives. Sue was also asked to make contact with the AIEP cultural education component and to keep a log on her feelings about American Indian identity. Mary also talked with Sue about an American Indian drug intervention program that could be implemented on the reservation. Sue expressed an interest in the program for her family members.

During the twelve weeks of intervention, Sue's situation improved greatly. She had been successful in turning in assignments except for weeks 12 and 13 when she began to neglect assignments again. Through interviews with Sue's mother, Mary gained additional insight about the homework assignments. Mary learned that during those two weeks Sue's mother had been too busy to engage Sue in conversations about her progress. In the next family session, Sue and her mother were able to discuss their reciprocal relationship and its impact on Sue's school success.

Sue's flashbacks had also tapered off and, after weeks of journal entries about Indian identity, Sue had decided to talk further with others about the drug intervention program for the reservation. With Mary's help, Sue began to connect with others who also supported the intervention program. Sue had been very motivated to resolve her issues.

PRACTICE EVALUATION SKILLS

We now discuss the application of the seven-step process to practice evaluation in this case study.

STEP 1: ESTABLISHING TRUST

In building rapport with Sue, Mary used the initial session to establish trust by demonstrating competence and openness to learning as much as possible about

Sue's background, her cultural orientation, and her major concerns. Mary collaborated with Sue about the evaluation process.

STEP 2: CONCEPTUALIZING THE PROBLEMS
From a systems–ecological framework, Mary used an ecomap to help gather information about Sue and her environment. The main problems were identified as Sue's (1) flashbacks, (2) concern about the inhalant use of extended family members, (3) identity conflict and ambivalence toward cultural activities, and (4) missed school assignments. Mary helped Sue to establish the following goals for each of these concerns: (1) to complete 100 percent of her assignments, (2) to experience no flashbacks, (3) to attend at least one cultural function, and (4) to take a step toward helping her family on the reservation.

STEP 3: BEHAVIORAL DEFINITIONS AND MEASUREMENTS
Sue's teachers had indicated that Sue "appeared depressed." Mary considered asking Sue to take a standardized depression scale, but ruled this out because of cultural bias. For example, references to crying were not culturally appropriate because, among some Kickapoo people, crying is viewed negatively as "dirtying the soul," something that should be avoided. Instead, Mary used an ethnographic interviewing approach and asked Sue to define her own meaning regarding her sadness and dysphoria. Mary asked Sue to complete a brief self-report scale based on Sue's language and references to negative feelings associated with the flashbacks.

STEP 4: SELECTING A MEASUREMENT STRATEGY
By the fourth session, Mary had a good handle on the "who, how, and what" of measuring the outcomes of the interventions. During the week, Sue was asked to keep a log or journal about thoughts, feelings, and events related to cultural identity. Mary also planned to include Sue's mother in some sessions and to conduct brief, informal interviews with her about Sue's demeanor at home. Data on school assignments would be gathered from Sue's teachers. Mary would also create content-analysis scales to examine Sue's references to negative feelings associated with the flashbacks during sessions.

STEP 5: SELECTING AN EVALUATION PLAN
Mary realized that the information she had collected during the first: two sessions about flashbacks could serve as baseline data for a single-subject design. She noted the frequency of flashbacks per week as well as the percent of missed school assignments and continued to monitor these weekly. Based on Sue's log entries, Mary planned to compare Sue's references to positive ethnic and cultural identity to her own case notes. Mary monitored these targets over the next sixteen weeks of intervention.

STEP 6: ANALYSIS AND REPORTING
After the twelfth week of intervention, Mary and Sue agreed that things seemed to be stabilized. Mary discussed the visual analysis, which indicated great improvement (see Figures 28.1 and 28.2). Flashbacks had decreased to none a week over the past three weeks and Sue's teachers had reported no missed assignments during the past three weeks. Through her involvement with pursuing the drug intervention program for the reservation, Sue felt empowered by the experience of helping her

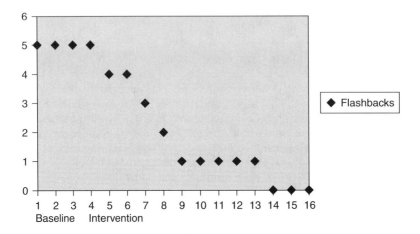

FIGURE 28.1   Number of Flashbacks per Week

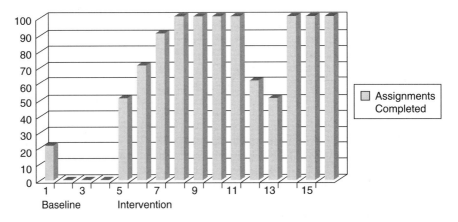

FIGURE 28.2   Percentage of Completed Assignments per Week

extended family. Sue's positive Indian identity was also restored and Sue had renewed her commitment to cultural activities.

STEP 7: EXAMINING EMPOWERMENT GOALS
Mary was effective in helping Sue in claiming a positive identity as American Indian, and assisted her in reestablishing mutually empathic relationships with her extended family. Mary's work to bring the substance abuse program to the reservation reflected mobilizing resources and power to respond to oppression and its consequences for Indian people. Finally, Mary assisted Sue in increasing proactive behavior in seeking change, evident from Sue's efforts to help her family members access the substance abuse program.

SUMMARY

This chapter presents a framework to guide practice evaluation with American Indian individuals and families. The seven guidelines presented allow social workers to examine whether culturally sensitive interventions have translated into positive outcomes for clients. Evaluating practice with American Indian clients requires social workers to combine generic evaluative research skills with culture-specific knowledge and critical thinking skills. How and to what extent generic practice principles are modified depends on knowledge about the potential cultural dynamics, theoretical approaches, and the social worker's ability to adjust evaluation techniques to match the client.

Assuming that all social workers are implementing culturally sensitive interventions with clients, the next step is to demonstrate that these interventions have been effective with various client populations, including the American Indians. This guide serves as a beginning step. More effort is needed to uncover other variables that may impact evaluation methods with American Indian clients.

REFERENCES

Armstrong, T. L., Guilfoyle, M. H., & Melton, A. P. (1996). Traditional approaches to tribal justice: History and current practice. In M. Nielsen & R. Silverman (Eds.), Native Americans, crime and justice. (pp. 46–53). Boulder, CO: Westview.

Bachman, R. (1992). Death and violence on the reservation: Homocide, family violence, and suicide in American Indian populations. New York: Auburn House.

Bechtold, D. W. (1994). Indian adolescent suicide: Clinical and developmental considerations [Monograph]. American Indian and Alaska Native Mental Health Research, 4 Mono, 71–81.

Berg, I. K. (1994). *Family based services: A solution-focused approach.* New York: W. W. Norton.

Berg, I. & DeJong, P. (1996). Solution-building conversations: Co-constructing a sense of competence with clients. *Families in Society, 77* (6), 376–390.

Bloom, M., Fischer, L., & Orme, J. G. (1999). *Evaluating practice: Guidelines for the accountable professional,* 3rd ed., Boston: Allyn & Bacon.

Bloom, M. & Orme, J. G. (1993). Ethics and the single-system design. *Journal of Social Service Research, 18,* 161–180.

Blount, M., Thyer, B. A., & Frye, T. (1992). Social work practice with Native Americans. In D. F. Garrison, J. S. Wodarski, & B. A. Thyer (Eds.), *Cultural diversity and social work* (pp. 107–119). Springfield, IL: Charles C. Thomas.

Broken Nose, M. A. (1992, June). Working with the Oglala Lakota: An outsider's perspective. *Families in Society: The Journal of Contemporary Human Services,* Vol # 380–384.

Choney, S. K., Berryhill-Paapke, E., & Robbins, R. R. (1995). The acculturation of American Indians: Developing frameworks for research and practice. In J. G. Ponterotto, J. M. Casas, L. A. Suzuki, & C. M. Alexander (Eds.), *Handbook of multicultural counseling* (pp. 73–92). Thousand Oaks, CA: Sage.

Cowger, C. (1994). Assessing client strengths: Clinical assessment for client empowerment. *Social Work, 39,* 262–267.

Dana, R. H. (1993). *Multicultural assessment perpsectives for professional psychology.* Boston, MA: Allyn & Bacon.

Dana, R. H. (1998). Understanding cultural identity in intervention and assessment. *Multicultural aspects of Counseling Series,* Vol. 9. Thousand Oaks, CA: Sage.

Davis, M. (1994). *Native America in the twentieth century.* New York: Garland.

Devore, W. & Schlesinger, E. G. (1996). Ethnic-sensitive social work practice, 4th ed. Boston, MA: Allyn & Bacon.

DuBois, B. & Miley, K. (1996). *Social work: An empowering profession,* 2nd ed. Boston, MA: Allyn & Bacon.

Franklin, C. (1996) Solution-focused therapy: A marital case study using recursive dialectic analysis. *Journal of Family Psychotherapy 7,* 31–51.

Franklin, C. & Jordan, C. (1999). Rapid assessment in family practice. In C. Franklin & C. Jordan (Eds.), *Family Practice: Brief systems methods for social work* (pp. 225–256). Pacific Grove, CA: Brooks/Cole.

Franklin C., Waukechon, J., & Larney, P. S. (1995). Culturally relevant school programs for American Indian children and families. *Social Work in Education, 17,* 183–192.

Garbarino, J. (1982). *Children and families in the social environment.* New York:Aldine.

Germain, C. B. (1991). *Human behavior in the social environment.* New York: Columbia University Press.

Gilbert, D. J. (1997, June). The culturegram: A graphical, interactive approach to appreciating the complexity of culture. Paper presented at The National Conference on Race and Ethnicity in American Higher Education. Orlando, FL.

Gross, E. (1995). Deconstructing politically correct practice literature: The American Indian case. *Social Work, 40,* 206–213.

Ho, M. K. (1987). *Family therapy with ethnic minorities.* Newberry Park, CA: Sage.

Jordan, C. & Franklin, C. (1995). *Clinical assessment for social workers: Quantitative and qualitative methods.* Chicago, IL: Lyceum.

LeCroy, C. W. 1992. *Case studies in social work practice.* Pacific Grove, CA: Brooks/Cole.

Liebow, E. R. (1989). Category or community? Measuring urban Indian social cohesion with network sampling. *Journal of Ethnic Studies, 16,* 67–100.

Lum, D. (1992). *Social work practice and people of color: A process-stage approach,* 2nd ed. Pacific Grove, CA: Brooks/Cole.

May, P. A. & Smith, M. B. (1988). Some Navajo Indian opinions about alcohol abuse and prohibition: A survey and recommendations for policy [Monograph]. *Journal of Studies on Alcohol, 49,* 324–334.

May, P. A., & Van Winkle, N. W. (1994). Indian adolescent suicide: The epidemiologic picture in New Mexico [Monograph]. *American Indian and Alaska Native Mental Health Research Journal of the National Center, 4 (Mono),* 2–35.

McDonnell, J. A. (1991). *The Dispossession of the American Indian, 1887–1934.* Bloomington, IN: Indiana University Press.

McGrane, B. (1989). *Beyond anthropology: Society and the other.* New York: Columbia University Press.

McLemore, S. D. & Romo, H. D. (1998). *Racial and ethnic relations in America.* Boston, MA: Allyn & Bacon.

Mihesuah, D. A. (1993). Suggested Guidelines for institutions with scholars who conduct research on American Indians. *American Indian Culture and Research Journal, 17,* 131–139.

Mohawk, J. (1992). Looking for Columbus: Thoughts on the past, present, and future of humanity. In M. A. Jaimes (Ed.), *The state of Native America: Genocide, colonization, and resistance* (pp. 439–444). Boston, MA: South End.

Nagel, J. (1996). *American Indian ethnic renewal: Red power and the resurgence of identity and culture.* New York: Oxford University Press.

Nel, J. (1994). Preventing school failure: The Native American child. *Clearinghouse, 67* (3), 169–174.

Paniagua, F. A. (1994). *Assessing and treating culturally diverse clients: A practical guide* (Multicultural aspects of counseling series, 4). Thousand Oaks, CA: Sage.

Pinderhughes, E. (1989). *Understanding race, ethnicity, and power: The key to efficacy in clinical practice.* New York: Free Press.

Rubin, A. & Babbie, E. (1998). *Research methods for social work,* 3rd ed. Pacific Grove, CA: Brooks/Cole.

Russell, C. (1998). *Racial and ethnic diversity: Asians, Blacks, Hispanics, Native Americans, and Whites.* Ithaca, NY: New Strategist.

Sale, K. (1990). *The conquest of paradise.* New York: Knopf.

Saleebey, D. (1996). The strengths perspective in social work practice: Extensions and cautions. *Social Work, 41,* 296–305.

Snipp, M. C. (1989). *American Indians: The first of this land.* New York: Russell Sage Foundation.

Statistical Abstract of the United States: 1997 (117th edition). U.S. Bureau of the Census. Washington, DC.

Staudt, M. (1997). Pseudoissues in practice evaluation: Impediments to responsible practice. *Social Work, 42,* 99–105.

Stiffarm, L. A., & Lane, P., Jr. (1992). The demography of native North America: A question of American Indian survival. In M. A. Jaimes (Ed.), *The state of Native America* (pp. 23–53). Boston, MA: South End.

Sue, D. W. & Sue, D. (1990). *Counseling the culturally different: Theory and practice,* 2nd ed. New York: John Wiley.

Thompson, J. W., Walker, R. D., & Silk-Walker, P. (1993). Psychiatric care of American Indians and Alaska Natives. In Albert C. Gaw (Ed.), *Culture, ethnicity, and mental illness* (pp. 189–241). Washington, DC: American Psychiatric Press.

Todorov, T. (1984). *The conquest of America.* New York: Harper & Row.

Van Voorhis, R. M. (1998). Culturally relevant practice: A framework for teaching the psychosocial dynamics of oppression. *Journal of Social Work Education, 34,* 121–133.

Viney, L. L. (1993). Listening to what my clients and I say: Content analysis categories and scales. In B. Fretz (Series Ed.) & G. Neimeyer (Vol. Ed.), *Constructivist assessment: A casebook:* Vol. 2. *The counseling psychologist casebook series* (pp. 104–142). Newbury, CA: Sage.

Walters, K. (1999). Urban American Indian Identity attitudes and acculturation styles. *Journal of Human Behavior in the Social Environment, 2* (½), 163–178.

Wambach, K. & Van Soest, D. (1997). Oppression. 1997 Supplement, *Encyclopedia of Social Work,* 19th ed. Washington, DC: National Association of Social Workers Press.

Weaver, H. N. (1996). Social work with American Indian youth using the orthogonal model of cultural identification. *Families in Society: The Journal of Contemporary Human Services, 77,* 98–107.

Weaver, H. N. (1997). The challenges of research in Native American communities: Incorporating principles of cultural competence. *Journal of Social Service Research, 23* (2), 1–15.

Weaver, H. & White, B. (1997). The Native American family circle: Roots of resiliency. *Journal of Family Social Work, 2* (1), 67–79.

ENDNOTE

[1]The term *Native American* can be extended to include all descendants of the pre-Columbian inhabitants of North America, including American Indian, Alaska Native, and Canadian and Mexican Indian people. There is an enormous amount of diversity both within and between each of these groups; thus, for the purpose of this chapter, the authors will focus on the American Indian population.

CHAPTER 29

PROGRAM EVALUATION WITH NATIVE AMERICAN/ AMERICAN INDIAN ORGANIZATIONS

LORRE G. LEWIS

Culturally appropriate program evaluations are vital to the health of social and human services programs within Native American/American Indian (Native/ Indian) communities. The purposes of program evaluation include ensuring that programs are effective, culturally sensitive, contribute to tribal revitalization (Fleming, 1992), and meet the needs of as many community members as possible, especially those who are vulnerable.

This chapter will concentrate on program evaluation in reservation-based settings; however, it should be acknowledged that more than half, 51 percent, of Natives/Indians live in urban environments. Though most large metropolitan areas have an agency or several agencies that seek to meet the needs of urban Natives/Indians, the largest Native/Indian social service agencies continue to be tribal governments. These governments administer multiple programs addressing the needs of tribal members who are geographically centered on or near their home reservations.

This chapter will focus on issues related to culturally appropriate evaluations, but will not address the technical aspects of conducting evaluations, leaving that to a number of available excellent texts (Berk & Rossi, 1999; Patton, 1986, 1990).

SOCIODEMOGRAPHIC OVERVIEW

The variability of Native/Indian peoples provides the first difficulty in discussing how to incorporate cultural considerations in well-designed program evaluations. There are currently over 540 federally recognized and over 300 state recognized

Native/Indian tribes or Alaska Native organizations, each with a distinct history. These tribes range in size from under a 100 members to over 200,000 in the case of the Oklahoma Cherokee, with the next largest being the approximately 120,000 Dine (Navaho). Over 200 American Indian languages continue to be spoken (Fleming, 1992). Cultures in distinct geographic regions result from the interaction between human physical, emotional, and spiritual needs and environmental resources, and vary greatly.

SOCIAL AND POLITICAL ISSUES: TRIBAL MEMBERSHIP AND DISTINCTIVENESS OF EACH TRIBE

The methods by which tribal membership is determined also vary considerably. While in the United States census self-identification is used to determine the number of American Indians, tribal membership is more properly seen as a determination of citizenship within a tribal nation. Enrollment is used to determine who is eligible for tribal services and for services from the Indian Health Service and the Bureau of Indian Affairs. American Indians often differ greatly by degree of Indian ancestry and, since 1930, the majority of Indian people have been of mixed heritage (Wilson, 1992).

The determination of eligibility of tribal membership is often based on blood quantum with 25 percent Indian blood a commonly accepted minimum for official tribal membership. However, this is not the case for many Indian nations. For example, among the Haudenosaunee (or Iroquois Confederacy), enrollment is determined by whether the birth mother is a member or not. Among other nations, there is no blood quantum requirement, and in still others both parents must be members of the tribe for the child to be a tribal member, ensuring that most members are "full-blood."

This brief discussion of enrollment underscores an important point: Even a matter as seemingly simple as tribal membership may be hard for those on the outside to understand. Additionally, what one has learned from one tribe may not be applicable to another tribe due to the distinctiveness of each tribe.

RESERVATION-BASED NATIVE AMERICAN/ AMERICAN INDIAN PROGRAMS: ORGANIZATION AND FUNDING

Enormous variability exists in Native/Indian governmental organizations, their available resources, their cultural attributes, and their assimilation with the non-Native society. The organization of tribal governments is complex and may range from traditional forms of governance to constitutional systems loosely modeled on the U.S. federal government. The variety of tribal programs can be compared to a small-scale state system in which social services, resource management, housing, utilities, and educational services for children, youth, and adults are all under the control of tribal governments.

Tribal and U.S. Federal government relations are determined by many laws and regulations, and only the few that affect policy and procedure at the local level will be discussed here. The Indian Self-Determination and Education Assistance Act of 1975 allows tribes to contract with the Federal Government through the Bureau of Indian Affairs (BIA) to provide social, educational, and health services to their tribal members. Some of the regulatory functions of this law require quarterly reports, which should be included in program evaluations. This allows the tribes to plan and implement their own programs rather than have the BIA do so.

The 1978 Indian Child Welfare Act (ICWA) gives tribes some jurisdiction over child welfare cases concerning children of their tribal members and requires that states make reasonable efforts to place Native/Indian children in Native/Indian homes. The ICWA also provides the rationale for tribal child welfare programs and their funding; such programs are usually housed in the BIA.

Federal agencies other than the BIA provide funding for various tribal programs including Housing and Urban Development, the Department of Education, and various discretionary grant programs that are funded through agencies such as the Center for Substance Abuse and Prevention and the Department of Justice. Moreover tribal programs may also be funded by private agencies.

Tribal governments often must conduct program evaluations as a requirement of a funding agency. At times, these funding agencies and the tribal governments have different goals. While it is preferable for program evaluation to occur as an aspect of program development, and the evaluation should be seen as an integral component of the program, all too often program evaluation is an afterthought (Beauvais & Trimble, 1992), something that must be done to appease a funding agency.

Given the importance of this funding to people's livelihoods, as well as the political costs of program unresponsiveness and failure, tribal governments are often interested in the small details of every program. Additionally, these programs are under the daily scrutiny of tribal members, who often express their concerns to the tribal council. Sensitivity to the political aspects of evaluation is a must in these circumstances. In some ways, managing the politics can take as much time as engaging in those activities that are usually considered "the evaluation." Added to the dimension of tribal politics are cultural differences that are likely to cause the outside evaluator some consternation as he or she attempts to perform an evaluation.

CULTURAL VALUES AND NORMS TO CONSIDER IN THE PERFORMANCE OF PROGRAM EVALUATION FOR NATIVE AMERICAN/AMERICAN INDIAN COMMUNITIES

Culture is a large construct, including not only the outward elements that strangers can see, such as clothing and ceremonies, but also the inner life of communities, families within those communities, and the individuals within those families. Culture has been described as the customs, beliefs, values, and knowledge of a people (Linton, 1947), and it also includes norms, mores, and sanctions (Orlandi, 1992).

Moreover, cultures are not static but, rather, change in response to interactions with other cultures and as a result of choices that people make over time. Nor is this process of change in one direction. Just as the Native/Indian cultures have changed as a result of interacting with the general U.S. culture, they have also been a potent force in changing the Euro-American culture in turn (Weatherford, 1991). The orthogonal cultural identification theory suggests that people are able to identify with more than one culture at a time and independently of each other (Oetting & Beauvais, 1990). Natives/Indians are both Native/Indian and American at the same time.

For program developers and evaluators, this means that, in essence, Native/Indian programs must integrate Native/Indian cultures with the best practices of a particular field. As an example, for many Native/Indian people, mental heath is spiritual and holistic. While healing occurs for the individual, that healing takes place in the context of the individual's community. Not only the client, but also his or her family and community members must be involved in the healing process (Wilkinson, 1980). An important feature of any mental health program, then, would be the inclusion of such cultural features with the best possible social work, psychological, and psychiatric services. An evaluator cannot ignore these cultural features while choosing outcome measures of a program evaluation.

Cultural variability complicates any discussion of program evaluation in Native/Indian communities. In addition to an extensive literature review, the individual wishing to perform such evaluations must spend a great deal of time in the individual Native/Indian community in order to become acquainted with the particulars of that community. These particulars include, at a minimum: a basic understanding of the history of the specific Native/Indian nation; identification of informal and formal leaders; and an understanding of the proper protocol in gaining access and permission to conduct evaluation activities.

Learning about the Native/Indian community in which one is working is important because of the concern many Native/Indian people have that non-Native/Indian or Natives/Indians from other tribes will try to influence tribal members to adopt a value perspective other than their own (LaFromboise, Trimble, & Mohatt, 1990). Additionally, Natives/Indians have often been exposed to outside researchers who are meeting their own needs without consideration of the needs and values of the Native/Indian community (Beauvais & Trimble, 1992). Therefore, it is important to work within the perspective of specific tribal traditions and beliefs (Weaver, 1997).

This may be seen as a process of acculturation in which the outside evaluator is learning the symbols and customs, as well as the tribal and personal history, of the particular Native/Indian tribe with whom he or she is working (Heinrich, Corbine, and Thomas, 1990). Community resources, such as tribal leaders, elders, medicine people, and local Indian professionals, can be a part of accessing this information as well as historical and anthropological literature specific to the community within which one is working (Fleming, 1992).

The importance of the evaluator addressing his or her own biases, values, and beliefs has been stressed by Weaver (1997). The evaluation questions that are asked, the way in which those questions are asked, and the assumptions underlying those questions are all likely to be formed by the evaluator's personal perceptions. For this reason, the evaluator must be particularly self-aware when working across cultures.

Moreover, an outside evaluator must also understand that acculturation and assimilation include violent and forceful acts against Native/Indian people. Because acculturation and assimilation were forced on Natives/Indians and their communities, positive and negative effects have been experienced by all individuals and communities in Indian country. Understanding the historical process that has shaped Indian communities is an important part of understanding the Indian worldview and value system and why social services are conducted in certain ways. A knowledge of the historical background will help shape questions by providing a framework and working knowledge of why Native/Indian people live today as they do.

THE VALUE AND CHALLENGES OF PROGRAM EVALUATION IN NATIVE AMERICAN/AMERICAN INDIAN COMMUNITIES

Evaluation can take place in many different program areas in Native/Indian urban and reservation communities:

- Educational programs
- Head Start
- Natural Resources Management
- Employment Programs for various Native/Indian populations (Roberts, Harper, & Preszler, 1997)
- Administrative Reviews
- Health Behaviors (Weaver, 1997)
- Alcohol and Substance Abuse Treatment and Prevention Programs (Baldwin, 1999; Brindis, Berkowitz, & Peterson, 1995; Rowe, 1997)

and many others.

Program evaluations can have more than one purpose. In formative evaluations, one is attempting to improve the program, while in summative evaluations the purpose is to determine whether the program has been effective, and, hence, should be continued (Orlandi, 1992). The confusion of these two types of program evaluation is especially problematic within Native organizations, which are all too likely to hear criticism rather than praise and to interpret that criticism as a threat to the survival of program and staff.

In evaluating Native/Indian programs, it is important to look at the strengths as well as the problems in these communities. It is easy to focus on the very severe problems of poverty, alcoholism, and family violence that exist in many Native/Indian communities, but this focus misses most of the picture, which is one of strength and resilience. Social stressors such as poverty, racism, hostile educational systems, hunger, and poor housing must be understood in the context of historical and current oppression that continues to affect all aspects of Native/Indian life (Chester, Robin, Koss, Lopez, & Goldman, 1994; Dufrene & Coleman, 1992). Many of these problems can be understood best as coping mechanisms for this oppression.

Indicators of health and indicators of dysfunction, from high school graduation to dropout, from income to rates of unemployment, from use of alcohol to abstinence, vary considerably from tribe to tribe (Fleming, 1992). As a result of historical, geographic, and political factors, the sociodemographic factors of tribes can differ remarkably. While some tribes have valuable natural resources with which to fund tribal objectives, others have only federal or state funding.

Despite the social problems that Natives/Indians often face, evaluators new to the Native/Indian scene are likely to be surprised by the lack of research available in key areas. For example, the literature related to alcohol and substance abuse treatment for Native/Indian women is limited (Brindis, Berkowitz, & Peterson, 1995), as is that related to employment programs (Roberts, Harper, & Preszler, 1997).

The challenges of doing program evaluations in Native/Indian communities are many. As mentioned, the substantive areas in which Natives/Indians are involved are diverse. One person may be called on to work in areas not his or her first area of expertise.

The difficulties inherent to doing program evaluation with Natives/Indians does not excuse the evaluator from using the best possible methods. While compromises must always be made in research, due to restrictions of resources such as time and expense, Natives/Indians deserve nothing less than the best possible methods that are culturally sensitive.

PRACTICE FOCUS: EVALUATION

Ecological Strengths and Empowerment Perspectives

An ecological framework adds to the process of program evaluation by directing the evaluator to consider the environment in which the program exists. A central feature of Native/Indian communities is the existing community talent and energy possessed by community members. Calling on the strengths of Native/Indian community members in all parts of program development and evaluation can only strengthen the process. Outside evaluators, even if Native/Indian themselves, need to have community members in positions of real responsibility, rather than simply as staff members (Beauvais & Trimble, 1992). The contributions of community members are likely to prevent the evaluators from committing avoidable mistakes as well as empowering community members to "own" the evaluation and have a stake in the recommendations.

Having a purpose for the evaluation that emerges from the Native/Indian community and its leadership is the first step to empowering the community to make use of the results of the evaluation. A process in which the Native/Indian community determines the evaluation's purpose is especially important, given that outside evaluators may be thought by the community to be using their own values rather than the values of the specific community (Orlandi, 1992). Empowering community members requires skill not only in facilitating the process of community decision making, but also a sensitivity to the political and social realities of a particular system. While difficult, it is important to make attempts to include the often disenfranchised groups within a tribal community.

Finally, an evaluator is likely to find resources in terms of talents, a willingness to work toward the community good, and valuable inside knowledge within the Native/Indian community's members. The strength and resilience of Native/Indian people has been tempered by years of oppression, and that strength and resilience is the basis of community empowerment.

Utilization-Focused Evaluation

Program evaluations performed with Native/Indian organizations are most helpful if they are utilization-focused, as described by Patton (1986). These program evaluations provide feedback to tribal organizations about how the program can better serve tribal members. Therefore, the evaluation is helping the tribe rather than serving the needs of outside researchers and policymakers. This focus on utilization begins with identifying the principal users of the results of the evaluation. A tribal council's purpose in authorizing an evaluation may differ markedly from the purpose that a funder may have, and these purposes may differ yet again from those of the program participants. While one group may be interested in barriers to participation, another may be looking for cost-effectiveness as related to participant change, and a third may be concerned about cultural appropriateness.

Moreover, it is only by providing information helpful to a primary intended user that it is likely that the results of the evaluation will be utilized. Both the primary users of the evaluation results and the evaluator are essential to the process of making choices about the nature, purpose, content, and methods of the evaluation.

In fact, it is only after the primary users have been identified that one can move to the second stage of utilization-focused evaluation: identifying and focusing on questions with "high utilization potential" (Patton, 1986, p. 75). Such questions seek information that the primary users will use in making decisions. The process of identifying utilizable questions will also lead to a focusing of the evaluation because it is impossible to obtain information on every subject of interest. The goal of utilization-focused evaluation is strengthening the program in question rather than engaging in a research project, which, though interesting, may not mean much to program participants, staff, or decision makers.

PRACTICE SKILLS: ACCESSING AND WORKING COOPERATIVELY WITH NATIVE/INDIAN COMMUNITIES FOR PROGRAM DEVELOPMENT AND PURPOSEFUL EVALUATION

Understanding barriers to access and working cooperatively with community members to overcome those barriers is a necessary step in program evaluation. A common barrier is the understandable cynicism with which Natives/Indians greet one more new program. An unfortunate dynamic operates in Native/Indian and other communities in which a problem is identified: Political leaders express concern and provide funding for numerous programs in many locations, but, though the problem is chronic, the funding dries up when a quick solution is not forthcoming (Beauvais & Trimble, 1992). Another issue that may arise is the lack of inclusion of people from the community who have been working on the problem for years, with little in the way of resources, but whose efforts are overlooked when new funding sources become available.

Given the history of oppression that Natives/Indians have faced, and the problems that researchers have caused in the past, it should come as no surprise that Native/Indian governments now extend significant oversight to any kind of research on Native/Indian reservations, including program evaluation. While it is likely that such an evaluation is often a requirement of a funding agency, the purposes of program evaluation are often unclear and, therefore, it will be necessary to explain in detail why the evaluator is doing things in a particular way.

Additionally, many tribal governments have established protocols for doing research in Native communities (Beauvais & Trimble, 1992). These may include a tribal human subjects review committee that will need to approve the research design, including participant selection and the instrument(s) to be used. Additionally, some tribes may require editorial approval over reports, controlling the dissemination of research results, and retaining ownership of raw data and findings. As Beauvais and Trimble note: "Indian communities recognize all too well that the research process can be intrusive and the results invidious, divisive, and scandalous" (p. 175).

It is insufficient to simply involve highly visible tribal leadership. Identifying informal leaders and gatekeepers who may have traditional or familial bases of support and eliciting advice from them about the program and its evaluation is more likely to lead to the ability to adequately carry out the program and evaluate it. The amount of time needed to apprise the community about the nature of the program and its evaluation will likely surprise those outside the community, but the process of information sharing, community input, implementing suggested modifications, and consensus building cannot be rushed. Moreover, there may be political issues of which the researcher/evaluator is unaware, and such issues cannot be resolved by those who are outside the community. Such frustrations are best endured if one has allowed sufficient time, several months at a minimum.

A complete and truthful presentation of the program and agreement based on that presentation are vital to the future success of the program. Without such understanding and agreement, the project could be summarily discontinued (Beauvais & Trimble, 1992).

PRACTICE SKILLS: CULTURALLY APPROPRIATE DATA COLLECTION

Clearly defining the program participants is an important aspect of the data collection process. A common mistake is to use community-wide indicators rather than to evaluate the experiences or behavior changes of the people to whom the program was delivered (Orlandi, 1992). Most importantly, questions must also be directed towards the strengths of program participants as well as the difficulties that may have brought them to the program in the first place.

The necessity for modifying instruments for cultural sensitivity and conceptual equivalence is a difficult prospect (Beauvais & Trimble, 1992), especially given the lack of reliability and validity testing across cultures. Behaviors in a non-Native/Indian culture may have quite different meanings in the Native/Indian culture: For example, it is common for Natives/Indians to quietly observe new situations and people. For non-Natives/Indians, this can be interpreted as quietness, passivity, and lack of interest. However, for Native/Indian people, this behavior is often a mark of politeness. Evaluators must also be aware of this style of communication when they speak to Natives/Indians for fear of mistaking their silence for agreement; it may be that the evaluator has not provided enough time and silence for Native/Indian people to begin to speak without interrupting someone else.

While it is unlikely that an evaluator will be able to undertake the rigorous process of establishing conceptual or functional equivalence across measures, it is necessary to probe the proposed instruments. Doing this involves discussing research design and instrumentation with community members who are very knowledgeable about the traditional culture, the effects of assimilation and acculturation on that culture, and the local people. Examining the purposes of the instrument, the reason for each item, and how the instrument, in light of the particular Native/Indian culture's beliefs and values, is integral to this process of cultural oversight. An item-by-item examination of each instrument is important, given that people from different cultures are likely to understand concepts and questions differently. This different understanding could lead to the reliability of the instrument being compromised. Beauvais and Trimble (1992) suggest utilizing factor analysis, in addition to the usual reliability and validity measures, to identify items that may not be functionally or conceptually equivalent across cultures. Instruments normed on other populations cannot be assumed to have similar properties with Natives/Indians.

The data collection measures must also be sensitive to other aspects of the community. Native/Indian people are often asked to fill out any number of surveys, from biannual needs assessments asking, for example, about who has indoor plumbing to one's educational attainment to various surveys related to health. Therefore, a program evaluator must be careful to ask only questions related to the program evaluation rather than to give in to curiosity. Curiosity, while understandable, may also be intrusive.

Some measures to insure that participants will complete instruments include respecting the participants' time constraints by not overburdening them with over-lengthy instruments, making it convenient for them to complete the survey, and paying participant incentives. It is also helpful to do structured or semistructured interviews rather than to ask participants to fill out pencil-and-paper surveys, because these are likely to be identified with an impersonal, distant approach (Weaver, 1997), and are not likely to successfully obtain the needed return rate. Surveys should not be conducted without adequate pilot testing in which knowledgeable community members give feedback about the survey and its individual items.

Data must be collected with an awareness of the geographical features of the reservation, because, on some reservations, there are concentrations of people in towns, but in others considerable distances may separate tribal members. Visiting the site in which the program is to be conducted and meeting the people who will run the program will apprise the evaluator of the resources, both personnel and material, that actually exist (Beauvais & Trimble, 1992).

Moreover, while considering cultural issues during the process of designing a program is important, it is equally necessary to consider whether the program as conducted was culturally appropriate. Once again, this involves a discussion with community elders and members. While this data is not quantifiable, it is qualitative in nature and has important implications for the conduct of future programs and replication in other Native/Indian settings. Even though a program may be effective according to certain sorts of outcome measures, it may be so contrary to the Native/Indian community's values as to be unworkable in that community.

PRACTICE SKILLS: INCLUDING THE NATIVE/INDIAN COMMUNITY IN DATA ANALYSIS AND PUBLICATION

The dissemination of results is best negotiated in the earliest stages of program development. Some of the issues that need to be discussed include whether the tribe or Native/Indian nation will be identified by name or concealed in some mutually agreed-on way. Results should be published first in the community, with an opportunity to voice concerns prior to public dissemination. These concerns will preferably accompany the evaluator's subsequent public presentation of results, their interpretation, and the discussion of the evaluator's findings. Considerable community involvement will enhance the accuracy of findings (Weaver, 1997). In a focus group, one cannot only check with the community about one's interpretations but also can begin the publication process in a way that is respect-ful of the community.

Two reports may be more useful than one in presenting evaluation results on Native/Indian programs as suggested by Beauvais and Trimble (1992). The first report addresses questions of whether the program is valuable to and well received by the community, culturally appropriate, and perceived by the commu-nity as useful or making a difference. In a technical report, one is more likely to answer questions of particular interest to or provide quantitative data required by a funding agency.

Finally, in publishing results one must be aware of the power issues involved. Quite clearly, research results, especially in the area of social science, have been used to stigmatize Native/Indian people. Social science often concentrates on the most problematic of human experiences. It is not surprising that this is the infor-mation non-Natives/Indians are most likely to hear and remember about Native/Indian people. But this kind of one-sided reporting is not only shaming, it also inaccurately represents Native/Indian people.

CASE VIGNETTE

The following case vignette is a combination of the author's experiences but has been partially fabricated in order to illustrate some of the principles and pitfalls dis-cussed above. The vignette describes the process but no findings.

In order to apply for funding for a domestic violence program on a reserva-tion within its jurisdiction, a local law enforcement agency (LEA) found it necessary to invite faculty members from a local university to perform a program evaluation. This was an unusual and uncomfortable relationship for the LEA.

It was also an unusual and uncomfortable experience for the tribal council, which had not been consulted before the application for funding was submitted. In its favor, the project included two deputies who were members of the local Indian nation.

At the same time, the Indian nation had independently obtained funding for two domestic violence programs that were to run simultaneously. In order to coor-dinate these programs and the program by the Indian Nation, a task force was insti-tuted and the faculty and deputies joined this group on those occasions when the tribal task force members thought it appropriate.

Once funding was obtained for the LEA's domestic violence program, the deputies and evaluators began the process of obtaining approval from tribal lead-ership. This process was complicated by the preoccupation of the tribal council with internal tribal political controversies. The evaluators sought the advice of social services personnel in the tribe regarding individuals to contact and the best method of approaching these individuals and the tribal council as a whole.

The evaluators had three goals in these meetings: The first was to gain approval for their presence on the reservation; the second was to gain approval for collecting data from tribal members about an extremely sensitive subject; and the third was to gain input about the research instrument and to modify it as needed. Approval for each of these goals was linked: if the tribal council felt that the evalu-ators were insensitive to tribal concerns, they would be unlikely to allow them on the reservation and no evaluation could take place; if tribal council members felt uncomfortable about the instrument, they would be unlikely to allow the evaluators to speak to tribal members.

This process was assisted by the presence of two tribal members, the deputies, who were a part of the program, and by the presence of the evaluators at tribal domestic violence task force meetings. Such personal contacts and relationships were vitally important in enabling the evaluators to do their job. Additionally, the evaluators were not evaluating a tribal program but a program being conducted by the local LEA. Identifying the primary users of the evaluation was problematic, given that two different entities with different interests had a stake in the evaluation.

This program would involve having two deputies, members of the tribal nation, respond to domestic violence calls on the reservation as well as conduct educational programming. They would be supported in their work by a program coordinator, who would provide case management services to domestic violence victims.

The methodology of the evaluation was planned to include a survey that victims of domestic violence would be asked to fill out. At first contact, the deputy or the program coordinator would ask the victim whether the evaluators could contact her and how it would be safe for her to be contacted. The evaluators, or their research assistant, would then contact the victim to ask permission to fill out the survey. The survey would take place in person or over the phone. Additionally, files maintained by the program coordinator were reviewed for disposition of the case—services to which the individual had been referred and utilized. A follow-up survey was also conducted to verify this information. Survey participants were paid $20 for each interview.

In reviewing the instrument, the evaluators agreed to language changes on items that were considered overly intrusive. They also agreed to identify tribal members (collectively), as distinguished from nontribal members who might reside on the reservation, and to share the data so that the tribal nation could apply for funding independently, using the collected data for needs assessment. Concerns about confidentiality were addressed. The evaluators and their research assistant were the only ones able to link names and identification numbers on the survey. Information collected by law enforcement and by the domestic violence program coordinator were compiled by the research assistant and were stripped of identifying information.

One concern that quickly emerged was how progress was going to be shared on an ongoing basis. This was a particularly tricky process because of the concerns of two powerful political agencies, the tribal council and the LEA. This issue was partially addressed when a tribal council member was designated as a contact person for the evaluators, who then made monthly or more contacts with the council member to discuss developments and concerns as they arose. Additionally, the mechanism of reporting to the tribal domestic violence task force was emphasized.

Having deputies ask the victims to participate in the survey turned out to be problematic on several levels. On one hand, it wasn't clear that the women didn't feel coerced to participate, but, on the other, having the deputies involved may have made the women less inclined to participate.

Findings from the evaluation were first shared with the LEA. Because this program was politically sensitive, it was necessary to share them first with the office that had authorized the evaluation. The comments and input of LEA personnel and the domestic violence program coordinator were added to the report. Findings were then shared with tribal domestic violence task force members and the tribal council at a public meeting; however, it was not expected that study participants, domestic violence victims, would wish to go to such a meeting. No other way of disseminating the data to the victims was arranged. The tribal council and domestic violence task force members provided different interpretations to the evaluator's findings, which added to the accuracy and richness of the report. This input was provided to the LEA and a final report, including the comments of these different groups, was included.

Perhaps the most problematic aspect of this evaluation was the lack of participation by domestic violence victims in designing the study and being given an opportunity to comment on the findings. Another problem was in identifying users of the evaluation. Nevertheless, the evaluation provided information of use both to the LEA and the Indian nation.

CONCLUSION

It is hoped that this chapter has illuminated the rewards as well as the risks of program evaluations with American Indian organizations and programs. Such evaluations require the evaluator to have multiple skill sets, to not only understand the science of evaluation but also the social skills to work across cultures. Skillfully and sensitively performed, program evaluation has an important role in providing effective social work services to Native/Indian populations.

REFERENCES

Baldwin, J. A. (1999). Conducting drug abuse prevention research in partnership with Native American communities: Meeting challenges through collaborative approaches. *Drugs & Society, 14* (½), 77–92.

Beauvais, F. & Trimble, J. E. (1992). The role of the researcher in evaluating American Indian alcohol and other drug abuse prevention programs. In M. A. Orlandi, R. Weston, & L. G. Epstein, (Eds.), *Cultural competence for evaluators: A guide for alcohol and other drug abuse prevention practitioners working with ethnic/racial communities* (pp. 173–201). Rockville, MD: U.S. Department of Health and Human Services, Public Health Service, Alcohol, Drug Abuse, and Mental Health Administration.

Berk, R. A. & Rossi, P. H. (1999). *Thinking about program evaluation,* 2nd ed. Thousand Oaks, CA: Sage.

Brindis, C., Berkowitz, G., & Peterson, S.(1995). *Evaluating the effectiveness of alcohol and substance abuse services for American Indian/Alaska Native women: Phase 2 final report: Executive summary.* Washington, DC: Indian Health Service.

Chester, B., Robin, R. W., Koss, M. P., Lopez, J., & Goldman, D. (1994). Grandmother dishonored: Violence against women by male partners in American Indian communities. *Violence and Victims, 9* (3), 249–258.

Dufrene, P. M. & Coleman, V. D. (1992). Counseling Native Americans: Guidelines for group practice. *The Journal for Specialists in Group Work, 17* (4), 229–234.

Fleming, C. M. (1992). American Indians and Alaska Natives: Changing societies past and present. In M. A. Orlandi, R. Weston, & L. G. Epstein, (Eds.), *Cultural competence for evaluators:*

A guide for alcohol and other drug abuse prevention practitioners working with ethnic/racial communities (pp. 147–171). Rockville, MD: U.S. Department of Health and Human Services, Public Health Service, Alcohol, Drug Abuse, and Mental Health Administration.

Heinrich, R. K., Corbine, J. L., & Thomas, K. R. (1990). Counseling Native Americans. *Journal of Counseling and Development, 69* (1), 128–133.

LaFromboise, T. D., Trimble, J. E., & Mohatt, G. V. (1990). Counseling intervention and American Indian tradition: An integrative approach. *The Counseling Psychologist, 18* (4), 628–654.

Linton, R. (1947). *The study of man.* New York: Appleton.

Oetting, E. R. & Beauvais, F. (1990). Orthogonal cultural identification theory: The cultural identification of minority adolescents. *International Journal of the Addictions, 25,* 655–685.

Orlandi, M. A. (1992). The challenge of evaluating community-based prevention programs: A cross-cultural perspective. In M. A. Orlandi, R. Weston, & L. G. Epstein, (Eds.), *Cultural competence for evaluators: A guide for alcohol and other drug abuse prevention practitioners working with ethnic/racial communities* (pp.1–22). Rockville, MD: U.S. Department of Health and Human Services, Public Health Service, Alcohol, Drug Abuse, and Mental Health Administration.

Patton, M. Q. (1986). *Utilization-focused evaluation.* Thousand Oaks, CA: Sage.

Patton, M. Q. (1990). *Qualitative evaluation and research methods.* Thousand Oaks, CA: Sage.

Roberts, R. L., Harper, R., Preszler, B. (1997). The effects of the Fresh Start Program on Native American parolees' job placement. *Journal of Employment Counseling, 34* (3), 115–122.

Rowe, W. E. (1997). Changing ATOD norms and behaviors: A Native American community commitment to wellness. *Evaluation and Program Planning, 20* (3), 323–333.

Weatherford, J. (1991). *Native roots: How the Indians enriched America.* New York: Fawcett Columbine.

Weaver, H. N. (1997). The challenges of research in Native American communities: Incorporating principles of cultural competence. *Journal of Social Service Review, 23* (2), 1–15.

Wilkinson, G. T. (1980). On assisting Indian people. *Social Casework: The Journal of Contemporary Social Work, 61,* 451–454.

Wilson, T. P. (1992). Blood quantum: Native American mixed blood. In M. P. P. Root (Ed.), *Racially mixed people in America.* Newbury Park, CA: Sage.

CHAPTER 30

COMPETENCIES IN PRACTICE EVALUATIONS WITH ASIAN AMERICAN INDIVIDUALS AND FAMILIES

PATRICK LEUNG

MONIT CHEUNG

Although Asian and Pacific Island Americans (APIs)[1] represent at least twenty-three ethnic groups with thirty-two linguistic groups and more than one hundred dialects, these culturally diverse populations have been conveniently grouped for statistical purposes (Inouye, 1999). Though culturally diverse, the family concept among Asian Americans is important and strong. Because of the commonality among APIs in maintaining their family ties, this chapter will focus on a generic discussion based on the family concept, with the understanding that clients come from various cultural backgrounds. The major premise of this chapter is that evaluation of clinical practice is essential. Practice issues related to API groups have been addressed, but practice evaluation methods have not been systematically studied due to the fact that the meaning of mental health may not be uniform across these groups (English & Le, 1999; Marsella & Kameoka, 1989). When working with API clients and their families, clinical practitioners must remember three principles. First, it is important to positively convey the concept of mental health and address the purpose of counseling services according to clients' family and cultural expectations (as supported by a study on self-reinforcement by Wong, et al., 1999; see also Flaskerud & Liu, 1990; Kline & Huff, 1999). Second, clinicians must evaluate clients' decision to seek, or not to seek, family support (see Ishida, 1999; Leung, 1985; Yang, 1991). Third, mental health professionals must help clients recognize their strengths as well as evaluate their limitations that may block the optimal use of their potential in the environment (see Kline & Huff, 1999; McGoldrick, et al., 1999).

Applying the above principles in practice, this chapter will: (1) focus on issues of evaluating practice, (2) describe areas of practice competencies that require constant evaluations when the practitioner is working with the API populations, (3) use an actual case to address the importance of evaluating cultural competencies, and (4) identify evaluation formats for practice considerations. When we discuss the issues facing API clients and families, we are by no means trying to generalize about all API populations. On the contrary, it is our intent to address common issues to API populations that can be analyzed in any cultural context. In addition, although this chapter is written in the context of social work practice, it is also applicable to all helping professions.

ISSUES IN EVALUATING PRACTICE
WITH ASIAN AMERICANS

From observations and research studies, scholars and practitioners suggest different models for counseling API individuals. For example, the "variations model" (Kitano, 1989) focuses on addressing the differences in terms of expectations across cultures. The "empathic–introspective approach" (Yi, 1995) suggests that the helping professionals should develop a culturally sensitive awareness toward the internal experiential world of Asian individuals. The "multimodal assessment" approach (Yu, 1999) includes acculturation, role expectations, communication style, and emotional expressiveness in the social work assessment process. However, it is seldom that we find "models" of evaluating social and counseling services provided.

Although evaluation models are not specific to social services for APIs, studies related to outcome success have been documented. For instance, Flaskerud and Liu (1990) evaluate outcome measures in their practice evaluations with Southeast Asian clients. They emphasize in the assessment three concrete aspects of evaluation: (1) number of sessions with the counselor; (2) dropout incidences or rates from therapy; and (3) the admission–discharge difference in standardized scores. However, these evaluative measures are practitioner-oriented, i.e., measures based on the practitioner's experience rather than based on the client's own evaluation of self-achievement. In another study, English and Le (1999) use needs assessment to identify community problems when evaluating a health care program for Vietnamese Americans in California. The use of evaluation in practice with the API clientele seems to focus mainly on the needs of providing more services due to the fact that these services have been underutilized by these clients.

In terms of evaluation method, several evaluation approaches have been proposed, but many of these approaches are not written with reference to API populations. One of these approaches specific to APIs is to directly involve clients in satisfaction surveys (for example, English & Le, 1999). In the Asian context, however, such an approach can be misinterpreted as either a dissatisfaction assessment or a means for pleasing others. Some API individuals may think that they should only report something that is undesirable and disregard the survey even if satisfaction is found. Others may solely focus on positives even if dissatisfaction is evident. No literature has addressed these phenomena because cultural factors are mixed with situational factors in Asian clients' responses to surveys (Morris & Peng, 1994).

Cheung (1999) identifies obstacles in clinical practice evaluations. One obstacle is that clients may not understand the importance of keeping their data. Second, a commitment to conducting evaluations seems to be absent in many clinical settings. Additionally, clients' anticipation of positive outcomes may also contaminate the evaluation results. It is suggested that improvement should be based on the individual plan observed and implemented by both the social worker and the client. Among the API populations, positive attitude and acceptance are important measures of success. Strengths-based approaches are highly recommended.

NORMS AND MEANING OF CLINICAL PRACTICE AND MENTAL HEALTH

In the API community, the most common stereotype of mental health is that it is a Western study of mental illness, and that a typical Asian individual would not and should not have mental health problems. If Asian clients were diagnosed as having a mental health problem, they would be perceived as being controlled by some unknown social or spiritual forces (see a recent discussion on Asian women in Edman & Kameoka, 1997). With this belief, five issues arise in relation to service utilization. First, API people seldom pay attention to, or simply do not recognize, mental health problems. Many Asian Americans who believe in body–mind harmony do not distinguish between mental health and physical health. When they face a mental health problem, they first seek help within their family network. When the problem becomes severe, they then seek help from a herbal doctor, a traditional healer, or a physician. However, they only identify the physical or psychosomatic symptoms such as headache and back pain. Very few would mention their mental health distress, because they are supposed to keep quiet in front of authority figures (Chan, 1987; Ho, 1984). Even after the selected helper has identified possible mental health problems, the individual or his or her family may refuse to seek help from mental health professionals, either trying to avoid shame or thinking that the problem would naturally heal (Kim, 1995).

A second issue facing APIs is that most of them do not seek help at all. One of the main reasons is that they do not want to be stigmatized. Another reason is related to the internal locus-of-control characteristic commonly recognized by Asian cultures (Ho, 1984). When facing a mental health problem, they usually internalize the problem and try to avoid talking about it. Even though some may tell their family about the problem, their family members would also keep it internal and seldom talk to a mental health professional.

The perception about Western medicine contributes to the third issue. Many API families learn the Asian practice of treatment and think that mental health services are Western methods. When an Asian American family uses traditional healing methods or seeks help from a religious leader or a shaman, the family members do not want to disclose to their physician or social worker what they have done. Whether they believe in their traditional methods or not, their intent is to avoid negative comments about their culture. Furthermore, they may also believe that these traditional methods cannot be combined with Western methods. Many times, clients' hesitation in sharing their personal, familial, or environmental problems can make the social worker's assessment unable to reflect accurately what the actual picture might be. In addition, the basis of Western treatment is dependent on an open acknowledgment of the problem and an individual's resolve to seek some form of assistance, which is uncommon to some of these clients. Some API clients cannot accept this individualistic concept. Therefore, although they might agree to seek help from a counselor, resistance is often evident.

Language barriers are the fourth issue. When API individuals are ready to seek help, they often face the problem of service providers who are unable to provide bicultural, bilingual services to accommodate their language (Cheung, 1989; Kline & Huff, 1999). Sometimes a translator is used when services are provided. However, many API clients feel uncomfortable in the treatment process because they cannot communicate directly and effectively with the counselors (Kaneshige, 1973). In other words, without appropriate language skills, social workers may find rapport building, which requires listening skills and cultural sensitivity, difficult to achieve (Tsui & Schultz, 1985).

The fifth issue is the cultural competence of the service providers. Even though the API client may have a good command of English, some of them may not know how to include their cultural heritage to enhance assessment. Similarly, a social worker who speaks the client's language may not fully understand the culture of this client. For example, a Chinese counselor from Hong Kong may not fully understand the culture of a Chinese client from Taiwan. A second-generation American-born Vietnamese therapist may not understand the cultural issues facing first-generation Vietnamese immigrants. Perceptions of needs may vary based on how well the client–worker relationship is established (Hatton, et al., 1998).

In a recent study of the perceived needs among the diverse Asian population in Houston, Texas, Leung (1999) found that most of the 323 respondents did not see mental health as a problem affecting themselves or their families. When asked to rank the needs of Asian people living in the United States in six areas of concerns (basic needs, community and social issues, family and relationship issues, health and mental health issues, type of hardship, and immigration issues), most of the needs were ranked with either "no concern (0)" or "mild (1)" on a 4-point scale. This finding illustrates that many Asian people either do not have many mental health needs in these areas or do not perceive the existence of such needs. Their response may be explained by two strong beliefs, that "no need is better than asking for help" and "self is represented by a collective culture rather than an individual." In a study of treatment strategies, Ino and Glicken (1999) found that a collectivist approach that includes the assessment of family and cultural influences is far more effective than the "Western" approach of assessing the individualistic definition of a crisis.

PRACTICE PRINCIPLES AND
SKILLS IN EVALUATION

Before evaluating clinical practice, social workers must evaluate their own cultural values and competencies so that they do not feel overwhelmed by the demand of cultural sensitivity (Hu & Chen, 1999). The University of Kentucky (1989) describes social work competencies in five "I" categories: Informational Competencies, Intellectual Competencies, Interpersonal Competencies, Intrapersonal Competencies, and Intervention Competencies. Cultural consideration is incorporated in all five areas. In self-assessment, all these areas assume that self-awareness is a prerequisite to cultural competencies (Cheung, Stevenson, & Leung, 1992; Stevenson, Cheung, & Leung, 1992). The authors of this chapter suggest the use of questioning techniques to identify areas of improvement and awareness in knowledge, skills, and attitude development. In combining the five "I" areas and the questioning idea to identify cultural competencies, it is suggested that social workers and other helping professionals must evaluate themselves before assessing their work with Asian American clients and families. These five areas are specified in terms of self-evaluation questions relevant to the clients' cultural expectations.

Informational Competencies

Knowledge about Asian Americans in terms of:

1. Ethnic differences
   - Do I know that diversity exists among these clients and their families in terms of languages, customs, values, religions, communication patterns, food preferences, and other cultural components?

2. Family History
   - Do I know that these clients and their families may be American-born citizens, legal or illegal immigrants, or permanent residents who do or do not want to claim their U.S. citizenship?
   - Do I know that some of the family members may be visa holders, such as students, exchange scholars, job hunters, or visitors?
   - Do I know how many generations of these families have been residing in the United States?
   - Do I know that these clients have a family history and immigration background that may require special attention?

3. Minority Identity Development
   - Do I know that individual clients establish their personal identity through a variety of means that may include their families of origin, ethnic history, immigration, peers, schools, jobs, friends, neighbors, or people of the same or different ethnic backgrounds?
   - Do I know that some clients may choose to work with social workers of different ethnic backgrounds than they are?

4. Specific Information
   - Do I know that I can learn from clients about their specific needs and ethnic interests?
   - Do I know that clients have their legal, ethical, and political rights in my practice?
   - Do I know that there are many social policies in this country that affect the clients and their families because of their ethnic background?
   - Do I know what the client's major purpose for seeking help is?
   - Do I know that the clients may have access to receiving social services that they are not aware of or not willing to be exposed to?

Intellectual Competencies

Application of knowledge to work with Asian Americans in terms of:

1. Information Gathering
   - What means do I use to determine the information required to assess the needs of these individuals and families?
   - How do I use psychosocial assessments, genograms, or other tools to assess the impact of family history on current individual and family functioning with reference to the Asian background of the client?

2. Assessment
   - How do I help these individuals and families analyze their past (such as immigration, war trauma) and current situations (such as migration, cultural adjustment) in order to make future decisions?
   - How do I help clients analyze resources and strengths?
   - How do I offer suggestions without imposing certain values on my clients?
   - How do I interpret data with reference to the client's cultural expectations?

3. Goal Setting
   - How do I help clients prioritize their mental health concerns in relation to their cultural needs?
   - How do I set mutual goals with my clients with a balanced perspective between client's demand and social worker's mission?
   - How do I help clients evaluate their cultural constraints in achieving these goals?
   - How do I identify alternatives within the formal and informal systems that the client is affiliated with?
   - How do I help clients select their options?

Interpersonal Competencies

1. Relationship Building
   - Do I feel comfortable about my ethnicity, which is different from my clients?

- Can I show genuineness even though my clients do not want to work with me initially because we are culturally different?
- How do I show my positive regard when the clients see me as an authority figure?
- Do I spend time in rapport-building even though my goal is to intervene?
- Do I understand that a trusting relationship with Asian clients will help them come out from silence after hiding their problems within the family?

2. Communication Skills
   - How do I communicate with my clients to make them feel safe and at ease?
   - Do I pay attention to nonverbal communications between my clients and me?
   - How do I invite family members to attend our sessions?
   - How do I communicate with the family to ensure trust and safety?
   - How do I negotiate with family members to resolve disagreements among them?
   - How do I exercise my assertiveness without intimidating my clients and their family members?
   - How do I encourage family members to speak when there is a spokesperson within this family?

Intrapersonal Competencies

1. Values and Attitudes
   - Am I willing to work with individuals and families whose values and beliefs are different from mine?
   - Do I represent clients and their families in all system levels to help them voice their concerns?
   - Am I flexible in adapting to the clients' situations and circumstances when making assessment?
   - Am I objective in assessing clients' needs in reference to their cultural beliefs and values?

2. Personal Qualities and Characters
   - Am I creative in planning services for these clients?
   - Am I aware of my own biases toward API?
   - Am I being open to lifestyle variations?
   - Do I accept the clients when they do not agree with me?
   - Do I respect the kinship solidarity system and the need to maintain balance and harmony within the client's family?
   - Do I value the practice of "filial piety"?
   - Do I address only men and elders in the family in initial contacts?
   - Do I respect women's decision made with reference to their traditionally inherited role to remain silent?

Intervention Competencies

1. Intervention
   - Do I plan services according to the needs, constraints, and cultural expectations of these families?
   - Do I seek to learn about the cultural expectations that may influence the service plan?
   - How do I seek formal and informal support systems for my clients?
   - Do I acknowledge the importance of measuring the various rates of acculturation within the family?
   - Do I analyze and support the client's wish to seek, or not to seek, family advice?
   - Do I help clients balance their interpersonal relationships rather than confront them about their conflict avoidance behavior?

2. Termination
   - How do I prepare my clients for termination?
   - Am I aware of the fact that termination may mean another starting point to many API clients?
   - Am I aware of any cultural rituals that the clients would perform for termination?

The need for self-evaluation must be ever present in the helping profession for enhancing worker–client interactions. Without this self-evaluation, the social worker loses his or her objectivity and ability to connect with the client.

> **CONNECTING EVALUATION TO PRACTICE: A CASE STUDY**
> In a child abuse situation, a Chinese mother stated that the discipline on her child was harsh but she had to do so to chase away a bad spirit. Without examining the mother's definition within the context of her culture and belief system, the social worker might immediately react to this explanation as rationalization or denial. The next set of responses might include several service-oriented steps: giving this mother information regarding what ought to be done when disciplining a child, teaching her about the child protection law, and telling her what the social worker would do next (such as reporting to CPS, asking the mother to attend parenting workshops, etc.).
>
> Although many of these service-oriented steps may be necessary, the social worker in this case first adopted a culturally sensitive customized framework that was followed by two additional steps: (1) having the mother to define "bad spirit" in her cultural context, and (2) having the mother to identify alternative ways to chase this bad spirit away. By doing these two steps, the worker was able to assess that, in the mother's belief system, the dark and hairy birthmark that covered half of her son's back signified some evil power. During the intervention, the social worker helped the family reframe this bad spirit into a challenge to the family. The mother was then able to see the suffering of the son who had fought with this spirit before birth and got his body bruised with the birthmark.

Although the belief systems of the family and the worker were quite different, the worker saw her role as a facilitator, not as an interpreter or critic of the family's religious definitions. When the mother reevaluated her abusive behavior, she became aware of her overreactions to the son's behaviors and praised the son's courage to chase the spirit away while bearing with the mother's irrational responses. As a result, she was encouraged to ask the son questions about discipline and talk about feelings. She was then able to see the son's birthmark as a positive energy to fight against bad spirits. She wanted to help the son to rebuild his self-image. Given the legal limits in social service provisions, empowering clients to design alternative methods within the context of their belief system is a way to help them evaluate the intervention. Also, it is the clients' view that creates the variables for evaluation, such as the son's involvement, the meaning of the bad spirit, and so on. On closure with this family, the mother was able to improve her relationship with her son and her family. The social worker also learned about the family's religion and the son's involvement in the rituals. Without being judgmental about the family's belief system, the worker was successful in her role as an enabler and educator.

EVALUATION CONSIDERATIONS

After self-evaluation, the practitioner must also consider the reluctance to utilize formal mental health services in the API community. Many API individuals prefer handling their problems on their own. They often feel that these services do not help them due to different cultural expectations or misunderstanding (Kline & Huff, 1999). The feeling of "losing face" is another significant obstacle. As a result, the planning and implementation of services should be target-specific and result-oriented, not focusing solely on the problem. Therefore, it is of paramount importance to involve clients from the very beginning in *defining* their issues or problems.

In general, Americans believe that a problem is not a problem if it does not require a solution. However, many Asian Americans believe that a problem is a problem and that it is not supposed to be shared with others because it does not yet have a solution. To change this view requires reframing of the problem to reach a target that is perceived by the client as achievable. Based on a general API belief, concreteness is a major concept in learning. When social workers reframe the helping process into a learning process, they now focus on how concrete the plan is and what measurable outcomes the clients could accomplish within a limited time period. Nonetheless, many of the problems API clients are facing are abstract in nature, such as anxiety and alienation. The reframing of these problems into numbers or occurrences of physical indicators, such as shortness of breath, may fit the clients' view of maintaining harmony between the the physical world and the abstract feelings, i.e., mind-body connections.

In addition to reframing problems based on a vision of change, it is essential to encourage clients to view the newly defined target from a positive perspective. Social workers constantly encourage their clients to accept themselves and see their family problems as a source of positive energy that draws special attention, rather than as a negative force that produces ill health.

CONCLUSION

When working with API clients and families, a social worker uses rapport-building skills and interpersonal relationships to model how the clients could analyze various perceptions of the same problem and start making changes for themselves. When drawing from data to make recommendations with API clients, the social worker may need to do the following:

1. encourage the clients to share their perceptions about any change in the stated issue or problem;
2. summarize what has been done in terms of individual actions, interactions with others, and the building of interpersonal relationships;
3. identify data based on clients' input;
4. complete data collection based on observations;
5. compare the data between clients and the practitioners to achieve objectivity;
6. analyze what could have been done to achieve better outcomes;
7. empower the clients to continue what has worked best for them; and
8. continue the assessment for follow-up purposes.

There are two dimensions in clinical evaluations with the diverse API populations: client's definition and practitioner's integrative perspective. On these two dimensions, concreteness and sensitivity are the major components in conducting effective clinical evaluations. This model of clinical evaluation with API clients includes a variety of views and perspectives based on concrete definitions and sensitive evaluations of cultural expectations of self and others.

REFERENCES

Chan, C. S. (1987). Asian-American women: Psychological responses to sexual exploitation and cultural stereotypes. *Asian American Psychological Association Journal, 12* (1), 11–15.

Cheung, M. (1989). The elderly Chinese living in the United States: Assimilation or adjustment? *Social Work, 34* (5), 457–461.

Cheung, K. M. (1999). Effectiveness of social work treatment and massage therapy for nursing home clients. *Research on Social Work Practice, 9* (2), 229–247.

Cheung, K. M., Stevenson, K. M., & Leung, P. (1991, July/August). Competency-based evaluation of case management skills in child sexual abuse intervention. *Child Welfare, 70*(4), 425–435.

Edman, J. L. & Kameoka, V. A. (1997). Cultural differences in Illness schemas: An analysis of Filipino and American illness attributions. *Journal of Cross-Cultural Psychology, 28* (3), 252–265.

English, J. G. & Le, A. (1999). Assessing needs and planning, implementing, and evaluating health promotion and disease prevention programs among Asian American population groups. In R. M. Huff & M. V. Kline (Eds.), *Promoting health in multicultural populations: A handbook for practitioners* (pp. 357–373). Thousand Oaks, CA: Sage.

Flaskerud, J. H. & Liu, P. Y. (1990). Influence of therapist ethnicity and language on therapy outcomes of Southeast Asian clients. *International Journal of Social Psychiatry, 36* (1), 18–29.

Fong, R. (1994). Family preservation: Making it work for Asians. *Child Welfare, 73* (4), 331–341.

Hatton, C., Azmi, S., Caine, A., & Emerson, E. (1998). Informal careers of adolescents and adults with learning difficulties from the South Asian communities: Family circumstances, service support and carer stress. *British Journal of Social Work, 28* (6), 821–837.

Ho, M. K. (1984). Social group work with Asian/Pacific-Americans. *Social Work with Groups, 7* (3), 49–61.

Hu, X. & Chen, G. (1999). Understanding cultural values in counseling Asian families. In K. S. Ng (Ed.), *Counseling Asian families from a systems perspective* (pp. 27–37). Alexandria, VA: American Counseling Association.

Ino, S. M. & Glicken, M. D. (1999). Treating Asian American clients in crisis: A collectivist approach. *Smith College Studies in Social Work, 69* (3), 525–540.

Inouye, J. (1999). Asian American health and disease. In R. M. Huff & M. V. Kline (Eds.), *Promoting health in multicultural populations: A handbook for practitioners* (pp. 337–356). Thousand Oaks, CA: Sage.

Ishida, D. N. (1999). Promoting health among Asian American population groups: A case study from the field. In R. M. Huff & M. V. Kline (Eds.), *Promoting health in multicultural populations: A handbook for practitioners* (pp. 375–381). Thousand Oaks, CA: Sage.

Kaneshige, E. (1973). Cultural factors in group counseling and interaction. *Personnel and Guidance Journal, 51* (6), 407–412.

Kim, Y. O. (1995). Cultural pluralism and Asian Americans: Culturally sensitive social work practice. *International Social Work, 38* (1), 69–78.

Kitano, H. H. L. (1989). A model for counseling Asian Americans. In P. B. Pedersen, J. G. Draguns, et al. (Eds.), *Counseling across cultures* (pp. 139–151). Honolulu, HI: University of Hawaii Press.

Kline, M. V. & Huff, R. M. (1999). Tips for working with Asian American populations. In R. M. Huff & M. V. Kline (Eds.), *Promoting health in multicultural populations: A handbook for practitioners* (pp. 383–394). Thousand Oaks, CA: Sage.

Leung, E. (1985). Family support and postnatal emotional adjustment. *Bulletin of the Hong Kong Psychological Society, 14,* 32–36.

Leung, P. (1999). Stress and mental health issues: A needs assessment survey of Asians in the Houston area. Houston, TX: University of Houston Graduate School of Social Work.

Marsella, A. J. & Kameoka, V. A. (1989). Ethnocultural issues in the assessment of psychopathology. In S. Welzler (Ed.), *Measuring mental illness: Psychometric assessment for clinicians* (pp. 231–256). Washington, DC: American Psychiatric Press.

McGoldrick, M., Almeida, R., Preto, N. G., Bibb, A., Sutton, C., Hudak, J., & Hines, P. M. (1999). Efforts to incorporate social justice perspectives into a family training program. *Journal of Marriage and Family Counseling, 25* (2), 191–209.

Morris, M. W. & Peng, K. (1994). Culture and cause: American and Chinese attributions for social and physical events. *Journal of Personality and Social Psychology, 67* (6), 949–971.

Stevenson, K. M., Cheung, K. M., & Leung, P. (1992, July/August). A new approach to training child protective service workers for ethnically sensitive practice. *Child Welfare, 71* (4), 291–305.

Tsui, P. & Schultz, G. L. (1985). Failure of rapport: Why psychotherapeutic engagement fails in the treatment of Asian clients. *American Journal of Orthopsychiatry, 55* (4), 561–569.

University of Kentucky. (1989). *Collaboration for competency: Examining social work curriculum in the perspective of current practice with children and families.* Lexington, KY: University of Kentucky College of Social Work.

Wong, S. S., Heiby, E. M., Kameoka, V. A., & Dubanoski, J. P. (1999). Perceived control, self-reinforcement, and depression among Asian American and Caucasian American elders. *Journal of Applied Gerontology, 18* (1), 46–62.

Yang, J. (1991). Career counseling of Chinese American women: Are they in limbo? *Career Development Quarterly, 39* (4), 350–359.

Yi, K. (1995). Psychoanalytic psychotherapy with Asian clients: Transference and therapeutic considerations. *Psychotherapy, 32* (2), 308–316.

Yu, M. M. (1999). Multimodel assessment of Asian families. In K. S. Ng (Ed.), *Counseling Asian families from a systems perspective* (pp. 15–26). Alexandria, VA: American Counseling Association.

E N D N O T E

1. Asian Americans (AA) and Pacific Islander Americans (PIA) are grouped under the same category in the Census. In this chapter, the terms *Asian Americans* and *Asians and Pacific Islanders* (API) are used interchangeably to include both AA and PIA.

CHAPTER 31

EVALUATION AND ASSESSMENT IN HAWAIIAN AND PACIFIC COMMUNITIES

JON K. MATSUOKA

The Pacific Ocean is home to numerous archipelagoes that have long been settled by humans. The diaspora of Pacific peoples coincided with developments in navigational technologies. Polynesians, in particular, honed their seafaring skills, which allowed them to develop new settlements throughout the South Pacific and, perhaps, even the Americas. They brought with them knowledge, beliefs, skills, and organic materials that promoted their survival in new, yet familiar physiographies. The psyche of island dwellers emerged from the exigent need to practice sustainability (Halapua, 1993). Indigenous science was built on notions of resource sustainability and an understanding of constraints governing carrying capacities on islands. Healthy island economies were built on the principle of sustainability; that is, resource use levels did not surpass rates of natural replenishment. Human survival and quality of life was contingent on highly developed indigenous science and technology that was steeped in an understanding of organismic reproductive rates and ecologies, providing optimal conditions for species reproduction and survival. This knowledge served as a basis for laws governing human behavior. Prescriptive and proscriptive norms were consistent with conservation practices (Matsuoka & McGregor, 1994). Transgressive behaviors posed a threat to the sustainability of vital resources and the overall well-being of the community.

CULTURAL VALUES AND NORMS

Indigenous Pacific settlements occurred adjacent to freshwater sources, where people cultivated taro and other staple crops. Other communities occurred further downstream, near the coastline, where inhabitants harvested marine resources. Trading between mountain and coastal settlers within the same district was a major activity in a thriving subsistence economy. Subsistence economies were sustainable. For example, when fishers observed their fish stocks dwindling, they moved on to another area within the reef. Resources were managed in a sustainable way by rotating fishing activities to areas that were allowed to regenerate, and by observing certain seasonal conditions (e.g., not harvesting during breeding season). Resource management was essential. Any mismanagement would leave communities vulnerable to the unforgiving forces of nature. Pacific Island people developed an indigenous science and epistemology from direct and systematic observations. Knowledge was conveyed through an oral tradition.

Although social stratification occurred along with advances in technology, especially those related to greater food production (e.g., fishponds for aquaculture), work roles were generally undifferentiated and commensalistic (Diamond, 1998). Communal life was defined by a high degree of participation, protocol, and solidarity. Fertility rates and human population levels were determined by the availability of food and space (Hawley, 1986).

Families were viewed as "superorganic" systems spanning across time. Genealogy and place were synonymous, as families remained in the same locale across generations. Thus, family psyche and disposition were molded by the evolutionary forces of the environment and a locale's unique physiography. A spirituality emanated from the intimacy between people and the natural elements. The qualities of the environment were thought to be infused into the identities of long-term residents.

CONTEMPORARY ISSUES AND PROBLEMS

Traditional practices and organic relationships are still present today, especially in the remote rural areas of Hawai'i. Families cling to their genealogy and vigorously protect the secrecy of their family's burial grounds. Some are able to chant their genealogy, which dates back hundreds of years. Elders, or *kupuna,* are the proprietors of cultural traditions and the transmitters of the *mo'olelo* (stories of a place) to younger generations. A continued reliance on natural resources for sustenance bonds people to the land and to each other. Fishing, hunting, and gathering practices are the basis for a conservation ethic and an indigenous spirituality. Typically, resources that are caught (e.g., fish) by younger cohorts are shared throughout the community, especially with those who are older and less adept at strenuous physical activity (Matsuoka, McGregor, & Minerbi, 1994). This type of resource sharing and mutual support strengthens community bonds and reinforces a collective mentality. Gathering resources is also a means for encouraging family cohesion and cooperation. Family members are designated age-appropriate role prescriptions related to a subsistence activity. The utility of all members, despite their age, signifies the importance of everyone and teaches a sense of responsibility to the young.

Although very few families are wholly dependent on subsistence activities, it remains a vital link to tradition and a healthy lifestyle. Most Hawaiian families that engage in subsistence are also gainfully employed. Resources derived from subsistence supplement diet and offset the costs of expensive food items. Ironically, many food items that were once abundant (e.g., fish, taro) are relatively expensive in Hawai'i. Thus, those on fixed incomes will opt for cheaper, less healthy foods, which leads to health problems. In a contemporary society, where there are numerous social and psychological forces that pose constant threats to indigenous identity and well-being, the essential means to cultural survival is through an organic connection.

Amid drastic environmental and economic changes, an organic connection has become difficult to maintain. Almost from the point of Western contact, resources vital to sustainable subsistence economies have been diverted for other uses. Water, which was vital to Hawaiian agriculture, was diverted to sugar and pineapple fields. Plantation agriculture, logging, and ranching destroyed native ecosystems, such as lowland forested and nearshore ocean areas. Runoff from disturbed lands settled on critical marine habitats, such as coral reefs, turning them into underwater deserts.

Westerners brought with them their own organic materials, which wreaked havoc on the vulnerable native species. Hawaiian organisms that had evolved in a remote and protected environment were no match for the aggressive alien species from the continent.[1] Hawai'i now has more rare and endangered species than anywhere else in the United States (Lauren, 1993). The intrusion of alien species leading to the decimation of native ones is a metaphor for what also happened in the human sphere. As referred to previously, native Hawaiians underwent a genocidal reduction in their original population levels, and are also at the top or overrepresented on virtually every social and health problem indicator in the state (Mokuau & Matsuoka, 1995).

Throughout the Pacific region, the sanctity of communities has been disturbed by foreign interests. In Hawai'i and other Pacific islands, surviving indigenous populations have been displaced and dispossessed. The Hawaiian Homestead Act in 1920 has provided lands and homes to thousands of Hawaiian families, yet thousands more are on a waiting list (Native Hawaiian Study Commission, 1983).

Approximately a third of all Hawaiians have moved to the North American continent (Stannard, 1985). In many communities, young people leave reluctantly because of a lack of viable job opportunities. And, in many instances, such migrations lead to substantial population reductions, resulting in an imbalanced age ratio as only the older age cohorts remain. The probability that Hawaiian culture can be maintained and perpetuated over several generations on the continent is very low. Although expatriates may maintain strong localities to Hawai'i, their spirit and psyche are not being replenished by the natural forces of the islands. The biophysical environment of Hawai'i (landscape, climate) is an omnipresent force that bonds people to the land and shapes their attitudes and lifeways. The people of Hawai'i draw their sense of identity from natural symbolism (mountains, seascapes), and, when they leave Hawai'i, they detach themselves from these elements.

The loss of a nature-based economy has meant different things to different people. For some, the transition from subsistence to employment and a cash-based economy has occurred over a protracted period across generations. Thus, change occurred incrementally without severe disruption. On the other end, Hawaiians who have resisted change, because they found Western ideals inferior to their own or were thrust into a Western lifestyle because traditional ways were disrupted, may have suffered the worst. The later cohort has been relegated to poverty, is predisposed to health and mental health problems, and displacement due to insurmountable cost-of-living demands and landlessness has meant community dissolution (Matsuoka, 1988).

In rural locales, some families were able to retain their ancestral lands amid the onslaught of massive foreign takeover, but Hawaiian communities in both rural and urban settings face many challenges. Hawaiians in urban areas are far removed from the nature-based economies practiced by their forebears as little as a generation ago. Rural dwellers must contend with the political battles raging over land use and resource diversion. Many pristine rural areas are poised for development because they are well suited for resort and luxury housing. The systematic devolution away from nature-based or subsistence economies has relegated many Hawaiians to poverty status. Consequently, the indigenous populace is afflicted with the highest rates of health and mental health problems, and the highest rate of incarceration (Papa Ola Lokahi, 1992).

Over time, sustainable economies have been replaced by transnational corporate activity. It began with large-scale agricultural production for the purpose of exportation. When foreign competition led to a reduction in profits, landowners converted their lands into tourist-related ventures. Under subsistence, resources such as fish and forests were essential elements to a thriving economic system and were effectively managed. Under capitalism, they were either commodified or disregarded, and, thus, were exploited. Prior to the European discovery of the Hawaiian Islands, a self-contained society produced enough food to sustain a population of 600,000 to 1 million. Under a capitalistic system, contemporary Hawai'i must import 90 percent of its food to support a comparable population.

SOCIODEMOGRAPHIC OVERVIEW

When British sea captain James Cook first sailed to the Hawaiian Islands in 1778, his demographer estimated a native population of approximately 300,000. Later estimates based on archaeological evidence determined the population to be between 800,000 to 1 million (Stannard, 1989). From the point of first contact, Hawaiians were exposed to infectious diseases that they had no immunity to (Fuchs, 1961). Epidemics raged through the population and, by the turn of the nineteenth century, less than 40,000 Hawaiians remained.

Hawaiian demographic shifts coincided with economic and political changes occurring in the islands. In 1848, under heavy pressure from foreigners, the system of land ownership changed. Foreigners were allowed to obtain lands for the first time. Hawaiians, unfamiliar with the Western policies and procedures for retaining their lands, were quickly dispossessed of their lands and economies. By the end of the century, white men owned four acres of land for every one owned by a native (Daws, 1974).

The decline in the indigenous populace was inversely related to the massive in-migration of laborers from Asia. Large landowners from the United States exploited the land and cheap labor to amass fortunes in agribusiness. Foreign immigration continued to climb as sugar and pineapple production soared. As the cost of labor and land escalated and the profit margin decreased, landowners looked to new ventures to make greater profits. Hawai'i's climate and environment offered qualities that were highly conducive to developing a tourist industry. Since 1960, the income generated from tourism has increased more than 2,000 percent (Matsuoka, 1988).

The gradual shift from an agricultural economy to tourism has hastened the shift in the island's demographic makeup. The flow of immigrants, particularly from the Philippines, has filled Hawai'i's growing service sector needs. In-migrants from the North American continent have come to Hawai'i in unprecedented numbers (also to support the burgeoning tourism industry) (Matsuoka, Lum, and Ome, 1998).

The resident population of Hawai'i underwent a 44 percent increase during the twenty-year period between 1970 and 1990. Caucasians have been and remain the largest group in Hawai'i, accounting for about a third of the population in 1990. Their percentage of the state's population has increased by 24 percent over the twenty-year period. Japanese residents declined by 6 percent (22 percent of the population) during the same period, Filipinos increased by over 80 percent (15 percent of the state's population), and Hawaiians (part and full-blooded) grew by 94 percent (13 percent of the population). Chinese also experienced a 32 percent increase, but comprised only 6 percent of the state's population in 1990 (State of Hawai'i, 1990).

In analyzing population growth, it is important to distinguish between growth attributed to immigration and growth attributed to fertility rates. Growth in the number of Caucasians was attributable to a steady flow of migrants from the continent. In 1990, 71 percent of Caucasians were born in a different state. Growth among the Filipino and Chinese groups was attributable to immigrants arriving in Hawai'i from their homelands. The Japanese population in Hawai'i is primarily locally born and raised. Increases in the Hawaiian population were based almost entirely on increased birthrates in Hawai'i. In 1990, 3 percent of Asian and Pacific Islanders were born in a different state, while 21 percent were born in a foreign country.

The movement and exchange of people between Hawai'i, the United States, and Asia (primarily the Philippines) is highly related to economic conditions. The bulk of the immigrants from Asia arrive in Hawai'i to assume low-wage, service sector employment. On the other hand, the bulk of westbound resident partyheads to Hawai'i (heads of households from North America moving to Hawai'i) are assuming managerial and professional positions. When excluding military personnel, 43 percent of westbound residents fall into this employment category.

The history of imperialism and colonization has led to an infusion of immigrants to many Pacific locales from around the world. Hawai'i serves as an example of the relationship between political and economic upheaval and demographic change. The depopulation of native Hawaiians coincided with the loss of culture and a sovereign government. The growing influence of Westerners and transnational interests has meant wholesale structural changes to Hawaiian society.

PRACTICE PRINCIPLES AND SKILLS: A COMMUNITY ASSESSMENT MODEL

An epistemological quest must begin with an understanding of the form and nature of reality as defined by the knower. Research paradigms must be based on indigenous realities that are embedded in fluid and meaningful exchanges between people and their environment. The methodological question centers around creating an approach to gathering evidence that provides an explanation for social action that not only has predictive value but resonates with the knower.

Communities will be affected differently, depending on the nature of development and change and the culture and lifeways of the community. Traditional Pacific communities are particularly vulnerable to changing economic and environmental conditions because the integrity of their culture is tied directly to the quality of, and access to, natural resources. The long-term effects of inappropriate development are often associated with varying degrees of community dissolution and social problems.

Environmental shifts set in motion changes that reverberate throughout systems in the human ecology (e.g., family community). This pattern of change provides insights into the scope of issues to be considered and assessed, causal relationships, conditions related to the etiology of social problems, and adaptation and coping mechanisms. Human ecology provides an analytic framework for understanding person-in-environment congruity, or *goodness-of-fit*, and assessments of how social change impacts people differently, depending on their cultural perspective and psychological constitution.

Participatory Action Research

Empirical data is a critical resource within a technocracy and can be used to affect change through the validation of worldviews and lifeways. The significance of Participatory Action Research (PAR) is brought to light because of cultural chasms leading to discrepant ways of understanding and valuing phenomena. In most cases, the *dominant* cultural perspective prevails over minority or indigenous perspectives in decision-making arenas. Western ideology is supported and reinforced by social science and the political infrastructure. Contributing to the injustice and the onslaught of change is a general lack of *cultural interpreters* who are capable of posing the experiences of minority and indigenous peoples in ways that are not only accurate, but palatable to decision makers. PAR offers a means for scientifically documenting and translating non-Western experiences. Empirical data can also be used to structure issues that appeal to the sensibilities of decision makers.

PAR is conducted for the purpose of documenting particular social realities in order to enable constituencies/communities to advocate for communities and the resources needed to sustain them (Whyte, Greenwood, & Lazes, 1991). A basic premise stemming from this model is that research can be a catalyst for social action. PAR can be viewed as a process that involves establishing networks between representatives of a locale or community, research consultants, and bureaucrats. The goal of this process is to discover and document aspects of a community in order to preserve or ameliorate such aspects in an effort to sustain or improve the quality of life. Program and policy implications are drawn from the data and social action and implementation strategies are developed by community planners.

The role of the researcher needs to be redefined in the context of working with indigenous Pacific groups. The conventional model of pure research, in which participants are treated as passive subjects and kept at a distance throughout the technical and interpretive stages of research, is antithetic to the goal of documenting indigenous realities. According to Whyte and colleagues (1991), the greatest conceptual and methodological challenges come from engagement with the world. Thus, a prerequisite to PAR for any researcher is to be able to connect on a personal level with members of the community under study. Developing an appreciation for and sensitivity to the subjective realities of residents of a locale is essential to humanizing or indigenizing scientific inquiry. Engagement also refers to the ability of the researcher to elicit and incorporate indigenous concepts into measures and methods, while maintaining a high level of scientific rigor and objectivity. The results must be able to stand up to the scrutiny of hostile reviews.

Multimethod Approach

A multimethod approach offers many advantages over conventional research (Brewer & Hunter, 1989). The blending of quantitative and qualitative methods provides a basis for understanding the multiple dimensions of social phenomena. A multimethod research approach is consistent with an ecological orientation and the goal of assembling multiple social dimensions into a mosaic form.

Quantitative research is useful in terms of assessing community behaviors, sentiments, and statuses, distinguishing subgroup patterns and outcomes; and exploring causal relationships. Qualitative research is critical to understanding group dynamics, the role of history and the interpretation of events, and organic person-in-environment relations. While quantitative data provides a skeletal framework for understanding social phenomena, qualitative data is the substance for understanding the inner workings of human systems. Together, they provide a holistic impression of reality.

Another advantage of the multimethods approach is that it allows investigators to compare related sets of data derived from different methods. Results that concur with each other serve the purpose of triangulation or cross-validation. Results that are incongruous lead to questions concerning the psychometric properties of measures, conceptual equivalence, or provide new clues pertaining to the complexity of a phenomenon. They also signal the need to be cautious in interpreting the significance of any one set of data.

Indices and Measures

An indicator is a measurable characteristic that is observed from a change phenomenon. It is generally associated with a time-series process to reflect the degree to which an outcome has been achieved. Indicators can be viewed as variables that are numerically represented. The starting point is a baseline that represents the nature (e.g., degree, frequency, quality) of a phenomenon at preintervention. The phenomenon is measured at subsequent points following an intervention (program) to evaluate its effectiveness and the degree to which the program has achieved its goals.

Indicators of community change can be represented through elements of well-being. The elements that comprise various aspects of communal life can be conceptualized in terms of a human ecology, and they must also be "localized" or "indigenized." Communities are extremely diverse systems that require a process of analysis that is commensurate with their complexities. I would like to propose the following constructs as a frame of reference for analyzing community change:[2]

- Family: Refers to the extended family; conjugal support systems, sharing, exchange of services, and child-rearing networks;
- Community Life: Refers to the cohesion and integrity of local communities; the continuity of life-cycle events; community services; and any displacement of people;
- Human Well-Being and Spirituality: Refers to physical health in relation to cultural loss/stress syndrome; the impact of changes on mental and cultural health, and identity and pride; community-based health care;
- Natural Environment, Cultural, and Ecological Resources: Refers to areas to gather; sense of place; legendary or sacred places where spiritual ties to ancestors, deities, life forces are experienced; healing places; and hunting areas, fishing zones, and access; integrity of traditional socioeconomic zones (*ahupua'a* resources from the mountain to the sea);
- Rights: Refers to the exercise of rights defined in the Hawai'i State Constitution, the Hawai'i Revised Statutes, the American Indian Religious Freedom Act, and common law;
- Economics and Indigenous Land: Refers to employment, wages, purchasing power, socioeconomic status, and cost-of-living; value of subsistence activities; and benefit to community-based and culturally appropriate economic development initiatives. Hawaiian lands include lands and natural resources in their ecological *ahupua'a* setting used for homesteading, farming, ranching, aquaculture, fishing, income-generating activities, and for subsistence

gathering; community land trusts as land base for group-oriented activities; and government land held in trust for the benefit of Hawaiians.

Each construct may represent a set of variables that can be operationalized in ways that allow for measurement. With this broad scope of analysis as a backdrop, evaluative designs and methods can be streamlined according to the unique characteristics of the community and the programs established to serve them.

The following approaches to community assessment, planning, and evaluation are drawn from human ecological principles. In some cases, depending on the nature and scope of research, they may be used sequentially as a package. But, for the most part, they represent different types of methods used in the process of community-building.

Ecological Framework Using GIS Mapping

The centerpiece of this analysis is the Geographic Information System (GIS), which comprises computer programs that can visually place statistical data into the geographic landscape when the spatial location of the data is known. This process produces base maps that are used to understand spatial relations among human and environmental variables. This process can assist in decision making that is oriented to taking the condition of the human/natural ecosystems into account. Given the interrelationship between subsistence, cultural, and religious customs and practices to natural resources, the GIS mapping method can assist in the rendering of Native Hawaiian indices (McGregor, Matsuoka, & Minerbi, 1997).

> **VIGNETTE**
> The GIS method was used in an island-wide project that examined Native Hawaiian externalities. The overlay method was used to identify areas that were sensitive to land development when taking into consideration critical cultural factors. A map of the island of Moloka'i is used as an example of how this technique is applied (see Map 31.1).
> The areas with a lot of "graphic congestion" suggest that they should be off-limits to land development as it would disrupt critical cultural habitats. Areas that are generally devoid of graphic symbols need to also be considered in terms of their contiguous relationship to critical areas and site-specific investigations. Such open areas do not necessarily represent those that can be readily developed or exploited.

Community-Based Planning and Visioning

An aspect of community evaluation is planning. There are many different approaches to community-based planning. The community-based perspective suggests that the vision and goals of the community are derived from residents. It requires an organizational process that provides a systematic approach to data collection. It might begin with identifying constituencies within the community. They may include formalized or informal groups as well as age and gender cohorts. Var-

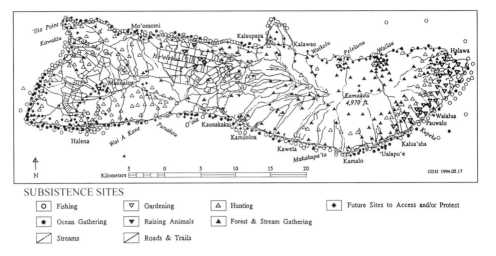

SUBSISTENCE SITES

⊡ Fishing	▽ Gardening	△ Hunting	◆ Future Sites to Access and/or Protect
⊙ Ocean Gathering	▼ Raising Animals	▲ Forest & Stream Gathering	
⟋ Streams	⟋ Roads & Trails		

MAP 31.1   Map of Hawaiian Subsistence Sites.

From Matsuka, J. & McGregor, D. (1998). Moloka'i: A Study of Hawaiian subsistence and community sustainability. In M.D. Hoff (ed.). *Sustainable community development: Studies in economic, environmental, and cultural revitalization.* New York: Lewis.

ious techniques can be used to draw out information from participants. Each technique can be streamlined according to the proclivities of the group. For example, youth may be more inclined to respond to visual approaches, such as drawing their vision of a future community. Other groups may be more responsive to a guided dialogue format.

Community visioning often leads to thematic representations of what residents want to see occur in their future. Themes tend to revolve around environmental or structural changes or improvements (e.g., new facilities), economic opportunities through community-based economic development, cultural and recreational offerings, and developing new programs and services for special cohorts (e.g., youth, the elderly). Once the community enhancement themes are identified, they are discussed before a larger community forum for the purpose of gaining consensus and discussing details.

The process of assessing the feasibility of "community building" ideas begins. A feasibility study is conducted in order to determine their logistics, including such things as cost, location, permitting process, market, grant/loan opportunities, and time frame. If the feasibility study concludes that it is worth the effort to pursue the project, then subsequent steps (e.g., business plan) towards operationalizing the plan will follow.

VIGNETTE
A visioning project was employed in a collaborative effort between a private, nonprofit children's center, a university, and a Hawaiian community association (Department of Urban & Regional Planning, University of Hawai'i, 1998). The

intent of the project was to assist the community in identifying its issues, assets, and a vision for the future. It identified and contacted ten groups in the community (e.g., youth, *kupuna* [elderly], *hula halau* [troupe]) in order to conduct focus group sessions. In the sessions, various techniques were used to elicit information from participants. For example, senior residents were asked to engage in an exercise whereby they developed a time line for the community. They were asked to identify important events in the life of the community. They were also asked to create a vision for the community's tomorrow. Other groups were asked to draw a map of the community's assets. The data was analyzed in terms of five themes including culture, *'ohana*, education, environment, and economic development. Each area was assessed in terms of strengths, challenges, and goals (see Table 31.1).

Community Evaluation Method: Logic Modeling

Every Pacific community is different in terms of demography, locale and physiography, proximity to government and business centers, history, and problems and assets. The program initiatives aimed at addressing issues in the community carry measurable objectives. In some situations, the real challenge is to extrapolate from indicators a sense as to whether the real goals are being met. For example, if one's intent to is address substance abuse through community-building efforts, it may be difficult to assume that programs aimed generally at community-building are

TABLE 31.1   Economic Development

To enhance self-reliance, we bring together the resources and talents of our community to create jobs and economic opportunities.

STRENGTHS	CHALLENGES	GOALS
■ Many professionals living in Papakolea ■ Presence of entrepreneurs	■ Welfare Reform ■ Financial security ■ Cottage Industries	■ Community based jobs/employment ■ Create Community-based Economic Development ■ Self-reliance ■ Increase wealth and happiness

ECONOMIC DEVELOPMENT PROJECTS:

1. Vending wagon
2. Certified Community Kitchen
3. Concession stands (Hookui & Puowaina)
4. Day care service
5. Culinary Academy

6. Clothing Manufacturing business
7. Craft Fair and Crafter's network
8. Native plant cultivation
9. Resource Directory

Hill, E., Lange, K., Olson-Orr, & Valles, K. (1998). A Vision for the Future: A Project Report on the Papakolea Visioning Project. University of Hawai'i, Department of Urban and Regional Planning.

affecting rates of substance abuse. Yet, if rates decline during the same period in which the programs occurred, and there were specific program components aimed at addressing substance abuse, then one can infer (short of a controlled, experimental design) that there was an impact. It may be dubious to consider one-to-one correlations between interventions/program and outcomes. Rather, positive movement towards community-building may be reflected in changes in several social indicators.

Program evaluators can identify indicators and devise measures to collect data at designated time periods. Qualitative methods can be used to elicit information from administrators, line staff, and clients or service recipients/participants in order to gain personal, in-depth knowledge of program effectiveness, especially as it refers to specific outcomes. The use of different evaluation methodologies in community and program assessments is critical given the range of epistemological styles of residents, program personnel, and funders. Notions of success or effectiveness should not hinge solely on one indicator or data source. Rather, data from multiple sources should be pooled together (triangulated) in order to cross-reference notions and seek to more wholly understand the process as it relates to outcomes.

Logic models are a useful means for assessing program/community outcomes. It provides a progressive description of how a program theoretically works in order to achieve its objectives (United Way, 1996). The various components are as follows:

Issues → Inputs → Activity → Outputs → Outcomes

Community *issues* are those that are identified as aspects or phenomena within the community that either detract from or enhance its well-being. Issues are usually those that are identified by the residents themselves. Issues can be conceptualized in terms of problems and assets. Problems might include crime, substance abuse, domestic violence, youth problems, unemployment, environmental pollution, lack of services, lack of educational or employment opportunities, and so forth. Issues might be identified through formal or informal mechanisms. Equally critical to identifying community issues is identifying its strengths and assets. These qualities, once identified, can be a cornerstone or catalyst for community-building. Assets include qualities such as community cohesion and pride, knowledgeable elders, educational and sports programs, strong leadership, churches, the existence of cottage industries, and close proximity to natural resources.

Inputs refers to the resources that are allocated to the program. They might include grant monies, personnel time and expertise devoted to designing and running the program, volunteer or community service time spent by residents, facilities and equipment, and even laws and regulations.

An *activity* is the actual "doing" part of a program. They include strategies, techniques, and types of treatment that comprise the program's service methodology. Offering low-interest loans and business consultation to microenterprises, specialized legal services to indigenous practitioners, and job training and educational services to high-risk youth are examples of activities.

Outputs are the products of program activities and are usually measured in terms of the volume of work accomplished. They might refer to the number of residents served, the number of sessions held, and the number of courses taught. They have little inherent value except that they are a mechanism for supporting change in the community.

The most critical aspect of logic modeling are *outcomes.* They are the changes or benefits resulting from the community-based programs. They reflect the program's effectiveness in achieving its objectives in the community-building process. Outcomes might include declining rates of neighborhood crime, residents who graduated from a substance abuse program who remain drug-free over time, higher rates of employment and small business success among residents, and laws and regulations passed that protect indigenous gathering rights.

Indicators and Measures

An indicator is a measurable characteristic that is observed from a change phenomenon. It is generally associated with a time-series process to reflect the degree to which an outcome has been achieved. Indicators can be viewed as variables that are numerically represented. The starting point is a baseline that represents the nature (e.g., degree, frequency, quality) of a phenomenon at preintervention. The phenomenon is measured at subsequent points following an intervention (program) to evaluate its effectiveness and the degree to which the program has achieved its goals.

Indicators of community change can be represented through elements of well-being. The elements that comprise various aspects of communal life can be conceptualized in terms of a human ecology, and they must also be "localized" or "indigenized." Communities are extremely diverse systems that require a process of analysis that is commensurate with their complexities.

Data Sources

Surveys and focus groups are methods used to collect data in a systematic manner in order to gain a clearer understanding of the sentiments of residents regarding problems. Social indicators that are often kept by government services on an annual basis represent actual or at least documented evidence of epidemiology, rates, and changes over time of social problems. Public forums where residents voluntarily come to express their viewpoints are another means, although less scientific, of identifying community issues. These processes are used to assess the status of communities and determine what issues exist, and to develop strategies for addressing them. Once problems or assets are documented through empirical data, they can be monitored over time. Initial data collection can serve as baselines reflecting current statuses that are used to determine the impacts of an intervention or community building activity.

VIGNETTE

A logic model was used to plan an economic development project that was drawn from the aforementioned community visioning project. Nine ideas on economic development were drawn from the visioning. Following the completion of a feasibility study, the cultivation of native Hawaiian plants was deemed one of the most viable.

The native plants project began with the recruitment of families in the community. Once identified, they were involved in a "community day" when they given a tray of native plants of their choice and university students assisted in clearing land and planting in the recipients' yards. Resources for the project (plants, soil, personnel) originally came from a native plants organization in charge of reforesting damaged ecosystems.

Following the planting, a series of workshops were held for the participants on how to grow and nurture the plants. Ultimately, the organizers of the project hope to teach residents how to mass-produce native plants, provide greenhouses to facilitate their propagation, teach them business and marketing skills, and provide the pathway for commercial plant-raising. A logic model is provided in Table 31.2.

CONCLUSION

As in most types of research on Pacific and/or indigenous communities, traditional approaches to community assessment and evaluation must be modified according to the unique characteristics, histories, and perspectives of residents. Research of this nature begins with developing a framework around the worldviews and sentiments of island people, and is based on an understanding of the organic sociocultural process that evolves from an environmental kinship. It is also based on the principle of empowerment through community-based initiatives. Each form of community-based research needs to be highly participatory and lead to some type of action, planning, or program enhancement. There must be a blending of flexibility with scientific rigor. Of course, degree of "rigor" is relative to the measurability of the phenomenon under examination. The difficulty in measuring cultural phenomena should not diminish its significance.

The social challenges facing Pacific and Hawaiian communities are so immense that it is difficult to decide where to begin. One issue that is becoming increasingly clear is that the unit of analysis and the target for system intervention is the community. Community development programs are generally aimed at restoring well-being through economic development, cultural revitalization, access to the environment and the assertion of native rights, and the strengthening of families. Innovative and culturally appropriate approaches to community assessment and program evaluation are critical to planning, implementation, and determining whether the efforts are making a difference.

TABLE 31.2   Logic Model for Native Plants Project

INPUTS	ACTIVITIES	OUTPUTS	OUTCOMES	INDICATORS	DATA SOURCE	DATA COLLECTION METHOD
Plant project provides plants, soil, pots, and technical assistance	Project provides workshops on caring for native plants	Residents attend, participate in meetings and field trips	Increase knowledge of native plants	Number of plants produced	Program evaluation; monitoring of project participants	Interviews; self-report measures State-sponsored studies of native plant restitution efforts
University provides technical assistance and grant-writing support	Field trips to native ecosystem areas to observe plants growing in wild; collect seeds		High survival rate of seedlings and cuttings	Number of plants sold commercially at a profit	Scientific studies of health of reintroduced native plant species	
Private, nonprofit children's center provides grant and organizational support	Establish partnership with other native plant growers; exchange stock, knowledge		Mass production of native plants and building of greenhouses	Increased income for participating households		
Support from community foundations			Increase knowledge of marketing and business know-how	Number of small native plants businesses in operation		
Community provides classroom space			Increase the number of endangered native plant species	Survival rate and biostatistics on native plants/reforested areas		
			Reforestation of denuded areas			

NOTES

1. The threat of alien species is present in other Pacific island locales that evolved in relative isolation.

2. The indices were drawn from a community-based effort to develop new impact research paradigms. It is published in a technical report: Minerbi, L., McGregor, D., & Matsuoka, J. (1993). Native Hawaiian and Local Cultural Assessment Project. Hawai'i Environmental Risk Ranking Project, State Department of Health, Honolulu, Hawai'i.

REFERENCES

Brewer, J. & Hunter, A. (1989). *Multimethods research: A synthesis of styles.* Newbury Park, CA: Sage.

Daws, G. (1974). *Shoal of time: A history of the Hawaiian islands.* Honolulu: University Press of Hawai'i.

Department of Urban & Regional Planning, University of Hawai'i. (April, 1998). A vision for the future: A report on the Papakolea Visioning project. Honolulu, Hawai'i.

Diamond, J. (1998). *Guns, Germs, & Steel.* New York: Norton Press.

Fuchs, L. H. (1961). *Hawai'i pono.* San Diego: Harcourt Brace Jovanovich.

Halapua, S. (1993). Sustainable development: From ideal to reality in the Pacific Islands. Paper presented at the Fourth Pacific Islands Conference of Leaders, Tahiti, French Polynesia, June 24–26.

Hawley, A. H. (1986). *Human ecology: A theoretical essay.* Chicago: University of Chicago Press.

Lauren, N. (1993). Preserving paradise. *Spirit of Aloha, 18*(1), 17–18.

Matsuoka, J. (1988). Tourism development in Hawai'i: An examination of some critical social impacts. *Social Development Issues, 12* (1), 81–91.

Matsuoka, J., Lum, C., & Ome, S. (1998). *Brain drain or cultural drain: The waning of Hawai'i's local populace.* University of Hawai'i, School of Social Work.

Matsuoka, J. & McGregor, D. (1994). Endangered culture: Hawaiians, nature, and economic development. In M. Hoff and J. McNutt (Eds.), *Social work and the environment.* London: Avebury/Gower House.

Matsuoka, J., McGregor, D., & Minerbi, L. (1994). Governor's Moloka'i subsistence task force, final report. Department of Business, Economic Development, & Tourism, Honolulu, HI.

McGregor, D., Matsuoka, J., & Minerbi. L. (1997). *Hawai'i Externalities Workbook.* Honolulu: Hawaiian Electric Company.

Mokuau, N. & Matsuoka, J. (1995). Turbulence among a native people: Social work practice with Hawaiians. *Social Work, 40*(4), 465–472.

Native Hawaiian Study Commission. (1983). Report on the culture, needs, and concerns of Native Hawaiians. Honolulu, HI.

Papa Ola Lokahi, (1992). *Native Hawaiian health data book.* Honolulu: Author.

Stannard, D. (1985). Tourism and the destruction of Hawai'i: Part I. *Save Hawai'i,* 3–9.

Stannard, D. (1989). *Before the horror: The population of Hawai'i on the eve of Western contact.* Honolulu: University of Hawai'i, Social Science Research Institute.

State of Hawai'i. (1990). *Hawai'i State data book.* Department of Business, Economic development and Tourism. Honolulu, HI.

United Way of America. (1996). *Measuring program outcomes: A practical approach.* Honolulu: Author.

Whyte, W. F., Greenwood, D. J., Lazes, P. (1991). Participatory action research: Through practice to science in social research. In W. P. Whyte (Ed.), *Participatory action research.* Newbury Park, CA: Sage.

CHAPTER 32

FUTURE DIRECTIONS FOR CULTURALLY COMPETENT SOCIAL WORK PRACTICE

ROWENA FONG

SHARLENE B.C.L. FURUTO

Culturally competent social work practice is being challenged and forced to change to meet the needs of ethnic minority individuals, families, and communities in the twenty-first century. Changing demographics dictate an examination of social work practice in order to provide effective services to clients of color. Census projections continue to predict that families of color in the United States will represent more than 50 percent of the total population by the year 2050 (McAdoo, 1999). Diversity within the major ethnic groups (African Americans, Latinos, First Nations Peoples, and Asians and Pacific Islanders) is becoming complex and calls for a reexamination of social work practice with individuals, families, communities, and organizations.

This concluding chapter will highlight some of the values that strengthen ethnic groups and ethical dilemmas that challenge the same. We refer you to the individual chapters in this text that stress various ethnic values. This will be followed by a review of culturally competent assessment, intervention, and evaluation with multilevel ethnic groups. Our final remarks will propose recommendations for future practice with ethnic groups.

The varying client systems are surrounded by unique values and ethical dilemmas. The values of a culture are the underpinnings necessary to success and are to be used as strengths and empowerment tools (Brown, Chapter 2); unfortunately, values systems are underused. It is important to know the values of not only each ethnic group but also the similar values among the ethnic groups. Within each culture there are many values to choose from, and those selected reflect the authors' perspectives. Values shared in the Latino population are spirituality, family, community, children, cooperation, respect, and interpersonal relations (Zuniga, Chapter 4). First Nations Peoples value identity, spirituality, sharing and generosity, respect for elders, noninterference or self-reliance, present time anonymity, and submission or nonconfrontation (Yellow Bird, Chapter 5). Examples of the values of African Americans are family and descendent connectedness, closeness to community, kinship care, and father involvement (Devore, Chapter 3). Values cited for Asians and Pacific Islanders include family and kin responsibility, obligation and filial piety, hierarchical order, respect and loyalty, as well as identity—sometimes interwoven with shame (Ross-Sheriff & Husain, Chapter 6).

These values and others should guide the formulation and design of assessments, interventions, and evaluations in culturally competent social work practice (Fong, Chapter 1; Rayama, Furuto, Edmondson, Chapter 7). Cultural values as strengths and resources have been underused, and social workers have not maximized the potential of this empowerment tool. Cultural values are seen as strengths by ethnic groups and need to be better used by the social work profession to empower communities.

ASSESSMENTS FOR CULTURALLY COMPETENT PRACTICE

There are few assessment models designed for use with ethnic groups. Furthermore, those few assessment tools for ethnic individuals, families, and communities are challenged by changing subgroups within the various minority groups. Existing tools, approaches, and cultural resources need to be reexamined and more culturally competent ones need to be developed.

There needs to be a reexamination of assessment tools for ethnic minority individuals and families. Westbrooks and Starks (Chapter 8) challenge the Person-in-Environment (PIE) tool and advocate for one that goes beyond the PIE, highlights the strengths, and thereby empowers the ethnic community. They propose the Strengths-Perspective-Inherent-in-Cultural-Empowerment (SPICE) model that empowers while incorporating cultural resources. The major premise is that the deleterious effects of oppression on African Americans need to be reversed and used instead to empower this ethnic group. Assessments can be tools that facilitate social justice (Weaver, Chapter 13; Morelli, Chapter 14).

Assessment issues need to address migration or immigration experiences, levels of acculturation, social class and racism, natural support systems, belief systems, cultural values as strengths (Negroni-Rodriguez & Morales, Chapter 10), and oppression (Westbrooks & Starks, Chapter 8; Negroni-Rodriguez, Chapter 10). Micro-level assessments need to incorporate cultural and historical perspectives (Devore, Chapters 3; Brave Heart, Chapter 12). Brave Heart discusses Historical Trauma Theory to guide the assessment of trauma across generations and within current lifespans. Assessment needs to include "indigenous interpretations of symptoms" (Brave Heart, Chapter 12) and the examining of the cultural milieu to understand psychosocial stressors (Brave Heart, Chapter 12; Morelli, Chapter 14). In summary, at the micro-and-mezzo levels, assessment of individuals and families needs to reexamine the tools, the purposes, and the perspectives or theories that guide assessments. Lacking is the consistent use of cultural resources as strengths. This needs to be further developed in the twenty-first century.

When assessing communities, the community members themselves need to define their own problems, and stakeholders should be involved. Cultural strengths such as the elders (Acevedo & Morales, Chapter 11; Weaver, Chapter 13), cultural continuity, and traditions (Weaver, Chapter 13), and important cultural resources, such as cultural activities, need to play a vital role in the assessment process (Acevedo & Morales, Chapter 11). Communities may differ and have unique experiences because of historical, migration, and immigration factors. Some ethnic communities may not be able to unify (Manning, Chapter 9), limiting the exercise of power and access to resources. The resulting inequity among community members is a reminder that all community members, including small subgroups, need to be represented (Chow, Chapter 15). Methods of assessment should complement the culture of the community, and communities, agencies, or organizations in the African American culture are to "determine the level of Afrocentric replenishment" (Manning, Chapter 9). In summary, we need to solicit and encourage the participation of representative community members, cultural traditions, cultural activities, and cultural resources when assessing ethnic organizations and communities in the new millennium.

INTERVENTIONS REFLECTING CULTURALLY COMPETENT PRACTICE

Despite the progress made in social work practice with ethnic groups in the United States, much more needs to be done. There are few comprehensive ethnic intervention models in the literature that are specific to the major ethnic groups and their subgroups. Brave Heart (Chapter 20) reminds practitioners working with Native clients that "the uniqueness of each Native culture must be respected and practice must be modified accordingly." In addition, interventions should also take into account the historical and cultural perspectives in practice development and implementation.

The theoretical frameworks for intervention must be based on that client's specific ethnic or cultural group. In African American culture there is an Africentric theoretical and practice orientation (Harvey, Chapter 16) that assumes the individual identity is a collective identity, the spiritual component is essential, and affect knowledge relates to epistemology (Schiele, cited in Chapter 16). Examples of cultural interventions are heritage-reminding, retreats and naming ceremonies, family enhancement, and empowerment dinners (Harvey, Chapter 16).

Intervention frameworks for some ethnic groups, such as Mexican Americans, may need to include a bicultural/bilingual component. Galan (Chapter 18) however, advises us to maintain a balance between value–behavior congruence. Galan describes the "processing of cultural beliefs" whereby the client weighs cultural information, prioritizes to choose appropriate behavior, and maintains integrity in belief and behavior. Kanuha (Chapter 22) reminds us that for Asian and Pacific Island American lesbians and gay men it is very important to remember that there is a dual tension of being A/PIA gay men and lesbians and it is important to "make links between the relevant concepts of gay/lesbian culture and A/PIA culture."

Sensitivities about linkages and making culturally appropriate connections at the micro and mezzo levels also continue at the macro level. When intervening with African American communities, Daly (Chapter 17) stresses the need for communication skills in multicultural situations. Puig (Chapter 19) expands on communication skills with Hispanic Americans and warns, "any communication should take into consideration the underlying significances of messages, as practitioners have to rely on their ability to decode between the literal and the analogic meanings in these cross-cultural exchanges." Furuto, San Nicolas, Kim, and Fiaui, (Furuto, San Nicolas, Kim, & Fiaui, Chapter 23) warn macro-practitioners that they must be aware of "allegorical and metaphorical communication, realizing that comments, seemingly unrelated, are actually significant."

Indigenous communities need to organize themselves around the issue of sovereignty as a means by which to develop themselves and their communities (Furuto, San Nicolas, Kim, & Fiaui, Chapter 23). Brown and Gundersen (Chapter 21) describe the importance of sovereignty and including sovereign powers when developing American Indian Tribal Communities. They emphasize that "tribal communities must be able to exercise the full extent of their tribal sovereign powers and authority in the development of tribal health and welfare systems, regulations, standards and practices."

EVALUATIONS OF CULTURALLY COMPETENT PRACTICES

Most evaluations for ethnic groups on the micro-, mezzo-, and macro-levels are inappropriate and incomplete. While ethnic families and communities live in environments very different from the mainstream United States, most evaluations fail to factor in "the social, economic, psychological, and political context in which they survive" (Davis, Chapter 24). Grant (Chapter 25), therefore, promotes use of an "Afrocentric perspective" that highlights African beliefs, values, and mores that have survived historical times and events. This and other perspectives from the different ethnic groups should be part of the evaluation process.

Evaluations need to include strengths of the culture available to them and used by them, in particular cultural values and norms (Villa, Chapter 26; Colon, Chapter 27; Lewis, Chapter 29). Evaluations often ignore what works or is effective in ethnic communities (Matsuoka, Chapter 31). Indigenous evaluations do exist. Villa has developed the *La Fe de la Gente* (the people's faith/spirituality) framework to evaluate the role of spirituality in a Mexican American's coping strategy.

Evaluation of clinical practice with Asian and Pacific Islander individuals and families challenges problem definitions. According to Cheung and Leung (Chapter 30), many Asian Americans believe that "a problem is a problem because it does not yet have a solution; whereas Americans tend to believe that a problem is not a problem if it does not require a solution." This difference in problem defining impacts the solution required and, thus, the evaluation of the process or outcome. While it is not possible to have the same worldview, it is mandatory that culturally competent social workers not only recognize but also account for these differences when evaluations are being conducted. Social workers are also reminded to evaluate our commitment to social justice when working with American Indians (Weaver, Chapter 13; Gilbert & Franklin, Chapter 28) and other minority groups (Morelli, Chapter 14; and Furuto, San Nicolas, Kim, & Fiaui, Chapter 23).

FUTURE DIRECTIONS

Culturally competent social work practice in the twenty-first century challenges social work practice at all levels. As practitioners, cultural awareness and sensitivity dictate our knowledge of cultural values and norms. However, to be culturally competent, practitioners need to go beyond knowledge attainment and consistently use cultural traditions and activities in assessment, intervention, and evaluation on all levels of practice. The knowledge of cultural norms and values from each particular ethnic group, acknowledging the different subgroupings, is to be the baseline information to guide practice. Western norms and values are no longer the guideposts. The compromise is biculturalization of assessments and interventions but the starting point must be the indigenous culture itself.

Assessments need to include theoretical frameworks that encompass oppression, sovereignty, historical trauma, and cultural perspectives. Assessing for cultural strengths in the form of traditions and cultural activities and empowering ethnic families have been underutilized. Intervention frameworks specifically for ethnic groups and their subgroups across generations are needed. Spirituality, sovereignty, and ethnic resources should be considered for inclusion in intervention plans and implementation for ethnic and cultural groups. Ethnic values, strengths, and perspectives need to direct intervention on all levels. Evaluations of ethnic groups must be based on that specific ethnic worldview to be valid and meaningful. The Africentric models should be further developed and Latinocentric, First Nationscentric, and Asian and Pacificentric models are overdue. Such models, for example an Asiancentric model for practice, would start at the macro level and identify the key societal cultural values important to the different Asian groups. There would be within-group variations on the choice of values because of acculturation, gender, social class, sexual orientation, sibling order, and regional location. Once these cultural values were identified, they would be used as strengths in assessments and intervention planning and implementation. Intervention selection would involve a biculturalization process where an indigenous intervention would be matched with a western one with congruent theoretical underpinnings. The evaluations of the interventions would consider cultural contexts and not be driven by culturally inappropriate outcome measures.

In conclusion, social work education in the twenty-first century needs a reexamination of practice teaching and research to fully acknowledge and respect the ethnic individuals, families, and communities in the United States. To be cultural competent, practitioners are challenged to recreate a new worldview in approaching and applying effective practices to an increasingly diverse population.

REFERENCES

MacAdoo, H. Ed. (1999). *Family Ethnicity: Strength in diversity.* 2nd edition. Thousand Oaks: Sage.

Schiele, J. (1994). Afrocentricity as an alternative worldview for equality. *Journal of Progressive Human Services, 5,* 5-25.

INDEX

CHAPTERS ORGANIZED BY ETHNIC GROUPINGS, PRACTICE METHODS AND LEVELS OF PRACTICE

ETHNIC GROUPINGS:

African Americans: 3, 8, 9, 16, 17, 24, 25
Asians/South Asians/Pacific Islanders: 6, 14, 15, 22, 23, 30, 31
First Nations Peoples/Native Clients/Native Americans: 5, 12, 13, 20, 21, 28, 29
Latinos/ Mexican Americans/Hispanic Americans: 4, 10, 11, 18, 19, 26, 27

PRACTICE METHOD AND LEVELS OF PRACTICE

Assessment:

Individuals and Families: 8, 10, 12, 14
Communities and Organizations: 9, 11, 13, 15

Intervention:

Individuals and Families: 16, 18, 20, 22
Communities and Organizations: 17, 19, 21, 23

Evaluation:

Individuals and Families: 24, 26, 28, 30
Communities and Organizations: 25, 27, 29, 31